BILL BRYSON

WALKABOUT

Also by Bill Bryson

THE LOST CONTINENT

MOTHER TONGUE

NEITHER HERE NOR THERE

MADE IN AMERICA

NOTES FROM A SMALL ISLAND

NOTES FROM A BIG COUNTRY

BILL BRYSON
WALKABOUT

A WALK in the WOODS
&
DOWN UNDER

Doubleday

LONDON · NEW YORK · TORONTO · SYDNEY · AUCKLAND

TRANSWORLD PUBLISHERS
61–63 Uxbridge Road, London W5 5SA
a division of The Random House Group Ltd

RANDOM HOUSE AUSTRALIA (PTY) LTD
20 Alfred Street, Milsons Point, Sydney,
New South Wales 2061, Australia

RANDOM HOUSE NEW ZEALAND LTD
18 Poland Road, Glenfield, Auckland 10, New Zealand

RANDOM HOUSE (PTY) LTD
Endulini, 5a Jubilee Road, Parktown 2193, South Africa

A Walk in the Woods first published 1997 by Doubleday
A division of Transworld Publishers

Down Under first published 2000 by Doubleday
A division of Transworld Publishers

This omnibus edition published 2002

A catalogue record for this book is available
from the British Library.
ISBN 0385 604831

Typeset in 11/13pt Sabon by
Falcon Oast Graphic Art Ltd.

Printed in Great Britain by
Mackays of Chatham plc, Chatham, Kent

3 5 7 9 10 8 6 4

CONTENTS

A WALK IN THE WOODS

To Katz,
of course

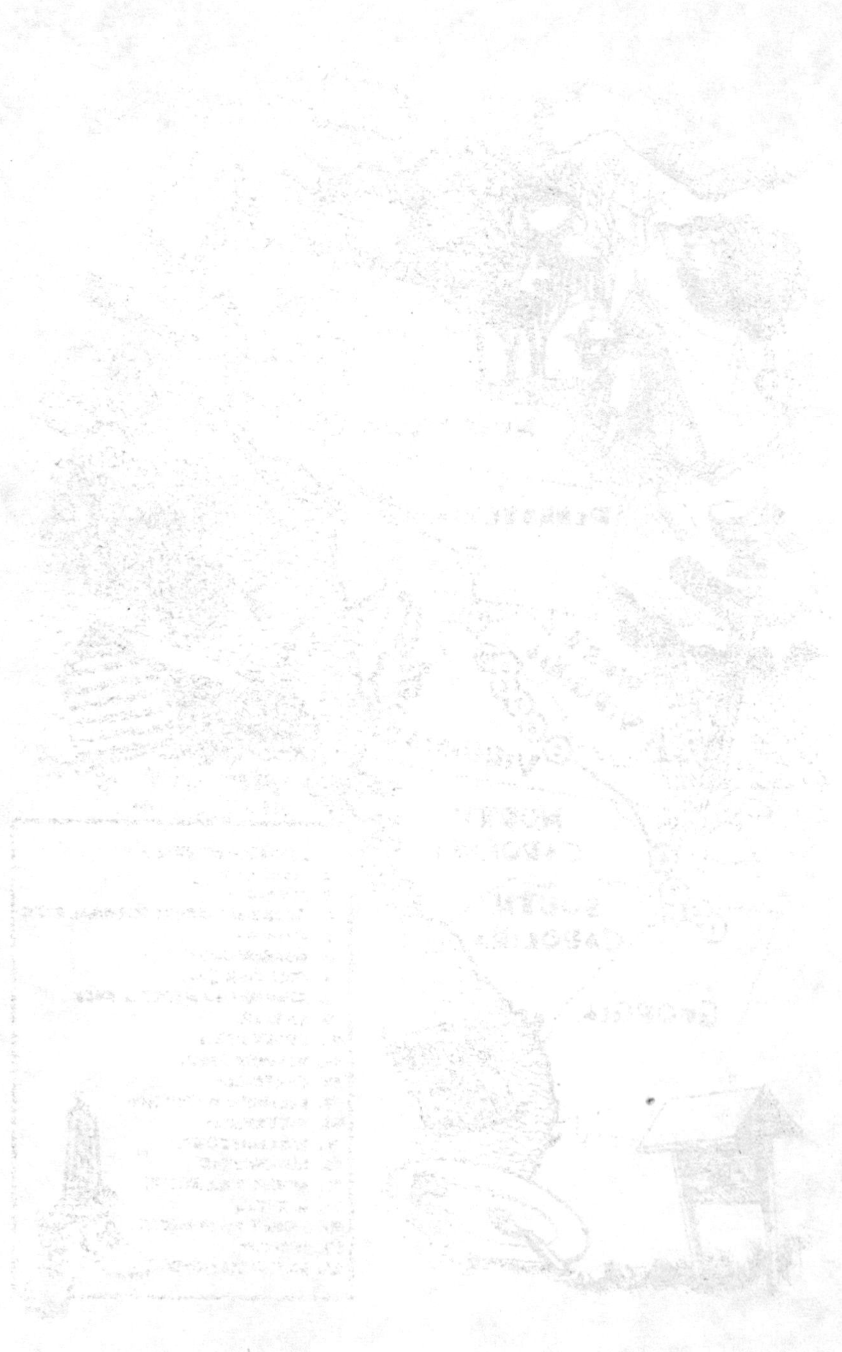

MAINE
VT.
N.H.
MASS.
NEW YORK
PENNSYLVANIA
WEST VIRGINIA
VIRGINIA
NORTH CAROLINA
SOUTH CAROLINA
GEORGIA
MAINE
NOODLES
1. SPRINGER MOUNTAIN
2. HIAWASSEE
3. FRANKLIN
4. SMOKY MOUNTAINS NATIONAL PARK
5. ROANOKE
6. WAYNESBORO
7. ROCKFISH GAP
8. SHENANDOAH NATIONAL PARK
9. SKYLAND
10. FRONT ROYAL
11. HARPERS FERRY
12. CENTRALIA
13. DELAWARE WATER GAP
14. PITTSFIELD
15. WILLIAMSTOWN
16. MANCHESTER
17. MOUNT KILLINGTON
18. HANOVER
19. MOUNT WASHINGTON
20. MONSON
21. MOUNT KATAHDIN

CHAPTER ONE

NOT LONG AFTER I MOVED WITH MY FAMILY TO A SMALL TOWN IN NEW Hampshire I happened upon a path that vanished into a wood on the edge of town.

A sign announced that this was no ordinary footpath, but the celebrated Appalachian Trail. Running more than 2,100 miles along America's eastern seaboard, through the serene and beckoning Appalachian Mountains, the AT is the granddaddy of long hikes. The Virginia portion alone is twice the length of the Pennine Way. From Georgia to Maine, it wanders across fourteen states, through plump, comely hills whose very names – Blue Ridge, Smokies, Cumberlands, Catskills, Green Mountains, White Mountains – seem an invitation to amble. Who could say the words 'Great Smoky Mountains' or 'Shenandoah Valley' and not feel an urge, as the naturalist John Muir once put it, to 'throw a loaf of bread and a pound of tea in an old sack and jump over the back fence'?

And here it was, quite unexpectedly, meandering in a dangerously beguiling fashion through the pleasant New England community in which I had just settled. It seemed such an extraordinary notion – the idea that I could set off from home and walk 1,800 miles through woods to Georgia, or turn the other way and clamber over the rough and stony White Mountains to the fabled prow of Mount Katahdin floating in forest 450 miles to the north in a wilderness few have seen. A little voice in my head said: 'Sounds neat! Let's do it!'

I formed a number of rationalizations. It would get me fit after years of waddlesome sloth. It would be useful – I wasn't quite sure in what way, but I was sure none the less – to learn to fend for myself in the wilderness. When guys in camouflage pants and hunting hats sat around in the Four Aces Diner talking about fearsome things done out of doors I would no longer have to feel like such a cupcake. I wanted a little of that swagger that comes with being able to gaze at a far horizon through eyes of chipped granite and say with a slow, manly sniff, 'Yeah, I've shit in the woods.'

And there was a more compelling reason to go. The Appalachians are the home of one of the world's great hardwood forests – a relic of the richest, most diversified sweep of woodland ever to grace the temperate world – and that forest is in trouble. If the global temperature rises by 4°C over the next fifty years, as is evidently possible, then the whole of the Appalachian wilderness below New England could become savannah. Already trees are dying in mysterious and frightening numbers. The elms and chestnuts are long gone, the stately hemlocks and flowery dogwoods are going, and the red spruces, Fraser firs, hickories, mountain ashes and sugar maples may be about to follow. Clearly if ever there was a time to experience this singular wilderness, it was now.

So I decided to do it. More rashly, I announced my intention – told friends and neighbours, confidently informed my publisher, made it common knowledge among those who knew me. Then I bought some books and talked to people who had done the trail in whole or in part and came gradually to realize that this was way beyond – *way* beyond – anything I had attempted before.

Nearly everyone I talked to had some gruesome story involving a guileless acquaintance who had gone off hiking the trail with high hopes and new boots and come stumbling back two days later with a bobcat attached to his head or dripping blood from an armless sleeve and whispering '*Bear!*' in a hoarse voice, before sinking into a troubled unconsciousness.

The woods were full of peril – rattlesnakes and water moccasins and nests of copperheads; bobcats, bears, coyotes, wolves, and wild boar; loony hillbillies destabilized by gross quantities of impure corn liquor and generations of profoundly unbiblical sex; rabies-crazed skunks, raccoons and squirrels; merciless fire ants and ravening blackfly; poison ivy, poison sumac, poison salamanders; even a scattering of moose lethally deranged by a parasitic worm that burrows a nest in their brains and befuddles them into chasing hapless hikers through remote, sunny meadows and into glacial lakes.

Literally unimaginable things could happen to you out there. I heard of a man who had stepped from his tent for a midnight pee and was swooped upon by a short-sighted hoot owl – the last he saw of his scalp it was dangling from talons prettily silhouetted against a harvest moon – and of a young woman who was woken by a sinuous tickle across her belly and peeked into her sleeping bag to find a copperhead bunking down in the warmth between her legs. I heard four separate stories (always related with a chuckle) of campers and bears sharing tents for a few confused and lively moments; of people abruptly vaporized ('tweren't nothing left of him but a scorch mark') by body-sized bolts of lightning when caught in sudden storms on high ridgelines; of tents crushed beneath falling trees, or eased off precipices on ballbearings of beaded rain and sent paragliding onto distant valley floors, or swept away by the watery wall of a flash flood; of hikers beyond counting whose last experience was trembling earth and the befuddled thought 'Now what the f—?'

It required only a little light reading in adventure books and almost no imagination to envision circumstances in which I would find myself caught in a tightening circle of hunger-emboldened wolves, staggering and shredding clothes under an onslaught of pincered fire ants, or dumbly transfixed by the sight of enlivened undergrowth advancing towards me, like a torpedo through water, before being bowled backwards by a sofa-sized boar with cold beady eyes, a piercing squeal, and a slaverous, chomping appetite for pink, plump, city-softened flesh.

Then there were all the diseases lurking in the woods – *Giardia lamblia*, Eastern equine encephalitis, Rocky Mountain spotted fever, Lyme disease, *Helicobacter pylori*, *Ehrlichia chaffeenis*, schistosomiasis, brucellosis, and shigella, to offer but a sampling. Eastern equine encephalitis, caused by the prick of a mosquito, attacks the brain and central nervous system. If you are very lucky you can hope to spend the rest of your life propped in a chair with a bib round your neck, but generally it will kill you. There is no known cure. No less arresting is Lyme disease, which comes from the bite of a deer tick smaller than a pinhead. If undetected, it can lie dormant in the human body for years before erupting in a positive fiesta of maladies. This is a disease for the person who wants to experience it all. The symptoms begin with headaches, fatigue, fever, chills, shortness of breath, dizziness, and shooting pains in the extremities, then march on to cardiac irregularities, facial paralysis, muscle spasms, severe mental impairment, loss of control of body functions, and – not surprising in the circumstances – chronic depression.

Then there is the little-known family of organisms called hantaviruses, which swarm in the micro-haze above the faeces of mice and rats, and are hoovered into the human respiratory system by anyone unlucky enough to stick a breathing orifice near them – by lying down, say, on a sleeping platform over which infected mice have recently scampered. In 1993 a single outbreak of hantavirus killed thirty-two people in the southwestern United States, and the following year the disease claimed its first victim on the AT when a hiker contracted it after sleeping in a 'rodent-infested shelter'. (All AT shelters are rodent infested.) Among viruses, only rabies, Ebola and HIV are more certainly lethal. Again, there is no treatment.

Finally, this being America, there is the constant possibility of murder. At least nine hikers – the actual number depends on which source you consult and how you define a hiker – have been murdered along the trail since 1974. Two young women would die while I was out there.

For various practical reasons, principally to do with the long, punishing winters of northern New England, there are only so many available months to hike the trail each year. If you start at the northern end, at Mount Katahdin in Maine, you must wait for the snows to clear in late May or June. If, on the other hand, you start in Georgia and head north, you must time it to finish before mid-October when the snows blow back in. Most people hike from south to north with spring, ideally keeping one step ahead of the worst of the hot weather and the more irksome and infectious of insects. My intention was to start in the south in early March. I put aside six weeks for the first leg.

The precise length of the Appalachian Trail is a matter of interesting uncertainty. The US National Park Service, which constantly distinguishes itself in a variety of alarming ways, manages in a single leaflet to give the length of the trail as 2,155 miles and 2,200 miles. The official Appalachian Trail Guides, a set of eleven books each dealing with a particular state or section, variously give the length as 2,144 miles, 2,147 miles, 2,159 miles and 'more than 2,150 miles'. The Appalachian Trail Conference, the governing body, in 1993 put the trail length at exactly 2,146.7 miles, then changed for a couple of years to a hesitantly vague 'more than 2,150 miles', but has recently returned to confident precision with a length of 2,160.2 miles. In 1993, three people rolled a measuring wheel along its entire length and came up with a distance of 2,164.9 miles. At about the same time a careful measure based on a full set of US Geological Survey maps put the distance at 2,118.3 miles.

What is certain is that it is a long way, and from either end it is not easy. The peaks of the Appalachian Trail are not particularly formidable as mountains go – the highest, Clingmans Dome, in Tennessee, tops out at a little under 6,700 feet – but they are big enough and they go on and on. There are more than 350 peaks over 5,000 feet along the AT, and perhaps a thousand more in the vicinity. In a week you can cross fifty Snowdons. Altogether, it takes about five months, and five million steps, to walk the trail from end to end.

And of course on the AT you must lug on your back everything you need. It may seem obvious, but it came as a small shock to me to realize that this wasn't going to be even remotely like an amble through the Lake District, where you head off for the day with a haversack containing a packed lunch and a copy of Wainwright, and at day's end retire from the hills to a convivial inn. Here you sleep out of doors and cook your own food. Few people manage to carry less than 40 pounds and when you are hauling that kind of weight, believe me, never for a moment does it escape your notice. It is one thing to walk 2,000 miles; quite another to walk 2,000 miles with a wardrobe on your back.

My first inkling of just how daunting an undertaking it was to be came when I went to our local outfitters, the Dartmouth Co-Op, to purchase equipment. My son had just got an after-school job there, so I was under strict instructions of good behaviour. Specifically, I was not to say or do anything stupid, try on anything that would require me to expose my stomach, say 'Are you shitting me?' when informed of the price of a product, be conspicuously inattentive when a sales assistant was explaining the correct maintenance or aftercare of a product, and above all not to don anything inappropriate, like a woman's ski hat, in an attempt to amuse.

I was told to ask for Dave Mengle because he had walked large parts of the trail himself and was something of an encyclopedia of outdoor knowledge. A kindly and deferential sort of fellow, Mengle could talk for perhaps four days solid, with interest, about any aspect of hiking equipment.

I have never been so simultaneously impressed and bewildered. We spent a whole afternoon going through his stock. He would say things to me like: 'Now this has a 70-denier high-density abrasion-resistant fly with a ripstop weave. On the other hand, and I'll be frank with you here' – and he would lean towards me and reduce his voice to a low, candid tone, as if disclosing that it had once been arrested in a public toilet with a sailor – 'the seams are lap-felled rather than bias-taped and the vestibule is a little cramped.'

I think because I mentioned that I had done a bit of hiking in England, he assumed some measure of competence on my part. I didn't wish to alarm or disappoint him, so when he asked me questions like 'What's your view on carbon fibre stays?' I would shake my head with a rueful chuckle, in recognition of the famous variability of views on this perennially thorny issue, and say, 'You know, Dave, I've never been able to make up my mind on that one – what do you think?'

Together we discussed and gravely considered the relative merits of side compression straps, spindrift collars, crampon patches, load transfer differentials, airflow channels, webbing loops, and something called the occipital cutout ratio. We went through that with every item. Even an aluminium cookset offered considerations of weight, compactness, thermal dynamics, and general utility that could occupy a mind for hours. In between there was lots of discussion about hiking generally, mostly to do with hazards like rockfalls, bear encounters, cookstove explosions, and snakebites, which he described with a certain misty-eyed fondness, before coming back to the topic at hand.

With everything, he talked a lot about weight. It seemed to me a trifle overfastidious to choose one sleeping bag over another because it weighed three ounces less, but as equipment piled up around us I began to appreciate how ounces accumulate into pounds. I hadn't expected to buy so much – I already owned hiking boots, a Swiss army knife and a plastic map pouch that you wear round your neck on a piece of string, so I had felt I was pretty well there – but the more I talked to Dave the more I realized that I was shopping for an expedition.

The two big shocks were how expensive everything was – each time Dave dodged into the storeroom or went off to confirm a denier rating, I stole looks at price tags and was invariably appalled – and that every piece of equipment appeared to require some further piece of equipment. If you bought a sleeping bag, then you needed a stuff sack for it. The stuff sack cost $29. I found this an increasingly difficult concept to warm to.

When after much solemn consideration I settled on a backpack – a very expensive Gregory, top of the range, no-point-in-stinting-here sort of thing – he said, 'Now what kind of straps do you want with that?'

'I beg your pardon?' I said, and recognized at once that I was on the brink of a dangerous condition known as retail burnout. No more now would I blithely say, 'Better give me half a dozen of those, Dave. Oh, and I'll take eight of these – what the heck, make it a dozen. You only live once, eh?' The mound of provisions that a minute ago had looked so pleasingly abundant and exciting – all new! all mine! – suddenly seemed burdensome and extravagant.

'Straps,' Dave explained. 'You know, to tie on your sleeping bag and lash things down.'

'It doesn't come with straps?' I said in a new, level tone.

'Oh, no.' He surveyed a wall of products, and touched a finger to his nose. 'You'll need a raincover too, of course.'

I blinked. 'A raincover? Why?'

'To keep out the rain.'

'The backpack's not rainproof?'

He grimaced as if making an exceptionally delicate distinction. 'Well, not a hundred per cent . . .'

This was extraordinary to me. 'Really? Did it not occur to the manufacturer that people might want to take their packs outdoors from time to time? Perhaps even go camping with them. How much is this pack anyway?'

'Two hundred and fifty dollars.'

'Two hundred and fifty dollars! Are you shi—' I paused and put on a new voice. 'Are you saying, Dave, that I pay two hundred and fifty dollars for a pack and it doesn't have straps and it isn't waterproof?'

He nodded.

'Does it have a bottom in it?'

Mengle smiled uneasily. It was not in his nature to grow critical or weary in the rich, promising world of camping equipment. 'The straps come in a choice of six colours,' he offered helpfully.

I ended up with enough equipment to bring full employment to a vale of sherpas – a three-season tent, self-inflating sleeping pad, nested pots and pans, folding cutlery, plastic dish and cup, complicated pump-action water purifier, stuff sacks in a rainbow of colours, seam sealer, patching kit, sleeping bag, bungee cords, water bottles, waterproof poncho, waterproof matches, pack cover, a rather nifty compass/ thermometer keyring, a little collapsible stove that looked frankly like trouble, gas bottle and spare gas bottle, a hands-free torch that you wear on your head like a miner's lamp (this I liked very much), a big knife for killing bears and hillbillies, insulated long johns and vests, four bandannas, and lots of other stuff, some of which I had to go back again and ask what it was for exactly. I drew the line at buying a designer groundcloth for $59.95, knowing I could acquire a lawn tarp at K-Mart for $5. I also said no to a first-aid kit, sewing kit, anti-snakebite kit, $12 emergency whistle and small orange plastic shovel for burying one's poop, on the grounds that these were unnecessary, too expensive or invited ridicule. The orange spade in particular seemed to shout: 'Greenhorn! Sissy! Make way for Mr Buttercup!'

Then, just to get it all over and done with at once, I went to the local bookshop and bought books – *The Thru-Hiker's Handbook*, *Walking the Appalachian Trail*, several books on wildlife and the natural sciences, a geological history of the Appalachian Trail by the exquisitely named V. Collins Chew, and the complete, aforementioned set of official Appalachian Trail Guides, consisting of eleven small paperback books and fifty-nine maps in different sizes, styles and scales covering the whole trail from Springer Mountain to Mount Katahdin, and ambitiously priced at $233.45 the set. On the way out I noticed a volume called *Bear Attacks: Their Causes and Avoidance*, opened it up at random, found the sentence 'This is a clear example of the general type of incident in which a black bear sees a person and decides to try to kill and eat him', and tossed that into the shopping basket, too.

I took all this home and carried it down to the basement in several trips. There was such a lot, nearly all of it technologically unfamiliar to me, which made it both exciting and daunting, but mostly daunting. I put the hands-free torch on my head, for the heck of it, and pulled the tent from its plastic packaging and erected it on the floor. I unfurled the self-inflating sleeping pad and pushed it inside and followed that with my fluffy new sleeping bag. Then I crawled in and lay there for quite a long time trying out for size the expensive, confined, strangely new-smelling, entirely novel space that was soon to be my home from home. I tried to imagine myself lying not in a basement beside the reassuring, cosily domesticated roar of the furnace, but rather outside, in a high mountain pass, listening to wind and tree noise, the lonely cry of doglike creatures, the hoarse whisper of a Georgia mountain accent saying: 'Hey, Virgil, there's one over here. Y'all remember the rope?' But I couldn't really.

I hadn't been in a space like this since I stopped making dens with blankets and card tables at about the age of nine. It was really quite snug and, once you got used to the smell, which I naively presumed would dissipate over time, and the fact that the fabric gave everything inside a sickly greenish pallor, like the glow off a radar screen, it was not so bad. A little claustrophobic perhaps, a little odd-smelling, but cosy and sturdy even so.

This wouldn't be so bad, I told myself. But secretly I knew that I was quite wrong.

CHAPTER TWO

ON THE AFTERNOON OF 5 JULY 1983, THREE ADULT SUPERVISORS AND A group of youngsters set up camp at a popular spot beside Lake Canimina in the fragrant pine forests of western Quebec, about 80 miles north of Ottawa, in a park called La Vérendrye Provincial Reserve. They cooked dinner and afterwards, in the correct fashion, secured their food in a bag and carried it a hundred or so feet into the woods, where they suspended it above the ground between two trees, out of the reach of bears.

About midnight, a black bear came prowling around the margins of the camp, spied the bag and brought it down by climbing one of the trees and breaking a branch. He plundered the food and departed, but an hour later he was back, this time entering the camp itself, drawn by the lingering smell of cooked meat in the campers' clothes and hair, in their sleeping bags and tent fabric. It was to be a long night for the Canimina party. Three times between midnight and 3.30 a.m. the bear came to the camp.

Imagine, if you will, lying in the dark alone in a little tent, nothing but a few microns of trembling nylon between you and the chill night air, listening to a 400-pound bear moving around your campsite. Imagine its quiet grunts and mysterious snufflings, the clatter of upended cookware and sounds of moist gnawings, the pad of its feet and the heaviness of its breath, the singing brush of its haunch along your tent side. Imagine the hot flood of adrenalin, that unwelcome tingling in the back of your arms, at the sudden rough bump of its snout against the foot of your tent, the alarming wild wobble of your frail shell as it roots through the backpack that you left casually propped by the entrance – with, you suddenly recall, a Snickers bar in the pouch. Bears adore Snickers bars, you've heard.

And then the dull thought – oh, God – that perhaps you brought the Snickers bar in here with you, that it's somewhere in here, down by your feet or underneath you or – oh, shit, here it is. Another bump of grunting head against the tent, this time near your shoulders. More crazy wobble. Then silence, a very long silence, and – wait, shhhhh . . . yes! – the unutterable relief of realizing that the bear has withdrawn to the other side of the camp or shambled back into the woods. I tell you right now. I couldn't stand it.

So imagine then what it must have been like for poor little David Anderson, aged twelve, when at 3.30 a.m., on the third foray, his tent of all tents was abruptly rent with a swipe of claw and the bear, driven to distraction by the rich, unfixable, everywhere aroma of hamburger, bit hard into a flinching limb and dragged him shouting and flailing through the camp and into the woods. In the few moments it took the boy's fellow campers to unzip themselves from their accoutrements – and imagine, if you will, trying to swim out of suddenly voluminous sleeping bags, take up flashlights and makeshift cudgels, undo tent zips with helplessly fumbling fingers, and give chase – in those few moments, poor little David Anderson was dead.

Now imagine reading a nonfiction book packed with stories such as this – true tales soberly related – just before setting off alone on a camping trip of your own into the North American wilderness. The book to which I refer is *Bear Attacks: Their Causes and Avoidance* by a Canadian academic named Stephen Herrero. If it is not the last word on the subject, then I really, really, really do not wish to hear the last word. Through long winter nights in New Hampshire, while snow piled up outdoors and my wife slumbered peacefully beside me, I lay saucer-eyed in bed reading clinically precise accounts of people gnawed pulpy in their sleeping bags, plucked whimpering from trees, even noiselessly stalked (I didn't know this happened!) as they sauntered unawares down leafy paths or cooled their feet in mountain streams. People whose one fatal mistake was to smooth their hair with a dab of aromatic gel, or eat juicy meat, or tuck a Snickers bar in their shirt pocket for later, or have sex, or even, possibly, menstruate, or in some small, inadvertent way pique the olfactory properties of the hungry bear. Or, come to that, whose fatal failing was simply to be very, very unfortunate – to round a bend and find a moody male blocking the path, head rocking appraisingly, or wander unwittingly into the territory of a bear too slowed by age or idleness to chase down fleeter prey.

Now it is important to establish right away that the possibility of a serious bear attack on the Appalachian Trail is remote. To begin with, the really terrifying American bear, the grizzly – *Ursus horribilis* as it is so vividly and correctly labelled – doesn't range east of the Mississippi, which is good news because grizzlies are large, powerful and ferociously bad-tempered. When Lewis and Clark went into the wilderness, they found that nothing unnerved the native Indians more than the grizzly, and not surprisingly since you could riddle a grizzly with arrows – positively porcupine it – and it would still keep coming. Even Lewis and Clark with their big guns were astounded and unsettled by the ability of the grizzly to absorb volleys of lead with barely a wobble.

Herrero recounts an incident that nicely conveys the near indestructibility of the grizzly. It concerns a professional hunter in Alaska named Alexei Pitka, who stalked a big male through snow and finally felled it with a well-aimed shot to the heart from a large-bore rifle. Pitka should probably have carried a card with him that said: 'First make sure bear is dead. Then put gun down.' He advanced cautiously and spent a minute or two watching the bear for movement, but when there was none he set the gun against a tree – big mistake – and strode forward to claim his prize. Just as he arrived, the bear sprang up, clapped its expansive jaws around the front of Pitka's head, as if giving him a big kiss, and with a single jerk tore off his face.

Miraculously, Pitka survived. 'I don't know why I set that durn gun against the tree,' he said later. Actually what he said was, 'Mrffff mmmpg nnnmmm mffffffn,' on account of having no lips, teeth, nose, tongue or other vocal apparatus.

If I were to be pawed and chewed – and this seemed to me entirely possible, the more I read – it would be by a black bear, *Ursus americanus*. There are at least 500,000 black bears in North America, possibly as many as 700,000. They are notably common in the hills along the Appalachian Trail (indeed, they often *use* the trail, for convenience), and their numbers are growing. Grizzlies, by contrast, number no more than 35,000 in the whole of North America, and just 1,000 in the mainland United States principally in and around Yellowstone National Park. Of the two species, black bears are generally smaller (though this is a decidedly relative condition; a male black bear can still weigh up to 650 pounds) and unquestionably more retiring.

Black bears rarely attack. But here's the thing. Sometimes they do. All bears are agile, cunning and immensely strong, and they are always hungry. If they want to kill you and eat you, they can, and pretty much whenever they want. That doesn't happen often, but – and here is the absolutely salient point – once would be enough.

Herrero is at pains to stress that black bear attacks are infrequent, relative to their numbers. In the eight decades to 1980 he found just twenty-three confirmed black bear killings of humans (about half the number of killings by grizzlies), and most of these were out west or in Canada. In New Hampshire there has not been an unprovoked fatal attack on a human by a bear since 1784. In Vermont, there has never been one.

I wanted very much to be calmed by these assurances but could never quite manage the necessary leap of faith. After noting that just 500 people were attacked and hurt by black bears between 1960 and 1980 – twenty-five attacks a year from a resident population of at least half a million bears – Herrero adds that most of these injuries were not severe. 'The typical black bear-inflicted injury', he writes blandly, 'is minor and usually involves only a few scratches or light bites.'

Pardon me, but what exactly is a light bite? Are we talking a playful wrestle and gummy nips? I think not. And is 500 certified attacks really such a modest number, considering how few people go into the North American woods? And how foolish must one be to be reassured by the information that no bear has killed a human in Vermont or New Hampshire in 200 years? That's not because the bears have signed a treaty, you know. There's nothing to say that they won't start a modest rampage tomorrow.

So let us imagine that a bear does go for us out in the wilds. What are we to do? Interestingly, the advised stratagems are exactly opposite for grizzly and black bear. With a grizzly, you should make for a tall tree, since grizzlies aren't much for climbing. If a tree is not available, then you should back off slowly, avoiding direct eye contact. All the books tell you that if the grizzly comes for you on no account should you run. This is the sort of advice you get from someone who is sitting at a keyboard when he gives it. Take it from me, if you are in an open space with no weapons and a grizzly comes for you, run. You may as well. If nothing else, it will give you something to do with the last seven seconds of your life. However, when the grizzly overtakes you, as it most assuredly will, you should fall to the ground and play dead. A grizzly may chew on a limp form for a minute or two, but generally will lose interest and shuffle off. With black bears, however, playing dead is futile since they will continue chewing on you until you are considerably past caring. It is also foolish to climb a tree because black bears are adroit climbers and, as Herrero drily notes, you will simply end up fighting the bear in a tree.

To ward off an aggressive black bear, Herrero suggests making a lot of noise, banging pots and pans together, throwing sticks and rocks, and 'running at the bear'. (Yeah, right. You first, Professor.) On the other hand, he then adds judiciously, these tactics could 'merely provoke the bear'. Well, thanks. Elsewhere he suggests that hikers should consider making noises from time to time – singing a song, say – to alert bears to their presence, since a startled bear is more likely to be an angry bear, but then a few pages later cautions that 'there may be danger in making noise', since that can attract a hungry bear that might otherwise overlook you.

The fact is, no one can tell you what to do. Bears are unpredictable, and what works in one circumstance may not work in another. In 1973, two teenagers, Mark Seeley and Michael Whitten, were out for a hike in Yellowstone when they inadvertently crossed between a mother and her cubs. Nothing worries and antagonizes a female bear more than to have people between her and her brood. Furious, she turned and gave chase – despite the bear's lolloping gait it can move at up to 35 miles an hour – and the two boys scrambled up trees. The bear followed Whitten up his tree, clamped her mouth round his right foot, and slowly and patiently tugged him from his perch. (Is it me, or can you feel your fingernails scraping through the bark?) On the ground, she began mauling him extensively. In an attempt to distract the bear from his friend, Seeley shouted at it, whereupon the bear came and pulled him out of his tree, too. Both young men played dead – precisely the wrong thing to do, according to all the instruction manuals – and the bear left.

I won't say I became obsessed by all this, but it did occupy my thoughts a great deal in the months while I waited for spring to come. My particular dread – the vivid possibility that left me staring at tree shadows on the bedroom ceiling night after night – was having to lie in a small tent, alone in an inky wilderness, listening to a foraging bear outside, and wondering what its intentions were. I was especially riveted by an amateur photograph in Herrero's book, taken late at night by a camper with a flash at a campground out west. The photograph caught four black bears as they puzzled over a suspended food bag. The bears were clearly startled but not remotely alarmed by the flash. It was not the size or demeanour of the bears that troubled me – they looked almost comically unaggressive, like four guys who had got a Frisbee caught up a tree – but their numbers. Up to that moment it had not occurred to me that bears might prowl in parties. What on earth would I do if *four* bears came into my camp?

Why, I would die, of course. Literally shit myself lifeless. I would blow my sphincter out of my backside like one of those unrolling paper streamers you get at children's parties – I dare say it would even give a merry toot – and bleed to a messy death in my sleeping bag.

Herrero's book was written in 1985. Since that time, according to an article in the *New York Times*, bear attacks in North America have increased by 25 per cent. The *Times* article also noted that bears are far more likely to attack humans in the spring following a bad berry year. The previous year had been a very bad berry year. I didn't like the feel of any of this.

Then there were all the problems and particular dangers of solitude. I still have my appendix, and any number of other organs that might burst or sputter in the empty wilds. What would I do then? What if I fell from a ledge and broke my back? What if I lost the trail in a blizzard or fog, or was seized at the throat by a venomous snake, or lost my footing on moss-slickened rocks crossing a stream and cracked my head a concussive blow? You could drown in three inches of water on your own. You could die from a twisted ankle. No, I didn't like the feel of this at all.

At Christmas, I put notes in lots of cards inviting people to come with me on the trail, if only part of the way. Nobody responded, of course. Then one day in late February, with departure nigh, I got a call. It was from an old school friend named Stephen Katz. Katz and I had grown up together in Iowa, but I had pretty well lost touch with him. Those of you who have read *Neither Here Nor There* may recall Katz as my youthful travelling companion round Europe. In the twenty-five years since, I had run into him three or four times on visits home, but hadn't seen him otherwise.

'I've been hesitating to call,' he said slowly. He seemed to be searching for words. 'But this Appalachian Trail deal – do you think maybe I could come with you?'

I couldn't believe it. 'You want to come with me?'

'If it's a problem, I understand.'

'No,' I said. 'No, no, no. You're very welcome. You are extremely welcome.'

'Really?' He seemed to brighten.

'Of course.' I really could not believe it. I wasn't going to have to walk alone. I did a little jig. *I wasn't going to have to walk alone.* 'I can't tell you how welcome you would be.'

'Oh, great,' he said in a flood of relief, then added in a confessional tone, 'I thought maybe you might not want me along.'

'Why ever not?'

'Because, you know, I still owe you six hundred dollars from Europe.'

'Hey, jeez, certainly not – you owe me six hundred dollars?'

'I still intend to pay you back.'

'Hey,' I said, 'hey.' I couldn't remember any $600. I had never released anyone from a debt of this magnitude before and it took me a moment to get the words out. 'Listen, it's not a problem. Just come hiking with me. Are you sure you're up for this?'

'Absolutely.'

'What kind of shape are you in?'

'Real good. I walk everywhere these days.'

'Really?' This is most unusual in America.

'Well, they repossessed my car, you see.'

'Ah.'

We talked a little more about this and that – his mother, my mother, Des Moines. I told him what little I knew about the trail and the wilderness life that awaited us. We settled that he would fly to New Hampshire the next Wednesday, we would spend two days making preparations, and then hit the trail. For the first time in months I felt positively positive about this enterprise. He seemed remarkably upbeat, too, for someone who didn't have to do this at all.

My last words to him were, 'So, how are you with bears?'

'Hey, they haven't got me yet!'

That's the spirit, I thought. Good old Katz. Good old anyone with a pulse and a willingness to go walking with me. After he rang off, it occurred to me I hadn't asked him why he wanted to come. Katz was the one person I knew on earth who might be on the run from guys with names like Julio and Mr Big. Anyway, I didn't care. I wasn't going to have to walk alone.

I found my wife at the kitchen sink and told her the good news. She was more reserved in her enthusiasm than I had hoped.

'You're going into the woods for weeks and weeks with a person you have barely seen for twenty-five years. Have you really thought this through?' (As if I have ever thought anything through.) 'I thought you two ended up getting on each other's nerves in Europe.'

'No.' This was not quite correct. 'We started off on each other's nerves. We ended up despising each other. But that was a long time ago.'

She gave me her pull-the-other-one look. 'You have nothing in common.'

'We have everything in common. We're forty-four years old. We'll talk about haemorrhoids and lower back pain and how we can't remember where we put anything, and the next night I'll say, "Hey, did I tell you about my back problems?" and he'll say, "No, I don't think so," and we'll do it all over again. It'll be great.'

'It'll be hell.'

'Yeah, I know,' I said.

And so I found myself, six days later, standing at our local airport watching a tin commuter plane containing Katz touch down and taxi to a halt on the tarmac twenty yards from the terminal. The hum of the propellers intensified for a moment, then gradually stuttered to a halt and the plane's door-cum-stairway fell open. I tried to remember the last time I had seen him. After our summer in Europe, Katz had gone back to Des Moines and devoted himself single-handedly to ensuring that Iowa had a thriving drug culture. He had partied for years, until there was no one left to party with, then he had partied with himself, alone in small apartments, in T-shirt and boxer shorts, with a bottle and a baggie of pot and a TV with rabbit ears. I remembered now that the last time I had seen him was about five years before in a Denny's restaurant where I was taking my mother for breakfast. He was sitting in a booth with a haggard fellow who looked as if his name would be Virgil Starkweather, tucking into pancakes and taking occasional illicit nips from a bottle in a paper bag. It was eight in the morning and Katz looked very happy. He was always happy when he was drunk, and he was always drunk.

Two weeks after that, I later heard, police found him in an upside-down car in a field outside Mingo, hanging by his seatbelt, still clutching the steering wheel and saying, 'Well, what seems to be the problem, officers?' There was a small quantity of cocaine in the glovebox and he was despatched to a minimum security prison for eighteen months. While there, he started attending AA meetings. To everyone's surprise, not least his own, he had not touched alcohol or an illegal substance since.

After his release, he got a little job, went back to college part time and settled down for a while with a hairdresser named Patty. For the past three years he had devoted himself to rectitude and – I instantly saw now as he stooped out of the door of the plane – growing a stomach. Katz was arrestingly larger than when I had last seen him. He had always been kind of fleshy, but now he brought to mind Orson Welles after a very bad night. He was limping a little and breathing harder than one ought to after a walk of 20 yards.

'Man, I'm hungry,' he said without preamble, and let me take his carry-on bag, which instantly jerked my arm to the floor.

'What have you got in here?' I gasped.

'Ah, just some tapes and shit for the trail. There a Dunkin' Donuts anywhere around here? I haven't had anything to eat since Boston.'

'Boston? You've just come from Boston.'

'Yeah, I gotta eat something every hour or so or I have, whaddayacallit, seizures.'

'Seizures?' This wasn't quite the reunion scenario I had envisioned. I imagined him bouncing around on the Appalachian Trail like some wind-up toy that had fallen on its back.

'Ever since I took some contaminated phenylthiamines about ten years ago. If I eat a couple of doughnuts or something I'm usually OK.'

'Stephen, we're going to be in the wilderness in three days. There won't be doughnut stores.'

He beamed proudly. 'I thought of that.' He indicated his bag on the carousel – a green army surplus duffel – and let me pick it up. It weighed at least seventy-five pounds. He saw my look of wonder. 'Snickers,' he explained. 'Lots and lots of Snickers.'

We drove home by way of Dunkin' Donuts. My wife and I sat with him at the kitchen table and watched him eat five Boston cream doughnuts, which he washed down with two glasses of milk. Then he said he wanted to go and lie down awhile. It took him whole minutes to get up the stairs.

My wife turned to me with a look of perfect blankness.

'Please just don't say anything,' I said.

In the afternoon, after Katz had rested, he and I visited Dave Mengle and got him fitted with a backpack and a tent and sleeping bag and all the rest of it, and then went to K-Mart for a groundsheet and thermal underwear and some other small things. After that he rested some more.

The following day we went to the supermarket to buy provisions for our first week on the trail. I knew nothing about cooking, but Katz had been looking after himself for years and had a repertoire of dishes, principally involving peanut butter, tuna and noodles stirred together in a pot, that he thought would transfer nicely to a camping milieu, but he also piled lots of other things into the trolley – four large pepperoni sausages, five pounds of rice, assorted packets of cookies, oatmeal, raisins, M&Ms, Spam, more Snickers, sunflower seeds, Graham crackers, instant mashed potatoes, two large bags of brown sugar – these, he said confidingly, were absolutely vital – several sticks of beef jerky, a couple of bricks of cheese, a tinned ham, and the full range of gooey and evidently imperishable cakes and doughnuts produced by a company called Little Debbie.

'You know, I don't think we'll be able to carry all this,' I suggested as he placed a horsecollar-shaped bologna in the trolley.

Katz surveyed the trolley grimly. 'Yeah, you're right,' he agreed. 'Let's start again.'

He abandoned the trolley there and went off for another one. We went round again, this time trying to be more intelligently selective, but we still ended up with clearly too much.

We took everything home, divided it up, and went off to pack – Katz to the bedroom where all his other stuff was, I to my basement HQ. I packed for two hours, but I couldn't begin to get everything in. I put aside books and notebooks and nearly all my spare clothes, and tried lots of different combinations, but every time I finished I would turn to find something large and important left over. Eventually I went upstairs to see how Katz was doing. He was lying on the bed, listening to his Walkman. Stuff was scattered everywhere. His backpack was limp and unattended. Little percussive hisses of music were leaking from his ears.

'Aren't you packing?' I said.

'Yeah.'

I waited a minute, thinking he would bound up, but he didn't move. 'Forgive me, Stephen, but you give the impression that you are lying down.'

'Yeah.'

'Can you actually hear what I'm saying?'

'Yeah, in a minute.'

I sighed and went back down to the basement.

Katz said little during dinner and afterwards returned to his room. We heard nothing more from him throughout the evening, but about midnight, as we lay in bed, noises began to float to us through the walls – clompings and mutterings, sounds like furniture being dragged across the floor, and brief enraged outbursts, interspersed with long periods of silence. I held my wife's hand and couldn't think of anything to say.

In the morning, I tapped on Katz's door and eventually put my head in. He was asleep, fully dressed, on top of a tumult of bedding. The mattress was partway off the bed, as if he had been engaged in the night in some scuffle with intruders. His pack was full, but unsecured, and personal effects were still liberally distributed around the room. I told him we had to leave in an hour to catch our plane.

'Yeah,' he said.

Twenty minutes later, he came downstairs, laboriously and with a great deal of soft cursing. Without even looking you could tell he was coming down sideways and with care, as if the steps were glazed with ice. He was wearing his pack. Things were tied to it all over – a pair of grubby sneakers and what looked like a pair of dress boots, his pots and pans, a Laura Ashley carrier bag evidently appropriated from my wife's wardrobe and filled now with God knows what. 'This is the best I could do,' he said. 'I had to leave a few things.'

I nodded. I'd left a few things, too – notably the oatmeal, which I didn't like anyway, and the more disgusting-looking of the Little Debbie cakes, which is to say all of them.

My wife drove us to the airport in Manchester, through blowing snow, in the kind of awkward silence that precedes a long separation. Katz sat in the back and ate doughnuts. At the airport, she presented me with a knobbly walking stick the children had bought me. It had a red bow on it. I wanted to burst into tears – or, better still, climb in the car and speed off while Katz was still frowning over his new, unfamiliar straps. She squeezed my arm, gave a weak smile and went.

I watched her go, then went into the terminal with Katz. The man at the check-in desk looked at our tickets to Atlanta and our packs and said – quite alertly, I thought, for a person wearing a short-sleeved shirt in winter – 'You fellows hiking the Appalachian Trail?'

'Sure are,' said Katz proudly.

'Lot of trouble with wolves down in Georgia, you know.'

'Really?' Katz was all ears.

'Oh, yeah. Coupla people been attacked recently. Pretty savagely, too, from what I hear.' He messed around with tickets and luggage tags for a minute. 'Hope you brought some long underwear.'

Katz screwed up his face. 'For *wolves*?'

'No, for the weather. There's gonna be record cold down there over the next four or five days. Gonna be *well* below zero in Atlanta tonight.'

'Oh, great,' Katz said and gave a ruptured, disconsolate sigh. He looked challengingly at the man. 'Any other news for us? Hospital call to say we got cancer or anything?'

The man beamed and slapped the tickets down on the counter. 'No, that's about it, but you have a real good trip. And hey' – he was addressing Katz now, in a lower voice – 'you watch out for those wolves, son, because between you and me you look like pretty good eating.' He gave a wink.

'Jesus,' said Katz in a low voice, and looked deeply, deeply gloomy.

We took the escalator up to our gate. 'And they won't feed us on this plane either, you know,' he announced with a curious bitter finality.

CHAPTER THREE

IT STARTED WITH BENTON MACKAYE, A MILD, KINDLY, INFINITELY well-meaning visionary who in the summer of 1921 unveiled an ambitious plan for a hiking trail to his friend Charles Harris Whitaker, editor of a leading architectural journal. To say that MacKaye's life at this point was not going well would be to engage in heartless understatement. In the previous decade he had been fired from a job at Harvard, eased out of a position at the National Forest Service, and eventually, for want of a better place to stick him, given a desk at the Labor Department, a federal agency, with a vague assignment to come up with ideas to improve efficiency and morale. There, he dutifully produced ambitious, unworkable proposals which were received with amused tolerance and promptly binned. In April 1921 his wife, a well-known pacifist and suffragette named Jessie Hardy Stubbs, flung herself off a bridge over the East River in New York and drowned.

It was against this background, just ten weeks later, that he offered Whitaker his idea for an Appalachian Trail, and the proposal was published in the somewhat unlikely forum of Whitaker's *Journal of the American Institute of Architects* the following October. A hiking trail was only part of MacKaye's grand vision. He saw the AT as a thread connecting a network of mountaintop work camps where pale, depleted urban workers in their thousands would come and engage in healthful toil in a selfless spirit and refresh themselves on nature. There were to be hostels and inns and seasonal study centres, and eventually permanent woodland villages – 'self-owning' communities whose inhabitants would support themselves with co-operative 'non-industrial activity' based on forestry, farming and crafts. The whole would be, as MacKaye ecstatically described it, 'a retreat from profit' – a notion that others saw as 'smacking of Bolshevism', in the words of one biographer.

At the time of MacKaye's proposal there were already several hiking clubs in the eastern United States – the Green Mountain Club, the Dartmouth Outing Club, the venerable Appalachian Mountain Club, among others – and these mostly patrician organizations already owned and maintained hundreds of miles of mountain and woodland trails, mostly in New England. In 1925 representatives of the leading clubs met in Washington and founded the Appalachian Trail Conference with a view to constructing a 1,200-mile-long trail connecting the two highest peaks in the east: 6,684-foot Mount Mitchell in North Carolina and the slightly smaller (by 396 feet) Mount Washington in New Hampshire. In fact, however, for the next five years nothing happened, largely because MacKaye occupied himself with refining and expanding his vision until he and it were only tangentially connected to the real world.

Not until 1930, when a young admiralty lawyer in Washington and keen hiker named Myron Avery took over the development of the project, did work actually begin, but suddenly it moved on apace. Avery was not evidently a lovable fellow. As one contemporary put it, he left two trails from Maine to Georgia: 'One was of hurt feelings and bruised egos. The other was the AT.' He had no patience with MacKaye and his 'quasi-mystical epigrams', and the two never got along. In 1935, they had an acrimonious falling out over the development of the trail through Shenandoah National Park – Avery was willing to accommodate the building of a scenic highway through the mountains; MacKaye thought it a betrayal of founding principles – and they never spoke again.

MacKaye always gets the credit for the trail, but largely this was because he lived to be ninety-six and had a good head of white hair; he was always available in later years to say a few words at ceremonies on sunny hillsides. Avery on the other hand died in 1952, a quarter-century before MacKaye and when the trail was still little known. But it was really Avery's trail. He mapped it out, bullied and cajoled clubs into producing volunteer crews, and personally superintended the construction of hundreds of miles of path. He extended its planned length from 1,200 miles to well over

2,000, and before it was finished had walked every inch of it. In under seven years, using volunteer labour, he built a 2,000-mile trail through mountain wilderness. Armies have done less.

The Appalachian Trail was formally completed on 14 August 1937 with the clearing of a two-mile stretch of woods in a remote part of Maine. Remarkably, the building of the longest footpath in the world attracted almost no attention. Avery was not one for publicity and by this time MacKaye had retired in a funk. No newspapers noted the achievement. There was no formal celebration to mark the occasion.

The path they built had no historical basis. It didn't follow any Indian trails or colonial post roads. It didn't even seek out the best views, or highest hills or most notable landmarks. In the end, it went nowhere near Mount Mitchell, though it did take in Mount Washington and then carried on another 350 miles to Mount Katahdin in Maine. (Avery, who had grown up in Maine and done his formative hiking there, was most insistent on this.) Essentially it went where access could be gained, mostly high up on the hills, over lonely ridges and forgotten hollows that no one had ever used or coveted, or sometimes even named. It fell short of the actual southern end of the Appalachian Mountain chain by 150 miles, and of the northern end by nearer 700. The work camps and chalets, the schools and study centres, were never built.

Still, quite a lot of the original impulse behind MacKaye's vision survives. All 2,100 miles of the trail, as well as side trails, footbridges, signs, blazes, and shelters, are impeccably maintained by volunteers – indeed, the Appalachian Trail is said to be the largest volunteer-run undertaking on the planet. It remains gloriously free of commercialism. The Appalachian Trail Conference didn't hire its first paid employee until 1968, and retains the air of a friendly, accessible, well-intentioned outfit. The AT is no longer the longest long-distance footpath in the world – the Pacific Crest and Continental Divide trails, both out west, are slightly longer – but it will always be the first and greatest. It has a lot of friends. It deserves them.

Almost from the day of its opening, the trail has had to be moved around. First, 118 miles in Virginia were rerouted to accommodate the construction of Skyline Drive through Shenandoah National Park. Then, in 1958, overdevelopment on and around Mount Oglethorpe in Georgia necessitated lopping 20 miles off the trail's southern end and moving the start to Springer Mountain, in the protected wilderness of the Chattahoochee National Forest. Ten years later, the Maine Appalachian Trail Club rerouted 263 miles of trail – half its total length across the state – removing the trail from logging roads and putting it back in the wilds. Even now the trail is never quite the same from one year to the next.

The hardest part about hiking the Appalachian Trail is getting onto it, nowhere more than at its ends. Springer Mountain, the launching-off point in the south, is seven miles from the nearest highway, at a place called Amicalola Falls State Park, which in turn is a good way from anywhere. From Atlanta, the nearest outlet to the wider world, you have a choice of one train or two buses a day to Gainesville, and then you are still 40 miles short of being 7 miles short of the start of the trail, as it were. (To and from Katahdin in Maine is even more problematic.) Fortunately, there are people who will pick you up at Atlanta and take you to Amicalola for a fee. Thus it was that Katz and I delivered ourselves into the hands of a large, friendly guy in a baseball cap named Wes Wisson, who had agreed to take us from the airport in Atlanta to Amicalola Falls Lodge, our setting-off point for Springer, for $60.

Every year between early March and late April, about 2,000 hikers set off from Springer, most of them intending to go all the way to Katahdin. Only about 10 per cent actually make it. Half don't make it past central Virginia, less than a third of the way. A quarter get no further than North Carolina, the next state. Ten per cent drop out the first week. Wisson has seen it all.

'Last year, I dropped a guy off at the trailhead,' he told us as we tooled north through darkening pine forests towards the rugged hills of north Georgia. 'Three days later he calls me from the payphone at Woody Gap – that's the first payphone you come to. Says he wants to go home, that the trail wasn't what he expected it to be. So I drive him back to the airport. Two days after that he's back in Atlanta. Says his wife made him come back because he'd spent all this money on equipment and she wasn't going to let him quit so easy. So I drop him off at the trailhead. Three days later he phones from Woody Gap again. He wants to go to the airport. "Well, what about your wife?" I says. And he says, "This time I'm not going home."'

'How far is it to Woody Gap?' I asked.

'Twenty-one miles from Springer. Doesn't seem much, does it? I mean, he'd come all the way from Ohio.'

'So why did he quit so soon?'

'He said it wasn't what he expected it to be. They all say that. Just last week I had three ladies from California – middle-aged gals, real nice, kind of giggly but, you know, *nice* – I dropped them off and they were in real high spirits. About four hours later they called and said they wanted to go home. They'd come all the way from California, you understand, spent God knows how much on airfares and equipment – I mean, they had the nicest stuff you ever saw, all brand new and top of the range – and they'd walked maybe a mile and a half before quitting. Said it wasn't what they expected.'

'What do they expect?'

'Who knows? Escalators maybe. It's hills and rocks and woods and a trail. You don't got to do a whole lot of scientific research to work that out. But you'd be amazed how many people quit. Then again, I had a guy, oh about six weeks ago, who shoulda quit and didn't. He was coming off the trail. He'd walked from Maine on his own. It took him eight months, longer than it takes most people, and I don't think he'd seen anybody for the last several weeks. When he came off he was just a trembling wreck. I had his wife with me. She'd come to meet him, and he just fell into her arms and started weeping. Couldn't talk at all. He was like that all the way to the airport. I've never seen anybody so relieved to have anything done with, and I kept thinking, "Well, you know, sir, hiking the Appalachian Trail is a voluntary endeavour," but of course I didn't say anything.'

'So can you tell when you drop people off whether they're gonna make it?'

'Pretty generally.'

'And do you think we'll make it?' said Katz.

He looked at us each in turn. 'Oh, you'll make it all right,' he replied, but his expression said otherwise.

Amicalola Falls Lodge was an eyrie high on a mountainside, reached up a long, winding road through the woods. The man at the airport in Manchester had certainly seen the right weather forecast. It was piercingly, shockingly cold when we stepped from the car. There was a treacherous, icy wind that seemed to dart round from every angle and then zip up sleeves and trouser legs. 'Jee-zuss!' Katz cried in astonishment, as if somebody had just thrown a bucket of ice water over him, and scooted inside. I paid up and followed.

The lodge was modern, posh and very warm, with an open lobby dominated by a stone fireplace, and the sort of anonymously comfortable rooms you would find in a Holiday Inn. We parted for our rooms and agreed to rendezvous at seven. I got a Coke from a machine in the corridor, had a lavishly steamy shower involving many towels, inserted myself between crisp sheets – how long would it be till I enjoyed this kind of comfort again? – watched discouraging reports by happy, mindless people on the Weather Channel, and slept hardly at all.

I was up before daybreak and sat by the window watching as a pale dawn grudgingly exposed the surrounding landscape – a stark and seemingly boundless expanse of thick, rolling hills covered in ranks of bare trees and the meagrest dusting of snow. It didn't look terribly forbidding – these weren't the Himalayas – but it didn't look like anything you would particularly want to walk out into.

On my way to breakfast, the sun popped out, filling the world with encouraging brightness, and I stepped outside to check out the air. The cold was startling, like a slap to the face, and the wind was still bitter. Dry little pellets of snow, like tiny spheres of polystyrene, chased around in swirls. A big wall thermometer by the entrance read 11°F.

'Coldest ever for this date in Georgia,' a hotel employee said with a big pleased smile as she hurried in from the car park, then stopped and said: 'You hiking?'

'Yeah.'

'Well, better you'n me. Good luck to ya. Brrrrrrr!' And she dodged inside.

To my surprise, I felt a certain springy keenness. I was ready to hike. I had waited months for this day, after all, even if it had been mostly with foreboding. I wanted to see what was out there. All over America today people would be dragging themselves to work, stuck in traffic jams, wreathed in exhaust smoke. I was going for a walk in the woods. I was more than ready for this.

I found Katz in the dining room and he was looking laudably perky, too. This was because he had made a friend – a waitress named Rayette, who was attending to his dining requirements in a distinctly coquettish way. Rayette was six feet tall and had a face that would frighten a baby, but she seemed good-natured and was diligent with the coffee. She could not have signalled her availability to Katz more clearly if she had thrown her skirt over her head and lain across his Hungry Man Breakfast Platter. Katz in consequence was pumping testosterone.

'Ooh, I like a man who appreciates pancakes,' Rayette cooed.

'Well, honey, I sure appreciate *these* pancakes,' Katz responded, face agleam with syrup and early-morning happiness. It wasn't exactly Hepburn and Tracy, but it was strangely touching none the less.

She went off to deal with a distant customer and Katz watched her go with something like paternal pride. 'She's pretty ugly, isn't she?' he said with a big incongruous beam.

I sought for tact. 'Well, only compared with other women.'

Katz nodded thoughtfully, then fixed me with a sudden fearful look. 'You know what I look for in a female these days? A heartbeat and a full set of limbs.'

I made a sympathetic expression.

'And that's just my starting point, you understand. I'm prepared to compromise on the limbs. You think she's available?'

'I believe you might have to take a number.'

He nodded soberly. 'Probably be an idea if we ate up and got out of here.'

I was very happy with that. I drained a cup of coffee and we went off to get our things. But when we met up outside ten minutes later, togged up and ready to go, Katz was looking miserable. 'Let's stay here another night,' he said.

'What? Are you kidding?' I was completely taken aback by this. 'Why?'

'Because it's warm in there and it's cold out here.'

'We've gotta do it.'

He looked to the woods. 'We'll freeze out there.'

I looked to the woods, too. 'Yeah, probably. We've still gotta do it.'

I hoisted my pack, and took a backward stagger under the weight – it would be days before I could do this with anything approaching aplomb – jerked tight the belt and trudged off. At the edge of the woods, I glanced back to make sure Katz was following. Ahead of me spread a vast, stark world of winter-dead trees. I stepped portentously onto the path, a fragment of the original Appalachian Trail from the days when it passed here en route from Mount Oglethorpe to Springer.

The date was 9 March. We were on our way.

The route led down into a wooded valley with a chuckling

stream edged with brittle ice, which the path followed for perhaps half a mile before taking us steeply up into denser woods. This was, it quickly became evident, the base of the first big hill, Frosty Mountain, and it was immediately taxing. The sun was shining and the sky was a hearty blue, but everything at ground level was brown – brown trees, brown earth, frozen brown leaves – and the cold was unyielding. I trudged perhaps a hundred feet up the hill, then stopped, bug-eyed, breathing hard, heart kabooming alarmingly. Katz was already falling behind and panting even harder. I pressed on.

It was hell. First days on hiking trips always are. I was hopelessly out of shape – hopelessly. The pack weighed way too much. Way too much. I had never encountered anything so hard, for which I was so ill prepared. Every step was a struggle.

The hardest part was coming to terms with the constant dispiriting discovery that there is always more hill. The thing about being on a hill, as opposed to standing back from it, is that you can almost never see exactly what's to come. Between the curtain of trees on every side, the ever-receding contour of rising slope before you, and your own plodding weariness, you gradually lose track of how far you have come. Each time you haul yourself up to what you think must surely be the crest, you find that there is in fact more hill beyond, sloped at an angle that kept it from view before, and that beyond that slope there is another, and beyond that another and another, and beyond each of those more still, until it seems impossible that any hill could run on this long. Eventually you reach a height where you can see the tops of the topmost trees, with nothing but clear sky beyond, and your faltering spirit stirs – nearly there now! – but this is a pitiless deception. The elusive summit continually retreats by whatever distance you press forward, so that each time the canopy parts enough to give a view you are dismayed to see that the topmost trees are as remote, as unattainable, as before. Still you stagger on. What else can you do?

When, after ages and ages, you finally reach the tell-tale world of truly high ground, where the chilled air smells of pine sap and the vegetation is gnarled and tough and wind-bent, and push through to the mountain's open pinnacle, you are, alas, past caring. You sprawl face down on a sloping pavement of gneiss, pressed to the rock by the weight of your pack, and lie there for some minutes, reflecting in a distant, out-of-body way that you have never before looked this closely at lichen, not in fact looked this closely at anything in the natural world since you were four years old and had your first magnifying glass. Finally, with a weary puff, you roll over, unhook yourself from your pack, struggle to your feet and realize – again in a remote, light-headed, curiously not-there way – that the view is sensational: a boundless vista of wooded mountains, unmarked by human hand, marching off in every direction. This really could be heaven. It's splendid, no question, but the thought you cannot escape is that you have to walk this view – and this is the barest fraction of what you will traverse before you've finished.

You compare your map with the immediate landscape and note that the path ahead descends into a steep valley – a gorge really, not unlike the gorges the coyote is forever plunging into in Roadrunner cartoons; gorges that have actual vanishing points – which will deliver you to the base of a hill even more steep and formidable than this, and that when you scale that preposterously taxing peak you will have done 1.7 miles since breakfast, while your schedule (blithely drawn up at a kitchen table and jotted down after perhaps three seconds' consideration) calls for 8.9 miles by lunch, 16.8 by teatime, and even greater distances tomorrow.

But perhaps it is also raining, a cold, slanting, merciless rain, with thunder and lightning playing on the neighbouring hills. Perhaps a troop of Eagle Scouts comes by at a depressing trot. Perhaps you are cold and hungry and smell so bad that you can no longer smell yourself. Perhaps you want to lie down and be as the lichen: not dead exactly but just very still for a long, long time.

But of course I had all this ahead of me. Today I had nothing to do but traverse four middling mountains over seven miles of well-marked trail in clear, dry weather. It didn't seem too much to ask. It was hell.

I don't know when I lost track of Katz, but it was in the first couple of hours. At first I would wait for him to catch up, bitching every step of the way and pausing after each three or four shuffling paces to wipe his brow and look sourly at his immediate future. It was painful to behold in every way. Eventually I waited to see him pull into view, just to confirm that he was still coming, hadn't fallen to the path palpitating or thrown down his pack in disgust and gone looking for Wes Wisson. I would wait and wait and eventually his shape would appear among the trees, breathing heavily, moving with incredible slowness, and talking in a loud, bitter voice to himself. Halfway up the third big hill, the 3,400-foot-high Black Mountain, I stood and waited a long while, and thought about going back, but eventually turned and struggled on. I had enough small agonies of my own.

Seven miles seems so little, but it's not, believe me. With a pack, even for fit people it is not. You know what it's like when you're at a zoo or amusement park with a small child who won't walk another step? You hoist him lightly onto your shoulders and for a while – for a couple of minutes – it's actually kind of fun to have him up there, pretending you're going to tip him off or cruising his head towards some low projection before veering off (all being well) at the last instant. But then it starts to get uncomfortable. You feel a twinge in your neck, a tightening between your shoulder blades, and the sensation seeps and spreads until it is quite decidedly uncomfortable, and you announce to little Jimmy that you're going to have to put him down for a bit.

Of course, Jimmy bawls and won't go another step, and your partner gives you that disdainful, I-should-have-married-the-quarterback look because you haven't gone 400 yards. But, hey, it hurts. Hurts a lot. Believe me, I understand.

OK, now imagine *two* little Jimmies in a pack on your back, or, better still, something inert but weighty, something that doesn't want to be lifted, that makes it abundantly clear to you as soon as you pick it up that what it wants is to sit heavily on the ground – say, a bag of cement or a box of medical textbooks, in any case 40 pounds of profound heaviness. Imagine the jerk of the pack going on, like the pull of a down elevator. Imagine walking with that weight for hours, for days, and not along level asphalt paths with benches and refreshment kiosks at thoughtful intervals, but over a rough trail, full of sharp rocks and unyielding roots and staggering ascents that transfer enormous amounts of strain to your pale, shaking thighs. Now tilt your head back – please, this is the last thing I'll ask of you – until your neck is taut and fix your gaze on a point two miles away. That's your first climb. It's 4,682 steep feet to the top and there are lots more like it. Don't tell me that seven miles is not far.

Oh, and here's the other thing. You don't have to do this. You're not in the army. You can quit right now. Go home. See your family. Sleep in a bed. Or alternatively, you poor, sad schmuck, you can walk 2,169 miles through mountains and wilderness to Maine.

And so I trudged along for hours, in a private little world of weariness and woe, up and over imposing hills, through an endless cocktail party of trees, all the time thinking: 'I must have done seven miles by now, *surely*.' But always the wandering trail ran on.

At half past three, I climbed some steps carved into granite and found myself on a spacious rock overlook: the summit of Springer Mountain. I shed my pack and sat down heavily against a tree, astounded at how weary I was. The view was splendid – the rolling swell of the Cohutta Mountains, brushed with a bluish haze the colour of cigarette smoke, running away to a far-off horizon. The sun was already low in the sky. I rested for perhaps ten minutes, then got up and had a look around. There was a bronze plaque screwed into a boulder announcing the start of the Appalachian Trail and nearby on a post was a wooden box containing a Bic pen on a length of string and a standard spiral notebook, its pages curled from the damp air. The notebook was the trail register – I had somehow expected it to be leatherbound and funereal – and it was filled with eager entries, nearly all written in a youthful hand. There were perhaps twenty-five pages of entries since 1 January – eight entries on this day alone. Most were hurried and cheery – 'March 2nd. Well, here we are and man it's *cold*! See y'all on Katahdin! Jaimie and Spud' – but about a third were longer and more carefully reflective, with messages along the lines of 'So here I am at Springer at last. I don't know what the coming weeks hold for me, but my faith in the Lord is strong and I know I have the love and support of my family. Mom and Pookie, this trip is for you', and so on.

I waited for Katz for three-quarters of an hour, then went looking for him. The light was fading and the air was growing sharp. I walked and walked, down the hill and through the endless trees, back over ground that I had gratefully put behind me for ever, I thought. Several times I called his name and listened, but there was nothing. I walked on and on, over fallen trees I had struggled over hours ago, down slopes I could only dimly recall. My grandmother could have got this far, I kept thinking. Finally, I rounded a bend and there he was stumbling towards me, wild-haired and one-gloved, and nearer hysteria than I have ever seen a grown person.

It was hard to get the full story out of him in a coherent flow, because he was so furious, but I gathered he had thrown many items from his pack over a cliff in a temper. None of the things that had been dangling from the outside were there any longer, including his water bottle.

'What did you get rid of?' I asked, trying not to betray too much alarm.

'Heavy fucking shit, that's what. The pepperoni, the rice, the brown sugar, the Spam, I don't know what all. Lots. Fuck.' Katz was almost cataleptic with displeasure. He acted as if he had been deeply betrayed by the trail. It wasn't, I guess, what he had expected.

I saw his glove lying in the path 30 yards back and went to retrieve it.

'OK,' I said when I returned, 'you haven't got too far to go.'

'How far?'

'Maybe a mile.'

'Shit,' he said bitterly.

'I'll take your pack.' I lifted it onto my back. It wasn't exactly empty now, but it was decidedly moderate in weight. God knows what he had thrown out.

We trudged up the hill to the summit in the enveloping dusk. A few hundred yards beyond the summit was a campsite with a wooden shelter in a big grassy clearing against a backdrop of black trees. There were a lot of people there, far more than I'd expected this early in the season. The shelter – a basic, three-sided affair with a sloping roof – looked crowded and there were a dozen or so tents scattered around the open ground. Nearly everywhere there was the hiss of little campstoves, threads of rising food smoke and the movements of lanky young people.

I found us a site on the edge of the clearing, almost in the woods, off by ourselves.

'I don't know how to put up my tent,' Katz said in a petulant tone.

'Well, I'll put it up for you then.' You big soft flabby baby. Suddenly I was very tired.

He sat on a log and watched me put up his tent. When I finished, he pushed in his pad and sleeping bag and crawled in after. I busied myself with my tent, fussily made it into a little home. When I completed my work and straightened up I realized there was no sound or movement from within his.

'Have you gone to bed?' I said, aghast.

'Yump,' he replied in a kind of affirmative growl.

'That's it? You've retired? With no dinner?'

'Yump.'

I stood for a minute, speechless and flummoxed, too tired to be indignant. Too tired to be hungry either, come to that. I crawled into my tent, brought in a water bottle and book, laid out my knife and torch for purposes of nocturnal illumination and defence, and finally shimmied into the bag, more grateful than I have ever been to be horizontal. I was asleep in moments. I don't believe I have ever slept so well.

When I awoke it was daylight. The inside of my tent was coated in a curious flaky rime, which I realized after a moment was all my night-time snores, condensed and frozen and pasted to the fabric, as if into a scrapbook of respiratory memories. My water bottle was frozen solid. This seemed gratifyingly macho, and I examined it with interest, as if it were a rare mineral. I was surprisingly snug in my bag and in no hurry at all to put myself through the foolishness of climbing hills, so I just lay there as if under grave orders not to move. After a while I became aware that Katz was moving around outside, grunting softly as if from aches and doing something that sounded improbably industrious.

After a minute or two, he came and crouched by my tent, his form a dark shadow on the fabric. He didn't ask if I was awake or anything, but just said in a quiet voice: 'Was I, would you say, a complete asshole last night?'

'Yes you were, Stephen.'

He was quiet a moment. 'I'm making coffee.' I gathered this was his way of an apology.

'That's very nice.'

'Buggering cold out here.'

'And in here.'

'My water bottle froze.'

'Mine, too.'

I unzipped myself from my nylon womb and emerged on creaking joints. It seemed very strange – very novel – to be standing outdoors in long johns. Katz was crouched over the campstove, boiling a pan of water. We seemed to be the only campers awake. It was cold, but perhaps just a trifle warmer than the day before and a low dawn sun burning through the trees looked cautiously promising.

'How do you feel?' he said.

I flexed my legs experimentally. 'Not too bad, actually.'

'Me either.'

He poured water into the filter cone. 'I'm going to be good today,' he promised.

'Good.' I watched over his shoulder. 'Is there a reason', I asked, 'why you are filtering the coffee with toilet paper?'

'I, oh . . . I threw out the filter papers.'

I gave a sound that wasn't quite a laugh. 'They couldn't have weighed two ounces.'

'I know, but they were great for throwing. Fluttered all over.' He dribbled on more water. 'The toilet paper seems to be working OK, though.'

We watched it drip through and were strangely proud. Our first refreshment in the wilderness. He handed me a cup of coffee. It was swimming in grounds and little flecks of pink tissue, but it was piping hot, which was the main thing.

He gave me an apologetic look. 'I threw out the brown sugar too, so there won't be any sugar for the oatmeal.'

Ah. 'Actually, there won't be any oatmeal for the oatmeal. I left it in New Hampshire.'

He looked at me. 'Really?' Then he added, as if for the record: 'I love oatmeal.'

'What about some of that cheese?'

He shook his head. 'Flung.'

'Peanuts?'

'Flung.'

'Spam?'

'Really flung.'

This was beginning to sound a trifle grave. 'What about the baloney?'

'Oh, I ate that at Amicalola,' he said, as if it had been weeks ago, then added in a tone of sudden magnanimous concession, 'Hey, I'm happy with a cup of coffee and a couple of Little Debbies.'

I gave a small grimace. 'I left the Little Debbies, too.'

His face expanded. 'You left the Little Debbies?'

I nodded apologetically.

'*All* of them?'

I nodded.

He breathed out hard. This really was grave – a serious challenge, apart from anything else, to his promised equanimity. We decided we had better take inventory. We cleared a space on a groundsheet and pooled our commissary. It was startlingly austere – some dried noodles, one bag of rice, raisins, coffee, salt, a good supply of chocolate bars, and toilet paper. That was about it.

We breakfasted on a Snickers bar and coffee, packed up our

camp, hoisted our packs with a sideways stagger and set off once again.

'I can't believe you left the Little Debbies,' Katz said, and immediately began to fall behind.

CHAPTER FOUR

WOODS ARE NOT LIKE OTHER SPACES. TO BEGIN WITH THEY ARE CUBIC. Their trees surround you, loom over you, press in from all sides. Woods choke off views, and leave you muddled and without bearings. They make you feel small and confused and vulnerable, like a small child lost in a crowd of strange legs. Stand in a desert or prairie and you know you are in a big space. Stand in a wood and you only sense it. They are a vast, featureless nowhere. And they are alive.

So woods are spooky. Quite apart from the thought that they may harbour wild beasts and armed, genetically challenged fellows named Zeke and Festus, there is something innately sinister about them – some ineffable thing that makes you sense an atmosphere of pregnant doom with every step and leaves you profoundly aware that you are out of your element and ought to keep your ears pricked. Though you tell yourself it's preposterous, you can't quite shake the feeling that you are being watched. You order yourself to be serene – it's just a wood for goodness' sake – but really you are jumpier than Don Knotts with pistol drawn. Every sudden noise – the crack of a falling limb, the crash of a bolting deer – makes you spin in alarm and stifle a plea for mercy. Whatever mechanism within you is responsible for adrenalin, it has never been so sleek and polished – so keenly poised to pump out a warming squirt of adrenal fluid. Even asleep you are a coiled spring.

The American woods have been unnerving people for 300 years. The inestimably priggish and tiresome Henry David Thoreau thought nature was splendid, splendid indeed, so long as he could stroll to town for cakes and barley wine, but when he experienced real wilderness, on a visit to Katahdin in 1846, he was unnerved to the core. This wasn't the tame world of overgrown orchards and sun-dappled paths that passed for wilderness in suburban Concord, Massachusetts, but a forbidding, oppressive, primeval country that was 'grim and wild . . . savage and dreary', fit only for 'men nearer of kin to the rocks and wild animals than we'. The experience left him, in the words of one biographer, 'near hysterical'.

But even men far tougher and more attuned to the wilderness than Thoreau were sobered by its strange and palpable menace. Daniel Boone, who not only wrestled bears but tried to date their sisters, described corners of the southern Appalachians as 'so wild and horrid that it is impossible to behold them without terror'. When Daniel Boone is uneasy, you know it is time to watch your step.

When the first Europeans arrived in the New World there were perhaps 950 million acres of woodland in what would become the lower forty-eight states. The Chattahoochee National Forest through which Katz and I now trudged was part of an immense unbroken canopy stretching from southern Alabama to Canada and beyond, and from the shores of the Atlantic to the distant grasslands of the Missouri River.

Most of that forest is now gone, but what survives is more impressive than you might expect. The Chattahoochee is part of four million acres – 6,000 square miles – of federally owned forest stretching up to the Great Smoky Mountains and beyond, and spreading sideways across four states. On a map of the United States it is an incidental smudge of green, but on foot the scale of it is colossal. It would be four days before Katz and I crossed a public highway, eight days till we came to a town.

And so we walked. We walked up mountains and through high, forgotten hollows, along lonesome ridges with long views of more ridges, over grassy balds and down rocky, twisting, jarring descents, and through mile after endless mile of dark, deep, silent woods, on a wandering trail eighteen inches wide and marked with rectangular white blazes (two inches wide, six long) slapped at intervals on the grey-barked trees. Walking is what we did.

Compared with most other places in the developed world, America is still to a remarkable extent a land of forests. One third of the landscape of the lower forty-eight states is covered in trees – 728 million acres in all. Maine alone has ten million uninhabited acres. That's 15,600 square miles – an area considerably bigger than Belgium – without a single permanent resident. Altogether just 2 per cent of the United States is classified as built up.

About 240 million acres of America's forests are owned by the government. The bulk of this – 191 million acres, spread over 155 parcels of land – is held by the US Forest Service under the designations of National Forests, National Grasslands, and National Recreation Areas. All this sounds soothingly untrampled and ecological, but in fact a great deal of Forest Service land is designated 'multiple-use', which is generously interpreted to allow any number of boisterous activities – mining, oil and gas extraction, ski resorts (137 of them), condominium developments, snowmobiling, off-road vehicle scrambling, and lots and lots and lots of logging – that seem curiously incompatible with woodland serenity.

The Forest Service is truly an extraordinary institution. It was conceived a century ago as a kind of woodland bank, a permanent repository of American timber, when people grew alarmed at the rate at which American forests were falling. Its remit was to manage and protect these resources for the nation. These were not intended to be parks. Private companies would be granted leases to extract minerals and harvest timber, but they would be required to do so in a restrained, intelligent way.

That was the plan. In the event, mostly what the Forest Service did was build roads. I am not kidding. There are 378,000 miles of roads in America's national forests. That may seem a meaningless figure, so look at it this way. It is eight times the total mileage of America's interstate highway system. It is the largest road system in the world in the control of a single body. The Forest Service has the second highest number of road engineers of any government institution on the planet. To say that these guys like to build roads barely hints at their level of dedication. Show them a stand of trees anywhere and they will regard it thoughtfully for a long while, and say, 'You know, we could put a road here.' It is the avowed aim of the US Forest Service to construct 580,000 miles of additional forest road by the middle of the next century.

The reason the Forest Service builds these roads, quite apart from the deep pleasure of doing noisy things in the woods with big yellow machines, is to allow private timber companies to get to previously inaccessible stands of trees. Of the Forest Service's 150 million acres of loggable land, about two-thirds is held in store for the future. The remaining one-third – 49 million acres, or an area roughly twice the size of Ohio – is available for logging. It allows huge swathes of land to be clear cut, including (to take one recent example) 209 acres of thousand-year-old redwoods in Oregon's Umpqua National Forest.

In 1987, it casually announced that it would allow private timber interests to remove hundreds of acres of wood a year from the venerable and verdant Pisgah National Forest, next door to the Great Smoky Mountains National Park, and that 80 per cent of that would be through what it calls 'scientific forestry' – clear cutting – which is not only a brutal visual affront to any landscape, but brings huge, reckless washoffs that gully the soil, robbing it of nutrients and disrupting ecologies further downstream, sometimes for miles. This isn't science. It's rape.

And yet the Forest Service grinds on. By the late 1980s – this is so extraordinary I can hardly stand it – it was the only significant player in the American timber industry that was cutting down trees faster than it replaced them. Moreover it was doing this with the most sumptuous inefficiency. Eighty per cent of its leasing arrangements lost money, often vast amounts of it. In one typical deal, the Forest Service sold hundred-year-old lodgepole pines in the Targhee National Forest in Idaho for about $2 each after spending $4 per tree surveying the land, drawing up contracts and – of course – building roads. Between 1989 and 1997, it lost an average of $242 million a year – almost $2 billion all told, according to the Wilderness Society. This is all so discouraging that I think we'll leave it here and return to our two lonely heroes trudging through the lost world of the Chattahoochee.

In 1890, a railway man from Cincinnati named Henry C. Bagley came to this part of Georgia, saw the stately white pines and poplars, and was so moved by their towering majesty and abundance that he decided to chop them all down. They were worth a lot of money. Besides, freighting the timber to northern mills would keep his railway cars puffing. In consequence over the next thirty years nearly all the hills of north Georgia were turned into sunny groves of stumps. By 1920, foresters in the South were taking away 15.4 billion board feet of timber a year. It wasn't until the 1930s, when the Chattahoochee National Forest was officially formed, that nature was invited back in, so the forest we walked through now was really just a strapping adolescent.

There is a strange frozen violence in a forest out of season. Every glade and dale seemed to have just completed some massive cataclysm. Downed trees lay across the path every fifty or sixty yards, often with great bomb craters of dirt around their splayed roots. Dozens more lay rotting on the slopes, and every third or fourth tree, it seemed, was leaning steeply on a neighbour. It was as if the trees couldn't wait to fall over, as if their purpose in the universal scheme of things was to grow big enough to topple with a really good, splintering crash. I was forever coming up to trees so precariously and weightily tipped over the path that I would waver, then scoot under, fearing the crush of really unfortunate timing and imagining Katz coming along a few minutes later, regarding my wriggling legs and saying, 'Shit, Bryson, what're you doing under there?' But no trees fell. Everywhere the woods were still and preternaturally quiet. Except for the occasional gurgle of running water and the shuffle of fallen leaves in the wind, there was almost never a sound.

The woods were silent because spring had not yet come. In a normal year we would be walking into the zestful bounty of a southern mountain spring, through a radiant, productive, newborn world alive with the zip of insects and the fussy twitter of birds; a world bursting with fresh wholesome air and that rich, velvety, lung-filling smell of chlorophyll you get when you push through low branches. Above all there would be wild flowers in dazzling profusion, blossoming from every twig, pushing valiantly through the fertile litter on the forest floor, carpeting every sunny slope and stream bank – trillium and trailing arbutus, Dutchmen's breeches, jack-in-the-pulpit, mandrake, violets, snowy bluets, buttercups and bloodroot, dwarf iris, columbine and wood sorrel, and other cheerful nodding wonders almost beyond counting. There are 1,500 types of wild flower in the southern Appalachians, forty rare types in the north Georgia woods alone. They are a sight to lift the hardest heart. Instead we trudged through a cold, silent world of bare trees, beneath pewter skies, on ground like iron.

We fell into a simple routine. Each morning we rose at first light, shivering and rubbing arms, made coffee, broke camp, ate a couple of fistfuls of raisins, and set off into the silent woods. We would walk from about half past seven to four. We seldom walked together – our paces didn't match – but every couple of hours I would sit on a log (always surveying the surrounding undergrowth for the rustle of bear or boar) and wait for Katz to catch up, to make sure everything was OK. Sometimes other hikers would come along, and they would tell me where Katz was and how he was progressing, which was nearly always slowly but gamely. The trail was much harder for him than for me, and to his credit he tried not to bitch. It never escaped me for a moment that he didn't have to be there.

I had thought we would have a jump on the crowds, but there was a fair scattering of other hikers – three students from Rutgers University in New Jersey; an astoundingly fit older couple with tiny packs hiking to their daughter's wedding in far-off Virginia; a gawky kid from Florida named Jonathan; perhaps two dozen of us altogether in the same general neck of the woods, all heading north. Because everyone walks at different rates and rests at different times, three or four times a day you bump into some or all of your fellow hikers, especially on mountaintops with panoramic views or beside streams with good water, and above all at the wooden shelters that stand at distant intervals, ostensibly but not always actually, a day's hike apart in clearings just off the trail. In consequence you get to know your fellow hikers at least a little, quite well if you meet them nightly at the shelters. You become part of an informal clump, a loose and sympathetic affiliation of people from different age groups and walks of life but all experiencing the same weather, same discomforts, same landscapes, same eccentric impulse to hike to Maine.

Even at busy times, however, the woods are great providers of solitude, and I encountered long periods of perfect aloneness, when I didn't see another soul for hours, and many times when I would wait for Katz for a long spell and no other hiker would come along. When that happened, I would leave my pack and go back and find him, to see that he was all right, which always pleased him. Sometimes he would be proudly bearing my stick, which I had left by a tree when I had stopped to tie my laces or adjust my pack. We seemed to be looking out for each other. It was very nice. I can put it no other way.

Around four we would find a spot to camp, and pitch our tents. One of us would go off to fetch and filter water while the other prepared a sludge of steamy noodles. Sometimes we would talk, but mostly we existed in a kind of companionable silence. By six o'clock, dark and cold and weariness would force us to our tents. Katz went to sleep instantly, as far as I could tell. I would read for an hour or so with my curiously inefficient little miner's lamp, its beam throwing quirky, concentric circles of light onto the page, like the light of a bicycle lamp, until my shoulders and arms grew chilly out of the bag, and heavy from tilting the book at awkward angles to catch the nervous light. So I would put myself in darkness and lie there listening to the peculiarly clear, articulated noises of the forest at night, the sighs and fidgets of wind and leaves, the weary groan of boughs, the endless murmurings and stirrings, like the noises of a convalescent ward after lights out, until at last I fell heavily asleep. In the morning we would rise shivering and rubbing arms, wordlessly repeat our small chores, fill and hoist our packs and venture into the great entangling forest again.

On the fourth evening we made a friend. We were sitting in a nice little clearing beside the trail, our tents pitched, eating our noodles, savouring the exquisite pleasure of just sitting, when a plumpish, bespectacled young woman in a red jacket and the customary out-sized pack came along. She regarded us with the crinkled squint of someone who is either chronically confused or can't see very well. We exchanged hellos and the usual banalities about the weather and where we were. Then she squinted at the gathering gloom and announced she would camp with us.

Her name was Mary Ellen. She was from Florida, and she was, as Katz for ever after termed her in a special tone of awe, a piece of work. She talked nonstop, except when she was clearing out her Eustachian tubes, which she did frequently, by pinching her nose and blowing out with a series of violent and alarming snorts of a sort that would make a dog leave the sofa and get under a table in the next room. I have long known that it is part of God's plan for me to spend a little time with each of the most stupid people on earth, and Mary Ellen was proof that even in the Appalachian woods I would not be spared. It became evident from the first moment that she was a rarity.

'So what are you guys eating?' she said, plonking herself down on a spare log and lifting her head to peer into our bowls. 'Noodles? Big mistake. Noodles have got like no energy. I mean like zero.' She unblocked her ears. 'Is that a Starship tent?'

I looked at my tent. 'I don't know.'

'Big mistake. They must have seen you coming at the camping store. What did you pay for it?'

'I don't know.'

'Too much, that's how much. You should have got a three-season tent.'

'It is a three-season tent.'

'Pardon me saying so, but it is like seriously dumb to come out here in March without a three-season tent.' She unblocked her ears.

'It is a three-season tent.'

'You're lucky you haven't froze yet. You should go back and like punch out the guy that sold it to you because he's been like, you know, negligible selling you that.'

'Believe me, it is a three-season tent.'

She unblocked her ears and shook her head impatiently. 'That's a three-season tent.' She indicated Katz's tent.

'*That*'s exactly the same tent.'

She glanced at it again. 'Whatever. How many miles did you do today?'

'About ten.' Actually we had done eight point four – but this had included several formidable escarpments, including a notable wall of hell called Preaching Rock, the highest eminence since Springer Mountain, for which we had awarded ourselves bonus miles, for purposes of morale.

'Ten miles? Is that all? You guys must be like *really* out of shape. I did fourteen-two.'

'How many have your lips done?' said Katz, looking up from his noodles.

She fixed him with one of her more severe squints. 'Same as the rest of me, of course.' She gave me a private look as if to say, 'Is your friend like seriously *weird* or something?' She cleared her ears. 'I started at Gooch Gap.'

'So did we. That's only eight point four miles.'

She shook her head sharply, as if shooing a particularly tenacious fly. 'Fourteen-two.'

'No, really, it's only eight point four.'

'Excuse me, but I just *walked* it. I think I ought to know.' And then suddenly: 'God, are those Timberland boots? *Mega* mistake. How much did you pay for them?'

And so it went. Eventually I went off to swill out the bowls and hang the food bag. When I came back, she was fixing her own dinner, but still talking away at Katz.

'You know what your problem is?' she was saying. 'Pardon my French, but you're too fat.'

Katz looked at her in quiet wonder. 'Excuse me?'

'You're too fat. You should have lost weight before you came out here. Shoulda done some training, 'cause you could have like a serious, you know, heart thing out here.'

'Heart thing?'

'You know, when your heart stops and you like, you know, die.'

'Do you mean a heart attack?'

'That's it.'

Mary Ellen, it should be noted, was not short on flesh herself, and unwisely at that moment she leaned over to get something from her pack, displaying an expanse of backside on which you could have projected motion pictures for, let us say, an army base. It was an interesting test of Katz's forbearance. He said nothing, but rose to go for a pee and out of the side of his mouth as he passed me he rendered a certain convenient expletive as three low, dismayed syllables, like the call of a freight train in the night.

The next day, as always, we rose chilled and feeling wretched, and set about the business of attending to our small tasks, but this time with the additional strain of having our every move examined and rated. While we ate raisins and drank coffee with flecks of toilet paper in it, Mary Ellen gorged on a multi-course breakfast of oatmeal, Pop Tarts, trail mix and a dozen small squares of chocolate, which she lined up in a row on the log beside her. We watched like orphaned refugees while she plumped her jowls with food and enlightened us as to our shortcomings with regard to diet, equipment and general manliness.

And then, now a trio, we set off into the woods. Mary Ellen walked sometimes with me and sometimes with Katz, but always with one of us. It was apparent that for all her bluster she was majestically inexperienced and untrailworthy – she hadn't the faintest idea how to read a map, for one thing – and ill at ease on her own in the wilderness. I couldn't help feeling a little sorry for her. Besides, I began to find her strangely entertaining. She had the most extraordinarily redundant turn of phrase. She would say things like 'There's a stream of water over there', and 'It's nearly ten o'clock a.m.'. Once, in reference to winters in central Florida, she solemnly informed me, 'We usually get frosts once or twice a winter, but this year we had 'em a couple of times.' Katz for his part clearly dreaded her company and winced beneath her tireless urgings to smarten his pace.

For once, the weather was kindly – more autumnal than spring-like in feel, but gratifyingly mild. By ten o'clock, the temperature was comfortably in the sixties. For the first time since Amicalola I took off my jacket, and realized with mild perplexity that I had absolutely no place to put it. I tied it to my pack with a strap and trudged on.

We laboured four miles up and over Blood Mountain, at 4,461 feet the highest and toughest eminence on the trail in Georgia, then began a steep and exciting two-mile descent towards Neels Gap. Exciting because there was a shop at Neels Gap, at a place called the Walasi-Yi Inn, where you could buy sandwiches and ice cream. At about half past one, we heard a novel sound – motor traffic – and a few minutes later we emerged from the woods onto US Highway 19 and 129, which despite having two numbers was really just a back road through a high pass between wooded nowheres. Directly across the road was the Walasi-Yi Inn, a splendid stone building constructed by the Civilian Conservation Corps, a kind of army of the unemployed, during the Great Depression in the 1930s, and now a combination of hiking outfitters, grocery, bookshop and youth hostel. We hastened across the road – positively scurried across – and went inside.

Now it may seem to stretch credibility to suggest that things like a paved highway, the whoosh of passing cars and a proper building could seem exciting and unfamiliar after a scant five days in the woods, but in fact it was so. Just passing through a door, being inside, surrounded by walls and a ceiling, was novel. And the Walasi-Yi's stuff was – well, I can't begin to describe how wonderful it was. There was a single modest-sized chilled cabinet filled with fresh sandwiches, soft drinks, cartons of juice and perishables like cheese, and Katz and I stared into it for ages, dumbly captivated. I was beginning to learn that the central feature of life on the Appalachian Trail is deprivation, that the whole point of the experience is to remove yourself so thoroughly from the conveniences of everyday life that the most ordinary things – processed cheese, a can of pop gorgeously beaded with condensation – fill you with wonder and gratitude. It is an intoxicating experience to taste Coca-Cola as if for the first time and to be conveyed to the very brink of orgasm by white bread. Makes all the discomfort worthwhile.

Katz and I bought two egg salad sandwiches each, some crisps, chocolate bars and soft drinks, and went with them to a picnic table outside, where we ate with greedy smackings and expressions of rapture, then returned to the chill cabinet to stare in wonder some more. The Walasi-Yi, we discovered, provided other services to bona fide hikers for a small fee – laundry centre, showers, towel hire – and we greedily availed ourselves of all those. The shower was a dribbly, antiquated affair, but the water was hot and I have never, and I mean never, enjoyed a grooming experience more. I watched with the profoundest satisfaction as five days of grime ran down my legs and into the drainhole, and noticed with astonished gratitude that my body had taken on a noticeably svelter profile. We did two loads of laundry, washed out our cups and food bowls and pots and pans, bought and sent postcards, phoned home, and stocked up liberally on fresh and packaged foods in the shop.

The Walasi-Yi was run by an Englishman named Justin and his American wife Peggy, and we fell into a running conversation with them as we drifted in and out through the afternoon. Peggy told me that already they had had a thousand hikers through since 1 January, with the real start of the hiking season still to come. They were a kindly couple, and I got the sense that Peggy in particular spends a lot of her time talking people into not quitting. Only the day before a young man from Surrey had asked them to call him a cab to take him to Atlanta. Peggy had almost persuaded him to persevere, to try for just another week, but in the end he had broken down and wept quietly and asked from the heart to be let go home.

My own feeling was that for the first time I really wanted to keep going. The sun was shining. I was clean and refreshed. There was ample food in our packs. I had spoken to my wife by phone and knew that all was well. Above all, I was starting to feel fit. I was sure I had lost half a stone already. I was ready to go. Katz, too, was aglow with cleanness and looking chipper.

We packed our purchases on the porch and realized together in the same instant, with joy and amazement, that Mary Ellen was no longer part of our retinue. I put my head in the door and asked if they had seen her.

'Oh, I think she left about an hour ago,' Peggy said.

Things were getting better and better.

It was after four o'clock by the time we set off again. Justin had said there was a natural meadow ideal for camping about an hour's walk further on. The trail was warmly inviting in late afternoon sunlight – there were long shadows from the trees and expansive views across a river valley to stout, charcoal-coloured mountains – and the meadow was indeed a perfect place to camp. We pitched our tents and ate sandwiches, crisps and soft drinks we had bought for dinner.

Then, with as much pride as if I had baked them myself, I brought out a little surprise – two packets of Hostess cupcakes.

Katz's face lit up like the birthday boy in a Norman Rockwell painting.

'Oh, wow!'

'They didn't have any Little Debbies,' I apologized.

'Hey,' he said, 'hey.' He was lost for greater eloquence. Katz loved cakes.

We ate three of the cupcakes between us, and left the last one on the log, where we could admire it, for later. We were lying there, propped against logs, burping, smoking, feeling rested and content, talking for once – in short, acting much as I had envisioned it in my more optimistic moments back home – when Katz let out a low groan. I followed his gaze to find Mary Ellen striding briskly down the trail towards us from the wrong direction.

'I *wondered* where you guys had got to,' she scolded. 'You know, you are like *really* slow. We could've done another four miles by now easy. I can see I'm going to have to keep my eyes on you from now— Say, is that a Hostess cupcake?' Before I could speak or Katz could seize a log with which to smite her dead, she said, 'Well, I don't mind if I do,' and ate it in two bites.

It would be some days before Katz smiled again.

CHAPTER FIVE

'SO WHAT'S YOUR STAR SIGN?' SAID MARY ELLEN.

'Cunnilingus,' Katz answered and looked profoundly unhappy.

She looked at him. 'I don't know that one.' She made an I'll-be-darned frown and said, 'I thought I knew them all. Mine's Libra.' She turned to me. 'What's yours?'

'I don't know.' I tried to think of something. 'Necrophilia.'

'I don't know that one either. Say, are you guys having me on?'

'Yeah.'

It was two nights later. We were camped at a lofty spot called Indian Grave Gap, between two brooding summits, the one tiring to recollect, the other dispiriting to behold. We had hiked 22 miles in two days – a highly respectable distance for us – but a distinct listlessness and sense of anticlimax, a kind of midmountain lassitude, had set in. We spent our days doing precisely what we had done on previous days and would continue to do on future days, over the same sorts of hills, along the same wandering track, through the same endless woods. The trees were so thick that we hardly ever got views, and when we did get views it was of infinite hills covered in more trees. I was discouraged to note that I was grubby again already and barking for white bread. And then of course there was the constant, prattling, awesomely brainless presence of Mary Ellen.

'When's your birthday?' she said to me.

'December the eighth.'

'That's Virgo.'

'No, actually it's Sagittarius.'

'Whatever.' And then abruptly: 'Jeez, you guys stink.'

'Well, uh, we've been walking.'

'Me, I don't sweat. Never have. Don't dream either.'

'Everybody dreams,' Katz said.

'Well, I don't.'

'Except people of extremely low intelligence. It's a scientific fact.'

Mary Ellen regarded him expressionlessly for a moment, then said abruptly, to neither of us in particular: 'Do you ever have that dream where you're like at school and you look down and like you haven't got any clothes on?' She shuddered. 'I hate that one.'

'I thought you didn't dream,' said Katz.

She stared at him for a very long moment, as if trying to remember where she had encountered him before. 'And falling,' she went on, unperturbed. 'I hate that one, too. Like when you fall into a hole and just fall and fall.' She gave a brief shiver, and then noisily unblocked her ears.

Katz watched her with idle interest. 'I know a guy who did that once and one of his eyes popped out,' he said.

She looked at him doubtfully.

'It rolled right across the living room floor and his dog ate it. Isn't that right, Bryson?'

I nodded.

'You're making that up.'

'I'm not. It rolled right across the floor and before anybody could do anything, the dog gobbled it down in one bite.'

I confirmed it for her with another nod.

She considered this for a minute. 'So what'd your friend do about his eye hole? Did he have to get a glass eye or something?'

'Well, he wanted to, but his family was kind of poor, you know, so what he did was he got a ping-pong ball and painted an eye on it and he used that.'

'Ugh,' said Mary Ellen softly.

'So I wouldn't go blowing out your ear holes any more.'

She considered again. 'Yeah, maybe you're right,' she said at length, and blew out her ear holes.

In our few private moments, when Mary Ellen went off to tinkle in distant shrubs, Katz and I had formed a secret pact that we would hike 14 miles on the morrow to a place called Dicks Creek Gap, where there was a highway to the town of Hiawassee, 11 miles to the north. We would hike to the gap if it killed us, and then try to hitchhike into Hiawassee for dinner and a night in a motel.

Plan B was that we would kill Mary Ellen and take her Pop Tarts.

And so the next day we hiked, really hiked, startling Mary Ellen with our thrusting strides. There was a motel in Hiawassee – clean sheets! shower! colour TV! – and a reputed choice of restaurants. We needed no more incentive than that to perk our step. Katz flagged in the first hour, and I felt tired too by afternoon, but we pushed determinedly on. Mary Ellen fell further and further off the pace, until she was behind even Katz. It was a kind of miracle in the hills.

At about four o'clock, tired and overheated and streaked about the face with rivulets of gritty sweat, I stepped from the woods onto the broad shoulder of US Highway 76, an asphalt river through the woods, pleased to note that the road was wide and reasonably important-looking. A half-mile down the road there was a clearing in the trees and a drive – a hint of civilization – before the road curved away invitingly. Several cars passed as I stood there.

Katz tumbled from the woods a few minutes later, looking wild of hair and eye, and I hustled him across the road against his voluble protests that he needed to sit down *immediately*, but I wanted to try to get a lift before Mary Ellen came along and screwed things up. I couldn't think how she might, but I knew she would.

'Have you seen her?' I asked anxiously.

'Miles back, sitting on a rock with her boots off rubbing her feet. She looked real tired.'

'Good.'

Katz sagged onto his pack, grubby and spent, and I stood beside him on the shoulder with my thumb out, trying to project an image of wholesomeness and respectability, making private irked tutting noises at every car and pickup that passed. I had not hitchhiked in twenty-five years, and it was a vaguely humbling experience. Cars shot past very fast – unbelievably fast to us who now resided in Foot World – and gave us scarcely a glance. A very few approached more slowly, always occupied by elderly people – little white heads, just above the window line – who stared at us without sympathy or expression, as they would at a field of cows. It seemed unlikely that anyone would stop for us. I wouldn't have stopped for us.

'We're never going to get picked up,' Katz announced despondently after cars had forsaken us for fifteen minutes.

He was right, of course, but it always exasperated me how easily he gave up on things. 'Can't you try to be a little more positive?' I said.

'OK, I'm positive we're never going to get picked up. I mean, look at us.' He smelled his armpits with disgust. 'Jesus, I smell like Jeffrey Dahmer's refrigerator.'

There is a phenomenon called Trail Magic, known and spoken of with reverence by everyone who hikes the trail, which holds that often when things look darkest some little piece of serendipity comes along to put you back on a heavenly plane. Ours was a baby-blue Pontiac TransAm, which flew past, then screeched to a stop on the shoulder a hundred yards or so down the road, in a cloud of gravelly dust. It was so far beyond where we stood that we didn't think it could possibly be for us, but then it jerked into reverse and came at us, half on the shoulder and half off, moving very fast and a little wildly. I stood transfixed. The day before we had been told by a pair of seasoned hikers that sometimes in the South drivers will swerve at AT hitchhikers, or run over their packs, for purposes of hilarity, and I supposed this was one of those moments. I was about to fly for cover, and even Katz was halfway to his feet, when it stopped just before us, with a rock and another cloud of dust, and a youthful female head popped out of the passenger side window.

'Yew boys wunna rod?' she called.

'Yes ma'am, we sure do,' we said, putting on our best behaviour.

We hastened to the car with our packs and bowed down at the window to find a very handsome, very happy, very drunk young couple, who didn't look to be more than eighteen or nineteen years old. The woman was carefully topping up two plastic cups from a three-quarters-empty bottle of Wild Turkey. 'Hi!' she said. 'Hop in.'

We hesitated. The car was packed nearly solid with stuff – suit-cases, boxes, assorted black plastic bags, hangerloads of clothes. It was a small car to begin with and there was barely room for them.

'Darren, why'n't you make some room for these gentlemen,' the young woman ordered and then added for us: 'This yere's Darren.'

Darren got out, grinned a hello, opened the boot and stared blankly at it while the perception slowly spread through his brain that it was also packed solid. He was so drunk that I thought for a moment he might fall asleep on his feet, but he snapped to and found some rope and quite deftly tied our packs on the roof. Then, ignoring the vigorous advice and instructions of his partner, he tossed stuff around in the back until he had somehow created a small cavity into which Katz and I climbed, puffing out apologies and expressions of the sincerest gratitude.

Her name was Donna, and they were on their way to some

desperate-sounding community – Turkey Balls Falls or Coon Slick or some place – another 50 miles up the road, but they were pleased to drop us in Hiawassee, if they didn't kill us all first. Darren drove at 127 miles an hour with one finger on the wheel, his head bouncing to the rhythm of some internal song, while she twirled in her seat to talk to us. She was stunningly pretty, entrancingly pretty.

'Y'all have to excuse us. We're celebrating.' She held up her plastic cup as if in toast.

'What're you celebrating?' asked Katz.

'We're gittin' married tomorrah,' she announced proudly.

'No kidding,' said Katz. 'Congratulations.'

'Yup. Darren yere's gonna make a honest woman outta me.' She tousled his hair, then impulsively lunged over and gave the side of his head a kiss, which became lingering, then probing, then frankly lascivious, and concluded, as a kind of bonus, by shooting her hand into a surprising place – or at least so we surmised because Darren abruptly banged his head on the roof and took us on a brief but exciting detour into a lane of oncoming traffic. Then she turned to us with a dreamy, unabashed leer, as if to say, 'Who's next?' It looked, we reflected later, as if Darren might have his hands full, though we additionally concluded that it would probably be worth it.

'Hey, have a drink,' she offered suddenly, seizing the bottle round the neck and looking for spare cups on the floor.

'Oh, no thanks,' Katz said, but looked tempted.

'G'*won*,' she encouraged.

Katz held up a palm. 'I'm reformed.'

'Yew *are*? Well, good for you. Have a drink then.'

'No really.'

'How 'bout *yew*?' she said to me.

'Oh, no thanks.' I couldn't have freed my pinned arms even if I had wanted a drink. They dangled before me like Tyrannosaurus limbs.

'*Yer* not reformed, are ya?'

'Well, kind of.' I had decided, for purposes of solidarity, to forswear alcohol for the duration.

She looked at us. 'You guys like Mormons or something?'

'No, just hikers.'

She nodded thoughtfully, satisfied with that, and had a drink. Then she made Darren jump again.

They dropped us at Mull's Motel in Hiawassee, an

old-fashioned, nondescript, patently non-chain establishment on a bend in the road near the centre of town. We thanked them profusely, went through a little song-and-dance of trying to give them petrol money, which they stoutly refused, and watched as Darren returned to the busy road as if fired from a rocket launcher. I believe I saw him bang his head again as they disappeared over a small rise.

And then we were alone with our packs in an empty motel car park in a dusty, forgotten, queer-looking little town in north Georgia. The word that clings to every hiker's thoughts in north Georgia is *Deliverance*, the 1974 novel by James Dickey and subsequent film. It concerns, as you may recall, four middle-aged men from Atlanta who go on a weekend canoeing trip down the fictional Cahulawasee River (but based on the real, nearby Chattooga) and find themselves severely out of their element. 'Every family I've ever met up here has at least one relative in the penitentiary,' a character in the book remarks forebodingly as they drive up. 'Some of them are in for making liquor or running it, but most of them are in for murder. They don't think a whole lot about killing people up here.' And so of course it proves, as our urban foursome find themselves variously buggered, murdered and hunted by a brace of demented backwoodsmen.

Early in the book Dickey has his characters stop for directions in some 'sleepy and hookwormy and ugly' town, which for all I know could have been Hiawassee. What is certainly true is that the book was set in this part of the state, and the movie was filmed in the area. The famous banjo-plucking albino who played Dueling Banjos in the movie still apparently lives in Clayton, just down the road.

Dickey's book, as you might expect, attracted heated criticism in the state when it was published – one observer called it 'the most demeaning characterization of southern highlanders in modern literature', which if anything was an understatement – but in fact it must be said people have been appalled by northern Georgians for 150 years. One nineteenth-century chronicler described the region's inhabitants as 'tall, thin, cadaverous-looking animals, as melancholy and lazy as boiled cod-fish', and others freely employed words like 'depraved', 'rude', 'uncivilized' and 'backward' to describe the reclusive, underbred folk of Georgia's deep, dark woods and desperate townships. Dickey, who was himself a Georgian and knew the area well, swore that his book was a faithful description.

Perhaps it was the lingering influence of the book, perhaps simply the time of day, or maybe nothing more than the unaccustomedness of being in a town, but Hiawassee did feel palpably weird and unsettling – the kind of place where it wouldn't altogether surprise you to find your gasoline being pumped by a cyclops. We went into the motel reception, which was more like a small, untidy living room than a place of business, and found an aged woman with lively white hair and a bright cotton dress sitting on a sofa by the door. She looked happy to see us.

'Hi,' I said. 'We're looking for a room.'

The woman grinned and nodded.

'Actually, two rooms if you've got them.'

The woman grinned and nodded again. I waited for her to get up, but she didn't move.

'For tonight,' I said encouragingly. 'You do have rooms?' Her grin became a kind of beam and she grasped my hand, and held on tight; her fingers felt cold and bony. She just looked at me intently and eagerly, as if she thought – hoped – that I would throw a stick for her to fetch.

'Tell her we come from Reality Land,' Katz whispered in my ear.

At that moment a door swung open and a grey-haired woman swept in, wiping her hands on an apron.

'Oh, ain't no good talking to her,' she said in a friendly manner. 'She don't know nothing, don't say nothing. Mother, let go the man's hand.' Her mother beamed at her. 'Mother, let *go* the man's hand.'

My hand was released and we booked into two rooms. We went off with our keys and agreed to meet in half an hour. My room was basic and battered – there were cigarette burns on every possible surface, including the toilet seat and door lintels, and the walls and ceiling were covered in big stains that suggested a strange fight to the death involving lots of hot coffee – but it was very heaven to me. I called Katz, for the novelty of using a telephone, and learned that his room was even worse. We were very happy.

We showered, put on such clean clothes as we could muster and eagerly repaired to a popular nearby bistro called the Georgia Mountain Restaurant. The car park was crowded with pickup trucks and inside it was busy with meaty people in baseball caps. I had a feeling that if I'd said 'Phone call for you, Bubba', every man in the room would have risen. I won't say the Georgia Mountain had food I would travel for, even within Hiawassee, but it was certainly reasonably priced. For $5.50 each, we got 'meat and three' (three being the number of vegetables) as they call it here, a trip to the salad bar and dessert. I ordered fried chicken, black-eyed peas, roast potatoes and 'ruterbeggars', as the menu had it. I had never had them before, and can't say I will again. We ate noisily and with gusto, and ordered many refills of iced tea.

Dessert was of course the highlight. Everyone on the trail dreams of something, usually a sweet, and my sustaining vision had been an outsized slab of pie. It had occupied my thoughts for days and when the waitress came to take our order I asked her, with beseeching eyes and a hand on her forearm, to bring me the largest piece she could slice without losing her job. She brought me a vast, viscous, canary-yellow wedge of lemon pie. It was a monument to food technology, yellow enough to give you a headache, sweet enough to make your eyeballs roll up into your head – everything, in short, you could want in a pie so long as taste and quality didn't enter into your requirements. I was just plunging into it when Katz broke a long silence by saying, with a strange kind of nervousness, 'You know what I keep doing? I keep looking up to see if Mary Ellen's coming through the door.'

I paused, a forkful of shimmering goo halfway to my mouth, and noticed with passing disbelief that his dessert plate was already empty. 'You're not going to tell me you miss her, Stephen?' I said drily and pushed the food home.

'No,' he responded tartly, not taking this as a joke at all. He took on a frustrated look from trying to find words to express his complex emotions. 'We did kind of ditch her, you know,' he finally blurted.

I considered the charge. 'Actually, we didn't kind of ditch her. We ditched her.' I wasn't with him at all on this. 'So?'

'Well, I just, I just feel kind of bad – just *kind* of bad – that we left her out in the woods on her own.' Then he crossed his arms as if to say: 'There, I've said it.'

I put my fork down and considered the point. 'She came into the woods on her own,' I said. 'We're not actually responsible for her, you know. I mean, it's not as if we signed a contract to look after her.'

I said these things, but even as I said them I realized with a kind of horrible seeping awareness that he was right. We had ditched her, left her to the bears and wolves and chortling mountain men. I had been so completely preoccupied with my own savage lust for food and a real bed that I had not paused to consider what our abrupt departure would mean for her – a night alone among the whispering trees, swaddled in darkness, listening with involuntary keenness for the tell-tale crack of branch or stick under a heavy foot or paw. It wasn't something I would wish on anyone. My gaze fell on my pie, and I realized I didn't want it any longer. 'Maybe she'll have found somebody else to camp with,' I suggested lamely, and pushed the pie away.

'Did *you* see anybody today?'

He was right. We had seen hardly a soul.

'She's probably still walking right now,' Katz said with a hint of sudden heat. 'Wondering where the hell we got to. Scared out of her chubby little wits.'

'Oh, don't,' I half pleaded, and distractedly pushed the pie a half-inch further away.

He nodded an emphatic, busy, righteous little nod, and looked at me with a strange, glowing, accusatory expression that said, 'And if she dies let it be on your conscience.' And he was right; I was the ringleader here. This was my fault.

Then he leaned closer and said in a completely different tone of voice, 'If you're not going to eat that pie, can I have it?'

In the morning we breakfasted at a Hardee's across the street and paid for a taxi to take us back to the trail. We didn't speak about Mary Ellen or much of anything else. Returning to the trail after a night's comforts in a town always left us disinclined to talk.

We were confronted with an immediate steep climb, and walked slowly, almost gingerly. I always felt terrible on the trail the first day after a break. Katz, on the other hand, just always felt terrible. Whatever restorative effects a town visit offered always vanished with astounding swiftness on the trail. Within two minutes it was as if we had never been away – actually worse, because on a normal day I would not be labouring up a steep hill with a greasy, leaden Hardee's breakfast threatening at every moment to come up for air.

We had been walking for about half an hour when another hiker – a fit-looking middle-aged guy – came along from the other direction. We asked him if he had seen a girl named Mary Ellen in a red jacket with kind of a loud voice.

He made an expression of possible recognition and said: 'Does she – I'm not being rude here or anything – but does she do this a lot?' and he pinched his nose and made a series of horrible honking noises.

We nodded vigorously.

'Yeah, I stayed with her and two other guys in Plumorchard Gap Shelter last night.' He regarded us closely, dubiously. 'She a friend of yours?'

'Oh, no,' we said, disavowing her entirely, as any sensible person would. 'She just sort of latched on to us for a couple of days.'

He nodded in understanding, then grinned. 'She's a piece of work, isn't she?'

We grinned, too. 'Was it bad?' I said.

He made a look that showed genuine pain, then abruptly, as if putting two and two together, said, 'So you must be the guys she was talking about.'

'Really?' Katz said. 'What'd she say?'

'Oh, nothing,' he said, but he was suppressing a small smile in that way that makes you say:

'What?'

'Nothing. It was nothing.' But he was smiling.

'*What?*'

He wavered. 'Oh, all right. She said you guys were a couple of overweight wimps who didn't know the first thing about hiking and that she was tired of carrying you.'

'She said *that*?' Katz said, scandalized.

'Actually I think she called you pussies.'

'She called us *pussies*?' Katz said. 'Now I will kill her.'

'Well, I don't suppose you'll have any trouble finding people to hold her down for you,' the man said absently, scanning the sky, and added: 'Supposed to snow.'

I made a crestfallen noise. This was the last thing we wanted. 'Really? Bad?'

He nodded. 'Six to eight inches. More on the higher elevations.' He lifted his eyebrows stoically, agreeing with my dismayed expression. Snow wasn't just discouraging, it was dangerous.

He let the prospect hang there for a moment, then said, 'Well, better keep moving.' I nodded in understanding, for that was what we did in these hills. I watched him go, then turned to Katz, who was shaking his head.

'Imagine her saying that after all we did for her,' he said, then noticed me staring at him, and said in a kind of squirmy way, 'What?' and then, more squirmily, '*What?*'

'Don't you ever, *ever*, spoil a piece of pie for me again. Do you understand?'

He winced. 'Yeah, all right. Jeez,' he said and trudged on muttering.

Two days later we heard that Mary Ellen had dropped out with blisters after trying to do 35 miles in two days. Big mistake.

CHAPTER SIX

DISTANCE CHANGES UTTERLY WHEN YOU TAKE THE WORLD ON FOOT. A mile becomes a long way, two miles literally considerable, ten miles whopping, 50 miles at the very limits of conception. The world, you realize, is enormous in a way that only you and a small community of fellow hikers know. Planetary scale is your little secret.

Life takes on a neat simplicity, too. Time ceases to have any meaning. When it is dark you go to bed and when it is light again you get up, and everything in between is just in between. It's quite wonderful, really.

You have no engagements, commitments, obligations or duties; no special ambitions and only the smallest, least complicated of wants; you exist in a tranquil tedium, serenely beyond the reach of exasperation, 'far removed from the seats of strife', as the early explorer and botanist William Bartram put it. All that is required of you is a willingness to trudge.

There is no point in hurrying because you are not actually going anywhere. However far or long you plod, you are always in the same place: in the woods. It's where you were yesterday, where you will be tomorrow. The woods is one boundless singularity. Every bend in the path presents a prospect indistinguishable from every other, every glimpse into the trees the same tangled mass. For all you know, your route could describe a very large, pointless circle. In a way, it would hardly matter.

At times, you become almost certain that you slabbed this hill-side three days ago, crossed this stream yesterday, clambered over this fallen tree at least twice today already. But most of the time you don't think. No point. Instead you exist in a kind of mobile zen mode, your brain like a balloon tethered with string, accompanying but not actually part of the body below. Walking for hours and miles becomes as automatic, as unremarkable, as breathing. At the end of the day you don't think, 'Hey, I did sixteen miles today,' any more than you think, 'Hey, I took 8,000 breaths today.' It's just what you do.

And so we walked, hour upon hour, over rollercoaster hills, along knife-edge ridges and over grassy balds, through depthless ranks of oak, ash, chinkapin and pine. The skies grew sullen and the air chillier, but it wasn't until the third day that the snow came. It began in the morning as thinly scattered flecks, hardly noticeable, but then the wind rose, then rose again, until it was blowing with an end-of-the-world fury that seemed to have even the trees in a panic, and with it came snow, great flying masses of it. By midday we found ourselves plodding into a stinging, cold, hard-blowing storm. Soon after, we came to a narrow ledge of path along a wall of rock called Big Butt Mountain.

Even in ideal circumstances the path round Big Butt would have required delicacy and care. It was like a window ledge on a skyscraper, no more than fourteen or sixteen inches wide, and crumbling in places, with a sharp drop on one side of perhaps 80 feet and long, looming stretches of vertical granite on the other. Once or twice I nudged foot-sized rocks over the side and watched with faint horror as they crashed and tumbled to improbably remote resting places. The trail was cobbled with rocks and threaded with wandering tree roots against which we constantly stubbed and stumbled, and veneered everywhere with polished ice under a thin layer of powdery snow. At exasperatingly frequent intervals, the path was broken by steep, thickly bouldered streams, frozen solid and ribbed with blue ice, which could only be negotiated in a crablike crouch. And all the time, as we crept along on this absurdly narrow, dangerous perch, we were half blinded by flying snow and jostled by gusts of wind, which roared through the dancing trees and shook us by our packs. This wasn't a blizzard; it was a tempest. We proceeded with painstaking deliberativeness, placing each foot solidly before lifting the one behind. Even so, twice Katz made horrified, heartfelt, comic-book noises as his footing went – 'AIEEEEE!' noises and 'EEEARGH!' noises – and I turned to find him hugging a tree, feet skating, his expression bug-eyed and fearful.

It was deeply unnerving. It took us over two hours to cover six-tenths of a mile of trail. By the time we reached solid ground at a place called Bearpen Gap, the snow was four or five inches deep and accumulating fast. The whole world was white, filled with dime-sized snowflakes that fell at a slant before being caught by the wind and hurled in a variety of directions. We couldn't see more than 15 or 20 feet ahead, often not that.

The trail crossed a logging road, then led straight up Albert Mountain, a bouldered summit 5,250 feet above sea level, where the winds were so wild and angry that they hit the mountain with an actual walloping sound, and forced us to shout to hear each other. We started up and hastily retreated. Hiking packs leave you with no recognizable centre of gravity at the best of times; here we were literally being blown over. Confounded, we stood at the bottom of the summit and looked at each other. This was really quite grave. We were caught between a mountain we couldn't climb and a ledge we had no intention of trying to renegotiate. Our only apparent option was to pitch our tents – if we could in this wind – crawl in and hope for the best. I don't wish to reach for melodrama, but people have died in less trying circumstances.

I dumped my pack and searched through it for my trail map. Appalachian Trail maps are so monumentally useless that I had long since given up using them. AT maps vary somewhat, but most are on an abysmal scale of 1:100,000, which ludicrously compresses every kilometre of real world into a mere centimetre of map. Imagine a square kilometre of physical landscape and all that it might contain – logging roads, streams, a mountaintop or two, perhaps a fire tower, a knob or grassy bald, the wandering AT and maybe a pair of important side trails – and imagine trying to convey all that information on an area the size of the nail on your little finger. That's an AT map.

Actually, it's far, far worse than that because AT maps – for reasons that bewilder me beyond speculation – provide less detail than even their meagre scale allows. For any ten miles of trail, the maps will name and identify perhaps only three of the dozen or more peaks you cross. Valleys, lakes, gaps, creeks and other important, possibly vital, topographical features are routinely left unnamed. Forest Service roads are often not included and, if included, inconsistently identified. Even side trails are frequently left off. There are no co-ordinates, no way of directing rescuers to a particular place, no pointers to towns just off the map's edge. These are, in short, seriously inadequate maps.

In normal circumstances, this is merely irksome. Now, in a blizzard, it seemed closer to negligence. I dragged the map from the pack and fought the wind to look at it. It showed the trail as a red line. Nearby was a heavy, wandering black line, which I presumed to be the Forest Service road we stood beside, though there was no actual telling. According to the map, the road – if a road is what it was – started in the middle of nowhere and finished half a dozen miles later equally in the middle of nowhere, which clearly made no sense – indeed wasn't even possible. (You can't start a road in the middle of forest; earth-moving equipment can't spontaneously appear among the trees. Anyway, even if you could build a road that didn't go anywhere, why would you?) There was, obviously, something deeply and infuriatingly wrong with this map.

'Cost me eleven bucks,' I said to Katz a little wildly, shaking the map at him and then crumpling it into an approximately flat shape and jabbing it into my pocket.

'So what're we going to do?' he said.

I sighed, unsure, then yanked the map out and examined it again. I looked from it to the logging road and back. 'Well, it looks as if this logging road curves around the mountain and comes back near the trail on the other side. If it does and we can find it, then there's a shelter we can get to. If we can't get through, I don't know, I guess we take the road back downhill to lower ground and see if we can find a place out of the wind to camp.' I shrugged a little helplessly. 'I don't know. What do you think?'

Katz was looking at the sky, watching the flying snow. 'Well, I think', he said thoughtfully, 'that I'd like to have a long hot soak in a Jacuzzi, a big steak dinner with a baked potato and lots of sour cream, and I mean lots of sour cream, and then sex with the Dallas Cowboys cheerleaders on a tigerskin rug in front of a roaring fire in one of those big stone fireplaces like you get in a lodge at a ski resort. You know the kind I mean?' He looked at me. I nodded. 'That's what *I'd* like. But I'm willing to try your plan if you think it will be more fun.' He flicked snow from his brow. 'Besides, it would be a shame to waste all this delightful snow.' He issued a single bitter guffaw, and returned to the hysterical snow. I hoisted my pack and followed.

We plodded up the road, bent steeply, buffeted by winds. Where it settled, the snow was wet and heavy and getting so deep that soon it would be impassable and we would have to take shelter whether we wanted to or not. There was no place to pitch a tent here, I noticed uneasily – only steep, wooded slope going up on one side and down on the other. For quite a distance – far longer than it seemed it ought to – the road stayed straight. Even if, further on, it did curve back near the trail, there was no certainty – or even perhaps much likelihood – that we would spot it. In these trees and this snow you could be ten feet from the trail and not see it. It would be madness to leave the logging road and try to find it. Then again, it was probably madness to be following a logging road to higher ground in a blizzard.

Gradually, and then more decidedly, the road began to hook round behind the mountain. After about an hour of dragging sluggishly through ever-deepening snow we came to a high, windy level spot where the trail – or at least a trail – emerged down the back of Albert Mountain and continued on into level woods. I regarded my map with bewildered exasperation. It didn't give any indication of this whatever, but Katz spotted a white blaze 20 yards into the woods, and we whooped with joy. We had refound the AT. A shelter was only a few hundred yards further on. It looked as if we would live to hike another day.

The snow was nearly knee-deep now and we were tired, but we all but pranced through it, and Katz whooped again when we reached an arrowed sign on a low limb that pointed down a side trail and said BIG SPRING SHELTER. The shelter, a simple wooden affair, open on one side, stood in a snowy glade – a little winter wonderland – 150 yards or so off the main trail. Even from a distance we could see that the open side faced into the wind and that the drifting snow was nearly up to the lip of the sleeping platform. Still, if nothing else it offered at least a sense of refuge.

We crossed the clearing, heaved our packs onto the platform and in the same instant discovered that there were two people there already – a man and a boy of about fourteen. They were Jim and Heath, father and son, they were from Chattanooga and they were cheerful, friendly, and not remotely daunted by the weather. They had come hiking for the weekend, they told us (I hadn't even realized it was a weekend), and knew the weather was likely to be bad, though not perhaps quite this bad, and so were well prepared. Jim had brought a big clear plastic sheet, of the sort decorators use to cover floors, and was trying to rig it across the open front of the shelter. Katz, uncharacteristically, leapt to his assistance. The plastic sheet didn't quite reach, but we found that with one of our groundcloths lashed alongside it we could cover the entire front. The wind walloped ferociously against the plastic and from time to time tore part of it loose, where it fluttered and snapped, with a retort like gunshot, until one of us leapt up and fought it back into place. The whole shelter was in any case incredibly leaky of air – the plank walls and floors were full of cracks through which icy wind and occasional blasts of snow shot – but we were infinitely snugger than we would have been outside.

So we made a little home of it for ourselves, spread out our sleeping pads and bags, put on all the extra clothes we could find, and fixed dinner from a reclining position. Darkness fell quickly and heavily, which made the wildness outside seem even more severe. Jim and Heath had some chocolate cake which they shared with us – a treat beyond heaven – and then the four of us settled down to a long, cold night on hard wood, listening to a banshee wind and the crash of angry branches.

When I awoke, all was stillness – the sort of stillness that makes you sit up and take your bearings. The plastic sheet before me was peeled back a foot or so and weak light filled the space beyond. Snow was over the top of the platform and lying an inch deep over the foot of my sleeping bag. I shooed it off with a toss of my legs. Jim and Heath were already stirring to life. Katz slumbered heavily on, an arm flung over his forehead, his mouth a great open hole. It was not quite six.

I decided to go out to reconnoitre and see how stranded we might be. I hesitated at the platform's edge, then jumped out into the drift – it came up over my waist and made my eyes fly open where it slipped under my clothes and found bare skin – and pushed through it into the clearing, where it was slightly – but only slightly – shallower. Even in sheltered areas, under an umbrella of conifers, the snow was nearly knee-deep and tedious to churn through. But everywhere it was stunning. Every tree wore a thick cloak of white, every stump and boulder a jaunty snowy cap, and there was that perfect, immense stillness that you get nowhere else but in a big wood after a heavy snowfall. Here and there clumps of snow fell from the branches, but otherwise there was no sound or movement. I followed the side trail up and under heavily bowed limbs to where it rejoined the AT. The AT was a plumped blanket of snow, round and bluish, in a long, dim tunnel of overbent rhododendrons. It looked deep and hard going. I walked a few yards as a test. It was deep and hard going.

When I returned to the shelter, Katz was up, moving slowly and going through his morning groans, and Jim was studying his maps, which were vastly better than mine. I crouched beside him and he made room to let me look with him. It was 6.1 miles to Wallace Gap and a paved road, old US 64. A mile down the road from there was Rainbow Springs Campground, a private campsite with showers and a store. I didn't know how hard it would be to walk seven miles through deep snow and had no confidence that the campground would be open this early in the year. Still, it was obvious this snow wasn't going to melt for days and we would have to make a move sometime; it might as well be now when at least it was pretty and calm. Who knew when another storm might blow in and really strand us?

Jim had decided that he and Heath would accompany us for the first couple of hours, then turn off on a side trail called Long Branch, which descended steeply through a ravine for 2.3 miles and emerged near a car park where they had left their car. He had hiked the Long Branch trail many times and knew what to expect. Even so, I didn't like the sound of it, and asked him hesitantly if he thought it was a good idea to go off on a little-used side trail, into goodness knows what conditions, where no one would come across him and his son if they got in trouble. Katz, to my relief, agreed with me. 'At least there's always other people on the AT,' he said. 'You don't know what might happen to you on a side trail.' Jim considered the matter and said they would turn back if it looked bad.

Katz and I treated ourselves to two cups of coffee, for warmth, and Jim and Heath shared with us some of their oatmeal, which made Katz intensely happy. Then we all set off together. It was cold and hard going. The tunnels of bowed rhododendrons, which often ran on for great distances, were exceedingly pretty, but when our packs brushed against them they dumped volumes of snow onto our heads and down the back of our necks. The three adults took it in turns to walk in front because the lead person always received the heaviest dumping, as well as having all the hard work of dibbing holes in the snow.

The Long Branch trail, when we reached it, descended steeply through bowed pines – too steeply, it seemed to me, to come back up if the trail proved impassable, and it looked as if it might. Katz and I urged them to reconsider, but Jim said it was all downhill and well marked and he was sure it would be all right.

'Hey, you know what day it is?' said Jim suddenly and, seeing our blank faces, supplied the answer: 'March the twenty-first.'

Our faces stayed blank.

'First day of spring,' he said.

We smiled at the irony of it, shook hands all round, wished each other luck and parted.

Katz and I walked for three hours more, silently and slowly through the cold, white forest, taking it in turns to break snow. At about one o'clock we came at last to Old 64, a lonesome, superannuated two-lane road through the mountains. It hadn't been cleared and there were no tyre tracks through it. It was starting to snow again, steadily, prettily. We set off down the road for the campground, and had walked about a quarter of a mile when from behind there was the crunching sound of a motorized vehicle proceeding cautiously through snow. We turned to see a big jeep-type car rolling up beside us. The driver's window hummed down. It was Jim and Heath. They had come to let us know they had made it, and to make sure we had likewise. 'Thought you might like a lift to the campground,' Jim said.

We climbed gratefully in, filling their nice car with snow, and rode down to the campsite. Jim told us that they had passed it on the way up and it looked open, but that they would take us to Franklin, the nearest town, if it wasn't. They had heard a weather forecast. More snow was expected over the next couple of days.

They dropped us at the campground – it was open – and departed with waves. Rainbow Springs was a small private campsite with several small overnight cottages, a shower block, and a couple of other indeterminate buildings scattered around a big level open area clearly intended for camper vans and recreational vehicles. By the entrance, in an old white house, was the office, which was really a general store. We went in and found that every hiker for 20 miles was already there, several of them sitting round a wood stove eating chilli or ice cream and looking rosy-cheeked and warm and clean. Three or four of them we knew already. The campground was run by Buddy and Jensine Crossman, who seemed friendly and welcoming. If nothing else, it was probably not often that business was this good in March. I enquired about a cabin.

Jensine stubbed out a cigarette and laughed at my naivety, which caused her a small coughing attack. 'Honey, the cabins went two days ago. There's two places left in the bunkhouse. After that people are going to have to sleep on floors.'

Bunkhouse is not a word I particularly want to hear at my time of life, but we had no choice. We signed in, were given two very small, stiff towels for the shower, and trudged off across the grounds to see what we got for our $11 apiece. The answer was very little.

The bunkhouse was basic and awesomely unlovely. It was dominated by twelve narrow wood bunks stacked in tiers of three, each with a thin bare mattress and a grubby bare pillow lumpily filled with shreds of styrofoam. In one corner stood a potbellied stove, hissing softly, surrounded by a semicircle of limp boots and draped with wet woollen socks, which steamed foully. A small wooden table and a pair of broken-down easy chairs, both sprouting stuffing, completed the furnishings. Everywhere there was stuff – tents, clothes, backpacks, raincovers – hanging out to dry, dripping sluggishly. The floor was bare concrete, the walls uninsulated plywood. It was singularly uninviting, like camping in a garage.

'Welcome to the Stalag,' said a man with an ironic smile and an English accent.

His name was Peter Fleming and he was a lecturer at a college in New Brunswick who had come south for a week's hiking but, like everyone else, had been driven in by the snow. He introduced us around – each person greeted us with a friendly but desultory nod – and indicated which were the spare bunks, one on the top level, nearly up at the ceiling, the other on the bottom on the opposite side of the room.

'Red Cross parcels come on the last Friday of the month, and there'll be a meeting of the escape committee at nineteen hundred hours this evening. I think that's about all you need to know.'

'And don't order the Philly cheese steak sandwich unless you want to puke all night,' said a wan but heartfelt voice from a shadowy bunk in the corner.

'That's Tex,' Fleming explained. We nodded.

Katz selected the topmost bunk and set about the long challenge of trying to get into it. I turned to my own bunk and examined it with a kind of appalled fascination. If the mattress stains were anything to go by, a previous user had not so much suffered from incontinence as rejoiced in it. He had evidently included the pillow in his celebrations. I lifted it and sniffed it, then wished I hadn't. I spread out my sleeping bag, draped some socks over the stove, hung up a few things to dry, then sat on the edge of the bed and passed a pleasant half-hour with the others watching Katz's dogged struggle to the summit, which mostly involved deep grunts, swimming legs, and invitations to all onlookers and well-wishers to go fuck themselves. From where I sat, all I could see was his expansive butt and homeless lower limbs. His posture brought to mind a shipwreck victim clinging to a square of floating wreckage on rough seas, or possibly someone who had been lifted unexpectedly into the sky by a weather balloon he was preparing to hoist – in any case, someone holding on for dear life in dangerous circumstances. I grabbed my pillow and climbed up alongside him to ask why he didn't just take the bottom bunk.

His face was wild and flushed; I'm not even sure he recognized me at that moment. 'Because heat rises, buddy,' he said, 'and when I get up here – if I fucking ever do – I'm going to be *toast*.' I nodded – there was seldom any point in trying to reason with Katz when he was puffed out and fixated – and used the opportunity to switch pillows on him.

Eventually, when it became unsustainably pathetic to watch, three of us pushed him home. He flopped heavily and with an alarming crack of wood which panicked the poor, quiet man in the bunk underneath, and announced he had no intention of leaving this spot until the snows had melted and spring had come to the mountains. Then he turned his back and went to sleep.

I trudged through the snow to the shower block for the pleasure of dancing through ice water, then went to the general store and hung out by the stove with half a dozen others. There was nothing else to do. I ate two bowls of chilli – the house speciality – and listened to the general conversation. This mostly involved Buddy and Jensine bitching about the previous day's customers, but it was nice to hear some voices other than Katz's.

'You shoulda seen 'em,' Jensine said with distaste, picking a fleck of tobacco off her tongue. 'Didn't say please, didn't say thank you. Not like you guys. You guys are a breath of fresh air in comparison, believe me. And they made a complete pigpen of the bunkhouse, didn't they, Buddy?' She passed the baton to Buddy.

'Took me an hour to clean it this morning,' he said grimly, which surprised me because the bunkhouse didn't look as if it had been cleaned this century. 'There were puddles all over the floor and somebody, I don't know who, left a filthy old flannel shirt, which was just disgusting. *And* they burned all the firewood. Three days' worth of firewood I took down there yesterday and they burned every stick of it.'

'We were real glad to see 'em go,' said Jensine. 'Real glad. Not like you guys. You guys are a breath of fresh air, believe me.' Then she went off to answer a ringing phone.

I was sitting next to one of the three kids from Rutgers University whom we had been running into off and on since the second day. They had a cabin now, but had been in the bunkhouse the night before. He leaned over and in a whisper said: 'She said the same thing yesterday about the people the day before. She'll be saying the same thing tomorrow about us. Do you know, there were fifteen of us in the bunkhouse last night.'

'Fifteen?' I repeated, in a tone of wonder. It was intolerable enough with twelve. 'Where on earth did the extra three sleep?'

'On the floor – and they were still charged eleven bucks for it. How's your chilli?'

I looked at it as if I hadn't thought about it, as in fact I hadn't. 'Pretty terrible, actually.'

He nodded. 'Wait till you've been eating it for two days.'

When I left to walk back to the bunkhouse, it was still snowing, but peacefully. Katz was awake and up on one elbow, smoking a cadged cigarette, and asking people to pass things up to him – scissors, a bandanna, matches – as the need arose and to take them away again as he finished with them. Three people stood at the window watching the snow. The talk was all of the weather. There was no telling when we would get out of here. It was impossible not to feel trapped.

We spent a wretched night in our bunks, faintly lit by the dancing glow of the stove, which the timid man (unable or reluctant to sleep with the restless mass of Katz bowing the slats just above his head) diligently kept stoked, and wrapped in a breathy, communal symphony of night-time noises – sighs, weary exhalations, dredging snores, a steady dying moan from the man who had eaten the Philly cheese steak sandwich, the monotone hiss of the stove, like the soundtrack of an old movie – and woke, stiff and unrested, to a gloomy dawn of falling snow and the dispiriting prospect of a long, long day with nothing to do but hang out at the camp store or lie on a bunkbed reading old *Reader's Digest*s which filled a small shelf by the door. Then word came that an industrious youth named Zack from one of the cabins had somehow got to Franklin and rented a minivan, and was offering to take anyone to town for $5. There was a virtual stampede. To the dismay and disgust of Buddy and Jensine, practically everyone paid up and left. Fourteen of us packed into the minivan and started on the long descent to Franklin, in a snowless valley far below.

And so we had a little holiday in Franklin, which was small, dull and cautiously unattractive, but mostly dull – the sort of place where you find yourself, for want of anything better to do, strolling out to the lumberyard to watch guys on forklifts shunting wood about. There wasn't a thing in the way of diversions, nowhere to buy a book or even a magazine that didn't involve speedboats, customized cars or guns and ammo. The town was full of hikers like us who had been driven down from the hills and had nothing to do but hang out listlessly in the diner or launderette, and two or three times a day make a pilgrimage to the far end of Main Street to stare forlornly at the distant, snow-draped, patently impassable peaks. The outlook was not good. There were rumours of seven-foot drifts in the Smokies. It could be days before the trail was passable again.

I was plunged into a restless depression by this, heightened by the realization that Katz was verily in heaven at the prospect of several days idling in a town, on vacation from purpose and exertion, trying out various attitudes of repose. To my intense vexation, he had even bought a *TV Guide*, to plan his viewing more effectively over the coming days.

I wanted to get back on the trail, to knock off miles. It was what we did. Besides, I was bored to a point somewhat beyond being bored out of my mind. I was reading restaurant place mats, then turning them over to see if there was anything on the back. At the lumberyard I talked to workmen through the fence. Late on the third afternoon I stood in a Burger King and studied, with absorption, the photographs of the manager and his executive crew (reflecting on the curious fact that people who go into hamburger management always look as if their mother slept with Goofy), then slid one pace to the right to examine the employee of the month awards. It was then I realized I had to get out of Franklin.

Twenty minutes later I announced to Katz that we were returning to the trail in the morning. He was of course astounded and dismayed. 'But it's *The X Files* on Friday,' he sputtered. 'I just bought cream soda.'

'The disappointment must be crushing,' I replied with a thin, heartless smile.

'But the snow. We'll never get through.'

I gave a shrug that was meant to look optimistic, but was probably closer to indifferent. 'We might,' I said.

'But what if we don't? What if there's another blizzard? We were very lucky, if you ask me, to escape with our lives last time.' He looked at me with desperate eyes. 'I've got eighteen cans of cream soda in my room,' he blurted and then wished he hadn't.

I arched an eyebrow. 'Eight*een*? Were you planning to settle here?'

'It was on special,' he muttered defensively and retreated into a sulk.

'Look, Stephen, I'm sorry to spoil your festive arrangements, but we didn't come all the way down here to drink pop and watch TV.'

'Didn't come down here to die either,' he said, but he argued no more.

So we went, and were lucky. The snow was deep, but passable. Some lone hiker, even more impatient than I, had pushed through ahead of us and compacted the snow a little, which helped. It was slick on the steep climbs – Katz was forever sliding back, falling down, cursing mightily – and occasionally on higher ground we had to detour round expansive drift fields, but there was never a place where we couldn't get through.

And the weather perked up. The sun came out; the air grew milder and heavier; the little mountain streams became lively with the tumble and gurgle of meltwater. I even heard the tentative twitter of birds. Above 4,500 feet, the snow lingered and the air felt refrigerated, but lower down the snow retreated in daily bounds until by the third day it was no more than scrappy patches on the darkest slopes. It really wasn't bad at all, though Katz refused to admit it. I didn't care. I just walked. I was *very* happy.

CHAPTER SEVEN

FOR TWO DAYS KATZ BARELY SPOKE TO ME. ON THE SECOND NIGHT, AT 9 p.m. an unlikely noise came from his tent – the punctured-air click of a beverage can being opened – and he said in a pugnacious tone, 'Do you know what that was, Bryson? Cream soda. You know what else? I'm drinking it right now, and I'm not giving you any. And you know what else? It's delicious.' There was a slurpy, intentionally amplified drinking noise. 'Mmmm-mmmm. Dee-*light*-ful.' Another slurp. 'And do you know why I'm drinking it now? Because it's nine p.m. – time for *The X Files*, my favourite programme of all time.' There was a long moment's drinking noise, the sound of a tent zip parting, the *tink* of an empty can landing in undergrowth, the tent zip closing. 'Man, that was so good. Now fuck you and good night.'

And that was the end of it. In the morning he was fine.

Katz never really did get into hiking, though goodness knows he tried. From time to time, I believe, he glimpsed that there was something – some elusive, elemental something – that made being out in the woods almost gratifying. Occasionally, he would exclaim over a view or regard with admiration some passing marvel of nature, but mostly to him hiking was a tiring, dirty, pointless slog between distantly spaced comfort zones. I, meanwhile, was wholly, mindlessly, very contentedly absorbed with the business of just pushing forward. My congenital distraction sometimes fascinated him and sometimes amused him, but mostly it just drove him crazy.

Late on the morning of the fourth day after leaving Franklin, I was perched on a big green rock waiting for Katz after it dawned on me that I had not seen him for some time. When at last he came along, he was even more dishevelled than usual. There were twigs in his hair, an arresting new tear in his flannel shirt, and a trickle of dried blood on his forehead. He dropped his pack and sat heavily beside me with his water bottle, took a long swig, mopped his forehead, checked his hand for blood, and finally said, in a conversational tone: 'How did you get around that tree back there?'

'What tree?'

'The fallen tree, back there. The one across the ledge.'

I thought for a minute. 'I don't remember it.'

'What do you mean you don't remember it? It was blocking the path, for crying out loud.'

I thought again, harder, and shook my head with a look of feeble apology. I could see he was heading towards exasperation.

'Just back there four, five hundred yards.' He paused, waiting for a spark of recognition, and couldn't believe that it wasn't forthcoming. 'One side a sheer cliff, the other side a thicket of brambles with no way through, and in the middle a big fallen tree. You *had* to have noticed it.'

'Whereabouts was it exactly?' I asked, as if stalling for time.

Katz couldn't contain his irritation. 'Just back *there*, for Christ's sake. One side cliff, other side brambles, and in the middle a big fallen-down oak with about this much clearance.' He held his hand about 14 inches off the ground, and was dumbfounded by my blank look. 'Bryson, I don't know what you're taking, but I gotta have some of it. The tree was too high to climb over and too low to crawl under and there wasn't any way round it. It took me a half-hour to get over it, and I cut myself all to shit in the process. How could you not remember it?'

'It might come to me after a bit,' I said hopefully. Katz shook his head sadly. I was never entirely certain why he found my mental absences so irritating – whether he thought I was being wilfully obtuse to annoy him or whether he felt I was unreasonably cheating hardship by failing to notice it – but I made a private pledge to remain alert and fully conscious for a while, so as not to exasperate him. This was a fortunate thing because two hours later we had one of those hallelujah moments that come but rarely on the trail. We were walking along the lofty breast of a mountain called High Top when the trees parted at a granite overlook and we were confronted with an arresting prospect – a sudden new world of big, muscular, comparatively craggy mountains, steeped in haze and nudged at the distant margins by moody-looking clouds, at once deeply beckoning and rather awesome.

We had found the Smokies.

Far below, squeezed into a narrow valley, was Fontana Lake, a long, fjord-like arm of pale green water. At the lake's western end, where the Little Tennessee River flows into it, stands a big hydroelectric dam, 480 feet high, built by the Tennessee Valley Authority in the 1930s. It is the biggest dam in America east of the Mississippi, and something of an attraction for people who like concrete in volume. We hastened down the trail to it as we had an inkling that there was a visitors' centre there, which meant the possibility of a cafeteria and other gratifying contacts with the developed world. At the very least, we speculated excitedly, there would be vending machines and rest rooms, where we could wash and get fresh water, look in a mirror – briefly be groomed and civilized.

There was indeed a visitors' centre, but it was shut. A peeling notice taped to the glass said it wouldn't open for another month. The vending machines were empty and unplugged, and to our dismay even the rest rooms were locked. Katz found a tap on an outside wall and turned it, but the water had been shut off. We sighed, exchanged stoic, long-suffering looks, and pushed on.

The trail crossed the lake on the top of the dam. The mountains before us didn't so much rise from the lake as rear from it, like startled beasts. It was clear at a glance that we were entering a new realm of magnificence and challenge. The far shore of the lake marked the southern boundary of Great Smoky Mountains National Park. Ahead lay 800 square miles of dense, steeply mountainous forest, with seven days and 71 miles of rigorous hiking before we came out the other end and could dream again of cheeseburgers, Cokes, flush toilets and running water. It would have been nice, at the very least, to have set off with clean hands and faces. I hadn't told Katz, but we were about to traverse sixteen peaks above 6,000 feet, including Clingmans Dome, the highest point on the AT at 6,643 feet (just 41 feet less than nearby Mount Mitchell, the highest mountain in the eastern United States). I was eager and excited – even Katz seemed cautiously keen – for there seemed a good deal to be excited about.

For one thing, we had just picked up our third state, Tennessee, which always brings a sense of achievement on the trail. For nearly its whole length through the Smokies, the AT marks the boundary between North Carolina and Tennessee. I liked this very much – the idea of being able to stand with my left foot in one state and my right foot in the other whenever I wanted, which was often, or to choose at rest breaks between sitting on a log in Tennessee and a rock in North Carolina, or to pee across state lines, or many other variations. Then there was the excitement of all the new things we might see in these rich, dark, storied mountains – giant salamanders and towering tulip trees and the famous jack-o'-lantern mushroom, which glows at night with a greenish phosphorescent light called foxfire. Perhaps we would even see a bear (downwind, from a safe distance, oblivious of me, interested *exclusively* in Katz if either of us). Above all, there was the hope – the conviction – that spring could not be far off, that every passing day had to bring us closer to it, and that here in the natural Eden of the Smokies it would surely, at last, burst forth.

For the Smokies are indeed a very Eden. We were entering what botanists like to call 'the finest mixed mesophytic forest in the world'. The Smokies harbour an astonishing range of plant life – over 1,500 types of wild flower, 1,000 varieties of shrub, 530 mosses and lichen, 2,000 types of fungi. They are home to 130 native species of tree. The whole of Europe has just 85.

They owe this lavish abundance to the deep, loamy soils of their sheltered valleys, known locally as coves, to their warm, moist climate (which produces the natural bluish haze from which they get their name), and above all to the happy accident of the Appalachians' north–south orientation. During the last ice age, you see, as glaciers and ice sheets spread down from the Arctic, northern flora all over the world naturally fled southwards. In Europe, untold numbers of native species were crushed against the impassable barrier of the Alps and its cousins, and fell into extinction. In eastern North America, there was no such impediment to retreat, so trees and other plants found their way through river valleys and over the mountains until they arrived at a congenial refuge in the Smokies, and there they have remained ever since. (When at last the ice sheets drew back, the native northern trees began the long process of returning to their former territories. Some, like the white cedar and rhododendron, are only now reaching home – a reminder that, geologically speaking, the ice sheets have only just gone.)

Rich plant life naturally brings rich animal life. The Smokies are home to 67 varieties of mammal, over 200 types of bird, and 80 species of reptile and amphibian – all larger numbers than are found in comparable-sized areas almost anywhere else in the temperate world. Above all, the Smokies are famous for their bears. There are an estimated 400 to 600 black bears in the park, not a large number, but they are a chronic problem because so many of them have lost their fear of people. Almost nine million people a year come to the Smokies, many of them to picnic. So bears have learned to associate people with food. Indeed, to them people are overweight creatures in baseball caps who spread lots and lots of food out on picnic tables and then shriek a little and waddle off to get their video cameras when old Mr Bear comes along and climbs onto the table and starts devouring their potato salad and chocolate cake. Since the bear doesn't mind being filmed and indeed seems indifferent to his audience, pretty generally some fool will come up to it and try to stroke it or feed it a cupcake or something. There is one recorded instance of a woman smearing honey on her toddler's fingers so that the bear would lick it off for the video camera. Failing to understand this, the bear ate the baby's hand.

When this sort of thing happens – and about a dozen people a year are injured, usually at picnic sites, usually by doing something dumb – or when a bear becomes persistent or aggressive, park rangers shoot it with a tranquillizer dart, truss it up and take it into the depths of the backcountry, far from roads and picnic sites, and let it loose. Of course by now the bear has become thoroughly habituated both to human beings and to human beings' food. And whom will they find to take food from out in the backcountry? Why, me and Katz, of course, and others like us. The annals of Appalachian Trail hikes are full of tales of hikers being mugged by bears in the backcountry of the Smokies. And so as we plunged into the steep, dense, covering woods of Shuckstack Mountain, I stayed closer than usual to Katz and carried my walking stick like a cosh. He thought I was a fool, of course.

The true creature of the Smokies, however, is the reclusive and little-appreciated salamander. There are twenty-five varieties of salamander in the Smokies, more than anywhere else on earth. Salamanders are interesting, and don't let anyone tell you otherwise. To begin with, they are the oldest of all land vertebrates. When creatures first crawled from the seas, this is what came up, and they haven't changed a great deal since. Some varieties of Smokies salamander haven't even evolved lungs. (They breathe through their skin.) Most salamanders are tiny, only an inch or two long, but the rare and startlingly ugly hellbender salamander can attain lengths of over two feet. I ached to see a hellbender.

Even more varied and under-appreciated than the salamander is the freshwater mussel. Three hundred types of mussel, a third of the world's total, live in the Smokies. Smokies mussels have terrific names, like purple wartyback, shiny pigtoe and monkeyface pearly-mussel. Unfortunately, that is where all interest in them ends. Because they are so little regarded, even by naturalists, mussels have vanished at an exceptional rate. Nearly half of all Smokies mussel species are endangered; twelve are thought to be extinct.

This ought to be a little surprising in a national park. I mean it's not as if mussels are flinging themselves under the wheels of passing cars. Still, the Smokies seem to be in the process of losing most of their mussels. The National Park Service actually has something of a tradition of making things extinct. Bryce Canyon National Park is perhaps the most interesting – certainly the most enthusiastic – example. It was founded in 1923, and in less than half a century under the Park Service's careful stewardship had lost seven species of mammal – the white-tailed jackrabbit, prairie dog, pronghorn antelope, flying squirrel, beaver, red fox and spotted skunk – quite an achievement. Altogether, forty-two species of mammal have disappeared from America's national parks this century.

Here in the Smokies, not far from where Katz and I now trod, the Park Service in 1957 decided to 'reclaim' Abrams Creek, a tributary of the Little Tennessee River, for rainbow trout. To that end, biologists dumped extravagant quantities of a poison called rotenone into 15 miles of creek. Within hours, tens of thousands of dead fish were floating on the surface like autumn leaves – what a proud moment that must be for a trained naturalist. Among the thirty-one species of Abrams Creek fish that were wiped out was one called the smoky madtom, which scientists had never seen before. Thus the Park Service biologists managed the wonderfully unusual accomplishment of discovering and eradicating a new species of fish in the same instant. (In 1980, another colony of smoky madtoms was found in a nearby stream.)

Of course, that was forty years ago and such foolishness would be unthinkable in these more enlightened times. Today the National Park Service employs a much more subtle approach to endangering wildlife: neglect. It spends almost nothing – less than 3 per cent of its budget – on research of any type, which is why no one knows how many mussels are extinct or even why they are going extinct. Everywhere you look in the eastern forests, trees are dying in colossal numbers. In the Smokies, over 90 per cent of Fraser firs – a noble tree, unique to the southern Appalachian highlands – are sick or dying, from a combination of acid rain and the depredations of an insect called the balsam woolly adelgid. Ask a park official what they are doing about it and he will say, 'We are monitoring the situation closely.' For this read: 'We are watching them die.'

Or consider the grassy balds – treeless, meadowy expanses of mountaintop, up to 250 acres in extent, which are quite unique to the southern Appalachians. No one knows why the balds are there, or how long they have existed, or why they appear on some mountains but not others. Some believe they are natural features, perhaps relics of lightning fires, and some that they are man-made, burned or cleared to provide land for summer grazing. What is certain is that they are central to the character of the Smokies. To climb for hours through cool, dark forest and emerge at last onto the liberating open space of a sunny bald, under a dome of blue sky, with views to every horizon, is an experience not to be forgotten. But they are far more than just grassy curiosities. According to the writer Hiram Rogers, grassy balds cover just 0.015 per cent of the Smokies landscape, but hold 29 per cent of its flora. For unknown numbers of years they were used first by Indians and then by European settlers for grazing summer livestock, but now, with graziers banished and the Park Service doing nothing, woody species like hawthorn and blackberry are steadily reclaiming the mountaintops. Within twenty years, there may be no balds left in the Smokies. Ninety plant species have disappeared from the balds since the park was opened in the 1930s. At least twenty-five more are expected to go in the next few years. There is no plan to save them.

Now you might conclude from this that I don't much admire the Park Service and its people, and that's not exactly true. I never met a ranger who wasn't helpful and dedicated and generally well informed. Mind you, I hardly ever met a ranger because most of them have been let go, but the ones I encountered were entirely all right. No, my problem is not with the people on the ground, it is with the Park Service itself. A lot of people point out in defence of the national parks that they have been starved of funds, and this is indubitably so. Adjusted for inflation, the Park Service budget today is $200 million a year less than it was a decade ago. In consequence, even as visitor numbers have soared – from 207 million in 1983 to nearly 300 million today – campsites and interpretation centres have been shut, warden numbers slashed, and essential maintenance deferred to a positively ludicrous degree. By 1997, the repair backlog for the national parks had reached $6 billion. All quite scandalous.

But consider this. In 1991, as its trees were dying, its buildings crumbling, its visitors being turned away from campgrounds it could not afford to keep open, and its employees being laid off in record numbers, the National Park Service threw a seventy-fifth anniversary party for itself in Vail, Colorado. It spent $500,000 on the event. That may not be quite as moronically negligent as tipping hundreds of gallons of poison into a wilderness stream, but it is certainly in the right spirit.

But, hey, let's not lose our perspective here. The Smokies achieved their natural splendour without the guidance of a national park service and don't actually need it now. Indeed, given the Park Service's bizarre and erratic behaviour throughout its history (here's another one for you: in the 1960s it invited the Walt Disney Corporation to build an amusement complex in Sequoia National Park in California) it is perhaps not an altogether bad idea to starve it of funds. I am almost certain that if that $200 million a year were restored to the budget, nearly all of it would go into building more car parks and RV facilities, not into saving trees, and certainly not into restoring the precious, lovely grassy balds. It is actually Park Service policy to let the balds vanish. Having got everyone agitated by interfering with nature for years, it has decided now not to interfere with nature at all, even when that interference would be demonstrably beneficial. I tell you, these people are a wonder.

Dusk was settling in when we reached Birch Spring Gap Shelter, standing on a slope beside a muddy stream a couple of hundred feet downhill from the trail. In the silvery half-light it looked wonderful. In contrast to the utilitarian plywood structures found elsewhere on the trail, the shelters of the Smokies were solidly built of stone in an intentionally quaint, rustic style, so from a distance Birch Spring Gap Shelter had the snug, homey, inviting look of a cabin. Up close, however, it was somewhat less enthralling. The interior was dark and leaky, with a mud floor like chocolate pudding, a cramped and filthy sleeping platform, and scraps of wet litter everywhere. Water ran down the inside of the walls and trickled into pools on the sleeping ledge. Outside there was no picnic table, as at most other shelters, and no privy. Even by the austere standards of the Appalachian Trail, this was grim. But at least we had it to ourselves.

Like other AT shelters, it had an open front – I never really understood the thinking behind this – but this one was covered with a modern chain link fence. A sign on the fence said: BEARS ARE ACTIVE IN THIS AREA. DO NOT LEAVE DOOR OPEN. Interested to see just how active, I had a look at the shelter register while Katz boiled water for noodles. Every shelter has a register in which visitors make diary-like entries on the weather or their state of mind, if any, and note any unusual occurrences. This one mentioned only a couple of odd bearlike noises outside in the night, but what really caught the attention of the shelter's chroniclers was the unusual liveliness of its resident mice and even rats, and this, I can now attest, was so.

From the moment – the moment – we put our heads down that night there were the scurryings and scutterings of rodents. They were absolutely fearless and scampered freely over our bags and even across our heads. Cursing furiously, Katz banged around at them with his water bottle and whatever else came to hand. Once I turned on my headlamp to find a packmouse on top of my sleeping bag, high up on my chest, not six inches from my chin, sitting up on its haunches, and regarding me with a gimlet eye. Reflexively, I hit the bag from inside, flipping him into a startled oblivion.

'Got one!' cried Katz.

'Me, too,' I said, rather proudly.

Katz was scrabbling around on his hands and knees, as if trying to pass for a mouse himself, enlivening the dark with a flying flash-light beam and pausing from time to time to hurl a boot or bang down his water bottle. Then he would crawl back in his bag, be still for a time, curse abruptly, fling off encumbrances and repeat the process. I buried myself in my bag and pulled the drawstring tight over my head. And thus passed the night, with repeated sequences of Katz being violent, followed by silence, followed by scamperings, followed by Katz being violent. I slept surprisingly well, all things considered.

I expected Katz to wake in a foul temper, but in fact he was chipper.

'There's nothing like a good night's sleep and that was nothing like a good night's sleep,' he announced when he stirred, and gave an appreciative snort. His happiness, it turned out, was because he had killed seven mice, and was feeling very proud – not to say pumped up and gladiatorial. Some fur and a nubbin of something pink and pulpy still adhered to the bottom of his water bottle, I noticed when he raised it to his lips. Occasionally it troubled me – I presume it must trouble all hikers from time to time – just how far one strays from the normal measures of civility on the trail. This was such a moment.

Outside, fog was stealing in, filling the spaces between the trees. It was not an encouraging morning. A drizzle hung in the air when we set off and before long it had turned into a steady, merciless, deadfall rain.

Rain spoils everything. There is no pleasure in walking in waterproofs. There is something deeply dispiriting about the stiff rustle of nylon and the endless, curiously amplified patter of rain on fabric. Worst of all you don't even stay dry; the waterproofs keep out the rain, but make you sweat so much that soon you are clammily sodden. By afternoon, the trail was a running stream. My boots gave up the will to stay dry. I was soaked through and squelching with every step. It rains up to 120 inches a year in some parts of the Smokies. That's ten feet. That's a lot of rain. We had a lot of it now.

We walked 9.7 miles to Spence Field Shelter, a modest distance even for us, but we were wet through and chilled, and anyway it was too far to hike to the next one. The Park Service – why does this seem so inevitable? – imposes a host of petty, inflexible, exasperating rules on AT hikers, among them that you must move smartly forward at all times, never stray from the trail, and camp each night at a shelter. It means effectively not only that you must walk a prescribed distance each day, but then spend the night penned up with strangers. We peeled off the worst of our wet clothes and rooted for dry ones in our packs, but even stuff from deep in the middle felt damp. There was a stone fireplace built into the shelter wall, and some kindly soul had left a pile of twigs and small logs by the side. Katz tried to light a fire, but everything was so wet that it wouldn't burn. Even his matches wouldn't strike. Katz exhaled in disgust and gave up. I decided to make some coffee, to warm us up, and the stove proved equally temperamental.

As I fiddled with it, there was the singing rustle of nylon from without and two young women entered, blinking and bedraggled.

They were from Boston and had hiked in on a side trail from Cades Cove. A minute or two later four guys on spring break from Wake Forest University came in, then a lone young hiker who proved to be our acquaintance Jonathan, and finally a couple of bearded middle-aged guys. After four or five days in which we had seen scarcely a soul, suddenly we were inundated with company.

Everyone was considerate and friendly, but there was no escaping the conclusion that we were hopelessly overcrowded. It occurred to me, not for the first time, how delightful, how truly delightful, it would be if MacKaye's original vision had been realized – if the shelters along the trail were proper hostels, with hot showers, individual bunks (with curtains for privacy and reading lights, please), and a resident caretaker/cook who would keep a cheery fire dancing in the grate and invite us, any minute now, to take our places at a long table for a dinner of stew and dumplings, cornbread and, oh, let us say, peach cobbler. Outside there would be a porch with rocking chairs, where you could sit and smoke your pipe and watch the sun sink into the lovely distant hills. What bliss it would be. I was perched on the edge of the sleeping platform lost in a little reverie along these lines and absorbed with trying to get a small volume of water to boil – quite happy really – when one of the middle-aged guys drifted over and introduced himself as Bob. I knew with a sinking heart that we were going to talk equipment. I could just see it coming. I hate talking equipment.

'So what made you buy a Gregory pack?' he said.

'Well, I thought it would be easier than carrying everything in my arms.'

He nodded thoughtfully, as if this were an answer worth considering, then said: 'I've got a Kelty.'

I wanted to say – ached to say – 'Well, here's an idea to try to get hold of, Bob. I don't remotely give a shit.' But talking equipment is one of those things you just have to do, like chatting to your mother's friends in the supermarket, so I said: 'Oh, yeah? You happy with it?'

'Oh, *yeah*,' was the deeply sincere reply. 'Tell you why.' He brought it over to show me its features – its snap pockets, its map pouch, its general miraculous ability to hold contents. He was particularly proud of a dropdown inner stowage pouch, bulging with little plastic bottles of vitamins and medicines, with a transparent window built into it. 'It lets you see what you've got in there, without having to undo the zipper,' he explained and looked at me with an expression that invited staggered admiration.

Just at that moment Katz stepped up. He was eating a carrot – nobody could cadge food like Katz – and was about to ask me something, but when his eye lit on Bob's transparent pouch, he said: 'Hey, look – a pouch with a window. Is that for people who are so stupid they can't figure out how to get it open?'

'Actually, it's a very useful feature,' said Bob in a carefully measured tone. 'It lets you check the contents without having to undo the zipper.'

Katz gave him a genuinely incredulous look. 'What – like you're so busy on the trail you can't spare the three seconds it takes to open a zipper and look inside?' He turned to me. 'These college kids are willing to trade Pop Tarts for Snickers. What do you think?'

'Well, I actually find it quite useful,' Bob said quietly, to himself, but he took his pack away and bothered us no more. I'm afraid my equipment conversations nearly always ended up like that somehow, with the talker retiring with hurt feelings and a piece of formerly prized equipment cradled to his chest. It was never my wish, believe me.

The Smokies went downhill from there. We walked for four days and the rain fell tirelessly, with an endless, typewriter patter. The trail everywhere became boggy and slick. Puddles filled every dip and trough. Mud became a feature of our lives. We trudged through it, stumbled and fell in it, knelt in it, set our packs down in it, left a streak of it on everything we touched. And always when you moved there was the maddening, monotonous sound of your nylon going *wiss, wiss, wiss* until you wanted to take a gun and shoot it. I didn't see a bear, didn't see a salamander, didn't see foxfire, didn't see anything actually – just perpetual dribbles and droplets of rain adhering to my glasses.

Each night we stopped in leaky byres, and cooked and lived with strangers – crowds of them, all cold and damp and shuffling, and gaunt and half mad from the ceaseless rain and the cheerlessness of wet hiking. It was awful. And the worse the weather got the more crowded the shelters grew. It was spring break – half term – at colleges all over the east, and scores and scores of young people had had the idea to come hiking in the Smokies. The Smokies shelters are supposed to be for thru-hikers, not casual drop-ins, and words were sometimes exchanged. It was not like the AT at all. It was worse than awful.

By the third day, Katz and I both had nothing dry and were shivering constantly. We slopped up to the summit of Clingmans Dome – a high point of the trip, by all accounts, with views in clear weather to make the heart take wing – and saw nothing, nothing whatever, but the dim shapes of dying trees in a sea of swirling fog.

We were soaked and filthy, desperately needed a launderette, clean, dry clothes, a square meal, and a Ripley's Believe It or Not Museum. It was time to go to Gatlinburg.

CHAPTER EIGHT

BUT FIRST WE HAD TO GET THERE.

It was eight miles from Clingmans Dome to US 441, the first paved road since Fontana Dam four days before. Gatlinburg lay fifteen long, twisting, downhill miles to the north. It was too far to walk and it didn't seem likely that we would get a lift hitching in a national park, but in a parking area nearby I noticed three homeward-bound youths loading packs into a large, fancy car with New Hampshire number plates, and impulsively I went and introduced myself to them as a fellow citizen of the Granite State and asked them if they could find it in their hearts to take two weary old guys into Gatlinburg. Before they could demur, which was clearly their instinct, we thanked them profusely and climbed into the back seat. And thus we secured a stylish but rather sullen passage to Gatlinburg.

Gatlinburg is a shock to the system from whichever angle you survey it, but never more so than when you descend upon it from a spell of moist, grubby isolation in the woods. It sits just outside the main entrance to Great Smoky Mountains National Park and specializes in providing all those things that the park does not, principally slurpy food, motels, gift shops and sidewalks on which to waddle and dawdle, nearly all of it strewn along a single astoundingly ugly main street. For years it has prospered on the confident understanding that when Americans load up their cars and drive enormous distances to a setting of rare natural splendour what most of them want when they get there is to play a little crazy golf and eat dribbly food. Great Smoky Mountains National Park is the most popular national park in America, but Gatlinburg – this is so unbelievable – is more popular than the park.

So Gatlinburg is appalling. But that's OK. After eight days on the trail we were ready to be appalled, eager to be appalled. We checked into a motel, where we were received with a palpable lack of warmth, got honked at twice as we crossed the main street (one rather loses the knack of crossing roads on the trail) and finally presented ourselves at an establishment called Jersey Joe's Restaurant, where we ordered cheeseburgers and Cokes from a charmless, gum-popping waitress who declined to be heartened by our wholesome smiles. We were halfway through this simple, disappointing repast when the waitress dropped the bill on the table as she passed. It came to $20.74.

'You're joking,' I spluttered.

The waitress – let's call her Betty Slutz – stopped and looked at me, then slowly swaggered back to the table, staring at me with majestic disdain the while.

'You got a problem here?'

'Twenty dollars is a bit much for a couple of burgers, don't you think?' I squeaked in a strange, never-before-heard Bertie Wooster voice. She held her stare for another moment, then picked up the bill and read it through aloud for our benefit, smacking each item as she read.

'Two burgers. Two sodas. State sales tax. City sales tax. Beverage tax. Inclusive gratuity. Grand total: twenty dollars and seventy-four cents.' She let it fall back onto the table and graced us with a sneer. 'Welcome to Gatlinburg, gentlemen.'

Welcome, indeed.

And then we went out to see the town. I was particularly eager to have a look at Gatlinburg because I had read about it in a wonderful book called *The Lost Continent*. In it the author describes the scene on the main street thus: 'Walking in an unhurried fashion up and down the street were more crowds of overweight tourists in boisterous clothes, with cameras bouncing on their bellies, consuming ice-creams, cotton candy and corn dogs, sometimes simultaneously,' and so it was today. The same throngs of pear-shaped people in Reeboks wandered between food smells, clutching grotesque comestibles and bucket-sized soft drinks. It was still the same tacky, horrible place. Yet I would hardly have recognized it from just nine years before. Nearly every building I remembered had been torn down and replaced with something new, principally mini-malls and shopping courts, which stretched back from the main street and offered a whole new galaxy of shopping and eating opportunities.

In *The Lost Continent* I gave a specimen list of Gatlinburg's attractions as they were in 1987 – the Elvis Presley Hall of Fame, National Bible Museum, Stars Over Gatlinburg Wax Museum, Ripley's Believe It or Not Museum, American Historical Wax Museum, Gatlinburg Space Needle, Bonnie Lou and Buster Country Music Show, Carbo's Police Museum, Guinness Book of Records Exhibition Center, Irlene Mandrell Hall of Stars Museum and Shopping Mall, a pair of haunted houses, and three miscellaneous attractions, Hillbilly Village, Paradise Island, and World of Illusions. Of these fifteen diversions, just three appeared to be still in existence nine years later. They had of course been replaced by other things – a Mysterious Mansion, Hillbilly Golf, a Motion Master ride – and these in turn will no doubt be gone in another nine years, for that is the way of America.

I know the world is ever in motion, but the speed of change in the United States is simply dazzling. In 1951, the year I was born, Gatlinburg had just one retail business – a general store called Ogle's. Then, as the postwar boom years quickened, people began coming to the Smokies by car, and motels, restaurants, gas stations and gift shops popped up to serve them. By 1987, Gatlinburg had 60 motels and 200 gift shops. Today it has 100 motels and 400 gift shops. And the remarkable thing is that there is nothing remotely remarkable about that.

Consider this: half of all the offices and malls standing in America today have been built since 1980. Half of them. Eighty per cent of all the housing stock in the country dates from 1945. Of all the motel rooms in America, 230,000 have been built in the last fifteen years. Just up the road from Gatlinburg is the town of Pigeon Forge, which twenty years ago was a sleepy hamlet – nay, which *aspired* to be a sleepy hamlet – famous only as the hometown of Dolly Parton. Then the estimable Ms Parton built an amusement park called Dollywood. Now Pigeon Forge has 200 outlet shops stretched along three miles of highway. It is bigger and uglier than Gatlinburg, and has better parking, and so of course it gets more visitors.

Now compare all this with the Appalachian Trail. At the time of our hike, the Appalachian Trail was fifty-nine years old. That is, by American standards, incredibly venerable. The Oregon and Santa

Fe trails didn't last as long. Route 66 didn't last as long. The old coast-to-coast Lincoln Highway, a road that brought transforming wealth and life to hundreds of little towns, so important and familiar that it became known as 'America's Main Street', didn't last as long. Nothing in America does. If a product or enterprise doesn't constantly reinvent itself it is superseded, cast aside, abandoned without sentiment in favour of something bigger, newer and, alas, always, always uglier. And then there is the good old AT, still quietly ticking along after six decades, unassuming, splendid, faithful to its founding principles, sweetly unaware that the world has quite moved on. It's a miracle really.

Katz needed bootlaces, so we went to an outfitter's and while he was off in the footwear section, I had an idle shuffle around. Pinned to a wall was a map showing the whole of the Appalachian Trail on its long march through fourteen states, but with the eastern seaboard rotated to give the AT the appearance of having a due north–south orientation, allowing the mapmaker to fit the trail into an orderly rectangle, about six inches wide and four feet high. I looked at it with a polite, almost proprietorial interest – it was the first time since leaving New Hampshire that I had considered the trail in its entirety – and then inclined closer, with bigger eyes and slightly parted lips. Of the four feet of trail map before me, reaching approximately from my knees to the top of my head, we had done the bottom two inches.

I went and got Katz and brought him back with me, pulling on a pinch of shirtsleeve. 'What?' he said. 'What?'

I showed him the map. 'Yeah, what?' Katz didn't like mysteries.

'Look at the map, and then look at the part we've walked.'

He looked, then looked again. I watched closely as the expression drained from his face. 'Jesus,' he breathed at last. He turned to me, full of astonishment. 'We've done *nothing*.'

We went and got a cup of coffee, and sat for some time in a kind of dumbfounded silence. All that we had experienced and done – all the effort and toil, the aches, the damp, the mountains, the horrible stodgy noodles, the blizzards, the dreary evenings with Mary Ellen, the endless, wearying, doggedly accumulated miles – all that came to two inches. My hair had grown more than that.

One thing was obvious. We were never going to walk to Maine.

*

In a way it was a liberation. If we couldn't walk the whole trail, we also didn't have to, which was a novel thought that grew more attractive the more we considered it. We had been released from our obligations. A whole dimension of drudgery – the tedious, mad, really quite pointless business of stepping over every inch of rocky ground between Georgia and Maine – had been removed. We could enjoy ourselves.

So the next morning, after breakfast, we spread maps out across my motel-room bed and studied the possibilities. In the end we decided to return to the trail not at Newfound Gap, where we had left it, but a little further on at a place called Spivey Gap, near Ernestville. This would take us beyond the Smokies, with its crowded shelters and stifling regulations, and put us back in a world where we could please ourselves. I got out the Yellow Pages and looked up cab companies. There were three in Gatlinburg. I called the first one.

'How much would it be to take two of us to Ernestville?' I enquired.

'Dunno,' came the reply.

This threw me slightly. 'Well, how much do you think it would be?'

'Dunno.'

'But it's just down the road.'

There was a considerable silence and then the voice said: 'Yup.'

'Haven't you ever taken anybody there before?'

'Nope.'

'Well, it looks to me on my map like it's about twenty miles. Would you say that's about right?'

Another pause. 'Might be.'

'And how much would it be to take us twenty miles?'

'Dunno.'

I looked at the receiver. 'Excuse me, but I just have to say this. You are more stupid than a paramecium.'

Then I hung up.

'Maybe not my place to say,' Katz offered thoughtfully, 'but I'm not sure that's the best way to ensure prompt and cheerful service.'

I called up another cab company and asked how much it would be to Ernestville.

'Dunno,' said the voice.

Oh, for Christ's sake, I thought.

'What do you wanna go there for?' demanded the voice.

'Pardon?'

'What do you wanna go to Ernestville for? 'Tain't nothin' there.'

'Well, actually we want to go to Spivey Gap. We're hiking the Appalachian Trail, you see.'

'Spivey Gap's another five miles.'

'Yeah, I was just trying to get an idea . . .'

'You shoulda said so 'cause Spivey Gap's another five miles.'

'Well, how much would it be to Spivey Gap then?'

'Dunno.'

'Excuse me, but is there some kind of gross stupidity requirement to be a cab driver in Gatlinburg?'

'What?'

I hung up again and looked at Katz. 'What *is* it with this town? I've blown more intelligent life into a handkerchief.'

I called up the third and final company and asked how much it would be to Ernestville.

'How much you got?' barked a feisty voice.

Now here was a guy I could do business with. I grinned and said, 'I don't know. A dollar fifty?'

There was a snort. 'Well, it's gonna cost you more than that.' A pause and the creak of a chair going back. 'It's gonna go on what's on the meter, you understand, but I expect it'll be about twenty bucks, something like that. What do you wanna go to Ernestville for anyway?'

I explained about Spivey Gap and the AT.

'Appalachian Trail? You must be a danged fool. What time you wanna go?'

'I don't know. How about now?'

'Where y'at?'

I told him the name of the motel.

'I'll be there in ten minutes. Fifteen minutes at the outside. If I'm not there in twenty minutes, then go on ahead without me and I'll meet you at Ernestville.' He hung up. We had not only found a driver; we'd found a comedian.

While we waited on a bench outside the motel office, I bought a copy of the *Nashville Tennessean* newspaper out of a metal box, just to see what was happening in the world. The principal story indicated that the state legislature, in one of those moments of enlightenment with which the Southern states often distinguish themselves, was in the process of passing a law banning schools from teaching evolution. Instead they were to be required to instruct that the Earth was created by God, in seven days, sometime before the turn of the century. The article reminded us that this was not a new issue in Tennessee. The little town of Dayton – not far from where Katz and I now sat, as it happened – was the scene of the famous Scopes trial in 1925, when the state prosecuted a schoolteacher named John Thomas Scopes for rashly promulgating Darwinian hogwash. As nearly everyone knows, Clarence Darrow, for the defence, roundly humiliated William Jennings Bryan, for the prosecution, but what most people don't realize is that Darrow lost the case. Scopes was convicted and the law wasn't overturned in Tennessee until 1967. And now the state was about to bring the law back, proving conclusively that the danger for Tennesseans isn't so much that they may be descended from apes as that they may be overtaken by them.

Suddenly – I can't altogether explain it, but suddenly – I had a powerful urge not to be this far south any longer. I turned to Katz.

'Why don't we go to Virginia?'

'What?'

Somebody in a shelter a couple of days before had told us how delightful – how gorgeously amenable to hiking – the mountains of the Virginia Blue Ridge were. Once you got up into them, he had assured us, it was nearly all level walking with sumptuous views over the broad valley of the Shenandoah River. People routinely knocked off 25 miles a day up there. From the vantage of a dank, dripping Smokies shelter, this had sounded like Xanadu, and the idea had stuck. I explained my thinking to Katz.

He sat forward intently. 'Are you saying we leave out all the trail between here and Virginia? Not walk it? Skip it?' He seemed to want to make sure he understood this exactly.

I nodded.

'Well, shit yes.'

So when the cab driver pulled up a minute later and got out to look us over, I explained to him, hesitantly and a bit haplessly – for I had really not thought this through – that we didn't want to go to Ernestville at all now, but to Virginia.

'*Virginia?*' he said, as if I had asked him if there was anywhere local we could get a dose of syphilis. He was a little guy, short but built like iron, and at least seventy years old, but real bright, smarter than me and Katz put together, and he grasped the notion of the enterprise before I had halfway explained it.

'Well, then you want to go to Knoxville and rent a car and drive up to Roanoke. That's what you want to do.'

I nodded. 'How do we get to Knoxville?'

'How's a *cab* sound to you?' he barked at me as if I were three-quarters stupid. I think he might have been a bit hard of hearing, or else he just liked shouting at people. 'Probably cost you about fifty bucks,' he said speculatively.

Katz and I looked at each other. 'Yeah, OK,' I said and we got in.

And so, just like that, we found ourselves heading for Roanoke and the sweet green hills of old Virginny.

CHAPTER NINE

IN THE SUMMER OF 1948, EARL V. SHAFFER, A YOUNG MAN JUST OUT OF the army, became the first person to hike the Appalachian Trail from end to end in a single summer. With no tent, and often navigating with nothing better than roadmaps, he walked for 123 days, from April to August, averaging 17 miles a day. Coincidentally, while he was hiking, the *Appalachian Trailway News*, the journal of the Appalachian Trail Conference, ran a long article by Myron Avery and the magazine's editor, Jean Stephenson, explaining why an end-to-end hike was probably not possible.

The trail Shaffer found was nothing like the groomed and orderly corridor that exists today. Though it was only eleven years since the trail's completion, by 1948 it was already subsiding into oblivion. Shaffer found that large parts of it were overgrown or erased by wholesale logging. Shelters were few, blazes often non-existent. He spent long periods bushwhacking over tangled mountains or following the wrong path when the trail forked. Occasionally he stepped onto a highway to find that he was miles from where he ought to be. Often he discovered that local people were not aware of the trail's existence or, if they knew of it, were amazed to be told that it ran all the way from Georgia to Maine. Frequently he was greeted with suspicion.

On the other hand, even the dustiest little hamlets nearly always had a store or café, unlike now, and generally when he left the trail he could count on a country bus to flag down for a lift to the nearest town. Although he saw almost no other hikers in the four months, there was other, real life along the trail. He often passed small farms and cabins, or found graziers tending herds on sunny balds. All those are long gone now. Today the AT is a wilderness by design – actually, by fiat, since many of the properties Shaffer passed were later compulsorily purchased and quietly returned to woodland. There were twice as many songbirds in the eastern United States in 1948 as now. Except for the chestnuts, the forest trees were healthy. Dogwood, elms, hemlocks, balsam firs and red spruces still thrived. Above all, he had 2,000 miles of trail almost entirely to himself.

When Shaffer completed the walk in early August, four months to the day after setting off, and reported his achievement to Conference headquarters, no one there actually believed him. He had to show officials his photographs and trail journal, and undergo a 'charming but thorough cross-examination', as he put it in his later account of the journey, *Walking with Spring*, before his story was finally accepted.

When news of Shaffer's hike leaked out, it attracted a good deal of attention – newspapers came to interview him, the *National Geographic* ran a long article – and the AT underwent a modest revival. But hiking has always been a marginal pursuit in America, and within a few years the AT was once more largely forgotten except among a few diehards and eccentrics. In the early 1960s a plan was put forward to extend the Blue Ridge Parkway, a scenic highway, south from the Smokies by building over the southern portion of the AT. That plan failed (on grounds of cost, not because of any particular outcry), but elsewhere the trail was nibbled away or reduced to a rutted, muddy track through zones of commerce. In 1958, as we've seen, 20 miles were lopped off the southern end from Mount Oglethorpe to Springer Mountain. By the mid-1960s it looked to any prudent observer as if the AT would survive only as scattered fragments – in the Smokies and Shenandoah National Park, from Vermont across to Maine, as forlorn relic strands in the odd state park, but otherwise buried under shopping malls and housing developments. Much of the trail crossed private land and new owners often revoked informal rights-of-way agreements, forcing confused and hasty relocations onto busy highways or other public roads – hardly the tranquil wilderness experience envisioned by Benton MacKaye. Once again, the AT looked doomed.

Then, in a timely piece of fortuitousness, America got a Secretary of the Interior, Stewart Udall, who actually liked hiking. Under his direction a National Trails System Act was passed in 1968. The law was ambitious and far-reaching – and largely never realized. It envisioned 25,000 miles of new hiking trails across America, most of which were never built. However, it did produce the Pacific Crest Trail and secured the future of the AT by making it a de facto national park. It also provided funds – $170 million since 1978 – for the purchase of private land to provide a wilderness buffer alongside it. Now nearly all the trail passes through protected wilderness. Just 21 miles of it – less than 1 per cent of the total – is on public roads, mostly on bridges and where it passes through towns.

In the half-century since Shaffer's hike, about 4,000 others have repeated the feat. There are two kinds of end-to-end hikers – those who do it in a single season, known as 'thru-hikers', and those who do it in chunks, known as 'section hikers'. The record for the longest section hike is forty-six years. The Appalachian Trail Conference doesn't recognize speed records, on the grounds that that isn't in the spirit of the enterprise, but that doesn't stop people from trying. In the 1980s a man named Ward Leonard, carrying a full pack and with no support crew, hiked the trail in 60 days 16 hours – an incredible feat when you consider that it would take you about five days to drive an equivalent distance. In May 1991, an 'ultra-runner' named David Horton and an endurance hiker named Scott Grierson set off within two days of each other. Horton had a network of support crews waiting at road crossings and other strategic points, and so needed to carry nothing but a bottle of water. Each evening he was taken by car to a motel or private home. He averaged 38.3 miles a day with ten or eleven hours of running. Grierson, meanwhile, merely walked, but he did so for as much as eighteen hours a day. Horton finally overtook Grierson in New Hampshire on the thirty-ninth day, and reached his goal in 52 days 9 hours. Grierson came in a couple of days later.

All kinds of people have completed thru-hikes. One man hiked it in his eighties. Another did it on crutches. A blind man named Bill Irwin hiked the trail with a seeing-eye dog, and fell down an estimated 5,000 times in the process. Probably the most famous, certainly the most written about, of all thru-hikers was Emma 'Grandma' Gatewood, who successfully hiked the trail twice in her late sixties despite being eccentric, poorly equipped, a tad stupid (actually very stupid, but I don't want to seem unkind), and a danger to herself. (She was forever getting lost.) My own favourite, however, is a guy named Woodrow Murphy from Pepperell, Massachusetts, who did a thru-hike in the summer of 1995. I would have liked him anyway, just for being called Woodrow, but I especially admired him when I read that he weighed 350 pounds and was doing the hike to lose weight. In his first week on the trail, he managed just five miles a day, but he persevered and by August, when he reached his home state, he was up to a dozen miles a day. He had lost 53 pounds – a trifle, all things considered – and at last report was considering doing it all over again the following year.

A significant fraction of thru-hikers reach Katahdin, then turn around and start back to Georgia. They just can't stop walking, which kind of makes you wonder. In fact, the more you read about thru-hikers the more you end up being filled with a kind of wonder. Take Bill Irwin, the blind man. After his hike he said: 'I never enjoyed the hiking part. It was something I felt compelled to do. It wasn't my choice.' Or David Horton, the ultra-runner who set the speed record in 1991. Horton by his own account became 'a mental and emotional wreck' and spent most of the period crossing Maine weeping copiously. Well, then why do it, you stupid tit? Even good old Earl Shaffer ended up as a recluse in the backwoods of Pennsylvania. I don't mean to suggest that hiking the AT drives you potty, just that it takes a certain kind of person to do it.

And how did I feel about giving up the quest when a granny in plimsolls, a human beachball named Woodrow and over 3,990 others had made it to Katahdin? Well, pretty good, as a matter of fact. I was still going to hike the Appalachian Trail; I just wasn't going to hike all of it. Katz and I had already walked half a million steps, if you can believe it. It didn't seem altogether essential to do the other 4.5 million to get the idea of the thing.

So we rode to Knoxville with our comical cab driver, acquired a hire car at the airport, and found ourselves, shortly after midday, heading north out of Knoxville through a half-remembered world of busy roads, dangling traffic signals, vast intersections, huge signs, and acre upon acre of shopping malls, gas stations, discount stores, exhaust centres, car lots and all the rest. Even after a day in Gatlinburg, the transition was dazzling. I remember reading once how some Stone Age Indians from the Brazilian rainforest with no knowledge or expectation of a world beyond the jungle were taken to São Paulo or Rio, and when they saw the buildings and cars and passing aeroplanes they wet themselves, lavishly and in unison. I had some idea how they felt.

It is such a strange contrast. When you are on the AT, the forest is your universe, infinite and entire. It is all you experience day after day. Eventually it is about all you can imagine. You are aware, of course, that somewhere over the horizon there are mighty cities, busy factories, crowded freeways, but here in this part of the country, where woods drape the landscape for as far as the eye can see, the forest rules. Even the little towns like Franklin and Hiawassee and even Gatlinburg are just way stations scattered helpfully through the great cosmos of woods.

But come off the trail, properly off, and drive somewhere, as we did now, and you realize how magnificently deluded you have been. Here, the mountains and woods were just backdrop – familiar, known, nearby, but no more consequential or noticed than the clouds that scudded across their ridgelines. Here the real business was up close and on top of you: gas stations, Wal-Marts, K-Marts, Dunkin' Donuts, Blockbuster Videos, a ceaseless unfolding pageant of commercial hideousness.

Even Katz was unnerved by it. 'Jeez, it's ugly,' he breathed in wonder, as if he had never witnessed such a thing before. I looked past him, along the line of his shoulder, to a vast shopping mall with a prairie-sized car park, and agreed. It was horrible. And then, lavishly and in unison, we wet ourselves.

CHAPTER TEN

THERE IS A PAINTING BY ASHER BROWN DURAND CALLED *KINDRED Spirits*, which is often reproduced in books when the subject turns to the American landscape in the nineteenth century. Painted in 1849, it shows two men standing on a rock ledge in the Catskills in one of those sublime lost world settings that look as if they would take an expedition to reach, though the two figures in the painting are dressed, incongruously, as if for the office, in long coats and plump cravats. Below them, in a shadowy chasm, a stream dashes through a jumble of boulders. Beyond, glimpsed through a canopy of leaves, is a long view of gorgeously forbidding blue mountains. To right and left, jostling into frame, are disorderly ranks of trees which immediately vanish into consuming darkness.

I can't tell you how much I would like to step into that view. The scene is so manifestly untamed, so full of an impenetrable beyond, as to present a clearly foolhardy temptation. You would die out there for sure – shredded by a cougar or thudded with a tomahawk or just lost and wandering to a stumbling, confounded death. You can see that at a glance. But never mind. Already you are studying the foreground for a way down to the stream over the steep rocks and wondering if that notch ahead will get you through to the neighbouring valley. Farewell, my friends. Destiny calls. Don't wait supper.

Nothing like that view exists now, of course. Perhaps it never did. Who knows how much licence these romantic johnnies took with their stabbing brushes? Who after all is going to struggle with an easel and campstool and box of paints to some difficult overlook, on a hot July afternoon, in a wilderness filled with danger, and not paint something exquisite and grand?

But even if the pre-industrialized Appalachians were only half as wild and dramatic as in the paintings of Durand and others like him, they must have been something to behold. It is hard to imagine now how little known, how full of possibility, the world beyond the eastern seaboard once was. When Thomas Jefferson sent Lewis and Clark into the wilderness he confidently expected them to find woolly mammoths and mastodons. Had dinosaurs been known, he would almost certainly have asked them to bring him home a triceratops.

The first people to venture deep into the woods from the east (the Indians, of course, had got there perhaps as much as 20,000 years before them) weren't looking for prehistoric creatures or passages to the west or new lands to settle. They were looking for plants. America's botanical possibilities excited Europeans inordinately, and there was both glory and money to be made out in the woods. The eastern woods teemed with flora unknown to the old world and there was a huge eagerness, from scientists and amateur enthusiasts alike, to get a piece of it. Imagine if tomorrow a spaceship found a jungle growing beneath the gassy clouds of Venus. Think what Bill Gates, say, would pay for some tendrilled, purply-lobed piece of Venusian exotica to put in a pot in his greenhouse. That was the rhododendron in the eighteenth century – and the camellia, the hydrangea, the wild cherry, the rudbeckia, the azalea, the aster, the ostrich fern, the catalpa, the spice bush, the Venus flytrap, the Virginia creeper, the euphorbia. These and hundreds more were collected in the American woods, shipped across the ocean to England and France and Russia, and received with greedy keenness and trembling fingers.

It started with John Bartram – actually, it started with tobacco, but in a scientific sense it started with John Bartram – a Pennsylvania Quaker, born in 1699, who grew interested in botany after reading a book on the subject, and began sending seeds and cuttings to a fellow Quaker in London. Encouraged to seek out more, he embarked on increasingly ambitious journeys into the wilderness, sometimes travelling over a thousand miles through the rugged mountains. Though he was entirely self-taught, never learned Latin, and had scant understanding of Linnaean classifications, he was a prize plant collector, with an uncanny knack for finding and recognizing unknown species. Of the 800 plants discovered in America in the colonial period, Bartram was responsible for about a quarter. His son William found many more.

Before the century was out, the eastern woods were fairly crawling with botanists – Peter Kalm, Lars Yungstroem, Constantine Samuel Rafinesque-Schmaltz, John Fraser, André Michaux, Thomas Nuttall, John Lyon, and others pretty much beyond counting. There were so many people out there, hunting so competitively, that it is often not possible to say with any precision who discovered what. Depending on which source you consult, Fraser found either forty-four new plants or 215, or something in between. One of his uncontested discoveries was the fragrant southern balsam, the Fraser fir, so characteristic of the high ranges of North Carolina and Tennessee, but it bears his name only because he scrambled to the top of Clingmans Dome just ahead of his keen rival Michaux.

These people covered astonishing sweeps, for considerable periods. One of the younger Bartram's expeditions lasted over five years and plunged him so deeply into the woods that he was long given up for lost; when he emerged he discovered that America had been at war with Britain for a year, and he had lost his patrons. Michaux's voyages took him from Florida to Hudson's Bay; the heroic Nuttall ventured as far as the shores of Lake Superior, going much of the way on foot for want of funds.

They often collected in prodigious, not to say rapacious, quantities. Lyon pulled 3,600 *Magnolia macrophylla* saplings from a single hillside, and thousands of plants more, including a pretty red thing which left him in a fevered delirium and covered 'almost in one continued blister all over my body'; he had found, it turned out, poison sumac. In 1765, John Bartram discovered a particularly lovely camellia, *Franklinia altamaha*; already rare, it was hunted to extinction in just twenty-five years. Today it survives only in cultivation – thanks entirely to Bartram. Rafinesque-Schmaltz, meanwhile, spent seven years wandering through the Appalachians, didn't discover much, but brought in 50,000 seeds and cuttings.

How they managed it is a wonder. Every plant had to be recorded and identified, its seeds collected or a cutting taken; if the latter, it had to be potted up in stiff paper or sailcloth, kept watered and tended, and somehow transported through a trackless wilderness to civilization. The privations and perils were constant and exhausting. Bears, snakes and panthers abounded. Michaux's son was severely mauled on one expedition when a bear charged him from the trees. (Black bears seem to have been notably more ferocious in former times; nearly every journal has accounts of sudden, unprovoked attacks. It seems altogether likely that eastern bears have become more retiring because they have learned to associate humans with guns.) Indians, too, were commonly hostile – though just as often bemused at finding European gentlemen carefully collecting and taking away plants that grew in natural abundance – and then there were all the diseases of the woods, like malaria and yellow fever. 'I can't find one [friend] that will bear the fatigue to accompany me in my peregrinations,' John Bartram complained wearily in a letter to his English patron. Hardly surprising.

But evidently it was worth it. A single, particularly valued seed could fetch up to five guineas. On one trip, John Lyon cleared £900 after expenses, a considerable fortune, then returned the next year and made nearly as much. Fraser made one long trip under the sponsorship of Catherine the Great of Russia and emerged from the wilderness only to find that there was a new tsar who had no interest in plants, thought he was mad, and refused to honour his contract. So Fraser took everything to Chelsea, where he had a little nursery, and made a good living selling azaleas, rhododendrons and magnolias to the English gentry.

Others did it for the simple joy of finding something new – none more admirably than Thomas Nuttall, a bright but unschooled journeyman printer from Liverpool who came to America in 1808 and discovered an unexpected passion for plants. He undertook two long expeditions, which he paid for out of his own pocket, made many important discoveries, and generously gave to the Liverpool Botanic Gardens plants that might have made him rich. In just nine years, from a base of zero, he became the leading authority on American plants. In 1817, he produced (literally, for he not only wrote the text but set most of the type himself) the seminal *Genera of North American Plants*, which stood for the better part of a century as the principal encyclopedia of American botany. Four years later he was named curator of the Botanic Garden at Harvard University, a position he held with distinction for a dozen years, and somehow also found time to become a leading authority on birds, producing a celebrated text on American ornithology in 1832. He was, by all accounts, a kindly man who gained the esteem of everyone who met him. Stories don't get a great deal better than that.

Already in Nuttall's day the woods were being transformed. The panthers, elk and timberwolves were being driven to extinction, the beaver and bear nearly so. The great first-growth white pines of the north woods, some of them 220 feet high – that's the height of a twenty-storey building – had mostly been felled to make ships' masts or simply cleared away for farmland, and nearly all the rest would go before the century was out. Everywhere there was a kind of recklessness born of a sense that the American woods were effectively inexhaustible. Two-hundred-year-old pecan trees were commonly chopped down just to make it easier to harvest the nuts on their topmost branches. With each passing year the character of the woods changed perceptibly. But until quite recent times – painfully recent times – one thing remained in abundance that preserved the primeval super-Eden feel of the original forest: the massively graceful American chestnut.

There has never been a tree like it. Rising a hundred feet from the forest floor, its soaring boughs spread out in a canopy of incomparable lushness, an acre of leaves per tree, a million or so in all. Though only half the height of the tallest eastern pines, the chestnut had a weight and mass and symmetry that put it in another league. At ground level, a full-sized tree would be 10 feet through its bole, more than 20 feet around. I have seen a photograph, taken at the start of this century, of people picnicking in a grove of chestnuts not far from where Katz and I now hiked, in an area known as the Jefferson National Forest. It is a happy Sunday party, in heavy clothes, the ladies with clasped parasols, the men with bowler hats and walrus moustaches, all handsomely arrayed on a blanket in a clearing, against a backdrop of steeply slanting shafts of light and trees of unbelievable grandeur. The people are so tiny, so preposterously out of scale to the trees around them, as to make you wonder for a moment if the picture has been manipulated as a kind of joke, like those old postcards that show watermelons as big as barns or an ear of corn that entirely fills a wagon under the droll legend A TYPICAL IOWA FARM SCENE. But this is simply the way it was – the way it was over tens of thousands of square miles of hill and cove, from the Carolinas to New England. And it is all gone now.

In 1904, a keeper at the Bronx Zoo in New York noticed that the zoo's handsome chestnuts had became covered in small orange cankers of an unfamiliar type. Within days they began to sicken and die. By the time scientists identified the source as an Asian fungus called *Endothia parasitica*, probably introduced with a shipment of trees or infected lumber from the Orient, the chestnuts were dead and the fungus had escaped into the great sprawl of the Appalachians, where one tree in every four was a chestnut.

For all its mass, a tree is a remarkably delicate thing. All of its internal life exists within three paper-thin layers of tissue, the phloem, xylem and cambium, just beneath the bark, which together form a moist sleeve around the dead heartwood. However tall it grows, a tree is just a few pounds of living cells thinly spread between roots and leaves. These three diligent layers of cells perform all the intricate science and engineering needed to keep a tree alive, and the efficiency with which they do it is one of the wonders of life. Without noise or fuss, every tree in a forest lifts massive volumes of water – several hundred gallons in the case of a large tree on a hot day – from its roots to its leaves, where it is returned to the atmosphere. Imagine the din and commotion, the clutter of machinery, that would be needed for a fire department to raise a similar volume of water to that of a single tree. And lifting water is just one of the many jobs that the phloem, xylem and cambium perform.

They also manufacture lignin and cellulose, regulate the storage and production of tannin, sap, gum, oils and resins, dole out minerals and nutrients, convert starches into sugars for future growth (which is where maple syrup comes into the picture), and goodness knows what else. But because all this is happening in such a thin layer, it also leaves the tree terribly vulnerable to invasive organisms. To combat this, trees have formed elaborate defence mechanisms. The reason a rubber tree seeps latex when cut is that this is its way of saying to insects and other organisms, 'Not tasty. Nothing here for you. Go away.' Trees can also deter destructive creatures like caterpillars by flooding their leaves with tannin, which makes the leaves less tasty and so inclines the caterpillars to look elsewhere. When infestations are particularly severe, some trees can even communicate the fact. Some species of oak release a chemical that tells other oaks in the vicinity that an attack is under way. In response, the neighbouring oaks step up their tannin production the better to withstand the coming onslaught.

By such means, of course, does nature tick along. The problem arises when a tree encounters an attacker for which evolution has left it unprepared, and seldom has a tree been more helpless against an invader than the American chestnut against *Endothia parasitica*. It enters a chestnut effortlessly, devours the cambium cells and positions itself for attack on the next tree before the tree has the faintest idea, chemically speaking, what hit it. It spreads by means of spores, which are produced in the hundreds of millions in each canker. A single woodpecker can transfer a billion spores on one flight between trees. At the height of the American chestnut blight, every woodland breeze would loose spores in uncountable trillions to drift in a pretty, lethal haze onto neighbouring hillsides. The mortality rate was 100 per cent. In just over thirty-five years the American chestnut became a memory. The Appalachians alone lost four billion trees, a quarter of its cover, in a generation.

A great tragedy, of course. But how lucky, when you think about it, that these diseases are at least species specific. Instead of a chestnut blight or Dutch elm disease or dogwood anthracnose, what if there was just a tree blight – something indiscriminate and unstoppable that swept through whole forests? In fact there is. It's called acid rain.

But let's stop there. I think we've both had enough science for one chapter. But hold that thought, please, and bear it in mind when I tell you that there wasn't a day in the Appalachian woods when I didn't give passing thanks for what there was.

So the forest through which Katz and I passed now was nothing like the forest that was known even to people of my father's generation, but at least it was a forest. It was splendid in any case to be enveloped once more in our familiar surroundings. It was in every detectable respect the same forest that we had left in North Carolina – same violently slanted trees, same narrow brown path, same expansive silence, broken only by our tiny grunts and laboured breaths as we struggled up hills that proved to be as steep, if not quite as lofty, as those we had left behind. But, curiously, though we had come a couple of hundred miles north, spring seemed further advanced here. The trees, predominantly oak, were more fully in bud and there were occasional clumps of wild flowers – bloodroot and trillium and Dutchmen's breeches – rising through the carpet of last year's leaves. Sunlight filtered through the branches overhead, throwing spotlights on the path, and there was a certain distinctive, heady spring lightness in the air. We took off first our jackets and then our sweaters. The world seemed altogether a genial place.

Best of all, there were views, luscious and golden, to left and right. For 400 miles through Virginia, the Blue Ridge is essentially a single long fin, only a mile or two wide, notched here and there with deep, V-shaped passes called gaps, but otherwise holding generally steady at about 3,000 feet, with the broad green Valley of Virginia stretching off to the Allegheny Mountains to the west and lazy pastoral piedmont to the east. So here each time we hauled ourselves to a mountaintop and stepped onto a rocky overlook, instead of seeing nothing but endless tufted green mountains stretching to the horizon, we got airy views of a real, lived-in world: sunny farms, clustered hamlets, clumps of woodland and winding highways, all made exquisitely picturesque by distance. Even an interstate highway, with its cloverleaf interchanges and parallel carriageways, looked benign and thoughtful, like the illustrations you used to get in children's books in my boyhood, showing an America that was busy and on the move, but not too busy to be attractive.

We walked for a week and hardly saw a soul. One afternoon I met a man who had been section hiking for twenty-five years with a bicycle and a car. Each morning he would drop the bike at a finishing point ten miles or so down the trail, drive the car back to the start, hike between the two and cycle back to his car. He did this for two weeks every April and figured he had about another twenty years to go. Another day I followed an older man, lean and rangy, who looked to be well into his seventies. He had a small, old-fashioned day pack of tawny canvas and moved with extraordinary swiftness. Two or three times an hour I would sight him just ahead, 50 or 60 yards away, vanishing into the trees. Though he moved much faster than I did and never seemed to rest, he was always there. Wherever there was 50 or 60 yards of view, there he would be – just the back of him, just disappearing. It was like following a ghost. I tried to catch him up and couldn't. He never looked at me that I could see, but I was sure he was aware of me behind him. You get a kind of sixth sense for the presence of others in the woods, and when you realize people are near you always pause to let them catch up, just to exchange pleasantries and say hello and maybe find out if anyone has heard a weather forecast. But the man ahead never paused, never varied his pace, never looked back. In the late afternoon he vanished and I never saw him again.

In the evening, I told Katz about it.

'Jesus,' he muttered privately, 'now he's hallucinating on me.' But the next day Katz saw him all day – but behind him, following, always near but never overtaking. It was very weird. After that, neither of us saw him again. We didn't see anyone.

In consequence, we had shelters to ourselves each night, which was a big treat. You know your life has grown pathetic when you are thrilled to have a covered wooden platform to call your own, but there you are – we were thrilled. The shelters along this section of trail were mostly new and spanking clean. Several were even provisioned with a broom – a cosy, domestic touch. Moreover, the brooms were used – we used them, and whistled while we did it – proving that if you give an AT hiker an appliance of comfort he will use it responsibly. Each shelter had a nearby privy, a good water source, and a picnic table, so we could prepare and eat our meals in a more or less normal posture instead of squatting on damp logs. All of these are great luxuries on the trail. On the fourth night, just as I was facing the dismal prospect of finishing my only book and thereafter having nothing to do in the evenings but lie in the half-light and listen to Katz snore, I was delighted, thrilled, sublimely gratified to find that some earlier user had left a Graham Greene paperback. If there is one thing the AT teaches, it is low-level ecstasy – something we could all do with more of in our lives.

So I was happy. We were doing 15 or 16 miles a day, nothing like the 25 miles we had been promised we would do, but still a perfectly respectable distance by our lights. I felt springy and fit and for the first time in years had a stomach that didn't look like a ball bag. I was still weary and stiff at the end of the day – that never stopped – but I had reached the point where aches and blisters were so central a feature of my existence that I ceased to notice them. Each time you leave the cosseted and hygienic world of towns and take yourself into the hills you go through a series of staged transformations – a kind of gentle descent into squalor – and each time it is as if you have never done it before. At the end of the first day, you feel mildly, self-consciously, grubby; by the second day disgustingly so; by the third you are beyond caring; by the fourth you have forgotten what it is like not to be like this. Hunger, too, follows a defined pattern. On the first night you are starving for your noodles; on the second night you are starving but wish it wasn't noodles; on the third you don't want the noodles but know you had better eat something; by the fourth you have no appetite at all but just eat because that is what you do at this time of day. I can't explain it, but it's strangely agreeable.

And then something happens to make you realize how much – how immeasurably much – you want to revisit the real world. On our sixth night, after a long day in uncharacteristically dense woods, we emerged towards evening at a small grassy clearing on a high bluff with a long, sensational, unobstructed view to the north and west. The sun was just falling behind the distant blue-grey Allegheny ridge, and the country between – a plain of broad, orderly farms, each with a clump of trees and a farmhouse – was just at that point where it was beginning to drain of colour. But the feature that made us gawp was a town – a real town, the first we had seen in a week – that stood perhaps six or seven miles to the north. From where we stood we could just make out what were clearly the large, brightly lit, coloured signs of roadside restaurants and big motels. I don't think I have ever seen anything that looked half so beautiful, a quarter so tantalizing. I would almost swear to you I could smell the steaks grilling. We stared at it for ages, as if it were something we had read about in books but had never expected to see.

'Waynesboro,' I said to Katz at last.

He nodded solemnly. 'How far?'

I pulled out my map and had a look. 'About eight miles by trail.'

He nodded solemnly again. 'Good,' he said. It was, I realized, the longest conversation we had had in two or three days, but there was no need to say anything more. We had been a week on the trail and were going to town the next day. That was self-evident. We would hike eight miles, get a room, have a shower, phone home, do laundry, eat dinner, buy groceries, watch TV, sleep in a bed, eat breakfast, return to the trail. All this was known and obvious. Everything we did was known and obvious. It was wonderful really.

So we pitched our tents and fixed noodles with the last of our water, then sat side by side on a log, eating in silence, facing Waynesboro. A full moon rose in the pale evening sky, and glowed with a rich white inner light that brought to mind, but perfectly, the creamy inside of an Oreo cookie. (Eventually on the trail everything reminds you of food.) After a long period of silence, I turned to Katz and asked him abruptly, in a tone that was hopeful rather than accusatory, 'Do you know how to make anything besides noodles?' I had been thinking, I guess, about resupplying the next day.

He thought about this for a good while. 'French toast,' he said at last, and grew silent for a long period before inclining his head towards me very slightly and saying: 'You?'

'No,' I said at length. 'Nothing.'

Katz considered the implications of this, looked for a moment as if he might say something, then shook his head stoically, and returned to his dinner.

CHAPTER ELEVEN

NOW HERE'S A THOUGHT TO CONSIDER. EVERY TWENTY MINUTES ON the Appalachian Trail, Katz and I walked further than the average American walks in a week. For 93 per cent of all trips outside the home, for whatever distance or whatever purpose, Americans now get in a car. That's ridiculous. When we moved to the States one of the things we wanted was to live in a town, where we could walk to the shops and post office and library. We found such a place in Hanover, New Hampshire. It's a small, pleasant college town, with a big green, leafy residential streets, an old-fashioned main street. Nearly everyone in town is within an easy level walk of the centre, and yet almost no one walks anywhere ever for anything. I have a neighbour who drives 800 yards to work. I know another – a perfectly fit woman – who will drive 100 yards to pick up her child from a friend's house. When school lets out here, virtually every child (except for four bitching kids with English accents) gets picked up and driven from a few hundred yards to three-quarters of a mile home. (Those who live further away get a bus.) Most of the children sixteen years or older have their own cars. That's ridiculous, too. On average the total walking of an American these days – that's walking of all types: from car to office, from office to car, round the supermarket and shopping malls – adds up to 1.4 miles a week, barely 350 yards a day.

At least in Hanover we can walk. In many places in America now, it is not actually possible to be a pedestrian, even if you want to be. I had this brought home to me the next day in Waynesboro, after we had got a room and treated ourselves to an extravagant late breakfast. I left Katz at a launderette (he loved doing laundry, for some reason – loved to read the tattered magazines and experience the miracle of stiff, disgusting clothes emerging from big machines fluffed and sweet-smelling) and set off to find some insect repellent for us.

Waynesboro had a traditional, vaguely pleasant central business district covering five or six square blocks, but, as so often these days, most retail businesses had moved out to shopping centres on the periphery, leaving little but a sprinkling of banks, insurance offices and dusty thrift stores or secondhand shops in what presumably was once a thriving downtown. Lots of shops were dark and bare, and there was nowhere I could find to get insect repellent, but a man outside the post office suggested I try K-Mart.

'Where's your car?' he said, preparatory to giving directions.

'I don't have a car.'

That stopped him. 'Really? It's over a mile, I'm afraid.'

'That's OK.'

He gave his head a little dubious shake, as if disowning responsibility for what he was about to tell me. 'Well, then what you want to do is go up Broad Street, take a right at the Burger King and keep on going. But, you know, when I think about it, it's *well* over a mile – maybe a mile and a half, mile and three-quarters. You walking back as well?'

'Yeah.'

Another shake. 'Long way.'

'I'll take emergency provisions.'

If he realized this was a joke he didn't show it. 'Well, good luck to you,' he said.

'Thank you.'

'You know, there's a cab company around the corner,' he offered helpfully as an afterthought.

'I actually prefer to walk,' I explained.

He nodded uncertainly. 'Well, good luck to you,' he said again.

So I walked. It was a warm afternoon, and it felt wonderful – you can't believe how wonderful – to be at large without a pack, bouncy and unburdened. With a pack you walk at a tilt, hunched and pressed forward, your eyes on the ground. You trudge; it is all you can do. Without, you are liberated. You walk erect. You look around. You spring. You saunter. You amble.

Or at least you do for four blocks. Then you come to a mad junction at Burger King and discover that the new six-lane road to

K-Mart is long, straight, very busy and entirely without facilities for pedestrians – no sidewalks, no zebra crossings, no central refuges, no buttons to push for a WALK signal at lively intersections. I walked through gas station and motel forecourts, across restaurant car parks, clambered over concrete barriers, crossed lawns, and pushed through neglected ranks of privet or honeysuckle at property boundaries. At bridges over creeks and culverts – and goodness me how developers love a culvert – I had no choice but to walk on the road, pressed against the dusty railings and causing less attentive cars to swerve to avoid me. Four times I was honked at for having the temerity to proceed through town without benefit of metal. One bridge was so patently dangerous that I hesitated at it. The creek it crossed was only a reedy trickle, narrow enough to step across, so I decided to go that way. I slid and scampered down the bank, found myself in a hidden zone of sucking grey mud, pitched over twice, hauled myself up the other side, pitched over again, and emerged at length streaked and speckled with mud and extravagantly decorated with burrs. When I finally reached the K-Mart Plaza I discovered that I was on the wrong side of the road and had to dash through six lanes of hostile traffic. By the time I crossed the car park and stepped into the air-conditioned, Muzak-happy world of K-Mart I was as grubby as if I had been on the trail and trembling all over.

The K-Mart, it turned out, didn't stock insect repellent.

So I turned round and set off back to town, but this time, in a burst of madness I don't even want to go into, I headed home cross country, over farm fields and a zone of light industry. I tore my jeans on barbed wire and got muddier still. When finally I got back to town, I found Katz sitting in the sun on a metal chair on the motel lawn, freshly showered, dressed in newly laundered attire and looking intensely happy in a way that only a hiker can look when he is in a town, at ease. Technically, he was waxing his boots, but really he was just sitting watching the world go by and dreamily enjoying the sunshine. He greeted me warmly. Katz was always a new man in town.

'Good lord, look at you!' he cried, delighted at my grubbiness. 'What have you been doing – you're *filthy*.' He looked me up and down admiringly, then said in a more solemn tone: 'You haven't been screwing hogs again, have you, Bryson?'

'Ha ha ha.'

'They're not clean animals, you know, no matter how attractive they may look after a month on the trail. And don't forget we're not in Tennessee any more. It's probably not even legal here – at least without a note from the vet.' He patted the chair beside him, beaming all over, happy with his quips. 'Come and sit down and tell me all about it. So what was her name – Bossy?' He leaned closely and confidentially. 'Did she squeal a lot?'

I sat in the chair. 'You're only jealous.'

'Well, as a matter of fact, I'm not. I made a friend of my own today. At the laundromat. Her name's Beulah.'

'Beulah? You're joking.'

'I may wish I was, but it's a fact.'

'Nobody's named Beulah.'

'Well, she is. And real nice, too. Not real smart, but real nice, with cute little dimples just here.' He poked his cheeks to show me where. 'And she has a terrific body.'

'Oh, yes?'

He nodded. 'Of course,' he added judiciously, 'it's buried under two hundred and twenty pounds of wobbling fat. Fortunately I don't mind size in a woman as long as, you know, you don't have to remove a wall or anything to get her out of the house.' He gave his boot a thoughtful swipe.

'So how did you meet her?'

'As a matter of fact,' he said, sitting forward keenly, as if this was a story worth telling, 'she asked me to come and look at her panties.'

I nodded. 'Of course.'

'They'd got caught in the washing-machine agitator,' he explained.

'And was she wearing them at the time? You said she wasn't real smart.'

'No, she was washing them and the elastic got stuck in the spindle thing and she asked me to come and help extract them. Big panties,' he added thoughtfully, and fell into a brief reverie at the memory of it, then continued: 'I got 'em out, but they were shredded all to hell, so I said, kind of droll like, "Well, miss, I sure hope you've got another pair, because these are shredded all to hell."'

'Oh, Stephen, the wit.'

'It'll do for Waynesboro, believe me. And *she* said – now here's the thing, my grubby, hog-humping friend – *she* said, "Well, wouldn't you like to know, honey."' He made his eyebrows bounce. 'I'm meeting her at seven outside the fire station.'

'What, she keeps her spare knickers there?'

He gave me an exasperated look. 'No, it's just a place to meet. We're going to Pappa John's Pizza for dinner. And then, with any luck, we'll do what you've been doing all day. Only I won't have to climb a fence and lure her with alfalfa. Well, I hope not anyway. Hey, look at this,' he said, and reached down to a paper bag at his feet. He brought out a pair of pink female knickers that could fairly be called capacious. 'I thought I'd give them to her. As a kind of joke, you understand.'

'In a restaurant? Are you sure that's a good idea?'

'Discreetly, you know.'

I held up the knickers with outstretched arms. They really were quite arrestingly jumbo-sized. 'If she doesn't like them, you can always use them as a groundsheet. Are these – I have to ask – are these this big as part of the joke, or—'

'Oh, she's a big woman,' Katz said and bounced his eyebrows again happily. He put them neatly, reverently back in the bag. '*Big* woman.'

So I dined alone at a place called the Coffee Mill Restaurant. It felt a little odd to be without Katz after so many days of constant companionship, but agreeable as well, for the same reason. I was eating a steak dinner, my book propped against a sugar shaker, entirely content, when I glanced up to find Katz stalking towards me across the restaurant, looking alarmed and furtive.

'Thank God I found you,' he said, and took a seat opposite me in the booth. He was sweating freely. 'There's some guy looking for me.'

'What're you talking about?'

'Beulah's husband.'

'Beulah has a husband?'

'I know. It's a miracle. There can't be more than two people on the planet who'd be willing to sleep with her and here we are both in the same town.'

This was all going too fast for me. 'I don't understand. What happened?'

'I was standing outside the fire station, you know, like we'd agreed, and a red pickup truck screeches to a stop and this guy gets out looking real angry and saying he's Beulah's old man and he wants to talk to me.'

'So what did you do?'

'I ran. What do you think?'

'And he didn't catch you?'

'He weighed about six hundred pounds. He wasn't exactly the sprinting type. More the shoot-your-balls-off type. He's been cruising round for a half-hour looking for me. I've been running through back yards and crashing into clothes lines and all kinds of shit. I ended up with some other guy chasing me because he thought I was a prowler. What the hell am I supposed to do now, Bryson?'

'OK, first you stop talking to fat ladies in laundromats.'

'Yeah yeah yeah yeah yeah.'

'Then I go out of here, see if the coast is clear, and give you a signal from the window.'

'Yeah? And then?'

'Then you walk very briskly back to the motel, with your hands over your balls, and hope this guy doesn't spot you.'

He was quiet a moment. 'That's it? That's your best plan? That's your very best plan?'

'Have you got a better one?'

'No, but I didn't go to college for four years.'

'Stephen, I didn't study how to save your ass in Waynesboro. I majored in political science. If your problem was to do with proportional representation in Switzerland, I might be able to help you.'

He sighed and sat back heavily with his arms crossed, bleakly considering his position and how he'd got himself into this fix. 'You don't let me talk to any women again, of any size, at least until we get out of the Confederacy. These guys have all got guns down here. You promise?'

'Oh, it's a promise.'

He sat in edgy silence while I finished my dinner, swivelling his head to check out all the windows, expecting to see a fat, angry face pressed against the glass. When I had finished and paid the bill, we went to the door.

'I could be dead in a minute,' he said grimly, then clutched my forearm. 'Look, if I get shot, do me a favour. Call my brother and tell him there's ten thousand dollars buried in a coffee can under his front lawn.'

'You buried ten thousand dollars under your brother's front lawn?'

'No, of course not, but he's a little prick and it would serve him right. Let's go.'

I stepped outside and the street was clear – completely empty of traffic. Waynesboro was at home, in front of the TV. I gave him a nod. His head came out, looked cautiously left and right, and he tore off down the street at a rate that was, all things considered, astounding. It took me two or three minutes to stroll to the motel. I didn't see anyone. At the motel, I knocked on his door.

Instantly a preposterously deep, authoritative voice said, 'Who is it?'

I sighed. 'Bubba T. Flubba. I wanna talk to yew, boy.'

'Bryson, don't fuck around. I can see you through the peephole.'

'Then why are you asking who it is?'

'Practising.'

I waited a minute. 'Are you going to let me in?'

'Can't. I got a chest of drawers in front of the door.'

'Are you serious?'

'Go to your room and I'll call you.'

My room was next door, but the phone was already ringing when I got there. Katz wanted every detail of my walk home, and had elaborate plans for his defence involving a heavy ceramic lamp base and, ultimately, escape out of the back window. My role was to create a diversion, ideally by setting the man's truck alight, then running in a contrary direction. Twice more in the night, once just after midnight, he called me to tell me that he had seen a red pickup truck cruising the streets. In the morning, he refused to go out for breakfast, so I went to the supermarket for groceries and brought us both a bag of food from Hardee's. He wouldn't leave the room until the cab was waiting by the motel office with the motor running. It was four miles back to the trail. He looked out of the back window the whole way.

The cab dropped us at Rockfish Gap, southern gateway to Shenandoah National Park. I was looking forward to the park because it is exceptionally beautiful – that is why it is a national park, of course – but filled with mild disquiet at the prospect of spending the next seven or eight nights and 101 miles under the yoke of National Park Service rules. At Rockfish Gap, there is a tollbooth manned by rangers where motorists have to pay an entrance fee and thru-hikers have to acquire a backcountry hiking permit. The permit doesn't cost anything – one of the noblest traditions of the Appalachian Trail is that every inch of it is free – but you have to complete a lengthy form giving your personal details, your itinerary through the park and where you plan to camp each night, which is a little ridiculous because you haven't seen the terrain and don't know what kind of mileage you might achieve. Appended to the form were the usual copious regulations and warnings of severe fines and immediate banishment for doing, well, pretty much anything. I filled out the form as best I could and handed it in at the window to a lady ranger.

'So you're hiking the trail?' she said brightly, if not terribly astutely, accepted the form without looking at it, banged it severely with rubber stamps and tore off the part that would serve as our licence to walk on land that, in theory, we owned anyway.

'Well, we're trying,' I said.

'I must get up there myself one of these days. I hear it's real nice.'

This took me aback. 'You've never been on the trail?' But you're a ranger, I wanted to say.

'No, afraid not,' she answered wistfully. 'Lived here all my life, but haven't got to it yet. One day I will.'

Katz, mindful of Beulah's husband, was practically dragging me towards the safety of the woods, but I was curious.

'How long have you been a ranger?' I called back.

'Twelve years in August,' she said proudly.

'You ought to give it a try sometime. It's real nice.'

'Might get some of that flab off your butt,' Katz muttered privately, and stepped into the woods. I looked at him with interest and surprise – it wasn't like Katz to be so uncharitable – and put it down to lack of sleep, profound sexual frustration and a surfeit of Hardee's sausage biscuits.

Shenandoah National Park is a park with problems. More even than the Smokies, it suffers from a chronic shortage (though a cynic might say a chronic misapplication) of funds. Several miles of side trails have been closed and others are deteriorating. If it weren't that volunteers from the Potomac Appalachian Trail Club maintain 80 per cent of the park's trails, including the whole of the AT through the park, the situation would be much worse. Mathews Arm Campground, one of the park's main recreational areas, was closed for lack of funds in 1993 and hasn't been open since. Several other recreation areas are closed for most of the year. For a time in the 1980s, even the trail shelters – or huts as they are known here – were shut. I don't know how they did it – I mean to say, how exactly do you close a wooden structure with a 15-foot-wide opening at the front? – and still less why, since forbidding hikers from resting for a few hours on a wooden sleeping platform is hardly going to transform the park's finances. But then making things difficult for hikers is something of a tradition in the eastern parks. A couple of months earlier, all the national parks, along with all other non-essential government departments, had been closed for a couple of weeks during a budget impasse between President Clinton and Congress. Yet Shenandoah, despite its perennial want of money, found the funds to post a warden at each AT access point to turn back all thru-hikers. In consequence, a couple of dozen harmless people had to make lengthy, pointless detours by road before they could resume their long hike. This vigilance couldn't have cost the Park Service less than $20,000, or the better part of $1,000 for each dangerous thru-hiker deflected.

On top of its self-generated shortcomings, Shenandoah has a lot of problems arising from factors largely beyond its control. Overcrowding is one. Although the park is over a hundred miles long, it is almost nowhere more than a mile or two wide, so all its two million annual visitors are crowded into a singularly narrow corridor along the ridgeline. Campgrounds, visitor centres, car parks, picnic sites, the AT, and Skyline Drive – the scenic road that runs down the spine of the park – all exist cheek by jowl. One of the most popular (non-AT) hiking routes in the park, up Old Rag Mountain, has become so much in demand that on summer weekends people sometimes have to queue to get on it.

Then there is the vexed matter of pollution. Thirty years ago it was still possible, on especially clear days, to see the Washington Monument, 75 miles away. Now, on hot, smoggy summer days, visibility can be as little as two miles and never more than 30. Acid rain in the streams has nearly wiped out the park's trout. Gypsy moths arrived in 1983 and have since ravaged considerable acreages of oaks and hickories. The Southern pine beetle has done similar work on conifers and the locust leaf miner has inflicted disfiguring (but mercifully usually non-fatal) damage on thousands of locust trees. In just seven years, the woolly adelgid has fatally damaged more than 90 per cent of the park's hemlocks. Nearly all the rest will be dying by the time you read this. An untreatable fungal disease called anthracnose is wiping out the lovely dogwoods not just here but everywhere in America. Before long, the dogwood, like the American chestnut and American elm, will effectively cease to exist. It would be hard, in short, to conceive a more stressed environment.

And yet here is the thing. Shenandoah National Park is lovely. It is possibly the most wonderful national park I have ever been in, and, considering the impossible and conflicting demands put on it, it is extremely well run. Almost at once it became my favourite part of the Appalachian Trail.

We hiked through deep-seeming woods, along gloriously untaxing terrain, climbing a gentle 500 feet in four miles. In the Smokies, you can climb 500 feet in, well, about 500 feet. This was more like it. The weather was kindly and there was a real sense of spring being on the turn. And there was life everywhere – zumming insects, squirrels scampering along boughs, birds twittering and hopping about, spiders' webs gleaming silver in the sun. Twice I flushed grouse – always a terrifying experience: an instantaneous explosion from the undergrowth at your feet, like balled socks fired from a gun, followed by drifting feathers and a lingering residue of fussy, bitching noise. I saw an owl, which watched me imperturbably from a near stout limb, and loads of deer, which raised their heads to stare, but otherwise seemed fearless, and casually returned to their browsing when I had passed. Sixty years ago, there were no deer in this neck of the Blue Ridge Mountains. They had been hunted out of existence. Then, after the park was created in 1936, thirteen white-tailed deer were introduced, and, with no one to hunt them and few predators, they thrived. Today there are 5,000 deer in the park, all descended from those original thirteen, or others that migrated from nearby.

Surprisingly, considering its modest dimensions and how little room there is for real backcountry, the park is remarkably rich in wildlife. Bobcats, bears, red and grey foxes, beaver, skunks, raccoons, flying squirrels, and our friends the salamanders exist in admirable numbers, though you don't often see them, as most are nocturnal or wary of people. Shenandoah is said to have the highest density of black bears anywhere in the world – slightly over one per square mile. There have even been reported sightings – including by park rangers, who perhaps ought to know better – of mountain lions, even though mountain lions haven't been confirmed in the eastern woods for almost seventy years. There is the tiniest chance that they may exist in pockets in the northern woods – we shall get to that in due course and I think you'll be glad you waited – but not in an area as small and hemmed in as Shenandoah National Park.

We didn't see anything terribly exotic, or even remotely exotic, but it was nice just to see squirrels and deer, to feel that the forest was lived in. Late in the afternoon, I rounded a bend to find a wild turkey and her chicks crossing the trail ahead of me. The mother was regal and unflappable; her chicks were much too busy falling over and getting up again even to notice me. This was the way the woods were supposed to be. I couldn't have been more delighted.

We hiked till five and camped beside a tranquil spring in a small, grassy clearing in the trees just off the trail. Because it was our first day back on the trail, we were flush for food, including perishables like cheese and bread that had to be eaten before they went off or were shaken to bits in our packs, so we rather gorged ourselves, then sat around smoking and chatting idly until persistent and numerous midgelike creatures – no-see-ums, as they are universally known along the trail – drove us into our tents. It was perfect sleeping weather, cool enough to need a bag, but warm enough to sleep in your underwear, and I was looking forward to a long night's snooze – indeed was enjoying a long night's snooze when, at some indeterminate dark hour, there was a sound nearby that made my eyes fly open. Normally, I slept through everything – through thunderstorms, through Katz's snoring and noisy midnight pees – so something big enough or distinctive enough to wake me was unusual. There was a sound of undergrowth being disturbed – a click of breaking branches, a weighty pushing through low foliage – and then a kind of large, vaguely irritable snuffling noise.

Bear!

I sat bolt upright. Instantly every neuron in my brain was awake and dashing around frantically, like ants when you disturb their nest. I reached instinctively for my knife, then realized I had left it in my pack, just outside the tent. Nocturnal defence had ceased to be a concern after many successive nights of tranquil woodland repose.

There was another noise, quite near.

'Stephen, you awake?' I whispered.

'Yup,' he replied in a weary but normal voice.

'What was that?'

'How the hell should I know?'

'It sounded big.'

'Everything sounds big in the woods.'

This was true. Once a skunk had come plodding through our camp and it had sounded like a stegosaurus. There was another heavy rustle and then the sound of lapping at the spring. It was having a drink, whatever it was.

I shuffled on my knees to the foot of the tent, cautiously

unzipped the mesh and peered out, but it was pitch black. As quietly as I could, I brought in my backpack and, with the light of a small torch, searched through it for my knife. When I found it and opened the blade I was appalled at how wimpy it looked. It was a perfectly respectable appliance for, say, buttering pancakes, but patently inadequate for defending oneself against 400 pounds of ravenous fur.

Carefully, very carefully, I climbed from the tent and put on the torch, which cast a distressingly feeble beam. Something about 15 or 20 feet away looked up at me. I couldn't see anything at all of its shape or size – only two shining eyes. It went silent, whatever it was, and stared back at me.

'Stephen,' I whispered at his tent, 'did you pack a knife?'

'No.'

'Have you got anything sharp at all?'

He thought for a moment. 'Nail clippers.'

I made a despairing face. 'Anything a little more vicious than that? Because, you see, there is definitely something out here.'

'It's probably just a skunk.'

'Then it's one big skunk. Its eyes are three feet off the ground.'

'A deer then.'

I nervously threw a stick at the animal, and it didn't move, whatever it was. A deer would have bolted. This thing just blinked once and kept staring.

I reported this to Katz.

'Probably a buck. They're not so timid. Try shouting at it.'

I cautiously shouted at it: 'Hey! You there! Scat!' The creature blinked again, singularly unmoved. 'You shout,' I said.

'Oh, you brute, go away, do!' Katz shouted in merciless imitation. 'Please withdraw at once, you horrid creature.'

'Fuck you,' I said and lugged my tent right over to his. I didn't know what this would achieve exactly, but it brought me a tiny measure of comfort to be nearer to him.

'What are you doing?'

'I'm moving my tent.'

'Oh, good plan. That'll really confuse it.'

I peered and peered, but I couldn't see anything but those two wide-set eyes staring from the near distance like eyes in a cartoon. I couldn't decide whether I wanted to be outside and dead or inside and waiting to be dead. I was barefoot and in my underwear and shivering. What I really wanted – really, really wanted – was for the animal to withdraw. I picked up a small stone and tossed it at it. I think it may have hit it because the animal made a sudden noisy start, which scared the bejesus out of me and brought a whimper to my lips, and then it emitted a noise – not quite a growl, but near enough. It occurred to me that perhaps I oughtn't to provoke it.

'What are you doing, Bryson? Just leave it alone and it will go away.'

'How can you be so calm?'

'What do you want me to do? You're hysterical enough for both of us.'

'I think I have a right to be a trifle alarmed, pardon me. I'm in the woods, in the middle of nowhere, in the dark, staring at a bear, with a guy who has nothing to defend himself with but a pair of nail clippers. Let me ask you this. If it is a bear and it comes for you, what are you going to do – give it a pedicure?'

'I'll cross that bridge when I come to it,' Katz said implacably.

'What do you mean you'll cross that bridge? We're *on* the bridge, you moron. There's a bear out here, for Christ's sake. He's looking at us. He smells noodles and Snickers and – oh, shit.'

'What?'

'Oh. Shit.'

'What?'

'There's two of them. I can see another pair of eyes.' Just then, the torch battery started to go. The light flickered and then vanished. I scampered into my tent, stabbing myself lightly but hysterically in the thigh as I went, and began a quietly frantic search for spare batteries. If I were a bear, this would be the moment I would choose to lunge.

'Well, I'm going to sleep,' Katz announced.

'What are you talking about? You can't go to sleep.'

'Sure I can. I've done it lots of times.' There was the sound of him rolling over and a series of snuffling noises, not unlike those of the creature outside.

'Stephen, you can't go to sleep,' I ordered. But he could and he did, with amazing rapidity.

The creature – creatures, now – resumed drinking, with heavy lapping noises. I couldn't find any replacement batteries, so I flung the torch aside and put my miner's lamp on my head, made sure it worked, then switched it off. Then I sat for ages on my knees, facing the front of the tent, listening keenly, gripping my walking stick like a club, ready to beat back an attack, and with my knife open and at hand as a last line of defence. The bears – animals, whatever they were – drank for perhaps twenty minutes more, then quietly departed the way they had come. It was a joyous moment – but I knew from my reading that they would be likely to return. I listened and listened, but the forest returned to silence and stayed there.

Eventually I loosened my grip on the walking stick and put on a sweater – pausing twice to examine the tiniest noises, dreading the sound of a revisit – and after a very long time got back into my sleeping bag for warmth. I lay there staring at total blackness, and knew that never again would I sleep in the woods with a light heart.

And then, irresistibly and by degrees, I fell asleep.

CHAPTER TWELVE

I'D EXPECTED KATZ TO BE INSUFFERABLE IN THE MORNING, BUT IN FACT he was surprisingly gracious. He called me for coffee and when I emerged, feeling wretched and cheated of sleep, he said to me: 'You OK? You look like shit.'

'Didn't get enough sleep.'

He nodded. 'So you think it really was a bear?'

'Who knows?' I suddenly thought of the food bag – that's what bears normally go for – and spun my head to see, but it was still suspended a dozen or so feet from the ground from a branch about twenty yards away. Probably a determined bear could have got it down. Actually, my grandmother could have got it down. 'Maybe not,' I said, disappointed.

'Well, you know what I've got in here, just in case?' Katz said and tapped his shirt pocket significantly. 'Toenail clippers – because you just never know when danger might arise. I've learned *my* lesson, believe me, buddy.' Then he guffawed.

And so we returned to the woods. For virtually the length of Shenandoah National Park, the AT closely parallels and often crosses Skyline Drive, though most of the time you would scarcely guess it. Often you will be plodding through the sanctuary of woods when suddenly a car will sail past through the trees only 40 or 50 feet away – a perennially startling sight.

In the early 1930s, the Potomac Appalachian Trail Club – which was Myron Avery's baby and for a time was virtually indistinguishable from the Appalachian Trail Conference itself – came under attack from other hiking groups, particularly the patrician

Appalachian Mountain Club in Boston, for not resisting the building of Skyline Drive through the park. Stung by these rebukes, Avery sent MacKaye a deeply insulting letter in December 1935, which effectively terminated MacKaye's official – but even then peripheral – relationship with the trail. The two men never spoke again, though to his credit MacKaye paid Avery a warm tribute on his death in 1952 and generously noted that the trail could not have been built without him. A lot of people still dislike the highway, but Katz and I quite warmed to it. Frequently we would leave the trail and hike on the road for an hour or two. This early in the season – it was still early April – there were hardly any cars on the road, so we treated Skyline Drive as a kind of broad, paved, alternative footpath. It was novel to have something firm underfoot and exceedingly agreeable to be out in the open, in warm sunshine, after weeks in impenetrable woods. Motorists certainly had a more cosseted, looked-after existence than we did. There were frequent expansive overlooks, with splendid views (though even now, in clear spring weather, blanketed with a dirty haze beyond about six or seven miles), information boards giving helpful facts on the park's wildlife and flora, and even litter bins. We could do with some of this on the trail, we agreed. And then, when the sun got too hot or our feet grew sore (for asphalt is surprisingly hard on the feet) or we just fancied a change, we would return to the familiar, cool, embracing woods. It was very agreeable – almost rakish – to have options.

At one of the Skyline Drive lay-bys we came to, an information board was angled to direct the reader's attention to a nearby slope handsomely spread with hemlocks, a very dark, almost black native conifer particularly characteristic of the Blue Ridge. All these hemlocks, and all the hemlocks everywhere along the trail and far beyond, are being killed by an aphid introduced accidentally from Asia in 1924. The National Park Service, the board noted sadly, could not afford to treat the trees. There were too many of them over too wide an area to make a spraying programme practicable. Well, here's an idea. Why not treat *some* of the trees? Why not treat *a* tree? The good news, according to the board, was that the National Park Service hoped that some of the trees would stage a natural recovery over time. Well, whew! for that.

Sixty years ago, there were almost no trees on the Blue Ridge Mountains. All this was farmland. Often in the woods now the trail would follow the relics of old stone field walls and once we passed a small, remote cemetery – reminders that this was one of the few mountaintop areas in the entire Appalachian chain where people once actually lived. Unluckily for them, they were the wrong kind of people. In the 1920s, sociologists and other academics from the cities ventured into the hills, and they were invariably appalled at what they found. Poverty and deprivation were universal. The land was ridiculously poor. Many people were farming slopes that were practically perpendicular. Three-quarters of the people in the hills couldn't read. Most had barely gone to school. Illegitimacy was 90 per cent. Sanitation was practically unknown; only 10 per cent of households had even a basic privy. On top of that, the Blue Ridge Mountains were sensationally beautiful and conveniently sited for the benefit of a new class of motoring tourist. The obvious solution was to move the people off the mountaintops and into the valleys, where they could be poor lower down, build a scenic highway for people to cruise up and down on Sundays, and turn the whole thing into a great mountaintop fun zone, with commercial campgrounds, restaurants, ice cream parlours, crazy golf, helter-skelters, and whatever else might turn a snappy dollar.

Unfortunately for the entrepreneurs, then came the Great Depression and the commercial impulse withered. Instead, under that dizzying socialist impulse (though you must never use that term) that marked the presidency of Franklin Roosevelt, the land was bought for the nation. The people were moved out, and the Civilian Conservation Corps was put to work building pretty stone bridges, picnic shelters, visitor centres, and much else, and the whole was opened to the public in July 1936. It is the quality of craftsmanship that accounts substantially for the glory of Shenandoah National Park. Indeed, it is one of the very few examples of human handiwork – Hoover Dam is another, and Mount Rushmore, I would submit, is a third – anywhere in the United States that complements, even enhances, a natural landscape. I suppose that, too, is one reason I liked walking along Skyline Drive, with its broad, lawnlike grass verges and stone retaining walls, its clusters of artfully planted birches, its gentle curves leading to arresting, thoughtfully composed panoramas. This is the way all highways should be. For a time it looked as if all highways *would* be like this. It is no accident that the first highways in America were called parkways. That's what they were envisioned to be – parks you could drive through.

Almost none of this spirit of craftsmanship is evident on the AT in the park – you wouldn't expect it to be on a trail devoted to wilderness – but it is agreeably encountered in the park's shelters, or huts, which have something of the picturesque rusticity of the Smokies shelters but are airier, cleaner, and better designed, and without those horrible, depressing chain-link fences across their fronts.

Though Katz thought I was preposterous, I insisted on sleeping at shelters after our night at the spring – I somehow felt I could defend a shelter against marauding bears – and in any case the Shenandoah shelters were too nice not to use. Every one of them was attractive, thoughtfully sited, had a good water source, and a picnic table and privy. For two nights we had shelters to ourselves, and on the third were just exchanging congratulations on this remarkable string of luck when we heard a cacophony of voices approaching through the woods. We peeked round the corner and found a Boy Scout troop marching into the clearing. They said hello and we said hello, and then we sat with our legs dangling from the sleeping platform and watched them fill the clearing with their tents and abundant gear, pleased to have something to look at other than each other. There were three adult supervisors and seventeen Boy Scouts, all charmingly incompetent. Tents went up, then swiftly collapsed or keeled over. One of the adults went off to filter water and fell in the creek. Even Katz agreed that this was better than TV. For the first time since we had left New Hampshire, we felt like masters of the trail.

A few minutes later, a cheerful lone hiker arrived. His name was John Connolly, and he was a high school teacher from upstate New York. He had been hiking the trail, evidently only a couple of miles behind us, for four days, and had been camping alone in the open each night, which struck me now as awfully brave. He hadn't seen any bears – indeed, had been section hiking the trail for years and had seen a bear only once, briefly, rump end and fleeing, deep in the Maine woods. He was followed shortly by two men about our age from Louisville – Jim and Chuck, both real nice fellows, self-effacing and funny. We hadn't seen more than three or four hikers since leaving Waynesboro, and now suddenly we were inundated.

'What day is it?' I asked, and everyone had to stop and think.

'Friday,' someone said. 'Yeah, Friday.' That explained it – the start of a weekend.

We all sat around the picnic table, cooking and eating. It was wonderfully convivial. The three others had hiked a great deal and told us all about the trail ahead as far as Maine, which still seemed as distant as the next cosmos. Then the conversation turned to a perennial favourite among hikers – how crowded the trail had become. Connolly talked about how he had hiked nearly half the trail in 1987, at the height of summer, and had gone days without seeing anyone, and Jim and Chuck heartily seconded this.

This is something you hear a lot, and it is certainly true that more people are hiking than ever before. Until the 1970s, fewer than fifty people a year thru-hiked the AT. As recently as 1984, the number was just 100. By 1990, it had pushed past 200, and today it is approaching 300. These are big increases, but they are also still tiny, tiny numbers. Just before we set off, my local newspaper in New Hampshire had an interview with a trail maintainer who noted that twenty years ago the three campsites in his section averaged about a dozen visitors a week in July and August and that now they sometimes got as many as a hundred in a week. The amazing thing about that, if you ask me, is that they got so few for so long. Anyway, a hundred visitors a week for three campsites at the height of summer hardly seems overwhelming.

Perhaps I was coming at this from the wrong direction, having hiked in crowded little England for so long, but what never ceased to astonish me throughout our long summer was how empty the trail was. Nobody knows how many people hike the Appalachian Trail, but most estimates put the number at around three or four million a year. If four million is right, and we assume that probably three-quarters of that hiking is done during the six warmest months, that means an average of 16,500 people on the trail a day in season, or 7.5 people for each mile of trail, one person every 700 feet. In fact, few sections will experience anything like that high a density. A very high proportion of those four million annual hikers will be concentrated in certain popular places for a day or a weekend – the Presidential Range in New Hampshire, Baxter State Park in Maine, Mount Greylock in Massachusetts, in the Smokies and Shenandoah National Park. That four million will also include a high proportion of what you might call Reebok hikers – people who park their car, walk 400 yards, get back in their car and drive off, and never do anything as breathtaking as that again. Believe me, no matter what anyone tells you the Appalachian Trail is not crowded.

When people bleat on about the trail being too crowded, what they mean is that the shelters are too crowded, and this is indubitably sometimes so. The problem, however, is not that there are too many hikers for the shelters, but too few shelters for the hikers. Shenandoah National Park has just eight huts, each able to accommodate no more than eight people in comfort, ten at a pinch, in 101 miles of national park. That's about average for the trail overall. Although the distances between shelters can vary enormously, there is on average an AT shelter, cabin, hut or lean-to (240 of them altogether) about every ten miles. That means adequate covered sleeping space for just 2,500 hikers over 2,200 miles of trail. When you consider that more than 100 million Americans live within a day's drive of the Appalachian Trail, it is hardly surprising that 2,500 sleeping spaces is sometimes not enough. Yet, perversely, pressure is growing in some quarters to reduce the number of shelters to discourage what is seen – amazingly to me – as overuse of the trail.

So, as always when the conversation turned to the crowdedness of the trail and the fact that you now sometimes see a dozen people in a day when formerly you would have been lucky to see two, I listened politely and said, 'You guys ought to try hiking in England.'

Jim turned to me and said, in a kindly, patient way, 'But you see, Bill, we're not *in* England.' Perhaps he had a point.

Now here is another reason I am very, very fond of Shenandoah National Park, and why I am probably not cut out to be a proper American trail hiker – cheeseburgers. You can get cheeseburgers quite regularly in Shenandoah National Park, and Coca-Cola with ice and French fries and ice cream, and a good deal else. Although the rampant commercialization I spoke of a moment ago never happened – and thank goodness, of course – something of that *esprit de commerce* lives on in Shenandoah. The park is liberally sprinkled with public campgrounds and rest stops with restaurants and shops – and the AT, God bless it, pays nearly every one of them a call. It is entirely against the spirit of the AT to have restaurant breaks along the trail, but I never met a hiker who didn't appreciate it to bits.

Katz, Connolly and I had our first experience of it the next morning, after we had said farewell to Jim and Chuck and the Boy Scouts, who were all headed south, when we arrived about lunchtime at a lively commercial sprawl called Big Meadows.

Big Meadows had a campground, a lodge, a restaurant, a gift

shop/general store, and lots and lots of people spread around a big sunny grassy space. (Although it is a big meadow, it was actually named for a guy named Meadows, which pleased me very much for some reason.) We dropped our packs on the grass outside and hastened into the busy restaurant where we greedily partook of everything greasy, then repaired to the lawn to smoke and burp and enjoy a spell of tranquil digestion. As we lay there propped against our packs, a tourist in an unfortunate straw hat, clutching an ice cream, came up and looked us over in a friendly manner. 'So you fellas hiking?' he said.

We said we were.

'And you carry those packs?'

'Until we find someone to carry them for us,' said Katz cheerfully.

'How far you come this morning?'

'Oh, about eight miles.'

'Eight miles! Lord. And how far'll you go this afternoon?'

'Oh, maybe another eight miles.'

'No kidding! Sixteen miles on foot? With those things on your back? *Man* – ain't that a kick.' He called across the lawn: 'Bernice, come here a minute. You gotta see this.' He looked at us again. 'So whaddaya got in there? Clothes and stuff, I suppose?'

'And food,' said Connolly.

'You carry your own food, huh?'

'Have to.'

'Well, ain't that a kick.'

Bernice arrived and he explained to her that we were using our legs to proceed across the landscape. 'Ain't that something? They got all their food and everything in those packs.'

'Is that a fact?' Bernice said with admiration and interest. 'So, you're like *walkin'* everywhere?' We nodded. 'You walked here? All the way up here?'

'We walk everywhere,' said Katz solemnly.

'You never walked all the way up here!'

'Well, we did,' said Katz, for whom this was becoming one of the proudest moments of his life.

I went off to call home from a payphone and use the gents. When I returned a few minutes later, Katz had accumulated a small, appreciative crowd and was demonstrating the use and theory of various straps and toggles on his backpack. Then, at someone's behest, he put the pack on and posed for pictures. I had never seen him so happy.

While he was still occupied, Connolly and I went into the little grocery part of the complex to have a look around, and I realized just how little regarded and incidental hikers are to the real business of the park. Only 3 per cent of Shenandoah's two million annual visitors go more than a few yards into what is generously termed the backcountry. Ninety per cent of visitors arrive in cars or motor homes. This was a store for them. Nearly everything in the store required microwaving or oven heating or scrupulous refrigeration or came in large, family-sized quantities. (It's a rare hiker who wants twenty-four hamburger buns, I find.) There was not a single item of conventional trail food – raisins or peanuts or small, portable quantities of packets or tinned goods – which was a little dispiriting in a national park.

With no choice, and desperate not to eat noodles again if we could possibly help it (Connolly, I was delighted to learn, was also a noodles man), we bought twenty-four hot dogs and matching buns, a two-litre bottle of Coke, and a couple of large packets of cookies. Then we collected Katz, who announced regretfully to his adoring audience that he had to go – there were mountains still to climb – and stepped valiantly back into the woods.

We stopped for the night at a lovely, secluded spot called Rock Spring Hut, perched on a steep hillside with a long view over the Shenandoah Valley far below. The shelter even had a swing – a two-seater that hung on chains from the shelter overhang, put there in memory of one Theresa Affronti, who had loved the trail, according to a plaque on its back – which I thought was rather splendid. Earlier visitors to the shelter had left behind an assortment of tinned foods – beans, corn, Spam, baby carrots – which were lined up carefully along one of the support rafters. You find this sort of thing quite a lot on the trail. In some places, friends of the trail will hike up to shelters with home-made cookies or platters of fried chicken. It's quite wonderful.

While we were cooking dinner, a young southbound thru-hiker – the first of the season – arrived. He had hiked 26 miles that day and thought he had died and gone to heaven when he learned that hot dogs were on the menu. Six hot dogs apiece was more than Katz and Connolly and I could eat, so we ate four, and a quantity of cookies, and saved the rest for breakfast. But the young southbounder ate as if he had never eaten before. He downed six hot dogs, then a tin of baby carrots, and gratefully accepted a dozen or so Oreos, one after the other, and ate them with great savour and particularity. He told us he had started in Maine in deep snow, had been endlessly caught in blizzards, but was still averaging 25 miles a day. He was only about five foot six and his pack was enormous. No wonder he had an appetite. He was trying to hike the trail in three months, mostly by putting in very long days. When we woke in the morning, dawn was only just leaking in, but he had already gone. Where he had slept there was a brief note thanking us for the food and wishing us luck. We never did learn his name.

Late the next morning, when I realized that I had considerably outstripped Katz and Connolly, who were talking and not making very good time, I stopped to wait for them in a spacious, sun-dappled dell tucked into a bowl of small hills, which gave it an enchanting, secretive feel. Everything you might ask of a woodland scene was there – musical brook, carpet of lush ferns, elegant, well-spaced trees – and it struck me in passing what a nice place this would be to camp.

Just over a month later, two young women, Lollie Winans and Julianne Williams, evidently had the same thought. They pitched their tents somewhere in this tranquil, airy grove, then hiked the short way through the woods to Skyland Lodge, another commercial complex, to eat in its restaurant. No one knows exactly what happened, but some person at Skyland presumably watched them dine, then followed them back to their campsite. They were found three days later in their tents with their hands bound and their throats cut. There was no apparent motive. There has never been a suspect. Their deaths will almost certainly forever be a mystery. Of course I had no idea of this at the time, so when Katz and Connolly caught up I simply observed to them what a lovely spot it was. They looked at it and agreed, and then we moved on.

We had lunch with Connolly at Skyland, and then he left us to hitchhike back to his car at Rockfish Gap and return home. Katz and I bade him farewell and then pushed on, for that was what we did. We walked for three days more, stopping at restaurants when we came to them, and camping in shelters, which once again we had mostly to ourselves.

On our next to last day in the park, our sixth since setting off from Rockfish Gap, we awoke to chill, gloomy weather. The wind freshened and then it began to rain, steadily and heavily, a really cold, penetrating rain. It turned out to be an awful day in nearly every way. In the early afternoon, I discovered that I had lost my backpack raincover – which, may I just say here, was a completely useless, ill-designed piece of crap anyway, for which I had paid $25 – and that nearly everything in my pack now ranged from sodden to damp. I had, fortunately, taken to wrapping my sleeping bag in a double thickness of trash bags (cost 35 cents), so it at least was dry. Twenty minutes later, as I sheltered under a bough waiting for Katz, he arrived and immediately said, 'Hey, where's your stick?' I had lost my beloved walking stick – I suddenly remembered propping it against a tree when I had stopped to tie a lace – and was filled with despair. That stick had seen me through six and a half weeks of mountains, had become all but part of me. It was a link with my children, whom I missed more than I can tell you. I felt like weeping. I told Katz where I thought I'd left it, at a place called Elkwallow Gap, about four miles back.

'I'll get it for you,' he said without hesitation and started to drop his pack. I could have wept again – he really meant it – but I wouldn't let him go. It was too far and besides Elkwallow Gap was a public place. Someone would have taken it as a souvenir by now.

So we pressed on to a spot called Gravel Springs Hut. It was only half past two when we got there. We had planned to go at least six miles further, but we were so soaked and the rain was so unrelenting that we decided to stop. I had no dry clothes, so I stripped to my boxer shorts and climbed into my sleeping bag. We spent the longest afternoon I can ever remember listlessly reading and staring out at the pattering rain.

At about five o'clock, just to make our day complete, a group of six noisy people arrived, three men and three women, dressed in the most preposterously Ralph Lauren-style hiking clothes – safari jackets and broad-brimmed canvas hats and suede hiking boots. These were clothes for sauntering along the veranda at Mackinac or perhaps going on a jeep safari, but patently not for hiking. One of the women, arriving a few paces behind the others and walking through the mud as if it were radioactive, peered into the shelter at me and Katz and said with undisguised distaste, 'Ooh, do we have to *share*?'

They were, to a degree that would have been fascinating in less trying circumstances, stupid, obnoxious, cheerfully but astonishingly self-absorbed, and not remotely acquainted with trail etiquette. Katz and I found ourselves carelessly bumped and jostled into the darkest corners, sprayed with water from clothes being shaken out, and knocked on the head with casually discarded equipment. In astonishment we watched as clothes we had hung up to dry on a small clothes line were pushed and bunched to one side to make abundant room for their stuff. I sat sullenly, unable to concentrate on my book, while two of the men crouched beside me, in my light, and had the following conversation:

'I've never done this before.'

'What – camp in a shelter?'

'No, look through binoculars with my glasses on.'

'Oh, I thought you meant camp in a shelter – ha! ha! ha!'

'No, I meant look through binoculars with my glasses on – ha! ha! ha!'

After about a half an hour of this Katz came over, knelt beside me and said in a whisper, 'One of these guys just called me "Sport". I'm getting the fuck out of here.'

'What're you going to do?'

'Pitch my tent in the clearing. You coming?'

'I'm in my underpants,' I said pathetically.

Katz nodded in understanding and stood up. 'Ladies and gentlemen,' he announced, 'can I have your attention for a minute? Excuse me, Sport, can I have your attention? We're going to go out and pitch our tents in the rain, so you can have *all* the space in here, but my friend here is in his boxer shorts, and is afraid of offending the ladies – and maybe exciting the gentlemen,' he added with a brief, sweet leer, 'so could you turn your heads for a minute while he puts his wet clothes back on? Meanwhile, I'll say goodbye and thank you for allowing us to share a few inches of your space for a little while. It's been a slice.'

Then he jumped down into the rain. I dressed hastily, surrounded by silence and self-consciously averted gazes, then bounded down with a small, wimpily neutral goodbye. We pitched our tents about 30 yards away – not an easy or enjoyable process in the driving rain, believe me – and climbed in. Before we had finished, voices from the shelter had resumed and were succeeded by peals of triumphant laughter. They were noisy until dark, then drunkenly noisy until the small hours. I wondered if at any point they would experience some twinge of charity or remorse and send over a peace offering – a brownie, perhaps, or a hot dog – but they did not.

When we woke in the morning, the rain had stopped, though the world was still insipid and drear, and water was dripping from the trees. We didn't bother with coffee. We just wanted to get out of there. We broke down our tents and packed away our stuff. Katz went to get a shirt from the line, and reported that our six friends were sleeping heavily. There were two empty bourbon bottles, he reported in a tone of disdain.

We hefted our packs and set off down the trail. We had walked perhaps 400 yards, out of sight of the camp, when Katz stopped me.

'You know that woman who said "Ooh, do we have to share?" and shoved our clothes to the end of the clothes line?' he asked.

I nodded. Of course I remembered her.

'Well, I'm not real proud of this. I want you to understand that. But when I went to get my shirt, I noticed her boots were right by the edge of the platform and, well, I did something kind of bad.'

'What?' I tried to imagine, but couldn't.

He opened his hand and there were two suede shoelaces. Then he beamed – a big, winning beam – and stuck them in his pocket and walked on.

CHAPTER THIRTEEN

AND THAT WAS ABOUT IT FOR THE START OF OUR GREAT ADVENTURE. We walked 18 miles to Front Royal, where my wife was to pick us up in two days if she managed to find her way by car from New Hampshire in an unfamiliar country.

I had to go off for a month to do other things – principally, try to persuade Americans to buy a book of mine even though it had nothing to do with effortless weight loss, running with the wolves, thriving in an age of anxiety, or the O.J. Simpson trial. (Even so, it sold over sixty copies.) Katz was going back to Des Moines, where he had the offer of a job for the summer building houses, though he promised to come back in August and hike the famous and forbidding Hundred Mile Wilderness in Maine with me.

At one point, very early in the trip, he had talked earnestly of doing the whole trail, pushing on alone until I was able to rejoin him in June, but when I mentioned this now he just gave a hollow laugh and invited me to join him in the real world when I felt up to it.

'To tell you the truth, I'm amazed we've come this far,' he said, and he was right. We had hiked 500 miles, a million and a quarter steps, since setting off from Amicalola. We had grounds to be proud. We were real hikers now. We had shit in the woods and slept with bears. We had become, we would forever be, mountain men.

We reached Front Royal about seven, dead tired, and went to the first motel we came to. It was arrestingly dire, but cheap. The bed sagged, the TV picture jumped as if it were being mercilessly goosed by an electronic component, and my door didn't lock. It pretended to lock, but if you pushed on it from outside with a finger, it popped open. This perplexed me for a moment until I realized that no one could possibly want any of my possessions, so I just pulled it shut and went off to find Katz and go to dinner. We ate at a steakhouse down the street and retired happily to our televisions and beds.

In the morning, I went early to K-Mart and bought two complete new sets of clothes – socks, underwear, blue jeans, sneakers, handkerchiefs, and the two liveliest shirts I could find (one with boats and anchors, the other with a famous-monuments-of-Europe motif). I returned to the motel, presented Katz with half – he couldn't have been more thrilled – then went to my room and put on my new attire. We met in the motel car park ten minutes later, looking crisp and stylish, and exchanged many flattering comments. With a day to kill, we went for breakfast, had an idle, contented saunter through the modest central business district, poked around in thrift shops for something to do, found a camping store where I bought a replacement hiking stick exactly like the one I had lost, had lunch, and in the afternoon decided naturally to go for a walk. It was, after all, what we did.

We found some railroad tracks, which followed the stately curves of the Shenandoah River. There is nothing more agreeable, more pleasantly summery, than to stroll along railroad tracks in a new shirt. We walked without haste or particular purpose, mountain men on holiday, chatting seamlessly about nothing in particular, stepping aside from time to time to let a freight train lumber past, and generally enjoying the abundant sunshine, the beckoning infinite gleam of silver track, and the simple pleasure of moving forward on legs that felt tireless. We walked almost till sunset. It was a happy way to conclude the trip.

In the morning we went to breakfast and then there was the three hours of fidgety torture of standing at the edge of a motel drive watching traffic for a particular car filled with beaming, much-missed faces. Well, you can imagine the reunion scene, I'm sure – the exuberant hugs, the tumble of information about the confusion of finding the right turnoff and motel, the impressed appraisal of dad's new body, the less impressed appraisal of his new shirt, the sudden remembering to include Katz (bashfully grinning on the margins) in the celebrations, the tousling of hair, the whole transcendently happy business of being back together.

We took Katz to National Airport in Washington, where he was booked on a late afternoon flight to Des Moines. At the airport, I realized we were already in different universes – he in a 'Where do I go to check in?' sort of distraction, I in the distraction of knowing that my family waited, that the car was badly parked, that it was nearly rush hour in Washington – so we parted awkwardly, almost absently, with hasty wishes for a good flight and promises to meet again in August. When he was gone I felt bad, but then I turned to the car, saw my family, and didn't think about him again for weeks.

It was the end of May, almost June, before I got back on the trail. I went for a walk in the woods near our home, with a day pack containing a bottle of water, two peanut butter sandwiches, a map (for form's sake), and nothing else. It was summer now, so the woods were alive with green and heavy with birdsong and swarming mosquitoes and blackfly. I walked five miles over low hills through the woods to the town of Etna, where I sat beside an old cemetery and ate my sandwiches, then packed up and walked home. I was back before lunch. It didn't feel right at all.

The next day I drove to Mount Moosilauke, 50 miles from my home on the southern edge of the White Mountains. Moosilauke is a wonderful mountain, one of the most beautiful in New England, with a certain leonine grandeur and weighty majesty, but it is rather in the middle of nowhere so it doesn't attract a great deal of attention. It belongs to Dartmouth College, of Hanover, whose famous Outing Club has been looking after it in a commendably low-key way since the early years of this century. Dartmouth introduced the sport of downhill skiing to America on Moosilauke, and the first national championships were held there in 1933. But it was too remote, and soon the sport in New England moved to other mountains nearer main highways, and Moosilauke returned to a splendid obscurity. Today you would never guess that it had ever known fame.

I parked in a small dirt car park, the only car that day, and set off into the woods. This time I had water, peanut butter sandwiches, a map, and insect repellent. Mount Moosilauke is 4,802 feet high, and steep. Without a full pack, I walked straight up it without stopping – a novel and gratifying experience. The view from the top was gorgeously panoramic, but it still didn't feel right without Katz, without a full pack. I was home by 4 p.m. This didn't feel right at all. You don't hike the Appalachian Trail and then go home and cut the grass.

So I decided to return to the trail properly, far away from home. The problem was that it is almost impossible nearly everywhere along the AT to get on and off the trail without assistance. I could fly to Washington or Newark or Scranton or Wilkes-Barre, or any of several other places in the *region* of the trail, but in each case I would still be scores of miles short of the trail itself. I couldn't ask my wife to drive me back to Virginia or Pennsylvania, any more than you could ask your wife to drop you in Düsseldorf. So I decided to drive myself. I would, I figured, park at a likely-looking spot, hike for a day or two into the hills, hike back and drive on a bit. I suspected this would turn out to be fairly unsatisfying, possibly even imbecilic, and I was right on both counts, but I didn't have a better alternative.

And thus I was to be found in the first week of June standing on the banks of the Shenandoah again, in Harpers Ferry, West Virginia.

Harpers Ferry is an interesting place and for a number of reasons. First, it is quite pretty. This is because it is a National Historical Park, which means it is owned by the nation as a treasured monument, so there are no Pizza Huts, McDonald's, Burger Kings or even residents, at least in the lower, older part of town. Instead, you get restored or recreated buildings with plaques and interpretation boards, so it doesn't have much, or indeed any, real life, but it still has a kind of polished prettiness. You can see that it would be a truly nice place to live if only people could be trusted to reside there without succumbing to the urge to have Pizza Huts and Taco Bells (and personally I believe they could, for up to eighteen months), so instead you get a pretend town, attractively tucked between steep hills at the confluence of the Shenandoah and Potomac rivers.

It is a National Historical Park because, of course, it is a historic place. It was at Harpers Ferry that the abolitionist John Brown decided to liberate America's slaves and set up a new nation of his own in northwestern Virginia, which was a pretty ambitious undertaking considering that he had an army of just twenty-one people. To that end, on 16 October 1859, he and his little group stole into town under cover of darkness, captured the federal armoury without resistance (it was guarded by a single nightwatchman), yet still managed to kill a hapless passer-by – who was, ironically, a freed black slave. When news got out that a federal armoury with 100,000 rifles and a great deal of ammunition was in the hands of a small band of lunatics, the President, James Buchanan, despatched Lieutenant-Colonel Robert E. Lee – at that time still a loyal Union soldier – to sort things out. It took Lee and his men less than three minutes of fighting to overcome the hapless rebellion. Brown was captured alive, swiftly tried and sentenced to be hanged a month hence.

One of the soldiers sent to oversee the hanging was Thomas J. Jackson – soon to become famous as Stonewall Jackson – and one of the eager onlookers in the crowd was John Wilkes Booth. So the capture of the federal armoury at Harpers Ferry served as quite a neat overture for all that followed.

Meanwhile, in the wake of Brown's little adventure, all hell was breaking loose. Northern abolitionists like Ralph Waldo Emerson made Brown a martyr, and Southern loyalists got up in arms, quite literally, at the idea that this might be the start of a trend. Before you knew it, the nation was at war.

Harpers Ferry remained at the centre of things throughout the wildly bloody conflict that followed. Gettysburg was just 30 miles to the north, Manassas a similar distance to the south, and Antietam (where, it is worth noting, twice as many men died in one day as the total American losses in the War of 1812, Mexican War and Spanish–American War combined) was just ten miles away. Harpers Ferry itself changed hands eight times during the war, though the record in this regard belongs to Winchester, Virginia, a few miles south, which managed to be captured and recaptured seventy-five times.

These days Harpers Ferry passes its time accommodating tourists and cleaning up after floods. With two temperamental rivers at its feet and a natural funnel of bluffs before and behind, it is forever being inundated. There had been a bad flood in the town six months before, and the park's staff were still busy mopping out, repainting and carrying furnishings, artefacts and displays down from upstairs storage rooms. (Three months after my visit, they would have to take everything back up again.) At one of the houses, two of the rangers came out of the door and down the walk, and nodded smiles at me as they passed. Both of them, I noticed, were packing sidearms. Goodness knows what the world is coming to when park rangers carry service revolvers.

I had a poke around the town, but nearly every building I went to had a locked door and a notice saying CLOSED FOR FLOOD REPAIRS. Then I went and looked at the spot where the two rivers flow together. There was an Appalachian Trail noticeboard there. Although it had been only about ten days since the two women were murdered in Shenandoah National Park, there was already a small poster appealing for information. It had colour photographs of them both. They were clearly photos taken by the women themselves along the trail, in hiking gear, looking happy and healthy, radiant even. It was hard to look at them, knowing their doom. It occurred to me, with a small inward start, that had the two women lived they would very probably be arriving in Harpers Ferry just about now, that instead of standing here looking at a poster of them I could be chatting with them – or indeed, given a slight alteration of luck and fate, that it could be they looking at a poster of me and Katz looking trail-happy and confident.

In one of the few houses open I found a friendly, well-informed, happily unarmed ranger named David Fox, who seemed surprised and pleased to have a visitor. He bobbed up instantly from his stool when I came in and was clearly eager to answer any questions. We got to talking about preservation, and he mentioned how hard it was for the Park Service with so few funds to do a proper job. When the park had been formed, there had been money enough to buy only about half of the Schoolhouse Ridge Battlefield above town – one of the most important if least celebrated of Civil War battle sites – and now a developer was in the process of building houses and shops on what Fox clearly saw as hallowed ground. The developer had even started running pipes across National Park land in the confident – but, as it happened, mistaken – presumption that the Park Service wouldn't have the will or money to stop him. Fox told me I should go up and look at it. I said I would.

But first I had a more important pilgrimage to make. Harpers Ferry is the headquarters of the Appalachian Trail Conference, overseers of the noble footpath to which I had dedicated my summer. The ATC occupies a modest white house on a steep hill above the old part of town. I trudged up and went in. The HQ was half office/half shop – the office portion commendably busy-looking, the shop half arrayed with AT guides and keepsakes. At one end of the public area was a large-scale model of the entire trail, which, had I seen it before I started, would very possibly have dissuaded me from attempting such an undertaking. It was perhaps 15 feet long and conveyed instantly and arrestingly what a hard hike the AT is. The rest of the public area was filled with AT goods – T-shirts, postcards, bandannas, books, miscellaneous publications. I chose a couple of books and some postcards, and was served at the counter by a friendly young woman named Laurie Potteiger, whose label described her as an Information Specialist, and they seem to have chosen the right person for she was a mine of information.

She told me that the previous year 1,500 prospective thru-hikers had started the trail, 1,200 had made it to Neels Gap (that's a drop-out rate of 20 per cent in the first week, from a corps of people who had intended to hike for five or six months!), about a third had made it to Harpers Ferry, roughly halfway, and about 300 had reached Katahdin, a higher success rate than usual. Sixty or so people had successfully hiked the trail from north to south. This year's crop of thru-hikers had been passing through for the past month. It was too early to say what the final figure for the year would be, but it would certainly be higher. It rose, in any case, almost every year.

I asked her about the dangers of the trail, and she told me that in the eight years she had worked for the ATC, there had been just two confirmed cases of snakebite, neither fatal, and one person killed by lightning.

I asked her about the recent murders.

She gave a grimace. 'It's awful. Everyone's really upset about it, because trust is such a kind of bedrock part of hiking the AT, you know? I thru-hiked myself in 1987, so I know how much you come to rely on the goodness of strangers. The trail is really all about that, isn't it? And to have that taken away, well . . .' Then, remembering her position, she gave me a little bit of the official line – a brief, practised, articulate spiel to the effect that one should never forget that the trail is not insulated from the larger ills of society but that statistically it remains extremely safe compared with most places in America. 'It's had nine murders since 1937 – about the same as you would get in many small towns.' This was correct, but a wee bit disingenuous. The AT had no murders in its first thirty-six years and nine in the past twenty-two. Still her larger point was unarguable. You are more likely to be murdered in your bed in America than on the AT. Or as an American friend put it to me much later: 'Look, if you draw a two-thousand-mile-long line across the United States at any angle, it's going to pass through nine murder victims.'

'If you're interested, there's a book about one of the murders,' she said and reached below the counter. She rooted for a moment in a box and brought out a paperback called *Eight Bullets*, which she passed to me for examination. It was about two women who were shot in Pennsylvania in 1988. 'We don't keep it out because, you know, it's kind of upsetting, especially now,' she said apologetically.

I bought it, and as she handed me my change I mentioned to her the thought that if the women had survived they would be passing through about now. 'Yeah,' she said, 'I'd thought about that.'

It was drizzling when I stepped back outside. I went up to Schoolhouse Ridge to have a look at the battlefield. It was a large, park-like hilltop with a wandering path lined at intervals with information boards describing charges and last-ditch stands and other confused, noisy action. The battle for Harpers Ferry was the finest moment for Stonewall Jackson – he who had last come to town to hang John Brown – because it was here, through some deft manoeuvring and a bit of luck, that he managed to capture 12,500 Union troops, more American soldiers than would be captured in a single action until Bataan and Corregidor in the Second World War.

Now Stonewall Jackson is a man worth taking an interest in. Few people in history have achieved greater fame in a shorter period with less useful activity in the brainbox than General Thomas J. Jackson. His idiosyncrasies were legendary. He was hopelessly, but inventively, hypochondriacal. One of his more engaging physiological beliefs was that one arm was bigger than the other, and in consequence he always walked and rode with that arm held straight up, so that his blood would drain into his body. He was a champion sleeper. More than once he fell asleep at the dinner table with food in his mouth. At the Battle of White Oak Swamp, his lieutenants found it all but impossible to rouse him and lifted him, insensible, onto his horse where he continued to slumber while shells exploded around him. His obtuseness was famed. Once when a celebrated singer sang 'Dixie' for him and his officers, then asked if he had any special requests, he told her he had just one – would she sing 'Dixie' for him? He showed excessive zeal in recording captured goods, and would defend them at all costs. His list of materiel liberated from the Union Army during the 1862 Shenandoah campaign included 'six handkerchiefs, two and three-quarter dozen neckties, and one bottle of red ink'. He constantly drove his superiors, fellow commanders and junior officers to enraged frustration, partly by repeatedly disobeying instructions and partly by his paranoid habit of refusing to divulge his strategies, such as they were, to anyone. One officer under his command was ordered to withdraw from the town of Gordonsville, where he was on the brink of a signal victory, and march at the double to Staunton. Arriving in Staunton, he found fresh orders to go at once to Mount Crawford. There he was told to return to Gordonsville.

It was largely because of his habit of marching troops all over the Shenandoah Valley in an illogical and inexplicable fashion that Jackson earned a reputation among bewildered enemy officers for wiliness. His ineradicable fame rests almost entirely on the fact that he had a couple of small victories when other Southern troops were being slaughtered and routed, and by dint of having the best nickname any soldier has ever enjoyed. He was unquestionably brave, but in fact it is altogether possible that he was given that nickname not for gallantry and daring, but for standing inert, like a stone wall, when a charge was called for. General Barnard Bee, who gave him the name at the First Battle of Manassas, was killed before the day was out, so the matter will remain forever unresolvable.

His victory at Harpers Ferry, the greatest triumph for the Confederacy in the Civil War, was almost entirely because for once he followed the instructions of Robert E. Lee. It sealed his fame. A few months later he was accidentally shot by his own troops at the Battle of Chancellorsville, and died eight days later. The war was barely half over. He was just thirty-nine.

Jackson spent much of the war in and around the Blue Ridge Mountains, camping in and marching through the very woods and high gaps through which Katz and I had lately passed, so I was interested to see the scene of his greatest triumph, and followed the path around the undulating field reading the information boards with dutiful attention and peering unsuccessfully through the trees for a sign of the new housing development. It was late and the light was going, and anyway, to be perfectly frank, I have never been much good at battlefields. It was, I suppose, theoretically interesting to know that Captain Poague's battery stood just here and Colonel Grigsby's troops were arrayed in a thin, wavery line over there, but really there is no getting round the fact that today it is just a pleasant grassy field on a West Virginia hill.

I was hungry and had driven a long way, so I didn't have the necessary energy to imagine the noise and smoke and carnage. Besides, I had had enough death for one day. So I tramped back to the car and continued on.

CHAPTER FOURTEEN

IN THE MORNING, I DROVE ON TO PENNSYLVANIA, 30 MILES OR SO TO the north. The Appalachian Trail runs for 230 miles in a northeasterly arc across the state, like the broad end of a slice of pie. I never met a hiker with a good word to say about the trail in Pennsylvania. It is, as someone told a *National Geographic* reporter in 1987, the place 'where boots go to die'. During the last ice age it experienced what geologists call a periglacial climate – a zone at the edge of an ice sheet characterized by frequent freeze–thaw cycles that fractured the rock. The result is mile upon mile of jagged, oddly angled slabs of stone strewn about in wobbly piles known to science as *Felsenmeer* (literally, 'sea of rocks'). These require constant attentiveness if you are not to twist an ankle or sprawl on your face – not a pleasant experience with 50 pounds of momentum on your back. Lots of people leave Pennsylvania limping and bruised. Pennsylvania also has what are reputed to be the meanest rattlesnakes anywhere along the trail, and the most unreliable water sources, particularly in high summer. The AT in the state passes through no national parks or forests, traverses no notable eminences, offers no particularly memorable vistas, is untouched by history. It is essentially just the central part of a very long, taxing haul between the South and New England. It is little wonder that most people dislike it.

Oh, and it also has the very worst maps ever produced for hikers anywhere. The six sheets – maps is really much too strong a word for them – produced for Pennsylvania by a body called the Keystone Trails Association are small, monochrome, appallingly printed, inadequately keyed, and astoundingly vague – in short, completely useless: comically useless, heartbreakingly useless, dangerously useless. No one should be sent into a wilderness with maps this bad.

I had this brought home to me with a certain weep-inducing force as I stood in a car park in a place called Caledonia State Park looking at a section of map that was simply a blurred smear of whorls, like a poorly taken thumb print. A single contour line was interrupted by a printed number in microscopic type. The number said either 1800 or 1200 – it wasn't possible to tell – but it didn't actually matter because there was no scale indicated anywhere, nothing to denote the height interval from one contour line to the next, or whether the packed bands of lines indicated a steep climb or precipitous descent. Not one single thing – not one single thing – within the entire park and for some miles around was denoted. From where I stood, I could be 50 feet or two miles from the Appalachian Trail, in any direction. There was simply no telling.

Foolishly, I had not looked at these maps before setting off from home. I had packed in a hurry, simply noted that I had the correct set, and stuck them in my pack. I looked through them all now with a sense of dismay, as you might a series of compromising pictures of a loved one. I had known all along that I was never going to walk across Pennsylvania – I had neither the time nor the spirit for it – but I had thought I might find some nice circular walks that would give me something of the challenging flavour of the state without making me endlessly retrace my steps. It was clear now, looking through the complete set, that not only were there no circular hikes to be had, but it was going to be the next thing to pure luck any time I stumbled on the trail at all.

Sighing, I put the maps away and set off through the park on foot looking for the familiar white blazes of the AT. It was a pleasant park in a wooded valley, quite empty on this fine morning. I walked for perhaps an hour along a network of winding paths through trees and over wooden footbridges, but I failed to find the AT, so I returned to the car, and pushed on, along a lonely highway through the dense flying leaves of Michaux State Forest and on to Pine Grove Furnace State Park, a large recreation area built around a nineteenth-century stone kiln, now a picturesque ruin, from which it takes its name. The park had snack huts, picnic tables and a lake with a swimming area, but all were shut and there wasn't a soul about. On the edge of the picnic area was a big dumpster with a sturdy metal lid that had been severely – arrestingly – mangled and dented, and half wrenched from its hinges, presumably by a bear trying to get at park rubbish. I examined it with the deepest respect; I hadn't realized black bears were quite that strong.

Here at least the AT blazes were prominent. They led around the lake and up through steep woods to the summit of Piney Mountain, which wasn't indicated on the map and isn't really a mountain since it barely rises to 1,500 feet. Still, it was challenging enough on a hot summer's day. Just outside the park there is a board marking the traditional, but entirely notional, midpoint of the Appalachian Trail, with 1,080.2 indicated miles of hiking in either direction. (Since no one can say exactly how long the AT is, the real midpoint could be anywhere within 50 miles or so; in any case, it would change from year to year because of reroutings.) Two-thirds of thru-hikers never see it anyway, because they have dropped out by this point. It must actually be quite a depressing moment – to have slogged through a mountainous wilderness for ten or eleven weeks and to realize that for all that effort you are still but halfway there.

It was also round here that one of the trail's more notorious murders took place, the one at the heart of the book *Eight Bullets*, which I had bought at ATC headquarters the day before. The story is simply told. In May 1988, two young hikers, Rebecca Wight and Claudia Brenner, who were lesbians, excited the attention of a disturbed young man with a rifle, who shot them eight times from a distance as they made love in a leafy clearing beside the trail. Wight was killed. Brenner, seriously wounded, managed to stumble down the mountain to a road and was rescued by some passing teenagers in a pickup truck. The murderer was swiftly caught and convicted.

The next year a young man and woman were killed by a drifter at a shelter just a few miles to the north, which rather gave Pennsylvania a bad reputation for a while, but then there were no murders anywhere along the AT for seven years until the recent deaths of the two young women in Shenandoah National Park. Their deaths brought the official murder toll to nine – quite a large number for any footpath, no matter how you look at it – though in fact there probably have been more. Between 1946 and 1950 three people vanished while hiking through one small area of Vermont, but they aren't included in the tally; whether because it happened so long ago or because it was never conclusively proved they were murdered I couldn't say. I was also told by an acquaintance in New England of an older couple who were killed by a deranged axe murderer in Maine sometime in the 1970s, but again it doesn't appear in any records because, evidently, they were on a side trail when they were attacked.

I had read *Eight Bullets*, Brenner's account of the murder of her friend, overnight, so I was generally acquainted with the circumstances, but I intentionally left the book in the car as it seemed a little morbid to go looking for a death site nearly a decade after the event. I wasn't remotely spooked by the murder, but even so I felt a vague, low-grade unease at being alone in a silent wood so far from home. I missed Katz, missed his puffing and bitching and unflappable fearlessness, hated the thought that if I sat on a rock waiting he would never come. The woods were in full chlorophyll-choked glory now, which made them seem even more pressing and secretive. Often, I couldn't see five feet into the dense foliage on either side of the path. If I did happen on a bear, I would be quite helpless. No Katz would come along after a minute to smack it on the snout for me and say, 'Jesus, Bryson, you cause me a lot of trouble.' No one at all would come to share the excitement, it appeared. There didn't seem to be another person within 50 miles. The woods belonged to me and whatever else was out there.

So I walked the 3.5 miles to the top of Piney Mountain with a certain purposeful briskness. At the summit, I stood uncertainly, unable to decide whether to go on a bit further or turn back and perhaps try somewhere else, when there was a dry crack of wood and a careless rustle of undergrowth perhaps 50 feet into the woods – something good-sized and unseen. I stopped everything – moving, breathing, thinking – and stood on tiptoe peering into the leafy void. The noise came again, nearer. Whatever it was, it was coming my way! Whimpering quietly but sincerely, I ran a hundred yards, daypack bouncing wildly, glasses jiggling, then turned, heart stopped, and looked back. A deer, resplendently antlered, stepped onto the path, gazed at me for a moment without concern, and sauntered on. I took a long moment to catch my breath and wiped a river of sweat from my brow. I wasn't sure I was cut out for this sort of thing. I returned to the car without further incident.

I stopped the night near Harrisburg, and in the morning drove north and east across the state on back highways, trying to follow the trail as closely as I could by road, and stopping once or twice where possible to sample the trail, but without finding anything that looked remotely rewarding, so mostly I drove. Pennsylvania is not an easy place to characterize, partly because it is big and populous – 400 miles across from east to west; twelve million inhabitants – and partly because it is such a peculiar, patternless mix of ugly, half-dead factory towns, sweet little college communities, rolling farmland, and industrially scarred hillsides – a place equally at home to Rocky Balboa, Dwight Eisenhower, Andrew Carnegie and an Amish farmer. In the space of five miles it can go from hideous to gorgeous to hideous to more hideous to gorgeous again. I know a man who bought an old farmhouse in a remote, storybook vale as a weekend home. He awoke one Sunday to explosive booms and the tinkle of ceiling plaster and discovered that a gravel company was quarrying right up to his property line. He sold the house at a staggering loss, bought another, even more remote property, and awoke there to the sound of a phalanx of bulldozers preparing the farmland next door for a giant polypropylene plant. So he moved to Virginia. But that's Pennsylvania for you.

I passed through a long tight valley, enclosed by dark hills. Every farm on both sides of the road grew Christmas trees – endless, genetically identical rows of them that presented an infinite variety of straight lines from whatever angle you viewed them. At the end of each drive there was a mailbox with a name neatly lettered on the side, and every name without exception sounded comical and made up – Pritz, Putz, Mootz, Snootz, Schlepple, Klutz, Kuntz, Kunkle – and the scattered towns were just the same but for the addition of a place suffix: Funksville, Crumsville, Kutztown. Then, little by little, the town names began to take on a frank industrial tone – Port Carbon, Minersville, Lehigh Furnace, Slatedale – and I realized I was entering the strange, half-forgotten world of Pennsylvania's Anthracite Region. At Minersville, I turned onto a back highway and headed through a landscape of overgrown slag heaps and rusting machinery towards Centralia, the strangest, saddest town I believe I have ever seen.

Eastern Pennsylvania sits on one of the richest coalbeds on Earth. Almost from the moment Europeans arrived, they realized there was coal out there in quantities almost beyond conception. The trouble was it was virtually all anthracite, a coal so immensely hard – it is 95 per cent carbon – that for a very long time no one could figure out how to get it to light. It wasn't until 1828 that an enterprising Scot named James Neilson had the simple but effective idea of injecting heated air rather than cold air into an iron furnace by means of a bellows. The process became known as a hot blast and it transformed the coal industry all over the world (Wales, too, had a lot of anthracite), but especially in the United States. By the end of the century America was producing 300 million tons of coal a year, about as much as the rest of the world put together, and the great bulk of it came from Pennsylvania's anthracite belt.

Meanwhile, to its intense gratification, Pennsylvania had also discovered oil – not only discovered it, but devised ways to make it industrially useful. Petroleum – or rock oil – had been a curiosity of western Pennsylvania for years. It emerged in seeps along riverbanks where it was blotted up with blankets to be made into patent medicines esteemed for their value to cure everything from scrofula to diarrhoea. In 1859, a mysterious figure named Colonel Edwin Drake – who wasn't a colonel at all but a retired railway conductor, with no understanding of geology – developed, from goodness knows where, the belief that oil could be extracted from the ground via wells. At Titusville, he bored a hole to a depth of 69 feet and got the world's first gusher. Quickly it was realized that petroleum in volume could be not just used to bind bowels and banish scabby growths, but refined into lucrative products like paraffin and kerosene. Western Pennsylvania boomed inordinately. In three months, as John McPhee notes in *In Suspect Terrain*, the endearingly named Pithole City went from a population of zero to 15,000, and other towns throughout the region sprang up – Oil City, Petroleum Center, Red Hot. John Wilkes Booth came and lost his savings, then went off to kill a president, but others stayed and made a fortune.

For one lively half-century Pennsylvania had a virtual monopoly on one of the most valuable products in the world, oil, and an overwhelmingly dominant role in the production of a second, coal. Because of the proximity of rich supplies of fuel the state became the centre of big, fuel-intensive industries like steelmaking and chemicals. Lots of people became colossally rich.

But not the mineworkers. Mining has of course always been a wretched line of work everywhere, but nowhere more so than in the United States in the second half of the nineteenth century. Thanks to immigration, miners were infinitely expendable. When the Welsh got bolshie, you brought in Irish. When they failed to satisfy, you brought in Italians or Poles or Hungarians. Workers were paid by the ton, which meant not only that they were given an incentive to hack out coal with reckless haste, but also that any labour they expended making their environment safer or more comfortable went uncompensated. Mine shafts were bored through the earth like holes through Swiss cheese, often destabilizing whole valleys. In 1846, at Carbondale, almost 50 acres of mine shafts collapsed simultaneously without warning, claiming hundreds of lives. Explosions and flash fires were common. Mine dust is incredibly volatile – and most of this at a time, remember, when the only illumination was open flames. Between 1870 and the outbreak of the First World War, 50,000 people died in American mines.

The great irony of anthracite is that, tough as it is to light, once you get it lit it's nearly impossible to put out. Stories of uncontrolled mine fires are legion in eastern Pennsylvania. One fire at Lehigh began in 1850 and didn't burn itself out until the Great Depression – eighty years after it started.

And thus we come to Centralia. For a century Centralia was a sturdy little pit community. However difficult life may have been for the early miners, by the second half of the twentieth century Centralia was a reasonably prosperous, snug, hardworking town with a population approaching 2,000. It had a thriving business district with banks and a post office and the normal range of shops and small department stores, a high school, four churches, an Odd Fellows Club, a town hall – in short, a typical, pleasant, contentedly anonymous small American town.

Unfortunately, it also sat on 24 million tons of anthracite. In 1962, a fire in a tip on the edge of town ignited a coal seam. The fire department poured thousands of gallons of water onto the fire, but each time they seemed to have it extinguished it came back, like those trick birthday candles that go out for a moment and then spontaneously reignite. And then, very slowly, the fire began to eat its way along the subterranean seams. Smoke began to rise eerily from the ground over a wide area, like steam off a lake at dawn. On Highway 61, the asphalt grew warm to the touch, then began to crack and settle, rendering the road unusable. The smoking zone passed under the highway and fanned out through a neighbouring woodland and up towards St Ignatius Catholic Church on a knoll above the town.

The US Bureau of Mines brought in experts, who proposed any number of possible remedies – digging a deep trench through the town, deflecting the course of the fire with explosives, flushing the whole thing out hydraulically – but the cheapest proposal would have cost at least $20 million with no guarantee that it would work, and in any case no one was empowered to spend that kind of money. So the fire slowly burned on.

In 1979, the owner of a petrol station near the centre of town found that the temperature in his underground tanks was registering 172°F. Sensors sunk into the earth showed that the temperature 13 feet under the tanks was almost 1,000 degrees. Elsewhere people were discovering that their cellar walls and floors were hot to the touch. Smoke by now was seeping from the ground all over town, and people were beginning to grow nauseated and faint from the increased levels of carbon dioxide in their homes. In 1981, a twelve-year-old boy was playing in his grandmother's back garden when a plume of smoke suddenly appeared in front of him. As he stared at it, the ground opened around him. He clung to tree roots until someone heard his calls and hauled him out. The hole was found to be 80 feet deep. Within days, similar cave-ins were appearing all over town. It was about then that people started getting serious about the fire.

The federal government came up with $42 million to evacuate the town. As people moved out, their houses were bulldozed and the rubble was neatly, fastidiously, cleared away until there were almost no buildings remaining. So today Centralia isn't really even a ghost town. It's just a big open space with a grid of empty streets still surreally furnished with stop signs and fire hydrants. Every 30 feet or so there is a neat, paved driveway going 15 or 20 yards to nowhere. There are still a few houses scattered around – all of them modest, narrow, woodframed structures stabilized with brick buttresses – and a couple of buildings in what was once the central business district.

I parked outside a building with a faded sign that said, rather grandly, CENTRALIA MINE FIRE PROJECT OFFICE OF THE COLUMBIA REDEVELOPMENT AUTHORITY. The building was boarded and all but falling down. Next door was another, in better shape, called Speed Stop Car Parts, overlooking a neatly groomed park with an American flag on a pole beside a bench. The shop appeared to be still in business, but the interior was darkened and there was no one around. There was no one anywhere, come to that – no passing traffic, not a sound but the lazy clank of a metal ring knocking against the flagpole. Here and there in the vacant lots were metal cylinders, like oil drums, that had been fixed in the ground and were silently venting smoke.

Up a slight slope, across an expanse of vacant lots, a modern church, quite large, stood in a lazy pall of white smoke – St Ignatius, I assumed. I walked up. The church looked sound and usable – the windows were not boarded and there were no KEEP OUT signs – but it was locked and there was no board announcing services or anything even to indicate its name or denomination. All around it smoke was hovering wispily off the ground, but just behind it great volumes of smoke were billowing from the earth over a large area. I walked over and found myself on the lip of a vast cauldron, perhaps an acre in extent, which was emitting thick, cloudlike, pure white smoke – the kind of smoke you get from burning tyres or old blankets. It was impossible to tell through the stew of smoke how deep the hole was. The ground felt warm and was loosely covered in a fine ash.

I walked back to the front of the church. A heavy metal crash barrier stood across the old road and a new highway curved off down a hillside away from the town. I stepped round the barrier and walked down old Highway 61. Clumps of weedy grass poked through the surface here and there, but it still looked a serviceable road. All around on both sides for a considerable distance the land smoked broodingly, like the aftermath of a forest fire. About 50 yards along, a jagged crack appeared down the centre of the highway and quickly grew into a severe gash several inches across, emitting still more smoke. In places the road on one side of the gash had subsided a foot or more, or slumped into a shallow, bowl-shaped depression. From time to time I peered into the crack, but couldn't gauge anything of its depth for the swirling smoke, which proved to be disagreeably acrid and sulphurous when the breeze pushed it over me.

I walked along for some minutes, gravely examining the scar as if I were some kind of official inspector of highways before I spread my gaze more generally and it dawned on me that I was in the middle – very much in the middle – of an extensively smoking landscape, on possibly no more than a skin of asphalt, above a fire that had been burning out of control for thirty-four years – not, I'm bound to say, the smartest place in North America to position oneself. Perhaps it was no more than a literally heated imagination, but the ground suddenly seemed distinctly spongy and resilient, as if I were walking across a mattress. I retreated in haste to the car.

It seemed odd on reflection that I, or any other severely foolish person, could drive in and have a look round a place as patently dangerous and unstable as Centralia, and yet there was nothing to stop anyone from venturing anywhere. What was odder still was that the evacuation of Centralia was not total. Those who wanted to stay and live with the possibility of having their houses fall into the earth were allowed to remain, and a few had evidently so chosen. I got back in the car and drove up to a lone house in the centre of town. The house, painted a pale green, was eerily neat and well maintained. A vase of artificial flowers and other modest decorative knick-knacks stood on a windowsill and there was a bed of marigolds by the freshly painted stoop. But there was no car in the drive and no one answered the bell.

Several of the other houses proved on closer inspection to be unoccupied. Two were boarded and had DANGER – KEEP OUT notices tacked to them. Five or six others, including a clutch of three on the far side of the central park, were still evidently lived in – one, amazingly, even had children's toys in the garden (who on earth would keep children in a place like this?) – but there was no answer at any of the bells I tried. Everyone was either at work or, for all I knew, lying dead on the kitchen floor. It seemed exceedingly odd that people would be permitted to remain here, but then America is a strange country where personal liberty is concerned. At one house I knocked at I fancied I saw a curtain move, but I couldn't be sure. Who knows how crazy these people might be after three decades of living on top of an inferno and breathing head-lightening quantities of CO_2, or how weary they might have grown of outsiders cheerfully poking around and treating their town as a curious diversion? I was privately relieved that no one answered my knocks because I couldn't for the life of me think what my opening question would be.

It was well past lunchtime, so I drove the five miles or so to Mount Carmel, the nearest town. Mount Carmel was mildly startling after Centralia – a busy little town, nicely old-fashioned, with traffic on Main Street and sidewalks full of shoppers and other townsfolk going about their business. I had lunch at the Academy Luncheonette and Sporting Goods Store – possibly the only place in America where you can gaze at jockstraps while eating a tuna salad sandwich – and was intending then to push on in search of the AT, but on the way back to the car I passed a public library and impulsively popped in to ask if they had any information on Centralia.

They did – three fat files bulging with newspaper and magazine cuttings, most dating from 1979–81 when Centralia briefly attracted national attention, particularly after the little boy, one Todd Dombowski, was nearly swallowed by the earth in his granny's garden.

There was also, quite poignantly now, a slender, casebound history of Centralia, prepared to mark the town's centenary just before the outbreak of the fire. It was full of photographs showing a bustling town not at all unlike the one that stood just outside the library door, but with the difference of thirty-some years. I had forgotten just how distant the 1960s have grown. All the men in the photograph wore hats; the women and girls were in billowy skirts. All, of course, were happily unaware that their pleasant, anonymous town was quite doomed. It was nearly impossible to connect the busy place in the photographs to the empty space from which I had just come.

As I put the things back in their folders, a cutting fluttered to the floor. It was an article from *Newsweek*. Someone had underlined a short paragraph towards the end of the article and put three exclamation marks in the margin. It was a quote from a mine fire authority observing that if the rate of burning held steady there was enough coal under Centralia to burn for a thousand years.

It happened that a few miles beyond Centralia there was another scene of unusual devastation that I had heard about and was keen to investigate – a mountainside in the Lehigh Valley that had been so lavishly polluted by a zinc mill that it had been entirely stripped of vegetation. I had heard about it from John Connolly, who recalled it as being near Palmerton, so I drove there the following morning. Palmerton was a good-sized town, grimy and industrial, but not without its finer points – a couple of solid turn-of-the-century civic buildings that gave it an air of consequence, a dignified central square, and a business district that was clearly depressed but gamely clinging to life. The background was dominated everywhere by big, prison-like factories all of which appeared to be redundant. At one end of town, I spotted what I had come to find – a steep, broad eminence, perhaps 1,500 feet high and several miles long, which was almost entirely naked of vegetation. There was a car park beside the road, and a factory a hundred yards or so beyond. I pulled into the car park and got out to gawp – it truly was an arresting sight.

As I stood there, some fat guy in a uniform stepped out of a security booth and waddled towards me looking cross and officious.

'The hell you think you're doing?' he barked.

'Pardon me?' I replied, taken aback, and then: 'I'm looking at that hill.'

'You can't do that.'

'I can't look at a hill?'

'Not here you can't. This is private property.'

'I'm sorry. I didn't know.'

'Well, it's private – like the sign says.' He indicated a post that was in fact signless and looked momentarily struck. 'Well, it's private,' he added.

'I'm sorry. I didn't know,' I said again, not appreciating yet how keenly this man took his responsibilities. I was still marvelling at the hill. 'That's an amazing sight, isn't it?' I said.

'What is?'

'That mountain. There isn't a scrap of vegetation on it.'

'I wouldn't know. I'm not paid to look at hillsides.'

'Well, you should look sometime. I think you'd be surprised. So is that the zinc factory then?' I said, with a nod at the complex of buildings over his left shoulder.

He regarded me suspiciously. 'What do you want to know for?'

I returned his stare. 'I'm out of zinc,' I replied.

He gave me a sideways look as if to say 'Oh, a wise guy, huh?' and said suddenly, decisively, 'I think maybe I'd better take your name.' With difficulty he extracted a notebook and a stubby pencil from a back pocket.

'What, because I asked you if that was a zinc factory?'

'Because you're trespassing on private property.'

'I didn't know I was trespassing. You don't even have a sign up.'

He had his pencil poised. 'Name?'

'Don't be ridiculous.'

'Sir, you are trespassing on private property. Now are you gonna tell me your name?'

'No.'

We went through a little back and forth along these lines for a minute. At last he shook his head regretfully and said, 'Play it your way then.' He dragged out some communication device, pulled up an antenna and got it to operate. Too late I realized that for all his air of exasperation this was a moment he had dreamed of during many long, uneventful shifts in his little glass booth.

'J.D.?' he said into the receiver. 'Luther here. You got the clamps? I got an infractor in Lot A.'

'What are you doing?'

'I'm impounding your vehicle.'

'Don't be ridiculous. I only pulled off the road for a minute. Look, I'm going, OK?'

I got in the car, started the engine and made to go forward, but he blocked the way. I leaned from the window. 'Excuse me,' I called, but he didn't move. He just stood with his back to me and his arms crossed, conspicuously disregarding me. I tooted the horn lightly, but he was not to be shifted. I put my head out of the window and said, 'All right, I'll tell you my name then.'

'It's too late for that.'

'Oh, for God's sake,' I muttered and then, out of the window, 'Please?' and then, whinily, 'Come on, buddy, *please*?' but he had set a course and was not to be deflected. I leaned out once more. 'Tell me, did they specify "asshole" on the job description, or did you go on a course?' Then I breathed a very bad word and sat and steamed.

Thirty seconds later a car pulled up and a man in sunglasses got out. He was wearing the same uniform, but was ten or fifteen years older and a whole lot trimmer. He had the bearing of a drill sergeant.

'Problem here?' he said, looking from one to the other of us.

'Perhaps you can help me,' I said in a tone of sweet reason. 'I'm looking for the Appalachian Trail. This gentleman here tells me I'm trespassing.'

'He was looking at the *hill*, J.D.,' the fat guy protested a little hotly, but J.D. raised a palm to still him, then turned to me.

'You a hiker?'

'Yes, sir.' I indicated the pack on the back seat. 'I just wanted directions and the next thing I know' – I gave a cheerfully dismayed laugh – 'this man's telling me I'm on private property and he's impounding my car.'

'J.D., the man was looking at the hill and asking questions.' But J.D. held up another calming hand.

'Where you hiking?'

I told him.

He nodded. 'Well, then you want to go up the road about four miles to Little Gap and take the right for Danielsville. At the top of the hill you'll see the trail crossing. You can't miss it.'

'Thank you very much.'

'Not a problem. You have a good hike, you hear.'

I thanked him again and drove off. In the rear-view mirror I noticed with gratification that he was remonstrating quietly but firmly with Luther – threatening, I very much hoped, to take his communication device away.

The route went steeply up to a lonesome pass where there was a dirt car park. I parked, found the AT and walked along it on a high exposed ridge through the most amazingly devastated terrain. For miles it was either entirely barren or covered in the spindly trunks of dead trees, a few still weakly standing but most toppled. It brought to mind a First World War battlefield after heavy shelling. The ground was covered in a gritty black dust, like iron filings.

The walking was uncommonly easy – the ridge was almost perfectly flat – and the absence of vegetation meant that there were boundless views. All the other visible hills, including those facing me across the narrow valley, looked to be in good health, except where they had been scarred and gouged by quarrying or strip mining, which was regularly. I walked for a little over an hour until I came to a sudden, almost absurdly steep descent to Lehigh Gap – almost a thousand feet straight down, or of course straight up for those coming from the other direction – gave small thanks that I didn't have to do either and trudged back to the car the way I had come.

It was almost four o'clock when I got back to the car. The afternoon was as good as shot. I had driven 350 miles to get to Pennsylvania, had spent four long days in the state and walked a net 11 miles of the Appalachian Trail. Never again, I vowed, would I try to hike the Appalachian Trail with a car.

Still, I did have the deep and lasting satisfaction of having got a fat guy named Luther in trouble. I have had worse trips.

CHAPTER FIFTEEN

ONCE, AEONS AGO, THE APPALACHIANS WERE OF A SCALE AND MAJESTY to rival the Himalayas – piercing, snow-peaked, pushing breathtakingly through the clouds to heights of four miles or more. New Hampshire's Mount Washington is still an imposing presence, but the stony mass that rises above the New England woods today represents, at most, the stubby bottom one-third of what was ten million years ago.

That the Appalachian Mountains present so much more modest an aspect today is because they have had so much time in which to wear away. The Appalachians are immensely old – older than the oceans and continents, far, far older than most other mountain chains. When simple plants colonized the land and the first creatures crawled blinking from the sea, the Appalachians were there. They are, in fact, among the oldest landscape features on Earth.

Something over a billion years ago, the continents of Earth were a single mass called Pangaea surrounded by the lonely Panthalassan Sea. Then some unexplained turmoil within the earth's mantle caused the land to break apart and drift off as vast asymmetrical chunks. From time to time over the ages since – three times at least – the continents have held a kind of grand reunion, floating back to some central spot and bumping together with slow but crushing force. It was during the third of these collisions, starting about 470 million years ago, that the Appalachians were first pushed up (like a rucked carpet, as the analogy nearly always has it). Four hundred and seventy million years is a mind-dulling number, but if you can imagine flying backwards through time at the rate of one year per second, it would take you about sixteen years to cover such a span. It's a long time.

The continents didn't just move in and out from each other in some kind of grand slow-motion square dance, but spun in lazy circles, changed their orientation, went on cruises to the tropics and poles, made friends with smaller landmasses and brought them home. Florida once belonged to Africa. A corner of Staten Island is, geologically, part of Europe. The seaboard from New England up to Canada appears to have originated in Morocco. Parts of Greenland, Ireland, Scotland and Scandinavia have the same rocks as the eastern United States – are, in effect, ruptured outposts of the Appalachians. There are even suggestions that mountains as far south as the Shackleton Range in Antarctica may be fragments of the Appalachian family.

The Appalachians were formed in three long phases, or orogenies as scientists like to call them, known as the Taconic, Acadian and Alleghenian. The first two were essentially responsible for the northern Appalachians, the third for the central and southern Appalachians. As the continents bumped and nudged, sometimes one continental plate would slide over another, pushing ocean floor before it, reworking the landscape for 150 miles or more inland. At other times it would plunge beneath, stirring up the mantle and resulting in long spells of volcanic activity and earthquakes. Sometimes the collisions would interleave layers of rock like shuffled playing cards.

It is tempting to think of this as some kind of giant continent-sized car crash, but of course it happened with imperceptible slowness. The Proto-Atlantic Ocean (sometimes more romantically called Iapetus), which filled the void between continents during one of the early splits, looks in most textbook illustrations like a transitory puddle – there in Fig. 9A; vanished in Fig. 9B, as if the sun had come out for a day or so and dried it up – yet it existed far longer, hundreds of millions of years longer, than our own Atlantic has. So it was with the formation of mountains. If you were to travel back to one of the mountain-building phases of the Appalachians, you wouldn't be aware of anything geologically grand going on, any more than we are sensible now that India is ploughing into Asia like a runaway truck into a snowbank, pushing the Himalayas up by a millimetre or so a year.

And as soon as the mountains were built, they began, just as ineluctably, to wear away. For all their seeming permanence, mountains are exceedingly transitory features. In *Meditations at 10,000 Feet*, the writer and geologist James Trefil calculates that a typical mountain stream will carry away about 1,000 cubic feet of mountain in a year mostly in the form of sand granules and other suspended particles. That is equivalent to the capacity of an average-sized dump truck – clearly not much at all. Imagine a dump truck arriving once each year at the base of a mountain, filling up with a single load and driving off, not to reappear for another twelve months. At such a rate it seems impossible that it could ever cart away a mountain, but in fact given sufficient time that is precisely what would happen. Assuming a mountain 5,000 feet high with 500,000 million cubic feet of mass – roughly the size of Mount Washington – a single stream would level it in about 500 million years.

Of course most mountains have several streams and moreover are exposed to a vast range of other reductive factors, from the infinitesimal acidic secretions of lichen (tiny but relentless) to the grinding scrape of ice sheets, so most mountains vanish very much more quickly – in a couple of hundred million years, say. Right now the Appalachians are shrinking on average by 0.03 millimetres per year. They have gone through this cycle at least twice, possibly more – rising to awesome heights, eroding away to nothingness, rising again, each time recycling their component materials in a dazzlingly confused and complex geology.

The detail of all this is theory, you understand. Very little of it is more than generally agreed upon. Some scientists believe the Appalachians experienced a fourth, earlier mountain-building episode, called the Grenville Orogeny, and that there may have been others earlier still. Likewise Pangaea may have split and reformed not three times but a dozen times, or perhaps a score of times. On top of all this, there are a number of lapses in the theory, chief of which is that there is little direct evidence of continental collisions, which is odd, even inexplicable, if you accept that at least three continents rubbed together with enormous force for a period of at least 150 million years. There ought to be a suture, a layer of scar tissue, stretching up the eastern seaboard of the United States. There isn't.

I am no geologist, God knows. Show me an unusual piece of greywacke or a handsome chunk of gabbro and I will regard it with respect and listen politely to what you have to say, but it won't actually mean anything to me. If you tell me that once it was seafloor ooze and that through some incredible sustained process it was thrust deep into the earth, baked and squeezed for millions of years, then popped back onto the surface, which is what accounts for its magnificent striations, its vitreous crystals and flaky biotite mica, I will say, 'Goodness!' and 'Is that a fact!' but I can't pretend that anything actual will be going on behind my game expression.

Just occasionally am I permitted an appreciative glimpse into the wonder that is geology, and such a place is the Delaware Water Gap. There, above the serene and stately Delaware River, stands Kittatinny Mountain, a wall of rock 1,300 feet high, consisting of resistant quartzite (or so it says here), that was exposed when the river cut a passage through softer rock on its quiet, steady progress to the sea. The result in effect is a cross-section of mountain, which is not a view you get every day, or indeed anywhere else along the Appalachian Trail that I am aware of, and here it is particularly impressive because the exposed quartzite is arrayed in long, wavery bands that lie at such an improbably canted angle – about 45° – as to suggest to even the dullest imagination that something very big, geologically speaking, happened here.

It is a very fine view. A century or so ago people compared it to the Rhine and even (a little ambitiously, I'm bound to say) the Alps. The artist George Innes came and made a famous painting called *Delaware Water Gap*. It shows the river rolling lazily between meadowy fields dotted with trees and farms, against a distant backdrop of sere hills, notched with a V where the river passes through. It looks like a piece of Yorkshire or Cumbria transplanted to the American continent. In the 1850s, a plush 250-room hotel called Kittatinny House rose on the banks of the river, and was such a success that others soon followed. For a generation after the Civil War, the Delaware Water Gap was the place to be in summer. Then, as is always the way with these things, the White Mountains came into fashion, then Niagara Falls, then the Catskills, then the Disneys. Now almost no one comes to the Water Gap to stay. People still pass through in large numbers, but they park in a lay-by, have a brief appreciative gaze, then get back in their cars and drive off.

Today, alas, you have to squint, and pretty hard at that, to get any notion of the tranquil beauty that attracted Innes. The Water Gap is not only the nearest thing to spectacle in eastern Pennsylvania, but the only usable breach in the Appalachians in the area of the Poconos. In consequence, its narrow shelf of usable land is packed with state and local roads, a railway line, and an interstate highway with a long, heartbreakingly uninteresting concrete bridge carrying streams of humming trucks and cars between Pennsylvania and New Jersey – the whole suggesting, as John McPhee neatly put it in *In Suspect Terrain*, 'a convergence of tubes leading to a patient in intensive care'.

Still, Kittatinny Mountain, towering above the river on the New Jersey side, is a compelling sight and you can't look at it – at least I couldn't, at least not this day – without wanting to climb it and see what is up there. I parked at an information centre at its base and set off into the welcoming green woods. It was a gorgeous morning – dewy and cool but with the kind of sunshine and sluggish air that promises a lot of heat later on – and I was early enough to be able to get a decent day's walk in. I was gratified to find that I was really looking forward to this. I was on the edge of several thousand acres of very pretty woodlands shared jointly by Worthington State Forest and the Delaware Water Gap National Recreation Area. The path was well maintained and just steep enough to feel like healthful exercise rather than some kind of obsessive torture.

And here was a final, joyful bonus: I had excellent maps. I was now in the cartographically thoughtful hands of the New York–New Jersey Trail Conference, whose maps are richly printed in four colours, with green for woodland, blue for water, red for trails and black for lettering. They are clearly and generously labelled and sensibly scaled (1:36,000), and they include in full all connecting roads and side trails. It is as if they want you to know where you are and to take pleasure in knowing it.

I can't tell you what a satisfaction it is to be able to say, 'Ah, Dunnfield Creek, I see,' and, 'So that must be Shawnee Island down there.' If all the AT maps were anything like as good as this, I would have enjoyed the experience appreciably more – say 25 per cent more. It occurred to me now that a great part of my mindless indifference to my surroundings earlier on was simply that I didn't know where I was, couldn't know where I was. Now for once I could take my bearings, perceive my future, feel as if I was somehow in touch with a changing and knowable landscape.

And so I walked five thoroughly agreeable miles up Kittatinny to Sunfish Pond, a very comely 41-acre pond surrounded by woods. Along the way, I encountered just two other people – both day hikers – and I thought again what a stretch it is to suggest that the Appalachian Trail is too crowded. Something like 30 million people live within an hour's drive of the Water Gap – New York is just 45 miles to the east, Philadelphia a little bit more to the south – and it was a flawless summer's day, and the whole of these majestic woods belonged to just three of us.

For northbound hikers Sunfish Pond is something of a glorious novelty, since nowhere south of here will you find a body of water on a mountaintop. It is in fact the first glacial feature northbound hikers come across. During the last ice age, this was about as far as the ice sheets got. The furthest advance in New Jersey was about 10 miles south of the Water Gap, though even here, where the climate would let it go no further, it was still at least 2,000 feet thick.

Imagine that! A wall of ice nearly half a mile high, and beyond it for thousands of square miles nothing but more ice, broken only by the peaks of a very few of the loftiest mountains. What a sight that must have been. And here is the thing. We are still in an ice age, only now we experience it for just part of the year. Snow and ice and cold are not really typical features of Planet Earth. Taking the long view, Antarctica is actually a jungle. (It's just having a chilly spell.) At the very peak of the last ice age 20,000 years ago, 30 per cent of Earth was under ice. Today 10 per cent still is.

There have been at least a dozen ice ages in the last two million years, each lasting in the neighbourhood of 100,000 years. The force of them is quite staggering. The most recent intrusion, called the Wisconsinian ice sheet, spread down from the polar regions over much of Europe and North America, growing to depths of up to two miles and advancing at an estimated rate of 200 to 400 feet a year. As it soaked up the Earth's free water, sea levels fell by 450 feet. Then, about 10,000 years ago, not abruptly exactly but near enough, it began to melt back. No one knows why. What it left in its wake was a landscape utterly transformed. It dumped Long Island, Cape Cod, Nantucket and most of Martha's Vineyard where previously there had just been sea, and it gouged out the Great Lakes, Hudson Bay, and little Sunfish Pond, among much else. Every foot of the landscape from here on north would be scored and scarred with reminders of glaciation – scattered boulders called erratics, drumlins, eskers, V-shaped valleys, high tarns. I was entering a new world.

No one knows much of anything about Earth's many ice ages – why they came, why they stopped, when they may return. One interesting theory, given our present-day concerns with global warming, is that the ice ages were caused not by falling temperatures but by rising ones. Warm weather would increase precipitation, which would increase cloud cover, which would lead to less snowmelt at higher elevations. You don't need a great deal of bad weather to get an ice age. As Gwen Schultz notes in *Ice Age Lost*, 'It is not necessarily the amount of snow that causes ice sheets, but the fact that snow, however little, lasts.' In terms of precipitation, she observes, Antarctica 'is the driest large area on Earth, drier overall than any large desert'.

Here's another interesting thought. If glaciers started re-forming, they would have a great deal more water now to draw on – Hudson Bay, the Great Lakes, the hundreds of thousands of lakes of Canada, none of which existed to fuel the last ice sheet – so they would grow much more quickly. And if they did start to advance again, what exactly would we do? Blast them with TNT or maybe nuclear warheads? Well, doubtless we would, but consider this. In 1964, the largest earthquake ever recorded in North America rocked Alaska with 200,000 megatons of concentrated might, the equivalent of 2,000 nuclear bombs. Almost 3,000 miles away in Texas water sloshed out of swimming pools. A street in Anchorage fell 20 feet. The quake devastated 24,000 square miles of wilderness, much of it glaciated. And what effect did all this might have on Alaska's glaciers? None.

Just beyond the pond was a side trail, the Garvey Springs Trail, which descended very steeply to an old paved road along the river, just below a spot called Tocks Island, which would take me in a lazy loop back towards the visitor centre where I had left the car. It was four miles and the day was growing warm, but the road was shaded and quiet – I saw only three cars in an hour or so – and so it was a pleasant stroll, with restful views of the river across overgrown meadows.

By American standards, the Delaware is not a particularly imposing waterway, but it has one almost unique characteristic. It is almost the last significant undammed river in the United States. Now this might seem an inestimable virtue – a river that runs as nature planned it. However, one consequence of its unregulated nature is that the Delaware regularly floods. In 1955 there was a flood that even now is remembered as 'the Big One'. In August of that year – ironically at the height of one of the most severe droughts in decades – two hurricanes hit North Carolina one after the other, disrupting and enlivening weather all up and down the east coast. The first dumped ten inches of rain in two days on the Delaware River Valley. Six days later the valley received ten inches in less than twenty-four hours. At a place called Camp Davis, a holiday complex, forty-six people, mostly women and children, took refuge from the rising flood waters in the camp's main building. As the waters rose, they fled first upstairs and then into the attic, but to no avail. Some time in the night a 30-foot wall of water came roaring through the valley and swept the house away. Amazingly, nine people survived.

Elsewhere, bridges were being brushed aside and riverside towns inundated. Before the day was out, the Delaware River would rise 43 feet. By the time the waters finally receded, 400 people were dead and the whole of the Delaware Valley was devastated.

Into this gooey mess stepped the US Army Corps of Engineers, with a plan to build a dam at Tocks Island, very near where I was walking now. The dam, according to the Corps' plan, would not only tame the river but allow the creation of a new national park, at the heart of which would be a recreational lake almost 40 miles long. Eight thousand residents were moved out. It was all done very clumsily. One of the people evicted was blind. Several farmers had only parts of their land bought, so that they ended up with farmland but no house or a farmhouse but no land. A woman whose family had farmed the same land since the eighteenth century was carried from her house kicking and bellowing, to the delight of newspaper photographers and film crews.

The thing about the Army Corps of Engineers is that they don't build things very well. A dam across the Missouri River in Nebraska silted up so catastrophically that a noisome blobby ooze began to pour into the town of Niobrara, eventually forcing its permanent abandonment. Then a Corps dam in Idaho failed. Fortunately it was in a thinly populated area and there was some warning. Even so, several small towns were washed away and eleven people lost their lives. But these were relatively small dams. Tocks Dam would have held one of the largest artificial reservoirs in the world, with 40 miles of water behind it. Four substantial cities – Trenton, Camden, Wilmington and Philadelphia – and scores of smaller communities stood downstream. A disaster on the Delaware would truly be a disaster.

And here was the nimble Army Corps of Engineers planning to

hold back 250 billion gallons of water with notoriously unstable glacial till. Besides that there were all kinds of environmental worries – that salinity levels below the dam would rise catastrophically, for example, devastating the ecology lower down, not least the valuable oyster beds of Delaware Bay.

In 1992, after years of growing protests that spread far beyond the Delaware Valley, the dam plan was finally put on hold, but by this time whole villages and farms had been bulldozed. A quiet, remote, very beautiful farming valley that had not changed a great deal in 200 years was lost for ever. 'One beneficial result of the [cancelled] project,' notes the *Appalachian Trail Guide to New York and New Jersey*, 'was that the land acquired by the federal government for the national recreation area has provided the Trail with a protected corridor.'

To tell you the truth I was getting seriously tired of this. I know the Appalachian Trail is supposed to be a wilderness experience and I accept that there are many places where it would be a shame for it to be otherwise, but sometimes, as here, the ATC seems to be positively phobic about human contact. Personally, I would have been pleased to be walking now through hamlets and past farms rather than through some silent 'protected corridor'.

Doubtless it is all to do with its historic impulse to tame and exploit the wilderness, but America's attitude to nature is, from all sides, very strange if you ask me. I couldn't help comparing my experience now with an experience I'd had three or four years earlier in Luxembourg when I went hiking with my son for a magazine assignment. Luxembourg is a much more delightful place to hike than you might think. It has lots of woods, but also castles and farms and steepled villages and winding river valleys – the whole, as it were, European package. The footpaths we followed spent a lot of time in the woods, but also emerged at obliging intervals to take us along sunny back roads and over stiles and through farm fields and hamlets. We were always able at some point each day to call in at a bakery or post office, to hear the tinkle of shop bells and eavesdrop on conversations we couldn't understand. Each night we slept in an inn and ate in a restaurant with other people. We experienced the whole of Luxembourg, not just its trees. It was wonderful, and it was wonderful because the whole charmingly diminutive package was seamlessly and effortlessly integrated.

In America, alas, beauty has become something you drive to, and nature an either/or proposition – either you ruthlessly subjugate it, as at Tocks Dam and a million other places, or you deify it, treat it as something holy and remote, a thing apart, as along the Appalachian Trail. Seldom would it occur to anyone on either side that people and nature could coexist to their mutual benefit – that, say, a more graceful bridge across the Delaware River might actually set off the grandeur around it, or that the AT might be more interesting and rewarding if it wasn't *all* wilderness, if from time to time it purposely took you past grazing cows and tilled fields.

I would have much preferred it if the AT guidebook had said: 'Thanks to the Conference's efforts, farming has been restored to the Delaware River Valley, and the footpath rerouted to incorporate 16 miles of riverside walking because, let's face it, you can get too much of trees sometimes.'

Still, we must look on the bright side. If the Army Corps of Engineers had had its foolish way, I'd have been swimming back to my car now, and I was grateful at least to be spared that.

Anyway, it was time to do some real hiking again.

CHAPTER SIXTEEN

IN 1983, A MAN WALKING IN THE BERKSHIRE HILLS OF MASSACHUSETTS just off the Appalachian Trail saw – or at least swears he saw – a mountain lion cross his path, which was a little unsettling and even more unexpected since mountain lions hadn't been seen in the northeastern United States since 1903, when the last one was shot in New York State.

Soon, however, sightings were being reported all over New England. A man driving a back road of Vermont saw two cubs playing at the roadside. A pair of hikers saw a mother and two cubs cross a meadow in New Hampshire. Every year there were half a dozen or more reports in similar vein, all by credible witnesses. In the late winter of 1994 a farmer in Vermont was walking across his property, taking some seed to a bird feeder, when he saw what appeared to be three mountain lions about 70 feet away. He stared dumbstruck for a minute or two, for mountain lions are swift, fierce creatures and here were three of them looking at him with calm regard, then he hightailed it to a phone and called a state wildlife biologist. The animals were gone by the time the biologist arrived, but he found some fresh scat, which he dutifully bagged up and despatched to a US Fish and Wildlife Laboratory. The lab report came back that it was indeed the scat of *Felis concolor*, the eastern mountain lion, also variously and respectfully known as the panther, cougar, puma and, especially in New England, catamount.

All this was of some interest to me, for I was hiking in about the same spot as that initial mountain lion sighting. I was back on the trail with a new keenness and a new plan. I was going to hike

New England, or at least as much of it as I could knock off till Katz came out in seven weeks to walk with me through Maine's Hundred Mile Wilderness. There were almost 700 miles of gorgeously mountainous Appalachian Trail in New England – about a third of the AT's total trail length – enough to keep me occupied till August. To that end, I had my obliging missus drive me to southwestern Massachusetts and drop me on the trail near Stockbridge for a three-day amble through the Berkshires. Thus it was that I was to be found, on a hot morning in mid-June, labouring sweatily up a steep but modest eminence called Becket Mountain, in a haze of repellent-resistant blackflies, and patting my pocket from time to time to check that my knife was still there.

I didn't really expect to encounter a mountain lion, but only the day before I had read an article in the *Boston Globe* about how western mountain lions – which indubitably are not extinct – had recently taken to stalking and killing hikers and joggers in the California woods, and even the odd poor soul standing at a backyard barbecue in an apron and funny hat. It seemed a kind of omen.

It's not entirely beyond the realm of possibility that mountain lions could have survived undetected in New England. Bobcats – admittedly much smaller creatures – are known to exist in considerable numbers and yet are so shy and furtive that you would never guess their existence. Many forest rangers go whole careers without seeing one. And there is certainly ample room in the eastern woods for large cats to roam undisturbed. Massachusetts alone has 250,000 acres of woodland, 100,000 in the Berkshires. From where I was now, I could, given the will and a more or less infinite supply of noodles, walk all the way to Cape Chidley in northern Quebec, 1,800 miles away on the icy Labrador Sea, and scarcely ever have to leave the cover of trees. Even so, it is unlikely that a large cat could survive in sufficient numbers to breed not just in one area but evidently all over New England and escape notice for nine decades. Still, there was that scat. Whatever it was out there, it shat like a mountain lion.

The most plausible explanation was that any lions out there – if lions they were – were released pets, bought in haste and later regretted. It would be just my luck, of course, to be savaged by an animal with a flea collar and a medical history. I imagined lying on my back, being ravaged, reading a dangling silver tag that said: 'My name is Mr Bojangles. If found please call Tanya and Gus at 924-4667.'

Like most large animals, and a good many small ones, the eastern mountain lion was wiped out because it was deemed to be a nuisance. Until the 1940s, many eastern states had well-publicized 'varmint campaigns', often run by state conservation departments, that awarded points to hunters for every predatory creature they killed, which was just about every creature there was – hawks, owls, kingfishers, eagles, and virtually any type of large mammal. West Virginia gave an annual college scholarship to the student who killed the most animals; other states freely distributed bounties and other cash rewards. Rationality didn't often come into it. Pennsylvania one year paid out $90,000 in bounties for the killing of 130,000 owls and hawks in order to save the state's farmers a slightly less than whopping $1,875 in estimated livestock losses. (It is not very often, after all, that an owl carries off a cow.)

As late as 1890 New York State paid bounties on 107 mountain lions, but within a decade they were virtually all gone. (The very last wild eastern mountain lion was killed in the Smokies in the 1920s.) The timberwolf and woodland caribou also disappeared from their last Appalachian fastnesses in the first years of this century, and the black bear very nearly followed them. In 1900, the bear population of New Hampshire – now over 3,000 – had fallen to just fifty.

There is still quite a lot of life out there, but it is mostly very small. According to a wildlife census by an ecologist at the University of Illinois named V. E. Shelford, a typical 10-square-mile block of eastern American forest holds almost 300,000 mammals – 220,000 mice and other small rodents, 63,500 squirrels and chipmunks, 470 deer, 30 foxes and 5 black bears.

The real loser in the eastern forests has been the songbird. One of the most striking losses was the Carolina parakeet, a lovely, innocuous bird whose numbers in the wild were possibly exceeded only by the unbelievably numerous passenger pigeon. (When the first pilgrims came to America there were an estimated nine billion passenger pigeons – more than twice the number of all birds found in America today.) Both were hunted out of existence – the passenger pigeon for pig feed and the simple joy of blasting volumes of birds from the sky with blind ease, the Carolina parakeet because it ate farmers' fruit and had a striking plumage that made a lovely lady's hat. In 1914, the last surviving members of each species died within weeks of each other in captivity.

A similar unhappy fate awaited the delightful Bachman's

warbler. Always rare, it was said to have one of the loveliest songs of all birds. For years it escaped detection, but in 1939 two birders, operating independently in different places, coincidentally saw a Bachman's warbler within two days of each other. Both shot the birds (nice work, boys) and that, it appears, was that for the Bachman's warbler. But there are almost certainly others that disappeared before anyone much noticed. John James Audubon's paintings include three birds – the small-headed flycatcher, the carbonated warbler and the Blue Mountain warbler – that have not been seen by anyone since. The same is true of Townsend's bunting, of which there is one stuffed specimen in the Smithsonian Institution in Washington.

What is certainly known is that between the 1940s and 1980s the populations of migratory songbirds fell by 50 per cent in the eastern US (in large part because of loss of breeding sites and other vital wintering habitat in Latin America), and by some estimates are continuing to fall by 3 per cent or so a year. Seventy per cent of all eastern bird species have seen population declines since the 1960s.

These days the woods are a pretty quiet place.

Late in the afternoon, I stepped from the trees onto what appeared to be a disused logging road. In the centre of the road stood an older guy with a pack and a distinctly bewildered look, as if he had just woken from a trance and found himself unaccountably in this place. He had, I noticed, a haze of blackflies of his own.

'Which way's the trail go, do you suppose?' he asked me. It was an odd question because the trail clearly and obviously continued on the other side. There was a three-foot gap in the trees directly opposite and, in case there was any possible doubt, a white blaze painted on a stout oak.

I swatted the air before my face for the twelve thousandth time that day and nodded at the opening. 'Just there, I'd say.'

'Oh, yes,' he answered. 'Of course.'

We set off into the woods together and chatted a little about where we had come from that day, where we were headed, and so on. He was a thru-hiker – the first I had seen this far north – and like me was making for Dalton. He had a curious puzzled look all the time, and regarded the trees in a peculiar way, running his gaze slowly up and down their lengths over and over again, as if he had never seen anything like them before.

'So what's your name?' I asked him.

'Well, they call me Chicken John.'

'Chicken John!' Chicken John was famous. I was quite excited. Some people on the trail take on an almost mythic status because of their idiosyncrasies. Early in the trip Katz and I kept hearing about a kid who had equipment so high-tech that no one had ever seen anything like it. One of his possessions was a self-erecting tent. Apparently he would carefully open a stuff sack and it would fly out, like joke snakes from a tin. He also had a satellite navigation system, and goodness knows what else. The trouble was his pack weighed about 95 pounds and he dropped out before he got to Virginia, so we never did see him. Woodrow Murphy, the walking fat man, had achieved this sort of fame the year before. Mary Ellen would doubtless have attracted a measure of it if she had not dropped out. Chicken John had it now – though I couldn't for the life of me recall why. It had been months before, way back in Georgia, that I had first heard of him.

'So why do they call you Chicken John?' I asked.

'You know, I don't honestly know,' he said, as if for some time he had been wondering that himself.

'When did you start your hike?'

'January the twenty-seventh.'

'January the twenty-seventh?' I said in small astonishment and did a quick private calculation on my fingers. 'That's almost five months.'

'Don't I know it,' he said with a kind of happy ruefulness.

He had been walking for the better part of half a year and he was still only three-quarters of the way to Katahdin.

'What kind of' – I didn't know quite how to put this – 'what kind of miles are you doing, John?'

'Oh, 'bout fourteen or fifteen if all goes well. Trouble is' – he slid me a sheepish look – 'I get lost a lot.'

That was it. Chicken John was forever losing the trail and ending up in the most improbable places. Goodness knows how anyone could manage to lose the Appalachian Trail. It is the most clearly defined, well-blazed footpath imaginable. Usually it is the only thing in the woods that isn't woods. If you can distinguish between trees and a long open corridor through the trees you will have no trouble finding your way along the AT. Where there might be any doubt at all – where a side trail enters or where the AT crosses a road – there are always blazes. Yet people do get lost. The famous Grandma Gatewood, for instance, was forever knocking on doors and asking where the heck she was.

I asked him what was the most lost he had ever been.

'Thirty-seven miles,' he said almost proudly, or if not proudly then fondly. 'I got off the trail on Blood Mountain in Georgia – still don't know how exactly – and spent three days in the woods before I came to a highway. I thought I was a goner that time. I ended up in Tallulah Falls, and even got my picture in the paper. Police gave me a ride back to the trail the next day, and pointed me the right way. They were real nice.'

'Is it true you once walked three days in the wrong direction?'

He nodded happily. 'Two and a half days to be precise. Luckily, I came to a town on the third day, and I said to a feller, "Excuse me, young feller, where is this?" and he said, "Why, it's Damascus, Virginia, sir," and I thought, well, that's mighty strange because I was in a place with the very same name just three days ago. And then I recognized the fire station.'

'How on earth do you—' I decided to rephrase the question. 'How does it happen, John, exactly?'

'Well, if I knew that I wouldn't do it, I suppose,' he said with a kind of chuckle. 'All I know is that from time to time I end up a long way from where I want to be. But it makes life interesting, you know. I've met a lot of nice people, had a *lot* of free meals. Excuse me,' he said abruptly, 'you sure we're going the right way?'

'Positive.'

He nodded. 'I'd hate to get lost today. There's a restaurant in Dalton.' I understood this perfectly. If you're going to get lost, you don't want to do it on a restaurant day.

We walked the last six miles together, but we didn't talk much after that. I was doing a 19-mile day, the longest I would do anywhere on the trail, and even though the grade was generally easy and I was carrying a light pack, I was real tired by late afternoon. John seemed content to have someone to follow, and in any case had his hands full scrutinizing the trees.

It was after six when we reached Dalton. John had the name of a man on Depot Street who let hikers camp in his back garden and use his shower, so I went with him to a gas station while he asked directions. When we emerged he started off in precisely the wrong direction.

'It's that way, John,' I said.

'Of course it is,' he agreed. 'And the name's Bernard, by the way. I don't know where they got that Chicken John from.'

I nodded and told him I would look for him the next day, but I never did see him again.

I spent the night in a motel, and the next day hiked on to Cheshire. It was only nine miles over easy terrain, but the blackfly made it a torment. I have never seen a scientific name for these tiny, vile, winged specks, so I don't know what they are other than a hovering mass that goes with you wherever you go and are forever in your ears and mouth and nostrils. Human sweat transports them to a realm of orgasmic ecstasy, and insect repellent only seems to excite them further. They are particularly relentless when you stop to rest or take a drink – so relentless that eventually you don't stop to rest and you drink while moving, and then spit out a tongueful of them. It's a kind of living hell. So it was with some relief that I stepped from their woodland domain in early afternoon and strolled into the sunny, dozing straggle that was the little community of Cheshire.

Cheshire had a free hostel for hikers in a church on the main street – Massachusetts people do a lot for hikers, it seems; elsewhere I had seen houses with signs inviting people to help themselves to water or pick apples from trees – but I didn't fancy a night in a bunkhouse, still less a long afternoon sitting around with nothing to do, so I pushed on to Adams, four miles away up a baking highway, but with at least the prospect of a night in a motel and a choice of restaurants.

Adams had just one motel, a dumpy place on the edge of town. I took a room and passed the rest of the afternoon strolling around, idly looking in store windows and browsing through boxes of books in a thrift shop, though of course there was nothing but *Reader's Digest* volumes and those strange books you only ever see in thrift shops with titles like *Home Drainage Encyclopedia: Volume One* and *Nod If You Can Hear Me: Living with a Human Vegetable*, and afterwards wandered out into the country to look at Mount Greylock, my destination for the next day. Greylock is the highest eminence in Massachusetts, and the first hill over 3,000 feet since Virginia for northbound hikers. It's just 3,491 feet to the top, but, surrounded as it is by much smaller hills, it looks considerably bigger. It has in any case a certain imposing majesty that beckons. I was looking forward to it.

And so early the next morning, before the day's heat had a chance to get properly under way – and a scorcher was forecast – I stopped in town for a can of pop and a sandwich for my lunch, and set off on a wandering dirt road towards the Gould Trail, a side trail leading steeply up to the AT and on to Greylock.

Greylock is certainly the most literary of Appalachian mountains. Herman Melville, living on a farm called Arrowhead on its western side, stared at it from his study window while he wrote *Moby-Dick,* and, according to Maggie Stier and Ron McAdow in their excellent *Into the Mountains*, a history of New England's peaks, claimed that its profile reminded him of a whale. When the book was finished, he and a group of friends hiked to the top and partied there till dawn. Nathaniel Hawthorne and Edith Wharton also lived nearby and set works there, and there was scarcely a literary figure associated with New England from the 1850s to 1920s who didn't at some time hike or ride up to admire the view.

Ironically, at the height of its fame, Greylock lacked much of the green-cloaked majesty it enjoys today. Its sides were mangy with the scars of logging, and the lower slopes gouged with holes for slate and marble quarries. Big, ramshackle sheds and sawhouses poked into every view. All that healed and grew over, and then in the 1960s, with the enthusiastic support of state officials in Boston, plans were drawn up to turn Greylock into a ski resort, with an aerial tram, a network of chairlifts, and a summit complex consisting of a hotel, shops and restaurants – all in 1960s *Jetsons*-style architecture – but luckily nothing ever came of it. Today Greylock sits on 11,600 acres of preserved land. It's a beauty.

The hike to the top was steep, hot and seemingly endless, but worth the effort. The open, sunny, fresh-aired summit of Greylock is crowned with a large, handsome stone building called Bascom Lodge, built in the 1930s by the tireless and ubiquitous cadres of the Civilian Conservation Corps. It now offers overnight accommodation to hikers and a restaurant. Also on the summit is a wonderful, wildly incongruous lighthouse (Greylock is 140 miles from the sea), which serves as the Massachusetts memorial for soldiers killed in the First World War. It was originally planned to stand in Boston Harbor, but for some reason ended up here.

I ate my lunch, treated myself to a wee and a wash in the lodge, and then hurried on, for I still had eight miles to go and I had a rendezvous arranged with my wife at four in Williamstown. For the next three miles, the walk was mostly along a lofty ridgeline connecting Greylock to Mount Williams. The views were sensational, across lazy hills to the Adirondacks half a dozen miles to the west, but really hot. Even up here the air was heavy and listless. And then it was a very steep descent – 3,000 feet in three miles – through dense, cool woods to a back road that led through exquisitely pretty open countryside.

Out of the woods it was sweltering. It was two miles along a road totally without shade and so hot I could feel the heat through the soles of my boots. When at last I reached Williamstown a sign on a bank announced a temperature of 97°. No wonder I was hot. I crossed the street and stepped into a Burger King, our agreed rendezvous. If there is a greater reason for being grateful to live in the twentieth century than the joy of stepping from the dog's breath air of a really hot summer's day into the crisp, clean, surgical chill of an air-conditioned establishment, then I can't think of it.

I bought a bucket-sized Coke and sat in a booth by the window, feeling very pleased. I had done 17 miles over a reasonably challenging mountain in hot weather. I was grubby, sweatstreaked, comprehensively knackered and rank enough to turn heads. I was a walker again.

In 1850, New England was 70 per cent open farmland and 30 per cent woods. Today the proportions are exactly reversed. Probably no area in the developed world has undergone a more profound change in just a century or so, at least not in a contrary direction to the normal course of progress.

If you were going to be a farmer, you could hardly choose a worse place than New England. (Well, the middle of Lake Erie maybe, but you know what I mean.) The soil is rocky, the terrain steep, and the weather so bad that people take actual pride in it. A year in Vermont, according to an old saw, is 'nine months of winter followed by three months of very poor sledding'.

But until the middle of the nineteenth century farmers survived in New England because they had proximity to the coastal cities like Boston and Portland and because, I suppose, they didn't know any better. Then two things happened: the invention of the McCormick reaper, which was ideally suited to the big, rolling farms of the Middle West but no good at all for the cramped, stony fields of New England, and the development of the railroads, which allowed the Midwestern farmers to get their produce to the East in a timely fashion. The New England farmers couldn't compete, and so they became Midwestern farmers, too. By 1860, nearly half of

Vermont-born people – 200,000 out of 450,000 – were living elsewhere.

In 1840, during the presidential election campaign, Daniel Webster gave an address to 20,000 people on Stratton Mountain in Vermont. Had he tried the same thing twenty years later (which admittedly would have been a good trick as he had died in the meantime) he would have been lucky to get an audience of fifty.

Today Stratton Mountain is pretty much all forest, though if you look carefully you can still see old cellar holes and the straggly remnants of apple orchards clinging glumly to life in the shady understorey beneath younger, more assertive birches, maples and hickories. Everywhere throughout New England you find old, tumbledown field walls, often in the middle of the deepest, most settled-looking woods – a reminder of just how swiftly nature reclaims the land in America.

And so I walked up Stratton Mountain on an overcast, mercifully cool June day. It was four steep miles to the summit at just under 4,000 feet. For a little over a hundred miles through Vermont the AT coexists with the Long Trail, which threads its way up and over the biggest and most famous peaks of the Green Mountains all the way to Canada. The Long Trail is actually older than the AT – it was opened in 1921, the year the AT was proposed – and I'm told that there are Long Trail devotees even yet who look down on the AT as a rather vulgar and overambitious upstart. In any case, Stratton Mountain is usually cited as the spiritual birthplace of both trails, for it was here that James P. Taylor and Benton MacKaye claimed to have received the inspiration that led to the creation of their wilderness ways – Taylor in 1909, MacKaye sometime afterwards.

Stratton was a perfectly fine mountain, with good views across to several other well-known peaks – Equinox, Ascutney, Snow and Monadnock – but I couldn't say that it was a summit that would have inspired me to grab a hatchet and start clearing a route to Georgia or Quebec. Perhaps it was just the dull, heavy skies and bleak light, which gave everything a flat, washed-out feel. Eight or nine other people were scattered around the summit, but there was one youngish, rather podgy man on his own in a very new and expensive-looking windcheater. He had some kind of hand-held electronic device with which he was taking mysterious readings of the sky or landscape.

He noticed me watching and said, in a tone that suggested he was hoping someone would take an interest, 'It's an Enviro Monitor.'

'Oh, yes?' I responded politely.

'Measures eighty values – temperature, UV index, dew point, you name it.' He tilted the screen so I could see it. 'That's heat stress.' It was some meaningless number that ended in two decimal places. 'It does solar radiation,' he went on, 'barometric pressure, wind chill, rainfall, humidity – ambient and active – even estimated burn time adjusted for skin type.'

'Does it bake cookies?' I asked.

He didn't like this. 'There are times when it could save your life, believe me,' he said, a little stoutly. I tried to imagine a situation in which I might find myself dangerously imperilled by a rising dew point, and could not. But I didn't want to upset the man, so I said: 'What's that?' and pointed at a blinking figure in the upper left-hand corner of the screen.

'Ah, I'm not sure what that is. But this' – he stabbed the console of buttons – 'now this is solar radiation.' It was another meaningless figure, to three decimal places. 'It's very low today,' he said and angled the machine to take another reading. 'Yeah, very low today.' Somehow I knew this already. In fact, although I couldn't attest any of it to three decimal places, I had a pretty good notion of the weather conditions generally, on account of I was out in them. The interesting thing about the man was that he had no pack, and so no waterproofs, and was wearing shorts and trainers. If the weather did swiftly deteriorate, and in New England it most assuredly can, he would probably die, but at least he had a machine that would tell him when and let him know his final dew point.

Call me a tiresome old fogey, but I hate all this technology on the trail. Some AT hikers, I had read, now carry laptop computers and modems, so that they can file daily reports to their family and friends. (If you are considering doing this yourself, here's a tip. Nobody cares that much. I'm sorry, that's not true. Nobody cares at all.) And now increasingly you find people with electronic gizmos like the Enviro Monitor or wearing sensors attached by wires to their pulse points so that they look as if they've come to the trail straight from some sleep clinic.

In 1996 the *Wall Street Journal* ran a splendid article on the nuisance of satellite navigation devices, cellphones and other such appliances in the wilderness. All this high-tech equipment, it appears, is drawing up into the mountains people who perhaps shouldn't be there. At Baxter State Park in Maine, the *Journal* reported, one hiker called up a National Guard Unit and asked them to send a helicopter to airlift him off Mount Katahdin because he was tired. On Mount Washington, meanwhile, 'two very demanding women', according to an official there, called the mountain patrol HQ and said they couldn't manage the last mile and a half to the summit even though there were still four hours of daylight left. They asked for a rescue team to come and carry them back to their car. The request was refused. A few minutes later, they called again and demanded in that case that a rescue team bring them some torches. That request was refused also. A few days later, another hiker called and requested a helicopter because he was a day behind schedule and was afraid he would miss an important business meeting. The article also described several people who had got lost with satellite navigation devices. They were able to report their positions as 36.2° north by 17.48° west or whatever, but unfortunately didn't have the faintest idea what that meant as they hadn't brought maps or compasses or, evidently, brains.

My new friend on Stratton, I believe, could have joined their club. I asked him whether he felt it was safe for me to make a descent with solar radiation showing 18.574.

'Oh, yeah,' he said quite earnestly. 'Solar radiationwise, today is very low risk.'

'Thank goodness,' I said, quite earnestly, too, and took my leave of him and the mountain.

And so I proceeded across Vermont, in a series of pleasant day hikes, without anything electronic but with some very nice packed lunches that my wife made for me each night before retiring and left in precisely the same spot on the top shelf in the fridge. Each morning I would rise at dawn, put my lunch in my pack, and drive off to Vermont. I would park the car and walk up a big mountain or across a series of rolling green hills.

At some point in the day when it pleased me, usually about 11 a.m., I would sit on a rock or a log, take out my packed lunch and examine the contents. I would go, as appropriate, 'Peanut butter cookies – my favourite!' or, 'Oh, hum, luncheon meat again,' and eat in a zestful chewy silence, thinking of all the mountaintops I had sat on with Katz where we would have killed for this. Then I would pack up everything very neatly, drop it in my pack and hike again till it was time to clock off and go home. And so passed late June and the first part of July.

I did Stratton Mountain and Bromley Mountain, Prospect Rock and Spruce Peak, Baker Peak and Griffith Lake, White Rocks Mountain, Button Hill, Killington Peak, Gifford Woods State Park, Quimby Mountain, Thistle Hill and finally concluded with a gentle 11-mile amble from West Hartford to Norwich. This took me past Happy Hill Cabin, the oldest shelter on the AT and possibly the most sweetly picturesque – it was torn down soon after by some foolishly unsentimental trail officials. The town of Norwich is notable for three things: for being pronounced 'Norwitch' (it used to be 'Norritch' before it got taken over by outsiders in the 1950s), for being the town that inspired the *Bob Newhart Show* on television (the one where he ran an inn and all the locals were charmingly imbecilic) and for being the home of the great Alden Partridge, of whom no one has ever heard, though of course you are about to.

Partridge was born in Norwich in 1755 and was a demon walker – possibly the first person on the whole planet who walked long distances for the pleasure of it. In 1785, he became superintendent of West Point at the unprecedentedly youthful age of thirty, then had some kind of falling out there, moved back to Norwich and set up a rival institution, the American Literary, Scientific and Military Academy. There he coined the term 'physical education' and took his appalled young charges on brisk rambles of 35 or 40 miles over the neighbouring mountains. In between times he went off on more ambitious hikes of his own. On a typical trip he strode 110 miles over the mountains from Norwich to Williamstown, Massachusetts – essentially the route I had just completed in gentle stages – trotted up Mount Greylock and came back home the same way. The trip there and back took him just four days – and this at a time, remember, when there were no maintained footpaths or helpful blazes. He did this sort of thing with virtually every peak in New England. There ought to be a plaque to him somewhere in Norwich to inspire the few hardy hikers still heading north at this point, but sadly there is none.

From Norwich, it is about a mile to the Connecticut River and a pleasant, unassuming 1930s bridge leading to the state of New Hampshire and the town of Hanover on the opposite bank. Once the road that led from Norwich to Hanover was a leafy, gently sinuous two-lane affair – the sort of tranquil, alluring byway you would hope to find connecting two old New England towns a mile apart. Then some highway official or other decided that what would be a really good idea would be to build a big, fast road between the two towns. That way people could drive the one mile from Norwich to Hanover perhaps as much as eight seconds faster and not have to suffer paroxysms of anguish if somebody ahead wanted to turn onto a side road because now there would be turning lanes everywhere – turning lanes big enough for a truck pulling a Titan missile to manoeuvre through without rolling over a kerb or disrupting the vital flow of traffic.

So they built a broad, straight highway, six lanes wide in places, with concrete dividers down the middle and outsized sodium street lamps that light the night sky for miles around. Unfortunately, this had the effect of making the bridge into a bottleneck where the road narrowed back to two lanes. Sometimes two cars would arrive simultaneously at the bridge and one of them would have to give way – well, imagine! – so, as I write, they are replacing that uselessly attractive old bridge with something much grander and in keeping with the Age of Concrete. For good measure they are widening the street that leads up a short hill to the centre of Hanover. Of course, that means chopping down trees all along the street and drastically foreshortening most of the front gardens with concrete retaining walls, and even a highway official would have to admit that the result is not exactly a picture, not something you would want to put on a calendar called 'Beautiful New England', but it will shave a further four seconds off that daunting trek from Norwich, and that's the main thing.

All this is of some significance to me partly because I live in Hanover, but mostly, I believe, because I live in the late twentieth century. Luckily I have a good imagination, so as I strode from Norwich to Hanover I imagined not a lively mini-expressway, but a country lane shaded with trees, bounded with hedges and wild flowers, and graced with a stately line of modestly scaled lamp-posts, from each of which was suspended, upside down, a highway official, and I felt much better.

CHAPTER SEVENTEEN

OF ALL THE CATASTROPHIC FATES THAT CAN BEFALL YOU IN THE OUT OF doors, perhaps none is more eerily unpredictable than hypothermia. There is scarcely an instance of hypothermic death that isn't in some measure mysterious and improbable. Consider a small story related by David Quammen in his book *Natural Acts*.

In the late summer of 1982, four youths and two men were on a canoeing holiday in Banff National Park when they failed to return to their base camp at the end of the day. The next morning a search party went out looking for them. They found the missing canoeists floating dead in their lifejackets in a lake. All were face-up and composed. Nothing about them indicated distress or panic. One of the men was still wearing his hat and glasses. Their canoes, drifting nearby, were sound, and the weather overnight had been calm and mild. For some unknowable reason, the six had carefully left their canoes and lowered themselves fully dressed into the cold water of the lake, where they had peacefully perished. In the words of one witness it was 'like they had just gone to sleep'. In a sense they had.

Popular impressions to the contrary, relatively few victims of hypothermia die in extreme conditions, stumbling through blizzards or fighting the bite of arctic winds. To begin with, relatively few people go out in that kind of weather and those that do are generally prepared. Most victims of hypothermia die in a much more dopey kind of way, in temperate seasons and with the air temperature nowhere near freezing. Typically, they are caught by an unforeseen change of conditions or combination of changes – a sudden drop in temperature, a cold pelting rain, the realization that they are lost – for which they are emotionally or physically under-equipped. Nearly always they compound the problem by doing something foolhardy – leaving a well-marked path in search of a short cut, blundering deeper into the woods when they would have been better off staying put, fording streams that only get them wetter and colder.

Such was the unfortunate fate of Richard Salinas. In 1990 Salinas went hiking with a friend in Pisgah National Forest in North Carolina. Caught by fading light, they headed back to their car, but somehow became separated. Salinas was an experienced hiker and all he had to do was follow a well-defined trail down a mountain to a car park. He never made it. Three days later, his jacket and knapsack were found abandoned on the ground miles into the woods. His body was discovered two months later snagged on branches in the little Linville River. As far as anyone can surmise, he had left the trail in search of a short cut, got lost, plunged deep into the woods, panicked and plunged deeper still, until at last hypothermia fatally robbed him of his senses. Hypothermia is a gradual and insidious sort of trauma. It overtakes you literally by degrees as your body temperature falls and your natural responses grow sluggish and disordered. In such a state, Salinas had abandoned his possessions, and soon after made the desperate and irrational decision to try to cross the rain-swollen river, which in normal circumstances he would have realized could only take him further away from his goal. On the night he got lost, the weather was dry and the temperature in the forties. Had he kept his jacket and stayed out of the water, he would have had an uncomfortably chilly night and a story to tell. Instead, he died.

A person suffering hypothermia experiences several progressive stages beginning, as you would expect, with mild and then increasingly violent shivering as the body tries to warm itself with muscular contractions, and proceeding on to profound weariness, heaviness of movement, a distorted sense of time and distance, and increasingly helpless confusion resulting in a tendency to make imprudent or illogical decisions and a failure to observe the obvious. Gradually the sufferer grows thoroughly disoriented and subject to increasingly dangerous hallucinations – including the decidedly cruel misconception that he is not freezing but burning up. Many victims tear off clothing, fling away their gloves or crawl out of their sleeping bags. The annals of trail deaths are full of stories of hikers found half naked lying in snowbanks just outside their tents. When this stage is reached, shivering ceases as the body just gives up and apathy takes over. The heart rate falls and brain-waves begin to look like a drive across the prairies. By this time, even if the victim is found the shock of revival may be more than his body can bear.

This was neatly illustrated by an incident reported in the January 1997 issue of *Outside* magazine. In 1980, according to the article, sixteen Danish seamen issued a mayday call, donned lifejackets and jumped into the North Sea as their vessel sank beneath them. There they bobbed for ninety minutes before a rescue ship was able to lift them from the water. Even in summer the North Sea is so perishingly cold that it can kill a person immersed in it in as little as thirty minutes, so the survival of all sixteen was a cause of some jubilation. They were wrapped in blankets and guided below, where they were given a hot drink, and abruptly dropped dead – all sixteen of them.

But enough of arresting anecdote. Let's toy with this fascinating malady ourselves.

I was in New Hampshire now, which pleased me, because we had recently moved to the state, so I was naturally interested to explore it. Vermont and New Hampshire are so snugly proximate and so similiar in size, climate, accent and livelihoods (principally skiing and tourism) that they are often bracketed as twins, but in fact they have quite different characters. Vermont is Volvos and antique shops and country inns with cutely contrived names like Quail Hollow Lodge and Fiddlehead Farm Inn. New Hampshire is guys in hunting caps and pickup trucks with number plates bearing the feisty slogan 'Live Free or Die'. The landscape too differs crucially. Vermont's mountains are comparatively soft and rolling and its profusion of dairy farms gives it a more welcoming and inhabited feel. New Hampshire is one big forest. Of the state's 9,304 square miles of territory, some 85 per cent – or an area somewhat larger than Wales – is woods, and nearly all the rest is either lakes or above treeline. So apart from the very occasional town or ski resort, New Hampshire is primarily, sometimes rather dauntingly, wilderness. And its hills are loftier, craggier, more difficult and forbidding.

In *The Thru-Hiker's Handbook* – the one indispensable guide to the AT, I might just say here – the great Dan 'Wingfoot' Bruce notes that when the northbound hiker leaves Vermont he has completed

80 per cent of the miles, but just 50 per cent of the effort. The New Hampshire portion alone, running 162 miles through the White Mountains, has thirty-five peaks over 3,000 feet. If Ben Nevis were on the Appalachian Trail in New Hampshire, it would just squeak into the top ten. Snowdon would be swallowed without trace. New Hampshire is hard.

I had heard so much about the ardours and dangers of the White Mountains that I was mildly uneasy about venturing into them alone – not terrified exactly, but prepared to be if I heard just one more bear-chase story – so you may conceive my quiet joy when a friend and neighbour named Bill Abdu offered to accompany me on some day hikes. Bill is a very nice fellow, amiable and full of knowledge, experienced on mountain trails, and with the inestimable bonus that he is a gifted orthopaedic surgeon – just what you want in a dangerous wilderness. I didn't suppose he'd be able to do much useful surgery up there, but if I fell and broke my back at least I'd know the Latin names for what was wrong with me.

We decided to start with Mount Lafayette, and to that end set off by car one clear July dawn and drove the two hours to Franconia Notch State Park – a notch in New Hampshire parlance is a mountain pass – a famous beauty spot at repose beneath commanding summits in the heart of the 700,000-acre White Mountain National Forest. Lafayette is 5,249 feet of steep, heartless granite. An 1870s account, quoted in *Into the Mountains*, observes: 'Mount Lafayette is . . . a true alp, with peaks and crags on which lightnings play, its sides brown with scars and deep with gorges.' All true. It's a beast. Only nearby Mount Washington exceeds it for both heft and popularity as a hiking destination in the White Mountains.

From the valley floor we had 3,700 feet of climb, 2,000 feet of it in the first two miles, and three smaller peaks en route – Mount Liberty, Little Haystack and Mount Lincoln – but it was a splendid morning, with mild but abundant sunshine and that invigorating minty-clean air you only get in northern mountains. It had the makings of a flawless day. We walked for perhaps three hours, talking little because of the steepness of the climb, but enjoying being out and keeping a good pace.

Every guidebook, every experienced hiker, every signboard beside every trailhead car park warns you that the weather in the White Mountains can change in an instant. Stories of campers who go for a stroll along sunny heights in shorts and sneakers only to find themselves, three or four hours later, stumbling to unhappy deaths in freezing fog are the stuff of every campfire, but they are also true. It happened to us when we were a few hundred feet shy of the summit of Little Haystack Mountain. The sunshine abruptly vanished, and from out of nowhere a swirling mist rolled into the trees. With it came a sudden fall in temperature, as if we had stepped into a cold store. Within minutes the forest was settled in a great foggy stillness, chill and damp. Timberline in the White Mountains occurs as low as 4,800 feet, about half the height in most other ranges, because the weather is so much more severe, and I began to see why. As we emerged from a zone of krummholz, the stunted trees that mark the last gasp of forest at treeline, and stepped onto the barren roof of Little Haystack we were met by a stiff, sudden wind – the kind that would snatch a hat from your head and fling it a hundred yards before you could raise a hand – which the mountain had deflected over us on the sheltered western slopes but which here was flying unopposed across the open summit. We stopped in the lee of some boulders to put on waterproofs, for the extra warmth as much as anything, for I was already quite damp from the sweat of effort and the moist air – a clearly foolish state to be in with the temperature falling and the wind whisking away any body heat. I opened my pack, rooted through the contents and then looked up with that confounded expression that comes with the discovery of a reversal. I didn't have my waterproofs. I rooted again, but there was hardly anything in the pack – a map, a light jumper, a water bottle and a packed lunch. I thought for a moment and with a small inward sigh remembered pulling the waterproofs out some days before and spreading them out in the basement to air. I hadn't remembered to put them back.

Bill, tightening a drawstring on his windcheater hood, looked over. 'Something wrong?'

I told him. He made a grave expression. 'Do you want to turn back?'

'Oh, no.' I genuinely didn't want to. Besides, it wasn't that bad. There wasn't any rain and I was only a little chilly. I put the jumper on and felt immediately better. Together we looked at his map. We had done almost all the height and it was only a mile and a half along a ridgeline to Lafayette, at which point we would descend steeply 1,200 feet to Greenleaf Hut, a mountain lodge with a cafeteria. If I did need to warm up, we would reach the hut a lot faster than if we went five miles back down the mountain to the car.

'You sure you don't want to turn back?'

'No,' I insisted. 'We'll be there in half an hour.'

So we set off again into the galloping wind and depthless grey murk. We cleared Mount Lincoln, at 5,100 feet, then descended slightly to a very narrow ridgeline. Visibility was no more than 15 feet and the winds were razor-sharp. Air temperature falls by about 2.5°F with every thousand feet of elevation, so it would have been chillier at this height anyway, but now it was positively uncomfortable. I watched with alarm as my jumper accumulated hundreds of tiny beads of moisture, which gradually began to penetrate the fabric and join the dampness of the shirt beneath. Before we had gone a quarter of a mile the jumper was wet through and hanging heavily on my arms and shoulders.

To make things worse, I was wearing blue jeans. Everyone will tell you that blue jeans are the most foolish item of clothing you can wear on a hike. I had contrarily become something of a devotee because they are tough and give good protection against thorns, ticks, insects and poison ivy – perfect for the woods. However, I freely concede they are completely useless in cold and wet. The cotton jumper was something I had packed as a formality, as you might pack anti-snakebite medicine or splints. It was July, for goodness' sake. I hadn't expected to need any kind of outerwear beyond possibly my trusty waterproofs, which of course I didn't have either. In short, I was dangerously misattired and all but asking to suffer and die. I certainly suffered.

I was lucky to escape with that. The wind was whooshing along noisily and steadily at a brisk 25 miles an hour, but gusting to at least double that, and from ever-shifting directions. At times, when the wind was head-on, we would take two steps forward and one back. When it came from an angle, it gave us a stiff shove towards the edge of the ridge. There was no telling in the fog how far the fall would be on either side, but it looked awfully steep, and we were after all a mile up in the clouds. If conditions had deteriorated just a little – if the fog had completely obscured our footing or the gusts had gathered just enough bump to knock a grown man over – we would have been pinned down up there, with me pretty well soaked through. Forty minutes before we had been whistling in sunshine. I understood now how people die in the White Mountains even in summer.

As it was, I was in a state of mild distress. I was shivering foolishly and feeling oddly lightheaded. There didn't seem to be any call to panic just yet, but I was clearly in bother. The ridge seemed to run on for ever, and there was no guessing in the milky void how long it would be till the form of Lafayette would rise to meet us. I glanced at my watch – it was two minutes to eleven; just right for lunch when and if we ever got to the godforsaken lodge – and took some comfort from the thought that at least I still had my wits about me. Or at least I felt as if I did. Presumably a confused person would be too addled to recognize that he was confused. Ergo if you know that you are not confused then you are not confused. Unless, it suddenly occurred to me – and here was an arresting notion – *unless* persuading yourself that you are not confused is merely a cruel, early symptom of confusion. Or even an advanced symptom. Who could tell? For all I knew I could be stumbling into some kind of helpless pre-confusional state characterized by the fear on the part of the sufferer that he may be stumbling into some kind of helpless pre-confusional state. That's the trouble with losing your mind; by the time it's gone, it's too late to get it back.

I glanced at my watch again and discovered with horror that it was still only two minutes to eleven. My sense of time was going! I might not be able to reliably assess my faltering brain, but here was proof on my wrist. How long would it be till I was dancing around half naked and trying to beat out flames, or seized with the brilliant notion that the best way out of this mess would be to glide to the valley floor on a magic, invisible parachute? I whimpered a little and scooted on, waited a good full minute and stole a glance at my watch again. Still two minutes to eleven! I was definitely in trouble.

Bill, who seemed serenely impervious to cold and of course had no idea that we were doing anything but proceeding along a high ridge in an unseasonal breeze, looked back from time to time to ask how I was doing.

'Great!' I'd say, for I was too embarrassed to admit that I was in fact losing my mind preparatory to stepping over the edge with a private smile and a cry of 'See you on the other side, old friend!' I don't suppose he had ever lost a patient on a mountaintop and I didn't wish to alarm him. Besides, I wasn't entirely convinced I was losing my grip; just severely uncomfortable.

I've no idea how long it took us to reach the windy summit of Lafayette other than that it was a double eternity. A hundred years ago there was a hotel on this bleak, forbidding spot and its wind-worn foundations are still a landmark – I have seen it in photographs – but I have no recollection of it now. My focus was entirely on descending the side trail to Greenleaf Hut. It led through a vast talus field and then, a mile or so further on, into woods. Almost as soon as we left the summit, the wind dropped and within 500 feet the world was quite calm, eerily so, and the dense fog was nothing more than straggly drifting shreds. Suddenly we could see the world below and how high up we were, which was a considerable distance, though all the nearby summits were wreathed in clouds. To my surprise and gratification, I felt much better. I stood up straight, with a sense of novelty, and realized that I had been walking in a severe hunch for some time. Yes, I definitely felt much better: hardly cold at all and agreeably clear-headed.

'Well, that wasn't so bad,' I said to Bill with a mountain man chuckle and pressed on to the hut.

Greenleaf Hut is one of ten picturesque and, in this case, brilliantly handy stone lodges built and maintained in the White Mountains by the venerable Appalachian Mountain Club. The AMC, founded over 120 years ago, is not only the oldest hiking club in America, but the oldest conservation group of any type. It charges a decidedly ambitious $50 a night for a bunk, dinner and breakfast, and consequently is known to thru-hikers as the Appalachian Money Club. Plus you have to make reservations days or sometimes weeks in advance. It doesn't really give the impression of being the thru-hiker's friend – more a hiking club for Cape Cod types. Still, to its credit, the AMC maintains 1,400 miles of trails in the Whites, runs an excellent visitor centre at Pinkham Notch, publishes worthwhile books and does let you come into its huts to use the toilets, get water or just warm up, which is what we gratefully did now.

We purchased cups of warming coffee and took them to a set of refectory tables, where we sat with a sprinkling of other steamy hikers and ate our packed lunches. The lodge was very congenial in a basic and rustic sort of way, with a high ceiling and plenty of room to move around. When we'd finished I was beginning to stiffen up, so I got up to move around and looked in on one of the two dormitories. It was a large room, packed with built-in bunks stacked four high. It was clean and airy, but startlingly basic, and presumably would be like an army barracks at night when it was full of hikers and their equipment. It didn't look remotely appealing to me. Benton MacKaye had nothing to do with these huts, but they were absolutely in accord with his vision – spare, rustic, wholesomely communal – and I realized with a kind of dull shock that if his dreams of a string of trailside hostels had been realized this is precisely how they would have been. My fantasy of a relaxed and cosy refuge with a porchful of rockers would actually have been rather more like a spell at boot camp – and an expensive one at that if the AMC's fees were anything to go by.

I did a quick calculation. Assuming $50 as the standard price, it would have cost the average thru-hiker somewhere between $6,000 and $7,500 to stay in a lodge each night along the trail. Clearly, it would never have worked. Perhaps it was better that things were as they were.

The sun was shining weakly when we emerged from the hut and set off back down the mountain on a side trail to Franconia Notch, and as we descended it gathered strength until we were back in a nice July day, with the air lazy and mild and the trees fetchingly speckled with sunlight and birdsong. By the time we reached the car, in late afternoon, I was almost completely dry, and my passing fright on Lafayette – now basking in hearty sunshine against a backdrop of vivid blue sky – seemed a remote memory.

As we climbed in, I glanced at my watch. It said two minutes to eleven. I gave it a shake and watched with interest as the second hand kicked back into motion.

CHAPTER EIGHTEEN

ON THE AFTERNOON OF 12 APRIL 1934, SALVATORE PAGLIUCA, A meteorologist at the summit weather observatory on Mount Washington, had an experience no one else has had before or since.

Mount Washington sometimes gets a little gusty, to put it mildly, and this was a particularly breezy day. In the previous twenty-four hours the wind speed had not fallen below 107 miles an hour, and often gusted much higher. When it came time for Pagliuca to take the afternoon readings, the wind was so strong that he tied a rope round his waist and had two colleagues take hold of the other end. As it was, the men had difficulty just getting the weather station door open and needed all their strength to keep Pagliuca from becoming a kind of human kite. How Pagliuca managed to reach his weather instruments and take readings is not known, nor are his words when he finally tumbled back in, though 'Jeeeeeeee*sus*!' would seem an apt possibility.

What is certain is that Pagliuca had just experienced a surface wind speed of 231 miles an hour. Nothing approaching that velocity has ever been recorded elsewhere.

In *The Worst Weather on Earth: A History of the Mount Washington Observatory*, William Lowell Putnam drily notes: 'There may be worse weather, from time to time, at some forbidding place on Planet Earth, but it has yet to be reliably recorded.' Among the Mount Washington weather station's many other records are: most weather instruments destroyed, most wind in twenty-four hours (nearly 3,100 miles of it), and lowest wind chill (a combination of 100 mph winds and a temperature of –47°F, a severity unmatched even in Antarctica).

Washington owes its curiously extreme weather not so much to height or latitude, though both are factors, as to its position at the precise point where high altitude weather systems from Canada and the Great Lakes pile into moist, comparatively warm air from the Atlantic or southern US. In consequence it receives 246 inches of snow a year and snowpacks of 20 feet. In one memorable storm in 1969, 98 inches of snow – that's eight feet – fell on the summit in three days. Wind is a particular feature; on average it blows at hurricane force (over 75 mph) on two winter days in three and on 40 per cent of days overall. Because of the length and bitterness of its winters, the average mean annual temperature at the summit is a meagre 27°F. The summer average is 52°F – a good 25°F lower than at its base. It is a brutal mountain, and yet people go up there – or at least try to – even in winter.

In *Into the Mountains*, Maggie Stier and Ron McAdow record how two University of New Hampshire students, Derek Tinkham and Jeremy Haas, decided to hike the entire Presidential Range – seven summits, including Washington, all named for US Presidents – in January 1994. Although they were experienced winter hikers and were well equipped, they couldn't have imagined what they were letting themselves in for. On their second night, the winds rose to 90 miles an hour and the temperature plummeted to –32°F. I have experienced –25°F in calm conditions and can tell you that even well wrapped and with the benefit of residual heat from indoors it becomes distinctly uncomfortable within a couple of minutes. Somehow the two survived the night, but the next day Haas announced he could go no further. Tinkham helped him into a sleeping bag, then stumbled on to the weather observatory a little over two miles away. He made it, just, though he was gravely frostbitten. His friend was found the next day, 'half out of his sleeping bag and frozen solid'.

Scores of others have perished in far less taxing conditions on Washington. One of the earliest and most famous deaths was that of a young woman named Lizzie Bourne who in 1855, not long after Mount Washington began to attract tourists, decided to amble up in the company of two male companions on a summery September afternoon. As you will have guessed already, the weather turned and they found themselves lost in fog. Somehow they got separated. The men made it after nightfall to a hotel on the summit.

Lizzie was found the next day just 150 feet from the front door, but quite dead.

Altogether 122 people have lost their lives on Washington. Until recently, when it was overtaken by Mount Denali in Alaska, it was the most murderous mountain in North America. So when the fearless Dr Abdu and I pulled up at its base a few days later for the second of our grand ascents I had brought enough backup clothes to cross the Arctic – waterproofs, woollen jumper, jacket, gloves, spare trousers and long underwear. Never again would I be chilled at height.

Washington, the highest peak north of the Smokies and east of the Rockies at a solidly respectable 6,288 feet, gets few clear days and this was a clear day, so the crowds were out in force. I counted over seventy cars at the Pinkham Notch Visitor Center car park at 8.10 in the morning when we arrived, and more pouring in every minute. Mount Washington is the most popular summit in the White Mountains and the Tuckerman Ravine Trail, our chosen route, is the most popular trail up Mount Washington. Some 60,000 hikers a year take to the Tuckerman route, though a good many of them get a lift to the top of the mountain and walk down, so the figures are perhaps a trifle skewed. In any case, it was no more than moderately busy on a good, hot, blue-skied, gorgeously promising morning in late July.

The walk up was much easier than I had dared hope. Even now, I could not quite get used to the novelty of walking big hills without a large pack. It makes such a difference. I won't say we bounded up, but considering that we had almost 4,500 feet of climb in a little over three miles, we walked at a pretty steady clip. It took us two hours and forty minutes (Bill's hiking guide to the White Mountains suggested a walking time of four hours and fifteen minutes), so we were pretty proud.

There may be more demanding and exciting summits to reach along the Appalachian Trail than Mount Washington but none can be more startling. You labour up the last steep stretch of rocky slope to what is after all a considerable eminence and pop your head over the edge and there you are greeted by, of all things, a vast terraced car park, full of automobiles gleaming hotly in the sun. Beyond stands a scattered complex of buildings among which move crowds of people in shorts and baseball caps. It has the air of a world fair bizarrely transferred to a mountaintop. You get so used along the AT to sharing summits with only a few other people, all of whom have worked as hard as you to get there, that this was positively dazzling. On Washington, visitors can arrive by car on a winding toll road or on a cog railway from the other side, and hundreds of people – hundreds and hundreds of them, it seemed – had availed themselves of these options. They were everywhere, basking in the sunshine, draped over the railings on the viewing terraces, wandering between various shops and food places. I felt for some minutes like a visitor from another planet. I loved it. It was a nightmare, of course, and a desecration of the highest mountain in the northeast, but I was delighted it existed in one place. It made the rest of the trail seem perfect.

The epicentre of activity was a monstrously ugly concrete building, the Summit Information Center, with big windows, broad viewing platforms and an exceedingly lively cafeteria. Just inside the door was a large list of all the people who had died on the mountain and the causes, beginning with one Frederick Strickland of Bridlington, Yorkshire, who lost his way while hiking in an October storm in 1849, and ran on through a quite breathtaking array of mishaps before concluding with the deaths of two hikers in an avalanche just three months earlier. Already six people had died on Washington's slopes in 1996, with the year barely half over – quite a sobering statistic – and there was plenty of room on the board for more.

In the basement was a small museum with displays on Washington's climate, geology and distinctive plant life, but what particularly captivated me was a comical short video called *Breakfast of Champions*, which I presume the meteorologists had made for their own amusement. It was filmed with a fixed camera on one of the summit terraces and showed a man sitting at a table, as if at an open-air restaurant, during one of its famous blows. While the man holds down the table with his arms, a waiter approaches against the wind with great and obvious difficulty, like someone wingwalking at 30,000 feet. He tries to pour the customer a bowl of cereal, and it all flies horizontally from the box. Then he adds milk, but this goes the same way (mostly over the customer – a particularly gratifying moment). Then the bowl flies away and the cutlery, as I recall, and then the table starts to go, and then the film ends. It was so good I watched it twice, then went off to find Bill so he could see it, but I couldn't spot him in the restless throngs, so I went outside onto the viewing platform and watched the cog railway train chuffing up the mountain, pouring out clouds of black smoke as it came. It stopped at the summit station and hundreds more happy tourists tumbled off.

Tourism goes back a long way on Mount Washington. As early as 1852 there was a restaurant at the summit and the proprietors were serving about a hundred meals a day. In 1853, a small stone hotel called Tip-Top House was built atop the mountain and was a huge and immediate success. Then in 1869 a local entrepreneur named Sylvester March built the cog railway, the first in the world. Everyone thought he was mad and that even if he succeeded in building the railway, which was doubtful, there wouldn't be any demand for it. In fact, as the disgorging throngs below me demonstrated now, people haven't tired of it yet.

Five years after the railway opened the old Tip-Top was succeeded by a much grander Summit House Hotel, and that was followed by a 40-foot tower with a multi-coloured searchlight, which could be seen all over New England and far out to sea. By late in the century a daily newspaper was being published on the summit as a summer novelty and American Express had opened a branch office.

Meanwhile back at ground level, things were also booming. The modern tourist industry, in the sense of people travelling en masse to a congenial spot and finding lots of diversions awaiting them when they get there, is essentially a White Mountains invention. Massive hotels, with up to 250 rooms, sprang up in every glen. Built in a jaunty domestic style, like cottages blown up to the scale of hospitals or sanatoria, these were exceedingly ornate and elaborate structures, among the largest and most complicated ever built of wood, with wandering rooflines robustly punctuated with towers and turrets and every other mark of architectural busyness the Victorian mind could devise. They had winter gardens and salons, dining rooms that could seat 200, and verandas like the promenade decks of ocean liners from which guests could drink in the wholesome air and survey nature's craggy splendour.

The finer hotels were very fine indeed. The Profile House at Franconia Notch had its own private railway line to Bethlehem Junction eight miles away; its grounds held twenty-one cottages, each with up to twelve bedrooms. The Maplewood had its own casino. Guests at the Crawford House could choose among nine daily newspapers from New York or Boston, shipped in specially. Whatever was new and exciting – lifts, gas lighting, swimming pools, golf courses – the White Mountain hotels were in the vanguard. By the 1890s, there were 200 hotels scattered through the

White Mountains. There has never been a collection of hotels of comparable grandeur anywhere, certainly not in a mountain setting. And now they are virtually all gone.

In 1902, the grandest of them all, the Mount Washington Hotel, opened at Bretton Woods, in an open, meadowy setting against the backdrop of the Presidential Range. Built in a commanding style described optimistically by the architect as 'Spanish Renaissance', it was the pinnacle of grace and opulence, with 2,600 acres of cultivated grounds, 235 guestrooms and every detail of finery that heaps of money could buy. For the plasterwork alone, the developers brought in 250 Italian artisans. But already it was something of an anachronism.

Fashion was moving on. American holidaymakers were discovering the seaside. The White Mountain hotels were a little too dull, a little too remote and expensive, for modern tastes. Worse, they had begun to attract the wrong sort of people – parvenus from Boston and New York. Finally, and above all, there was the automobile. The hotels were built on the assumption that visitors would come for a fortnight at least, but the motor car gave tourists a fickle mobility. In the 1924 edition of *New England Highways and Byways from a Motor Car*, the author gushed about the unrivalled splendour of the White Mountains – the tumbling cataracts of Franconia, the alabaster might of Washington, the secret charm of the little towns like Lincoln and Bethlehem – and encouraged visitors to give the mountains a full day and night. America was entering the age not just of the automobile but of the retarded attention span.

One by one the hotels closed down, became derelict or, more often, burned to the ground (often, miraculously, almost the only thing to survive was the insurance policy), and their grounds slowly returned to forest. Once I could have seen perhaps twenty large hotels from the summit. Today there is just one, the Mount Washington, still imposing and festive with its perky red roof, but inescapably forlorn in its solitary grandeur. (And even it has staggered along the edge of bankruptcy several times.) Elsewhere across the spacious valley far below, where once had proudly stood the Fabyan, the Mount Pleasant, the Crawford House and many others, today there was only forest, highways and motels.

From beginning to end the great age of the resort hotels in the White Mountains lasted just fifty years. Once again, I offer you the Appalachian Trail as a symbol of venerability. And with that in mind, I went off to find my friend Bill and complete our walk.

CHAPTER NINETEEN

'I'VE HAD A BRILLIANT IDEA,' SAID STEPHEN KATZ. WE WERE IN THE living room of my house in Hanover. It was two weeks later. We were leaving for Maine in the morning.

'Oh yeah?' I said, trying not to sound too wary, for ideas are not Katz's strongest suit.

'You know how awful it is carrying a full pack?'

I nodded. Of course I did.

'Well, I was thinking about it the other day. In fact I've been thinking about it a lot because to tell you the truth, Bryson, the idea of putting that pack on again filled me with' – he lowered his voice a tone – 'fucking dread.' He nodded with solemnity and repeated the two key words. 'And then I had a great idea. An alternative. Close your eyes.'

'What for?'

'I want to surprise you.'

I hate having to close my eyes for a surprise, always have, but I did it.

I could hear him rooting in his army surplus duffel bag. '"Who carries a lot of weight all the time?"' he continued. 'That was the question I asked myself. "Who carries a lot of weight day in and day out?" Hey, don't look yet. And then it occurred to me.' He was silent a moment, as if making some crucial adjustment that would assure a perfect impression. 'OK, now you can look.'

I uncovered my eyes. Katz, beaming immoderately, was wearing a *Des Moines Register* newspaper delivery bag – the kind of bright yellow pouch that paper boys in America traditionally sling over their shoulders before climbing on their bikes and riding off to do their rounds.

'You can't be serious,' I said quietly.

'Never been more serious in my life, my old mountain friend. I brought you one too.' He handed me one from his duffel bag, still pristinely folded and in a transparent wrapper.

'Stephen, you can't walk across the Maine wilderness with a newspaper delivery bag.'

'Why not? It's comfortable, it's waterproof – near enough – it's *capacious*, and it weighs all of about four ounces. It is the Perfect Hiking Accessory. Let me ask you this. When was the last time you saw a paper boy with a hernia?' He nodded sagely, as if he had foxed me with that one.

I made some tentative, preparatory shapes with my mouth prior to saying something, but Katz raced on before I could get a thought in order.

'Here's the plan,' he continued. 'We cut our load down to the bare minimum – no stoves, no gas bottles, no noodles, no coffee, no tents, no stuff sacks, no sleeping bags. We hike and camp like mountain men. Did Daniel Boone have a three-season fibre-fill sleeping bag? I don't think so. All we take is cold food, water bottles, maybe one change of clothes. I figure we can get the load down to five pounds. And' – he waggled his hand delightedly in the empty newspaper bag – 'we put it *all in here*.' His expression begged me to drape him with plaudits.

'Have you given any thought to how ridiculous you would look?'

'Yup. Don't care.'

'Have you considered what a source of uncontained mirth you would be to every person you met between here and Katahdin?'

'Don't give the tiniest shit.'

'Well, has it occurred to you what a ranger would say if he found you setting off into the Hundred Mile Wilderness with a newspaper delivery bag? Do you know they have the power to detain anyone they think is not mentally or physically fit?' This was actually a lie, but it brought a promising hint of frown to his brow. 'Also, has it also occurred to you that maybe the reason newspaper boys don't get hernias is that they only carry the bag for an hour or so a day – that maybe it might not be so comfortable lugging it for ten hours at a stretch over mountains – that maybe it would bang endlessly against your legs and rub your shoulders raw? Look how it's chafing against your neck already.'

His eyes slid stealthily down to the strap. The one positive thing about Katz and his notions was that it was never very hard to talk him out of them. He took the bag off over his head. 'OK,' he agreed, 'screw the bags. But we pack light.'

I was happy with that. In fact, it seemed a perfectly sensible proposal. We packed more than Katz wanted – I insisted on sleeping bags, warm clothes and our tents on the grounds that this could be a good deal more demanding than Katz appreciated – but I agreed to leave behind the stove, gas bottles and pots and pans. We would eat cold stuff – principally Snickers, raisins and an indestructible type of salami product called Slim Jims. It wouldn't kill us for a fortnight. Besides, I couldn't face another bowl of noodles. Altogether we saved perhaps five pounds of weight each – hardly anything really – but Katz seemed disproportionately happy. It wasn't often he got his way even in part.

And so the next day, my wife drove us deep into the boundless woods of northern Maine for our trek through the Hundred Mile Wilderness. Maine is deceptive. It is the twelfth smallest state, but it has more uninhabited forest – 10 million acres – than any other state but Alaska. In photographs it looks serene and beckoning, almost park-like, with hundreds of cool, deep lakes, and hazy, tranquil miles of undulating mountains. Only Katahdin, with its rocky upper slopes and startling muscularity, offers anything that looks faintly intimidating. In fact, it is all hard.

The trail maintainers in Maine have a certain hale devotion to seeking out the rockiest climbs and most forbidding slopes, and of these Maine has a breathtaking plenitude. In its 283 miles, the Appalachian Trail in Maine presents the northbound hiker with almost 100,000 feet of climb, the equivalent of three Everests. And at the heart of it all lies the famous Hundred Mile Wilderness – 99.7 miles of boreal forest trail without a shop, house or paved road, running from the village of Monson to a public campground at Abol Bridge, just below Katahdin. It is the remotest section of the entire AT. If something goes wrong in the Hundred Mile Wilderness, you are on your own. You could die of an infected blood blister out there.

It takes a week to ten days for most people to cross this fabled expanse. Because we had a fortnight, we had my wife drop us at Caratunk, a remote village on the Kennebec River, 38 miles short of Monson and the official start of the Wilderness. We would have three days of limbering up, and a chance to resupply at Monson before plunging irreversibly into the deepest woods. I had already done a little hiking to the west around Rangeley and Flagstaff lakes, in the week before Katz came, as a kind of reconnoitre, so I felt as if I knew the terrain. Even so it was a shock.

It was the first time in almost four months that I had hoisted a pack with a full load. I couldn't believe the weight, couldn't believe that there had ever been a time when I could believe the weight. The strain was immediate and discouraging. But at least I had been hiking. Katz, it was quickly evident, was starting from square one – actually, several score pancake breakfasts to the wrong side of square one. From Caratunk it was a long, gently upward haul of five miles to a big lake called Pleasant Pond, hardly taxing at all, but I noticed right away that he was moving with incredible deliberativeness, breathing very hard, and wearing a kind of shocked 'Where am I?' expression.

All he would utter was 'Man!' in an amazed tone when I asked him how he was, and a single heartfelt 'Fuhhhhhhhhck' – breathy and protracted, like the noise of a plumped cushion when someone sits on it – when he let his pack fall from his back at the first rest stop after forty-five minutes. It was a muggy afternoon and Katz was a river of sweat. He took a water bottle and downed nearly half of it. Then he looked at me with quietly desperate eyes, put his pack back on and wordlessly returned to his duty.

Pleasant Pond was a holiday spot – we could hear the happy shrieks of children splashing and swimming perhaps a hundred yards away, though we couldn't see anything of the lake through the trees. Indeed without their gaiety we wouldn't have known it was there, a sobering reminder of how suffocating the woods can be. Beyond rose Middle Mountain, just 2,500 feet high, but acutely angled and an entirely different experience on a hot day with a cumbersome pack sagging down on tender shoulders. I plodded joylessly on to the top of the mountain. Katz was soon far behind and moving with shuffling slowness.

It was after six o'clock when I reached the base of the mountain on the other side and found a decent campsite beside a grassy, little-used logging road at a place called Baker Stream. I waited a few minutes for Katz, then put up my tent. When he still hadn't come after twenty minutes, I went looking for him. He was almost an hour behind me when I finally found him, and his expression was glassy-eyed.

I took his pack from him and sighed at the discovery that it was light.

'What's happened to your pack?'

'Aw, I threw some stuff,' he said unhappily.

'What?'

'Oh, clothes and stuff.' He seemed uncertain whether to be ashamed or belligerent. He decided to try belligerence. 'That stupid sweater for one thing.' We had disputed mildly over the need for woollens.

'But it could get cold. It's very changeable in the mountains.'

'Yeah, right. It's August, Bryson. I don't know if you noticed.'

There didn't seem much point in trying to reason with him. When we reached the camp and he was putting up his tent I looked into his pack. He had thrown away nearly all his spare clothes and, it appeared, a good deal of the food.

'Where's the peanuts?' I said. 'Where's all your Slim Jims?'

'We didn't need all that shit. It's only three days to Monson.'

'Most of that food was for the Hundred Mile Wilderness, Stephen. We don't know what kind of supplies there'll be in Monson.'

'Oh.' He looked struck and contrite. 'I *thought* it was a lot for three days.'

I looked despairingly in the pack and then looked round. 'Where's your other water bottle?'

He looked at me sheepishly. 'I threw it.'

'You threw a water bottle?' This was truly staggering. If there is one thing you need on the trail in August, it is lots of water.

'It was heavy.'

'Of course it's heavy. Water's always heavy. But it is also kind of vital, wouldn't you say?'

He gave me a helpless look. 'I just had to get rid of some weight. I was desperate.'

'No, you were stupid.'

'Yeah, that too,' he agreed.

'Stephen, I wish you wouldn't do these things.'

'I know,' he said and looked sincerely repentant.

While he finished putting up his tent, I went off to filter water for the morning. Baker Stream was really a river – broad, clear and shallow – and very beautiful in the glow of a summery evening, with a backdrop of overhanging trees and the last rays of sunlight sparkling its surface. As I knelt by the water, I became curiously aware of something – some *thing* – in the woods beyond my left shoulder, which caused me to straighten up and peer through the clutter of foliage at the water's edge. Goodness knows what impelled me to look because I couldn't have heard anything over the musical tumult of water, but there about 15 feet away in the dusky undergrowth, staring at me with a baleful expression, was a moose – full-grown and female, or so I presumed since it had no antlers. It had evidently been on its way to the water for a drink when it was brought up short by my presence, and now clearly was undecided what to do next.

It is an extraordinary experience to find yourself face to face in the woods with a wild animal that is very much larger than you. You know these things are out there, of course, but you never expect at any particular moment to encounter one, certainly not up close – and this one was close enough for me to see the flea-like insects floating in circles about its head. We stared at each other for a good minute, neither of us sure what to do. There was a certain obvious and gratifying tang of adventure in this, but also something much more low-key and elemental – a kind of respectful mutual acknowledgement that comes with sustained eye contact. It was this that was unexpectedly thrilling – the sense that there was in some small measure a salute in our cautious mutual appraisal. Very slowly, so as not to alarm it, I crept off to get Katz.

When we returned, the moose had advanced to the water and was drinking about 25 feet upstream. 'Wow,' Katz breathed. He was thrilled, too, I was pleased to note. The moose looked up at us, decided we meant her no harm and went back to drinking. We watched her for perhaps five minutes, but the mosquitoes were chewing us up, so we withdrew and returned to our camp feeling considerably elated. It seemed a kind of confirmation – we *were* in the wilderness now – and an agreeable reward for a day of hard toil.

We ate a dinner of Slim Jims, raisins and Snickers, and retired to our tents to escape the endless assault of mosquitoes. As we lay there, Katz said, quite brightly: 'Hard day today. I'm beat.' It was unlike him to be chatty at tent time.

I grunted in agreement.

'I'd forgotten how hard it is.'

'Yeah, me, too.'

'First days are always hard, though, aren't they?'

'Yeah.'

He gave a settling-down sigh and yawned melodiously. 'It'll be better tomorrow,' he said, still yawning. By this he meant, I supposed, that he wouldn't fling anything foolish away. 'Well, good night,' he added.

I stared at the wall of my tent in the direction from which his voice had come. In all the weeks of camping together, it was the first time he had wished me a good night.

'Good night,' I said.

I rolled over on my side. He was right, of course. First days are always bad. Tomorrow would be better. We were both asleep in minutes.

Well, we were both wrong. The next day started well enough, with a sunny dawn that promised another hot day. It was the first time along the trail that we had woken to warmth and we enjoyed the novelty of it. We packed up our tents, breakfasted on raisins and Snickers, and set off into the deep woods.

By nine o'clock the sun was already high and blazing. Even on hot days, the woods are normally cool, but here the air was heavy and listless and steamy, almost tropical. About two hours after setting off, we came to a lagoon, about two acres in size, I would guess, and filled with papery reeds, fallen trees and the bleached torsos of dead trees that were still standing. Dragonflies danced across the surface. Beyond, waiting, rose a titanic heap called Moxie Bald Mountain. But what was of immediate note was that the trail ended, abruptly and puzzlingly, at the water's edge. Katz and I looked at each other: something wrong here surely. For the first time since Georgia, we wondered if we had lost the trail. (God knows what Chicken John would have made of it.) We retraced our steps a considerable distance, studied our map and trail guide, tried to find an alternative way round the pond through the hot and impenetrable undergrowth on every side, and finally concluded that we were intended to ford it. On the far shore, perhaps 80 yards away, Katz spied a white AT blaze. Clearly we had to wade across.

Katz led the way, barefoot and in boxer shorts, using a long stick like a punting pole to try to pick his way across on a jumble of submerged or half-submerged logs. I followed in a similar manner, but staying far enough back not to put my weight on a log he was using. They were covered in a slick moss and tended to bob or rotate alarmingly when stepped on. Twice he nearly toppled over. Finally, about 25 yards out, he lost it altogether and plunged with wheeling arms and an unhappy wail into the murky water. He went completely under, came up, went under again, and came up flailing and floundering with such wildness that for a few sincerely mortifying moments I thought he was drowning. The weight of his pack was clearly dragging him backwards and keeping him from gaining an upright position or even successfully keeping his head above water. I was about to drop my pack and plunge in to help when he managed to catch hold of a log and pull himself to a standing position. The water was up to his chest. He clung to the log and heaved visibly with the effort of catching his breath and calming himself down. He had obviously had a fright.

'You all right?' I said.

'Oh, peachy,' he replied. 'Just peachy. I don't know why they couldn't have put some crocodiles in here and made a real adventure of it.'

I crept on and an instant later I tumbled in, too. I had a few surreal, slow-motion moments of observing the world from the unusual perspective of the waterline or just below while my hand reached helplessly for a log that was just beyond my grasp – all this in a curious bubbly silence – before Katz sloshed to my assistance, firmly grabbed my shirt and thrust me back into a world of light and noise, and set me on my feet. He was surprisingly strong.

'Thank you,' I gasped.

'Don't mention it.'

We waded heavily to the far shore, taking it in turns to stumble and help each other up, and sloshed up onto the muddy bank trailing strands of half-rotted vegetation and draining huge volumes of water from our packs. We dumped our loads and sat on the ground, bedraggled and spent, and stared at the lagoon as if it had just played a terrible practical joke on us. I could not remember feeling this exhausted this early in the day anywhere along the trail. As we sat there, there were voices and two young hikers, hippyish and very fit, emerged from the woods behind us. They nodded hellos and looked appraisingly at the water.

'Afraid you gotta wade this one,' Katz said.

One of the hikers looked at him in a not unkindly way. 'This your first time hiking up here?' he said.

We nodded.

'Well, I don't want to discourage you, but mister you've only just *started* to get wet.'

With that he and his partner hoisted their packs above their heads, wished us luck and walked into the water. They waded skilfully across in perhaps thirty seconds – Katz and I had taken as many minutes – and stepped out on the other side, as if from a foot bath, put their dry packs back on, gave a small wave and disappeared.

Katz took a big thoughtful breath, partly sigh, partly just experimenting with the ability to breathe again. 'Bryson, I'm not trying to be negative – I swear to God I'm not – but I'm not sure I'm cut out for this. Could you lift your pack over your head like that?'

'No.'

And on that premonitory note, we strapped up and set squelchily off up Moxie Bald Mountain.

The Appalachian Trail was the hardest thing I have ever done, and the Maine portion was the hardest part of the Appalachian Trail, and by a factor I couldn't begin to compute. Partly it was the heat. Maine, that most moderate of states, was having a killer heatwave. In the baking sun, the shadeless granite pavements of Moxie Bald radiated an oven-like heat, but even in the woods the air was oppressive and close, as if the trees and foliage were breathing on us with a hot, vegetative breath. We sweated helplessly, copiously, and drank unusual quantities of water, but could never stop being thirsty. Water was sometimes plentiful, but more often non-existent for long stretches so that we were never sure how much we could prudently swallow without leaving ourselves short later on. Even fully stocked, we were short now thanks to Katz's dumping a bottle. Finally, there were the insects, which were relentless, the strangely unsettling sense of isolation, and the ever-taxing terrain.

Katz responded to this in a way that I had never seen. He showed a kind of fixated resolve, as if the only way to deal with this problem was to bull through it and get it over with.

The next morning we came very early to the first of several rivers we would have to ford. It was called Bald Mountain Stream, but in fact it was a river – broad, lively, strewn with boulders. It was exceedingly fetching – it glittered with dancing spangles in the early morning sun and was gorgeously clear – but the current seemed strong and there was no telling from the shore how deep it might be in the middle. Several large streams in the area, my *Appalachian Trail Guide to Maine* noted blithely, 'can be difficult or dangerous to cross in high water'. I decided not to share this with Katz.

We took off our shoes and socks, rolled up our trousers, and stepped gingerly out into the frigid water. The stones on the bottom were all shapes and sizes – flat, egg-shaped, domed – very hard on the feet, and covered with a filmy green slime that was ludicrously slippery. I hadn't gone three steps when my feet skated and I fell painfully on my ass. I struggled halfway to my feet, but slipped and fell again; struggled up, staggered sideways a yard or two and pitched helplessly forward, breaking my fall with my hands and ending up in the water doggie-style. As I landed, my pack slid forward and my boots, tied to its frame by their laces, were hurled into a kind of contained orbit; they flew round the side of the pack in a long, rather pretty trajectory, and came to a halt against my head, then plunked into the water where they dangled in the current. As I crouched there, breathing evenly and telling myself that one day this would be a memory, two young guys – clones almost of the two we had seen the day before – strode past with confident, splashing steps, packs above their heads.

'Fall down?' said one brightly.

'No, I just wanted a closer look at the water.' You moronic fit twit.

I went back to the riverbank, pulled on my soaked boots, and discovered that it was infinitely easier crossing with them on. I got a tolerable grip and the rocks didn't hurt as they had on my bare feet. I crossed cautiously, alarmed at the force of the current in the centre – each time I lifted a leg the current tried to reposition it downstream, as if it belonged to a gateleg table – but the water was never more than about three feet deep, and I reached the other side without falling.

Katz, meantime, had discovered a way across using boulders as stepping stones, but ended up stranded on the edge of a noisy torrent of what looked like deep water. He stood there covered with frowns. I couldn't for the life of me figure out how he had got up there – his boulder seemed isolated in an expanse of dangerously streaming water from all sides, and clearly he didn't know what to do now. He tried to ease himself into the water to wade the last ten yards to shore, and was instantly whisked away like a feather. For the second time in two days I sincerely thought he was drowning – he was certainly helpless – but the current carried him to a shallow bar of gleaming pebbles 20 feet further on, where he came up sputtering on his hands and knees, struggled up onto the bank, and continued on into the woods without a backward glance, as if this were the most normal thing in the world.

And so we pressed on to Monson, over hard trail and more rivers, collecting bruises and scratches and insect bites that turned our backs into relief maps. On the third day, forest-dazed and grubby, we stepped onto a sunny road, the first since Caratunk, and followed it on a hot ambulation into the forgotten hamlet of Monson. Near the centre of town was an old clapboard house with a painted wooden cut-out of a bearded hiker standing on the lawn bearing the message WELCOME AT SHAW'S.

Shaw's is the most famous guesthouse on the AT, partly because it's the last comfort stop for anyone going into the Hundred Mile Wilderness and the first for anyone coming out, but also because it's very friendly and good value. For $28 each we got a room, dinner and breakfast, and free use of the shower, laundry and guest lounge. The place was run by Keith and Pat Shaw, who started the business more or less by accident twenty years ago when Keith brought home a hungry hiker off the trail and the hiker passed on the word of how well he had been treated. Just a few weeks earlier, Keith told me proudly as we signed in, they had registered their 20,000th hiker.

We had an hour till dinner. Katz borrowed $5 – for pop, I presumed – and vanished to his room. I had a shower, put a load of washing in the machine and wandered out to the front lawn where there were a couple of Adirondack chairs on which I intended to park my weary butt, smoke my pipe and savour the blissful ease of late afternoon and the pleasant anticipation of a dinner earned. From a screened window nearby came the sounds of sizzling food and the clatter of pans. It smelled good, whatever it was.

After a minute, Keith came out and sat with me. He was an old guy, comfortably into his sixties, with almost no teeth and a body that looked as if it had put up with all kinds of tough stuff in its day. He was real friendly.

'You didn't try to pet the dog, did ya?' he said.

'No.' I had seen it from the window: an ugly, vicious mongrel that was tied up behind the house and got stupidly and disproportionately worked up by any noise or movement within a hundred yards.

'You don't wanna try to pet the dog. Take it from me: you do not wanna pet that dog. Some hiker petted him last week when I told him not to and it bit him in the balls.'

'Really?'

He nodded. 'Wouldn't let go neither. You shoulda heard that feller wail.'

'Really?'

'Had to hit the damn dog with a *rake* to get him to let go. Meanest damn dog I ever seen in my life. You don't wanna get near him, believe me.'

'How was the hiker?'

'Well, it didn't exactly make his day, I tell you that.' He scratched his neck contemplatively, as if he were thinking of having a shave one of these days. 'Thru-hiker, he was. Come all the way from Georgia. Long way to come to get your *balls* nipped.' Then he went off to check on dinner.

Dinner was at a big dining-room table that was generously covered in platters of meat, bowls of mashed potatoes and corn on the cob, a teetering plate of bread, a tub of butter. Katz arrived a few moments after me, looking freshly showered and very happy. He seemed unusually, almost exaggeratedly, energized, and gave me an impetuous tickle from behind as he passed, which was out of character.

'You all right?' I said.

'Never been better, my old mountain companion, never been better.'

We were joined by two others, a sweetly hesitant and wholesome-looking young couple, both tanned and fit and also very clean. Katz and I welcomed them with smiles, and started to pitch in, then paused and put back the bowls when we realized the couple were mumbling grace. This seemed to go on for ever. Then we pitched in again.

The food was terrific. Keith acted as waiter and was most insistent that we eat plenty. 'Dog'll eat it if you don't,' he said. I was happy to let the dog starve.

The young couple were thru-hikers, from Indiana. They had started at Springer on 28 March – a date that seemed impossibly snow-flecked and distant now in the full heat of an August evening – and had hiked continuously for 141 days. They had completed 2045.5 miles. They had 114.9 miles to go.

'So you've nearly done it, huh?' I said, a trifle inanely, but just trying to make conversation.

'Yes,' said the girl. She said it slowly, as two syllables, as if it hadn't previously occurred to her. There was something serenely mindless in her manner.

'Did you ever feel like giving up?'

The girl thought for a moment. 'No,' she said simply.

'Really?' I found this amazing. 'Did you never think, "Jeez, this is too much. I don't know that I want to go through with this"?'

She thought again, with an air of encroaching panic. These were obviously questions that had never penetrated her skull.

Her partner came to her rescue. 'We had a couple of low moments in the early phases,' he said, 'but we put our faith in the Lord and His will prevailed.'

'Praise Jesus,' whispered the girl, almost inaudibly.

'Ah,' I said, and made a mental note to lock my door when I went to bed.

'And God bless Allah for the mashed potatoes!' said Katz happily and reached for the bowl for the third time.

After dinner, Katz and I strolled to a general store up the road to get supplies for the Hundred Mile Wilderness, which we would start in the morning. He seemed odd in the grocery store – cheerful enough, but distracted and inattentive. We were supposed to be stocking up for ten days in the wilds – a fairly serious business – but he seemed unwilling to focus, and kept wandering off or picking up inappropriate things like chilli sauce and tin openers.

'Hey, let's get a sixpack,' he said suddenly, in a party voice.

'Come on, Stephen, get serious,' I said. I was looking at cheeses.

'I am serious.'

'Do you want cheddar or colby?'

'Whatever.' He wandered off to the beer cooler and came back carrying a sixpack of Budweiser.

'Hey, whaddaya say to a sixpack, bud – a sixpack of Bud, bud?' He nudged me in the ribs to emphasize the joke.

I pulled away from the nudge in distraction. 'Come on, Stephen, stop dicking around.' I had moved on to the chocolate bars and biscuits and was trying to figure out what might last us ten days without melting into a disgusting ooze or bouncing into a bag of crumbs. 'Do you want Snickers or do you want to try something different?' I asked.

'I want Budweiser.' He grinned, then, seeing this had passed me by, adopted a sudden, solemn, jokeless tone. 'Please, Bryson, can I borrow' – he looked at the price – 'four dollars and seventy-nine cents. I'm broke.'

'Stephen, I don't know what's come over you. Put the beer back. Anyway, what happened to that five dollars I gave you?'

'Spent it.'

'What on?' And then it occurred to me. 'You've been drinking already, haven't you?'

'No,' he said robustly, as if dismissing a preposterous and possibly slanderous allegation.

But he was drunk – or at least half drunk. 'You have,' I said in amazement.

He sighed and rolled his eyes slightly. 'Two quarts of Michelob. Big deal.'

'You've been drinking.' I was appalled. 'When did you start drinking again?'

'In Des Moines. Just a little. You know, a couple of beers after work. Nothing to get in a panic about.'

'Stephen, you know you can't drink.'

He didn't want to hear this. He looked like a fourteen-year-old who had just been told to clean up his room. 'I don't need a lecture, Bryson.'

'I'm not going to buy you beer,' I said evenly.

He grinned as if I were being unaccountably priggish. 'Just a six-pack. Come on.'

'*No!*'

I was furious, livid – more furious than I had been about anything in years. I couldn't believe he was drinking again. It seemed such a deep, foolish betrayal of everything – of himself, me, what we were doing out here.

Katz was still wearing half a grin, but it didn't belong to his emotions any longer. 'So you're not going to buy me a couple of lousy beers after all I've done for you?'

This seemed a low blow. 'No.'

'Then fuck you,' he said and turned on his heel and walked out.

CHAPTER TWENTY

WELL, THAT RATHER COLOURED THINGS, AS YOU CAN IMAGINE. WE never said another word about it. It just hung there. At breakfast, we exchanged good mornings, more or less as normal, but didn't speak beyond that and afterwards, as we waited by Keith's van for a promised lift to the trailhead, we stood in an awkward silence, like adversaries in a property dispute waiting to be summoned into the judge's chambers.

At the edge of the woods when we alighted there was a sign announcing that this was the start of the Hundred Mile Wilderness, with a long soberly phrased warning to the effect that what lay beyond was not like other stretches of the trail, and that you shouldn't proceed if you didn't have at least ten days' worth of food and weren't feeling pretty tip-top.

It gave the woods a more ominous, vaguely moody feel. They were unquestionably different from woods further south – darker, more shadowy, inclining more to black than green. There were different trees, too – more conifers at low levels and many more birches – and scattered through the undergrowth were large, rounded black boulders, like sleeping animals, which lent the still recesses a certain eeriness. When Walt Disney decided to make *Bambi*, he despatched his artists to the Maine woods to make sketches, but this was palpably not a Disney wood of roomy glades and cuddlesome creatures. This brought to mind the woods in *The Wizard of Oz*, where the trees have ugly faces and malign intent, and every step seems a gamble. This was a wood for looming bears, dangling snakes, wolves with laser-red eyes. I understood at once why the velvet-jacketed Henry David Thoreau shat himself here.

As ever, the trail was well blazed, but in places almost overgrown, with ferns and other low foliage almost meeting in the middle over the path. Since only 10 per cent of thru-hikers make it this far, and it is much too distant for most day hikers, the trail in Maine is more thinly used. Above all, what set the trail apart was the terrain. In profile, the topography of the AT over the 18-mile section from Monson to Barren Mountain looks reasonably undemanding, rolling along at a more or less steady 1,200 feet with just a few steep rises and falls. In fact, it was hell.

Within half an hour we had come to a wall of rock, the first of many, perhaps 400 feet high. The trail ran up its face along a slight depression, like a lift shaft. It was as near perpendicular as a slope can get without actually being a rock climb. Slowly and laboriously we picked our way between and over boulders, using our hands as much as our feet. Combined with our exertion, the cloying heat was almost unbearable. I found I had to stop every ten or twelve yards to draw breath and wipe burning sweat from my eyes. I was swimming in heat, bathed in heat, swaddled in it. I don't believe I have ever been so warm or sweated so freely. I drank three-quarters of a bottle of water on the way up and used much of the rest to wet a bandanna and try to cool my throbbing head. I felt dangerously overheated and faint. I began to rest more frequently and for longer periods, to try to cool down a little, but each time I set off again the heat came flooding back. I had never had to work so hard or so tiringly to clear an Appalachian impediment, and this was just the first of a series.

The top of the climb brought several hundred yards of bare, gently sloping granite, like walking along a whale's back. From each summit the panorama was sensational – for as far as the eye could see, nothing but heavy green woods, denim-blue lakes, and undulant mountains. Many of the lakes were immense – as big as Windermere at least – and nearly all of them had probably never felt so much as a human toe. There was a certain captivating sense of having penetrated into a secret corner of the world, but in the murderous sun it was impossible to linger.

Then came a difficult and unnerving descent down a rocky cliff face on the other side, a short walk through a dark, waterless valley, and delivery to the foot of another wall of rock. And so the day went, with monumental climbs and the hope of water over the next hill the principal thing drawing us on. Katz was soon out of water altogether. I gave him a drink of mine and he accepted it gratefully, with a look that asked for a truce. There was, however, still a kind of odour between us, an unhappy sense that things had changed and would not be the same again.

It was doubtless my fault. I pushed on further and longer than we would have normally, and without consulting him, unsubtly punishing him for having unbalanced the equilibrium that had existed between us, and Katz bore it silently as his due. We did 14 miles, an exceedingly worthy distance in the circumstances, and might have gone further, but at half past six we came to a broad ford called Wilber Brook and stopped. We were too tired to cross – that is to say, I was too tired – and it would be folly to get wet so near sundown. We made camp and shared out our cheerless rations with a kind of strained politeness. Even if we had not been at odds, we would scarcely have spoken. We were too tired. It had been a long day – the hardest of the trip – and the thought that hung over us was that we had 85 more miles of this before we got to the camp store at Abol Bridge, 100 miles till we reached the difficult summit of Katahdin.

Even then we had no prospect of real comfort. Katahdin is in Baxter State Park, which takes a certain hearty pride in its devotion to ruggedness and deprivation. There are no restaurants and lodges, no gift shops and hamburger stands, not even any paved roads. The park itself is in the middle of nowhere, a two-day hike from Millinocket, the nearest town. It could be ten or eleven days before we had a proper meal or slept in a bed. It seemed a long way off.

In the morning we silently forded the stream – we were getting pretty good at it now – and started up the long, slow climb to the roof of the Barren–Chairback Range, 15 miles of ragged summits that we had to cross before descending to a more tranquil spell in the valley of the Pleasant River. The map showed just three tarns in those mountains, glacial leftovers, all off the trail, but otherwise no indication of water at all. With less than four litres of water capacity between us and the day already warm, the long haul between water sources promised to be at the very least uncomfortable.

Barren Mountain was a strenuous slog, much of it straight up and all of it hot, though we seemed to be getting stronger. Even Katz was moving with a comparative lightness. The weather remained sultry. It took us nearly all the morning to hike the four and a half miles up. I reached the top some time ahead of Katz. The summit was sun-warmed granite, hot to the touch, but there was a wisp of breeze – the first in days – and I found a shady spot beneath a disused fire tower. It was the first time in what seemed like weeks that I had sat anywhere in relative comfort. I leaned back and felt as if I could sleep for a month. Katz arrived ten minutes later, puffing hard but pleased to be at the top. He took a seat on a boulder beside mine. I had about two inches of water left, and passed him the bottle. He took a very modest sip and made to hand it back.

'Go on,' I said, 'you must be thirsty.'

'Thanks.' He took a slightly less modest sip and put the bottle down. He sat for a minute, then got out a Snickers, broke it in two and extended half to me. It was a somewhat odd thing to do because I had Snickers of my own and he knew that, but he had nothing else to give.

'Thanks,' I said.

He gnawed off a bite of Snickers, ate for a minute and said from out of nowhere: 'Girlfriend and boyfriend are talking. The girlfriend says to the boyfriend, "Jimmy, how do you spell *paedophilia*?" The boyfriend looks at her in amazement. "Gosh, honey," he says "that's an *awfully* big word for an eight-year-old."'

I laughed.

'I'm sorry about the other night,' Katz said.

'Me too.'

'I just got a little . . . I don't know.'

'I know.'

'It's kind of hard for me sometimes,' he went on. 'I try, Bryson, I really do, but.' He stopped there and shrugged reflectively, a little helplessly. 'There's just this kind of hole in my life where drinking used to be.' He was staring at the view – the usual verdant infinity of woods and lakes, shimmering slightly in a heat haze. There was something in his gaze – a miles-away fixedness – that made me think for a minute he had stopped altogether, but he went on: 'When I went back to Des Moines after Virginia and got that job building houses, at the end of the day all the crew would go off to this tavern across the street. They'd always invite me, but I'd say' – he lifted two hands and put on a deep, righteous voice – '"No, boys, I'm reformed." And I'd go home to my little apartment and heat a TV dinner, and feel all virtuous, like I'm supposed to. But really, you know, when you do that night after night it's kind of hard to persuade yourself you're leading a rich and thrilling existence. I mean, if you had a Fun-o-Meter, the needle wouldn't exactly be jumping into the orgasmic zone because you've got your own TV dinner. You know what I'm saying?'

He glanced over, to see me nod.

'So anyway one day after work, they invited me for about the hundredth time and I thought, "Oh, what the hell. No law that says I can't go in a tavern like anybody else." So I went and had a Diet Coke and it was OK. I mean, it was nice just to be out. But you know how good a beer is at the end of a long day. And there was this *jerk* named *Dwayne* who kept saying, "Go on, have a beer. You *know* you want one. One little beer's not gonna hurt ya. You haven't had a drink for three years. You can handle it."' He looked at me again. 'You know?'

I nodded.

'Caught me when I was vulnerable,' Katz said with a hard, ironic smile. 'You know, when I was still breathing. I never had more than three, I swear to God. I know what you're going to say – believe me, everybody's said it already. I know I can't drink. I know I can't have just a couple of beers like a normal person, that pretty soon the number will creep up and up and spin out of control. I know that. But.' He stopped there again, shaking his head. 'But I love to drink. I can't help it. I mean, I *love* it, Bryson – love the taste, love that buzz you get when you've had a couple, love the smell and feel of taverns. I miss dirty stories and the click of pool balls in the background, and that kind of bluish, underlit glow of a bar at night.' He was quiet again for a minute, lost in a little reverie for a lifetime's drinking. 'And I can't have it any more. I know that.' He breathed out heavily through his nostrils. 'It's just that. It's just that sometimes all I see ahead of me is TV dinners – a sort of endless line of them dancing towards me like in a cartoon. You ever eat TV dinners?'

'Not for years and years.'

'Well, they're shit, believe me. And, I don't know, it's just kind of hard . . .' He trailed off. 'Actually, it's *real* hard.' He looked at me, on the edge of emotion, his expression frank and humble. 'Makes me kind of an asshole sometimes,' he said quietly but sincerely.

I gave him a smile. 'Makes you more of an asshole,' I said.

He grunted a laugh. 'Yeah, I guess.'

I reached over and gave him a stupidly affectionate jab on the shoulder. He received it with a flicker of appreciation.

'And do you know what the fuck of it is?' he said in a sudden pull-yourself-together voice. 'I could kill for a TV dinner right now. I really could.'

We laughed.

'Hungry Man Turkey Dinner with plastic giblets and forty-weight gravy. Hmmmm-mmmm. I'd leave your scrawny ass up here for just a *sniff* of that.' Then he brushed at a corner of his eye, said, 'Hoo, fuck,' and went to have a pee over the cliff edge.

I watched him go, looking old and tired, and wondered for a minute what on earth we were doing up here. We weren't boys any more.

I looked at the map. We were practically out of water, but it was less than a mile to Cloud Pond, where we could refill. We split the last half-inch, and I told Katz I would go on ahead to the pond, filter the water and have it waiting for him when he arrived.

It was an easy twenty-minute walk along a grassy ridgeline. Cloud Pond was down a steep side trail, about a quarter of a mile off the AT. I left my pack propped against a rock at the trailside, and went with our water bottles and the filter down to the pond edge and filled up.

It took me perhaps twenty minutes to walk down, fill the three bottles and walk back, so when I returned to the AT it had been about forty minutes since I had seen Katz. Even if he had tarried on the mountaintop, and even allowing for his modest walking speed, he should have reached here by now. Besides, it was an easy walk and I knew he was thirsty, so it was odd that he wasn't here more promptly. I waited fifteen minutes and then twenty and twenty-five, and finally I left my pack and went back to look for him. It was well over an hour since I had seen him when I reached the mountaintop, and he wasn't there. I stood confounded on the spot where we had last been together. His stuff was gone. He had obviously moved on, but if he wasn't on Barren Mountain and wasn't at Cloud Pond and was nowhere in between, then where was he? The only possible explanations were that he had gone back the other way, which was out of the question – Katz would never have left me without explanation; never – or that he had somehow fallen off the ridgeline. It was an absurd notion – there wasn't anything remotely challenging or dangerous about the ridgeline – but you never know. John Connolly had told us weeks before of a friend of his who had fainted in the heat and tumbled a few feet off a safe, level trail; he had lain unnoticed for hours in blazing sunshine and slowly baked to death. All the way back to the Cloud Pond turnoff I carefully surveyed the trail-edge brush for signs of disturbance and peered at intervals over the lip of the ridge, fearful of seeing Katz spread-eagled on a rock. I called his name several times, and got nothing in return but my own fading voice.

By the time I reached the turnoff it had been nearly two hours since I had seen him. This was becoming worryingly inexplicable. The only remaining possibility was that he had walked past the turnoff while I was down at the pond filtering water, but this seemed manifestly improbable. There was a prominent arrowed sign by the trail saying CLOUD POND and my pack had been clearly visible beside the trail. Even if he had somehow failed to notice these things, he knew that Cloud Pond was only a mile from Barren Mountain. When you have hiked the AT as much as we had, you get so you can judge a mile with considerable accuracy. He couldn't have gone too far beyond without realizing his mistake and coming back. This just didn't make sense.

All I knew was that Katz was alone in a wilderness with no water, no map, no clear idea of what terrain lay ahead, presumably no idea of what had become of me, and a worrying lack of sense. If there was ever one person who would decide while lost on the AT to leave the trail and try for a short cut, it was Katz. I began to feel extremely uneasy. I left a note on my pack and went off down the trail. A half-mile further on, the trail descended very steeply, almost perpendicularly, more than 600 feet to a deep, nameless valley. He had to have realized by this point, surely, that he had gone wrong. I had told him Cloud Pond was a level stroll.

Calling his name at intervals, I picked my way slowly along the path down the cliff face, fearing the worst at the bottom – for this was a precipice one could easily fall down, especially with a big ungainly pack and a preoccupied mind – but there was no sign of him. I followed the trail two miles through the valley and up onto the summit of a high pinnacle called Fourth Mountain. The view from the top was expansive in every direction; the wilderness had never looked so big. I called his name long and hard, and got nothing in return.

It was getting on for late afternoon by this time. He had been at least four hours without water. I had no idea how long a person could survive without water in this heat, but I knew from experience that you couldn't go for more than half an hour without experiencing considerable discomfort. It occurred to me with a sinking feeling that he might have seen another pond – there were half a dozen to choose from scattered across the valley 2,000 feet below – and decided in his perplexity that perhaps that was it, and tried to reach it cross country. Even if he wasn't confused, he might simply have been driven by thirst to try to reach one of those ponds. They looked wonderfully cool and refreshing. The nearest was only about two miles away, but there was no trail to it and it was down a perilous slope through the woods. Once you were in the woods and bereft of bearings, you could easily miss it by a mile. Conversely, you could be within 50 yards of it and not know, as we had seen at Pleasant Pond a few days before. And once you were lost in these immense woods, you would die. It was as simple as that. No one could save you. No helicopter could spot you through the cover of trees. No rescue teams could find you. None, I suspected, would even try. There would be bears down there, too – bears that had possibly never seen a human. All the possibilities made my head hurt.

I hiked back to the Cloud Pond turnoff, hoping more than anything I had hoped for in a long time that he would be sitting on the pack, and that there would be some amusing, unconsidered explanation – that we had kept just missing each other, like in a stage farce: him waiting bewildered at my pack, then going off to look for me; me arriving a moment later, waiting in puzzlement and going off – but I knew he wouldn't be there, and he wasn't. It was nearly dusk when I got back. I wrote a fresh note and left it under a rock in the middle of the AT, just in case, hoisted my pack and went down to the pond, where there was a shelter.

The irony was that this was the nicest campsite I experienced anywhere along the AT, and it was the one place I camped without Katz. Cloud Pond was a couple of hundred acres of exquisitely peaceful water surrounded by dark coniferous forest, the treetops pointy black silhouettes against a pale blue evening sky. The shelter, which I had to myself, was on a level area 30 or 40 yards back from the pond and slightly above it. It was practically new and spotless. There was a privy nearby. It was nearly perfect. I dumped my stuff on the wooden sleeping platform and went down to the water's edge to filter water, so I wouldn't have to do it in the morning, then stripped to my boxers and waded a couple of feet into the dark water to have a wash with a bandanna. If Katz had been there, I'd have had a swim. I tried not to think about him – certainly not to visualize him lost and bewildered. There was, after all, nothing I could do now.

Instead, I sat on a rock and watched the sunset. The pond was almost painfully beautiful. The long rays of the setting sun made the water shimmer golden. Offshore, two loons cruised, as if out for a spin after supper. I watched them for a long time, and thought about something I had seen on a BBC nature programme some time before.

Loons, according to the programme, are not social creatures. But towards the end of summer, just before they fly back to the North Atlantic, where they pass the winter bobbing on stormy waves, they host a series of get-togethers. A dozen or more loons from all the neighbouring ponds fly in, and they all swim around together for a couple of hours for no discernible reason other than the pleasure of being together. The host loon leads the guests on a proud but low-key tour of his territory – first to his favourite little cove, say, then perhaps over to an interesting fallen log, then on to a patch of lily pads. 'This is where I like to fish in the mornings,' he seems to be saying. 'And here's where we're thinking of moving our nesting site next year.' All the other loons follow him around with diligence and polite interest. No one knows why they do this (but then no one knows why one human being would want to show another his converted bathroom) or how they arrange their rendezvous, but they all show up each night at the right lake at the right time as certainly as if they had been sent a card that said: 'We're Having a Party!' I think that's wonderful. I would have enjoyed it more if I hadn't kept thinking of Katz stumbling and gasping and searching for a lake by moonlight.

Oh, and by the way, the loons are disappearing everywhere because their lakes are dying from acid rain.

I had a rotten night, of course, and was up before five and back on the trail at first light. I continued on north in the direction I guessed Katz had gone, but with the nagging thought that I was plunging ever further into the Hundred Mile Wilderness – not perhaps the best direction to go if he was somewhere nearby and in trouble. There was a certain incidental disquiet at the thought that I was on my own in the middle of nowhere – a disquiet briefly but vividly heightened when I stumbled in my haste on the return descent to the deep, nameless valley and came within a trice of falling 50 long feet, with a messy bounce at the bottom. I hoped I was doing the right thing.

Even flat out it would take me three days, perhaps four, to reach

Abol Bridge and the campground. By the time I alerted authorities, Katz would have been missing for four or five days. On the other hand, if I turned now and went back the way we had come, I could be in Monson by the following afternoon. What I really needed was to meet somebody coming south who could tell me if they had seen Katz, but there was no one out on the trail. I looked at my watch. Of course there wasn't. It was only a little after six in the morning. There was a shelter at Chairback Gap, six miles further on. I would reach it by eight or so. With luck, there might still be someone there. I pressed on with more care and a queasy uncertainty.

I clambered back over the pinnacle of Fourth Mountain – much harder with a pack – and into another wooded valley beyond. Four miles after leaving Cloud Pond, I came to a tiny stream, barely worthy of the term – really just a slick of moist mud. Speared to a branch beside the trail, in an intentionally prominent place, was an empty pack of Old Gold cigarettes. Katz didn't really smoke, but he always carried a pack of Old Golds. In the mud by a fallen log were three cigarette butts. He had obviously waited here. So he was alive and hadn't left the trail, and clearly had come this way. I felt immeasurably better. At least I was going in the right direction. As long as he stayed on the trail, I was bound eventually to overtake him.

I found him four hours after setting off, sitting on a rock by the turnoff for West Chairback Pond, head inclined to the sun as if working on his tan. He was extensively scratched and muddy, and wildly bedraggled, but otherwise looked OK. He was of course delighted to see me.

'Bryson, you old mountain man, you're a welcome sight. Where have you been?'

'I was wondering the same about you.'

'Guess I missed the last watering hole?'

I nodded.

He nodded, too. 'Knew I had, of course. Soon as I got down to the bottom of that big cliff, I thought, "Shit, this can't be right."'

'Why didn't you come back?'

'I don't know. I got it in mind somehow that you must have pushed on. I was real thirsty. I think I might have been a little confused – a little addled, as you might say. I was real thirsty.'

'So what did you do?'

'Well, I pushed on and kept thinking I had to come to water sooner or later, and eventually I came to a mud slick—'

'Where you left the cigarette pack?'

'You saw it? I'm so proud. Yeah, well, I soaked up some water there with my bandanna, because I remembered that's what Fess Parker did once on the *Davy Crockett Show*.'

'How very enterprising.'

He accepted the compliment with a nod. 'That took about an hour, and then I waited another hour for you and had a couple of smokes, and then it was getting dark so I put my tent up, ate a Slim Jim and went to bed. Then this morning I sponged up a little more water with my bandanna and I came on here. There's a real nice pond just down there, so I thought I'd wait here where there was water and hope that you'd come along eventually. I didn't think you'd leave me up here on purpose, but you're such a walking daydream I could just imagine you getting all the way to Katahdin before you noticed I wasn't with you.' He put on a poncey accent. '"Oh, I say, *delight*ful view – don't you agree, Stephen? Stephen? Stephen? Now where the *deuce* has he got to?"' He gave me a familiar smile. 'So I'm real glad to see you.'

'How'd you get so scratched up?'

He looked at his arm, which was covered in a zig-zag of dried blood. 'Oh that? It's nothing.'

'What do you mean it's nothing? It looks like you've been doing surgery on yourself.'

'Well, I didn't want to alarm you, but I also got kind of lost.'

'How?'

'Well, between losing you and coming upon the mud slick, I tried to get to a lake I saw from the mountain.'

'Oh, Stephen, you didn't.'

'Well, I was real thirsty, you know, and it didn't look too far. So I plunged off into the woods. Not real smart, right?'

'No.'

'Yeah, well, I learned that real fast because I hadn't gone more than half a mile before I was totally lost. I mean totally lost. It's weird, you know, because you're thinking all you've got to do is go downhill to the water and come back the same way, and that shouldn't be too tough as long as you pay attention. But the thing is, Bryson, there's nothing to pay attention to out there. It's just one big wood. So when I realized I didn't have the faintest idea where I was I thought, "OK, well, I got lost by going downhill, so I'd better go back up." But suddenly there's a *lot* of uphills, and a lot of downhills too, and it's real confusing. So I went up and up and up until I *knew* I'd gone a lot further than I'd come, and then I thought, "Well, Stephen, you stupid piece of shit" – 'cause I was getting a little cross with myself by this time, to tell you the truth – I thought, "you must have gone too far, you jackass," so I went back down a ways, and *that* didn't work, so then I tried going sideways for a while, and – well, you get the picture.'

'You should never leave the trail, Stephen.'

'Oh, now there's a timely piece of advice, Bryson. Thank you so much. That's like telling somebody who's died in a crash, "Drive safely now."'

'Sorry.'

'Forget it. I think maybe I'm still a little, you know, unsettled. I thought I was done for. Lost, no water – and you with the chocolate chip cookies.'

'So how did you get back to the trail?'

'It was a miracle, I swear to God. Just when I was about to lie down and give myself to the wolves and bobcats, I look up and there's a white blaze on a tree and I look down and I'm *standing* on the AT. At the mud slick, as a matter of fact. I sat down and had three smokes one after the other, just to calm myself down, and then I thought, "Shit, I bet Bryson's walked by here while I've been blundering around in the woods, and he'll never come back because he's already checked this section of trail." And then I began to worry that I never would see you again. So I really *was* glad when you turned up. To tell you the truth, I've never been so glad to see another person in my whole life, and that includes some naked women.'

There was something in his look.

'You want to go home?' I asked.

He thought for a moment. 'Yeah. I do.'

'Me, too.'

So we decided to leave the endless trail and stop pretending we were mountain men because we weren't. At the bottom of Chairback Mountain, four miles further on, there was a dirt logging road. We didn't know where it went other than that it must go somewhere. An arrow on the edge of the map pointed south to Katahdin Iron Works, site of an improbable nineteenth-century factory in the woods and now a state historical monument. According to my trail guide there was public parking at the old iron works, so there must be a road out. At the bottom of the mountain, we watered up at a brook that ran past, and then started off along the logging road. We hadn't been walking more than three or four minutes when there was a noise in the near distance. We turned to see a cloud of dust heading our way led by an ancient pickup truck moving at great speed. As it approached I instinctively put my thumb out, and to my astonishment it stopped about 50 feet past us.

We ran up to the driver's window. There were two guys in the cab, both in hard hats and dirty from work – loggers obviously.

'Where you going?' asked the driver.

'Anywhere,' I said. 'Anywhere but here.'

CHAPTER TWENTY-ONE

SO WE DIDN'T SEE KATAHDIN. WE DIDN'T EVEN SEE KATAHDIN IRON Works, except as a glimpsed blur, because we shot past it at about 70 miles an hour on the bounciest, most terrifyingly hasty ride I ever hope to have in the back of a pickup truck on a dirt road.

We held on for dear life in the open back, lifting our feet to let chainsaws and other destructive-looking implements slide past – first this way, then that – while the driver propelled us through the flying woods with reckless zest, bouncing over potholes with such vigour as to throw us a foot or two into the air, and negotiating curves as if in startled afterthought. In consequence we alighted at the little community of Milo, 20 miles to the south, on unsteady legs and blinking at the suddenness with which our circumstances had changed. One moment we were in the heart of the wilderness, facing at least a two-day hike to civilization, and now we were in the forecourt of a gas station on the edge of a remote little town. We watched the pickup truck depart, then took our bearings.

'You want to get a Coke?' I said to Katz. There was a machine by the gas station door.

He looked at it. 'No,' he said. 'Maybe later.'

It was unlike Katz not to fall upon soft drinks and junk food with exuberant lust when the opportunity presented itself, but I believed I understood. There is always a measure of shock when you leave the trail and find yourself parachuted into a world of comfort and choice, but it was different this time. This time it was permanent. We were hanging up our hiking boots. From now on, there would *always* be

Coke, and soft beds and showers and whatever else we wanted. There was no urgency now. It was a strangely subduing notion.

Milo had no motel, but we were directed to a place called Bishop's Boarding-house. It was a large old white house on a handsome street of substantial old houses, the kind where the garages were originally carriage houses with quarters upstairs for the servants.

We were received with warmth and bustling kindliness by the proprietor, Joan Bishop, a cheery, snowy-haired lady with a hearty Down East accent who came to the door wringing floury hands on an apron and waved us and our grubby packs into the spotless interior without a flicker of dismay.

The house smelled wholesomely of fresh-baked pastry, garden tomatoes, and air nobly unmodified by fans or air conditioners – old-fashioned summer smells. She called us 'you boys', and acted as if she had been expecting us for days, possibly years.

'Goodness me, just look at you boys!' she clucked in astonishment and delight. 'You look as if you've been wrestling bears!'

I suppose we must have looked a sight. Katz was liberally covered in blood from his fraught stumble through the woods, and there was tiredness all over us, even in our eyes.

'You boys go up and get yourselves cleaned up and come down to the porch afterwards and I'll have a nice jug of iced tea waiting for you. Or would you rather have lemonade? Never mind, I'll make both. Now go on!' And off she bustled.

'Thanks, Mom,' we muttered in a dazzled and grateful unison.

Katz was instantly transformed – so much so that he felt perhaps a trifle too much at home. I was wearily taking some things from my pack when he suddenly appeared in my room without knocking and hastily shut the door behind him, looking flummoxed. Only a towel, clutched not quite adequately around his waist, preserved his hefty modesty.

'Little old lady,' he said in amazement.

'Pardon?'

'Little old lady in the hallway,' he said again.

'It is a guesthouse, Stephen.'

'Yeah, I hadn't thought of that,' he said. He peeked round the door and disappeared without elaboration.

When we had showered and changed, we joined Mrs Bishop on the screened porch, where we slumped heavily and gratefully in the big old porch chairs, legs thrust out, the way you do when it's hot and you're tired. I was hoping that Mrs Bishop would tell us that she was forever putting up hikers who had been foiled by the Hundred Mile Wilderness, but in fact we were the first she could recall in that category.

'I read in the paper the other day that a man from Portland hiked Katahdin to celebrate his seventy-eighth birthday,' she said conversationally.

That made me feel immensely better, as you can imagine.

'I expect I'll be ready to try again by then,' Katz said, running a finger along the line of scratch on his forearm.

'Well, it'll still be there, boys, when you're ready for it,' she said. She was right, of course.

We dined in town at a popular restaurant, and afterwards, with the evening warm and congenial, went for a stroll. Milo was a sweetly hopeless town – commercially forlorn, far from anywhere and barely alive, but curiously likeable. Perhaps it was just that it was our last night away from home.

'So do you feel bad about leaving the trail?' Katz asked after a time.

I thought for a moment, unsure. I had come to realize that I didn't have any feelings towards the AT that weren't thoroughly contradictory. I was weary of the trail, but captivated by it; found the endless slog increasingly exhausting but ever invigorating; grew tired of the boundless woods but admired their boundlessness; enjoyed the escape from civilization and ached for its comforts. All of this together, all at once, every moment, on the trail or off.

'I don't know,' I said. 'Yes and no, I guess. What about you?'

He nodded. 'Yes and no.'

We walked along for some minutes, lost in small thoughts.

'Anyway, we did it,' Katz said at last, looking up. He noted my quizzical expression. 'Hiked Maine, I mean.'

I looked at him. 'Stephen, we didn't even see Mount Katahdin.'

He dismissed this as a petty quibble. 'Another mountain,' he said. 'How many do you need to see, Bryson?'

I gave a small laugh. 'Well, that's one way of looking at it.'

'It's the *only* way of looking at it,' Katz went on and quite earnestly. 'As far as I'm concerned, I hiked the Appalachian Trail. I hiked it in snow and I hiked it in heat. I hiked it in the South and I hiked it in the North. I hiked it till my feet bled. I *hiked* the Appalachian Trail, Bryson.'

'We missed out a lot of it, you know.'

'Details,' Katz sniffed.

I shrugged, not unhappily. 'Maybe you're right.'

'Of course I'm right,' he said, as if he were seldom otherwise.

We had reached the edge of town, by the little gas station/grocery store where the lumberjacks had dropped us. It was still open.

'So what do you say to some cream soda?' Katz said brightly. 'I'll buy.'

I looked at him with deepened interest. 'You don't have any money.'

'I know. I'll buy it with your money.'

I grinned and handed him a five-dollar bill from my wallet.

'*X Files* tonight,' Katz said happily – very, very happily – and disappeared into the store. I watched him go, shaking my head, and wondered how he always knew.

So that, I'm afraid, is how it ended for me and Katz – with a six-pack of cream soda in Milo, Maine.

I continued to hike, on and off, in a modest way, through the rest of summer and into autumn. In early November, when winter was blowing in and the hiking season was clearly at an end, I finally sat down at the kitchen table with my trail log and a calculator and totted up the miles I had done. I checked the numbers through twice, then looked up with an expression not unlike the one Katz and I had shared months before in Gatlinburg when we realized we were never going to hike the Appalachian Trail.

I had done 870 miles, considerably less than half, not a huge amount more than one-third. All that effort and sweat and disgusting grubbiness, all of those endless plodding days, the nights on hard ground – all that added up to just 39.5 per cent of the trail. Goodness knows how anyone ever completes the whole thing. I am filled with admiration and incredulity for those who see it through. But, hey and excuse me, 870 is still a lot of miles.

Stephen Katz returned to Des Moines, to a life of devoted sobriety. He calls from time to time and talks about coming out sometime to try the Hundred Mile Wilderness again, though I don't suppose he ever will.

I won't say that the experience changed our lives, and I can't speak for Katz, but I certainly gained an appreciation and respect for woods and wilderness and the colossal scale of America. I lost a lot of weight and for a time was remarkably fit.

Best of all, these days when I see a mountain, I look at it slowly and appraisingly, with a narrow, knowing gaze, and eyes of chipped granite.

DOWN UNDER

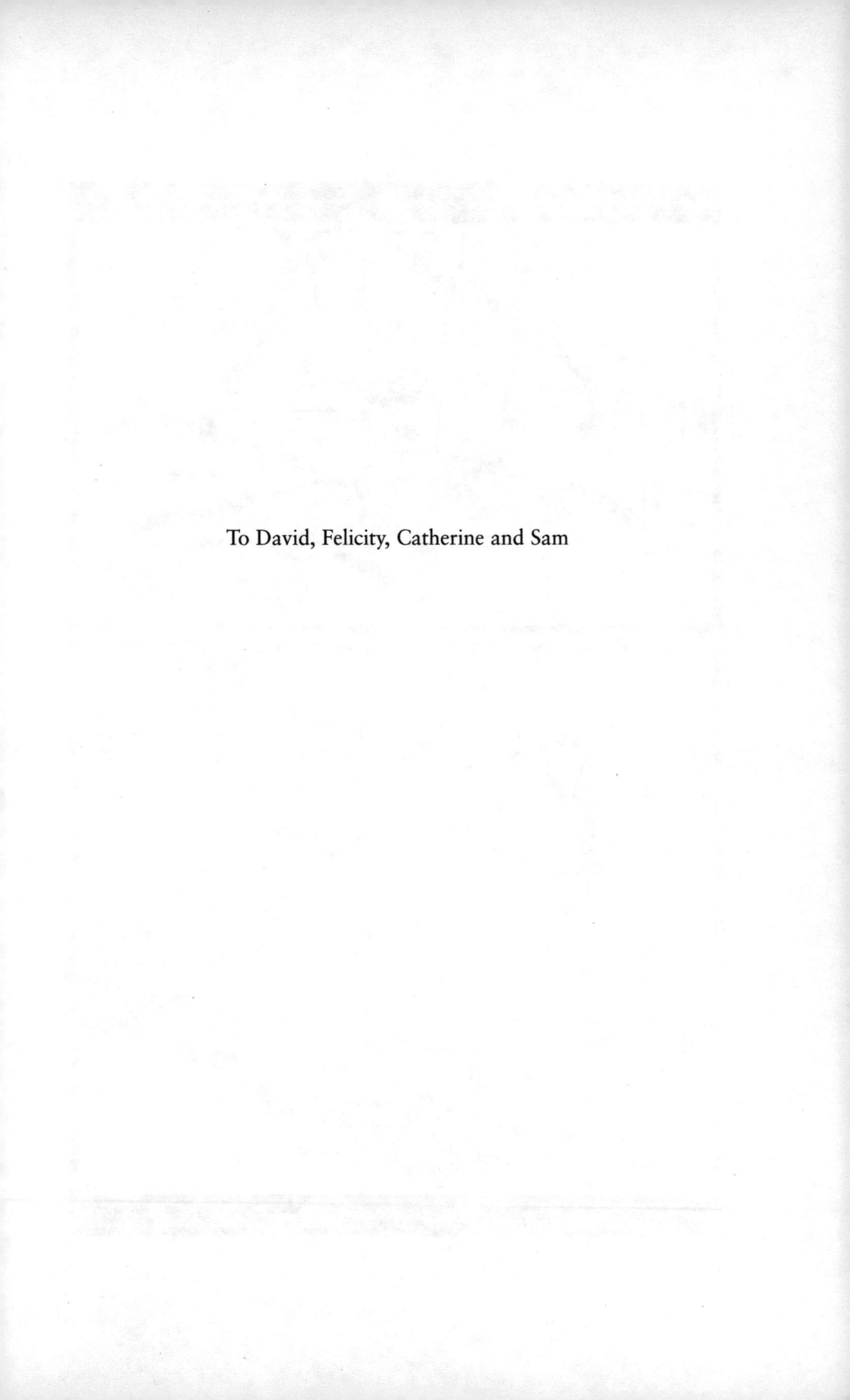

To David, Felicity, Catherine and Sam

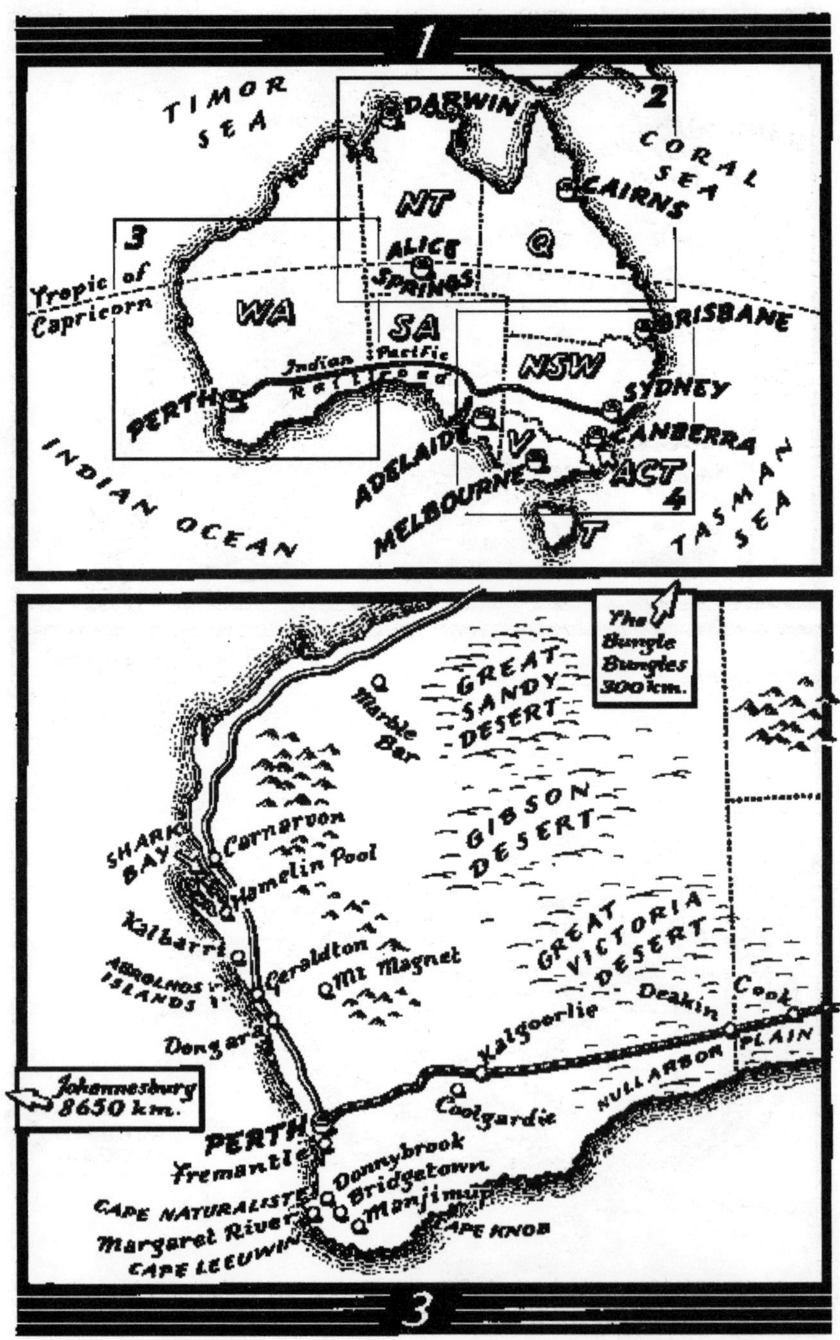
1
TIMOR SEA
DARWIN
2
CORAL SEA
CAIRNS
NT
Q
3
ALICE SPRINGS
Tropic of Capricorn
WA
SA
BRISBANE
Indian Pacific Railroad
NSW
SYDNEY
PERTH
CANBERRA
ADELAIDE
V
ACT
MELBOURNE
4
INDIAN OCEAN
T
TASMAN SEA
The Bungle Bungles 300 km.
Marble Bar
GREAT SANDY DESERT
GIBSON DESERT
SHARK BAY
Carnarvon
Hamelin Pool
Kalbarri
Geraldton
Mt Magnet
GREAT VICTORIA DESERT
ABROLHOS ISLANDS
Dongara
Deakin
Cook
Kalgoorlie
NULLARBOR PLAIN
Johannesburg 8650 km.
Coolgardie
PERTH
Fremantle
Donnybrook
Bridgetown
CAPE NATURALISTE
Manjimup
Margaret River
CAPE KNOB
CAPE LEEUWIN
3

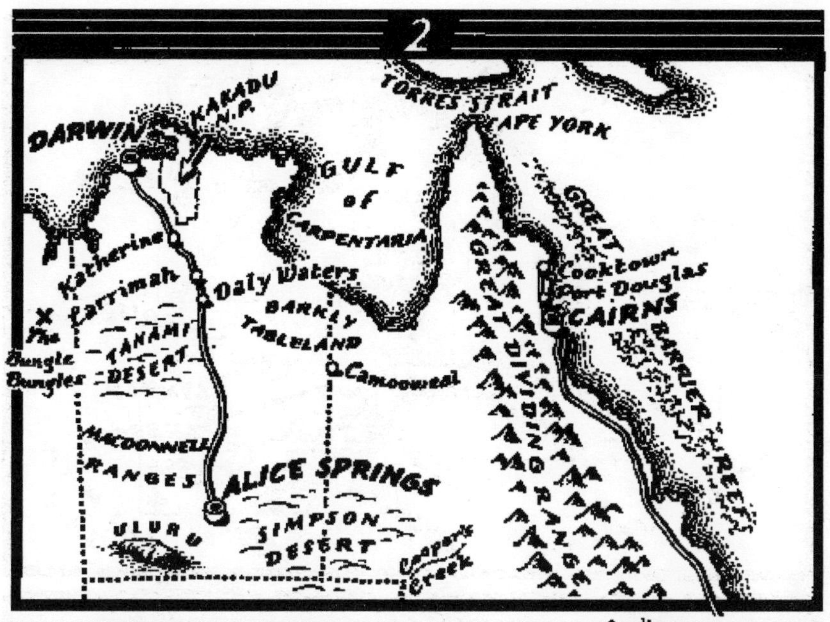
2
DARWIN
KAKADU N.P.
TORRES STRAIT
CAPE YORK
GULF of CARPENTARIA
GREAT BARRIER REEF
Katherine
Larrimah
Daly Waters
Cooktown
Port Douglas
CAIRNS
GREAT DIVIDING RANGE
BARKLY TABLELAND
The Bungle Bungles
TANAMI DESERT
Camooweal
MACDONNELL RANGES
ALICE SPRINGS
ULURU
SIMPSON DESERT
Cooper's Creek

STRZELECKI DESERT
Barringun
BRISBANE
Surfers Paradise
White Cliffs
Myall Creek
Silverton
Broken Hill
Darling River
FLINDERS RANGE
Grafton
Coffs Harbour
Bingara
Armidale
Macksville
Wilcannia
Bathurst
Newcastle
BAROSSA VALLEY
ADELAIDE
Menindee
Cowra
SYDNEY
Balranald
Hay
Young
Wollongong
CANBERRA
ALPINE N.P.
Des Moines 14100 km.
Lakes Entrance
MELBOURNE
Warrnambool
Portsea
4

Part One

INTO THE OUTBACK

CHAPTER ONE

I

FLYING INTO AUSTRALIA, I REALIZED WITH A SIGH THAT I HAD forgotten again who their Prime Minister is. I am forever doing this with the Australian PM – committing the name to memory, forgetting it (generally more or less instantly), then feeling terribly guilty. My thinking is that there ought to be one person outside Australia who knows.

But then Australia is such a difficult country to keep track of. On my first visit, some years ago, I passed the time on the long flight from London reading a history of Australian politics in the twentieth century, wherein I encountered the startling fact that in 1967 the Prime Minister, Harold Holt, was strolling along a beach in Victoria when he plunged into the surf and vanished. No trace of the poor man was ever seen again. This seemed doubly astounding to me – first that Australia could just *lose* a Prime Minister (I mean, come on) and second that news of this had never reached me.

The fact is, of course, we pay shamefully scant attention to our dear cousins Down Under – though not entirely without reason, I suppose. Australia is, after all, mostly empty and a long way away. Its population, about 19 million, is small by world standards – China grows by a larger amount each year – and its place in the world economy is consequently peripheral; as an economic entity, it is about the same size as Illinois. From time to time it sends us useful things – opals, merino wool, Errol Flynn, the boomerang – but nothing we can't actually do without. Above all, Australia doesn't misbehave. It is stable and peaceful and good. It doesn't have coups, recklessly overfish, arm disagreeable despots, grow coca in provocative quantities or throw its weight around in a brash and unseemly manner.

But even allowing for all this, our neglect of Australian affairs is curious. As you might expect, this is particularly noticeable when you are resident in America. Just before I set off on this trip I went to my local library in New Hampshire and looked up Australia in the *New York Times Index* to see how much it had engaged attention in my own country in recent years. I began with the 1997 volume for no other reason than that it was open on the table. In that year, across the full range of possible interests – politics, sport, travel, the coming Olympics in Sydney, food and wine, the arts, obituaries and so on – the *New York Times* ran 20 articles that were predominantly on or about Australian affairs. In the same period, for purposes of comparison, it found space for 120 articles on Peru, 150 or so on Albania and a similar number on Cambodia, more than 300 on each of the Koreas, and well over 500 on Israel. As a place that attracted American interest Australia ranked about level with Belarus and Burundi. Among the general subjects that outstripped it were balloons and balloonists, the Church of Scientology, dogs (though not dog sledding), and Pamela Harriman, the former ambassador and socialite who died in February 1997, a calamity that evidently required recording twenty-two times in the *Times*. Put in the crudest terms, Australia was slightly more important to Americans in 1997 than bananas, but not nearly as important as ice cream.

As it turns out, 1997 was actually quite a good year for Australian news in the United States. In 1996 the country was the subject of just nine news reports and in 1998 a mere six. Elsewhere in the world the news coverage may be more attentive, but with the difference, of course, that no one actually reads it. (Hands up, all those who can name the current Australian Prime Minister or say in which state you will find Melbourne or answer pretty much any antipodean question at all not involving cricket, rugby, Mel Gibson or *Neighbours*.) Australians can't bear it that the outside world pays so little attention to them, and I don't blame them. This is a country where interesting things happen, and all the time.

Consider just one of those stories that did make it into the *New York Times* in 1997, though buried away in the odd-sock drawer of

Section C. In January of that year, according to a report written in America by a *Times* reporter, scientists were seriously investigating the possibility that a mysterious seismic disturbance in the remote Australian outback almost four years earlier had been a nuclear explosion set off by members of the Japanese doomsday cult Aum Shinrikyo.

It happens that at 11.03 p.m. local time on the night of 28 May 1993 seismograph needles all over the Pacific region twitched and scribbled in response to a very large-scale disturbance near a place called Banjawarn Station in the Great Victoria Desert of Western Australia. Some long-distance lorry drivers and prospectors, virtually the only people out in that lonely expanse, reported seeing a sudden flash in the sky and hearing or feeling the boom of a mighty but far-off explosion. One reported that a can of beer had danced off the table in his tent.

The problem was that there was no obvious explanation. The seismograph traces didn't fit the profile for an earthquake or mining explosion, and anyway the blast was 170 times more powerful than the most powerful mining explosion ever recorded in Western Australia. The shock was consistent with a large meteorite strike, but the impact would have blown a crater hundreds of feet in circumference, and no such crater could be found. The upshot is that scientists puzzled over the incident for a day or two, then filed it away as an unexplained curiosity – the sort of thing that presumably happens from time to time.

Then in 1995 Aum Shinrikyo gained sudden notoriety when it released extravagant quantities of the nerve gas sarin into the Tokyo underground, killing twelve people. In the investigations that followed, it emerged that Aum's substantial holdings included a 500,000-acre desert property in Western Australia very near the site of the mystery event. There, authorities found a laboratory of unusual sophistication and focus, and evidence that cult members had been mining uranium. It separately emerged that Aum had recruited into its ranks two nuclear engineers from the former Soviet Union. The group's avowed aim was the destruction of the world, and it appears that the event in the desert may have been a dry run for blowing up Tokyo.

You take my point, of course. This is a country that loses a Prime Minister and that is so vast and empty that a band of amateur enthusiasts could conceivably set off the world's first non-governmental atomic bomb on its mainland and almost four years would pass before anyone noticed. Clearly this is a place worth getting to know.

And so, because we know so little about it, perhaps a few facts would be in order.

Australia is the world's sixth largest country and its largest island. It is the only island that is also a continent, and the only continent that is also a country. It was the first continent conquered from the sea, and the last. It is the only nation that began as a prison.

It is the home of the largest living thing on earth, the Great Barrier Reef, and of the most famous and striking monolith, Ayers Rock (or Uluru to use its now official, more respectful Aboriginal name). It has more things that will kill you than anywhere else. Of the world's ten most poisonous snakes, all are Australian. Five of its creatures – the funnel-web spider, box jellyfish, blue-ringed octopus, paralysis tick and stonefish – are the most lethal of their type in the world. This is a country where even the fluffiest of caterpillars can lay you out with a toxic nip, where seashells will not just sting you but actually sometimes *go* for you. Pick up an innocuous coneshell from a Queensland beach, as innocent tourists are all too wont to do, and you will discover that the little fellow inside is not just astoundingly swift and testy, but exceedingly venomous. If you are not stung or pronged to death in some unexpected manner, you may be fatally chomped by sharks or crocodiles, or carried helplessly out to sea by irresistible currents, or left to stagger to an unhappy death in the baking outback. It's a tough place.

And it is old. For 60 million years, since the formation of the Great Dividing Range, Australia has been all but silent geologically, which has allowed it to preserve many of the oldest things ever found on earth – the most ancient rocks and fossils, the earliest animal tracks and riverbeds, the first faint signs of life itself. At some undetermined point in the great immensity of its past – perhaps 45,000 years ago, perhaps 60,000, but certainly before there were modern humans in the Americas or Europe – it was quietly invaded by a deeply inscrutable people, the Aborigines, who have no clearly evident racial or linguistic kinship to their neighbours in the region, and whose presence in Australia can be explained only by positing that they invented and mastered ocean-going craft at least 30,000 years in advance of anyone else in order to undertake an exodus, then forgot or abandoned nearly all that they had learned and scarcely ever bothered with the open sea again.

It is an accomplishment so singular and extraordinary, so uncomfortable with scrutiny, that most histories breeze over it in a paragraph or two, then move on to the second, more explicable invasion – the one that begins with the arrival of Captain James Cook and his doughty little ship HMS *Endeavour* in Botany Bay in 1770. Never mind that Captain Cook didn't discover Australia and that he wasn't even a captain at the time of his visit. For most people, including most Australians, this is where the story begins.

The world those first Englishmen found was famously inverted – its seasons back to front, its constellations upside down – and unlike anything any of them had seen before, even in the near latitudes of the Pacific. Its creatures seemed to have evolved as if they had misread the manual. The most characteristic of them didn't run or lope or canter, but *bounced* across the landscape, like dropped balls. The continent teemed with unlikely life. It contained a fish that could climb trees; a fox that flew (it was actually a very large bat); crustaceans so big that a grown man could climb inside their shells.

In short, there was no place in the world like it. There still isn't. Eighty per cent of all that lives in Australia, plant and animal, exists nowhere else. More than this, it exists in an abundance that seems incompatible with the harshness of the environment. Australia is the driest, flattest, hottest, most desiccated, infertile and climatically aggressive of all the inhabited continents. (Only Antarctica is more hostile to life.) This is a place so inert that even the soil is, technically speaking, a fossil. And yet it teems with life in numbers uncounted. For insects alone, scientists haven't the faintest idea whether the total number of species is 100,000 or more than twice that. As many as a third of those species remain entirely unknown to science. For spiders, the proportion rises to 80 per cent.

I mention insects in particular because I have a story about a little bug called *Nothomyrmecia macrops* that I think illustrates perfectly, if a bit obliquely, what an exceptional country this is. It's a slightly involved tale but a good one, so bear with me please.

In 1931 on the Cape Arid peninsula in Western Australia, some amateur naturalists were poking about in the scrubby wastes when they found an insect none had seen before. It looked vaguely like an ant, but was an unusual pale yellow and had strange, staring, distinctly unsettling eyes. Some specimens were collected and these found their way to the desk of an expert at the National Museum of Victoria in Melbourne, who identified the insect at once as *Nothomyrmecia*. The discovery caused great excitement because, as far as anyone knew, nothing like it had existed on earth for a hundred million years. *Nothomyrmecia* was a proto-ant, a living relic from a time when ants were evolving from wasps. In entomological terms, it was as extraordinary as if someone had found a herd of triceratops grazing on some distant grassy plain.

An expedition was organized at once, but despite the most scrupulous searching no one could find the Cape Arid colony. Subsequent searches came up equally empty-handed. Almost half a century later, when word got out that a team of American scientists was planning to search for the ant, almost certainly with the kind of high-tech gadgetry that would make the Australians look amateurish and underorganized, government scientists in Canberra decided to make one final, pre-emptive effort to find the ants alive. So a party of them set off in convoy across the country.

On the second day out, while driving across the South Australia desert, one of their vehicles began to smoke and sputter, and they were forced to make an unscheduled overnight stop at a lonely pause in the road called Poochera. During the evening one of the scientists, a man named Bob Taylor, stepped out for a breath of air and idly played his torch over the surrounding terrain. You may imagine his astonishment when he discovered, crawling over the trunk of a eucalyptus beside their campsite, a thriving colony of none other than *Nothomyrmecia*.

Now consider the probabilities. Taylor and his colleagues were 800 miles from their intended search site. In the almost three million square miles of emptiness that is Australia, one of the handful of people able to identify it had just found one of the rarest, most sought-after insects on earth – an insect seen alive just once, almost half a century earlier – and all because their van had broken down where it did. *Nothomyrmecia*, incidentally, has still never been found at its original site.

You take my point again, I'm sure. This is a country that is at once staggeringly empty and yet packed with stuff. Interesting stuff, ancient stuff, stuff not readily explained. Stuff yet to be found.

Trust me, this is an interesting place.

II

Each time you fly from North America to Australia, and without anyone asking how you feel about it, a day is taken away from you when you cross the international dateline. I left Los Angeles on 3 January and arrived in Sydney fourteen hours later on 5 January. For me there was no 4 January. None at all. Where it went exactly I couldn't tell you. All I know is that for one twenty-four-hour period in the history of Earth, it appears I had no being.

I find that a little uncanny, to say the least. I mean to say, if you were browsing through your ticket folder and you saw a notice that said: 'Passengers are advised that on some crossings twenty-four-hour loss of existence may occur' (which is of course how they would phrase it, as if it happened from time to time) you would probably get up and make enquiries, grab a sleeve and say, 'Excuse me.' There is, it must be said, a certain metaphysical comfort in knowing that you can cease to have material form and it doesn't hurt at all, and, to be fair, they do give you the day back on the return journey when you cross the dateline in the opposite direction and thereby manage somehow to arrive in Los Angeles before you left Sydney, which in its way, of course, is an even neater trick.

Now I vaguely understand the principles involved here. I can see that there has to be a notional line where one day ends and the next begins, and that when you cross that line temporal oddities will necessarily follow. But that still doesn't get away from the fact that on any trip between America and Australia you will experience something that would be, in any other circumstance, the starkest impossibility. However hard you train or concentrate or watch your diet, no matter how many steps you take on the Stairmaster, you are never going to get so fit that you can cease to occupy space for twenty-four hours or be able to arrive in one room before you left the last one.

So there is a certain sense of achievement just in arriving in Australia – a pleasure and satisfaction to be able to step from the airport terminal into dazzling antipodean sunshine and realize that all your many atoms, so recently missing and unaccounted for, have been reassembled in an approximately normal manner (less half a pound or so of brain cells that were lost while watching a Bruce Willis action movie). In the circumstances, it is a pleasure to find yourself anywhere; that it is Australia is a positive bonus.

Let me say right here that I love Australia – adore it

immeasurably – and am smitten anew each time I see it. One of the effects of paying so little attention to Australia is that it is always such a pleasant surprise to find it there. Every cultural instinct and previous experience tells you that when you travel this far you should find, at the very least, people on camels. There should be unrecognizable lettering on the signs, and swarthy men in robes drinking coffee from thimble-sized cups and puffing on hookahs, and rattletrap buses and potholes in the road and a real possibility of disease on everything you touch – but no, it's not like that at all. This is comfortable and clean and familiar. Apart from a tendency among men of a certain age to wear knee-high socks with shorts, these people are just like you and me. This is wonderful. This is exhilarating. This is why I love to come to Australia.

There are other reasons as well, of course, and I am pleased to put them on the record here. The people are immensely likeable – cheerful, extrovert, quick-witted and unfailingly obliging. Their cities are safe and clean and nearly always built on water. They have a society that is prosperous, well ordered and instinctively egalitarian. The food is excellent. The beer is cold. The sun nearly always shines. There is coffee on every corner. Rupert Murdoch no longer lives there. Life doesn't get much better than this.

This was my fifth trip and this time, for the first time, I was going to see the real Australia – the vast and baking interior, the boundless void that lies between the coasts. I have never entirely understood why, when people urge you to see their 'real' country, they send you to the empty parts where almost no sane person would choose to live, but there you are. You cannot say you have been to Australia until you have crossed the outback.

Best of all, I was going to do it in the swankiest possible way: on the fabled Indian Pacific railway from Sydney to Perth. Running for 2,720 pleasantly meandering miles across the bottom third of the country, through the states of New South Wales, South Australia and Western Australia, the Indian Pacific is the queen of the southern hemisphere trainwise. From Sydney it climbs gently through the Blue Mountains, chunters across endless miles of big-sky sheep country, traces the Darling River to the Murray and the Murray on towards Adelaide, and finally crosses the mighty Nullarbor Plain to the goldfields around Kalgoorlie before sighing to a well-earned halt in distant Perth. The Nullarbor, an almost inconceivable expanse of murderous desert, was something I particularly longed to see.

The colour magazine of the *Mail on Sunday* was doing a special issue on Australia, and I had agreed to file a report. I had been planning for some time anyway to come out to write a book, so this was in the nature of a bonus trip – a chance to get the measure of the country in an exceedingly comfortable way at someone else's expense. Sounded awfully good to me. To that end, I would be travelling for the next week or so in the company of a young English photographer named Trevor Ray Hart, who was flying in from London and whom I would meet for the first time the next morning.

But first I had a day to call my own, and I was inordinately pleased about that. I had never been to Sydney other than on book tours, so my acquaintance with the city was based almost entirely on cab journeys through unsung districts like Ultimo and Annandale. The only time I had seen anything at all of the real city was some years before, on my first visit, when a kindly sales rep from my local publisher had taken me out for the day in his car, with his wife and two little girls in the back, and I had disgraced myself by falling asleep. It wasn't from lack of interest or appreciation, believe me. It's just that the day was warm and I was newly arrived in the country. At some unfortunate point, quite early on, jet lag asserted itself and I slumped helplessly into a coma.

I am not, I regret to say, a discreet and fetching sleeper. Most people when they nod off look as if they could do with a blanket; I look as if I could do with medical attention. I sleep as if injected with a powerful experimental muscle relaxant. My legs fall open in a grotesque come-hither manner; my knuckles brush the floor. Whatever is inside – tongue, uvula, moist bubbles of intestinal air – decides to leak out. From time to time, like one of those nodding-duck toys, my head tips forward to empty a quart or so of viscous drool onto my lap, then falls back to begin loading again with a noise like a toilet cistern filling. And I snore, hugely and helplessly, like a cartoon character, with rubbery flapping lips and prolonged steam-valve exhalations. For long periods I grow unnaturally still, in a way that inclines onlookers to exchange glances and lean forward in concern, then dramatically I stiffen and, after a tantalizing pause, begin to bounce and jostle in a series of whole-body spasms of the sort that bring to mind an electric chair when the switch is thrown. Then I shriek once or twice in a piercing and effeminate manner and wake up to find that all motion within 500 feet has stopped and all children under eight are clutching their mothers' hems. It is a terrible burden to bear.

I have no idea how long I slept in that car other than that it was not a short while. All I know is that when I came to there was a certain heavy silence in the car – the kind of silence that would close over you if you found yourself driving around your own city conveying a slumped and twitching heap from one unperceived landmark to another.

I looked around dumbly, not certain for the moment who these people were, cleared my throat and pulled myself to a more upright position.

'We were wondering if you might like some lunch,' my guide said quietly when he saw that I had abandoned for the moment the private ambition to flood his car with saliva.

'That would be very nice,' I replied in a small, abject voice, discovering in the same instant, with a customary inward horror, that while I had dozed a 400-pound fly had evidently been sick over me. In an attempt to distract attention from my unnatural moist sheen and at the same time re-establish my interest in the tour, I added more brightly: 'Is this still Neutral Bay?'

There was a small involuntary snort of the sort you make when a drink goes down the wrong way. And then with a certain strained precision: 'No, this is Dover Heights. Neutral Bay was' – a microsecond's pause, just to aerate the point – 'some time ago.'

'Ah.' I made a grave face, as if trying to figure out how we had managed between us to mislay such a chunk of time.

'Quite some time ago, in fact.'

'Ah.'

We rode the rest of the way to lunch in silence. The afternoon was more successful. We dined at a popular fish restaurant beside the pier at Watsons Bay, then went to look at the Pacific from the lofty, surf-battered cliffs that stand above the harbour mouth. On the way home the drive provided snatched views of what is unquestionably the loveliest harbour in the world – blue water, gliding sailboats, the distant iron arc of the Harbour Bridge with the Opera House squatting cheerfully beside it. But still I had not seen Sydney properly, and early the next day I departed for Melbourne.

So I was eager, as you may imagine, to make amends now. Sydneysiders, as they are rather quaintly known, have an evidently unquenchable desire to show their city off to visitors, and I had yet another kind offer of guidance before me, this time from a journalist on the *Sydney Morning Herald* named Deirdre Macken. An alert and cheerful lady of early middle years, Deirdre met me at my hotel with a young photographer named Glenn Hunt, and we set off on foot to the Museum of Sydney, a sleek and stylish new institution, which manages to look interesting and instructive without actually being either. You find yourself staring at artfully underlit displays – a caseful of immigrant artefacts, a room wallpapered with the pages of popular magazines from the 1950s – without being entirely certain what you are expected to conclude. But we did have a very nice latte in the attached café, at which point Deirdre outlined her plans for our busy day.

In a moment we would stroll down to Circular Quay and catch a ferry across the harbour to the Taronga Zoo wharf. We wouldn't actually visit the zoo, but instead would hike around Little Sirius Cove and up through the steep and jungly hills of Cremorne Point to Deirdre's house, where we would gather up some towels and boogie boards, and go by car to Manly, a beach suburb overlooking the Pacific. At Manly we would grab a bite of lunch, then have an invigorating session of boogie boarding before towelling ourselves down and heading for—

'Excuse me for interrupting,' I interrupted, 'but what is boogie boarding exactly?'

'Oh, it's fun. You'll love it,' she said breezily but, I thought, just a touch evasively.

'Yes, but what is it?'

'It's an aquatic sport. It's heaps of fun. Isn't it heaps of fun, Glenn?'

'Heaps,' agreed Glenn, who was, in the manner of all people whose film stock is paid for, in the midst of taking an infinite number of photographs. *Bizeet, bizeet, bizeet*, his camera sang as he took three quick and ingeniously identical photographs of Deirdre and me in conversation.

'But what does it entail exactly?' I persisted.

'You take a kind of miniature surfboard and paddle out into the sea, where you catch a big wave and ride it back to shore. It's easy. You'll love it.'

'What about sharks?' I asked uneasily.

'Oh, there's hardly any sharks here. Glenn, how long has it been since someone was killed by a shark?'

'Oh, ages,' Glenn said, considering. 'Couple of months at least.'

'Couple of months?' I squeaked.

'At least. Sharks are way overrated as a danger,' Glenn added. 'Way overrated. It's the rips that'll most likely get yer.' He returned to taking pictures.

'Rips?'

'Underwater currents that run at an angle to the shore and sometimes carry people out to sea,' Deirdre explained. 'But don't worry. That won't happen to you.'

'Why?'

'Because we're here to look after you.' She smiled serenely, drained her cup and reminded us that we needed to keep moving.

Three hours later, our other activities completed, we stood on a remote-seeming strand at a place called Freshwater Beach, near Manly. It was a big U-shaped bay, edged by low scrub hills, with what seemed to me awfully big waves pounding in from a vast and moody sea. In the middle distance several foolhardy souls in wet-suits were surfing towards some foamy outbursts on the rocky headland; nearer in a scattering of paddlers were being continually and, it seemed, happily engulfed by explosive waves.

Urged on by Deirdre, who seemed keen as anything to get into the briny drink, we began to strip down – slowly and deliberatively in my case, eagerly in hers – to the swimsuits she had instructed us to wear beneath our clothes.

'If you're caught in a rip,' Deirdre was saying, 'the trick is not to panic.'

I looked at her. 'You're telling me to drown calmly?'

'No, no. Just keep your wits. Don't try to swim against the current. Swim *across* it. And if you're still in trouble, just wave your arm like this' – she gave the kind of big, languorous wave that only an Australian could possibly consider an appropriate response to a death-at-sea situation – 'and wait for the lifeguard to come.'

'What if the lifeguard doesn't see me?'

'He'll see you.'

'But what if he doesn't?'

But Deirdre was already wading into the surf, a boogie board tucked under her arm.

Bashfully I dropped my shirt onto the sand and stood naked but for my sagging trunks. Glenn, never having seen anything quite this grotesque and singular on an Australian beach, certainly nothing still alive, snatched up his camera and began excitedly taking close-up shots of my stomach. *Bizeet, bizeet, bizeet, bizeet,* his camera sang happily as he followed me into the surf.

Let me just pause here for a moment to interpose two small stories. In 1935, not far from where we stood now, some fishermen captured a fourteen-foot beige shark and took it to a public aquarium at Coogee, where it was put on display. The shark swam around for a day or two in its new home, then abruptly, and to the certain surprise of the viewing public, regurgitated a human arm. When last seen the arm had been attached to a young man named Jimmy Smith, who had, I've no doubt, signalled his predicament with a big, languorous wave.

Now my second story. Three years later, on a clear, bright, calm Sunday afternoon at Bondi Beach, also not far from where we now stood, from out of nowhere there came four freak waves, each up to twenty-five feet high. More than 200 people were carried out to sea in the undertow. Fortunately, fifty lifeguards were in attendance that day, and they managed to save all but six people. I am aware that we are talking about incidents that happened many years ago. I don't care. My point remains: the ocean is a treacherous place.

Sighing, I shuffled into the pale green and cream-flecked water. The bay was surprisingly shallow. We trudged perhaps 100 feet out and it was still only a little over our knees, though even here there was an extraordinarily powerful current – strong enough to pull you off your feet if you weren't real vigilant. Another fifty feet on, where the water rose over our waists, the waves were breaking. If you discount a few hours in the lagoon-like waters of the Costa del Sol in Spain and an icy, instantly regretted dip once in Maine, I have almost no experience of the sea, and I found it frankly disconcerting to be wading into a rollercoaster of water. Deirdre shrieked with pleasure.

Then she showed me how the boogie board works. It was promisingly simple in principle. As a wave passed, she would leap aboard and skim along on its crest for many yards. Then Glenn had a turn and went even further. There is no question that it looked like fun. It didn't look too hard either. I was tentatively eager to have a try.

I positioned myself for the first wave, then jumped aboard and sank like an anvil.

'How'd you do that?' asked Glenn in wonder.

'No idea.'

I repeated the exercise with the same result.

'Amazing,' he said.

There followed a half-hour in which the two of them watched first with guarded amusement, then a kind of astonishment, and finally something not unlike pity, as I repeatedly vanished beneath the waves and was scraped over an area of ocean floor roughly the size of Polk County, Iowa. After a variable but lengthy period, I would surface, gasping and confused, at a point anywhere from four feet to a mile and a quarter distant, and be immediately carried under again by a following wave. Before long, people on the beach were on their feet and placing bets. It was commonly agreed that it was not physically possible to do what I was doing.

From my point of view, each underwater experience was essentially the same. I would diligently attempt to replicate the dainty kicking motions Deirdre had shown me and try to ignore the fact that I was going nowhere and mostly drowning. Not having anything to judge this against, I supposed I was doing rather well. I can't pretend I was having a good time, but then it is a mystery to me how anyone could wade into such a merciless environment and expect to have fun. But I was resigned to my fate and knew that eventually it would be over.

Perhaps it was the oxygen deprivation, but I was rather lost in my own little world when Deirdre grabbed my arm just before I was about to go under again and said in a husky tone: 'Look out! There's a bluey.'

Glenn took on an immediate expression of alarm. 'Where?'

'What's a bluey?' I asked, appalled to discover that there was some additional danger I hadn't been told about.

'A bluebottle,' she explained and pointed to a small jellyfish of the type (as I later learned from browsing through a fat book titled, if I recall, *Things That Will Kill You Horridly in Australia: Volume 19*) known elsewhere as a Portuguese man-of-war. I squinted at it as it drifted past. It looked unprepossessing, like a blue condom with strings attached.

'Is it dangerous?' I asked.

Now before we hear Deirdre's response to me as I stood there, vulnerable and abraded, shivering, nearly naked and half drowned, let me just quote from her subsequent article in the *Herald*:

> *While the photographer shoots, Bryson and boogie board are dragged 40 metres down the beach in a rip. The shore rip runs south to north, unlike the rip further out which runs north to*

south. Bryson doesn't know this. He didn't read the warning sign on the beach. Nor does he know about the bluebottle being blown in his direction – now less than a metre away – a swollen stinger that could give him 20 minutes of agony and, if he's unlucky, an unsightly allergic reaction to carry on his torso for life.*

'Dangerous? No,' Deirdre replied now as we stood gawping at the bluebottle. 'But don't brush against it.'

'Why not?'

'Might be a bit uncomfortable.'

I looked at her with an expression of interest bordering on admiration. Long bus journeys are uncomfortable. Slatted wooden benches are uncomfortable. Lulls in conversations are uncomfortable. The sting of a Portuguese man-of-war – even people from Iowa know this – is *agony*. It occurred to me that Australians are so surrounded with danger that they have evolved an entirely new vocabulary to deal with it.

'Hey, there's another one,' said Glenn.

We watched another one drift by. Deirdre was scanning the water.

'Sometimes they come in waves,' she said. 'Might be an idea to get out of the water.'

I didn't have to be told twice.

There was one more thing that Deirdre felt I needed to see if I was to have any understanding of Australian life and culture, so afterwards, as late afternoon gave way to the pale blush of evening, we drove out through the glittering sprawl of Sydney's western suburbs almost to the edge of the Blue Mountains to a place called Penrith. Our destination was an enormous sleek building, surrounded by an even more enormous, very full car park. An illuminated sign announced this as the Penrith Panthers World of Entertainment. The Panthers, Glenn explained, were a rugby league club.

Australia is a country of clubs – sporting clubs, workingmen's clubs, Returned Servicemen's League clubs, clubs affiliated to

* The statement is inarguable. However, the author would like the record to show that he did not have his glasses on; he trusted his hosts; he was scanning a large area of ocean for sharks; and he was endeavouring throughout not to excrete a large housebrick into his pants.

various political parties – each nominally, and sometimes no doubt actively, devoted to the well-being of a particular segment of society. What they are really there for, however, is to generate extremely large volumes of money from drinking and gambling.

I had read in the paper that Australians are the biggest gamblers on the planet – one of the more arresting statistics I saw was that the country has less than 1 per cent of the world's population but more than 20 per cent of its slot machines – and that between them Australians spend $11 billion* a year, or $2,000 per person, on various games of chance. But I had seen nothing to suggest such risky gusto until I stepped inside the World of Entertainment. It was vast and dazzling and immensely well appointed. The club movement in Australia is huge. In New South Wales alone, clubs employ 65,000 people, more than any other industry, and create an additional 250,000 jobs indirectly. They pay over $2 billion in wages and $500 million in gaming taxes. This is huge business and it is nearly all based on a type of slot machine popularly called a pokie.

I had assumed that we would have to bend the rules to get admitted – it was a club, after all – but in fact I learned that all Australian clubs allow instant membership to anyone, so keen are they to share the diverting pleasures of the poker machine. You just sign a temporary members' book by the door and in you go.

Surveying the crowds with a benign and cheerful eye was a man whose badge identified him as Peter Hutton, Duty Manager. In the manner of nearly all Australians, he was an easygoing and approachable sort. I quickly learned from him that this particular club has 60,000 members, of whom 20,000 will turn up on busy nights, like New Year's Eve. Tonight the figure would be more like 2,000. The club contained bars and restaurants almost beyond counting, sports facilities, a children's play area, and nightclubs and theatres. They were just about to build a thirteen-screen cinema and a crèche big enough to hold 400 infants.

'Wow,' I said, for I was impressed. 'So is this the biggest club in Sydney?'

'Biggest in the southern hemisphere,' Mr Hutton said proudly.

We wandered into the vast and tinkling interior. Hundreds of pokies stood in long straight lines, and at nearly every one sat an

* Unless otherwise indicated, all dollar signs refer to Australian dollars. As of early 2000, $1 was worth roughly 40 English pence (or £1 sterling to $2.50 Australian).

intent figure feeding in the mortgage money. They are essentially slot machines, but with a bewildering array of illuminated buttons and flashing lights that let you exercise a variety of options – whether to hold a particular line, double your stake, take a portion of your winnings, and goodness knows what else. I studied from a discreet distance several people at play, but couldn't begin to understand what they were doing, other than feeding a succession of coins into a glowing box and looking grim. Deirdre and Glenn were similarly unacquainted with the intricacies of pokies. We put in a $2 coin, just to see what would happen, and got an instant payout of $17. This made us immensely joyful.

I returned to the hotel like a kid who had had a very full day at the county fair – exhausted but deeply happy. I had survived the perils of the sea, been to a palatial club, helped to win $15 and made two new friends. I can't say I was a great deal closer to feeling that I had actually seen Sydney than I had been before, but that day would come. Meanwhile, I had a night's sleep to get and a train to catch.

CHAPTER TWO

I BELIEVE I FIRST REALIZED I WAS GOING TO LIKE THE AUSTRALIAN outback when I read that the Simpson Desert, an area bigger than some European countries, was named in 1932* after a manufacturer of washing machines. (Specifically, Alfred Simpson, who funded an aerial survey.) It wasn't so much the pleasingly unheroic nature of the name as the knowledge that an expanse of Australia more than 100,000 miles square didn't even *have* a name until less than seventy years ago. I have near relatives who have had names longer than that.

But then that's the thing about the outback – it's so vast and forbidding that much of it is still scarcely charted. Even Uluru was unseen by anyone but its Aboriginal caretakers until only a little over a century ago. It's not even possible to say quite where the outback is. To Australians anything vaguely rural is 'the bush'. At some indeterminate point 'the bush' becomes 'the outback'. Push on for another 2,000 miles or so and eventually you come to bush again, and then a city, and then the sea. And that's Australia.

And so, in the company of the photographer Trevor Ray Hart, an amiable young man in shorts and a faded T-shirt, I took a cab to Sydney's Central Station, an imposing heap of bricks on Elizabeth Street, and there we found our way through its dim and venerable concourse to our train.

* According to the Australian historian Geoffrey Blainey; but 1929 according to *National Geographic* magazine. There's hardly a fact about Australia that isn't significantly contradicted somewhere in print by somebody.

Stretching for a third of a mile along the curving platform, the Indian Pacific was everything the brochure illustrations had promised – silvery sleek, shiny as a new nickel, humming with that sense of impending adventure that comes with the start of a long journey on a powerful machine. Carriage G, one of seventeen on the train, was in the charge of a cheerful steward named Terry, who thoughtfully provided a measure of local colour by accompanying every remark with an upbeat Aussie turn of phrase.

Need a glass of water?

'No worries, mate. I'll get right on 'er.'

Just received word that your mother has died?

'Not a drama. She'll be apples.'

He showed us to our berths, a pair of singles on opposite sides of a narrow panelled corridor. The cabins were astoundingly tiny – so tiny that you could bend over and actually get stuck.

'This is it?' I said in mild consternation. 'In its entirety?'

'No worries.' Terry beamed. 'She's a bit snug, but you'll find she's got everything you need.'

And he was right. Everything you could possibly require in a living space was there. It was just very compact, not much larger than a standard wardrobe. But it was a marvel of ergonomics. It included a comfy built-in seat, a hideaway basin and toilet, a miniature cupboard, an overhead shelf just large enough for one very small suitcase, two reading lights, a pair of clean towels and a little amenity bag. In the wall was a narrow drop-down bed, which didn't so much drop down as fall out like a hastily stowed corpse as I, and I expect many other giddily experimental passengers, discovered after looking ruminatively at the door and thinking: 'Well, I wonder what's behind *there*?' Still, it did make for an interesting surprise, and freeing my various facial protuberances from its coiled springs helped to pass the half-hour before departure.

And then at last the train thrummed to life and we slid regally out of Sydney Central. We were on our way.

Done in one fell swoop, the journey to Perth takes nearly three days. Our instructions, however, were to disembark at the old mining town of Broken Hill to sample the outback and see what might bite us. So for Trevor and me the rail journey would be in two parts: an overnight run to Broken Hill and then a two-day haul across the Nullarbor. The train trundled out through the endless western suburbs of Sydney – through Flemington, Auburn, Parramatta, Doonside and the adorably named Rooty Hill – then picked up a little speed as we entered the Blue Mountains, where the houses thinned out and we were treated to long end-of-afternoon views over steep-sided vales and hazy forests of gum trees, whose quiet respirations give the hills their eponymous tinge.

I went off to explore the train. Our domain, the first-class section, consisted of five sleeping carriages, a dining carriage in a plush and velvety style that might be called *fin de siècle brothelkeeper*, and a lounge bar in a rather more modern mode. This was provisioned with soft chairs, a small promising-looking bar and low but relentless piped music from a twenty-volume compilation called, at a guess, 'Songs You Hoped You'd Never Hear Again'. A mournful duet from *Phantom of the Opera* was playing as I passed through.

Beyond first class was the slightly cheaper holiday class, which was much the same as ours except that their dining area was a buffet car with bare plastic tables. (These people apparently needed wiping down after meals.) The passage beyond holiday class was barred by a windowless door, which was locked.

'What's back there?' I asked the buffet-car girl.

'Coach class,' she said with a shudder.

'Is this door always locked?'

She nodded gravely. 'Always.'

Coach class would become my obsession. But first it was time for dinner. The tannoy announced the first sitting. Ethel Merman was belting out 'There's No Business Like Show Business' as I passed back through the first-class lounge. Say what you will, the woman had lungs.

For all its air of cultivated venerability, the Indian Pacific is actually an infant as rail systems go, having been created as recently as 1970 when a new standard-gauge line was built across the country. Before that, for various arcane reasons mostly to do with regional distrust and envy, Australian railway lines employed different gauges. New South Wales had rails 4 feet 8½ inches apart. Victoria opted for a more commodious 5 feet 3 inches. Queensland and Western Australia economically decided on a standard of 3 feet 6 inches (a width not far off that of amusement park rides; people must have ridden with their legs out of the windows). South Australia, inventively, had all three. Five times on any journey between the east and west coasts passengers and freight had to be offloaded from one train and redeposited on another, a mad and tedious process. Finally, sanity was mustered and an all-new line was built. It is the second longest line in the world, after Russia's Trans-Siberian.

I know all this because Trevor and I sat at dinner with a pair of quiet middle-aged teachers from rural north Queensland, Keith and Daphne. This was a big trip for them on teachers' salaries, and Keith had done his homework. He talked with enthusiasm about the train, the landscape, the recent bush fires – we were passing through Lithgow where hundreds of acres of bush had been scorched and two firefighters had lost their lives recently – but when I asked about Aborigines (the question of land reforms had been much in the news) he grew suddenly vague and flustered.

'It's a problem,' he said, staring hard at his food.

'At the school where I teach,' Daphne went on, hesitantly, 'the Aboriginal parents, well, they get their dole payment and spend it on drink and then go walkabout. And the teachers have to . . . well, *feed* the children. You know, out of their own pockets. Otherwise the children wouldn't eat.'

'It's a problem,' Keith said again, still fixed on his food.

'But they're lovely people really. When they're not drinking.'

And that pretty well killed the conversation.

After dinner Trevor and I ventured into the lounge carriage. While Trevor went to the bar to order I sank into an easy chair and watched the dusky landscape. It was farming country, vaguely arid. The background music, I noted with idle interest, had gone from 'Much Loved Show Tunes' to 'Party Time at the Nursing Home'. 'Roll Out the Barrel' was just finishing when we arrived and was swiftly succeeded by 'Toot Toot Tootsie Goodbye'.

'Interesting choice of music,' I observed drily to the young couple opposite me.

'Yes, lovely!' they replied with simultaneous enthusiasm.

Suppressing an urge to shriek, I turned to the man beside me – an educated-looking older man in a suit, which was striking because everyone else on the train was in casual wear. We chatted about this and that. He was a retired solicitor from Canberra on his way to visit a son in Perth. He seemed a reasonable and perceptive sort, so I mentioned to him, in a confiding tone, my puzzling conversation with the schoolteachers from Queensland.

'Ah, Aborigines,' he said, nodding solemnly. 'A great problem.'

'So I gather.'

'They want hanging, every one of them.'

I looked at him, startled, and found a face on the edge of fury.

'Every bloody one of them,' he said, jowls trembling, and without another word took his leave.

Aborigines, I reflected, were something I would have to look into. But for the moment I decided to keep the conversation to simple matters – weather, scenery, popular show tunes – until I had a better grasp of things.

The great if obvious feature of a train, as compared with a hotel room, is that your view is ever changing. In the morning I awoke to a new world: red soil, scrubby vegetation, huge skies and an encircling horizon broken only by an occasional skeletal gum tree. As I peered blearily from my narrow perch, a pair of kangaroos, flushed by the train, bounded across the foreground. It was an exciting moment. We were definitely in Australia now!

We arrived at Broken Hill just after eight and stepped blinking from the train. An airless heat hung over the land – the kind of heat that hits you when you open an oven door to check a roasting turkey. Waiting for us on the platform was Sonja Stubing, a good-natured young lady from the regional tourist office who had been sent to collect us from the station and take us to pick up a rental car for a drive around the outback.

'How hot does it get here?' I asked, breathing out hard.

'Well, the record's forty-eight.'

I thought for a minute. 'That's one hundred and eighteen degrees!' I said.

She nodded serenely. 'It was forty-two yesterday.'

Another brief calculation: 107 degrees. 'That's very hot.'

She nodded. 'Too hot.'

Broken Hill was a positively delightful little community – clean, trim, cheerfully prosperous. Unfortunately this was not at all what we wanted. We wanted proper outback: a place where men were men and sheep were nervous. Here there were cafés and a bookstore, travel agents offering enticing packages to Bali and Singapore. They were even doing a Noel Coward play at the civic centre. This wasn't the outback at all. This was Guildford with the heat turned up.

Things took a more hopeful turn when we went to Len Vodic Vehicle Hire to pick up a four-wheel drive for a two-day jaunt into the baking wilderness. The eponymous Len was a wiry old guy, energetic and friendly, who looked as if he had spent every day of his life doing tough stuff in the out of doors. He jumped behind the wheel and gave us the kind of swift, thorough rundown that people give when they assume they are dealing with intelligent and capable listeners. The interior presented a bewildering assortment of dials, levers, knobs, gauges and toggles.

'Now say you get stuck in sand and need to increase your offside differential,' Len was saying on one of the intermittent occasions I dipped into the lecture. 'You move this handle forward like so, select a hyperdrive ratio of between twelve and twenty-seven, elevate the ailerons and engage both thrust motors – but *not* the left-hand one. That's very important. And whatever you do, watch your gauges and don't go over one hundred and eighty degrees on the combustulator, or the whole thing'll blow and you'll be stuck out there.'

He jumped out and handed us the keys. 'There's twenty-five litres of spare diesel in the back. That should be more than enough if you go wrong.' He looked at us again, more carefully. 'I'll get you some more diesel,' he decided.

'Did you understand any of that?' I whispered to Trevor when he had gone.

'Not past the putting the key in the ignition part.'

I called to Len: 'What happens if we get stuck or lost?'

'Why, you die of course!' Actually, he didn't say that, but that's what I was thinking. I had been reading accounts of people who had been lost or stranded in the outback, like the explorer Ernest Giles who spent days wandering waterless and half dead before coming fortuitously on a baby wallaby that had tumbled from its mother's pouch. 'I pounced upon it,' Giles related in his memoirs, 'and ate it, living, raw, dying – fur, skin, bones, skull and all.' And this was one of the happier stories. Believe me, you don't want to get lost in the outback.

I began to feel a tremor of foreboding – a feeling not lightened when Sonja gave a cry of delight at the sight of a spider by our feet and said: 'Hey, look, a redback!' A redback, if you don't know already, is death on eight legs. As Trevor and I whimperingly tried to climb into each other's arms, she snatched it up and held it out to us on the tip of a finger.

'It's all right,' she giggled. 'It's dead.'

We peered cautiously at the little object on her fingertip, a telltale red hourglass shape on its shiny back. It seemed unlikely that something so small could deliver instant agony, but make no mistake, a single nip from a redback's malicious jaws can result within minutes in 'frenzied twitching, a profuse flow of body fluids and, in the absence of prompt medical attention, possible death'. Or so the literature reports.

'You probably won't see any redbacks out there,' Sonja reassured us. 'Snakes are much more of a problem.'

This intelligence was received with four raised eyebrows and expressions that said: 'Go on.'

She nodded. 'Common brown, western puff pastry, yellow-backed lockjaw, eastern groin groper, dodge viper . . .' I don't remember what she said exactly, but it was a long list. 'But don't worry,' she continued. 'Most snakes don't want to hurt you. If you're out in the bush and a snake comes along, just stop dead and let it slide over your shoes.'

This, I decided, was the least-likely-to-be-followed advice I had ever been given.

Our extra diesel loaded, we climbed aboard and, with a grinding of gears, a couple of bronco lurches and a lively but inadvertent salute of windscreen wipers, took to the open road. Our instructions were to drive to Menindee, 110 kilometres to the east, where we would be met by a man named Steve Garland. In the event, the drive to Menindee was something of an anticlimax. The landscape was shimmering hot and gorgeously forbidding, and we were gratified to see our first willy-willy, a column of rotating dust perhaps a hundred feet high moving across the endless plains to our left. But this was as close to adventure as we got. The road was newly paved and relatively well travelled. While Trevor stopped to take pictures, I counted four cars pass. Had we broken down, we wouldn't have been stranded more than a few minutes.

Menindee was a modest hamlet on the Darling River: a couple of streets of sun-baked bungalows, a petrol station, two shops, the Burke and Wills Motel (named for a pair of nineteenth-century explorers who inevitably came a cropper in the unforgiving outback) and the semi-famous Maidens Hotel, where in 1860 the aforementioned Burke and Wills spent their last night in civilization before meeting their unhappy fate in the barren void to the north.

We met Steve Garland at the motel and, to celebrate our safe arrival and recent discovery of fifth gear, crossed the road to Maidens and joined the noisy hubbub within. Maidens' long bar was lined from end to end with sun-leathered men in shorts and sweat-stained muscle shirts and wide-brimmed hats. It was like stepping into a Paul Hogan movie. This was more like it.

'So which window do they eject the bodies through?' I asked the amiable Steve when we were seated, thinking that Trevor would probably like to set up his equipment for a shot at chucking-out time.

'Oh, it's not like that here,' he said. 'Things aren't as wild in the outback as people think. It's pretty civilized really.' He looked around with what was clearly real fondness, and exchanged hellos with a couple of dusty-looking characters.

Garland was a professional photographer in Sydney until his partner, Lisa Menke, was appointed chief warden of Kinchega National Park up the road. He took a job as the regional tourism and development officer. His territory covered 26,000 square miles, an area half the size of England but with a population of just 2,500. His challenge was to persuade dubious locals that there are people in the world prepared to pay good money to holiday in a place that is vast, dry, empty, featureless and ungodly hot. The other part of his challenge was to find such people.

Between the merciless sun and the isolation, outback people are not always the most gifted of communicators. We had heard of one shopkeeper who, upon being asked by a smiling visitor from Sydney where the fish were biting, stared at the man incredulously for a long moment and replied: 'In the fucking river, mate, where do you think?'

Garland only grinned when I put the story to him, but conceded that there was a certain occasional element of challenge involved in getting the locals to see the possibilities inherent in tourism.

He asked us how our drive had been.

I told him that I had expected it to be a little more harsh.

'Wait till tomorrow,' he said.

He was right. In the morning we set off in mini convoy, Steve and his partner Lisa in one car, Trevor and I in the other, for White Cliffs, an old opal-mining community 250 kilometres to the north. Half a mile outside Menindee the asphalt ended and the surface gave way to a hard earthen road full of potholes, ruts and cement-hard corrugations, as jarring as driving over railway sleepers.

We jounced along for hours, raising enormous clouds of red dust in our wake, through a landscape brilliantly hot and empty, over tablelands flecked with low saltbush and spiky spinifex, the odd turpentine bush and weary-looking eucalypt. Here and there along the roadside were the corpses of kangaroos and the occasional basking goanna, a large and ugly type of monitor lizard. Goodness knows how any living things survive in that heat and aridity. There are creekbeds out there that haven't seen water in fifteen years.

The supreme emptiness of Australia, the galling uselessness of such a mass of land, was something it took the country's European settlers a long time to adjust to. Several of the earliest explorers were so convinced that they would encounter mighty river systems, or even an inland sea, that they took boats with them. Thomas Mitchell, who explored vast tracts of western New South Wales and northern Victoria in the 1830s, dragged two wooden skiffs over 3,000 miles of arid scrub without once getting them wet, but refused to the last to give up on them. 'Although the boats and their carriage had been of late a great hindrance to us,' he wrote with a touch of understatement after his third expedition, 'I was very unwilling to abandon such useful appendages to an exploring party.'

Reading accounts of early forays, it is clear that the first explorers were often ludicrously out of their depths. In 1802, in one of the earliest expeditions, Lieutenant Francis Barrallier described a temperature of 82.5 degrees F. as 'suffocating'. We can reasonably assume that he was recently arrived in the country. His men tried for days without success to hunt kangaroos before it occurred to them that they might stalk the creatures more effectively if they first removed their bright red jackets. In seven weeks they covered just 130 miles, an average of about one and a half miles a day.

In expedition after expedition the leaders seemed wilfully, almost comically, unable to provision themselves sensibly. In 1817, John Oxley, the surveyor-general, led a five-month expedition to explore the Lachlan and Macquarie rivers, and took only 100 rounds of ammunition – less than one shot a day from a single gun – and hardly any spare horseshoes or nails. The incompetence of the early explorers was a matter of abiding fascination for the Aborigines, who often came to watch. 'Our perplexities afforded them an inexhaustible fund of merriment and derision,' wrote one chronicler glumly.

It was into this tradition of haplessness that Burke and Wills improvidently stepped in 1860. They are far and away the most famous of Australian explorers, which is perhaps a little curious since their expedition accomplished almost nothing, cost a fortune and ended in tragedy.

Their assignment was straightforward: to find a route from the south coast at Melbourne to the Gulf of Carpentaria in the far north. Melbourne, at that time much larger than Sydney, was one of the most important cities in the British Empire, and yet one of the most isolated. To get a message to London and receive a reply took a third of a year, sometimes more. In the 1850s, the Philosophical Institute of Victoria decided to promote an expedition to find a way through the 'ghastly blank', as the interior was poetically known, which would allow the establishment of a telegraph line to connect Australia first to the East Indies and then onward to the world.

They chose as leader an Irish police officer named Robert O'Hara Burke, who had never seen real outback, was famous for his ability to get lost even in inhabited areas, and knew nothing of exploration or science. The surveyor was a young English doctor named William John Wills, whose principal qualifications seem to have been a respectable background and a willingness to go. A notable plus was that they both had outstanding facial hair.

Although by this time expeditions into the interior were hardly a novelty, this one particularly caught the popular imagination. Tens of thousands of people lined the route out of Melbourne when, on 19 August 1860, the Great Northern Exploration Expedition set off. The party was so immense and unwieldy that it took from early morning until 4 p.m. just to get it moving. Among the items Burke had deemed necessary for the expedition were a Chinese gong, a stationery cabinet, a heavy wooden table with matching stools, and grooming equipment, in the words of the historian Glen McLaren, 'of sufficient quality to prepare and present his horses and camels for an Agricultural Society show'.

Almost at once the men began to squabble. Within days, six of the party had resigned, and the road to Menindee was littered with provisions they decided they didn't need, including 1,500 pounds (let me just repeat that: 1,500 *pounds*) of sugar. They did almost everything wrong. Against advice, they timed the trip so that they would do most of the hardest travelling at the height of summer.

With such a burden, it took them almost two months to traverse the 400 miles of well-trodden track to Menindee; a letter from Melbourne normally covered the same ground in two weeks. At Menindee, they availed themselves of the modest comforts of Maidens Hotel, rested their horses and reorganized their provisions, and on 19 October set off into a blank ghastlier than they could ever have imagined. Ahead of them lay 1,200 miles of murderous ground. It was the last time that anyone in the outside world would see Burke and Wills alive.

Progress through the desert was difficult and slow. By December, when they arrived at a place called Cooper's Creek, just over the Queensland border, they had progressed only 400 miles. In exasperation Burke decided to take three men – Wills, Charles Gray and John King – and make a dash for the gulf. By travelling light he calculated that he could be there and back in two months. He left four men to maintain the base camp, with instructions to wait three months for them in case they were delayed.

The going was much tougher than they had expected. Daytime temperatures regularly rose to over 140 degrees F. It took them two months rather than one to cross the interior, and their arrival, when at last it came, was something of an anticlimax: a belt of mangroves along the shore kept them from reaching, or even seeing, the sea. Still, they had successfully completed the first crossing of the continent. Unfortunately, they had also eaten two-thirds of their supplies.

The upshot is that they ran out of food on the return trip and nearly starved. To their consternation, Charles Gray, the fittest of the party, abruptly dropped dead one day. Ragged and half delirious, the three remaining men pushed on. Finally, on the evening of 21 April 1861, they stumbled into base camp to discover that the men they had left behind, after waiting four months, had departed only that day. On a coolibah tree was carved the message:

DIG
3 FT. N.W.
APR. 21 1861

They dug and found some meagre rations and a message telling them what was already painfully evident – that the base party had given up and departed. Desolate and exhausted, they ate and turned in. In the morning they wrote a message announcing their safe return and carefully buried it in the cache – so carefully, in fact, that when a member of the base party returned that day to have one last look, he had no way of telling that they had made it back and had now gone again. Had he known, he would have found them not far away, plodding over rocky ground in the impossible hope of reaching a police outpost 150 miles away at a place called Mount Hopeless.

Burke and Wills died in the desert, far short of Mount Hopeless. King was saved by Aborigines, who nursed him for two months until he was rescued by a search party.

Back in Melbourne, meanwhile, everyone was still awaiting a triumphal return of the heroic band, so news of the fiasco struck like a thunderbolt. 'The entire company of explorers has been dissipated out of being,' the *Age* reported with frank astonishment. 'Some are dead, some are on their way back, one has come to Melbourne, and another has made his way to Adelaide . . . The whole expedition appears to have been one prolonged blunder throughout.'

When the final tally was taken, the cost of the entire undertaking, including the search to recover Burke's and Wills' bodies, came to almost £60,000, more than Stanley had spent in Africa to achieve far more.

Even now, the emptiness of so much of Australia is startling. The landscape we passed through was officially only 'semi-desert', but it was as barren an expanse as I had ever seen. Every twenty or twenty-five kilometres there would be a dirt track and a lonely mailbox signalling an unseen sheep or cattle station. Once a light truck flew past in a bouncing hell-for-leather fashion, spraying us with gravelly dinks and a coating of red dust, but the only other lively thing was the endless shaking flubbity-dubbing of the axles over the corduroy road. By the time we reached White Cliffs, in mid-afternoon, we felt as if we had spent the day in a cement mixer.

Seeing it today, it is all but impossible to believe that White Cliffs, a small blotch of habitations under a hard clear sky, was once a boom town, with a population of nearly 4,500, a hospital, a newspaper, a library and a busy core of general stores, hotels, restaurants, brothels and gaming houses. Today central White Cliffs consists of a pub, a launderette, an opal shop, and a grocery/café/petrol station. The permanent population is about eighty. They exist in a listless world of heat and dust. If you were looking for people with the tolerance and fortitude to colonize Mars this would be the place to come.

Because of the heat, most houses in town are burrowed into the faces of the two bleached hills from which the town takes its name. The most ambitious of these dwellings, and the principal magnet for the relatively few tourists who venture this far, is the Dug-Out Underground Motel, a twenty-six-room complex cut deep into the rocks on the side of Smith's Hill. Wandering through its network of rocky tunnels was like stepping into an early James Bond movie, into one of those subterranean complexes where the loyal minions of SMERSH are preparing to take over the world by melting Antarctica or hijacking the White House with the aid of a giant magnet. The attraction of burrowing into the hillside is immediately evident when you step inside – a constant year-round temperature of 67 degrees. The rooms were very nice and quite normal except that the walls and ceilings were cavelike and windowless. When the lights were off, the darkness and silence were total.

I don't know how much money you would have to give me to persuade me to settle in White Cliffs – something in the low zillions, I suppose – but that evening as we sat on the motel's lofty garden terrace with Leon Hornby, the proprietor, drinking beer and watching the evening slink in, I realized that my fee might be marginally negotiable. I was about to ask Leon – a city man by birth and, I would have guessed, inclination – what possessed him and his pleasant wife Marge to stay in this godforsaken outpost where even a run to the supermarket means a six-hour round trip over a rutted dirt road, but before I could speak a remarkable thing happened. Kangaroos hopped into the expansive foreground and began grazing picturesquely, and the sun plonked onto the horizon, like a stage prop lowered on a wire, and the towering western skies before us spread with colour in a hundred layered shades – glowing pinks, deep purples, careless banners of pure crimson – all on a scale that you cannot imagine, for there was not a scrap of intrusion in the forty miles of visible desert that lay between us and the far horizon. It was the most extraordinarily vivid sunset I believe I have ever seen.

'I came up here thirty years ago to build reservoirs on the sheep stations,' Leon said, as if anticipating my question, 'and never expected to stay, but somehow the place gets to you. I'd find these sunsets hard to give up, for one thing.'

I nodded as he got up to answer a ringing phone.

'Used to be even nicer once, a long time ago,' said Lisa, Steve's partner. 'There's been a lot of overgrazing.'

'Here or all over?'

'All over – well, nearly. In the 1890s there was a really bad drought. They say the land's never really recovered, and probably never will.'

Later, Steve, Trevor and I went down the hill to the White Cliffs Hotel, the local hostelry, and the appeal of the little town became more evident still. The White Cliffs was as nice a pub as I have ever been in. Not to look at, for Australian country pubs are nearly always austere and utilitarian places, with linoleum floors, laminated surfaces and glass-doored coolers, but rather for the congenial and welcoming atmosphere. Much of this is a tribute to the owner, Graham Wellings, a chipper man with a firm handshake, a matinee-idol hairstyle and a knack for making you feel as if he settled here in the hope that one day some folks like you would drop by.

I asked him what had brought him to White Cliffs. 'I was an itinerant sheep shearer,' he said. 'Came here in '59 to shear sheep and just never left. It was a lot more remote back then. Took us eight hours from Broken Hill, the roads were that bad. You can do it in three now, but back then the roads were rough as guts every inch of the way. We tumbled in here gasping for a cold beer, and of course there were no coolers in those days. Beer was room temperature – and room temperature was 110 degrees. No air conditioning either, of course. No electricity at all, unless you had your own generator.'

'So when did you get electricity in White Cliffs?'

He thought for an instant. 'Nineteen ninety-three.'

I thought I had misheard him. 'When?'

'Just about five years ago. We have telly now, too,' he added suddenly and enthusiastically. 'Got that two years ago.'

He seized a remote control unit and pointed it at a television mounted on the wall. When it warmed to life, he ran through their choice of three channels, turning to us at each with an expression that invited staggered admiration. I have been in countries where people still ride waggons and gather hay with forks, and countries where the per capita gross domestic product would not buy you a weekend at a Holiday Inn, but nowhere before had I been invited to regard television as a marvel.

He switched off and put the remote back on the shelf as if it were a treasured relic.

'Yeah, it was a different world,' he said musingly.

Still is, I thought.

CHAPTER THREE

IN THE MORNING STEVE AND LISA ESCORTED US BACK ALONG THE lonely dirt track to the paved highway at Wilcannia, where we parted ways – they to go left to Menindee, Trevor and I to go right to Broken Hill, 197 kilometres away down a straight and empty road, thus completing a large and irregular circle.

We had an afternoon in Broken Hill and spent it seeing the sights. We drove out to Silverton, once a rowdy mining town, now virtually derelict but for a big pub, which is said to be the most photographed and filmed in Australia. It's not that there is anything wildly special about the pub; it's more that it gives the appearance of being in the middle of nowhere while actually being conveniently handy to the air-conditioned amenities of Broken Hill. It's been used as a film location 142 times – in *A Town like Alice*, *Mad Max 2* and about every Australian beer commercial ever made. It now gets by, evidently, on the visits of film crews and of occasional tourists like us.

Broken Hill has had tough times, too. Even by Australian standards, it is a long way from anywhere – 750 miles from Sydney, the state capital, where all the decisions are made – and its citizens have an understandable tendency to think of themselves as neglected. As recently as the 1950s it had 35,000 people, against just 23,000 now. Its history dates from 1885, when a boundary rider checking fences chanced upon a lode of silver, zinc and lead in sumptuous proportions. Almost overnight Broken Hill became a boom town and gave birth along the way to Broken Hill Proprietary Ltd, still Australia's mightiest industrial colossus.

At its peak in 1893 Broken Hill had sixteen mines employing 8,700 miners. Today there is just one mine and 700 workers, which is the main reason for the population decline. Even so, that one mine produces more ore than all sixteen mines together at their peak. The difference is that whereas before you had thousands of men crawling about in poky shafts, today a handful of engineers with explosives blow out cathedral-sized chambers up to 300 feet high and the size of a football pitch and, when the dust has settled and everyone's ears have stopped ringing, a team of workers on giant bulldozers come along and scoop up all the ore. It's so vastly efficient that in only a decade or so all the ore will be gone, and quite what will become of Broken Hill is anyone's guess.

Meanwhile, it's a nice little town with an air of busyness and prosperity that brings to mind one of those establishing shots you'd see in a 1940s Hollywood movie featuring Jimmy Stewart or Deanna Durbin. Its main street is lined with handsome buildings in a modestly exuberant Victorian style. Seeking refreshment, Trevor and I ventured into one of the many imposing hotels – and I should just note that in an Australian context 'hotel' can signify many things: a hotel, a pub, a hotel *and* pub – that stand on nearly every corner. This one was called Mario's Palace Hotel, and it was very grand from without – it covered half a block and had a large wraparound balcony employing a lot of intricate ironwork – though inside it had an underlit and musty air. The bar seemed to be open – a TV was playing silently in the corner, the signs were illuminated – but there was no one in attendance and no sounds of anyone nearby. Leading off the bar were several large rooms – a ballroom, a dining room, perhaps another ballroom – all looking as if they had been decorated at considerable expense in 1953 and not used since.

A door led out into a hallway with a grand stairway. From the ground to the distant ceiling, a good three storeys above us, the stairwell walls were divided into panels of different sizes by strips of wood and some artist had filled each of them – scores in all – with a mural, some of them several feet across, some much smaller. They consisted entirely of romantic and idealized landscapes showing herds of kangaroos sipping at billabongs or swagmen gathered around a lonely coolibah tree. They were undeniably hokey, but charming even so and without question from a gifted hand. Almost involuntarily, we found ourselves advancing slowly up the stairs, moving with silent absorption from one image to the next.

'Good, eh?' came a voice after a minute and we turned to see a young man looking up at us and apparently not at all perturbed that we were making our way into the depths of his building. He was wiping his forearms with a cloth, as if he had been engaged in some large task like cleaning out a cauldron.

'They were done by a blackfella named Gordon Waye,' he went on. 'Pretty amazing bloke. He didn't sketch anything out or anything, didn't have any kind of a plan. He just picked up his paints and a brush and did it straight off. At the end of the day there'd be a finished painting. Then he'd collect his pay from the owner and clear off. Go walkabout, you know? Some time later – maybe a week or two, maybe a few months – he'd come back and knock off another one, collect some more money and clear off again, until eventually he'd done them all. Then he cleared off for good.'

'What became of him?'

'No idea. Don't think anyone knows. So where you fellas come from?'

'America and Britain,' I said, pointing appropriately.

'Long way to come. Expect you'll be wanting a cold beer then.'

We followed him into the bar, where he drew us two schooners of Victoria Bitter.

'Nice hotel,' I said, not really meaning it.

He looked at me faintly dubiously. 'Well, you can have it if you want. It's on the market.'

'Oh, yeah? How much for?'

'One million seven hundred and fifty thousand dollars.'

It took me a moment to form the words. 'That's a *lot* of money.'

He made a look of agreement. 'More than most people around here have got, that's for sure.' Then he disappeared with a crate through the door behind him.

We wanted to ask him more, and after a few minutes we wanted another beer, but he never did come back.

The following morning we caught the second of the twice-weekly Indian Pacifics to Perth. In the deliciously air-chilled bar car of the train, Trevor and I spread out a map of Australia and discovered with astonishment that for all our hours of driving over the previous days we had covered only the tiniest fraction of land surface – a freckle, almost literally, on the face of Australia. It is such an immense country, and we still had 3,227 kilometres of it to get through before we reached Perth. There was nothing to do but sit back and enjoy it.

After the heat and dust of the outback, I was glad to be back in the clean, regulated world of the train, and I fell into its gentle routines with gratitude and relish. Train life, I decided, takes some beating. At some point in the morning, generally when you have gone for breakfast, your bed vanishes magically into the wall, and in the evening just as magically reappears, crisply made with fresh sheets. Three times a day you are called to the dining car, where you are presented with a thoroughly commendable meal by friendly and obliging staff. In between times there is nothing to do but sit and read, watch the endlessly unfurling scenery or chat with your neighbour. Trevor, because he was young and full of life and unaccountably had failed to bring any of my books to make the hours fly, felt restless and cooped up, but I wallowed in every undemanding minute of it.

With all your needs attended to and no real decisions to make, you soon find yourself wholly absorbed with the few tiny matters that are actually at your discretion – whether to have your morning shower now or in a while, whether to get up from your chair and pour yourself another complimentary cup of tea or be a devil and have a bottle of Victoria Bitter, whether to stroll back to your cabin for the book you forgot or just sit and watch the landscape for emus and kangaroos. If this sounds like a living death, don't be misled. I was having the time of my life. There is something wonderfully lulling about being stuck for a long spell on a train. It was like being given a preview of what it will be like to be in your eighties. All those things eighty-year-olds appear to enjoy – staring vacantly out of windows, dozing in a chair, boring the pants off anyone foolish enough to sit beside them – took on a special treasured meaning for me. This was the life!

Our new complement of passengers seemed a livelier bunch. There was Phil, a printmaker from Newcastle in New South Wales; Rose and Bill, a sweet, quiet couple from England who were on their way to see their son, a mining engineer in Kalgoorlie; three white-haired guys from a lawn bowling club in Neutral Bay, who drank like sailors on shore leave; and a wonderful, rake-thin, chain-smoking, perpetually wobbly-drunk lady whose name no one seemed to know and whose response to any pleasantry of any type directed at her – 'Good morning,' 'Sleep well?', 'I'm Bill and this is Trevor' – was to cry 'Yes!' and give a prolonged, demented laugh, and take a sip of Shiraz. In such a crowd, the evenings tended to be nicely festive – so much so that my notes for the relevant periods are on matchbooks and the backs of beer mats, and show a certain measure of elevated incoherence ('G. attacked by camel in men's lav. Alice Springs 1947 – great!!!'). Still, my recollection is of having a jolly nice time and that is of course the main thing.

On our second day out from Broken Hill, we entered the mighty Nullarbor. Many people, even Australians, assume Nullarbor is an Aboriginal term, but in fact it is a corruption of the Latin for 'no trees', and the name could not be more apt. For hundreds of miles the landscape is as flat as a calm sea and unrelievedly barren – just glowing red soil, tussocky clumps of bluebush and spinifex, and scattered rocks the colour of bad teeth. In an area four times the size of Belgium there is not a scrap of shade. It is one of the most forbidding expanses on earth.

Just after breakfast, we entered the longest straight stretch of railway line in the world – 297 miles without a hint of deviation – and in mid-morning we heaved into Cook, a community that makes White Cliffs look accessible and urbane. Five hundred miles from any real town to east or west, a hundred miles from the nearest paved highway to the south and over a thousand to the north, Cook (pop. 40) exists solely to water, fuel and otherwise service the trains that pass through. Beside the track stood a sign that said: 'No Food or Fuel for Next 862 Kilometres' – rather a daunting thought, what?

We had two hours to kill in Cook – goodness knows why so long – and everyone was allowed to get off and look around. It was agreeable to move about without having to steady yourself against a swaying wall every couple of paces, but the thrill of Cook swiftly palls. There was nothing much to it – a railway station and post office, a couple of dozen prefabricated bungalows standing on dusty ground, a little shop whose shelves were mostly bare, a shuttered community centre, an empty school (it was the middle of school holidays), a small open-air swimming pool (also closed), and an airstrip with a limp windsock. The heat was terrific. On every side desert lapped at the town like floodwater.

I was standing there with a map of Australia, surveying the emptiness and trying to absorb the ungraspable fact that if I walked north from here I wouldn't come to a paved surface for 1,100 miles, when Trevor trotted up and told me we had been given permission to travel for an hour in the locomotive, so that he could take photos. This was a rare treat, and exciting news. Just before the train resumed its journey, we climbed aboard the locomotive with two replacement drivers, Noel Coad and Sean Willis, who would take the train on to Kalgoorlie.

They were genial and laid-back, in their late twenties or early thirties. Their cab was snug and comfy – homey even in a high-tech sort of way. It featured a fancy console with lots of switches and toggles, three shortwave radios and two computer screens, but also a number of domestic comforts: a kettle, a small refrigerator, an electric hotplate for cooking. Coad drove. He flipped a couple of switches, moved a gear lever a fraction of an inch, and we were off. Within a couple of minutes we were up to our cruising speed of 100 kilometres an hour.

I sat quite still, fearful of touching anything that would get us on the evening news, and enjoyed the novel perspective of looking straight ahead. And what an ahead it is on the boundless Nullarbor. Before us stretched a single-line track, two parallel bars of shining steel, dead straight and painfully shiny in the sunshine, and hatched with endless rungs of concrete sleepers. Somewhere in the vicinity of a preposterously remote horizon the two gleaming lines of steel met in a shimmery vanishing point. Endlessly, monotonously, we hoovered up sleepers as we progressed, but however much we pressed onward the vanishing point stayed always in the same place. You couldn't look at it – well, I couldn't look at it – without getting a headache.

'How far is it to the next curve?' I asked.

'Three hundred and sixty kilometres,' Willis answered.

'Don't you go crazy out here?'

'No,' they replied in unison and with evident sincerity.

'Do you ever see anything to break the monotony – animals and so forth?'

'A few 'roos,' Coad said. 'A camel from time to time. Once in a while somebody on a motorbike.'

'Really?'

'On that.' He indicated a rough dirt maintenance road that ran alongside the track. 'Very popular with the Japanese for some reason. Something to do with an initiation into a club or something.'

'We saw a bloke on a bicycle the other week,' Willis volunteered.

'No kidding?'

'Japanese bloke.'

'Was he all right?'

'Out of his mind if you ask me, but he seemed all right. He waved.'

'Isn't it awfully risky out there?'

'Nah – not if you keep to the track. There's fifty or sixty trains a week along this line, and nobody's going to leave you out here if you're in bother.'

We had arrived at a siding called Deakin, where the Indian Pacific had to pull over to let a freight train through, and where Trevor and I were to return to the passenger section. We hopped down from the locomotive and walked briskly back along the train towards the passenger carriages. (And you would walk briskly too, believe me, if you were outside a train with its motor running in the middle of a desert.) At the door of the first passenger carriage, David Goodwin, the train manager, was waiting for us.

He helped us up – it's a long way up onto a train when you haven't got a platform to start with – and we half fell in. Looking up, I discovered with a start that we were in the forbidden coach section. I have never felt so stared at in my life. As we followed David through the two coach carriages, 124 pairs of sunken eyes sullenly followed our every move. These were people who had no dining carriage, no lounge bar, no cosy berths to crawl into at night. They had been riding upright for two days since leaving Sydney, and still had twenty-four hours to go to Perth. I am almost certain that if we had not had the train manager as an escort they would have eaten us.

We arrived in Perth at first light and stepped from the train, glad to be back on solid ground and feeling disproportionately pleased with our achievement. I know that all that was required of us to get there was to sit passively for a total of seventy-two hours, but still we had done something that lots of Australians never do – namely, cross Australia.

It is a lame and obvious conclusion to draw, but Australia truly does exist on a unique scale. It's not just a question of brute distance – though goodness knows, there is plenty enough of that – but of the incredible emptiness that lies within all that distance. Five hundred miles in Australia is not like 500 miles elsewhere, and the only way to appreciate that is to cross the country at ground level.

I couldn't wait to see more.

Part Two

CIVILIZED AUSTRALIA

(The Boomerang Coast)

CHAPTER FOUR

I

YOU WOULDN'T THINK THAT SOMETHING AS CONSPICUOUS, AS PATENTLY *there*, as Australia could escape the world's attention almost to the modern age, but there you are. It did. Less than twenty years before the founding of Sydney it was still essentially unknown.

For nearly 300 years explorers had been looking for a conjectured southern continent, *Terra Australis Incognita* – some commodious mass that would at least partly counterbalance all that land that covered the northern half of the globe. In every instance one of two things happened: either they found it and didn't know they had or they missed it altogether.

In 1606, a Spanish mariner named Luis Vaez de Torres sailed across the Pacific from South America and straight into the narrow channel (now called the Torres Strait) that separates Australia from New Guinea without having the faintest idea that he had just done the nautical equivalent of threading a needle. Thirty-six years later the Dutchman Abel Tasman was sent to look for the fabled South Land and managed to sail 2,000 miles along the underside of Australia without detecting that a substantial land mass lay just over the left-hand horizon. Eventually he bumped into Tasmania (which he called Van Diemen's Land after his superior at the Dutch East India Company), and went on to discover New Zealand and Fiji, but it was not a successful voyage. In New Zealand, Maoris captured and ate some of his men – not the sort of thing that looks good in a report – and he failed to find anything in the way of riches. On the way home he passed within sight of the north coast of Australia, but, disheartened, accorded it no importance and sailed on.

That isn't to say that Australia had never felt a European footprint. From the early seventeenth century onwards mariners occasionally fetched up on its northern or western shores, often after running aground. These early visitors left a few names on maps – Cape Leeuwin, the Dampier Archipelago, the Abrolhos Islands – but saw no reason to linger in such a barren void and moved on. They knew there was something there – possibly a biggish island like New Guinea, possibly a mass of smaller islands like the East Indies – and they called this amorphous entity New Holland, but none equated it with the long-sought southern continent.

Because of the random and casual nature of these visits, no one knows when Australia first fell under a European gaze. The earliest recorded visit was in 1606, when a party of Dutch sailors under a Willem Jansz, or Janszoon, stepped briefly ashore in the far north (and as hastily retreated under a hail of Aboriginal spears), but it is evident that others had been there earlier still. A pair of Portuguese cannons, dating from no later than 1525, were found in 1916 at a place called Carronade Island on the northwest coast. Whoever left them would have been among the first Europeans to stray this far from home, but of this epochal visit not a thing is known. Even more intriguing is a map, drawn by a Portuguese hand and dating from roughly the same period, that shows not only a large land mass where Australia stands, but an apparent familiarity with the jogs and indentations of Australia's east coast – something supposedly not seen by outsiders for another two and a half centuries.

So when in April 1770 Lieutenant James Cook and his crew aboard HMS *Endeavour* sighted the southeast corner of Australia and followed the coast 1,800 miles north to Cape York, it wasn't so much a discovery as a confirmation.

Though Cook's voyage was unquestionably heroic, its first purpose was mundane. He had been sent halfway around the world, to Tahiti, to measure a transit of Venus across the sun. Combined with measurements taken at the same time elsewhere, this would permit astronomers to calculate the distance of the earth from the sun. It wasn't an especially complicated procedure but it was important to get it right. An attempt during the last transit eight years earlier had failed, and the next one wasn't due for another 105 years. Happily for science and for Cook, the skies stayed clear and the measurements were taken without setback or complication.

Cook was now free to go off and fulfil the second part of his assignment – to explore the lands of the South Seas and bring home anything that looked scientifically interesting. To this end, he had with him a brilliant and wealthy young botanist named Joseph Banks. To say that Banks was a dedicated collector is to indulge in the drollest understatement. In the course of the *Endeavour*'s three-year voyage, he gathered up some 30,000 specimens, including at least 1,400 plants never seen before – at a stroke increasing the world's stock of known plants by about a quarter. Banks brought back so many items that the Natural History Museum in London has whole drawers full of objects that, 220 years later, await cataloguing. The same voyage also made the first successful circumnavigation of New Zealand, confirming that it was not part of the fabled southern continent, as Tasman had optimistically concluded, but two islands. By any measure, it had been a good voyage and we can assume an air of satisfaction as the *Endeavour* turned at last for home.

So when, on 19 April 1770, three weeks out from New Zealand, Lieutenant Zachary Hicks cried 'Land ahoy!' at the sight of what turned out to be the extreme southeast tip of Australia, the *Endeavour* and its crew were already on something of a roll. Cook named the spot Point Hicks (it's now called Cape Everard) and turned the ship north.

The land they found was not only larger than had been supposed but more promising. For the whole of its length, the east coast was lusher, better watered and more congenially provisioned with harbours and anchorages than anything that had been reported elsewhere in New Holland. It presented, Cook recorded, a 'very agreeable and promising aspect . . . with hills, ridges, plains and valleys, with some grass but for the most part . . . covered with wood'. This was nothing like the barren and savage wastes that others had met.

For four months they headed up the coast. They stopped at a place Cook named Botany Bay, ran disastrously aground on the Great Barrier Reef, and finally, after making some urgent repairs, rounded the northernmost tip of the continent at Cape York. On the evening of 21 August, almost as an afterthought, he stepped ashore at a place he called Possession Island, planted a flag and claimed the east coast for Great Britain.

It was a remarkable achievement for a man who had been born a labourer's son in inland Yorkshire, hadn't been to sea until he was eighteen, and had joined the Navy only thirteen years before at the advanced age of twenty-seven. He would return twice more to the Pacific on even greater voyages – on the next he would sail 70,000 miles – before being murdered (and possibly eaten himself) by natives on a beach in Hawaii in 1779. Cook was a brilliant navigator and a conscientious observer, but he made one critical mistake on his first voyage: he took Australia's wet season for its dry one, and concluded that the country was more hospitable than it was.

The significance of this misapprehension became evident when Britain lost its American colonies, and, deciding it needed a new place to send its less desirable subjects, plumped for Australia. Remarkably, the decision was taken without any attempt at reconnoitring. When Captain Arthur Phillip at the head of a squadron of eleven ships – known reverentially ever after as the First Fleet – set sail from Portsmouth in May 1787, he and the 1,500-odd people in his care were heading off to start a colony in a preposterously remote, virtually unknown place that had been visited just once, briefly, seventeen years before and had not seen a European face since.

Never before had so many people been moved such a great distance at such expense – and all to be incarcerated. By modern standards (by any standards really), their punishments were ludicrously disproportionate. Most were small-time thieves. Britain wasn't trying to rid itself of a body of dangerous criminals so much as thin out an underclass. The bulk were being sent to the ends of the earth for stealing trifles. One famously luckless soul had been caught taking twelve cucumber plants. Another had unwisely pocketed a book called *A Summary Account of the Flourishing State of the Island of Tobago*. Most of the crimes smacked either of desperation or of temptation unsuccessfully resisted.

Generally, the term of transportation was seven years, but since there was no provision for their return and few could hope to raise the fare, passage to Australia was effectively a life sentence. But then this was an unforgiving age. By the late eighteenth century Britain's statute books were plump with capital offences; you could be hanged for any of 200 acts, including, notably, 'impersonating an Egyptian'. In such circumstances, transportation was quite a merciful alternative.

The voyage from Portsmouth took 252 days – eight months – and covered 15,000 miles of open sea (more than would seem strictly necessary, but they crossed the Atlantic in both directions to catch favourable winds). When they arrived at Botany Bay, they found it wasn't quite the kindly refuge they had been led to expect. Its exposed position made it a dangerous anchorage, and a foray ashore found nothing but sandflies and marsh. 'Of the natural meadows which Mr. Cook mentions near Botany Bay, we can give no account,' wrote a puzzled member of the party. Cook's descriptions had made it sound almost like an English country estate – a place where one might play a little croquet and enjoy a picnic on the lawn. Clearly he had seen it in a different season.

As they stood surveying their unhappy situation, there happened one of those coincidences in which Australian history abounds. On the eastern horizon two ships appeared and joined them in the bay. They were in the command of an amiable Frenchman, Count Jean-François de La Pérouse, who was leading a two-year journey of exploration around the Pacific. Had La Pérouse been just a little faster, he could have claimed Australia for France and saved the country 200 years of English cooking. Instead, he accepted his unlucky timing with the grace that marked the age. La Pérouse's expression when it was explained to him that Phillip and his crew had just sailed 15,000 miles to make a prison for people who had stolen lace and ribbons, some cucumber plants and a book on Tobago, must have been one of the great looks in history, but alas there is no record of it. In any case, after an uneventful rest at Botany Bay, he departed, never to be seen again. Soon afterwards his two ships and all aboard were lost in a storm off the New Hebrides.

Meanwhile, Phillip, seeking a more amenable location, sailed up the coast to another inlet, which Cook had noted but not explored, and ventured through the sandstone heads that form its mouth. There he discovered one of the great harbours of the world. At the point where Circular Quay now stands, he anchored his ships and started a city. It was 26 January 1788. The date would live for ever as Australia Day.

Among the many small and interesting mysteries of Australia in its early days is where so many of its names come from. It was

Cook who called the eastern coast New South Wales, and no one now has any idea why. Did he mean to signify that this would be a new Wales of the South or merely a new version of South Wales? If the latter, why just South Wales and not the whole of it? No one can say. What is certain is that he had no known connection to that verdant principality, southerly or otherwise.

Sydney likewise is a curious appellation. Phillip intended the name only to apply to the cove. He meant for the town to be known as Albion, but that name never took. We know for whom Sydney was named: Thomas Townshend, first Baron Sydney, who was Home and Colonial Secretary and therefore Phillip's immediate master. What we don't know is why Townshend, when he was ennobled, chose Sydney as his title. The reason died with him, and the title didn't last much longer; it was extinct by 1890. The harbour itself was called Port Jackson (it is officially still so known) after an admiralty judge, one George Jackson, who later abandoned his birth name in order to secure an inheritance from an eccentric relation and finished his life as Duckett.

Of the roughly one thousand people who shuffled ashore, about 700 were prisoners and the rest were marines and officers, officers' families and the governor and his staff. The exact numbers of each are not known,* but it hardly matters. They were all prisoners now.

They were, to put it mildly, a curious lot. The complement included a boy of nine and a woman of eighty-two – hardly the sort of people you would invite to help you through an ordeal. Though it had been noted in London that certain skills would be desirable in such a remote situation, no one had actually acted on that observation. The party included no one proficient in the natural sciences, no master of husbandry, not a soul who had the faintest understanding of growing crops in hostile climes. The prisoners were in nearly every practical respect woeful. Among the 700 there was just one experienced fisherman and no more than five people with a working knowledge of the building trade. Phillip was by all accounts a kindly man of even temper and natural honesty, but his situation was hopeless. Confronted with a land full of plants

* For the record, Captain Watkin Tench, who was there, recorded the numbers as 751 convicts and 211 marines landed, with 25 fatalities en route. Hughes in *The Fatal Shores* puts the number of convicts landed as 696 and the total number of fatalities as 48; he doesn't specify the number of marines. A *National Geographic* article I read put the number of prisoners at 775; a Penguin *Concise History* made it 529. I could go on and on.

he had never seen and knew nothing about, he recorded in despair: 'I am without one botanist, or even an intelligent gardener.'

Gamely, they made the best of things: they had no choice. Parties were sent into the countryside to see what they could find (essentially nothing); a government farm was set up on ground overlooking the harbour where the Botanic Gardens now stand; and attempts were made to establish friendly relations with the natives. The 'Indians', as they were at first generally called, were bewilderingly unpredictable. Generally friendly, they would nonetheless opportunistically attack settlers who ventured out of camp to fish or forage. In the first year, seventeen colonists were picked off in this way and scores more wounded, including Governor Phillip himself, who approached an Aborigine at Manly Cove in an attempt to converse and, to his consternation, had a spear thrust into his shoulder and out the back. (He recovered.)

Nearly everything was against them. They had no waterproof clothes to keep out the rain and no mortar to make buildings; no ploughs with which to till fields and no draught animals to pull the ploughs that they didn't have. The ground everywhere seemed cursed with an 'unconquerable sterility'. Such crops as managed to push through the soil were, more often than not, stolen under cover of darkness – by marines as often as by prisoners. For years, both groups would want not just for food but for nearly every basic commodity one could name: shoes, blankets, tobacco, nails, paper, ink, groundsheets, saddlery – whatever, in short, required manufacture. The soldiers did their best to evaluate their resources, but most had little idea of what they were looking for when they went after it, or at when they found it. The historian Glen McLaren quotes one report from a soldier sent to the Hunter River valley to see what might be there. 'The soil is black,' the soldier wrote hopefully, 'but mixed with a sort of sand or marly substance. Fish also are plenty, and I suppose, from their leaping, are of the trout kind.'

Development was further set back by the need to rely on prisoners, who clearly lacked any basis for devotion beyond self-interest. The cannier ones soon learned to lie their way to softer duties. One fellow named Hutchinson, coming across some scientific apparatus that had been packed away in one of the holds, persuaded his superiors that he knew all there was to know about dyestuffs, and spent months conducting elaborate experiments with beakers and scales, until it gradually became apparent that he didn't have the faintest idea what he was doing. When they couldn't fool their masters the prisoners could often fool their fellows. For years there existed an illicit commerce in which newly arrived convicts were sold maps showing them how to walk to China. Up to sixty at a time fled their captivity in the belief that that magically accommodating land lay just the other side of a vaguely distant river.

By 1790, the government farm had been abandoned and, with no sign of relief from England, they were desperately dependent on their dwindling supplies. It wasn't just that the food was short, but by now years old and barely edible, the rice so full of weevily grubs that 'every grain . . . was a moving body', as Watkin Tench queasily noted. At the height of their crisis they awoke one morning to find that half a dozen of their remaining cattle had wandered off, not to be seen again. These were seriously at-risk settlers.

There was at times a kind of endearing quality to their hopelessness. When Aborigines killed a convict named McEntire, Governor Phillip in an uncharacteristic fury (this was not long after he had been speared himself) despatched a band of marines on a punitive expedition with orders to bring back six heads – any six. The marines tramped about in the bush for a few days, but managed to capture just one Aborigine, and he was released when it was realized he was a friend. In the end they captured no one and the matter seems to have been quietly forgotten.

Exhausted by the stresses, Phillip was called home after four years, and retired to Bath. Apart from founding Sydney, he had one other notable achievement. In 1814, he managed to die by falling from a wheelchair and out of an upstairs window.

II

It is impossible in the frappaccino heaven that is modern Sydney to get the slightest sense of what life was like in those early years. Partly this is for the obvious reason that things have moved on a bit. Where, 200 years ago, there stood rude huts and sagging tents, today there rises a great and comely city, a transformation so total that it is impossible to see both ends at once, as it were. But there is also the consideration that the nature of Australia's beginnings is, even now, a tiny bit fudged, if not actually suppressed.

Nowhere in the city will you find a monument to the First Fleet. Go to the National Maritime Museum or Museum of Sydney and you will certainly get an impression that some of the early residents experienced privations – you might even deduce that their presence was not completely voluntary – but the idea that they arrived in chains is somewhat less than manifest. In his majestic history of the country's early years, *The Fatal Shore*, Robert Hughes notes that until as late as the 1960s Australia's convict beginnings were not deemed worthy of scholarly attention, and certainly not taught in school. John Pilger, in *A Secret Country*, writes that in his Sydney boyhood in the 1950s even among the family one never made reference to 'The Stain', the curiously menstrual euphemism by which convict antecedents were acknowledged. I can personally affirm that to stand before an audience of beaming Australians and make even the mildest quip about a convict past is to feel the air conditioning immediately elevated.

Personally, I think Australians ought to be extremely proud that from the most awkwardly unpropitious beginnings, in a remote and challenging place, they created a prosperous and dynamic society. That is exceedingly good going. So what if dear old gramps was a bit of a sticky-fingered felon in his youth? Look what he left behind.

And so once more to Circular Quay in Sydney, where Governor Phillip and his straggly, salt-encrusted band stepped ashore two centuries ago. I was back in Australia after a trip home to fulfil some other commitments and I was feeling, I have to say, pretty perky. The sun was gorgeously plump, the city coming to life – shutters were rattling open, chairs being set out at cafés – and I was basking in that sense of wonder and delight that comes with being freed from a sealed aeroplane and finding myself once again Down Under. I was about to see Sydney at last.

Life cannot offer many places finer to stand at eight thirty on a summery weekday morning than Circular Quay in Sydney. To begin with, it presents one of the world's great views. To the right, almost painfully brilliant in the sunshine, stands the famous Opera House with its jaunty, severely angular roof. To the left, the stupendous and noble Harbour Bridge. Across the water, shiny and beckoning, is Luna Park, a Coney Island-style amusement park with a maniacally grinning head for an entrance. Before you the spangly water is crowded with the harbour's plump and old-fashioned ferries, looking for all the world as if they have been plucked from the pages of a 1940s children's book with a title like *Thomas the Tugboat*, disgorging streams of tanned and lightly dressed office workers to fill the glass and concrete towers that loom behind.

An air of cheerful industriousness suffuses the scene. These are people who get to live in a safe and fair-minded society, in a climate that makes you strong and handsome, in one of the world's great cities – *and* they get to come to work on a boat from a children's story book, across a sublime plane of water, and each morning glance up from their *Heralds* and *Telegraphs* to see that famous Opera House and inspiring bridge and the laughing face of Luna Park. No wonder they look so damned happy.

It is the Opera House that gets all the attention, and you can understand why. It's so startlingly familiar, so hey-I'm-in-Sydney, that you can't stop looking at it. Clive James once likened the Opera House to 'a portable typewriter full of oyster shells', which is perhaps a tad severe. In any case, the Opera House is not about aesthetics. It's about being an icon.

That it exists at all is a small miracle. It's difficult to conceive now just what a backwater Sydney was in the 1950s, forgotten by the world and overshadowed even by Melbourne. As late as 1953, there were just 800 hotel rooms in the city, barely enough for one medium-sized convention, and not a thing to do in the evenings; even the bars closed at 6 p.m. The city's capacity for mediocrity cannot be better illustrated than by the fact that where the Opera House now stands, on as fine a situation as water and land afford, was then the site of a municipal tram garage.

Then two things happened. Melbourne was awarded the 1956 Summer Olympics – a call to action for Sydney if ever there was one – and Sir Eugene Goossens, head of the Sydney Symphony Orchestra, began to agitate for a concert hall in a city that didn't have a single decent orchestral space. Thus goaded, the city decided to tear down the ramshackle tram shed and build something glorious in its place. A competition was held for a suitable design and a panel of local worthies convened to select a winner. Unable to reach a consensus, the judges sought the opinion of the Finnish-born American architect Eero Saarinen, who sifted through the offerings and selected a design that the jurors had rejected. It was by a little-known 37-year-old Danish architect named Jørn Utzon. Possibly to the panel's relief, certainly to its credit, it deferred to Saarinen's opinion and Utzon was cabled with the news.

'The plan', in the words of John Gunther, 'was bold, unique, brilliantly chosen – and trouble – from its inception.' The problem was the famous roof. Nothing so daringly inclined and top-heavy had ever been built before and no one was sure that it could be. In retrospect, the haste with which the project was begun was probably its salvation. One of the lead engineers later noted that if anyone had realized at the outset how nearly impossible a challenge it would be, it would never have received the go-ahead. Just working out the principles necessary to build the roof took five years – the whole project had been intended to last no more than six – and construction in the end dragged on for almost a decade and a half. The final cost came in at a weighty $102 million, fourteen times the original estimate.

Utzon, interestingly, has never seen his prized creation. He was effectively dismissed in 1966 after an election brought in a change of state government, and has never been back. He also never designed anything else remotely as celebrated. Goossens, the man who started it all, likewise failed to see his dream realized. In 1956, while passing through customs at Sydney Airport, he was found to be carrying a large and diversified collection of pornographic material, and he was invited to take his sordid continental habits elsewhere. Thus, by one of life's small ironies, he was unable to enjoy, as it were, his own finest erection.

The Opera House is a splendid edifice and I wish to take nothing away from it, but my heart belongs to the Harbour Bridge. It's not as festive, but it is far more dominant – you can see it from every corner of the city, creeping into frame from the oddest angles, like an uncle who wants to get into every snapshot. From a distance it has a kind of gallant restraint, majestic but not assertive, but up close it is all might. It soars above you, so high that you could pass a ten-storey building beneath it, and looks like the heaviest thing on earth. Everything that is in it – the stone blocks in its four towers, the latticework of girders, the metal plates, the six million rivets (with heads like halved apples) – is the biggest of its type you have ever seen. This is a bridge built by people who have had an Industrial Revolution, people with mountains of coal and ovens in which you could melt down a battleship. The arch alone weighs 30,000 tons. This is a great bridge.

From end to end, it stretches 1,650 feet. I mention this not just because I walked every foot of it now, but because there is a certain poignancy in the figure. In 1923, when the city burghers decided to throw a bridge across the harbour, they determined to build not just any bridge, but the longest single-arch span ever constructed. It was a bold enterprise for a young country and it took longer to construct than expected – almost ten years. Just before it was completed, in 1932, the Bayonne Bridge in New York quietly opened and was found to be 25 inches – 0.121 per cent – longer.*

After such a long spell in an aeroplane I was eager to stretch my shapely limbs, so I crossed the bridge to Kirribilli and plunged into the old, cosily settled neighbourhoods of the lower north shore. And what a wonderful area it is. I wandered past the little cove where my hero, the aviator Charles Kingsford Smith (about whom much more anon), once impossibly took off in an aeroplane, and into the shaded hills above, through quiet neighbourhoods of cottagey homes buried in flowering jacaranda and fragrant frangipani (and in every front garden cobwebs like trampolines, in the centre of each the sort of spider that would make a brave man gasp). At every turn there was a glimpse of blue harbour – over a garden wall, at the bottom of a sloping road, suspended between close-set houses like a sheet hung to dry – and it was all the finer for being furtive. Sydney has whole districts filled with palatial houses that seem to consist of nothing but balconies and plate glass, with scarcely a leaf to block the beating sun or interrupt the view. But here on the north shore, wisely and nobly, they have sacrificed large-scale vistas for the cool shade of trees, and every resident will, I guarantee, go to heaven.

I walked for miles, through Kirribilli, Neutral Bay and Cremorne Point, and on through the prosperous precincts of Mosman, before at last I came to Balmoral with a sheltered beach overlooking Middle Harbour and a splendid waterfront park shaded with stout Moreton Bay figs, the loveliest tree in Australia by far. A sign by the water's edge noted that if you were eaten by sharks it wasn't because you hadn't been warned. Apparently shark attacks are much more likely inside the harbour than out. I don't know why. I had also read in Jan Morris's engaging and cheery book *Sydney* that the harbour teems with lethal goblinfish. What is notable about this is that in all my reading I never came across a single other reference to these rapacious creatures. This isn't to suggest, I

* This was not a good period for Australian pride vis-à-vis America. Just over two weeks after the bridge opened and was found to be tragically just short of superlative, Phar Lap, the greatest racehorse in Australian history, died in mysterious circumstances in California. There are still Australians who say we poisoned it. Australians are hugely proud of this horse, and will not thank you for pointing out that actually it was bred in New Zealand.

hastily add, that Ms Morris was being inventive; merely that it isn't possible in a single lifetime to read about all the dangers that lurk under every wattle bush or ripple of water in this wondrously venomous and toothy country.

These thoughts took on a certain relevance some hours later in the dry heat of afternoon when I returned to the city dog tired and pasted with sweat, and impulsively popped into the grand and brooding Australian Museum beside Hyde Park. I went not because it is fabulous, but because I was half crazed from the heat and it looked to be one of those old buildings that are dimly lit and gratifyingly cool inside. It was both of those, and fabulous as well. It is a vast and old-fashioned place – I mean that as the most admiring compliment; I know of no higher for a museum – with lofty galleried halls full of stuffed animals and long cases of carefully mounted insects, chunks of luminous minerals or Aboriginal artefacts. In a country such as Australia, every room is a wonder.

As you can imagine, I was particularly attracted to all those things that might hurt me, which in an Australian context is practically everything. It really is the most extraordinarily lethal country. Naturally, they play down the fact that every time you set your feet on the floor something is likely to jump out and seize an ankle. Thus my guidebook blandly observed that 'only' fourteen species of Australian snakes are seriously lethal, among them the western brown, desert death adder, tiger snake, taipan and yellow-bellied sea snake. The taipan is the one to watch out for. It is the most poisonous snake on earth, with a lunge so swift and a venom so potent that your last mortal utterance is likely to be: 'I say, is that a sn—'

Even from across the room you could see at once which was the display case containing the stuffed taipan, for it had around it a clutch of small boys held in rapt silence by the frozen gaze of its beady, lazily hateful eyes. You can kill it and stuff it and put it in a case, but you can't take away the menace. According to the label, the taipan carries a venom fifty times more deadly than that of the cobra, its nearest challenger. Amazingly, just one fatal attack is on record, at Mildura in 1989. But *we* knew the real story, my attentive little friends and I – that once you leave this building the taipans aren't stuffed and behind glass.

At least the taipan is five feet long and thick as a man's wrist, which gives you a reasonable chance of spotting it. What I found far more appalling was the existence of lethal small snakes, like the little desert death adder. Just eight inches long, it lies lightly buried in soft sand so that you have no hope of seeing it before setting your weary butt on its head. Even more worrying was the Point Darwin sea snake, which is not much larger than an earthworm but packs venom enough if not to kill you at least to make you very late for dinner.

But all of these are as nothing compared with the delicate and diaphanous box jellyfish, the most poisonous creature on earth. We will hear more of the unspeakable horrors of this little bag of lethality when we get to the tropics, but let me offer here just one small story. In 1992, a young man in Cairns, ignoring all the warning signs, went swimming in the Pacific waters at a place called Holloways Beach. He swam and dived, taunting his friends on the beach for their prudent cowardice, and then began to scream with an inhuman sound. It is said that there is no pain to compare with it. The young man staggered from the water, covered in livid whip-like stripes wherever the jellyfish's tentacles had brushed across him, and collapsed in quivering shock. Soon afterwards emergency crews arrived, inflated him with morphine, and took him away for treatment. And here's the thing. Even unconscious and sedated he was still screaming.

Sydney has no box jellyfish, I was pleased to learn. The famous local danger is the funnel-web spider, the most poisonous insect in the world with a venom that is 'highly toxic and fast-acting'. A single nip, if not promptly treated, will leave you bouncing around in the grip of seizures of an incomparable liveliness; then you turn blue; then you die. Thirteen deaths are on record, though none since 1981 when an antidote was devised. Also poisonous are white-tailed spiders, mouse spiders, wolf spiders, our old friend the redback ('hundreds of bites are reported each year . . . about a dozen known deaths') and a reclusive but fractious type called the fiddleback. I couldn't say for sure whether I had seen any of these in the gardens I had passed earlier in the day, but then I couldn't say I hadn't since they all looked essentially the same. No one knows, incidentally, why Australia's spiders are so extravagantly toxic; capturing small insects and injecting them with enough poison to drop a horse would appear to be the most literal case of overkill. Still, it does mean that everyone gives them lots of space.

I studied with particular alertness the funnel-web since this was the creature that I was most likely to encounter in the next few days. It was about 1.5 inches long, plump, hairy and ugly. According to the label, you can identify a funnel-web by 'the mating organ on the male palp, deeply curved fovea, shiny carapace and lower labium studded with short blunt spines'. Alternatively, of course, you can just let it sting you. I carefully copied all this down before it occurred to me that if I were to awake to find any large, furry creature advancing crablike across the sheets I was unlikely to note any of its anatomical features, however singular and telling. So I put away my notebook and went off to look at minerals, which aren't so exciting but do have the compensating virtue that almost never will they attack you.

I spent four days wandering around Sydney. I visited the principal museums with dutiful absorption and spent an afternoon in the admirably welcoming State Library of New South Wales, but mostly I just went wherever there was water. Without question, it is the harbour that makes Sydney. It's not so much a harbour as a fjord, sixteen miles long and perfectly proportioned – big enough for grandeur, small enough to have a neighbourly air. Wherever you stand, the people on the far shore are almost never so distant as to seem remote; often you could hail them if you wished. Because it runs through the heart of the city from east to west it divides Sydney into more or less equal halves, known as the northern and eastern suburbs. (And never mind that the eastern suburbs are actually in the south, or that many of the northern suburbs are decidedly eastern. Australians, never forget, started life as Britons.) To note that it is sixteen miles long barely hints at its extent. Because it constantly wanders off into arms that finish in the serenest little coves, the most gently scalloped bays, the harbour shoreline actually extends to 152 miles. The consequence of this wandering nature is that one moment you are walking beside a tiny sheltered cove that seems miles from anywhere, and the next you round a headland to find before you an open expanse of water with the Opera House and Harbour Bridge and clustered skyscrapers gleaming in airy sunshine and holding centre stage. It is endlessly and unbelievably beguiling.

On my last day I hiked out to Hunter's Hill, a treasured and secretive district about six miles from the city centre on a long finger of land overlooking one of the quieter inner reaches of the harbour. I chose it because Jan Morris had made it sound so delightful in her book. I dare say she reached it by water, as any sensible person would. I decided to walk out along Victoria Road, which may not be the ugliest road in Australia but must be the least agreeable to walk along.

I strode for shadeless miles through zones of factories, warehouses and railway lines, then miles more of marginal commercial districts of discount furnishers, industrial wholesalers and dingy pubs offering surreally unappealing inducements ('Meat Raffles 6–8 pm'). By the time I reached a small sign pointing down a side road to Hunter's Hill my expectations were flagging. Imagine then my satisfaction at discovering that Hunter's Hill was worth every steaming step – a lovely, hidden borough of plump stone mansions, pretty cottages and picturesquely clustered shops of an often impressive venerability. There was a small but splendid town hall dating from 1860 and a chemist's shop that had been in business since 1890, which must be a record in Australia. Every garden was a treasure and somewhere in almost every backdrop lurked a glimpse of harbour view. I could not have been more charmed.

Reluctant to retrace my steps, I decided to push on further, through Linley Point, Lane Cove, Northwood, Greenwich and Wollstonecraft, and rejoin the known world at the Harbour Bridge. It was a long way round and the day was sultry, but Sydney is such a constantly rewarding place and I was feeling ambitious. I suppose I walked for about an hour before it dawned on me that this was actually *quite* ambitious – I had barely penetrated Linley Point and was still miles from the central business district – but then I noticed on the map what appeared to be a worthwhile short cut through a place called Tennyson Park.

I followed a side road down to a residential street and about halfway along came to the entrance to the park. A wooden sign announced that what lay beyond was preserved bush land and politely requested users not to stray from the path. Well, this seemed a splendid notion – an expanse of native bush in the heart of a great city – and I ventured in eagerly. I don't know what image 'bush' conjures up in your mind, but this was not the brown and semi-barren tract I would have expected, but a wooded glade with a sun-dappled path and tinkling brook. It appeared to be scarcely used – every few yards I would have to duck under or walk around big spider webs strung across the path – which lent the whole enterprise a sense of lucky discovery.

I guessed it would take about twenty minutes to cut through the park – or 'the reserve', as Australians call these things – and I was probably about halfway along when from an indeterminate distance off to the right there came the bark of a dog, tentative and experimental, as if to say: 'Who's that?' It wasn't very close or intimidating, but it was clearly the bark of a big dog. Something in its timbre said: meat eater, black, very big, not too many generations removed from wolf. Almost in the same instant it was joined by the bark of a companion dog, also big, and this bark was decidedly less experimental. This bark said: 'Red alert! Trespasser on our territory!' Within a minute they had worked themselves up into a considerable frenzy.

Nervously I quickened my pace. Dogs don't like me. It is a simple law of the universe, like gravity. I am not exaggerating when I say that I have never passed a dog that didn't act as if it thought I was about to help myself to its Pedigree Chum. Dogs that have not moved from the sofa in years will, at the sniff of me passing outside, rise in fury and hurl themselves at shut windows. I have seen tiny dogs, no bigger than a fluffy slipper, jerk little old ladies off their feet and drag them over open ground in a quest to get at my blood and sinew. Every dog on the face of the earth wants me dead.

And now here I was alone in an empty wood, which suddenly seemed very large and lonely, and two big and angry-sounding dogs had me in their sights. As I pushed on, two things became increasingly apparent: I was definitely the target and these dogs were not messing around. They were coming towards me, at some speed. Now the barking said: 'We are going to have you, boy. You are dead meat. You are small, pulpy pieces.' You will note the absence of exclamation marks. Their barks were no longer tinged with lust and frenzy. They were statements of cold intent. 'We know where you are,' they said. 'You cannot make it to the edge of the woods. We will be with you shortly. Somebody call forensic.'

Casting worried glances at the foliage, I began to trot and then to run. It was now time to consider what I would do if the dogs burst onto the path. I picked up a rock for defence, then discarded it a few yards further on for a stick that was lying across the path. The stick was ludicrously outsized – it must have been twelve feet long – and so rotten that it fell in half just from being picked up. As I ran, it lost another half, and another, until finally it was no more than a soft spongy stub – it would have been like defending myself with a loaf of bread – so I threw it down and picked up a big jagged rock in each hand, and quickened my pace yet again. The dogs now seemed to be moving parallel to me, as if they couldn't find a way through, but at a distance of no more than forty or fifty yards. They were furious. My unease expanded, and I began to run a little faster.

In my stumbling haste, I rounded a bend too fast and ran headlong into a giant spider's web. It fell over me like a collapsing parachute. Ululating in dismay, I tore at the cobweb, but with rocks in my hands only succeeded in banging myself on the forehead. In a small, lucid corner of my brain I remember thinking: 'This really is very unfair.' Somewhere else was the thought: 'You are going to be the first person in history to die in the bush in the middle of a city, you poor, sad schlubb.' All the rest was icy terror.

And so I trotted along, wretched and whimpering, until I rounded a bend and found, with another small and disbelieving wail, that the path abruptly terminated. Before me stood nothing but impenetrable tangle – a wall of it. I looked around, astounded and appalled. In my panic – doubtless while I was scraping the cobwebs from my brow with the aid of lumps of granite – I had evidently taken a wrong turn. In any case, there was no way forward and nothing behind but a narrow path leading back in the direction of two surging streaks of malice. Glancing around in desperation, I saw with unconfined joy, at the top of a twenty-foot rise, a corner of rotary clothes line. There was a home up there! I had reached the edge of the park, albeit from an unconventional direction. No matter. There was a civilized world up there. Safety! I scrambled up the hill as fast as my plump little pins would carry me – the dogs were very close now – snagging myself on thorns, inhaling cobwebs, straining with every molecule of my being not to become a headline that said: 'Police find writer's torso; head still missing.'

At the top of the hill stood a brick wall perhaps six feet high. Grunting extravagantly, I hauled myself onto its flat summit and dropped down on the other side. The transformation was immediate, the relief sublime. I was back in the known world, in someone's much-loved back garden. There was a set of old swings that didn't look as if they had been used in some years, flower beds, a lawn leading to a patio. The garden appeared to be fully enclosed by brick wall on three sides and a big comfortable-looking house on the fourth, which I hadn't quite anticipated. I was trespassing, of course, but there wasn't any way I was going back into those woods. Part of the view was obscured by a shed or summerhouse. With luck there would be a gate beyond and I could let myself out and slip back into the world undetected. My most immediate concern was that there might be a big mean dog in here as well. Wouldn't that be richly ironic? With this in mind, I crept cautiously forward.

Now let us change the point of view just for a moment. Forgive me for getting you up, but I need to put you at the window beside the kitchen sink of this tranquil suburban home. You are a pleasant middle-aged homemaker going about your daily business – at this particular moment filling a vase with water to hold some peonies you have just cut from the bed by the drawing-room windows – and you see a man drop over your back wall and begin to move in a low crouch across your back garden. Frozen with fear and a peculiar detached fascination, you are unable to move, but just stand watching as he advances stealthily across the property in a commando posture, with short, frenzied dashes between covering objects, until he is crouched beside a concrete urn at the edge of your patio only about ten feet away. It is then that he notices you staring at him.

'Oh, hello!' says the man cheerfully, straightening up and smiling in a way that he thinks looks sincere and ingratiating, but in fact merely suggests someone who has failed to take his medication. Almost at once your thoughts go to a police mugshot you saw in the evening paper earlier in the week pertaining, if you recall, to a breakout at an institution for the criminally insane at Wollongong. 'Sorry to crash in on you like this,' the man is saying, 'but I was desperate. Did you hear all the racket? I thought they were going to *kill* me.'

He beams foolishly and waits for you to reply, but you say nothing because you are powerless to speak. Your eyes slide over to the open back door. If you both moved for it now, you would arrive together. All kinds of thoughts start to run through your head.

'I didn't actually *see* them,' the man goes on in a judicious but oddly pumped-up tone, 'but I know they were after me.' He looks as if he has been living rough. Smudges of dirt rim his face and one of his trouser legs is torn at the knee. 'They always go for me,' he says, earnest now, and puzzled. 'It's as if there's some kind of conspiracy to get me. I can be just walking down the street, you know, minding my own business, and suddenly from out of nowhere they just *come* for me. It's very unsettling.' He shakes his head. 'Is your gate unlocked?'

You haven't been listening to any of this because your hand has been moving almost imperceptibly towards the drawer containing the steak knives. As the question dawns on you, you find yourself giving a small, tight, almost involuntary nod.

'I'll just let myself out then. Sorry to have disturbed you.' At the gate he pauses. 'Take it from me,' he says, 'you don't ever want to go back in those woods alone. Something terrible could happen to you back there. I love your delphiniums by the way.' He smiles in a way that freezes your marrow, and says: 'Well, 'bye then.'

And he is gone.

Six weeks later you put the house on the market.

CHAPTER FIVE

I

WHEN AUSTRALIANS GET HOLD OF A NAME THAT SUITS THEM THEY TEND to stick with it in a big way. We can blame this unfortunate custom on Lachlan Macquarie, a Scotsman who was governor of the colony in the first part of the nineteenth century, and whose principal achievements were the building of the Great Western Highway through the Blue Mountains, the popularizing of Australia as a name (before him the whole country was indifferently referred to as either New South Wales or Botany Bay) and the world's first nearly successful attempt to name every object on a continent after himself.

You really cannot move in Australia without bumping into some reminder of his tenure. Run your eye over the map and you will find a Macquarie Harbour, Macquarie Island, Macquarie Marsh, Macquarie River, Macquarie Fields, Macquarie Pass, Macquarie Plains, Lake Macquarie, Port Macquarie, Mrs Macquarie's Chair (a lookout point over Sydney Harbour), Macquarie's Point and a Macquarie town. I always imagine him sitting at his desk, poring over maps and charts with a magnifying glass, and calling out from time to time to his first assistant: 'Hae we no' got a Macquarie Swamp yet, laddie? And look here at this wee copse. It has nae name. What shall we call *it*, do ye think?'

And that's just some of the Macquaries, by the way. Macquarie is also the name of a bank, a university, the national dictionary, a shopping centre, and one of Sydney's principal streets. That's not to mention the forty-seven other Roads, Avenues, Groves and Terraces in Sydney that, according to Jan Morris, are named for the man or his family. Nor have we touched on the Lachlan River, Lachlan Valley or any of the other first-name variations that sprang to his tireless mind.

You wouldn't suppose there would be much left after all that, but one of Macquarie's successors as governor, Ralph Darling, managed to get his name all over the place too. In Sydney you will find a Darling Harbour, Darling Drive, Darling Island, Darling Point, Darlinghurst and Darlington. Elsewhere Darling's modest achievements are remembered in the Darling Downs and Darling Ranges, a slew of additional Darlingtons, and the important Darling River. What isn't called Darling or Macquarie is generally called Hunter or Murray. It's awfully confusing.

Even when the names aren't exactly the same, they are often very similar. There is a Cape York Peninsula in the far north and a Yorke Peninsula in the far south. Two of the leading explorers of the nineteenth century were called Sturt and Stuart and their names are all over the place, too, so that you have constantly to stop and think, generally at busy intersections where an instant decision is required, 'Now did I want the Sturt Highway or the *Stuart* Highway?' Since both highways start at Adelaide and finish at places 3,994 kilometres apart, this can make a difference, believe me.

I was thinking about all this – the confusion of place names and monuments to Lachlan Macquarie – the following morning because I spent much of it in the grip of the first while in pursuit of the second. I was in a rental car, you see, trying to find my way out of the endless, bewildering sprawl of Sydney. According to the local telephone directory, there are 784 suburbs and other named districts in the city, and I believe I passed through every one of them as I sought in vain for a corner of Australia not covered by bungalows. Some neighbourhoods I visited twice, at opposite ends of the morning. For a time I thought about just abandoning the car at the kerb in Parramatta – I rather liked the name and people were beginning to wave to me familiarly – but eventually I shot out of the city, like a spat bug, pleased to find myself on the correct heading for Lithgow, Bathurst and points beyond, and filled with that sense of giddy delight that comes with finding yourself at large in a new and unknown continent.

My intention over the next couple of weeks was to wander through what I think of as Civilized Australia – the lower right-hand corner of the country, extending from Brisbane in the north to Adelaide in the south and west. This area covers perhaps 5 per cent of the nation's land surface but contains 80 per cent of its people and nearly all its important cities (specifically Brisbane, Sydney, Melbourne, Canberra and Adelaide). In the whole of the vast continent this is pretty much the only part that is conventionally habitable. Because of its curving shape, it is sometimes called the Boomerang Coast, though in fact my interest was largely internal. I was headed in the first instance for Canberra, the nation's interesting, parklike and curiously much scorned capital; thence I would cross 800 miles of lonely interior to distant Adelaide before finally fetching up, dusty but ever indomitable, in Melbourne, where I was to meet some old friends who would hose me down and take me off for a long-promised tour of the snake-infested, little-visited but gorgeously rewarding Victorian bush. There was much to see along the way. I was very excited.

But first I had to make my way through the Blue Mountains, the scenic and long-impassable hills lying just to Sydney's west. On approach the Blue Mountains don't look terribly challenging; they rise to no great height and everywhere wear a softening cloak of green. But in fact they are rent with treacherous gorges and bouldered canyons, some with walls rising sheer hundreds of feet, and that lovely growth proves on closer inspection to be of an unusually tangled and obscuring nature. For the first quarter of a century of European occupation, the Blue Mountains stood as an impenetrable barrier to expansion. Expeditions tried repeatedly to find a way through but were always turned back. Even if progress could be gained through the lacerating undergrowth, it was nearly impossible to maintain one's bearings amid the wandering gorges. Watkin Tench, a leader of one party, reported with understandable exasperation how he and his men struggled for hours to find a route to the top of one impossibly taxing defile, only to discover when they attained the summit that they were exactly opposite where they expected to be.

Finally, in 1813, three men, Gregory Blaxland, William Charles Wentworth and William Lawson, broke through – exhausted, tattered and 'ill with Bowel Complaints', as Wentworth glumly noted, then and on any occasion that anyone would listen for the rest of his long life. It had taken them eighteen days, but as they stepped onto the airy heights of Mount York they were rewarded with a view of pastoral splendour never before seen by European eyes. Below them, for as far as the gaze could reach, stretched a sunny, golden Eden, a continent of grass – enough, it seemed, to support a population of millions. Australia would be a mighty country. The news, when they returned to Sydney, was electrifying. In less than two years a road was cut through the wilderness and the westward peopling of Australia had begun.

Today the Great Western Highway, as it is grandly and romantically known, follows almost exactly the route taken by Blaxland and his companions nearly 200 years ago. It certainly feels venerable. The route goes up and through the mountains and for much of the way passes along such confined spaces that there is no room for a big modern road. So the Great Western has the tight bends and unyielding width of a road designed for an age when motorists clapped goggles over their eyes and started their cars with a crank. I had been through here not long before on the Indian Pacific, but the views from the train weren't good – glimpsed vistas seen through a picket fence of gum trees and then, each time, an abrupt veering away into denser woodland – and anyway I had been preoccupied with exploring the train. So I was eager now to see the mountains up close, in particular the famous, dreamy views from the little town of Katoomba.

Alas, luck was not with me. As I followed the tortuous road up into the distant hills, the windscreen became speckled with drizzle and a chill, swirling fog began to fill the spaces between the coachwood and sassafras trees that loomed up on every side. Very quickly the fog thickened to the density of woodsmoke. I had never been out in such fog. Within minutes, it was like piloting a small plane through cloud. There was a bonnet in front of me, and then just white. It was all I could do to keep the car affixed to its lane – the road was almost preposterously narrow and twisting, and with the visibility so low every sudden curve was received with a whoop of surprise.

At length I reached Katoomba where the fog was, if anything, worse. The town was reduced to spooky shapes that loomed out of the murk from time to time, like frights at a funfair ride. Twice, at no more than two miles an hour, I nearly drove into the backs of parked cars. I have no idea why I bothered but, having come this far, I found my way to a lookout spot called Echo Point, parked and got out. Not surprisingly, I was the only person there. I went and grasped the railing and gazed out, the way you do at a lookout point. Before me there stood nothing but depthless white and that peculiar twitchy stillness that fog brings. To my surprise, from out of the milky vapours there emerged an elderly couple, dapper and doddery and bundled up as if for a long winter. The man walked with a particularly unsteady gait, propped by a cane on one side and his wife on the other.

As they drew level he looked at me in surprise. 'You won't see anything today!' he barked as if I was wasting his time as well as my own. I guessed from the volume that he might be a little deaf. 'This won't clear for thirty-six hours.' More confidingly he added: 'Depression over the Pacific. Often happens.' He nodded sagely and joined me in contemplating the nothingness.

His wife gave me a tiny smile that was at once apologetic, long-suffering and a little wistful. 'It might clear after a bit,' she speculated hopefully.

He looked at her as if she had just announced an intention to have a shit on the pavement. '*Clear?* It's never going to *clear.* There's a depression over the Pacific.' He looked for a moment as if he might swipe her with his cane.

Her optimism was not lightly deflected, however. 'Don't you remember how it came out all lovely that time at Bunbury?' she said.

'Bunbury?' he replied incredulously. '*Bunbury?* That's the other side of the country. It's a different bloody ocean. What are you talking about? You're *mad*. You want putting away.' Suddenly I recognized the accent. He was a Yorkshireman, or at least once had been.

'It didn't look like it was going to turn out fine,' she went on to me, expecting a more sympathetic hearing, 'and then it *did* turn out—'

'It's a different ocean, woman! Are you deaf as well as mad?' It was clear that this was, at least in the fundamentals, a conversation that they had been having for years. 'You get a quite different set of meteorological conditions in the Indian Ocean – quite different. Any fool knows that.' He was quiet for half a second, and then said: 'I thought we were going for a cup of tea.'

'We are, dear. I just thought we'd have a little stroll.' Deftly she set him in motion again.

'A stroll? What *for*? There's bugger all to see. Are you blind as well as deaf and mad? This won't clear for thirty-six hours.'

'I know, dear, but—'

Within moments they were just voices floating out of a veil of white and then they were gone altogether.

*

Reluctant to leave the area, I spent the night in Blackheath, a pretty village in the woods a dozen miles further down the highway. My last view from my motel window before turning in was of a car passing slowly on the highway, its headlamps like searchlights, and the world settled under a thick eiderdown of murk. It didn't look terribly promising.

So you may imagine my surprise when I awoke in the morning to find bright sunshine spilled across my bed and filling the tops of the trees outside. I opened the door to a golden world, so bright it made me blink. Birds were singing in the exotic tones of the bush. I wasted not a moment getting back to Katoomba.

The view when I returned to Echo Point was outstanding – a broad vale of very green forest broken at intervals by square-topped outcrops and fractured pinnacles, the whole filled with a vast and imposing silence. The sky was a rich and all but cloudless blue. Even at nine in the morning you could tell it was going to be a really hot day. I spent ninety minutes or so walking along the clifftop, enjoying the view from various angles; I had a look at Katoomba Falls and the stranded sandstone uprights known as the Three Sisters, and at length, entirely satisfied, wandered back into town for coffee.

In the 1930s and 1940s, Katoomba was a popular retreat for people of a genteel and discriminating nature. It was much less raffish than Bondi or the other beach outposts, where there was always the danger that young Bruce and Noelene might be exposed to more flesh than was healthy at their ages or overhear strong language – men saying 'jeezums' and 'strewth' and so on. Katoomba offered more refined pursuits: strolls through the woods, a therapeutic dip in a hydro pool, orchestral dancing in the evenings. Today Katoomba clings, with a slight air of desperation, to its bygone glory. Its main street had a generous sprinkling of art deco buildings, notably a wonderful old movie house, though several, including the movie house, were closed.

I bought a morning newspaper and found my way into a café. It always amazes me how seldom visitors bother with local papers. Personally, I can think of nothing more exciting – certainly nothing you could do in a public place with a cup of coffee – than to read newspapers from a part of the world you know almost nothing about. What a comfort it is to find a nation preoccupied by matters of no possible consequence to oneself. I love reading about scandals involving ministers of whom I have never heard, murder hunts in communities whose names sound dusty and remote, features on revered artists and thinkers whose achievements have never reached my ears, whose talents I must take on faith. I love above all to venture into the colour supplements and see what's fashionable for the beach in this part of the world, what's new for the kitchen, what I might get for my money if I had A$400,000 to spare and a reason to live in Dubbo or Woolloomooloo. There is something about all this that feels privileged, almost illicit, like going through a stranger's drawers. Where else can you get this much pleasure for a trifling handful of coins?

At this time I was following with some devotion a libel trial in which two government ministers were suing a publisher over a book containing scurrilous and, as it proved, groundless allegations implying sexual indiscretions in times gone by. With each passing day the trial had taken on the most exhilarating air of farce. Just recently a former leader of the opposition had taken the stand and, for no reason that any sane person could deduce, had begun recounting lively stories of alleged sexual improprieties by other ministers who were not remotely connected to the book or trial. But what had attracted me to the case in the first place, and what made it all seem particularly special, was the simple happy coincidence that the two ministers at the heart of the affair were named Abbott and Costello.

So I was sitting happily absorbed in this when I heard a familiar voice say, quite loudly and in a discontented tone: 'This isn't strawberry jam. It's blackcurrant.'

I looked up to see my two little old friends from the day before. They were looking much smaller and frailer with their hats and coats and scarves off. These items, neatly folded, were stacked high on the chairs beside them, as if awaiting transfer to a linen cupboard. I wondered if perhaps they wore all those clothes not so much for warmth as because all the dressing and undressing helped them fill their days.

'They haven't got strawberry, dear,' said the wife in a quieter voice. 'The lady explained. They only have blackcurrant or marmalade.'

'Well, I don't want either.'

'Then don't have either.' This said with just a hint of weariness.

'But it's on my toast.'

'No, dear, that's my toast. I ordered you a jam doughnut.'

'Jam doughnut? *Jam doughnut?* Are you mad? I don't like jam doughnuts. This tea is cold.'

I lowered myself back into my paper, but on the way out I stopped to bid my elderly friends good day. The man clearly didn't have any very real notion who I was. The jam doughnut, I noticed, had been devoured; only a small purple dollop gleamed on the plate before him.

'It's the young man from Echo Point,' the woman explained, but her husband was too busy chasing the dollop of jam with a spoon to pay me any heed.

'I see the weather's cleared,' I observed cheerfully.

'Often happens like that,' the man said in a small shout, without looking up. 'I said it wouldn't last thirty-six hours.'

'We had an experience just like it at Bunbury once,' the wife said to me. 'Terrible fog and then all of a sudden it came out all lovely and clear. Do you remember that, dear?'

'Quite,' said the old man distractedly. Coaxing the elusive jam aboard with a forefinger, he lifted the spoon and bunged it in his mouth with a look of immense satisfaction. 'Quite.'

And so once more to the wandering road. Beyond Blackheath the highway began a steep and curvaceous descent towards Lithgow, where it skirted along the hem of the mountains before striking off cross country through grassy plains, towards the country town of Bathurst. I was now in the rural heartlands, in an area known to geology as the Murray–Darling Basin. The fields on all sides were filled with tall blond grass, which waved in a languid manner, and there were buttercups in the verges, the whole bathed in the sweetest, brightest sunlight. Here and there stately trees shaded a white farmhouse. There wasn't a gum tree in sight. I could almost have been in the American Midwest.

The welcoming world I was passing into now wasn't quite as virginal as Blaxland and his cronies had supposed when they first gazed down on it from the heights behind me. When the first settlers stepped from the wooded mountains they were startled to find herds of cows, numbering in the hundreds, grazing contentedly on the tall grasses – all offspring of the ones that had wandered off from Sydney Cove all those years before. The cows, it transpired, had gone *around* the mountains, through an open pass to the south. Why it had not occurred to a human being in twenty-five years to try to do likewise is a question that is rarely asked and has yet to be satisfactorily answered.

Nor were the fertile plains quite as boundless as had at first been supposed. Good grazing land extended only a few score miles inland from the coast and even that was subject to the dispiriting vagaries of nature. It still is. A hundred miles or so north of where I was driving now, on the edge of this grassy zone, stands the little town of Nyngan. In 1989, 1990, 1992, 1995, 1996 and 1998 it was devastated by torrential flash floods. For five years during this same period, while Nyngan was repeatedly inundated, the town of Cobar, just eighty miles to the west, recorded not a drop of rain. This is, if I haven't made it clear already, one tough country.

And yet the striking thing about this area was how thoroughly delightful and accommodating it appeared. The farms were neat and trim, and the towns I passed through gave every appearance of a comfortable prosperity. It was impossible to believe that a metropolis of four million people lay just over the hills behind. I felt as if I had stumbled into some forgotten, magically self-contained world. There were things out here I hadn't seen in years. Petrol stations with old-fashioned pumps and no canopies over the forecourt, so that you pumped your petrol in full sun, as I am sure God intended it. Metal pinwheel windmills of the sort that used to stand in every Kansas farm field. Little towns with people in them – people going about their business, greeting each other with a smile and a nod. It all had a familiarity about it, but the familiarity of something half forgotten. Gradually it dawned on me that I *was* in the American Midwest – but it was the American Midwest of long ago. I was, in short, in the process of making the marvellous and heart-warming discovery that outside the cities it is still 1958 in Australia. Hardly seems possible, but there you are. I was driving through my childhood.

Partly it was to do with that dazzling light. It was the kind of pure, undiffused light that can come only from a really hot blue sky, the kind that makes even a concrete highway painful to behold and turns every distant reflective surface into a little glint of flame. Do you know how sometimes on very fine days the sun will shine with a particular intensity that makes the most mundane objects in the landscape glow with an unusual radiance, so that buildings and structures you normally pass without a glance suddenly become arresting, even beautiful? Well, they seem to have that light in Australia nearly all the time. It took me a while to recognize that this was precisely the light of Iowa summers from my boyhood, and it was a shock to realize just how long it was since I had seen it.

Partly, too, it was to do with the road. Almost all Australian highways are still just two lanes wide, and what a difference that makes. You're not cut off from the wider world, as you are on a motorway, but part of it, intimately connected. All the million details of the landscape are there beside you, up close, not blurred into some distant, tediously epic backdrop. It changes your whole outlook. There's no point in hurrying when all it's going to do is put you in the feathery wake of that old chicken truck half a mile ahead. Might as well hold back and enjoy the scenery. So there's none of that mad, pointless urgency – gotta pass this guy, gotta keep pushing, gotta make some miles – that makes any drive on a motorway such an exhausting and unsatisfying business. When you come to a town on such a road it is an event. You don't fly through at speed, but slow down and *glide* through, in a stately manner, like a float in a parade, slow enough to nod to pedestrians if you wish and to check out the goods in the windows on Main Street. 'Oh, that's a good price on men's double-knit shirts,' you observe in a thoughtful tone, or 'Those lawn chairs were cheaper in Bathurst,' for, needless to say, you are talking to yourself by now. Sometimes – quite often, in fact – you stop for a coffee and a browse round the shops.

Afterwards you return to the open road and naturally at first you go a little too fast, for speed is an instinct, but then – whoops! – you round a bend to find yourself fast approaching the back of a tip lorry kicking out smoke and labouring heavily up a slope. So you drop back and take it easy. You lean an arm on the windowsill, lay a finger on the wheel and cruise. You haven't done this for years. You haven't been on a drive like this since you were a kid. You'd forgotten motoring could be fun. I loved it.

As if to underscore the agreeably retro nature of the driving experience in Australia, I began to discover that radio stations in country towns specialize in songs from yesteryear. I don't mean songs from the '60s and '70s, but much earlier. This may be the last country in the world where you can turn on a car radio and stand a more than passing chance of hearing Peggy Lee or Julie London, possibly even Gisele McKenzie, whose popularity in the 1950s can only be attributed to a winning smile and the luck to live in an undiscriminating age. It would be intemperate to make a sweeping generalization about rural Australian radio stations because I listened to no more than six or seven thousand hours of them in the time I was there, so I might have missed something good, but I will say this: when our modern monuments have crumbled to dust, when the careless hand of time has worn away all traces of the twentieth century, you can be certain that somewhere in an Australian country town there will be a disc jockey saying: 'And that was Doris Day with her classic hit "Que Sera Sera".' I even loved that too.

For a week or so.

And so by such happy means did I proceed through Lithgow, Bathurst, Blayney and Lyndhurst, and finally, in mid-afternoon, fetched up in Cowra, a compact and tidy community of 8,207 people in the Lachlan Valley on the Lachlan River – both named, of course, for our old friend Mr Macquarie. I knew nothing about Cowra, but I quickly learned that it is well known to Australians as the site of the infamous Cowra breakout.

During the Second World War, a large prisoner-of-war camp stood just outside Cowra. One side held 2,000 Italian POWs; on the other were 2,000 Japanese. The Italians were model prisoners. Overcoming the mortification of finding themselves taken from the front lines and transported to a distant, sunny land far from the roar of guns, they settled down and made the best of things. So gamely did they cover their disappointment that one might almost have thought they welcomed their new situation. They worked on local farms and were only lightly guarded. Their officers – I just love this – weren't guarded at all. They were free to come and go as they pleased, and asked only to close the door behind them to keep out the flies. Regularly they could be seen strolling into Cowra for cigarettes and newspapers, possibly an aperitif at the Lachlan Hotel.

The Japanese presented a sombre contrast. They refused to undertake work or offer any measure of cooperation. Most gave false names, so painful was the shame of capture. Ridiculously and tragically, in August 1944, in the middle of the night, 1,100 of them staged a suicidal mass breakout, bursting from their barracks with a banzai cry and charging en masse at the guard tower clutching baseball bats, chair legs and whatever other weapons they could contrive. The startled guards poured bullets into the mass but were quickly overwhelmed. Within minutes, 378 prisoners had escaped into the countryside. Quite what they expected to do out there is anyone's guess. It took nine days to round them all up. The furthest any of them had got was fifteen miles. The Japanese casualties were 231 killed and 112 wounded. The Australians suffered three killed on the night, and a fourth during the hunt afterwards.

All this is commemorated in photographs and other displays at Cowra's visitors' centre, which in itself was excellent, but in a room at the back was a small audio-visual theatre that was one of the most enchanting things I believe I have ever seen – certainly ever seen in a small country town in the middle of nowhere.

Behind glass on a kind of small stage were objects saved from the POW camp: some books and diaries, a couple of framed photographs, a baseball bat and glove, a medicine bottle, a Japanese board game. As I entered, the lights automatically dimmed in the room. A little introductory music played and then – this was the enchanting part – a young woman about six inches high stepped *out* of one of the framed photographs and began moving around among the objects and talking about Cowra in the 1940s and the prison breakout. My mouth fell open. She didn't just move about but interacted with the objects – stepped around books, idly leaned on a shell casing – as she went through her presentation. As you can imagine, I got up and had a closer look and I can tell you that no matter how close you got to the glass (and I had my head pressed up against it the way children do when they wish to be amusing) you couldn't see the artifice. She was a perfectly formed, full-colour, charmingly articulate, rather dishy three-dimensional person right in front of me and only six inches high. It was the most captivating thing I had seen in years. It was obvious that it was a film projected in some way from beneath, but there wasn't a stutter or bump, no scratchy lines or wriggly hairs. It was as real as an image can get. She was a perfect little hologram. The narrative, it is worth noting, was sympathetic and informative – a model of its type. I watched it three times and couldn't have been more impressed.

'Good, eh?' beamed a lady at the reception desk, seeing the amazed look on my face when I emerged.

'I'll say!'

Anticipating my questions, she passed me a laminated card that explained how it was all done. The display was created by a company in Sydney, employing an optical trick that has been around for well over a century. It was all to do with projecting an image onto a glass plate artfully positioned in such a way as to become invisible to the spectator. Beyond that the only real trick was taking fastidious care that the actress hit her marks exactly. It must have taken months. It was simply brilliant.

And I will say this. When they figure a way to get the little person to lap dance, they will make a *fortune*.

I ended the day at Young, a farming town in plum and cherry country forty miles down the Olympic Highway from Cowra in the direction of Canberra. I got a room in a motel on a side street not far from the town centre. The owner, a fit-looking fellow in shorts and a short-sleeved shirt, read my name off the registration card and said: 'G'day, Bill. Welcome to Young,' and gave my hand a powerful shake as if inducting me into a secret society. The friendliness of Australians – all of it quite sincere and spontaneous, as far as I could ever tell – never ceases to amaze or gratify. I had never had a motelier pump my hand before or act so pleased that fate had thrown us together. 'Glad to have you,' he went on, still pumping away. 'My name's Bruce' – or whatever it was, for I was too disarmed, in every sense, to catch it.

'Well, g'day, Bruce,' I stammered uncertainly. 'I'm Bill.'

'Yes, Bill, we've established that,' he said and dropped my hand abruptly. 'You're in room six.'

I took my key to my room, opened the door and stepped in. The room was, in every tiny particular, from 1958. I don't mean that it had not been decorated since 1958 or anything remotely disrespectful. I mean that inside that room it was 1958. The walls were panelled in knotty pine. The TV had a UHF dial on it. The toilet seat had been gift-wrapped with a 'sanitized for your convenience' wrapper. In a drawer in the bedroom were two complimentary postcards featuring views of the motel and a paper bag into which I was urged, for my further convenience, to place unflushable objects. The bag bore a drawing of a lady (to tip us off, presumably, that it was intended for female 'personal' things rather than, say, corn cobs or small engine parts). I could not have been happier. I dumped my stuff and walked into town through the baking end-of-day heat. Now I saw the 1950s everywhere. Even the 'children crossing' signs in Australia, I noticed, show kids in 1950s attire – a little girl in a party dress, a boy in short trousers.

Superficially, Young didn't look terribly much like the towns I had grown up with. The exceptionally wide streets (they love really wide streets in Australian country towns), the red tin roofs, the metal awnings that run like hat brims around every commercial building – all this was indubitably Australian. But in the way it worked, and what it contained, Young was uncannily familiar. This was a place where, when you had an errand to run, you drove into town, not out of it, and parked in an angled slot on Main Street. This alone was enough to hold me transfixed for some minutes. I had forgotten that there was a time when a little parking along Main Street was all a community needed. I walked around in a state of the profoundest admiration. Except for the banks and a supermarket, the businesses were locally owned, with all the peculiarities of taste and presentation that that implies. There were shops here of types I hadn't seen in years – fix-it shops and little electrical shops, bakeries, cobblers, tea rooms – and sometimes they sold the most extraordinary combinations of goods. At the far end of the main street, I came across one place so exceptional in this respect that it stopped me in my tracks.

It was a shop that sold pet supplies and pornography. I am quite genuine. I stood back to stare at the sign, then peered through the window and finally stepped inside. It was a smallish shop and I was the only customer. On a raised platform about halfway back sat a man beside a cash register, reading a newspaper. He didn't say hello or make any acknowledgement, which seemed odd – very un-Australian – until I realized he was being discreet. I imagine most of his customers do what I was doing now: wander around showing an unwonted interest in catnip and flea powders, pausing from time to time to study the labels on canisters of fish flakes and the like, before ending up, entirely by accident, at the back of the shop, in the heavy breathing section. Remarkably, this is what happened to me now. The adult section was partitioned into a little compound, with admission through a wooden gate. As I stood there, the gate made a small electronic buzzing sound – the kind of buzz that is made in office buildings when a door is opened from a remote location – and swung to in a provocative manner. I looked around, surprised. The man was still to all appearances absorbed in his newspaper. He seemed unaware that I was even in his shop, much less on the threshold of porno heaven. I grinned foolishly and thought about approaching him to explain that he had just made a quite understandable but nonetheless comical error – that I, far from being a desperate pervert in need of pictorial nutrition, was in fact a respectable travel writer drawn to his shop by the unusual juxtaposition of its contents. Then we would have a good laugh and possibly strike up a correspondence.

But then it occurred to me that if I *did* buy something – I am not suggesting for a moment that I would, but on the other hand I still had nothing for the kids – I probably wouldn't want my business card pinned to his bulletin board. It also occurred to me that I had a certain duty to find out if there was some unexpected connection between the two strands of his business. Perhaps *petting* had a whole different meaning in rural Australia. To say nothing of *dog fancier*. For all I knew the racks beyond the barrier were full of publications with frisky, animalistic titles – *Prime Mounts*, *Whip and Collar*, *Sheep Dip Frolics*. Who could say? Clearly I had a duty to find out, so I resumed my expression of sober perusal and stepped inside.

I had never actually been in one of these places before – and by that I don't mean a pet-supply porno parlour. I mean any kind of adult enclosure, and frankly I was shocked. The participants were human, not animal. More than that I am unwilling to specify. It certainly wasn't 1958 at the back of the pet-food shop in Young. That's all I'm saying.

II

Gratified though I was to find a pornographic pet-supply store in Young (or indeed anywhere), my business there was of a slightly more elevating nature. I had come to see the famous Lambing Flat Museum, which commemorates the town's days of glory as a gold-mining outpost. It was too late to visit the museum that afternoon, but I presented myself at the front door at 9 a.m. the next morning only to find that the museum didn't open till ten.

Never one to waste a living moment, I decided to repair to a town centre café for breakfast and prepare myself with a little background reading. Thus I was to be found ten minutes later sitting in a mostly empty establishment on Young's main drag, drinking coffee, waiting for eggs and bacon, and delving through a hefty one-volume paperback history of Australia by the noted historian Manning Clark, which I had purchased a few days earlier in Sydney.

The history of gold in Australia is a lively and generally heartwarming tale. It begins with a fellow named Edward Hargraves, who in 1849 travelled from Sydney to the California goldfields hoping to make his fortune. In two years of digging he found nothing but dirt, but he did notice an uncanny similarity between the gold-bearing terrain of California and the land of New South Wales beyond the Blue Mountains – the countryside I had just been driving through.

Hastening back to Australia before anyone else was struck by a similar thought, Hargraves began to hunt in the creekbeds around Orange and Bathurst, and very quickly found gold in payable quantities. Within a month of his discovery a thousand people were swarming through the district turning over rocks and banging away with picks. Once they knew what to look for, they began to find gold everywhere. Australia was swimming in the stuff. An Aboriginal farmworker tripped over one lump that yielded nearly eighty pounds of precious ore, an almost inconceivable amount to be found in one place. It was enough to ensure a life of princely splendour – or would have been except that as an Aborigine he wasn't allowed to keep it. The rock went instead to the property's owner.

Scarcely had this rush got under way than gold was found in even more luscious quantities over the border in the newly created colony of Victoria. Australia became seized with a gold fever that made the California rush seem almost pale and indecisive. Cities and towns became visibly depopulated as workers left to seek their fortunes. Shops lost all their clerks. Policemen walked off their posts. Wives came home to find a note on the table and the waggon gone. Before the year was out, it was estimated that half the men in Victoria were digging for gold, and thousands more were pouring into the country from abroad.

The gold rush transformed Australia's destiny. Before it, people could scarcely be induced to settle there. Now a stampede rose from every quarter of the globe. In less than a decade, the country took in 600,000 new faces, more than doubling its population. The bulk of that growth was in Victoria, where the richest goldfields were. Melbourne became larger than Sydney and for a time was probably the richest city in the world per head of population. But the real effect of gold was to put an end to transportation. When it was realized in London that transportation was seen as an opportunity rather than a punishment, that convicts *desired* to be sent to Australia, the notion of keeping the country a prison became unsustainable. A few boatloads of convicts were sent to Western Australia until 1868 (they would find gold there as well, in equally gratifying quantities) but essentially the gold rush of the 1850s marked the end of Australia as a concentration camp and its beginning as a nation.

Despite all the wealth that was to be found, things weren't always so easy for the diggers. In the hope of giving everyone a fair crack, prospectors were allowed to stake out only very modest claims – an area of just a few square yards – and here was where the problems began. When, in April 1860, gold was found at Lambing Flat, as Young was then known, fortune seekers turned up in quantity. By 1861, 22,000 people, among them 2,000 Chinese, were digging away, each on a plot of land about the size of a large throw rug. Inevitably most weren't finding much. Many of the miners began to cast resentful glances at the Chinese, who seemed to bear the heat and privations more cheerfully than their European counterparts, and who cooperated in a way that was felt to give them an unfair advantage. Also they seemed to be finding more gold. Also they were Chinese.

The upshot is that the white diggers decided to go and beat up the Chinese. That would make things much better surely. So in the middle of 1861 a substantial minority of the white miners – somewhere between 2,000 and 3,000, it appears – got together and staged a riot. It was a curiously organized affair. To begin with, the rioters brought in a brass band, which played 'Rule Britannia' and 'The Marseillaise' among other rousing songs deemed suitable for a civil disturbance. They also made and carried a large banner, which has since become something of an icon in Australian history. So, as the band played the kind of tunes normally heard at a Sunday afternoon park concert, the miners moved through the Chinese area beating people up with pickaxe handles or worse, robbing them and setting their tents alight. Then, just to make a day of it, they went on to burn down the courthouse. Afterwards, eleven of the rioters were tried but none was convicted. Obviously not Australia's proudest moment.

What was the immediate outcome of all this I can't tell you. Manning Clark, who is – I just have to say this – a most exasperating historian, mentions that one European miner was killed in the fray, but gives no hint as to how many Chinese died or were injured. Nor does he say what became of them afterwards – whether they were driven permanently from the site or whether things settled down and they returned to work. What is certain is that the Lambing Flat riot led to the adoption of what became known as the White Australia Policy, which essentially forbade the immigration of any non-European people until the 1970s. It would – and I really don't mean a pun here –

colour nearly every aspect of Australian life for over a century.

The Lambing Flat Museum was a large, old, single-storey brick building on a side street. I was there for the opening of the front door – an event that seemed to involve a great deal of unbolting and fiddling with a set of keys by someone on the inside. I began to suspect that it wasn't quite as popular or important an institution as I had supposed, for when the door swung open the lady nearly jumped out of her skin – 'Oh, you gave me such a start!' she said, chuckling merrily as if I had played a waggish joke on her – which left me with the impression that visitors were perhaps somewhat occasional. Anyway, she seemed glad to have me and, after accepting my $3 admission, urged me to take my time and come straight to her if I had any questions.

The museum was quite large and filled with the most extraordinary collection of stuff – flat irons, boot lasts, a buggy, old lanterns, odd fragments of machinery. Except for the absence of cobwebs, I could have been in my grandfather's barn. In a corner of the main room I found the centrepiece of the museum's collection – the large banner that the rioters carried in 1861. It is known as 'the roll-up flag' because neatly embroidered across it are the words: 'Roll Up. Roll Up. No Chinese.' In his book *A Secret Country*, which I had read before coming to Australia, the Australian journalist John Pilger suggests that the Lambing Flat Museum rather glorifies the event and offers nothing in the way of contrition. If that was true when Pilger visited – his book was published in 1991 – it no longer is. The labels give a balanced and thoughtful account of the riots, though again with a curious blankness regarding casualty numbers on either side.

The museum went on and on, and seemed to contain everything that everyone in Young had ever acquired and no longer wanted – sewing machines, adding machines, rifles, wedding albums, christening gowns. On a table was a large jar filled with small shiny black spheres, thousands of them. I peered at it, trying to figure out what it was.

'Canola seeds,' said a voice, quite near – so near it made me jump. I turned to find the lady who had let me in.

'Oh! You made me jump,' I said and she smiled in a way that made me suspect that that had been her intention. Perhaps, it occurred to me, that was how people passed the time in Young.

'Are you finding everything?' she asked.

I looked at her with interest. How would I know if I was or not?

But I replied: 'Yes, I am,' then added politely: 'It's very interesting.'

'Yes, there's a lot of history in Young,' she agreed, and looked around as if thinking perhaps there was too much.

My gaze returned to the jar of seeds. 'Do you grow a lot of canola around here?' I asked.

'No,' she said simply.

I considered this and tried to think of something more to say. 'Well, you've got the seeds if you decide to start,' I observed helpfully.

'Some people call it . . . *rape*,' she said, all but whispering the last word and raising her eyebrows significantly.

'Yes,' I agreed in what I believe was a concerned tone.

'I prefer canola.'

'Me, too.' I don't know why I said that. I have no position on seed names, however emotive, but it seemed prudent to agree with her.

Mercifully, just then a bell went – the kind of bell that sounds when someone comes in a shop entrance – and she excused herself. I waited half a dozen beats then followed her out, for I had seen all I needed to and I wanted to get a move on.

In the front hallway a middle-aged couple were in the process of buying tickets. The space was confined and I had to wait for them to step aside to let me out, and I thanked the white-haired lady as I passed.

'You enjoyed it, did you?' she asked.

'Very much,' I lied.

'Here on holiday?' asked the lady customer, presumably picking up on my accent.

'Yes, I am,' I lied again.

'How are you enjoying Australia?'

'I love it.' This was not a lie, but she looked at me doubtfully. 'Honestly,' I added.

Then a rather strange thing – well, I thought it was strange. The female customer placed a hand on my forearm and said, with a touch of real anxiety: 'I hope everyone is nice to you.'

I looked at her.

'Of course they will be,' I said. 'Australians are always nice.'

She gave me a look of imploring earnestness. 'Do you really think so?' Now don't get me wrong. Australians are the most wonderful people, but when they grow introspective it's sometimes a little strange.

I nodded. 'Really,' I said reassuringly. 'Australians are always nice.'

'Course they are, Maureen!' barked her husband. 'Salt of the earth. Now let the poor man go. I'm sure he has places he wants to be.' He was clearly from the other, heartier school of Australian archetypes – the one that thinks that any bloke not lucky enough to be born in Australia is tragically ill-favoured by fate and probably has a tiny dick as well, poor bastard.

And he was right, of course – about having places to be, I mean. It was time to move on to Canberra.

CHAPTER SIX

I

BEFORE AUSTRALIA'S SIX COLONIES FEDERATED IN 1901, THEY WERE, TO an almost ludicrous degree, separate. Each issued its own postage stamps, set clocks to its own time, had its own system of taxes and levies. As Geoffrey Blainey notes in *A Shorter History of Australia,* a pub owner in Wodonga, in Victoria, who wished to sell beer brewed in Albury, on the opposite bank of the Murray River in New South Wales, paid as much duty as he did on beer shipped from Europe. Clearly this was madness. So in 1891, the six colonies (plus New Zealand, which nearly joined, but later dropped out) met in Sydney to discuss forming a proper nation, to be known as the Commonwealth of Australia. It took some years to iron everything out, but on 1 January 1901 a new nation was declared.

Because Sydney and Melbourne were so closely matched in terms of pre-eminence, it was agreed in a spirit of compromise to build a new capital somewhere in the bush. Melbourne, meanwhile, would serve as interim capital.

Years were consumed with squabbles about where the capital should be sited before the selectors eventually settled on an obscure farming community on the edge of the Tidbinbilla Hills in southern New South Wales. It was called Canberra, though the name by then was often anglicized to Canberry. Cold in the winter, blazing hot in the summer, miles from anywhere, it was an unlikely choice of location for a national capital. About 900 square miles of surrounding territory, most of it pastoral and pretty nearly useless, was ceded by New South Wales to form the Australian Capital Territory, a federal zone on the model of America's District of Columbia.

So the young nation had a capital. The next challenge was what to call it, and yet more periods of passion and rancour were consumed with settling the matter. King O'Malley, the American-born politician who was a driving force behind federation, wanted to call the new capital Shakespeare. Other suggested names were Myola, Wheatwoolgold, Emu, Eucalypta, Sydmeladperbrisho (the first syllables of the state capitals), Opossum, Gladstone, Thirstyville, Kookaburra, Cromwell and the ringingly inane Victoria Defendera Defender. In the end, Canberra won more or less by default. At an official ceremony to mark the decision, the wife of the Governor-General stood up before a gathering of dignitaries and, 'in a querulous voice', announced that the winning name was the one that had been in use all along. Unfortunately, no one had thought to brief her, and she mispronounced it, placing the accent emphatically on the middle syllable rather than lightly on the first. Never mind. The young nation had a site for a capital and a name for a capital, and it had taken them just eleven years since union to get there. At this blistering pace, all being well, they might get a city going within half a century or so. In fact, it would take rather longer.

Although Canberra is now one of the largest cities in the nation and one of the most important planned communities on earth, it remains Australia's greatest obscurity. As national capitals go, it is still not an easy place to get to. It lies forty miles off the main road from Sydney to Melbourne, the Hume Highway, and is similarly spurned by the principal railway lines. Its main road to the south doesn't go anywhere much and the city has no approach at all from the west other than on a dirt track from the little town of Tumut.

In 1996 the Prime Minister, John Howard, caused a stir after his election by declining to live in Canberra. He would, he announced, continue to reside in Sydney and commute to Canberra as duties required. As you can imagine, this caused an uproar among Canberra's citizens, presumably because they hadn't thought of it themselves. What made this particularly interesting is that John Howard is by far the dullest man in Australia. Imagine a very committed funeral home director – someone whose burning ambition from the age of eleven was to be a funeral home director, whose proudest achievement in adulthood was to be elected president of the Queanbeyan and District Funeral Home Directors' Association – then halve his personality and halve it again, and you have pretty well got John Howard. When a man as outstandingly colourless as John Howard turns his nose up at a place you know it must be worth a look. I couldn't wait to see it.

You approach Canberra along a dual carriageway through rural woodland, which gradually morphs into a slightly more urban boulevard, though still in woodland, until finally you arrive at a zone of well-spaced but significant-looking buildings and you realize that you are there – or as near there as you can get in a place as scattered and vague as Canberra. It's a very strange city, in that it's not really a city at all, but rather an extremely large park with a city hidden in it. It's all lawns and trees and hedges and a big ornamental lake – all very agreeable, just a little unexpected.

I took a room in the Hotel Rex for no other reason than that I happened upon it and had never stayed in a hotel named for a family pet. The Hotel Rex was exactly what you would expect a large hotel built of concrete and called the Rex to be. But I didn't care. I was eager to stretch my legs and gambol about in all that green space. So I checked in, dumped my bags and returned at once to the open air. I'd passed a visitors' centre on the way in, and recollected it as being a short walk away, so I decided to start there. In the event, it was a long way – a very long way, as things in Canberra invariably prove to be.

The visitors' centre was almost ready to close when I got there, and in any case was just an outlet for leaflets and brochures for tourist attractions and places to stay. In a side room was a small cinema showing one of those desperately upbeat promotional films with a title like *Canberra – It's Got It All!* – the ones that boast how you can water-ski and shop for an evening gown *and* have a pizza all in the same day because this place has . . . *got it all*! You know the kind I mean. But I watched the film happily because the room was air conditioned and it was a pleasure to sit after walking so far.

It was just as well that I didn't require an evening gown or a pizza or water-skiing when I returned to the street because I couldn't find a thing anywhere. My one tip for you if you ever go to Canberra is don't leave your hotel without a good map, a compass, several days' provisions and a mobile phone with the number of a rescue service. I walked for two hours through green, pleasant, endlessly identical neighbourhoods, never entirely confident that I wasn't just going round in a large circle. From time to time I would come to a leafy roundabout with roads radiating off in various directions, each presenting an identical vista of antipodean suburban heaven, and I would venture down the one that looked most likely to take me to civilization only to emerge ten minutes later at another identical roundabout. I never saw another soul on foot or anyone watering a lawn or anything like that. Very occasionally a car would glide past, pausing at each intersection, the driver looking around with a despairing expression that said: 'Now where the fuck is my house?'

I had it in mind that I would find a handsome pub of the type that I had so often enjoyed in Sydney – a place filled with office workers winding down at the end of a long day, so popular at this hour that there would be an overspill of happy people on the pavement. This would be followed by dinner in a neighbourhood bistro of charm and hearty portions. But diversions of this or any other type seemed signally lacking in the sleepy streets of Canberra. Eventually, and abruptly, I turned a corner and was in the central business district. Here at last were stores and restaurants and all the other commercial amenities of a city, but all were closed. Downtown Canberra was primarily a series of plazas wandering between retail premises, and devoid of any sign of life but for a noise of slap and clatter that I recognized after a moment as the sound of skateboards. Having nothing better to do, I followed the sounds to an open square where half a dozen adolescents, all in backward-facing baseball caps and baggy shorts, were honing their modest and misguided skills on a metal railing. I sat for a minute on a bench and with morbid interest watched them risking compound fractures and severe testicular trauma for the fleeting satisfaction of sliding along a banister for a distance of from zero inches to a couple of feet before being launched by gravity and the impossibility of maintaining balance into space in the direction of an expanse of unyielding pavement. It seemed a remarkably foolish enterprise.

If there is anything more half-witted than asking six adolescents in backward-facing baseball caps for a dining recommendation then it doesn't occur to me just at the moment, but I'm afraid this is what I did now.

'Are you an American?' asked one of the kids in a tone of surprise that I wouldn't necessarily have expected to encounter in a world capital.

I allowed that I was.

'There's a McDonald's just around the corner.'

Gently I explained that it was not actually a condition of citizenship that I eat the food of my nation. 'I was thinking of maybe a nice Thai restaurant,' I suggested.

They looked at me with that flummoxed, dead-end expression that you have to be fourteen years old to produce with conviction.

'Or perhaps an Indian?' I offered hopefully and got the same no one-home look. 'Indonesian?' I went on. 'Vietnamese? Lebanese? Greek? Mexican? West Indian? Malaysian?'

As the list grew, they shifted uncomfortably, as if fearing that I was going to hold them individually accountable for the inadequacies of the local culinary scene.

'Italian?' I said.

'There's a Pizza Hut on Lonsdale Street,' piped up one with a look of triumph. 'They do an all-you-can-eat buffet on Tuesdays.'

'Thanks,' I said, realizing this was getting me nowhere, and started to leave, but then turned back. 'It's Friday today,' I pointed out.

'Yeah,' the kid agreed, nodding solemnly. 'They don't do it on Fridays.'

I found my way back to the Rex, but got only as far as the front entrance when I realized that I did not want to dine in my own hotel. It is such a tame and lonely thing to do – an admission that one has no life. As it happened, I had no life, but that wasn't quite the point. Do you know what is the most melancholy part of dining alone in your hotel? It's when they come and take away all the other place settings and wine glasses, as if to say: 'Obviously no one will be joining *you* tonight, so we'll just whip away all these things and seat you here facing a pillar, and in a minute we'll bring you a very large basket with just one roll in it. Enjoy!'

So I lingered by the entrance of the Rex for the merest moment, then returned to the street. I was on a boulevard built on an important scale, though it had almost no traffic and was mostly lined with darkened office buildings lurking in dense growth. Several hundred yards further on I came to a hotel not unlike the Rex. It contained an Italian restaurant with its own entrance, which was probably as good as I was going to get. I went in and was taken aback to realize that it was full of locals, dressed up as if for an occasion. Something in their familiar manner with the waiters, and with the surroundings generally, bespoke a more than transient relationship with the place. When locals eat in the restaurant of a big glass and concrete hotel, you know that the community must be in some measure wanting.

The waiter took away all the other place settings, but he brought me six breadsticks – enough to share if I made a friend. It was quite a jolly place with everyone around me getting comprehensively refreshed – the Australians do like a drink, bless them – and the food was outstanding, but it was nonetheless evident that we were dining in a hotel. Canberra has quite a lot of this, as I was to discover – eating and drinking in large, characterless hotels and other neutral spaces, so that you spend much of the time feeling as if you are on some kind of long layover at an extremely spacious international airport.

Afterwards, bloated with pasta, three bottles of Italian lager and all six of the breadsticks (I never did make a friend), I went for another exploratory amble, this time in a slightly contrary direction, certain that somewhere in Canberra there must be a normal pub and possibly a convivial restaurant for the following evening, but I passed nothing and once again found myself eventually on the threshold of the Rex. I looked at my watch. It was only nine thirty in the evening. I wandered into the cocktail lounge, where I ordered a beer and took a seat in a deep-backed chair. The lounge was empty but for a table with three men and a lady at it, getting boisterously merry, and a lone gent hunched over a tumbler at the bar.

I drank my beer and pulled out a small notebook and pen and placed them on the table in front of me in case I was taken with a sudden important observation, then followed that with a book I had bought at a second-hand bookshop in Sydney. Called *Inside Australia* and published in 1972, it was by the American journalist John Gunther, a name that once towered in the annals of travel journalism but is now, I fear, largely forgotten. It was his last book; it just about had to be as he died while preparing it, poor man.

I opened it to the chapter on Canberra, curious to see what he had to say about the place back then. The Canberra he describes is a small city of 130,000 people with the 'pastoral feeling of a country town' – an easygoing place with few traffic lights, little nightlife, a modest sprinkling of cocktail lounges and about 'half a dozen good' restaurants. In a word, it appeared actually to have gone backwards since 1972. I was proud to see that the Rex Hotel was singled out as a stylish address for visitors – always nice to see one's choices validated even when they are nearly thirty years out of date – and that its cocktail bar was adjudged one of the liveliest in the city. I looked up from my book and shrank at the thought that very possibly it still was.

At length I turned to the chapter on Australian politics – my reason for buying the book in the first place. Apart from the scoring of Australian Rules Football and the appeal of a much-esteemed dish called the pie floater (think of something unappetizing and brown floating on top of something unappetizing and green and you pretty well have it) there is nothing in Australian life more complicated and bewildering to the outsider than its politics. I had tried once or twice to wade through books on Australian politics written by Australians, but all these had started from the novel premise that the subject is interesting – a bold position, to be sure, but not a very helpful one – so I was hoping that the detached observations of a fellow American might be more instructive. Gunther gave it a game stab, I must say, but it was a challenge beyond even his talents for lucid compression. Here, for instance, is just a snippet of his attempt to explain Australia's system of preference voting:

> *If, after the second-preference votes are added to the first, there is still no candidate with a majority of the total ballots cast, the process is repeated: the ballots of the candidate trailing at this stage of the computation are divided up on the basis of second preference. If he inherited some second-preference votes from the first man eliminated, these are now redistributed on the basis of third preference. And so on.*

I particularly liked that casual concluding 'And so on.' It's a deft piece of work because it seems to say: 'I understand all this perfectly, but I see no need to tax you with the details,' whereas of course what he is really saying is: 'I haven't the faintest idea what any of this means and frankly I don't give two tiny mouse droppings because, as I pen these words, I am sitting in the lounge bar of a bush mausoleum called the Rex Hotel and it's a Friday night and I am half cut and bored out of my mind and now I am going to go and get another drink.' The uncanny thing was I knew the feeling exactly.

I glanced at my watch, appalled to realize it was only ten minutes after ten, and ordered another beer, then picked up the notebook and pen and, after a minute's thought, wrote: 'Canberra awfully boring place. Beer cold, though.' Then I thought for a bit more and wrote: 'Buy socks.' Then I put the notebook down, but not away, and tried without much success to eavesdrop on the conversation among the lively foursome across the room. Then I decided to come up with a new slogan for Canberra. First I wrote: 'Canberra – There's Nothing to It!' and then 'Canberra – Why Wait for Death?' Then I thought some more and wrote: 'Canberra – Gateway to Everywhere Else!', which I believe I liked best of all. Then I ordered another beer and drew a little cartoon. It showed two spawning salmon, halfway up a series of lively cascades, resting exhausted in a pool of calm water, when one turns to the other and says: 'Why don't we just stop here and have a wank?' This amused me very much and I put the page in my pocket against the day I learn to draw objects that people can actually recognize. Then I eavesdropped on the people some more, nodding and smiling appreciatively when they appeared to make a quip in the hope that they would see me and invite me over, but they didn't. Then I had another beer.

I think the last beer might have been a mistake because I don't remember much after that other than a sensation of supreme goodwill towards anyone who passed through the room, including a Filipino lady who came in with a hoover and asked me to lift my legs so that she could clean under my chair. My notes for the evening show only two other entries, both in a slightly unsteady hand. One says: 'Victoria Bitter – why called??? Not bitter at all. But quite nice!!!' The other said: 'I tell you, Barry, he was farting sparks!' I believe this was in reference to a colourful Aussie turn of phrase I overheard from the people at the next table rather than to any actual manifestation of flatulence of an electrical nature.

But I could be wrong. I'd had a few.

In the morning I woke to find Canberra puddled under a dull, persistent rain. My plan was to stroll across the main bridge over Lake Burley Griffin, to a district of museums and government buildings on the other side. It was a rotten morning, a foolish day to be out on foot, made more wretched by the slow-dawning realization, once I had set off from the hotel, that I was embarked on an expedition even more epic than the one the afternoon before. Canberra really is the most amazingly spacious city. On paper it looks quite inviting, with its serpentine lake, leafy avenues and

10,000 acres of parks (for purposes of comparison, Hyde Park in London is 340 acres), but at ground level it is simply a great deal of far-flung greenness, broken at distant intervals by buildings and monuments.

It is worth considering how it got this way. In 1911, with the capital site chosen, a competition was held for a design for it, which was won by Walter Burley Griffin of Oak Park, Illinois, a disciple of Frank Lloyd Wright. Griffin's design was unquestionably the best, but that doesn't necessarily mean a great deal. Another leading entrant, a Frenchman named Alfred Agache, failed to read the briefing notes carefully, or possibly at all, and placed Parliament and many other important buildings on a flood plain, guaranteeing that legislators would have to spend part of the year treading water while debating. Also, for reasons that can only invite wondered speculation, he placed the municipal sewage works in the very heart of the city, as a kind of centrepiece. Despite these quirky shortcomings, his entry came third. Second prize went to Eliel Saarinen, father of Eero, the man who later persuaded the Opera House judges to choose the bold design of Jørn Utzon. The elder Saarinen's design was perfectly workable, but it had a kind of brutal grandeur about it – a sort of proto-Third Reichish quality – that unsettled the Australian judges.

Griffin's plan, by contrast, was instantly engaging. It envisaged a garden city of 75,000 people, with tree-lined avenues angling through it and an ornamental lake at its heart. Handsome and confident, majestic but not imperious, it ideally suited the modest yearnings for respectability without fuss that marked the Australian character. Moreover, Griffin had an advanced understanding of the importance of presentation. His submissions were not modest sketches that looked as if they had been scribbled on the back of a cocktail napkin, but a series of large panoramic tableaux, exquisitely drafted on the finest stretched linen. In this he was assisted inestimably – totally, in fact – by his new bride, Marion Mahony Griffin, who was without doubt one of the great architectural artists of this century.

The drawings, all done by Marion, show a silhouetted skyline full of comely shapes – a dome here, a ziggurat there – but with surprisingly little in the way of committing details. They are tantalizing impressions – ethereal, cunningly distant. These are drawings you could gaze at for hours with pleasure, but turn your back for a moment and you cannot remember a thing that was in them, other than a vague sense of a pleasing composition. Although Griffin and his wife had never been to Australia (they worked from topographic maps) the drawings show an almost uncanny affinity for the landscape – an appreciation of its simple uncluttered beauty and big skies that you would swear was based on the closest acquaintanceship. Take nothing away from Walter: he was a gifted, occasionally even inspired, architect; but Marion was the genius of the outfit.

The Griffins had a decidedly bohemian bent – he liked big floppy hats and velvety ties; she had an unfortunate fondness for dancing through woodland glades in diaphanous gowns, in the manner of Isadora Duncan – and this no doubt counted against them in the rough and ready world of Australian politics in the second decade of the century. In any case, they found little in the way of funds or enthusiasm awaiting them when they arrived in Australia in 1913, and the outbreak of the First World War the following year made both scarcer still. Once on site, Griffin seemed unable to get to grips with things. He had no experience of managing a big project and clearly it did not suit his temperament. By 1920, no work at all had been done beyond a cursory staking out of the main roads. At the end of the year, more or less by mutual agreement, he left the project.

Griffin stayed in Australia another fifteen years and became one of the country's most illustrious architects, but nearly all the buildings he designed either were never built or have since been torn down. Increasingly beset by financial difficulties, he moved to India in 1935. There, in 1937 he contracted peritonitis after falling from some scaffolding and died, aged sixty. He was buried in an unmarked grave. Today almost all that remains from a long and busy career are Newman College at the University of Melbourne, a couple of municipal incinerators, and Canberra – and Canberra isn't really his at all.

Only the floor plan, so to speak, is his – the avenues, the roundabouts, the lake that cuts the city in half. The component parts fell to scores of other hands, none working together. An entirely new city was built on his layout, but it has none of the coherence that his design implied. It's really just a scattering of government buildings in a man-made wilderness. Even the lake, which winds a serpentine way between the commercial and parliamentary halves of the city, has a curiously dull, artificial feel. On a sloping promontory on its wooded north shore was a modestly sized building called the National Capital Exhibition, and I called there first, more in the hope of drying off a little than from any expectation of extending my education significantly.

It was quite busy. In the front entrance, two friendly ladies were seated at a table handing out free visitors' packs – big, bright yellow plastic bags – and these were accepted with expressions of gratitude and rapture by everyone who passed.

'Care for a visitors' pack, sir?' called one of the ladies to me.

'Oh, yes please,' I said, more thrilled than I wish to admit. The visitors' pack was a weighty offering, but on inspection it proved to contain nothing but a mass of brochures – the complete works, it appeared, of the visitors' centre I had visited the day before. The bag was so heavy that it stretched the handles until it was touching the floor. I dragged it around for a while, and then thought to abandon it behind a pot plant. And here's the thing. There wasn't room behind the pot plant for another yellow bag! There must have been ninety of them back there. I looked around and noticed that almost no one in the room still had a plastic bag. I leaned mine against the wall beside the plant and as I straightened up I saw that a man was advancing towards me.

'Is this where the bags go?' he asked gravely.

'Yes, it is,' I replied with equal gravity.

In my momentary capacity as director of internal operations I watched him lean the bag carefully against the wall. Then we stood for a moment together and regarded it judiciously, pleased to have contributed to the important work of moving hundreds of yellow bags from the foyer to a mustering station in the next room. As we stood, two more people came along. 'Place them just there,' we suggested, almost in unison, and indicated where we were sandbagging the wall. Then we exchanged satisfied nods and moved off into the museum.

The National Capital Exhibition was excellent. These things in Australia generally are. It wasn't a large building, but it gave a good grounding in the history and development of Canberra. What surprised me was how very recent most of it is. Several of the walls had blown-up photographs of Canberra as it was in times past, and most of these were arresting when compared with the present. Lake Burley Griffin,* for instance, wasn't filled until 1964. Before that,

* Whoever named the lake evidently didn't realize that Burley was Walter's middle name, not part of his surname.

for many years, it was just a muddy depression between the two halves of the city. On another wall a pair of matched aerial photographs showed Canberra in 1959 (pop. 39,000) and Canberra now (pop. 330,000). Apart from the addition of a few large buildings in what is known as the Parliamentary Zone and the filling of the lake, what was remarkable was how little changed the city looked.

Thus briefed, I was eager now to see it all with my own eyes, so I left the building and ventured along the wooded lakeside to the Commonwealth Avenue Bridge and set off for the distant and, as it were, official side of the city. The rain had stopped, but Lake Burley Griffin contains an engineering wonder (the wonder being why they bothered) called the Captain Cook Memorial Jet, a plume of water that shoots a couple of hundred feet into the air in a dazzlingly unarresting manner, then catches the prevailing breeze and drifts in a fine but drenching spray over the bridge and whatever is on it. Sighing, I pushed through it and emerged on the other side into an area of the most extravagantly spacious lawns, punctuated at distant intervals with government buildings and museums, each as remote as objects viewed through the wrong end of a telescope.

Even the National Capital Authority, the governing body for the city, admits in a promotional fact sheet that 'many people believe the Parliamentary Zone has an empty and unfinished character, where the vast distances between the institutions and other facilities discourage pedestrian movement and activity.' I'll say. It was like walking around the site of a very large world's fair that had never quite got off the ground.

I called first at the National Library because I wanted to see the *Endeavour* Journal, Captain Cook's famous diary of his voyage. Cook naturally took the journal home with him after his epic trip of discovery, but it was lost soon after his death and remained lost for almost one hundred and fifty years before it turned up unexpectedly at a Sotheby's auction in London in 1923. The Australian government hurriedly bought it for £5,000 (almost double what it was prepared to pay for the design of the city in which it sits) and it is now treated with the sort of reverence we in America reserve for ancient treasures like the Constitution and Nancy Reagan. Unfortunately, as I discovered when I presented myself at the information desk, it isn't out on display, but rather is shown just once a week by appointment.

I stared at the man in dismay. 'But I've travelled eight thousand miles,' I blurted.

'I'm sorry,' he said and seemed to mean it.

'I spent a night in the Rex,' I said, thinking surely that would clinch it, but he was powerless to help. He did, however, direct me to a leaflet in which I could see a picture of the journal and encouraged me to have a look round the public galleries. As it happened, these were splendid. One room held paintings showing Australians of note (well, of note to other Australians) and in another was an exhibition of the original drawings for the Sydney Opera House. These included not only Utzon's winning sketches, but the second- and third-place entries – both radiantly undistinguished. Second place went to a fat cylinder with a harlequin-style pattern in stainless steel. Third place looked like a large supermarket. In a glass case was a wooden model made by Utzon showing that the sails of the Opera House roof were not meant to echo the sailboats in the harbour (an assertion that is made over and over in books and articles, inside Australia and out) but are simply sections of a sphere.

Then it was across another thousand acres of undeveloped veldt to the National Gallery, a surprisingly big museum in a fortress-like building. It was airy and various and generally very good. I was particularly taken with the outback paintings of Arthur Streeton, of whom I had not heard, and with the large collection of Aboriginal paintings, mostly done on curled bark or other natural surfaces and covered in colourful dots and squiggles. It is a fact little noted that the Aborigines have the oldest continuously maintained culture on earth, and their art goes back to the very roots of it. Imagine if there were some people in France who could take you to the caves at Lascaux and explain in detail the significance of the paintings – why this bison is bolting from the herd, what these three wavy lines mean – because it is as fresh and sensible to them as if it were done yesterday. Well, Aborigines can do that. It is an unparalleled human achievement, scarcely appreciated, and I think that is worth a mention here, don't you agree?

I had intended to go on to Parliament House, but I emerged from the National Gallery to find that the afternoon was almost gone. I would have to leave that for the next day. I started back down the gentle slope towards the lake and bridge. The skies were clearing at last and on the far-off hills lay patches of silvery light. Now that the clouds had ceased their low-level assault and retired to fluffier heights, the view was really quite fine. Canberra is a city of memorials, most of them fairly grand and nearly all with a private avenue of trees, and from here I could take them in with a single panning motion of my head. It reminded me less of a city – much less – than of, say, a preserved battlefield. There was that sense of spaciousness and respectful greenness that you would expect to find at Gettysburg or Waterloo.

It was impossible to believe that 330,000 people were tucked into that view and it was this thought – startling when it hit me – that made me change my perception of Canberra completely. I had been scorning it for what was in fact its most admirable achievement. This was a place that had, without a twitch of evident stress, multiplied by a factor of ten since the late 1950s and yet was still a park.

I imagined some sweet little American community such as Aspen, Colorado, trying to absorb 300,000 additional residents in forty years and thought of the miles of random, carelessly dribbled infrastructure that that would require – the shopping malls and parking lots, the eight-lane roads stretching off into a forest of bright signs and elevated hoardings, the vast graded acres of housing ('bye, woods! 'bye, farm!), the distant plazas of supermarkets and box stores, the tangled ganglia of motels, petrol stations and fast food places. Well, there is virtually none of this in Canberra. What an accomplishment that is. My feeling for the place was transformed entirely.

Still, I must say a decent pub or two wouldn't go amiss.

II

Now here is why you will never understand Australian politics. In 1972, after twenty-three years of rule by the conservative Liberal Party, Australia elected a Labor government under the leadership of the dashing and urbane Gough Whitlam. At once Whitlam's government embarked on a programme of ambitious reforms – it gave Aborigines rights they had not previously enjoyed, began to disengage Australian troops from Vietnam, made university education free, and much more. But, as sometimes happens, the government gradually lost its majority and by 1975 Parliament was in a deadlock from which neither Whitlam nor the leader of the opposition, Malcolm Fraser, would budge.

Into this impasse stepped the Governor-General, Sir John Kerr, the Queen's official representative in Australia. Using a reserve privilege not before invoked, he dissolved Whitlam's government, placed Fraser in control and ordered a general election. The outrage and indignation Australians felt at this high-handed interference can scarcely be described. The country was thrown into a fury of resentment. Before they had had any real chance to sort out their differences themselves, an unelected representative of a government on the other side of the planet had taken the matter out of their hands. It was a humiliating reminder that Australia was still at root a colony, constitutionally subordinate to the United Kingdom. *

Nonetheless, as required, the Australians held a general election at which the voters overwhelmingly – overwhelmingly – turned Whitlam out of office and brought in Fraser. In other words, the electorate calmly endorsed the action that had so exercised the nation only a month before.

And that, as I say, is why you will never understand Australian politics.

Part of the problem, of course, is that it is nearly impossible to track Australian politics from abroad because so little news of the country's affairs leaks out into the wider world. But even when you are there and dutifully trying to follow it, you find yourself mired in a density of argument, a complexity of fine points, a skein of tangled relationships and enmities, that thwarts all understanding. Give Australians an issue and they will argue it so passionately and in such detail, from so many angles, with the introduction of so many loosely connected side issues, that it soon becomes impenetrable to the outsider.

At the time of my visit the big national issue was whether Australia was to become a republic – whether it was going to snip its last colonial ties to Britain and take the steps necessary to ensure that no future John Kerr ever similarly humbled the nation again. It seemed to me no issue. Surely any nation would want to have control of its own destiny? You would expect, at the very least, that the decision would be a straightforward one.

Yet for two years to my certain knowledge Australians had been tying themselves in knots over every possible objection to such a change. Who will be the new president under such a system and how can we guarantee that he never does anything he shouldn't do? What becomes of all those names like 'Royal Australian Air Force' and 'Royal Flying Doctor Service' if we're not actually royal any longer? What words shall we put in the new preamble to the constitution? Shall we refer to the Australian quality of 'mateship' as John Howard would like or shall we recognize that that is a fundamentally vacuous and embarrassing concept? Oh

* Not so! Kerr acted off his own bat and was not directed by the UK government or the Queen. A non-executive President could have the same reserve powers.

dear, this is awfully complicated. Maybe it would be better if we just left things as they are, and hope the British are good to us.

I don't mean to suggest that these are not important issues, of course. But it is an exhausting process to witness, and you do rather come away with two interlinked impressions – that Australians love to argue for argument's sake and that basically they would rather just leave everything as it is. In the end, of course, they voted against a republic, though at the time of my visit that seemed an extremely unlikely outcome. Yet another reason why outsiders will never understand Australian politics.

On the other hand, and what makes up for a lot, is that Australians have the best and most entertaining parliamentary debates anywhere. American and even British television news coverage would be vastly enlivened if it provided a nightly report from Australia's parliamentary chambers. You wouldn't have to explain what it was all about – it generally surpasses understanding anyway – but just allow the audience to savour the rich thrust and parry of Australian insult.

In his book *Among the Barbarians*, the Australian writer Paul Sheehan records an exchange in Parliament between a man named Wilson Tuckey and the then Prime Minister Paul Keating of which the following is a small part:

> *Tuckey: 'You are an idiot. You are just a hopeless nong . . .'*
> *Keating: 'Shut up! Sit down and shut up, you pig . . . Why do you not shut up, you clown? . . . This man has a criminal intellect . . . this clown continues to interject in perpetuity.'*

This was actually a fairly tame exchange for the linguistically versatile Mr Keating. Among the epithets that have taken flight from his tongue during the course of public debate, and are to be found gracing the pages of whatever is the Australian equivalent of *Hansard*, have been *scumbags*, *pieces of criminal garbage*, *sleazebags*, *stupid foul-mouthed grubs*, *piss-ants*, *mangy maggot*, *perfumed gigolos*, *gutless spivs*, *boxheads*, *immoral cheats*, and *stunned mullets*. And that was just to describe his mother. (I'm joking, of course!) Not all parliamentary invective is quite so ripe, but it is nearly all pretty good.

I had watched this sort of thing with the greatest of pleasure during my various Australian visits, so you can imagine the eagerness with which I parked my car in the visitors' area on Parliament Hill the next morning and proceeded across the manicured lawns for a quick look round before moving on to Adelaide.

Parliament House is a new building, which replaced an older, more modest Parliament House in 1988. It is a rather arrestingly horrible edifice, crowned with a ridiculous erection that looks like nothing so much as a very big Christmas-tree stand. On the way in, I stopped beside a large ornamental pool to have a look at the rooftop erection.

'Largest aluminium structure in the southern hemisphere,' declared, with evident pride, a man with a camera around his neck who saw me studying it.

'And are there many other aluminium structures competing for the honour?' I asked before I could stop myself.

The man looked flustered. 'Why, I don't know,' he said. 'But if there are they're smaller.'

I hadn't meant to offend. 'Well, it's certainly very . . . striking,' I offered.

'Yes,' he agreed. 'I think that's the word for it. Striking.'

'How much aluminium is in it?' I asked.

'Oh, I've no idea. But a great deal, you can be sure of that.'

'Enough to wrap a lot of sandwiches!' I suggested brightly.

He looked at me as if I were dangerously stupid. 'I don't know about that,' he said and, after a moment's befuddled hesitation, took his leave.

As it was a Sunday morning, I hadn't expected Parliament House to be open to visitors, but it was. I had to submit to a security inspection and had a small pocket-knife taken away from me and twenty minutes later was sawing away on a scone in the cafeteria with something far more lethal. The whole of Parliament House is rather like that – superficially grave and security-conscious, in keeping with the trappings of an important nation, but at the same time really quite relaxed, as if they know that no international terrorists are going to come storming over the parapets and that visitors are mostly just people like you and me who want to see where it all happens and then have a nice cup of tea and a cautiously flavourful treat in the cafeteria afterwards.

Inside it was much handsomer than the bland exterior had suggested, with a lot of native woods covering the floors and walls. Best of all, you weren't herded round in a group but left to explore on your own. I have never been in America's Capitol Building, but I dare say they don't just leave you to wander as whimsy takes you. I felt here as if I could go anywhere – that if I had known which was the right door I could have slipped into the Prime Minister's office and scribbled a note on his blotter or perhaps left my salmon cartoon to brighten his day. A couple of times I furtively tried door handles. They were always locked, but no alarms went off and no security people crashed through the windows to smother me with nets and take me away for interrogation. In the areas where security people were posted, they were always friendly and happy to answer any questions. I was very impressed.

Australia's Parliament is divided into two chambers, the House of Representatives and the Senate (interesting, in a very low-grade sort of way, that they use the British term for the institution and the American terms for the chambers), and both of these were open for inspection from the visitors' galleries. Both were quite small, but handsomer than I had expected. On television the green of the House of Representatives has a decidedly bilious look, as if the members are debating inside someone's pancreas, but in person it was much more tasteful and restrained. The Senate, which I had never seen on television (I believe because the Senators don't actually *do* anything – though I will check my John Gunther and get back to you on this), was in a restful ochre tone.

In a large upstairs foyer was a gallery containing portraits in oil of all the Prime Ministers, which I toured with interest. I had been doing quite a lot of reading, as you can imagine, so there was a real pleasure – a genuine oh-I've-heard-so-much-about-you quality – in seeing their faces at last. Here was kindly old Ben Chifley, a Labor PM just after the war and so much a man of the people that when in Canberra he stayed in the modest Kurrajong Hotel at a cost to the taxpayer of just six shillings a day, and could be found each morning strolling in his dressing gown to the communal bathroom to shave and wash with the other guests. Then there was the grand and leonine Robert Menzies, who was Prime Minister for twenty years but thought of himself as 'British to the bootstraps' and dreamed of retiring to a cottage in the English countryside, evidently happy to turn his back on his native soil for ever. And poor old Harold Holt whose fateful plunge into the sea in 1967 earned him my permanent devotion.

It's quite a small club. Since 1901 Australia has had just twenty-four Prime Ministers, and I was startled to realize how many of them remained unfamiliar to me. Of the twenty-four, I counted fourteen of whom I knew essentially nothing, including eight –

exactly one third – of whom I had not even heard. These included the festively named Sir Earle Christmas Grafton Page, who was, to be fair, Prime Minister for less than a month in 1939, but also William McMahon, who held the office for almost two years in the early 1970s and whose existence was until this moment quite unsuspected by me.

I would have felt worse about this except that only the day before I had read an article in the papers reporting a government study that had found that Australians themselves were essentially as ignorant of these men as I was – that indeed more people in Australia could identify and discuss the achievements of George Washington than could provide similar service for their own first elected head of state, Sir Edmund Barton.

And with that sobering thought to ponder, I left the nation's capital and set off for distant Adelaide.

CHAPTER SEVEN

IT IS 800 MILES FROM CANBERRA WEST TO ADELAIDE, MOST OF IT along a lonely, half-forgotten road called the Sturt Highway. The highway was named for Captain Charles Sturt, who explored the region in a series of expeditions between 1828 and 1845. Apart from charting the languid course of the Murray River and its tributaries, Sturt's principal distinction was in being the first of the early explorers to show a measure of competence. He knew, for instance, to secure his horses at night. This might seem a self-evident requirement for anyone hundreds of miles into a desolate void, but it was a skill indifferently applied before him. John Oxley, the leader of a slightly earlier expedition, failed to keep his horses tethered and woke up one morning to find them all gone. He and his men spent five days, mostly on foot, rounding them all up. Soon after, the horses wandered off again. Nonetheless, Oxley is commemorated with a highway of his own in northern New South Wales. Australians are very generous in this respect.

The Sturt Highway begins near Wagga Wagga, a hundred miles or so west of Canberra, and crosses broad, flat, dust-brown sheep country known as the Riverina, an area of plains cut by the fidgety meanderings of the Murrumbidgee River. It provides a perfect demonstration in three dimensions of how swiftly you can be in the middle of nowhere in Australia. One minute I was in a comely world of paddocks, meadows and pale green hills, with little country towns scattered at reliably accommodating intervals, and the next I was alone in an almost featureless nowhere – a disc of brown earth under a dome of blue sky, with only an occasional gum interposed between the two. Such habitations as I passed through weren't really communities at all, but just a couple of houses and a petrol station, occasionally a pub, and eventually even they all but ceased. Between Narrandera, the last outpost of civilization, and Balranald, the next, lay 200 miles of highway without a town or hamlet on it. Every hour or so I would pass a lonely roadhouse – a petrol station with an attached café of the sort known in the happy vernacular of Australia as a chew and spew – and occasionally an earthen track bumping off to a distant, unseen sheep station. Otherwise nothing.

As if to emphasize the isolation, all the area radio stations began to abandon me. One by one their signals faltered, and all those smoky voices so integral to Australian airwaves – Vic Damone, Mel Torme, Frank Sinatra at the mindless height of his doo-bee-doo phase – faded away, as if being drawn by some heavy gravity back into the hole from which they had escaped. Eventually the radio dial presented only an uninterrupted cat's hiss of static, but for one clear spot near the end of the dial. At first I thought that's all it was – just an empty clear spot – but then I realized I could hear the faint shiftings and stirrings of seated people, and after quite a pause a voice, calm and reflective, said:

'Pilchard begins his long run in from short stump. He bowls and . . . oh, he's out! Yes, he's got him. Longwilley is caught leg-before in middle slops by Grattan. Well, now what do you make of that, Neville?'

'That's definitely one for the books, Bruce. I don't think I've seen offside medium slow fast pace bowling to match it since Baden-Powell took Rangachangabanga for a maiden ovary at Bangalore in 1948.'

I had stumbled into the surreal and rewarding world of cricket on the radio.

After years of patient study (and with cricket there can be no other kind) I have decided that there is nothing wrong with the game that the introduction of golf carts wouldn't fix in a hurry. It is not true that the English invented cricket as a way of making all other human endeavours look interesting and lively; that was merely an unintended side effect. I don't wish to denigrate a sport that is enjoyed by millions, some of them awake and facing the right way, but it is an odd game. It is the only sport that incorporates meal breaks. It is the only sport that shares its name with an insect. It is the only sport in which spectators burn as many calories as players (more if they are moderately restless). It is the only competitive activity of any type, other than perhaps baking, in which you can dress in white from head to toe and be as clean at the end of the day as you were at the beginning.

Imagine a form of baseball in which the pitcher, after each delivery, collects the ball from the catcher and walks slowly with it out to centre field; and that there, after a minute's pause to collect himself, he turns and runs full tilt towards the pitcher's mound before hurling the ball at the ankles of a man who stands before him wearing a riding hat, heavy gloves of the sort used to handle radioactive isotopes, and a mattress strapped to each leg. Imagine moreover that if this batsman fails to hit the ball in a way that heartens him sufficiently to try to waddle sixty feet with mattresses strapped to his legs he is under no formal compulsion to run; he may stand there all day, and, as a rule, does. If by some miracle he is coaxed into making a misstroke that leads to his being put out, all the fielders throw up their arms in triumph and have a hug. Then tea is called and everyone retires happily to a distant pavilion to fortify for the next siege. Now imagine all this going on for so long that by the time the match concludes autumn has crept in and all your library books are overdue. There you have cricket.

But it must be said there is something incomparably soothing about cricket on the radio. It has much the same virtues as baseball on the radio – an unhurried pace, a comforting devotion to abstruse statistics and thoughtful historical rumination, exhilarating micro-moments of real action – but stretched across many more hours and with a lushness of terminology and restful elegance of expression that even baseball cannot match. Listening to cricket on the radio is like listening to two men sitting in a rowing boat on a large, placid lake on a day when the fish aren't biting; it's like having a nap without losing consciousness. It actually helps not to know quite what's going on. In such a rarefied world of contentment and inactivity, comprehension would become a distraction.

'So here comes Stovepipe to bowl on this glorious summer's afternoon at the MCG,' one of the commentators was saying now. 'I wonder if he'll chance an offside drop scone here or go for the quick legover. Stovepipe has an unusual delivery in that he actually leaves the grounds and starts his run just outside the Carlton & United Brewery at Kooyong.'

'That's right, Clive. I haven't known anyone start his delivery that far back since Stopcock caught his sleeve on the reversing mirror of a number 11 bus during the third test at Brisbane in 1957 and ended up at Goondiwindi four days later owing to some frightful confusion over a changed timetable at Toowoomba Junction.'

After a very long silence while they absorbed this thought, and possibly stepped out to transact some small errands, they resumed with a leisurely discussion of the England fielding. Neasden, it appeared, was turning in a solid performance at square bowel, while Packet had been a stalwart in the dribbles, though even these exemplary performances paled when set beside the outstanding play of young Hugh Twain-Buttocks at middle nipple. The commentators were in calm agreement that they had not seen anyone caught behind with such panache since Tandoori took Rogan Josh for a stiffy at Vindaloo in '61. At last Stovepipe, having found his way over the railway line at Flinders Street – the footbridge was evidently closed for painting – returned to the stadium and bowled to Hasty, who deftly turned the ball away for a corner. This was repeated four times more over the next two hours and then one of the commentators pronounced: 'So as we break for second luncheon, and with 11,200 balls remaining, Australia are 962 for two not half and England are four for a duck and hoping for rain.'

I may not have all the terminology exactly right, but I believe I have caught the flavour of it. The upshot was that Australia was giving England a good thumping, but then Australia pretty generally does. In fact, Australia pretty generally beats most people at most things. Truly never has there been a more sporting nation. At the 1996 Olympics in Atlanta, to take just one random but illustrative example, Australia, the fifty-second largest nation in the world, brought home more medals than all but four other countries, all of them much larger (the countries, of course, not the medals). Measured by population, its performance was streets ahead of anyone else. Australians won 3.78 medals per million of population, a rate more than two and a half times better than the next best performer, Germany, and almost five times the rate of the United States. Moreover, Australia's medal-winning tally was distributed across a range of sports, fourteen, matched by only one other nation, the United States. Hardly a sport exists at which the Australians do not excel. Do you know, there are even forty Australians playing baseball at the professional level in the United States, including five in the Major Leagues – and Australians don't even *play* baseball, at least not in any particularly devoted manner. They do all this on the world stage *and* play their own games as well, notably a very popular form of loosely contained mayhem called Australian Rules Football. It is a wonder in such a vigorous and active society that there is anyone left to form an audience.

No, the mystery of cricket is not that Australians play it well, but that they play it at all. It has always seemed to me a game much too restrained for the rough-and-tumble Australian temperament. Australians much prefer games in which brawny men in scanty clothing bloody each other's noses. I am quite certain that if the rest of the world vanished overnight and the development of cricket was left in Australian hands, within a generation the players would be wearing shorts and using the bats to hit each other.

And the thing is, it would be a much better game for it.

In the late afternoon, while the players broke for high tea or fifth snack or something – in any case, when the activity on the field went from very slight to non-existent – I stopped at a roadhouse for petrol and coffee. I studied my book of maps and determined that I would stop for the night in Hay, a modest splat in the desert a little off the highway a couple of hours down the road. As it was the only community in a space of 200 miles, this was not a particularly taxing decision. Then, having nothing better to do, I leafed through the index and amused myself, in a very low-key way, by looking for ridiculous names, of which Australia has a respectable plenitude. I am thus able to report that the following are all real places: Wee Waa, Poowong, Burrumbuttock, Suggan Buggan, Boomahnoomoonah, Waaia, Mullumbimby, Ewlyamartup, Jiggalong and the supremely satisfying Tittybong.

As I paid, the man asked me where I was headed.

'Hay,' I replied, and was struck by a sudden droll thought. 'And I'd better hurry. Do you know why?'

He gave me a blank look.

'Because I want to make Hay while the sun shines.'

The man's expression did not change.

'I want to make Hay while the sun shines,' I repeated with a slight alteration of emphasis and a more encouraging expression.

The blank look, I realized after a moment, was probably permanent.

'Aw, you won't have any trouble with that,' the man said after a minute's considered thought. 'It'll be light for hours yet.'

*

Hay was a hot and dusty but surprisingly likeable little town off the Sturt Highway across an old bridge over the muddy Murrumbidgee. In the motel, I dumped my bag and reflexively switched on the TV. It came up on the cricket, and I sat on the foot of the bed and watched it with unwonted absorption for some minutes. Needless to say, very little was happening on the pitch. An official in a white coat was chasing after a blown piece of paper and several of the players were examining the ground by the stumps, evidently looking for something. I couldn't think what, but then one of the commentators noted that England had just lost a wicket, so I supposed it was that. After a time a lanky young man in the outfield, who had been polishing a ball on his trouser leg as if about to take a bite from it, broke into a loping run. At length he hurled the ball at the distant batsman, who insouciantly lifted his bat an inch from the ground and putted it back to him. These motions were scrupulously replicated three times more, then the commentator said: 'And so at the end of the four hundred and fifty-second over, as we break for afternoon nap, England have increased their total to seventeen. So still quite a lot of work for them to do if they're going to catch Australia before fourth snack.'

I went out for a stroll over the terrestrial hotplate that is inland New South Wales in summer. The day was extravagantly warm. Every leaf on the kerbside trees was limp, like a tongue hanging out. I wandered up and down both sides of Lachlan Street, the main drag, and then some way out into the country to enjoy the sunset – an event always of calm and golden glory in the bush – and in the hope, ever unfulfilled, of seeing some kangaroos hopping picturesquely into frame. Kangaroos are commoner in Australia now than they were before Europeans came because all the rural improvements – the encouragement of grassland, the creating of ponds and so on – have benefited them in the same way they have sheep and cattle. Nobody knows how many kangaroos the country holds, but the number is generally assumed to be over 100 million, making them not much less numerous than sheep. But could I find even one out here? I could not.

So I strolled back into town and passed the evening in my usual gracious style – lager cocktails in a forlorn and nearly empty pub, dinner of steak and salad in a restaurant next door, another stroll to the edge of town to look, in vain, for kangaroos by moonlight. I was back in my room by about nine thirty. I switched on the TV and was impressed to see that play was still going on. Give the cricketers their due. It may be light work but they put in the hours. The man in the white coat was still chasing paper, though it wasn't possible to tell if it was the same piece. England, according to the commentator, had lost another three wickets, which seemed rather absent-minded of them. At this rate they would soon run out of equipment altogether and have to call it a day.

Perhaps, I decided as I switched the TV off, that was what they were hoping for.

In the morning I treated myself to a big breakfast to fortify myself for another long day's drive. Breakfast is, of course, our most savage event in Western society (if you hesitate to agree, then I urge you to name me another occasion – any occasion at all – when you would happily devour an embryo), and Australians seem to have a good fix on this. A lot of it comes down to a mastery of bacon. Unlike the curled shoe tongues that are consumed in Britain or the boringly crisp, regimented strips we go for in America, Australian bacon has a rough, meaty, fair dinkum heartiness. It looks as if it was taken off the pig while it was trying to escape. You can almost hear the squeal in every bite. Lovely. Also, they cut their toast thick. In short, the Australians know what they are about with breakfasts.

And so, radiant with cholesterol and contentment, I returned to the lonesome road. Beyond Hay, the landscape was even more impossibly flat, brown, empty and dull. The monumental emptiness of Australia is not easy to convey. It is far and away the most thinly peopled of nations. In Britain the average population density is 632 people per square mile; in the United States the average is 76; across the world as a whole it is 117. (And, just for interest, in Macau, the record holder, it is a decidedly snug 69,000 people per square mile.) The Australian average, by contrast, is six people per square mile. But even that modest figure is wildly skewed because Australians overwhelmingly live in a few clustered spots along the coast and leave the rest of the country undisturbed. Indeed, the proportion of people in Australia who live in urban areas is, at 86 per cent, about as high as in Holland and nearly as high as in Hong Kong. Out here if you found six people occupying the same square mile it would be either a family reunion or an Aum Shinrikyo planning session.

From time to time I passed through long miles of mallee scrub – low shrubs just bushy enough and high enough to strangle any view – and very occasionally, in the open plains, I would spy a low line of vivid green on the right-hand horizon, which I presumed marked an irrigated zone along the Murrumbidgee. Otherwise nothing. Just hard earth that strained to support a little dry grass and the odd thorny acacia or bent eucalypt.

It wasn't always so. Although inland Australia has never been exactly verdant, much of the marginal land once experienced periods of relative lushness, sometimes lasting years, occasionally lasting decades, and it enjoyed a natural resiliency that let it spring back after droughts. Then in 1859 a man named Thomas Austin, a landowner in Winchelsea, Victoria, a little south of where I was now, made a big mistake. He imported twenty-four wild rabbits from England and released them into the bush for sport. It is hardly a novel observation that rabbits breed with a certain keenness. Within a couple of years they had entirely overrun Austin's property and were spreading into neighbouring districts. Fifty million years of isolation had left Australia without a single predator or parasite able even to recognize rabbits, much less dine off them, and so they proliferated amazingly.

Collectively their appetite was essentially insatiable. By 1880, two million acres of Victoria had been picked clean. Soon they were pushing into South Australia and New South Wales, advancing over the landscape at a rate of seventy-five miles per year. Until the rabbits came, much of the countryside where I was driving now was characterized by lush groves of emu bush, a shrub that grew to a height of about seven feet and was in flower for most of the year. It was by all accounts a beauty and its leaves a boon to nibbling creatures. But rabbits fell on the emu bush like locusts, devouring every bit of it – leaves, flowers, bark, stems – until none was to be found. The rabbits ate so much of everything that sheep and other livestock were forced to extend both their range and their diet, punishing yet wider expanses. As sheep yields fell, farmers perversely compensated by increasing stocking levels, adding to the general devastation.

The problem would have been acute enough, but in the 1890s, after forty unusually green years, Australia fell into a murderous, decade-long drought – the worst in its recorded history. As the earth cracked and turned to dust, the topsoil – already the thinnest in the world – blew away, never to be replenished. In the course of the decade, some 35 million sheep, more than half the nation's total, perished; 16 million went in a single pitiless year, 1902.

The rabbits, meanwhile, hopped on. By the time science finally came up with a solution, almost a century had passed since Thomas Austin tipped his twenty-four bunnies out of the bag. The weapon deployed against the rabbits was a miracle virus from South America called myxomatosis. Harmless to humans and other animals, it was phenomenally devastating to rabbits, with a mortality rate of 99.9 per cent. Almost at once the countryside filled with twitching, stumbling, very sick rabbits, and then with tens of millions of little corpses. Although just one rabbit in a thousand survived, those few that did were naturally resistant to myxomatosis, and it was resistant genes that they passed on when they began to breed again. It took a while for things to get rolling, but today Australia's rabbit numbers are back up to 300 million and climbing fast.

At all events, the damage to the landscape, much of it irreversible, had already been done. And all so some clown could have something to pot at from his veranda.

Just as you plunge into emptiness with startling abruptness in Australia, so you plunge out of it again. Shortly after crossing into South Australia in mid-afternoon, I found myself entering rolling hills of orange groves. It was so startling I got out and had a look. On one side lay arid emptiness – a plain of stretched hessian spattered with clumps of mallee. But before me, filling the view to the distant horizon, spread a biblical-looking promised land – citrus groves and vineyards and vegetable patches in every lush shade of green. As I pushed on, the balance between orchards and vineyards tipped increasingly in favour of the latter until eventually there was nothing but vineyards and I realized I had reached the Barossa Valley, a quite spectacularly pretty corner of South Australia, with rolling hills of abundant green that gave it, literally and metaphorically, a Mediterranean air.

It was mostly settled by German farmers, who started Australia's wine industry here. Today Australians are among the most wine-savvy people on earth, but that development is quite recent. A story often recounted is how the British wine expert Len Evans, on a visit to the country in the 1950s, asked for a glass of wine in a country hotel. The hotelier regarded him narrowly for a long moment and asked: 'What are you, some kind of poof?' Even now the wines for which the Barossa is celebrated – Chardonnay, Cabernet Sauvignon and Shiraz – are all recent arrivals. Into the 1980s, the government was paying growers to uproot Shiraz vines and produce sticky sweet Rieslings. I've never quite understood why tourists from the more prosperous end of the market are so drawn to wine-growing areas. They wouldn't, presumably, want to go and see cotton before it became Gap slacks or caviar being gutted from sturgeon, but give them a backdrop of vines and they appear to think they have found heaven. Having said that, the Barossa Valley *is* awfully appealing, particularly after a couple of days on the lonely and far-flung Sturt Highway.

I stopped for the night in Tanunda, a handsome and well-touristed little town, mostly built along one very long street, fetchingly shadowed with leafy trees. Given its popularity with tourists and its Germanic beginnings, I had rather feared that Tanunda would be themed accordingly, but apart from one or two restaurants with 'Haus' in their titles and the odd mention of wurst in shop windows, there was mercifully little attempt to exploit its heritage. It was the eve of Australia Day, the big national holiday, and Tanunda was busy with people who had come for a mini-break.

I found a room, not without some difficulty, then wandered to the main street for a stroll before dinner. It was crowded with people who, like me, were trying to fill that empty hour between the shops' closing and the moment when one might with propriety start to drink. I walked among them, happy to be back in civilization – happy, above all, to be able to eavesdrop on conversations that didn't involve sheep dip, temperamental machinery, new wells or land clearance. (Or rumps, sumps, pumps and stumps, as I had begun to think of it.) It was clear from the conversations that I had landed in Yuppieville. Most were engaged in the interesting middle-class pastime of identifying all the objects in shop windows that looked like objects belonging to people they knew. Wherever I lingered I could hear someone observing, 'Oh, look. Sarah's got a bowl just like that,' or 'Your mother used to have a tea service like that one. I wonder whatever became of it. You don't suppose she gave it to Samantha, do you?' A few couples were playing a slightly edgier version of this game, which involved supplementary comments like 'No, the one *you* broke was *much* nicer' and 'But how many pairs of pearl earrings do you *need*, for God's sake?' and 'Well, if she did give it to Samantha, I'm going to be extremely pissed off, frankly, because she promised it to me. You'll just have to have a word with her.'

These were the people, I guessed, who had driven the furthest to get here and most needed a drink. Or possibly were just assholes.

I liked Tanunda and had a very pleasant evening there, but there was absolutely nothing exceptional or eventful in the experience, so I am going to tell you instead a little story related to me by a lovely woman named Catherine Veitch.

Catherine Veitch was my oldest friend in Australia, both in the sense that she was my first chum there and also that she was just about old enough to be my mother. I met her at the Melbourne Writers' Festival in 1992. I can't remember the circumstances now other than that she approached me after a reading either to set me straight with regard to some mistake I had made in one of my books on language – she was of a scholarly bent and impatient with sloppiness – or to enlighten me concerning some aspect of Australian life on which I had imprudently commented in the question and answer session. The upshot is that we had a cup of tea in the cafeteria and the next day I took a tram to her house in St Kilda for lunch, where I met most of her family. Her children, of whom she seemed to have a large but indeterminate number, were all grown and living away, but most of them called in at various points in the afternoon, to borrow a tool or check for messages or burrow in the fridge. It was just the kind of household I had always longed to grow up in – happy, comfortable, nicely chaotic, full of shouted conversations of the 'Try looking in the cupboard at the top of the stairs' type. And I liked Catherine very much. She was kind and funny and thoughtful and direct.

So we became great friends – though it was a friendship based almost entirely on correspondence. She had never been to America, and I went to Australia once a year if I was lucky, and not always to Melbourne. But three or four times a year she would send me long, wonderfully discursive letters hammered out on a jumpy and wilful typewriter. These letters seldom took less than an hour to read. In a single page they could range over a galaxy of subjects – her childhood in Adelaide, the inadequacies of certain politicians (actually, of most politicians), why Australians lack confidence, what her children had been up to. Generally she stuck in a wad of cuttings from the *Age*, the Melbourne newspaper. Much of what I know about Australia I learned from her.

I loved those letters. They came from so far away – just getting an envelope from Australia still seemed to me a faintly wondrous event – and described events and experiences that were unexceptional to her but breathtakingly exotic to me: taking a tram into the city, suffering through a heatwave in December, attending a lecture at the Royal Melbourne Institute, shopping for curtains at David Jones, the big local department store. I can't explain it except to say that, without giving up any part of the life I had already, I wanted intensely to have all that in my life as well. So it was through her letters, more than from almost anything else, that I consolidated my fixation with Australia.

Her letters were always happy, but the last one I received from her was especially sunny. She and John, her husband, were about to sell the house in St Kilda and move to the Mornington Peninsula, south of Melbourne, to take up a life of gracious retirement beside the sea, fulfilling a dream of many years' duration. Just after she sent that letter, to the shock of everyone who knew her, she suffered a sudden heart attack and died. I'd have been on my way to visit her now. Instead all I can offer is my favourite of the many stories she told me.

In the 1950s, a friend of Catherine's moved with her young family into a house next door to a vacant lot. One day some builders arrived to put up a house on the lot. Catherine's friend had a three-year-old daughter who naturally took an interest in all the activity going on next door. She hung around on the margins and eventually the builders adopted her as a kind of mascot. They chatted to her and gave her little jobs to do and at the end of the week presented her with a little pay packet containing a shiny new half crown, or something.

She took this home to her mother who made all the appropriate cooings of admiration and suggested that they take it to the bank the next morning to deposit it in her account. When they went to the bank, the cashier was equally impressed and asked the little girl how she had come by her own pay packet.

'I've been building a house this week,' she replied proudly.

'Goodness!' said the cashier. 'And will you be building a house next week, too?'

'I will if we ever get the fucking bricks,' answered the little girl.

CHAPTER EIGHT

SOUTH AUSTRALIANS ARE VERY PROUD THAT THEIRS IS THE ONLY Australian state that never received convicts. What they don't often mention is that it was planned by one. In the early 1830s, Edward Gibbon Wakefield, a man of independent means and unsavoury inclinations, was in Newgate Prison in London, on a charge of abducting a female child for sweaty and nefarious purposes, when he hatched the idea to found a colony of freemen in Australia. His plan was to sell parcels of land to sober, industrious people – farmers and capitalists – and use the funds raised to pay the passage of labourers to work for them. The labourers would gain ennobling employment; the investors would acquire a workforce and a market; everyone would benefit. The scheme never worked terribly well in practice, but the result was a new colony, South Australia, and a delightful planned city, Adelaide.

Whereas Canberra is a park, Adelaide is merely full of them. In Canberra you have the sense of being in a very large green space you cannot ever quite find your way out of; in Adelaide you are indubitably in a city, but with the pleasant option of stepping out of it from time to time to get a breath of air in a spacious green setting. Makes all the difference. The city was laid out as two distinct halves facing each other across the green plain of the Torrens River, with each half fully enclosed by parks. On a map, therefore, central Adelaide forms a large, plump, somewhat irregular figure of eight, with parks creating the figure and the two inner halves of the city filling the holes. It works awfully well.

I had no special destination in mind, but the next morning as I drove into the city from Tanunda I passed through North Adelaide, the handsome and prosperous zone inside the top half of the figure eight, spotted an agreeable-looking hotel and impetuously threw the car at the kerb. I was on O'Connell Street, in a neighbourhood of old, well-preserved buildings with lots of trendy restaurants, pubs and cafés. After Canberra, I wasn't going to let a slice of urban heaven like this slip past. So I procured a room and lost not a moment getting back into the open air.

Adelaide is the most overlooked of Australia's principal cities. You could spend weeks in Australia and never suspect it was there, for it rarely makes the news or gets a mention in anyone's conversation. It is to Australia essentially what Australia is to the world – a place pleasantly regarded but far away and seldom thought about. And yet it is unquestionably a lovely city. Everyone is agreed on that, including millions who have never been there.

I had been just once myself, on a book tour a few months before. What remained from that experience was an impression of physical handsomeness coupled with an oddly pleased sense of doom on the part of the inhabitants. Remark to anyone in Adelaide what an agreeable place it is, and you will be told at once, with a kind of eager solemnity: 'Yes, but it's dying, you know.'

'Is it?' you say in a tone of polite concern.

'Oh yes,' confides your informant, nodding with grim satisfaction. Then, if you are very unlucky, the person will tell you all about the collapse of the Bank of South Australia, an event of fiscal carelessness that took years to conclude and is nearly as long in the telling.

Adelaide's problem, it appears, is geographical. The city stands on the wrong edge of civilized Australia, far from the vital Asian markets and with nothing on its own doorstep but a great deal of nothing. To the north and west lie a million-odd square miles of searing desert; to the south nothing but open sea all the way to Antarctica. Only to the east are there any cities, but even Melbourne is 450 miles away and Sydney nearer a thousand. Why would anyone build a factory in Adelaide when it is so far from its markets? It is a reasonable question, but somewhat undermined by the consideration that Perth is even more remote – 1,700 miles more remote in its lonely outpost on the Indian Ocean – yet has a far more vibrant economy. At all events, the bottom line is that Adelaide seems stuck in an unhappy place, in every sense of the word.

Yet to the casual observer it seems quite as affluent as any other big city in Australia, possibly even more so. Its central shopping district is better looking and at least as well used as the equivalent zones in Sydney or Melbourne, and its pubs, restaurants and cafés appear to be as bustling and lively as any entrepreneur could wish. It has an outstanding stock of Victorian buildings, an abundance of parks and comely squares, and constant small touches – an ornate lamp-post here, a stone lion there – that give it a dash of classiness and respectful venerability that Sydney and Melbourne all too often discarded for the sequined glitter of skyscrapers. It feels rather like an urban version of a gentlemen's club – comfortable, old-fashioned, quietly grand, slightly drowsy by mid-afternoon, redolent of another age.

As I strolled downhill past Pennington Gardens, one of the central parks, I became gradually and then overwhelmingly aware of the tide of human activity all moving in a single direction – thousands and thousands of people converging on a stadium in the park. I asked two young men what was going on and was told there was a cricket match between England and Australia at the Oval.

'What – here in Adelaide? Today?' I said in surprise.

He considered the question with the bemusement it merited. 'Well, either that,' he replied drily, 'or thirty thousand people have made one pretty amazing bloody mistake, wouldn't you say?' Then he smiled to show that he wasn't being aggressive or anything. It appeared that he and his partner had stopped for a gallon or two of refreshment en route.

'Do you know, are there still tickets left?' I asked.

'Nah, mate, sold out. Sorry.'

I nodded and watched them go. That was another very British thing I'd noticed about Australians – they apologized for things that weren't their fault.

I found my way along North Terrace, the city's grandest thoroughfare, to the South Australian Museum, a stately pile devoted to natural and anthropological history. I was interested to see if it displayed a fossil called *Spriggina*, named for a minor hero of mine called Reginald Sprigg. In 1946, Sprigg, then a young government geologist, was poking around in the blisteringly inhospitable Ediacaran Hills of the Flinders Ranges, some 300 miles north of Adelaide, when he made one of those miraculous discoveries in which Australian natural history almost impossibly abounds. You will recall from an earlier chapter the case of the strange and long-lost proto-ant *Nothomyrmecia macrops* found unexpectedly at a dusty hamlet in the middle of nowhere. Well, Sprigg's find was in much the same general area and, in its way, no less remarkable.

His special moment came when he clambered a few yards up a rocky slope to find a piece of shade and a comfortable rock to lean against to have his lunch. As he sat eating his sandwiches he idly stretched out a toe and turned over a hunk of sandstone. Sprigg left no informal account of the event, but I think we can safely imagine him pausing in his chewing – pausing for a long moment, mouth slightly open – to stare at what he had just turned over, then slowly creeping nearer to have a closer look. What he had just found, you see, was something that wasn't thought to exist.

For almost a century, since the time of Charles Darwin, scientists had been puzzled by an evolutionary anomaly – that 600 million years ago complex life forms of an improbable variety had suddenly burst forth on earth (the famous Cambrian explosion), but without any evidence of earlier, simpler forms that might have paved the way for such an event. Sprigg had just found that missing link, a piece of rock swimming in delicate pre-Cambrian fossils. He was looking, in effect, at the dawn of visible life – at something no one had ever seen before or ever expected to see. It was a moment of supreme geological significance. And if he had sat anywhere else – anywhere at all in the infinite baking expanse that is the Australian outback – it would not have been made, certainly not then, possibly not ever.

That's the thing about Australia, you see. It teems with interesting stuff, but at the same time it's so vast and empty and forbidding that it generally takes a remarkable stroke of luck to find it.

Unfortunately, in 1946 the world scientific community paid little heed to news from Australia, and Sprigg's reports of his findings, duly recorded in the *Transactions of the Royal Society of South Australia*, languished for two decades before their significance became generally appreciated. But never mind. In the end, credit fell where it was due: Sprigg was immortalized with the name of a fossil, and the epoch he uncovered became known as the Ediacaran, after the hills through which he had tramped.

Alas, the museum was not open when I passed by – closed for the national holiday, I supposed – and so my hopes of glimpsing the dawn of life were dashed. Wandering on through shady side streets, however, I found a second-hand bookshop open and was happy to take that as a consolation prize. Probably because new books have always been expensive in Australia, the country has outstanding second-hand bookshops. These always have a large section devoted to 'Australiana' and these sections never fail to amaze, if only because they show you what a remarkably self-absorbed people the Australians are. I don't mean that as a criticism. If the rest of the world is going to pay them no attention, then they must do it themselves surely. That seems fair enough to me. But you do find in any trawl through the jumbled stacks the most wondrous titles. One of the first I took down now was called *That's Where I Met My Wife: A Story of the First Swimming Pool in the National Capital at Canberra.* Nearby was a plump volume entitled *A Sense of Union: A History of Sydney University Football Club*. Beside that was a history of the South Australia Ambulance Service. There were hundreds of titles like this – books about things that could never possibly have been of interest to more than a handful of people. It's quite encouraging that these books exist, but somehow faintly worrying as well.

Among them, however, you will often find the most rewarding surprises. This was so now when I took down a photographic history of Surfers Paradise, the famous Queensland beach resort, which caught my eye because I was heading there shortly. The book covered the story of the resort's development from the 1920s, when it was a flyblown coastal hamlet of neither fame nor consequence, to the early 1970s, when it abruptly burst forth as a kind of Miami Beach of the southern hemisphere. What particularly captivated me were the photographs of it during its intermediate phase, in the 1940s and '50s, when it was much closer in spirit and appearance to Coney Island or Blackpool. It is odd to be filled with a nostalgic longing for a place you have never known, but I was with Surfers Paradise and its innocent holidaymakers. I gazed enraptured at page after page of crisp black-and-white photographs showing happy people at play – strolling in groups along the Esplanade, jitterbugging in dance halls, sitting with drinks at surfside bars. How I envied them their snazzy outfits. I realize I may be in a minority here, but I would give almost anything to live in an age when I could put on two-tone shoes, red socks, a lively cotton shirt with a repeating pattern based on, say, baggage labels, hoist my baggy brown pants to *just* level with my nipples, drop a felt hat on my head and have people walking past look at me twice and think: '*Stylish guy!*'

There was something so marvellously innocent, so irretrievably lost, about the world back then. You could see it in the easy, confident gait and sun-drenched smiles of the holidaymakers in every photograph. These people were *happy*. I don't mean they were happy. They were *happy*. They were living at a good time in a lucky country and they knew it. They had good jobs, good homes, good families, good prospects, good holidays in cheerful, sunny places. I wouldn't suggest for an instant that Australians are unhappy people now – anything but, in fact – but they don't have that happiness in their faces any more. I don't think anybody does.

It was, it must be said, an age of the most dazzling primness. In the 1950s, Australia was probably the least confident nation in the English-speaking world. It was so far from everywhere that the authorities didn't seem to know quite what was acceptable, so essentially they played it safe and allowed nothing. One of the photographs in the Surfers Paradise book showed a souvenir emporium that had a very large billboard on its roof. The ad on the billboard was the famous Coppertone suntan lotion ad in which a small girl is having her swimsuit pulled down by an impish puppy, exposing an inch or two of sweet little bottom. And here's the thing. Someone had got out a ladder, climbed up with a bucket of paint and carefully painted panties over the little girl's crack. (Well, can't have people masturbating on the Esplanade, after all.) It wasn't just suntan lotion ads that were censored, but movies, plays, magazines and books in numbers unbelievable.

One thing you won't find much in Australian second-hand bookshops are 1950s or earlier editions of lots of books – *The Catcher in the Rye*, *A Farewell to Arms*, *Animal Farm*, *Peyton Place*, *Another Country*, *Brave New World* and hundreds and hundreds of others. The reason for this is simple: they were banned. Altogether, at its peak, 5,000 titles were forbidden to be imported into the country. By the 1950s this had fallen to a couple of hundred, but it still featured some extraordinary exclusions – *Childbirth Without Pain*, for instance, whose unflinching candour in describing where babies come from was considered a little too rich for Australian sensibilities. This was just conventional titles, by the way. The total doesn't include smutty stuff, which was of course banned outright. It wasn't just that you couldn't get certain books. You couldn't even find out which ones you couldn't get because the list of proscribed books was itself a secret.

It was Adelaide, interestingly, that put an end to all this. For decades it had been one of the more arrestingly unprogressive of Australian cities. The blame for this can be dropped in the lap of one Sir Thomas Playford, who for thirty-eight years, from the 1930s to the 1960s, was South Australia's premier. Playford was a man so parochial that once during a commodities crisis he suggested that the state might have to 'import wheat from Australia', and on another occasion remarked to the Vice Chancellor of the University of Adelaide that he couldn't see any point in universities at all. As you can imagine, he did not notably enrich the intellectual vigour of South Australia. Then in 1967 the state elected a youthful and charismatic Labor premier named Don Dunstan, and almost at once Adelaide and South Australia underwent a transformation. The city became a haven for artists and intellectuals. The Adelaide Festival blossomed into the nation's preeminent cultural event. Books that were still banned elsewhere in Australia – *Portnoy's Complaint* and *Naked Lunch*, for example – were freely available in Adelaide. Nude bathing beaches were allowed. Homosexuality was legalized. For one giddy decade or so, Adelaide was the hippest city in the country – the San Francisco of the antipodes.

In 1979, Dunstan's wife died and he abruptly retired from politics. Adelaide lost its momentum and began a gentle descent into obscurity. The artists and intellectuals drifted away; even Dunstan moved to Victoria. Under Playford South Australia had been backward but interestingly so. Under Dunstan it was racy and exhilaratingly so. The real problem with Adelaide these days, I suspect, is that it has just stopped being interesting.

Still, it's a lovely place for an amble on a summer's day. I made a couple of small purchases in the bookshop – an old hardback called *Australian Paradox*, which I bought for no more solid reason than that I rather liked the cover and it was attractively priced at $2, and a more recent volume entitled *Crocodile Attack in Australia*, which was nearly ten times dearer but had the compensating virtue of containing a great many gruesome anecdotes – then wandered off for a hike through the city's green and commodious parks.

Central Adelaide boasts almost 1,800 acres of parks, less than Canberra but a great deal more than most other cities of its size. As so often in Australia, they reflect an effort to recreate a familiarly British ambience in an antipodean setting. Of all the things people longed for when they first came to Australia, an English backdrop was perhaps the most outstanding. It is notable, when you look at early paintings of the country, how awkward, how strikingly un-Australian, the landscape so often appears. Even the gum trees look unusually lush and globular, as if the artists were willing them to take on a more English aspect. Australia was a disappointment to the early settlers. They ached for English air and English vistas. So when they built their cities, they laid them out with rolling English-style parks arrayed with stands of oak, beech, chestnut and elm in a way that recalled the dreamily bucolic efforts of Humphry Repton or Capability Brown. Adelaide is the driest city in the driest state on the driest continent, but you would never guess it from wandering through its parks. Here it is forever Sussex.

Unfortunately, such arrangements are out of fashion in the horticultural world. Since many of the original plantings are now coming to the end of their natural lives, the park authorities have instituted plans to sweep away the intruder species and recreate a riverine landscape dominated by mallee scrub and red river gums of the sort that existed here naturally before Europeans came along. Heart-warming though it is to see Australians taking pride in their native flora, the plan seems unfortunate to say the least. To begin with, Australia has several hundred thousand square miles of landscape featuring mallee scrub and red river gums; it is not as if this is a threatened environment. Worse, the parks as they are now are unusually fine, among the best in the world, and it would be a tragedy to lose them wherever they were. If you accept the logic that they are inappropriate because they are in a European style then clearly you would have to get rid of all of Adelaide's houses, streets, buildings and European-derived people. Unfortunately, as so often in a short-sighted world, no one asked me about any of this.

Still, the parks remain lovely for the moment and I was happy to pass into them now. They were packed with large family groups enjoying Australia Day, picnicking and playing cricket with tennis balls. Adelaide has miles of good beaches in its western suburbs, so it surprised me that such numbers of people had forsaken the shore to come into the city. It gave the day an engagingly old-fashioned air. This is how we spent the Fourth of July when I was a kid in Iowa – in parks, playing ball games. It seemed odd, too – but again pleasing – that in a country of so much space people chose to crowd together to relax. Perhaps it's all that intimidating emptiness that makes Australians such social creatures. The parks were so crowded, in fact, that it was often impossible to tell which ball game belonged to which group of onlookers, or even sometimes which fielders belonged to which ball game. When a ball bounced into a neighbouring party, as seemed to happen quite regularly, there was always an exchange of apologies on the one hand and a call of 'No worries' on the other as the ball was tossed back into play. It was effectively all one very large picnic, and I felt almost ridiculously pleased to be part of it even in such a marginal way.

It took about three hours, I suppose, to do the complete circuit of the parks. Quite often a roar would rise from the Oval. Cricket was obviously a livelier spectacle in person than on the radio. At length I emerged onto a street called Pennington Terrace, where a row of neat bluestone houses with shady lawns overlooked the Oval. At one a family had essentially moved its living room onto the front lawn. I know it can't have been so, but in my recollection they had brought out everything – floor lamps, coffee table, rug, magazine basket, coal scuttle. They had certainly brought out a sofa and a television on which they were watching the cricket. Behind the television, a couple of hundred yards away across open parkland, stood the Oval, so that whenever anything dramatic happened on their screen it was accompanied in real time by a roar from the stadium just beyond.

'Who's winning?' I called as I walked past.

'Bloody poms,' the man said, inviting me to share his amazement.

I trudged on uphill past the imposing hulk of St Peter's Cathedral. I was heading in a general way towards my hotel, intending to have a shower and a change of clothes before setting off to look for a pub and dinner. Out of the shade of the parks it was a blisteringly hot afternoon, and I was by now quite footsore, but I found myself drawn helplessly into the residential streets of North Adelaide. It was an area of quiet prosperity, settled under a Sunday serenity, with street after street of old houses, each buried under roses and frangipani, and every little plot a model of meticulously managed floral abundance.

At length I arrived at a place called Wellington Square, an open space overlooked by a grand pub of venerable aspect. I went straight over. Inside, it was cool and convivial, with gleaming fittings and a lot of burnished pale wood – nothing like the austere pubs of the bush. This was a place for cocktails, for talking about one's investment portfolio. It was busy, too, though most of the customers were eating rather than drinking – or at least eating as well as drinking. At nearly every table, they were hunched over steaks or battered portions of fish so hearty that they hung over the edge of the plates. On a large pulldown screen the cricket was showing, but with the sound turned down. I had found my home for the evening. I ordered a pint of Cooper's Draught and retired with it to a table overlooking the square. And there I sat for a good few minutes doing nothing at all, not even touching my glass, just savouring the pleasure of sitting down and finding myself in a far country with a glass of beer and cricket on the TV and a roomful of people enjoying the fruits of a prosperous age. I could not have been happier.

After a while I remembered my purchases from the second-hand bookshop and pulled them out for examination. I turned first to *Australian Paradox*, an account of a year-long stay in the country in 1959–60 written by an English journalist named Jeanne MacKenzie, and cracked it open, interested to see how Australia today compared with the Australia of forty years ago.

Well, what a different world it was. The Australia Ms MacKenzie describes is a place of boundless prosperity, full employment, twinkling wholesomeness and infinite optimism. In 1959–60, Australia was the third wealthiest country on the planet – I hadn't realized this – exceeded only by the United States and Canada. But what was particularly interesting was how modest were the components of material well-being back then. With admiration bordering on amazement, Ms MacKenzie notes that by the end of the 1950s three-quarters of city dwellers in Australia had a refrigerator and almost half had a washing machine (there wasn't yet enough electricity in most rural areas to run big appliances, so they didn't count). Nearly every home in the nation, she went on, had 'at least one radio' – gosh! – and 'most homes have other electrical appliances such as vacuum cleaners, irons and electric jugs'. Oh, to live in a world in which the ownership of an electric jug is a source of pride.

I spent a good hour reading through the book at random, spellbound by the simplicity of the age she described. In 1960, television was still an exciting novelty (it didn't reach Australia until 1956, and then only in Sydney and Melbourne at first), colour television a distant dream. In Melbourne on Sundays there were no newspapers, and cinemas and pubs were shut by law. Perth was still at the end of a very long dirt road and would remain so for many years. Adelaide was just half the size it is now and its famous festival was then brand new. Queensland was backward. (Still is!)

Even in the best restaurants, chicken Maryland and beef stroganoff were dishes of exotic distinction, and oysters were served with ketchup. For most people, foreign cuisine began and ended with spaghetti out of tins. Cheese came in two varieties – 'sharp' and 'tasty'. Supermarkets were a new and exciting concept. Five per cent of university-age kids in 1959 were actually in university – this also reported with admiration – up from 1.56 per cent twenty years before. It was, in every way, a different world.

What struck me in all this was not how much better off Australians are today, but how much worse they feel. One of the oddest things for an outsider to do is watch Australians assessing themselves. They are an extraordinarily self-critical people. You encounter it constantly in newspapers and on television and radio – a nagging conviction that no matter how good things are in Australia, they are bound to be better elsewhere. A curiously large proportion of books on Australian life and history bear grave, pessimistic titles: *Among the Barbarians*, *The Future Eaters*, *The Tyranny of Distance*, *This Tired, Brown Land*, *Fatal Impact*, *The Fatal Shore*. Even when the titles are neutral (they are never positive), they often contain the oddest, most startling conclusions. In *A Shorter History of Australia*, a thoughtful and unexceptionable survey of the country's considerable achievements over the past 200 years, the author, Geoffrey Blainey, finishes by noting that Australia has nearly completed its first century under peaceful federation. Then, out of the blue, he concludes with these words: 'Whether it will last for two centuries is not certain. In the sweep of human history no political boundary is permanent.'

Now is that very strange or what? You could understand a Canadian writing those words, or a Belgian or a South African. But an Australian? Please. This is a country that has never had a serious civil disturbance, never jailed a dissident, never shown the tiniest inclination to fray at the edges. Australia is the Norway of the southern hemisphere. And yet here is the country's foremost living historian suggesting that its continuation as a sovereign nation is by no means assured. Extraordinary.

If Australians lack one thing in their lonely eminence Down Under, it is perspective. For four decades they have watched in quiet dismay as one country after another – Switzerland, Sweden, Japan, Kuwait and many others – has climbed over them on the per capita GDP table. When news came out in 1996 that Hong Kong and Singapore had also squeezed ahead, you'd have thought from the newspaper editorials that Asian armies had come ashore somewhere around Darwin and were fanning out across the country, appropriating consumer durables as they went. Never mind that most of these countries were only marginally ahead and that much of it was to do with relative exchange rates. Never mind that when you take into account quality-of-life indicators such as cost of living, educational attainments, crime rates and so on Australia bounds back up near the top. (It ranks seventh on the United Nations' Human Development Index, a little behind Canada, Sweden, the United States and one or two others, but comfortably ahead of Germany, Switzerland, Austria, Italy and several other countries with stout economies and higher GDPs.) At the time of my visit, Australia was booming as never before. It was enjoying one of the fastest rates of economic growth in the developed world, inflation was invisible and unemployment was at its lowest level in years. Yet according to a study by the Australian Institute, 36 per cent of Australians felt life was getting worse and barely a fifth saw any hope of its getting better.

These days, it is true, in terms of gross dollars accumulated per head, Australia is no longer near the top. It comes in at number twenty-one, in fact. But I ask you, which would you rather be – third richest and thrilled because you have an electric jug and at least one radio, or twenty-first richest and living in a world where you can have everything a person could reasonably want?

On the other hand, in very few of these other countries do you run the slightest risk of being eaten by an estuarine crocodile, a thought that occurred to me now as I pulled out my second purchase, *Crocodile Attack in Australia* by Hugh Edwards, and waded chest deep into its 240 pages of gruesome, violent attacks by this most cunning and unsporting of creatures.

The saltwater crocodile is the one animal that has the capacity to frighten even Australians. People who would calmly flick a scorpion off their forearm or chuckle fearlessly at a pack of skulking dingoes will quake at the sight of a hungry croc, and I had not ventured far into the pages of Mr Edwards's chilling chronicles before I began to understand why. Consider this tale of an afternoon at play in northwestern Australia:

In March 1987, a motorcruiser with five people aboard was making its way along the Kimberley coast when it detoured up the Prince Regent River to visit Kings Cascade, a remote beauty spot where a tropical waterfall spills picturesquely over a granite outcrop. There they moored and went off variously to clamber over the cascades or have a swim. One of the swimmers was a young American model named Ginger Faye Meadows. As she and another young woman stood waist deep on a rock ledge under the waterfall, one of them noticed the cold, steady eyes and half-submerged snout of a crocodile coming towards them. Now imagine it. You are standing with your back to a rock wall much too steep and slippery to climb, with nowhere to retreat, and one of the deadliest creatures on earth is coming towards you – a creature so perfectly engineered to kill that it has scarcely changed in 200 million years. You are, in short, about to be killed by something from the age of the dinosaurs.

One of the two women took off a plastic shoe and threw it at the crocodile. It bounced off his head, causing him to blink and hesitate. In the same instant, Meadows decided to make a break for it. She dived into the water and tried to swim the twenty-five yards to safety. The friend stayed put. Meadows swam with strong strokes, but the crocodile followed on a line designed to intercept her. About halfway across it caught her round the middle and jerked her beneath the water.

According to the boat's skipper, Meadows stayed under for several seconds, then surfaced with 'her hands in the air and a really startled look on her face . . . She was looking right at me . . . but she didn't say a word.' Then she went under again and was seen no more. The next day would have been her twenty-fifth birthday.

This is probably the most famous crocodile attack in Australia in the last twenty-five years because it involved a well-known beauty spot, a luxury cruiser and a victim from America who happened to be young and very good looking. But here's the thing: there have been *lots* of others. What's more, Meadows's death was atypical because she saw it coming. For most people a crocodile attack comes completely unexpectedly. The chronicles of crocodile killings are full of stories of people standing in a few inches of water or sitting on a bank or strolling along an ocean beach when suddenly the water splits and, before they can even cry out, much less enter into negotiations, they are carried away for leisurely devouring. That is what is so scary about them.

Now I ask you. Who gives a stuff how much money people are making in Hong Kong or Singapore when you've got matters like that to worry about? That's all I'm saying.

CHAPTER NINE

I

I WOULD HAPPILY HAVE STAYED ANOTHER DAY OR TWO IN ADELAIDE, but I had tracks to make. It was almost time to meet my friends in Melbourne, but first I had a promise to myself of long standing to visit the Mornington Peninsula, a coastal area of beauty and charm just south of Melbourne. As ever in Australia, it would take some getting to. I left Adelaide early and was dismayed to discover, within an hour or so of setting off, that I was facing yet another long day of driving on empty roads through a featureless expanse. This seemed particularly unfair because, in the first place, I had supposed that I was heading back into civilization and, second, I had had quite enough of this sort of thing already and, third, I had intentionally chosen a slightly longer route along a coastal highway to avoid the prospect of overland visual tedium.

The road I was on was called the Princes Highway. The map showed it running in a graceful arc along the edge of a vast bay identified as the Younghusband Peninsula, and indeed it did present hours of sunny coastal views, but the tide was miles out, leaving the sea as a distant thread of bright blue on the far side of a million painfully reflective acres of saltpans. The inland side presented an equally featureless blankness filled with a single, infinitely repeated species of low shrub. For 146 kilometres the road was perfectly empty.

To pass the time, I sang Australia's unofficial national anthem, 'Waltzing Matilda'. It is an interesting song. It was written by Banjo

Paterson, who was not only Australia's greatest poet of the nineteenth century but also the only one named for a stringed instrument. It goes (and I think the record should show that these are the words precisely as set down by Paterson):

Oh! there once was a swagman camped in the Billabong
Under the shade of a Coolibah tree
And he sang as he looked at his old billy boiling
Who'll come a-waltzing Matilda with me.

The main distinguishing feature of 'Waltzing Matilda', you will notice, is that it makes no sense. Obviously it makes no sense to anyone not familiar with bush lingo – that part was intentional – but even when you understand the words it makes no sense. A *billabong*, for instance, is a waterhole. So a question that immediately arises, before you have even concluded the first line, is: Why was the swagman camped *in* it? I would camp beside it myself. You see what you are up against? The only possible conclusion is that Paterson had had a few when he grabbed his ink-pot and dashed off the words. Anyway, just to keep you fully informed, a *swagman* in Australian parlance is an itinerant traveller. The term comes from the rolled blanket, or *swag*, that he carried. Another name for a swag was a *Matilda*, evidently from the German *Mathilde*. (Don't ask me; my interest in this goes only so far.) A *billy* is a can for boiling water and a *coolibah tree* is a coolibah tree. There you have the terms. Why the swagman is a-waltzing with his bedroll and why above all he desires someone or something (in the second verse it's a sheep, for goodness' sake) to join him in this bizarre and possibly depraved activity are, of course, questions that cannot be answered.

On the other hand, it has a lovely tune (it's borrowed from an old Scottish air, 'Thou Bonnie Wood O' Craigielea'), which I render particularly melodically, if I say so myself, especially with my head out of the window to achieve that warbly effect that comes from singing into an onrush of air at speed. The problem with knowing only one verse, of course, is that it gets a trifle repetitive after a time. So you may conceive my satisfaction when I realized that if you changed 'billy boiling' to 'willy boiling' it put an entirely new slant on things, and I was able to come up with approximately forty-seven new stanzas, which not only extends the song to a length suitable for long bus journeys, but brings to it a dimension of coherence that it has lacked for almost a century.

I might have got the verse total even higher except that as I rounded the last sweep of bay and followed the road inland through a stretch of scrub, I came upon a sign announcing 'The Big Lobster' and in the excitement I abandoned my musical interests. The Big Lobster, you see, was something – or more properly a species of something – that I had longed to see ever since I had hit the road.

One of the more cherishable peculiarities of Australians is that they like to build big things in the shape of other things. Give them a bale of chicken wire, some fibreglass and a couple of pots of paint and they will make you, say, an enormous pineapple or strawberry or, as here, a lobster. Then they put a café and a gift shop inside, erect a big sign beside the highway (for the benefit of people whose acuity evidently does not extend to spotting a fifty-foot-high piece of fruit standing beside an otherwise empty highway), then sit back and wait for the money to roll in.

Some sixty of these objects are scattered across the Australian landscape, like leftover props from a 1950s horror movie. You can, if you have sufficient petrol money and nothing approaching a real life, visit a Big Prawn, a Big Koala, a Big Oyster (with searchlights for eyes, apparently), a Big Lawnmower, a Big Marlin, a Big Orange and a Big Merino Ram, among many others. The process, I am patriotically proud to tell you, was started by an American named Landy who built a Big Banana at Coff's Harbour, on the New South Wales coast, which proved so magically attractive to passing vehicles that it made Mr Landy, as it were, the big banana of the business.

Generally these objects are cannily set along a stretch of highway so astoundingly void and dull that you will stop for almost anything – as of course I did now when the road bent once again and I found looming before me a monstrously large, reddish pink, commendably lifelike lobster rearing up beside the road as if about to dine on a morsel of passing traffic. Owing to the peculiar shape of a lobster, the owners had decided (I imagine after quite a lot of thought) not to try to accommodate a gift shop and café inside, so the Big Lobster sat on the front lawn, secured with guy wires, while the retail facilities were in a separate building behind. I got out and approached for a closer look. It was impressively outsized. I learned from subsequent enquiry that it is fifty-six feet from the ground to the tip of its feelers – a good size even in the ambitious world of giant objects.

I was looking at it from various angles when I realized that I had wandered into someone's photograph.

'Oh, sorry!' I called.

'No worries, mate,' he replied with an easygoing air. 'You help to give it scale.'

He came up and stood beside me. He was in his early thirties and looked vaguely sad and dorky, like someone who worked in a low-grade job and still lived at home. He was dressed as if for a vacation, in shorts and a T-shirt that said 'Noosa' in large letters. Noosa is a Queensland resort. Together we stood and for quite a period silently admired the lobster.

'Big, isn't it?' I remarked at last, for very little escapes me in the world of fibreglass crustaceans.

'You wouldn't get a snap of me in front of it, would you?' he said in that curiously circular way in which Australians beg a favour.

'Of course.'

He went and stood beside it, a hand perched affectionately on a foreleg.

'You can tell people it's an engagement photo,' I suggested.

He liked that idea. 'Yeah!' he said keenly. 'Meet the fiancée. She's not much for looks or conversation, but jeez can she scuttle!'

I decided I liked this guy.

'So do you visit these things a lot?' I said, handing him back the camera.

'Only if I'm passing, you know. It's a pretty good one, though. Better than the Big Koala at Moyston.'

I didn't feel there was a great deal I could say to this.

'At Wauchope there's a Big Bull,' he added.

I raised my eyebrows in a way that said: 'Oh yes?'

He nodded fondly. 'Its testicles swing in the breeze.'

'It has testicles?' I said, impressed.

'I'll say. If they fell on you, you wouldn't get up in a hurry.'

We took an extended moment to savour this image. 'It would make an interesting insurance claim, I suppose,' I observed at last.

'Yeah!' He liked this idea, too. 'Or a newspaper headline: "Man crushed by falling bollocks."'

'"By falling bullock's bollocks",' I offered.

'Yeah!'

We were getting on like a house on fire. I hadn't had a conversation this long in days. What am I saying – I hadn't had this much *fun* in days. Unfortunately, neither of us could think of anything more to say, and so we just stood awkwardly for a while.

'Well, nice meeting you,' he said at last and with a shy smile shuffled off.

'Nice meeting *you*,' I said and meant it.

I went inside and bought a fridge magnet and about fifteen Big Lobster postcards, and returned to the road in a mellow frame of mind. I headed the car towards Warrnambool and the famous Great Ocean Road and drove some minutes in thoughtful silence. Then abruptly I thrust my head out of the window, and in a sweet but robust voice sang:

Forgetting that spoons stir hot liquids much better
The swagman immersed his tool in his tea
And he sighed as he spied his old willy boiling
Now I can't bugger you, so will you bugger me?

II

I spent the night in Port Fairy, and drove on the next day to the Mornington Peninsula along the Great Ocean Road, a tortuous, spectacularly scenic coastal highway built after the First World War as a make-work scheme for veterans. It took fourteen years to construct and you can see why at once because for most of its 187 miles it swoops along an impossibly challenging coastline in a hair-raising manner, barrelling around rocky headlands and clinging to the edges of sheer and crumbly cliffs. So demanding of attention are the endless hairpin bends that you scarcely have a moment to notice the views, but I figured an occasional glimpsed view was better than none. Here and there in the water stand pinnacles of rock created by the tireless erosive might of the sea. There used to be a natural rock arch called London Bridge over which you could stroll to stand above the sea, but in 1990 it collapsed, sending tons of debris into the surf below and stranding two startled but miraculously unharmed tourists on the seaward stub. London Bridge is now London Stacks.

The drive was as gorgeous as the guidebooks had promised: on one side the steep, wooded, semi-tropical hills of the Otway Range plunging straight into the sea, on the other foamy surf rolling onto long, curving beaches framed at either end by rocky outcrops. This stretch of Victoria is famous for two things: surfing and shipwrecks. With its wild currents and famous fogs, the south Victorian coast was long notorious to mariners. If you took all the water away, you would see 1,200 ships lying broken on the seabed, more than almost anywhere else in the world. I stopped from time to time to get out and take in the views – it really was the only way for a solitary driver to see them – and poked about in one or two of the sweetly old-fashioned little resort communities that lay along the way. These were surprisingly quiet, considering that it was the height of the Australian summer and the day after a national holiday. It struck me, not for the first time, that there seemed to be more places in Australia for tourists to go than there were tourists to fill them.

At a place called Torquay, the Great Ocean Road rejoined the main highway towards Melbourne. Twenty miles to the west, I noticed, was Winchelsea, where Thomas Austin set free the twenty-four rabbits that transformed the Australian landscape. The countryside roundabout looked vaguely arid and unpromising – it reminded me of Oklahoma or western Kansas – but I had no way of knowing, of course, how much of this could be attributed to the voracity of rabbits. Now you would think that people might have learned a lesson from Austin's experience, but amazingly no. At the very moment that rabbits were eating their way across the countryside, influential people were introducing other species of animals in great numbers – sometimes for sport, sometimes by accident, but mostly in an effort to liven things up a little. Precisely the same impulse that led people to build English-style parks in places like Adelaide led them to try to manipulate the countryside as well. Australia was deemed biologically deficient, its semi-arid plains too monotonous, its forests too silent. Gradually there arose acclimatization societies that made scores of eager introductions to fulfil a longing for the familiar. Before long it occurred to the societies that there was no reason to stop with British or even European animals. They began to dream of creating an African veldt in Australia, with giraffes, springboks and buffalo grazing the sunny plains. Their aspirations took on an almost surreal quality. In 1862, Sir Henry Barkly, governor of Victoria, called for the introduction of monkeys into the colony's forests 'for the amusement of wayfarers, whom their gambols would delight'. Before this could be acted on, Barkly had been replaced as governor by Sir Charles Darling, who said he didn't want monkeys but would be very pleased to see boa constrictors. He didn't get his way either, but scores of others did.

'Acclimatization was one of the most foolish and dangerous ideas ever to infect the thinking of nineteenth-century men,' writes Tim Low in the improbably gripping *Feral Future: The Untold Story of Australia's Exotic Invaders*, but infect them it did. Victoria, for some reason, became the hotbed of all this. Despite the experience with rabbits, dozens of other foolish introductions were made. In the 1860s the Ballarat Acclimatization Society loosed foxes into the landscape and they quickly became a scourge, a position from which they have not yet retreated. Other animals escaped or were abandoned and went wild. Camels were used to build the railway from Adelaide to Alice Springs, but were set free when the work was completed. Today 100,000 of them roam the central and western deserts, the only place in the world where one-humped dromedaries exist in the wild. Across the country there are up to five million wild donkeys, a million or more wild horses (called brumbies) and large numbers of water buffalo, cows, goats, sheep, pigs and dogs. Feral pigs have been caught in Melbourne suburbs. There are so many introduced species, in fact, that the red kangaroo, once the largest animal on the continent, is now only the thirteenth biggest.

The consequences for native species have often been devastating. About 130 mammals in Australia are threatened. Sixteen have become extinct – more than in any other continent. And guess what is the mightiest killer of all? According to the National Parks and Wildlife Service, it is the common cat. Cats love the Australian wild. There are 12 million of them out there, inhabiting every niche in the landscape from the driest deserts to the tallest mountains. With the fox they have driven many of Australia's smallest, cutest and most vulnerable native animals to the edge of extinction – numbats, bettongs, quolls, potoroos, bandicoots, rock wallabies, platypuses and many others. Since most of these creatures are nocturnal and rarely seen, most people don't notice their absence, but they are going fast.

As with animals, so with plants. In the 1850s, Victoria was unfortunate to have as chief botanist a dedicated acclimatizer with the imposing name of Baron Ferdinand Jacob Heinrich Von Mueller. As with animal acclimatizers, Von Mueller couldn't abide what he viewed as the impoverished nature of Australia's flora, and he spent much of his free time travelling the country sowing seeds of pumpkins, cabbages, melons and whatever else he thought might flourish. He had a special affection for blackberries, planting clumps of them all over. The blackberry is now Victoria's most pernicious weed, all but ineradicable and the bane of farmers everywhere. Where unmolested, it takes over whole landscapes. I saw some now as I drove along.

The lesson in this – that exotic species often thrive in Australia in a way that staggers belief – is one that Australians have had a curiously hard time fully grasping. Prickly pear, a type of pulpy cactus native to America, was introduced in Queensland early in the twentieth century as a potential stock feed and quickly went crazy. By 1925, 30 million acres were overrun with impenetrable groves of prickly pear up to six feet high. It is an almost absurdly dense plant – an acre of prickly pear weighs 800 tons, as against about fifteen tons for an acre of wheat – and a nightmare to clear. For a while it looked as if much of Queensland and beyond would simply become one Europe-sized bed of prickly pear. Fortunately it could be treated effectively with pesticides and a moth whose larvae relished its leaves, but it was a close-run thing and the cost was substantial.

Altogether, according to Low, Australia is now home to more than 2,700 foreign weeds. Interestingly, botanical gardens are among the worst offenders. Three escapees from Darwin's Botanic Gardens – mimosa bush, leucaena and crutch tree – threaten Kakadu National Park, a World Heritage site, and there have been others elsewhere.

Where these things come from is often a mystery. According to Low, in recent years a biting ant, from the species *Iridomyrmex*, has infested Brisbane. It has become a common nuisance. Interestingly, no one knows where it came from or how it got there. It just one day appeared. Nor, for obvious reasons, can anyone say where it will spread or what quiet havoc it might wreak. One thing alone is certain. As so often, it appears to be doing better in Australia than wherever it came from.

The Mornington Peninsula is a spur of land just south of Melbourne. It is, I suppose, Victoria's Cape Cod, in that it is coastal and very pretty and crowded with summer homes. It even has something of the same shape, curling around in a scorpion tail that almost encloses the considerable immensity of Port Phillip Bay, across which, at a distance of some fifty miles, stands Melbourne. I had two particular reasons for wanting to be here: Catherine Veitch had made it sound so appealing in her letters and it was here that Australia's tragically submersible Prime Minister, Harold Holt, went for his final swim.

Holt's fateful dip was at Portsea, at the peninsula's far end, so it was there I directed myself the next morning after overnighting in the little town of Mornington. Though I set off in watery sunshine, of the sort that seemed to promise a fine day later on, Portsea was settled under a heavy sea mist, and the temperature when I stepped out of the car was cooler than it had been twenty miles up the road. Most of the few people out in Portsea, I noticed, were wearing cotton jumpers or jackets.

Portsea is very small – a handful of shops and cafés against a larger backdrop of big houses looking aloof and broody in the wispy fog – but famously well heeled. A beach hut had just sold at auction here for $185,000. Not a beach house, you understand, but a beach hut – a simple wooden shed with no electricity, water or any features at all other than proximity to sand and sea. The purchaser didn't even actually get to own the hut. All his $185,000 bought him was the right in perpetuity to pay the council several hundred dollars in annual rent. The huts, which only locals are allowed to acquire, are immensely prized possessions. The one that had just been sold had been in the same family for fifty years.

I had coffee to warm up before continuing on to the Mornington Peninsula National Park, which covers the last nubbin of land before it meets the sea at a hilly outpost called Point Nepean, beyond which lies a notorious swirl of water called the Rip – a narrow passage forming the entrance to Port Phillip Bay. Only recently had this land become public. For a hundred years, the whole of this area – several hundred acres of the most glorious coastal property in Victoria – was off limits to the public because it was owned by the military, which used it as a firing range. Pause with me for a moment while we put this in perspective. Here you have a country of three million square miles, nearly all of it empty and eminently bombable. And here, just a couple of hours' drive from the country's second city, you have a headland of rare and sumptuous beauty, and of considerable ecological importance, and from this land you bar the public because you are trying to blow it to smithereens. Doesn't make much sense, what? The upshot is that after many years of wheedling and cajoling, the military was finally prevailed upon to yield a fragment of this land to form a national park. Even so, the army kept about two-thirds of the peninsula and still occasionally lofts bombs into it. In consequence, once you have acquired a ticket of admission at a visitors' centre on the edge of Portsea, you have to pass through a two-mile-long zone of military land on a road lined on both sides with tall fences bearing severe warnings of unexploded bombs and the folly of trespass. You can take a shuttle bus into the park or walk. I decided to walk, for the exercise, and set off through the cloaking mist. I appeared to have the place pretty much to myself.

I had gone no more than a dozen feet when I was joined by a fly – smaller and blacker than a housefly. It buzzed around in front of my face and tried to settle on my upper lip. I swatted it away, but it returned at once, always to the same spot. A moment later it was joined by another that wished to go up my nose. It also would not go away. Within a minute or so I had perhaps twenty of these active spots all around my head and I was swiftly sinking into the state of abject wretchedness that comes with a prolonged encounter with the Australian fly.

Flies are of course always irksome, but the Australian variety distinguish themselves by their very particular persistence. If an Australian fly wants to be up your nose or in your ear, there is no discouraging him. Flick at him as you will and each time he will jump out of range and come straight back. It is simply not possible to deter him. Somewhere on an exposed portion of your body is a spot about the size of a shirt button that the fly wants to lick and tickle and turn delirious circles upon. It isn't simply their persistence, but the things they go for. An Australian fly will try to suck the moisture off your eyeball. He will, if not constantly turned back, go into parts of your ears that a Q-tip can only dream about. He will happily die for the glory of taking a tiny dump on your tongue. Get thirty or forty of them dancing around you in the same way and madness will shortly follow.

And so I proceeded into the park, lost inside my own little buzzing cloud of woe, waving at my head in an increasingly hopeless and desultory manner – it is called the bush salute – blowing constantly out of my mouth and nose, shaking my head in a kind of furious dementia, occasionally slapping myself with startling violence on the cheek or forehead. Eventually, as the flies knew all along I would, I gave up and they fell upon me as on a corpse.

At length the flies and I reached the end of the military zone and the beginning of the park proper. Just inside this transition area was a signposted path leading up a medium-sized eminence called Cheviot Hill. This is what I had come to see, for it was at Cheviot Beach, on the other side, that Harold Holt went for the Swim That Needs No Towel. I followed the path upward through misty groves of low bushy trees – moonah, milkwort and tea trees, according to helpful noticeboards posted at intervals. At the top of the hill a stiff breeze was running, forceful enough to make me totter when I neglected to brace for it, and here at last the flies gave me a tiny bit of surcease. I stood with the wind full in my face, happier than I can tell you just to be left alone.

The view from the top of Cheviot Hill is said to be one of the finest in coastal Victoria, though I cannot vouch for this as I could see almost nothing. Across a grey-green vale, a mile or so distant, rose another hill at Point Nepean, covered in lazy cloud. Beyond was the notorious Rip, invisible from here. Below me, things were no less impenetrable. I appeared to be perhaps a hundred feet directly above Cheviot Beach, but it was like peering into a cauldron. All I could see through the drifting soup were some vague outlines of rocks and an indeterminate expanse of sand. Only the sounds of unseen waves flopping onto an unseen shore made it evident that I had found the sea.

Still, I felt a frisson of satisfaction at having reached the place of Holt's fateful swim. I tried to imagine the scene as it must have been, though it wasn't easy. On the day Holt waded into the surf, the weather was windy but fine. Things were not going very well for him as Prime Minister – his skills lay more in kissing babies and making the ladies tingle (he was evidently a bit of a hottie) than in running affairs of state – and we may safely assume that he was glad to be out of Canberra for the long Christmas break. Holt came to this beach because he had a weekend home at Portsea and the army let him stroll on its grounds for the sake of his privacy. So there were no lifeguards, members of the public or even security guards in attendance when, on 17 December 1967, Holt went for a breezy stroll with some friends among the rocks and pounding waves just below. Although the sea was lively and the tide dangerously high, and although Holt had almost drowned there six months earlier while snorkelling with some chums, he decided to go for a swim. Before anyone could react he had whipped off his shirt and plunged into the surf. He swam straight out from the beach a couple of hundred feet and almost instantly vanished, without fuss or commotion or even a languorous wave. He was fifty-nine years old and had been Prime Minister for not quite two years. His body was never found.

Cheviot Beach remains closed to the public, and in any case there was no way down to it from the clifftops, so I amused myself for a few minutes prowling through a complex of pillboxes and murky concrete bunkers left over from the Second World War until I walked into a large cobweb and, with an echoing shriek and a few moments of caroming about between walls, low lintels and other unyielding impedimenta, returned in subdued form to the open air. Rubbing my head and calling round the flies again, I followed the path back down to the road. At the bottom of the hill was a large and straggly cemetery, a relic from when this was a quarantine station. I tried to have a look around, but the flies would give me no peace. I had intended to stroll out to the headland where there was a nineteenth-century fort, but the thought of having the flies as my companions for another hour was more than I could endure, so I set off back along the empty road by which I had come.

At the visitors' centre I stopped in to have a look at the displays and got chatting with the park ranger. I asked him how dangerous this stretch of coastline was.

'Oh, very,' he said cheerfully. He showed me on a marine chart how the currents ran – which is to say all over the place. If they got hold of you, I gathered, they would pass you around like an unwanted parcel. Even the strongest swimmer would soon be exhausted by the fight. It was mostly to do with the Rip, where massive volumes of water rush through an opening only a few hundred yards across each time the tide rolls in or out. I hadn't realized until I saw the chart just how proximate Cheviot Beach was to this zone of watery turmoil. Even on a map it looked supremely foolhardy.

'So it wasn't a good idea for Harold Holt to go swimming out there?'

'Well, I wouldn't go swimming out there,' he replied. 'You know, there's about a hundred shipwrecks just along here.' He indicated an absurdly modest stretch of shoreline in the vicinity of Cheviot and the Rip. 'I think you can take it as read that when you've got a stretch of sea that sinks a hundred ships, it's probably not the most placid environment for a dip, you know?'

'Isn't it odd that they never found his body?'

'No.' This was said without hesitation.

'Really?' I don't understand the dynamics of the sea, but if driftwood and Coke cans are anything to go by, then I thought most buoyant objects ended up on a beach somewhere.

'Not to be too blunt about it, if you die out there it doesn't take too long to become part of the food chain.'

'Ah.'

'The thing you've got to remember,' he added with a sudden thoughtful air, 'is that the only thing unusual about the Harold Holt drowning was that he was Prime Minister when it happened. If it hadn't been for that the whole thing would have been completely forgotten. Mind you, it's pretty well forgotten anyway.'

'So you don't get a lot of people coming here in a kind of pilgrimage?'

'No, not at all. Most people barely remember it. A lot of people under thirty have never even heard of it.'

He broke off to issue tickets to some new arrivals and I drifted away to look at the displays of seagrasses and life in rockpools. But as I was leaving he called to me with an afterthought. 'They built a memorial to him in Melbourne,' he said. 'Know what it was?'

I indicated that I had no idea.

He grinned very slightly. 'A municipal swimming pool.'

'Seriously?'

His grin broadened, but the nod was sincere.

'This is a terrific country,' I said.

'Yeah,' he agreed happily. 'It is, you know.'

CHAPTER TEN

THROUGHOUT MY CHILDHOOD ON FRIDAY NIGHTS WHENEVER MY father was away, which was often (he was a sportswriter who travelled a lot for his work), my mother and I had an arrangement whereby I would take a bus downtown to meet her (she also worked for the local paper) and we would go to dinner at a cafeteria called Bishop's and then to a movie.

I don't wish to suggest that my mother abused the trust I placed in her with regard to the selection process, but it did seem uncanny that the movies I favoured had always just left town and that we ended up seeing something involving murder, passion and betrayal, usually starring Jeff Chandler, for whom my mother had a strange admiration, usually in a part that required him to spend a good deal of time bare-chested.

'Oh,' she would tut in a tone of shared chagrin, '*Twenty Thousand Leagues under the Sea* has just gone. But the Orpheum has the new Jeff Chandler movie, *Tame Lust*. Shall we go see that?'

I don't know if through the passage of time these movies have blurred into one in my memory or whether they actually were all identical, but they seemed always to have the same elements – way too much talking, lots of steamy embraces with Lana Turner or some other hard-looking blonde, very occasional gunfire resulting in a clutched belly, a staggered walk and a disappointingly modest seepage of blood, and a part for Chandler that put him frequently on a speedboat or lifeguard's stand dressed only in swimming trunks. (Without even looking at the screen you could tell which were the swimming trunks scenes because of the avidity with which my mother would begin to suck her lemon drops.) If a Jeff Chandler movie wasn't available – and amazingly sometimes whole weeks passed in which he didn't produce a picture – we would have to see something else.

Thus it was that one week when I was about nine we went to see *The Sundowners*, a Technicolor epic starring Robert Mitchum and Deborah Kerr in the story of a lovably feisty and indomitable couple making a life for themselves in the Australian bush. It was a memorable movie in many ways, not least in that it provided the endearing spectacle of Robert Mitchum doing an Aussie accent, and that it dealt with Australia at all, which made it, in Hollywood terms, essentially unique. Nearly forty years after the event I don't recall much of the detail of the film other than that Mitchum and Kerr spent every waking moment herding armies of sheep and fighting one discommoding peril of antipodean life after another – bushfires, dust storms, drought, locust infestations and pub brawls mostly. It was also evidently very hot in Australia: Mitchum never spoke without first taking off a dusty hat and running a forearm across his brow. Since my plans for myself, even at the age of nine, were to spend my adulthood driving an open-topped sports car through Europe with Jean Seberg at my side, I concluded that Australia was of essentially zero interest and did not actively think about it again for thirty years.

In consequence, when finally I made my first trip Down Under, to attend the 1992 Melbourne Writers' Festival, I was actually able to be astounded to find it there at all. I clearly recall standing on Collins Street in Melbourne, so freshly arrived that I still smelled of (possibly even glistened from) the insecticide with which the flight attendants sprayed the plane before arrival, watching the clanging trams and swirl of humanity, and thinking: 'Good lord, there's a country here.' It was as if I had privately discovered life on another planet, or a parallel universe where life was at once recognizably similar but entirely different.

I can't tell you how exciting it was. Insofar as I had accumulated any expectations of Australia at all in the intervening years, I had thought of it as a kind of alternative southern California, a place of constant sunshine and the cheerful vapidity of a beach lifestyle, but with a slight British bent – a sort of *Baywatch* with cricket, as I thought it. But this was nothing like that. Melbourne had a settled and gracious air that was much more European than North American, and it rained, rained the whole week, which delighted me inordinately because it was so totally not what I had expected.

What's more, and here we come to the real crux of things, I liked it, straight off, without quibble or doubt, in a way I had never expected to. Something about it just agreed with me. I suppose it helped that I had spent half my life in America and half in Britain because Australia was such a comfortable fusion of the two. It had a casualness and vivacity – a lack of reserve, a comfortableness with strangers – that felt distinctly American, but hung on a British framework. In their optimism and informality Australians could pass at a glance for Americans, but they drove on the left, drank tea, played cricket, adorned their public places with statues of Queen Victoria, dressed their children in the sort of school uniforms that only a Britannic people could wear without conspicuous regret. I felt extremely comfortable with this.

Almost at once I became acutely, and in an odd way delightedly, aware of how little I knew about the place. I didn't know the names of their newspapers or universities or beaches or suburbs, knew nothing of their history or private achievements, couldn't tell a policeman from a postman. I didn't even know how to order coffee. It appeared that you had to specify a length (principally long or short), a colour (black or white) and even an angle of orientation to the perpendicular (flat or not), and these could be put together in a multitude of permutations – 'long black', 'short black', even 'long short black'. My own preference, I discovered after many happy hours of experimentation, was 'flat white'. It was a moment of the sublimest happiness.

Because my responsibilities at the festival were extremely slight – one or two stage presentations and a little light sweeping afterwards – I was free to roam through the city and I did so with the greatest enthusiasm and devotion, eavesdropping on conversations, sitting in coffee bars with all the morning newspapers and half a dozen beverages (I was still in the experimental stage), devouring both, reading labels and hoardings and the signs in shop windows, asking questions of complete strangers: 'Excuse me, what's a Jacky Howe? What are norks? What's a Hills Hoist?'*

I loved – still do – Australian voices, the lilt and cadence, the effortlessly dry, direct way of viewing the world. At a reception for

* Respectively a singlet, a slang term for breasts (I saw it on the cover of a magazine and actually made a sales assistant blush in asking, but how else to learn?) and a type of rotary clothes line of which the Australians are mysteriously but touchingly proud.

some minor awards presentation – the East Gippsland Young Farmers First Novel Award or something, which I attended because I was just so pleased to get an invitation to anything and because cocktails were promised – I was standing with two female publicists from my publisher's when some obviously self-infatuated nork breezed in.

'Oh look, it's Bruce Dazzling,' observed one and then with a kind of distant, perfectly encapsulating disdain added: 'He'd go to the opening of an envelope.'

Someone else told me the story of an English friend of his who was flying to Australia when the stewardess tonged him a hot towel, which proved upon application to be cold. So he told her – not in complaint, but simply because he thought she might want to warm them up some more. The stewardess turned to him and, smiling sweetly, with only the tiniest trace of sarcasm, said: 'Well, why don't you sit on it a bit? That should warm it up.' I knew as soon as I heard that story that I was going to like this place. I haven't stopped yet.

Because my first exposure was to Melbourne, I formed a certain slavish attachment to the place. I still find it terribly exciting to arrive in Melbourne – not an emotion you will hear expressed often, but there you are – and driving now through the glossy high-rises of its central business district had something of the feeling of a homecoming. Over there was the first Australian hotel I'd stayed in, there the first coffee shop I'd tried, there the celebrated Melbourne Cricket Ground, where I once spent three hours happily bewildered by an Australian Rules Football match and dined on my first (and last) four-and-twenty pie ('made with real blackbirds', I was drolly assured). Insofar as such a statement could have meaning, this was my home in Australia.

Most people (and when I say 'most people' I mean of course me when I first got there) don't realize that for a long time Melbourne was much the most important city in Australia. Although Sydney has been slightly the bigger of the two for a century (Melbourne's population now is about 3.5 million to Sydney's 4 million), Melbourne was until relatively recently the centre of things, particularly in the realms of finance and culture. Sydney used to compensate by making up cruel but generally outstanding jokes about Melbourne's supposed lack of liveliness, like:

'Do you have any children?'
'Yes, two living and one in Melbourne.'

These days Sydney makes jokes about Melbourne *and* steals its thunder, which is naturally a little hard for Melbourne people to take. Nothing better illustrates the shift in the two cities' relative standings than that in 1956 the Olympics went to Melbourne and in 2000 they have gone to Sydney. Most things do nowadays. In 1956, Melbourne was headquarters to fifty of Australia's largest companies while Sydney had just thirty-seven. Today the proportions are almost exactly reversed. A generation ago, international companies routinely chose Melbourne for their Australian headquarters; today over two-thirds opt for Sydney. But far more galling to a city that has always viewed Sydney as having the intellectual vibrancy of, let us say, daytime television, Melbourne has had to watch as Sydney has appropriated chunks of its cultural pre-eminence – in publishing, fashion, film and television, all the performing arts. I used to visit my Australian publishers in Melbourne. Today I go to Sydney.

Having said all that, and once you strip out the huge visual advantage Sydney derives from its harbour, there is precious little to choose between the two in terms of quality of life or cultural satisfaction. Much less separates Melbourne from Sydney than separates Los Angeles from New York or Birmingham from London.

Melbourne may not have a Harbour Bridge or an Opera House like Sydney's but it has something in its way no less singular: the world's most bizarre right turns. If you are driving in central Melbourne and you wish to turn against the traffic, you don't get in the middle lane, but rather pull over to the kerb – as far as possible from where you want to be – and sit there for an indeterminate period (in my case until all the clubs and restaurants have shut and everyone has gone home for the night) and make your turn from there in a frantic moment just before the lights change. It's all to do with keeping out of the way of the trams – Melbourne's other speciality – which go down the middle of the road and can't have turning cars blocking their way. It's immensely confusing, not only to visitors from overseas but to other Australians – even, I suspect, to many Melbourne people.

But what really sets Melbourne apart is its love of Australian Rules Football, a sport little followed in Sydney or New South Wales, where rugby is the passion. It's interesting that Melburnians don't tell jokes about Sydney. They tell jokes about their beloved footy. To wit:

A man arriving for the Grand Final in Melbourne is surprised to find the seat beside his empty. Tickets for the Grand Final are sold out weeks in advance and empty seats unknown. So he says to the man on the other side of the seat: 'Excuse me, do you know why there is no one in this seat?'

'It was my wife's,' answers the second man, a touch wistfully, 'but I'm afraid she died.'

'Oh, that's terrible. I'm so sorry.'

'Yes, she never missed a match.'

'But couldn't you have given the ticket to a friend or relative?'

'Oh no. They're all at the funeral.'

I was on my way to meet an old friend named Alan Howe, who, it so happens, is the person who introduced me to the transfixing peculiarities of Australian Rules. I first met him nearly twenty years ago when I was working as a sub-editor on the business desk of *The Times* in London and he was a downy-faced recruit from Down Under. I had been there for a few months already when he arrived and was given a seat beside me on the subs' table. I don't want to say he was awfully young back then, but he was wearing a Cub Scout uniform. Anyway, I took him under my wing as a fellow colonial and taught him all I knew. Admittedly this was only three things – that Lloyd's the insurers had an apostrophe while Lloyds Bank did not; that the hyphen was oddly placed in the company name Rio Tinto-Zinc; and that the canteen was in the basement – but in those days that was all you needed to know to work on the business desk.

He was a quick learner and he soon outstripped us all. I remember one day I was having an argument with a colleague over whether the 'p/e' in 'p/e ratio' stood for penis envy or Prince Edward, when Howe told us it was short for 'price/earnings ratio', and that it was a staple measure of an equity's perceived worth arrived at by dividing its current value by its earnings per share over the previous twelve months, and I knew then that this was a guy who was going places. He hasn't disappointed us, I must say. After a distinguished spell at *The Times* he returned to Australia, where he became a rising star in the Murdoch firmament, fetching up in the early 1990s as editor of the *Sunday Herald-Sun*, over which popular publication he still presides. When I think of him sitting there at *The Times* in his little neckerchief and blue shirt, my old heart swells with pride.

He and his wife, a kindly and placid soul named Carmel Egan, live in South Melbourne in a lovely old house that was formerly a butcher's shop, of all things. I was late in arriving owing to a little inadvertent experiment I conducted to establish whether it is possible to find your way to an address in Melbourne using a street plan for Perth, but I found it at length. It was Carmel who received me.

'Howie's out,' she said, ushering me in. 'He's gone for a run.'

'A run?' I tried not to sound too astounded, but in the years I had known him Howe's idea of a whole-body workout was to drink standing up. Besides, he was one of those restless, high-energy people who are constitutionally incapable of putting on fat. He needed to run the way I needed to increase my children's college expenses. 'It's his heart,' she added.

I stared at her. 'He's got a heart problem?'

'No, of course not.' She laughed. 'He's just, you know, discovered it.'

I understood at once. Howe has long been one of the world's great hypochondriacs. For years he has been moving from organ to organ, certain that one of them is about to maim him in a painful and costly way. He is forever standing off in corners palpating himself for mysterious lumps and adjusting his lifestyle accordingly.

So Carmel and I sat and had a nice cup of tea, and I told her fond stories about her husband in those far-off London days before she had met him: how I taught him to use soap and wear matching socks, and helped him to find the treatments that made his gonads drop – the usual sort of thing. It was at this point that the great man himself flopped into the house, extravagantly flushed, breathless and sweaty. 'Hey, mate,' he managed to breathe out in what it looked like might be his dying words.

'Are you OK?'

'Never been better.'

'What are you running for?' I said.

'Ticker, mate.'

'There's nothing wrong with your heart.'

'That's right,' he said proudly. 'And do you know why? Because I look after it.' He nodded sagely, as if I hadn't thought of that, and cast a privately thoughtful glance at my bulk.

For dinner we walked to a local restaurant, where we talked agreeably about a million things – mutual friends, work, where I had been on this trip and where I was going, all the sorts of things you talk about when you get together with friends you rarely see. At one point Howe mentioned casually that he had recently been boogie boarding at Byron Bay, in New South Wales, when he had encountered a shark.

'Truly?' I said, impressed.

He nodded. 'It was a fair size, too – nine or ten footer, I'd say.'

'So how close was it?'

'Close. I could just about have touched it.'

'So what did you do?'

'Strategically retreated. What do you think?'

'Weren't you scared?'

He made a look of sudden enthusiasm, as if I had just put my finger on something. 'Yeah,' he said, 'I was a bit.'

'A bit?'

'Oh, yeah,' he returned wholeheartedly, as if being a bit scared was the maximum permitted in Australia, which I suppose it is.

This led to a fond recollection of other near-death experiences with animals, of which Australians always have a large fund – an encounter with a crocodile in Queensland, killer snakes nearly stepped on, waking up to find a redback abseiling on a thread towards one's face. Australians are very unfair in this way. They spend half of any conversation insisting that the country's dangers are vastly overrated and that there's nothing to worry about, and the other half telling you how six months ago their Uncle Bob was driving to Mudgee when a tiger snake slid out from under the dashboard and bit him on the groin, but that it's OK now because he's off the life-support machine and they've discovered he can communicate with eye blinks.

I was, of course, all ears for all this.

'So what's the story with the crocodile?' I asked eagerly.

Howe smiled with just a hint of sheepishness. 'Well, Carmel and I were on holiday up in Queensland, at a place called Port Douglas, when we decided' – he saw her about to correct him – 'when I decided that it would be fun to hire a boat and go out for a little fishing.'

'In a crocodile-infested estuary,' Carmel added. She turned to me. 'Alan was too cheap to pay for a big boat with a guide, so we got a little boat by ourselves. A very little boat.' She allowed him to continue.

'So we got this little boat,' he went on, with a magnanimous nod in her direction, 'with a little outboard motor on it, and we set off across this kind of estuary. The estuary was crowded with other boats, but I spotted an inlet, and I thought: "Oh, we'll try up there." Well, the inlet turns out to be a river – a really beautiful one. So we go cruising up this river and it's just wonderful, your quintessential tropical paradise – big green river, jungle backdrop, colourful birds flying through the trees. You can imagine it. Best of all, there's not a soul around. We've got it all to ourselves. So we find a nice spot and I cut the engine and we're sitting there with our fishing lines in the water having a nice relaxing time when Carmel points out a kind of muddy bare patch on the bank, and we realize it's a crocodile launching place. Couldn't be anything else. Then we notice that there are several of these launching places all along the bank. It starts to dawn on us that maybe this is why there is nobody else up here, because it's infested with crocodiles. Just as we are coming to this significant conclusion there's a splash off to one side, like something heavy going into the water, and then a line in the water moving vaguely towards us.'

'Whoa,' I said.

'My sentiments exactly, Bryson.' He grinned.

'So what did you do?'

'Well, like the good sailor I am, I hopped to the motor to get us out of there. Only the motor wouldn't start. It just would not go.'

'Meanwhile,' Carmel interjected, 'I'm sitting in the back of the boat watching this line coming towards us and saying, "Alan, the crocodile's coming. It's definitely coming our way. Let's get out of here, mate. What do you say?"'

'And I'm pulling on the cord, and pulling and pulling, and the engine is just going *putt putt putt pfffffft*. And all the while the crocodile's coming. *Finally*, miraculously, the engine catches and we're able to move off. Only we're pointing in the wrong direction, so we've got to go *up* the river, away from where we want to be, in order to turn around. Anyway, after much messing around and crashing into banks and a little affectionate discussion of how we're going to die in a minute and it's all my fault, we get turned around. Only to get out of there we've got to go towards where the crocodile is.'

'So where is the crocodile now?'

'No idea. There's no sign of him now. He's there somewhere, but we don't know where. He could be right alongside the boat for all we know. The water's so murky you can't see two inches into it. But we do know that sometimes crocodiles go for boats.'

'Especially little cheap tinny boats,' Carmel said, smiling at him.

Alan grinned happily. 'So I throw open the throttle,' he went on, 'and the boat putters along at about half a mile an hour because it is, I have to admit, a very small and cheap boat. We've got to go maybe a quarter of a mile through the crocodile's territory at crawling speed and all the while we're sitting there expecting to feel a bang against the hull and to be tipped into the water. It was a little unnerving.'

'Did you know,' I said, 'that an outboard motor engine sounds to a crocodile very like the territorial growl of another crocodile? That's why crocodiles so often go for small boats apparently.'

They looked at me with amazement. It's not often a foreigner gets to scare the crap out of Australian listeners, but I had just read the book after all.

'I'm so glad I didn't know that at Port Douglas,' Carmel said. She gave an expansive shiver.

'But you got back OK, I take it?' I asked.

Alan nodded happily. 'We went down the river, across the estuary and were out of that boat – and I mean clean out – before it touched the dock.' He looked at me with a very pleased and expectant smile. 'And how long do you think we'd had the boat out? We'd hired it for a half-day, bear in mind.'

I indicated that I couldn't guess.

Howe leaned towards me, beaming all over. 'Twenty-nine minutes,' he said with the supremest pride. 'Guy told us it was a record.'

'That's splendid,' I said.

'A proud achievement for the Howe family,' he added, and you could see that he meant it.

Howe had to put out a paper the next day, but Carmel offered to show me the sights. So late the next morning we drove into the city to drop off my rental car, and to do some shopping and have a look around. We were driving down Chapel Street looking for a place to park, and Carmel was telling me about her work – she is the Melbourne correspondent for News International – when she broke off and said brightly: 'Oh look, it's Jim Cairns.' She indicated a little old man crossing the road in front of us carrying a chair and a card table. He looked a touch timeworn, but otherwise unremarkable. 'He was Deputy Prime Minister in the Whitlam government,' she informed me. I looked at her to see if she was pulling my leg, but she smiled sincerely. 'He sells his autobiography at that market over there.' She indicated the sort of covered market where you would go to buy vegetables.

I looked at her. 'He sells books – his own book – from a card table?'

She smiled, cheerfully acknowledging that this might strike an outsider as just a trifle cheesy. 'I suppose it's a way for him to make a little pocket money,' she added.

This was a man, you understand, who had not so long ago held the second highest office in the land. The equivalent in America, I suppose, would be to find Walter Mondale sitting at a card table in a mall in Minneapolis selling White House coasters and other memorabilia.

'He does this regularly?' I asked.

'Oh, he's a fixture. You want to meet him?'

'Very much.'

We found a space and parked, but when we got to the market we discovered that he had gone. Evidently we had seen him on his way home. 'I think things are sometimes a little slow for him,' Carmel said sympathetically. 'He's been selling the book for a long time.'

I nodded and reflected, not for the first time, what a strange, small, distant country Australia is.

We were headed for the Immigration Museum but our route took us past the new Crown Casino, a gaming palace that all Melbourne people either loathe because it's tacky and tempts foolish people to lose their savings, or adore because it's tacky and sometimes pays out big. 'You want to have a look at it?' Carmel asked. I hesitated – I felt I had satisfied my gambling curiosity at the Penrith Panthers club in Sydney on my first trip – but she said with unusual certitude, 'I think it'll interest you,' and we went in.

She couldn't have been more right. It was an amazing place, vast in scale – it dwarfed by far even the Penrith club – and dripping with ornate fixtures. Some kind of frantic laser show involving synthesized music and lots of drifting smoke (the better to show up the dancing beams, I guess) was taking place in a lofty outer atrium, but almost nobody was watching. The real business was in the casino beyond, which was no less extravagant in decor and went on seemingly for ever. I can say with confidence that whoever won the contract for the carpet at the Crown Casino has not had to work since. It took twenty minutes to stroll from one end of the room to the other. The amazing thing was its busyness and strange intensity. It was barely lunchtime and perhaps 2,000 gamblers were already in devoted attendance. Hardly a pit or machine wasn't in fully active service. I had never seen anything on this scale outside Las

Vegas, and in Las Vegas a good chunk of the people are just fooling around and having a good time. The people here were merely intent. At one roulette table I saw a man distribute perhaps twenty chips around the baize, lose them all, then reach into a wallet and pluck out twenty $50 bills to buy more. Quite slowly – for urban Australia is such a multicultural place that you scarcely notice these things normally – it dawned on me that he and the overwhelming proportion of other patrons were Chinese. I may have misjudged his attire, but he looked like a waiter or cook – certainly not like someone who could afford to lose thousands in a session. I mentioned this to Carmel and she nodded.

'Spectacular gamblers,' she whispered. She gave a wan smile. 'It's huge business. A billion dollars a year goes through here. Victoria gets 15 per cent of all its revenues from gambling.'

I thought for a moment. That must be hundreds of millions of dollars. 'So how many casinos are there in the state?' I asked.

'You're in it,' she said.

The Immigration Museum, just over the Yarra River in a grand old edifice that was once the local Customs House, provided a calm and decidedly more cerebral contrast. It had only recently opened, and still gleamed with shiny newness. Howe had been particularly eager that I see it because in his capacity as pillar of the community he had been one of the driving forces behind its foundation. Since the immigrant experience is essentially the story of modern Australia, it was really a museum of social history and quite the best one I have seen anywhere.

In a cavernous central hall was a large walk-in display in the shape of an ocean liner and designed, with the help of replica cabins and various ephemera, to convey the flavour of shipboard life for immigrants at different periods. I was particularly taken with the 1950s portion. I suppose because I grew up a thousand miles from the sea and missed the great age of passenger liners, I have always been subject to a romantic longing for ocean travel. In any case, I found myself helplessly lingering over every trivial detail of shipboard life – studying a forty-year-old menu as if I would soon be making my choice between lamb cutlets and braised beef, imagining my own books and toiletries on the shelf beside the bunk, thinking whether for the tea dancing this afternoon I should wear my baggage label shirt or go for a wild-orchids-of-Hawaii motif.

I hadn't realized – or at least hadn't stopped to reflect in anything like an adequate manner – quite what an investment in both time and funds a trip to Australia represented in those days. Until as late as the early 1950s a round-trip aeroplane ticket from Australia to England cost as much as a three-bedroom suburban home in Melbourne or Sydney. With the introduction by Qantas of larger Lockheed Super Constellation airliners in 1954, prices began to fall, but even by the end of the decade travelling to Europe by air still cost as much as a new car. Nor was it a terribly speedy or comfortable service. The Super Constellations took three days to reach London and lacked the power or range to dodge most storms. When monsoons or cyclones were encountered, the pilots had no choice but to put on the seat-belt signs and bounce through them. Even in normal conditions they flew at a height guaranteed to produce more or less constant turbulence. (Qantas called it, without evident irony, the Kangaroo Route.) It was, by any modern measure, an ordeal.

So for nearly every immigrant throughout the 1950s, a trip to Australia meant a five-week sea cruise. Even now, of course, when you must allow yourself to be sealed into a winged canister for a full day in order to get there, Australia feels a long way away. But how infinitely remote it must have seemed when you stood on a ship's deck and watched the continents fall away one by one and measured out the distance in 12,000 miles of ship's wake. I studied the faces of the beaming people lounging on sunchairs or striding about on breezy decks. They wore expressions just like those on the faces of the people I'd seen in the Surfers Paradise book in Adelaide. These people were happy, too – radiantly so. They were on their way to a lucky country and they knew it. Awaiting them was a life of abundant sunshine and good jobs, good homes, good prospects, and electric jugs for all. They were going on a holiday and they were going *for ever.*

It was such an interesting age for Australia. It wasn't just millions of foreigners who became Australian in the 1950s but, in an odd way, Australians themselves. I had only just learned that until 1949 there was no such thing as Australian citizenship. People born in Australia were not in any technical sense Australians at all but Britons – as British as if they were from Cornwall or Scotland. They swore allegiance to king and country, and when Britain went to war they unhesitatingly went off to die in foreign fields for her. At school, they studied British history, geography and economics as assiduously as if they were growing up in Liverpool or Manchester.

I remember in one of her letters Catherine Veitch remarking to me on the surreal quality of sitting in an Adelaide classroom in the 1930s looking out on blazing waratah trees and flocks of kookaburras or whatever while learning the heights of Scottish mountains or the figures for barley production in East Anglia.

The absurdity of the situation wasn't lost on Australians, but Britain was all they had. As the historian Alan Moorehead once wrote: 'Australians of my generation grew up in a world apart. Until we went abroad we had never seen a beautiful building, hardly ever heard a foreign language spoken, or been to a well-acted play, or eaten a reasonably sophisticated meal, or listened to a good orchestra.' The oddest aspect of all was that millions of Australians, most of whom had never left the country, went through life thinking of England in some odd, ultimate sense as home. As late as 1957 in *On the Beach*, the Nevil Shute novel in which a nuclear war leaves Australia as the last inhabited place on earth, the author could have his Australian heroine lament: 'I was going home in March. To London. It's been arranged for years . . . It's so bloody unfair.' By 'home' she means a country she has never seen and now never will.

But even as Shute wrote Australia was in the process of becoming a very different country. In the Second World War it had suffered a kind of blunt trauma when, after the fall of Burma and Singapore, Britain pulled out of the Far East, leaving Australia suddenly alone and dangerously exposed. At the same time Winston Churchill, a man whose presumptuousness was never less than enthralling, asked Australia's military leaders to divert their troops to India – in effect, to abandon their wives and children and fight for the greater good of empire. The Australians decided they could not. Instead they stayed behind and fought a rearguard action to try to stop the Japanese advance across New Guinea.

Not many people outside Australia realize just how close the Japanese got. They had captured most of the Solomon Islands and much of New Guinea, just to the north, and seemed poised for an invasion. The Australian military, knowing the position was hopeless, drew up a plan to fall back to the southeast corner of the country, sacrificing nearly the whole of the continent in the hope of defending the main cities. It could have been no more than a delaying tactic. Luckily, the tide of battle moved elsewhere after the American naval victory at Midway and an Australian victory over Japan at Milne Bay. Australia was reprieved.

Australia escaped but it was left with two scars – a realization that Britain could not be counted on to come to its rescue in a crisis, and a sense of immense vulnerability to the teeming and unstable countries to the north. Both of these matters deeply influenced Australian attitudes in the post-war years – indeed still do. Australia became seized with the conviction that it must populate or perish – that if it didn't use all that empty land and fill all those empty spaces someone from outside might do it for them. So in the years after the war, the country threw open its doors. In the half-century after 1945 its population soared, from seven million to 18 million.

Britain alone couldn't provide the necessary bodies, so people were welcomed from all over Europe, particularly Greece and Italy in the immediate post-war years, making the nation vastly more cosmopolitan. Suddenly Australia was full of people who liked wine and good coffee and olives and aubergines, and realized that spaghetti didn't have to be a vivid orange and come from tins. The whole warp and rhythm of life changed. Good Neighbour Councils were established everywhere to help the immigrants settle and feel welcomed, and the Australian Broadcasting Corporation offered English language courses which were enthusiastically taken up by tens of thousands. By 1970, the country could boast of 2.5 million 'New Australians', as they were known.

Of course, it wasn't perfect. In the fever to populate, some migrants were accepted with less reflection than might have been wished. At least ten thousand children, many as young as four, were despatched from British orphanages between 1947 and 1967 by child welfare groups such as the Salvation Army, Barnardo's and the Christian Brothers. The impulse was genuinely altruistic – it was felt that the children would have a chance of a better life in a country that was warm and sunny and needed labour – but the execution often lacked subtlety. Siblings were frequently parted, never to meet again, and many of the children had essentially no notion of what was happening to them. In his book *Orphans of the Empire*, Alan Gill notes how one little boy, seeing a sign announcing the mustering point for 'the Barnardo's party', was thrilled because he presumed 'party' meant cake and ice cream. Another enquired, as the ship made its way up the Thames, whether they would be home in time for tea. Stories don't get a great deal more poignant than that.

There was also the deep odium of the White Australia Policy, which allowed immigration officials to keep out undesirables by requiring them to pass a literacy test in any European language of the authorities' choosing (including on one famous occasion Scottish Gaelic) and to deport non-whites with little thought of compassion. In the early 1950s, Arthur Calwell, the Minister for Immigration, tried to repatriate the Indonesian-born widow and eight children of an Australian citizen. If Australians have a single radiant virtue, it is the belief in a 'fair go' – a sense of the fundamental rightness of common justice – and the case caused an outcry. The courts told Calwell to get real, and the more insensitive side of the exclusion policy swiftly began to erode. Around 1970, as Australia increasingly recognized that it was, at least geographically, an Asian nation and not a European one, the colour bar came down and hundreds of thousands of immigrants were let in from across the region. Today Australia is one of the most multicultural countries on earth. A third of the people in Sydney were born in another country; in Melbourne the four most common surnames are Smith, Brown, Jones and Nguyen. Across the country as a whole almost a quarter of people have no British antecedents on either side of their families. For millions of people it truly was a chance of a new life – one that, on the whole, was generously extended and gratefully accepted.

In a single generation, Australia remade itself. It went from being a half-forgotten outpost of Britain, provincial, dull and culturally dependent, to being a nation infinitely more sophisticated, confident, interesting and outward looking. And it did all this, by and large, without discord or disturbance or serious mistakes – indeed often with a kind of grace.

By coincidence, a few nights earlier I had watched a television documentary about the immigrant experience in the 1950s. One of the people interviewed was a man who had arrived from Hungary as a teenager after the uprising there. On his first full day in the country he had gone as instructed to the local police station and explained in halting English that he was a new immigrant who had been told to register his address. The sergeant had stared at him for a moment, then risen from his seat and come around the desk. The Hungarian recalled that for one bewildered moment he thought the policeman might be about to strike him, but instead the sergeant thrust out a meaty hand and said warmly, 'Welcome to Australia, son.' The Hungarian recalled the incident with wonder even now, and when he finished there were tears in his eyes.

I tell you sincerely. It's a wonderful country.

CHAPTER ELEVEN

CARMEL GREW UP ON A FARM IN EASTERN VICTORIA ON THE SOUTHERN edge of the Great Dividing Range, in lovely country of green fields set against a backdrop of blue hills. Howe, a lifelong city boy whose notion of the bush was of a monotonous expanse filled with deathly creatures, had gone to visit the family farm out of a sense of husbandly duty and fallen for it at once – so much so that he and Carmel had bought a parcel of land high on a neighbouring hillside, trucked in a jaunty wooden cottage and placed it in a lofty spot giving views over miles of hills, woods and farms. Howe had been telling me about it with a certain repetitive rapture for years and was keen for me to see it. So the next day, after loading up with provisions, we set off in their car for the three-hour drive to their rural idyll.

'Bush' is such a vague word in Australia that I wasn't sure what to expect, but it became obvious once we had shrugged off the outer suburbs of Melbourne that eastern Victoria was a favoured corner of the world – greener than any part of Australia I had seen before and backed by mountains that attained a wholly respectable eminence. The road wound through meadowy landscapes in a charmingly indecisive manner and through a succession of small and pleasant little towns. With strange, unshakeable pride, Howe wore an arrestingly outsized and touchingly misguided bush hat he had lately acquired, which inclined Carmel and me, when we stopped for petrol or coffee, to signal to staring strangers that he was out on a visit and we'd be taking him back to the home at the end of the week, but otherwise the journey passed without incident or embarrassment.

Alan and Carmel's house stands in glorious seclusion on the brow of a steep hill. The view, over a snug and restful valley of tobacco fields and vineyards, was expansive and charming in a way that brought to mind a children's picture book. This was, I realized after a minute, the view from high up the beanstalk.

'Not bad, eh?' said Howe.

'Much too good for anyone in a hat like that. What's this area called?'

'The King Valley. Carmel's old man used to farm over there.' He pointed to a rolling piece of land nestled against a neighbouring hill. It recalled, almost impossibly, the landscapes of the American artist Grant Wood – gumdrop hills, rolling fields, plump trees – which depicted an idealized Iowa that never actually existed. It existed here.

Howe let us into the house and he and Carmel immediately began moving about in an impressively practised manner, opening windows, putting on the water heater, packing away groceries. I helped carry stuff in from the car, watching for snakes with every step, and when that was finished ventured onto the broad deck to take in the view. Howe came out after a minute bearing two cold beers, one of which he passed to me. I don't believe I had ever seen him looking so relaxed. Mercifully he had removed the hat.

He took a sip of beer, then said in an anecdotal tone: 'When I first met Carmel, she used to talk about one day buying a piece of land out here and putting a house on it and I thought: "Yes, dear." I mean, why would you want to own a house in the middle of the bush with all the costs and dangers of bush fires and everything? And then one day we came up to visit her family, and I took one look and I said: "Right, where do I sign?" Not long after that the family sold up and moved to Ballarat. So we bought this corner of the property, which they were happy to sell because it's too steep to farm, and had the house put up.' He nodded at Carmel, humming away in the kitchen. 'She loves it here. So do I, come to that. I never thought I'd say I loved the country but jeez you know it's a nice place to get away to.'

'Are bush fires a big worry?'

'Well, they are when they happen. Sometimes they're colossal. Gum trees just want to burn, you know. It's part of their strategy. How they outcompete other plants. They're full of oil, and once they catch fire they're a bugger to put out. You get a really big bush fire moving across the landscape at fifty miles an hour with flames leaping a hundred and fifty feet in the air and it's an awesome sight, believe me.'

'How often does that happen?'

'Oh, I suppose every ten years or so you get a really big one. There was one in 1994 that burned 600,000 hectares and threatened parts of Sydney. I was there at the time and in one direction there was this pall of black smoke that completely filled the sky. Burned for days. The biggest one ever was in 1939. People still talk about that one. It was during a heatwave so bad that department store mannequins' heads actually started to melt in the windows. Can you imagine that? That one burned up most of Victoria.'

'So how much at risk are you here?'

He shrugged philosophically. 'It's all in the lap of the gods. Could be next week, could be ten years from now, could be never.' He turned to me with an odd smile. 'You are totally at the mercy of nature in this country, mate. It's just a fact of life. But I tell you one thing.'

'What's that?'

'It sure makes you appreciate something like this when you know it could all go up in a puff of smoke.'

Howe is one of those people who can't stand to see anyone sleeping when there is daylight to be utilized, and he rousted me out early the next morning with the announcement that he had a busy day planned for us. For a terrible moment I thought he meant we were going to shingle the roof or dig up boulders or something, but then he noted that we were going to have a Ned Kelly day. Howe was immensely proud that Kelly came from this part of Victoria and wanted to show me several of the sights connected with his short and brutish life. This sounded somewhat more promising.

It is an interesting fact, and one that no doubt speaks much about the Australian character, that the nation never produced a law enforcement hero along the lines of Wyatt Earp or Bat Masterson in America. Australian folk heroes are all bad guys of the Billy the Kid type, only here they are known as bushrangers, and the most famous of them all was Ned Kelly.

The story of Kelly is easily told. He was a murderous thug who deserved to be hanged and was. He came from a family of rough Irish settlers, who made their living by stealing livestock and waylaying innocent passers-by. Like most bushrangers he was at pains to present himself as a champion of the oppressed, though in fact there wasn't a shred of nobility in his character or his deeds. He killed several people, often in cold blood, sometimes for no very good reason.

In 1880, after years on the run, Kelly was reported to be holed up with his modest gang (a brother and two friends) in Glenrowan, a hamlet in the foothills of the Warby Range in northeastern Victoria. Learning of this, the police assembled a large posse and set off to get him. As surprise attacks go, it wasn't terribly impressive. When the police arrived (on an afternoon train) they found that word of their coming had preceded them and that a thousand people were lined up along the streets and sitting on every rooftop eagerly awaiting the spectacle of gunfire. The police took up positions and at once began peppering the Kelly hideout with bullets. The Kellys returned the fire and so it went throughout the night. The next dawn during a lull Kelly stepped from the dwelling, dressed unexpectedly, not to say bizarrely, in a suit of home-made armour – a heavy cylindrical helmet that brought to mind an inverted bucket, and a breastplate that covered his torso and crotch. He wore no armour on his lower body, so one of the policemen shot him in the leg. Aggrieved, Kelly staggered off into some nearby woods, fell over and was captured. He was taken to Melbourne, tried and swiftly executed. His last words were: 'Such is life.'

Not exactly the stuff of legend, one would have thought, yet in his homeland Kelly is treated with deep regard. Sidney Nolan, one of Australia's most esteemed artists, did a famous series of paintings devoted to Kelly's life, and books abound on the subject. Even serious historians often accord him an importance that seems to the outsider curiously disproportionate. Manning Clark, for example, in his one-volume history of Australia, devotes just a paragraph to the design and foundation of Canberra, dispenses with federation in two pages, but gives a full nine pages to the life and achievements of Ned Kelly. He also allows Kelly some of his most florid and incoherent prose, which is saying a great deal, believe me. Manning Clark is an extraordinary stylist at the best of times – a man who would never call the moon 'the moon' when he might instead call it 'the lunar orb' – but with Kelly he was inspired to lofty allusions and cosmic musings of a rare impenetrability. Here is a small part of his description of Kelly's fateful emergence from the compound after the night-long shootout:

> *In the half light before that red disc [i.e., the sun] appeared again on the eastern horizon . . . a tall figure, encased in armour, came out of the mists and wisps of frosty air . . . Some thought it was a madman or a ghost; some thought it was the Devil, the whole atmosphere having stimulated in friend and foe alike a 'superstitious awe'.*

Personally – and this is just a stab in the dark – I think Manning Clark was taking way too much codeine. Here's another of his well-juiced creations, this the merest fragment of a much longer passage discussing Kelly's legacy:

> *He lived on as a man who had confronted the bourgeois calm-down with all the uproar of a magnificent Dionysian frenzy, a man who had taken down the mighty from their seat and driven the rich empty away. He lived on as a man who had savaged policemen in the old convict tradition . . . and denounced the brutal barbarism of those who clothed their sadism toward the common people in the panoply of the law.*

About 2,800 milligrams talking there, I would say.

Today Glenrowan is a one-street town with a couple of pubs, a scattering of houses and a short strip of enterprises dedicated to extracting a little cash from the Kelly legend. On this hot summer's day there were perhaps a dozen visitors in town, including Alan, Carmel and me. The biggest of the commercial establishments, a place called Ned Kelly's Last Stand, was covered in painted signs of a semi-professional quality. 'This is not a place for Whimps,' said one, promisingly. Another added: 'It is absolutely absurd that after allowing yourself 10 to 20 minutes to take photos, walk up and down the street and buy some souvenirs and then have the audacity to tell your friends – "Don't go to Glenrowan, for there is nothing to see." To be quite honest most visitors to Glenrowan wouldn't know if the country shithouse fell on them . . .'

The impression one derived from further study was that Ned Kelly's Last Stand contained some kind of animatronic show. Alan, Carmel and I exchanged happy looks and knew that this was a place for us. Inside, a friendly man presided over the till. We were mildly staggered to see that they wanted $15 a head for admission.

'It's good, is it?' said Howe.

'Mister,' said the man with the greatest sincerity, 'it's like Disneyland in there.'

We bought tickets and shuffled through a door into a dim room where the spectacle was to begin. The space was designed to look like an old saloon. In the middle were benches for the audience. Before us, in a deep gloom, we could just make out the shapes of furniture and seated dummies. After a few minutes, the lights dimmed altogether, there was a sudden startling bang of gunfire and the performance began.

Well, call me a Whimp, drop a brick shithouse on me, but I can honestly say that I have seldom seen anything so wonderfully, so delightfully, so monumentally bad as Ned Kelly's Last Stand. It was so bad it was worth every penny. Actually, it was so bad it was worth more than we paid. For the next thirty-five minutes we proceeded through a series of rooms where we watched home-made dummies, each with a frozen smile and a mop of hair that brought to mind wind-blown pubis, re-enacting various scenes from the famous Kelly shootout in a random and deliriously incoherent way. Occasionally one of them would turn a stiff head or jerk up a forearm to fire a pistol, though not necessarily in sync with the narrative. Meanwhile, around each room lots of other mechanical events were taking place – empty chairs rocked, cupboard doors mysteriously opened and shut, player pianos played, a figure of a boy on a trapeze (and why not?) swung back and forth amid the rafters. Do you know those fairground stalls where you fire a rifle at assorted targets to make an outhouse door swing open or a stuffed chicken fall over? Well, this reminded me of that, only much worse. The narrative, insofar as it could be heard above the competing noises, made no sense at all.

When at last we were liberated into the sunshine, we were so delighted that we considered going in again – but \$45 is a lot of money, after all, and we feared that with repeated exposure it might begin to make some sense. So instead we went and looked at a giant fibreglass Ned Kelly that stood outside one of the souvenir shops. It wasn't as big or as intimidating as the Big Lobster, and its testicles didn't swing in the breeze, but it was still a game stab at the genre. Then we had a look around a couple of the shops and bought some postcards, and returned to the car for the next part of our day's adventure.

This was to see the famous Kelly Tree at a remote spot called Stringybark Creek. This involved a long drive into a strange, spooky valley of abandoned and semi-abandoned farms, nearly all of them half buried under blackberry brambles, then up into dense and verdant rainforest, and finally into crowded groves of towering stringybark trees. Australia has some 700 varieties of eucalyptus trees and they have the most wonderfully expressive names – kakadu woollybutt, bastard tallow-wood, gympie messmate, candlebark, ghost gum – but the stringybark was the first that I could identify by sight. The bark peels off in long strips and hangs from the branches in fibrous tassels or lies in curled heaps on the ground, all the better to burn apparently. It was a handsome tree, too: tall, straight and exceptionally close-growing. Some miles into the woods we came to a parking area beside a sign announcing the Kelly Tree. We were the only visitors; it felt as if we might have been the only visitors in years. The forest was cool and noiseless, and with all the strands of bark hanging down it had a strange, unwelcoming, otherworldly feel. The Kelly Tree stood along a path through the woods, distinguished from the others by the stoutness of its trunk and by a metal plaque in the shape of Kelly's famous helmet.

'And what is the Kelly Tree exactly?' I asked.

'Well,' Alan said with a learned air, 'as the Kelly gang got more and more notorious the police started hunting them with greater determination, and so they had to hide out in increasingly remote and desperate places.'

'Such as here?'

He gave a nod. 'Can't get much lonelier than this.'

We took a moment to consider our surroundings. Because of the denseness with which the stringybarks grew beside each other, there was almost no space to stretch out or move around, and the air had a kind of dank, organic closeness. It was, I think, the least bucolic forest I have ever been in. Even the light seemed stale.

'For three years, Kelly and his gang laid low, but in 1878 four policemen tracked them here. Somehow Kelly and his men captured and disarmed the policemen. Then they murdered three of them in a slow and pretty horrible way.'

'Horrible in what way?' I asked, ever alert for the morbid detail.

'Shot them in the balls and let them bleed to death. To maximize the pain and indignity.'

'And the fourth policeman?'

'Scarpered. He hid overnight in a wombat's burrow and the next day he made his way back to civilization and raised the alarm. So it was the murder of three men here that led eventually to the shootout at Glenrowan, as so memorably depicted for us by the robotic wonders of Ned Kelly's Last Stand.'

'So how come you know so much about all this?'

He looked at me with a hint of disappointment. 'Because I know a great deal about many things, Bryson.'

'You haven't got a clue about hats, though,' said Carmel cheerfully.

He looked at her and decided that this was a comment not to be dignified with a response, then turned back to me. 'Now to Powers Lookout,' he announced with a certain resolve, and set off in a stately tramp for the car.

'And how many more Kelly sights will we be visiting?' I called, trying not to betray too much alarm as I followed him through the woods. I wish no disrespect to Australia's most treasured thug, nor to imply any disappointment at all in the Kelly Tree – quite the reverse – but we did seem to be hours from anywhere and fast approaching that time of day when one begins to think about the convivial possibilities of food and drink.

'Just one more and it's on the way home and you won't regret it, and then we'll have a pint.'

He was as good as his word. Powers Lookout was fabulous. A platform of rock hanging high in the sky, it was named for Harry Powers, another storied bushranger, who sometimes shared the view with Kelly and his gang. Some diligent crew had built sturdy wooden walkways up and around the craggy rocks, making it a simple if slightly taxing matter to get from the main body of the cliff to the rocky outcrop that was the lookout. The view was sensational: perhaps a thousand feet below spread the King Valley, a snug and tidy realm of small farms and white farmhouses. Beyond, across air of flawless clarity, rose waves of low mountains, culminating in the distinctive hump of Mount Buffalo some fifty kilometres away.

'You know, if you put this in Virginia or Vermont,' I mused, 'there would be scores of people here, even at this hour. There'd be souvenir stands and probably an Imax screen and an adventure park.'

Howe nodded. 'It'd be the same in the Blue Mountains. It's like I've been telling you. This corner of Victoria is a great secret. Don't put it in your book.'

'Certainly not,' I replied sincerely.

'And wait'll you see what we've got for you tomorrow. It's even better.'

'Not possible,' I said.

'No, it is. It's even better.'

What he had for us the next day was a place called Alpine National Park, and in fact it was even better. Covering 2,500 square miles of eastern Victoria, it was lofty, grand, cool and green. If ever there was a portion of Australia remote from all the clichéd images of red soil and baking sun, this was it. They even skied here in winter. Alpine is perhaps a somewhat ambitious term. You will find no craggy Matterhorns here. The Australian Alps have a gentler profile, more like the Appalachians of America or the Scottish Cairngorms. But they do attain entirely respectable heights – Kosciuszko, the tallest, tops out at something over 7,000 feet.

Howe, through one of his contacts, had got hold of a friendly and helpful warden named Ron Riley, who had agreed to show us round his airy domain. A genial man with a dapper grey beard, Ron had the lean bearing and far-off gaze of someone whose world is the outdoors. We met in the little town of Mount Beauty, where we decanted into one of the park's four-wheel-drive vehicles and set off on the long, twisting drive up Mount Bogong, Victoria's highest peak at 6,500 feet. I asked him if Mount Bogong was named for the famous bogong moths, which erupt in vast, fluttery multitudes every spring and for a day or two seem to be everywhere. Along with plump witchetty grubs and long, slimy mangrove worms, they are the delicacies of the Aboriginal diet most often noted by chroniclers – noted because of course they are so unappealing to the Western palate. The bogongs are roasted in hot ashes and eaten whole, or so I had read.

Ron acknowledged that this was where they came from.

'And the Aborigines really eat them?'

'Oh, yeah – well, traditionally anyway. A bogong moth is eighty-five per cent fat and they didn't get a lot of fat in their diet, so it was quite a treat for them. They used to come from miles.'

'Have you ever eaten one?'

'Once,' he said.

'And?'

'Once was enough.' He smiled.

'What did it taste like?'

He thought for a moment. 'Like a moth.'

I grinned. 'I read that it has a kind of buttery taste.'

He thought about that. 'No. It has a moth taste.'

We climbed up a steep, winding road through dense groves of an amazingly tall and beautiful tree. Ron told me they were mountain ashes.

I made an appropriately appreciative face. 'I didn't know you had ashes here.'

'We don't. They're eucalypts.'

I looked again, surprised. Everything else about it – its long, straight body, its height, its lushness – was completely at odds with the skeletal gums associated with the lowlands. It really was true that the eucalypts have filled every ecological niche in Australia. There never was a more various tree.

'Tallest tree in the world after the California redwoods,' Ron added with a nod at the ashes, causing me to make another appreciative face.

'How tall do they grow?'

'Up to three hundred feet. They average about two hundred.' Three hundred feet is about the height of a twenty-five-storey building. Big trees.

'Do you get many bush fires?'

Ron gave a regretful nod. 'Sometimes. We lost five hundred thousand hectares in this part of the Great Dividing Range in 1985.'

'Gosh,' I said, though the figure meant little to me. Later I looked in a book and discovered that 500,000 hectares is equivalent to the area covered by Yosemite, Grand Teton, Zion and Redwood national parks in America. In other words, it was a natural disaster on a scale almost inconceivable elsewhere. (I also looked in the *New York Times Index* to see what coverage it had been given: none.) Even without being able to conceive quite what 500,000 hectares is, I knew of course that it was a lot, so I added politely: 'That must have been awful.'

Ron nodded again. 'Yeah, it was a bit,' he said.

We passed through a zone of snow gums – yet another niche dominated by the versatile eucalypts – and emerged into a sunny world of high, gently undulant plains, covered everywhere in pale grass and spongy alpine plants, with long views to distant summits. Quite a few visitors were evident, most of them with the springy step and considered apparel of the serious walker. At every group we passed, Ron slowed and called, 'G'day,' and asked if they had everything they needed in the way of information. They always did, but it seemed an unusually welcoming gesture.

And then we had the most marvellous day. Sometimes we stopped and walked a little, and the rest of the time we drove. The weather was gorgeous – cool at these heights but sunny – and Ron was droll and good-natured. He knew every leaf and bud and insect, and seemed genuinely to enjoy showing off all the secret corners of the park. We bumped along overgrown tracks through meadowy vales and skittered up near-perpendicular gravel roads to hidden firetowers. At every turn there was a point of interest or a memorable view. Alpine National Park is immense. It extends to 6,460 square kilometres – the equivalent of about seventeen Isle of Wights – but it is actually vaster still because it is contiguous along its eastern border with the even larger Kosciuszko National Park in the Snowy Mountains just over the border in New South Wales. Ron pointed out Kosciuszko – 'Kozzie', he called it – almost exactly 100 kilometres away, but I couldn't see it even with binoculars.

We finished the day at an imposing eminence called Mount McKay, where there were yet more top-of-the-world views: range upon range of steep hills rolling away to a far-off horizon. He took in the view with the assessing gaze of someone watching for a telltale plume of smoke.

'So how much of all this are you responsible for?' I asked.

'A hundred thousand hectares,' he replied.

'Lot of ground,' I said, thinking of the responsibility.

'Yeah,' he replied, squinting thoughtfully at the vista before us, 'I'm very lucky.'

It would of course take something extremely exceptional to match Glenrowan and Powers Lookout and Alpine National Park, and frankly I am not sure that many other countries could have provided it, but Howe assured me that he had one last special something for us to see – something that existed nowhere else in the world but in one small corner of Victoria. Beyond that he would not be drawn. The next day, to add to the savour of pleasure deferred, we went to a sleepy, old-fashioned coastal resort called Lakes Entrance, where we stopped for the night and had a nice seafood supper and a shuffle around, and the day after set off for our mystery attraction en route to Melbourne.

For quite a spell we drove through flat, sunny, uneventful

farming country. I sat in the back in a state of tranquil mindlessness until Alan abruptly steered the car off the highway beside a big sign I couldn't see well enough to read and parked in a large and mostly empty car park. I unfolded myself from the back seat and stepped blinking from the car. Beside us was a long tubular building – rather like a very large cloche, but made of concrete and painted white.

I looked questioningly at Howe.

'The Giant Worm,' he announced.

I stared at him in wonder and admiration.

'Not as in the famous giant worms of southwest Gippsland?'

'The same. You're familiar with them then?'

I gave the hollow laugh that such a question deserved. I had been reading about these behemoths of the underworld for months, albeit mostly in footnotes and other passing references. I had never expected to find a shrine to them.

Even in a land of extraordinary creatures, the giant worms of Gippsland are exceptional. Called *Megascolides australis*, they are the world's largest earthworms, growing up to twelve feet in length and more than six inches in diameter. So substantial are they that you can actually hear them moving through the earth, with a gurgling sound, like bad plumbing. What it is about this one small corner of Victoria that led to the evolution of extremely outsized worms is a question that science has yet to answer – but then, it must be said, very few of the world's best minds are drawn to questions of earthworm physiology and distribution. However, Howe promised, such knowledge as the world holds was contained within the tubular structure before us.

We procured three tickets and stepped eagerly into the display areas. On the wall facing us as we entered was a blown-up photograph, taken early in the twentieth century, showing four ridiculously pleased-looking men holding a droopy twelve-footer, little thicker than a normal earthworm but clearly ambitious in the length department. This I studied with great interest until Carmel drew my attention to a display of living giant worms. These were in a large glass panel, half an inch thick and filled with earth, rather like a very large ant farm, which hung on the wall. According to a label, the case contained a pair of giant worms. In a couple of spots where the earth had come away from the glass, we could see a millimetre or two of living giant worm, but as they weren't moving or doing anything (*Megascolides* is extremely devoted to rest, it seems) the experience was, I confess, a trifle anticlimactic. I had rather hoped there would be a petting corner or perhaps a tamer with a whip and a chair getting them to go through hoops. Alan and I tried to enliven the worm by tapping lightly on the glass, but it declined to respond.

Beside the panel were two long glass tubes filled with formaldehyde and containing a pair of preserved giant worms, each of normal earthworm circumference but about four or five feet long – not exactly titans but long enough to impress. Worms don't preserve terribly well and the formaldehyde had horrible little bits of worm skin floating in it as if somebody had been shaking the tubes or, more probably (as Alan and I conclusively established by tapping on them), by tapping on them. It was hard to look at them without growing a little queasy.

In the next room was a short film that told all that was known about the giant earthworm, which is to say almost nothing. They are reclusive, delicate, not terribly numerous and deeply uncooperative creatures, and thus not easy to study, even assuming you had a mind to. As you may recall from childhood experiments, earthworms really don't wish to come out of their holes, and if you pull they tend to snap. Well, imagine trying to tug a twelve-foot-long worm out of its burrow. Nearly impossible.

The one thing the Giant Worm Museum establishes beyond question is that you can only get so much mileage out of giant worms. Recognizing this, the proprietors had provided many other displays. Next door were some glass cases containing live snakes, including the famous and fearsome taipan, Australia's deadliest snake. Alan and I conducted some further glass-tapping experiments, then retreated four yards together in a platonic embrace when the taipan snarled at us (or possibly just yawned), opening its jaws wide enough to swallow a human head, or so it seemed. Deciding that henceforth we would keep our hands in our pockets, we followed Carmel outdoors where there was a compound containing yet more animals – kangaroos and emus, a forlorn-looking dingo, some caged cockatoos, half a dozen curled and dozing wombats and a couple of koalas, also dozing. It was a very hot, still afternoon and evidently siesta time, so the enclosures had an air of profound inertness – even the cockatoos slept – but I strolled among them with fascination, delighted to see so much native exotica brought together in one place. I peered with particular interest at the wombats – 'a squat, thick, short-legged and rather inactive quadruped, with great appearance of stumpy strength', as the first Englishman to see one recorded in 1788 in words that could not be bettered. (The man, David Collins, was a little less reliable with the kangaroo, which he described as 'a small bird of beautiful plumage'.) Alan and Carmel looked on with the tolerant amusement with which an American might view a display of raccoons and chipmunks, for most of these were animals that they saw regularly in their natural state, but to me every one was a novelty, even the dingo, which is after all just a dog. I made two complete circuits of the menagerie, then with a look of satisfaction I gave a nod and we set off once again for Melbourne.

We went to dinner at a Vietnamese restaurant in the inner Melbourne suburb of Richmond, on a street lined seemingly for miles with exotic restaurants, and Alan made the point, with which I could not argue, that Melbourne is an infinitely better city than Sydney for dining out in. In the course of conversation Alan asked if I was going to the Great Barrier Reef, a place for which he had a special fondness. I said I wasn't on this trip, but I was when I came back in a few weeks.

'Just be careful they don't leave you out there.' He gave a thin smile.

'What do you mean?'

'There was a story here recently. An American couple were left out on the reef.'

'Left?' I said, puzzled but intrigued.

Howe nodded and speared at some pasta. 'Yeah. Somehow the boat went back to port two passengers short. Bit of a pisser for the people left behind, wouldn't you say? I mean, one minute you're swimming around looking at coral and fish, having the time of your life, and then you surface and discover that the boat has gone and you are all alone in a very large and empty ocean.'

'They couldn't swim to shore?'

He smiled tolerantly at my ignorance. 'Barrier Reef's a long way out, Bryson – something over thirty miles where they were. Long way to swim.'

'And there were no islands or anything?'

'Not where they were. They were effectively out to sea. Apparently there were a couple of things they could swim to – a big moored pontoon that the dive company used and some kind of a coral atoll, both a couple of miles away. So presumably they started swimming towards those. What they didn't know – couldn't know – was that they were swimming across a deep-water channel. And guess what lurks in deep-water channels?'

'Sharks,' I said.

He nodded at my perspicacity. 'So imagine it. You're miles out to sea, stranded. You're tired. You're swimming towards a coral outcrop and it's hard going because the tide is coming in. The light is fading. And you look around and see fins circling you, maybe half a dozen of them.' He gave me a moment to form a picture in my mind, then fixed me with a deadpan expression. 'I don't know about you, but I think I'd ask for my money back.' He laughed.

'So nobody came back to rescue them?'

'It was two days before anyone noticed they were missing,' said Carmel.

I turned to her in wonder. 'Two days?'

'By which time, of course, they were long gone.'

'Eaten by sharks?'

She shrugged. 'No way of knowing, but presumably. Anyway, they were never seen again.'

'Wow.'

We ate in thoughtful silence for a minute, then I mentioned that every time there was an odd story in Australia, it seemed to come out of Queensland. My favourite of the moment concerned a German man, recently detained outside Cairns, who had arrived on a tourist visa in 1982 and spent the past seventeen years wandering on foot through the northern deserts living almost exclusively off road kill. I was also extremely partial to the story of a group of illegal immigrants who were brought from China on an old fishing boat, which dropped them in shallow water a hundred yards off a beach near Cairns. They were caught when one of their members, carrying a suitcase, dripping water conspicuously from sodden trousers and squelching with every step, presented himself at a newsagent's shop and politely asked the proprietor if he would order a fleet of taxis to take him and some associates to the railway station at Cairns. Nearly every day, it seemed, the papers had a story of arresting improbability under a Queensland dateline.

Alan nodded in accord. 'There's a reason for that, of course.'

'What's that?'

'They're crazy in Queensland. Madder than cut snakes. You'll like it up there.'

In the morning, Alan ran me to the airport by way of his office. While he went off to hold the front page, or do whatever editors do, he left me to sit at his big desk and play in his swivel chair. When he returned he was carrying a folder, which he passed to me. 'I dug out some stuff on that American couple that disappeared. I thought it might be of use to you.'

'Thank you,' I said, quite touched.

'It should give you some tips on how not to get left on the reef. I know what a dozy bugger you are, Bryson.'

At the airport he jumped out of the car and helped me haul my bag out of the back. He shook my hand. 'And remember what I said about watching yourself up north,' he said.

'Madder than cut snakes,' I repeated, to show that I had been listening.

'Madder than a sack of them.'

He smiled, then jumped back in the car, waved and was gone.

CHAPTER TWELVE

IT IS POSSIBLE, I SUPPOSE, TO CONSTRUCT HYPOTHETICAL circumstances in which you would be pleased to find yourself, at the end of a long day, in Macksville, New South Wales – perhaps something to do with rising sea levels that left it as the only place on earth not under water, or maybe some disfiguring universal contagion from which it alone remained unscathed. In the normal course of events, however, it is unlikely that you would find yourself standing on its lonely main street at six thirty on a warm summer's evening gazing about you in an appreciative manner and thinking: 'Well, thank goodness I'm here!'

I was in Macksville owing to the interesting discovery that Brisbane is not three or four hours north of Sydney, as I had long and casually supposed, but the better part of a couple of days' drive. Well, if you look on the television weather map Brisbane and Sydney are practically neighbours, their little local suns and storm clouds all but bumping on the chart. But in Australia neighbourliness is of course a relative concept. In fact, it is almost 1,000 kilometres from Sydney to Brisbane, much of it along a cheerfully poky two-lane road. And so, in mildly confounded consequence, I was in Macksville for the night.

I don't wish to disparage a community that 2,811 people proudly call home (and what a miraculous notion that is), but as I had rather had it in mind that I would be dining on fresh-caught barramundi and watching a sunset emblazon the Pacific on Queensland's storied Gold Coast rather than stuck in an obscure backwater barely halfway there, my disappointment was real. My immediate preoccupation was that I was running out of time on this trip. I had a commitment of long standing to take part in a fund-raising hike in Syria and Jordan for a British children's charity. In three days I was to fly home from Sydney, to collect hiking gear and see how many of my children still recognized me, before flying off again to London and onward to Damascus. It was clear that I wasn't going to see as much of the northern reaches of the Boomerang Coast as I had hoped.

So my mood as I strolled into town from my motel was, let us say, restrained. Macksville wasn't so bad really. Set on the bank of the swift and muddy Nambucca River, it was essentially just a pause in the highway: a tentacle of neatly gardened bungalows and small office buildings leading to a very compact town centre. Though the road through town is the Pacific Highway, the main artery connecting Sydney and Brisbane, only two cars passed as I followed its dusty margin into town. At the heart of the modest community stood the large and fading Nambucca Hotel, and I stepped in, glad to escape the heat. It was a roomy place but nearly empty. Two older guys in singlets and battered bush hats propped up one end of the long bar. In a side room a man and a woman sat in silent absorption amid the soft, mechanical glow of pokies. I procured a beer, stood long enough to establish that no one was going to take any interest in me that might lead to a conversation, and retired to the central portion of the bar where I parked myself on a stool and idly watched the evening news on a silent TV mounted on the wall.

Somewhere police were out in the bush with a pack of straining sniffer dogs; there was no telling what the dogs were looking for, though if it was red clay soil they were doing extremely well. Somewhere else there appeared to be a fresh outbreak of Ross River fever – yet another previously unknown malady for me to worry about. Then there was Paul Keating, the former Prime Minister – he of the deeply expressive vocabulary, as you may recall from the Canberra chapter – standing on the steps of an office building answering questions from reporters and looking testy. It was impossible to determine what he was saying, but I imagined he was telling all those present that they were nongs and maggots. I decided I quite liked watching the news with the sound off.

Meanwhile, back in the Known World something was happening in Kosovo; convoys were rolling along country roads and mortars were throwing up puffs of smoke on distant hills. Bill Clinton was in some kind of moral hot water again, or so I assumed because he was shown strolling through the Rose Garden holding hands with Hillary and Chelsea, all of them looking mutually devoted. They had a lovable spaniel with them as well, which I took as a sign that the President had been very bad indeed. It hardly mattered. It all seemed so far away.

Then lots of sport, all of it featuring Australians performing commendably. Finally a weather chart came on and showed sun everywhere and then the newsreader tapped her papers square and smiled in a way that suggested that we could all go to bed happy because Greg Norman was winning the golf and everything else was a long, long way away and didn't really affect us.

It is amazingly easy in Australia to forget, or at least to reduce to a dim awareness, that there is a world out there. Australians work hard in their news coverage to overcome the handicap of distance, but even so sometimes around the margins of the news you get a curious sense of disconnectedness – little things that remind you that this is a far, far country. I had noticed, for instance, that Australian newspapers commonly run obituaries, particularly of foreign figures, weeks or even months after they die. That's fair enough in a sense, I suppose – these people are going to be dead for ever, after all – but it does lend the pages a curiously leisured air. Then the previous day on my flight from Melbourne to Sydney, while browsing through a copy of the *Bulletin*, the country's venerable news magazine, I read a section called 'Flashback', which recorded important events in history on that week's dates. For 22 January, it had this interesting entry: '1934: Actor Bill Bixby (died 1993) is born in Park Ridge, Illinois, US.'

Consider that just for a moment. In a column devoted to significant moments in world history, the birth date of an actor whose culminating achievement was to play the straight man in a 1960s television series called *My Favorite Martian* is still being recalled in Australia *six years after his death*. Well, I think that's kind of spooky, frankly. I appreciate, of course, that this was a filler item at the back of a magazine and one shouldn't read too much into it, so let me offer a rather more compelling piece of temporal eccentricity.

As I sat at the bar now I pulled out my one-volume history of Australia by Manning Clark and dutifully ploughed into it. I had only about thirty pages left and I would be less than candid if I didn't tell you that I couldn't wait to have Mr Clark and his extravagant dronings out of my life for ever. Still, Australia's history is an interesting one and I had a comfy stool and the prospect of as much beer as I wanted, so I wasn't unhappy.

So I sat and read the rest of the book, and here's the thing. It finished in 1935. After 619 pages of the densest exposition, the book terminates with the appointment of John Curtin as leader of the Australian Labor Party on 1 October 1935. This is, let me stress, the standard, current, one-volume history of Australia – the one to which you will be directed in every bookshop in the land – and it finishes in 1935. That's sixteen Prime Ministers ago!

I was so dumbfounded that I actually lifted the book over my head to see if some pages had fallen out, then looked on the floor around my bar stool. But no. The book finished by design in 1935. Manning Clark died – or yielded the final tortured spark of life, as I am sure he would have wished me to put it – in 1991, so I was prepared to excuse him the last decade or so of Australia's eventful saga, but I would have thought he would find space for, let us say, the Second World War. Although his history was written long after the war (specifically, between 1962 and 1987 as a series of six books, of which I held the distilled essence), it contains not one mention of the most important event of the twentieth century. There is not even a hint of gathering storm clouds. Nor does the text find room for the Cold War, Aboriginal land reforms, the emergence of a multicultural society, the fall of the Whitlam government, the move to become a republic or the life and times of Bill Bixby, among rather a lot else.

To cover this troubling gap, the publishers had introduced into the present edition an afterword – a 'coda' – written by the book's editor and abridger. This condensed the last sixty-five years of Australian history into thirty-four pages, which, as you can imagine, gave the whole a somewhat breathless and incidental flavour. And until the 1995 edition, it didn't even have that.

Well, I find that extremely odd. That's all I'm saying.

Sighing, I closed my book and realized I was famished. According to a sign on a door across the room, the Nambucca had a restaurant, so I wandered over to investigate. The door wouldn't open.

'Dining room's closed, mate,' said one of the two guys at the bar. 'Chef's crook.'

'Must've ate some of his own cooking,' came a voice from the pokie alcove, and we all had a grin over that.

'What else is there in town?' I asked.

'Depends,' said the man, scratching his throat thoughtfully. He leaned towards me slightly. 'You like good food?'

I nodded. Of course I did.

'Nothin' then.' He went back to his beer.

'Try the Chinese over the road,' said his companion. 'It's not too bad.'

The Chinese restaurant was just across the road as promised, but according to a sign in the window it was not licensed to serve alcohol and I couldn't face small-town Chinese food without the solace of beer. I have travelled enough to know that a chef does not, as a rule, settle in a place like Macksville because he has a lifelong yearning to share the subtleties of 3,500 years of Szechuan cuisine with sheep farmers. So I went off to see what else there might be in Macksville's compact heart. The answer was very little. Everything appeared to be shut except one small takeaway establishment called, not altogether promisingly, Bub's Hotbakes. I opened the door, briefly enlivening 5,000 flies that had dropped by to see what Bub and his team were up to, and stepped inside, knowing in my heart that this was almost certainly going to be a regretted experience.

Bub's had a substantial range of food, nearly all of it involving brown meat and gravy lurking inside pastry. I ordered a large sausage roll and chips.

'We don't do chips,' said the amply proportioned serving maiden.

'Then how did you get like that?' I wanted to say, but of course I suppressed this unworthy thought and revised my order to a large sausage roll and something called a 'continental cheesecake square' and went with them outside. I ate standing on the corner.

I take nothing away from Bub's culinary prowess, I trust, when I tell you that a large sausage roll and a continental cheesecake square was not the most satisfying possible culmination to a night on the town even in as remote and challenging a spot as Macksville. Besides, it was only seven thirty in the evening. I weighed my options – TV back in the motel, a sunset stroll along the highway or more beer in the Nambucca – and toddled back into the Nambucca.

The two men at the bar had departed, and their place had been taken by a lone woman who was engaged in some deep and earnest conversation with the barmaid. Judging from their pinched and animated faces, this clearly involved gossip. 'Aw, he's all right in his place – they just haven't dug it yet,' I heard one quip drily to the other.

I acquired another beer and retired with it to my favoured spot at the bar, where I cracked open my book of maps to see where exactly I stood. It had only begun to dawn on me in the last day or two just how much of this amazingly vast and ungainly country I had still to tackle. I had been driving around almost continuously now for four weeks and I had covered only the tiniest portion of it. What's more, I had done the easy parts – the parts that are well paved and reasonably inhabited. Altogether Australia has 180,000 miles of paved highway, enough to keep a dedicated driver occupied for about a year, but the great bulk of it is bundled into the populous eastern corridor. Elsewhere, over vast areas there is nothing. Not an inch of paved road exists along the nearly 2,000 miles of indented coastline from Darwin to Cairns, which must make it one of the longest, not to say comeliest, stretches of coastline in the world not touched by highway. Similarly, no road intrudes on the tropical lushness that stretches for 500 miles from just beyond Cairns to the tip of Cape York, Australia's northernmost point and another area of superlative beauty. In the whole of Queensland, an area into which you could comfortably fit most of Western Europe, just three paved roads venture into the state's vast and arid interior, and only one provides an outlet to the two-thirds of Australia that lies to the west. From Camooweal in the north to Barringun in the south, you could, if you were completely out of your mind, walk 1,400 miles of Queensland without once crossing a paved surface. Travel any distance into the interior and you are, with amazing swiftness, in an empty country.

The outback does have dirt tracks in relative abundance, 300,000 miles of them altogether, but standard rental cars aren't allowed on them and even in a fully equipped offroad vehicle it is a brave or foolhardy driver who ventures out on his own because it is so easy to get lost or stranded. Just recently a young couple from Austria, on a trip into the outback in a rented four-by-four, had sunk to their axles in sand on a lonely, nameless track in the Simpson Desert. When they realized they were hopelessly embedded, the woman decided to hike forty miles to the Oodnadatta Track, where rescue was more likely. Why the woman went and not the man I don't know. What is known is that she took nine of their twelve litres of water and set off into 140-degree F heat.

For most of us it is not possible to conceive just how punishing such heat is. Under a full sun with temperatures that high, it is actually possible to begin to cook, rather as you would in a microwave oven, from the inside out. The poor woman didn't stand a chance. Even with a good supply of water, she lasted less than two days and covered just eighteen miles, less than half the distance required. (Her partner, sitting in shade, survived and was rescued.) In short, you don't want to be caught in the outback.

My more immediate problem was what I was going to do with my last couple of days. My original programme called for me to go to Brisbane, Surfers Paradise and the Big Banana at Coff's Harbour. But I didn't really have time now to see Brisbane, at least in any meaningful way, and I wasn't all that excited about the Big Banana. I mean no disrespect to a national treasure, but my devotion to giant fruit goes only so far. So as I sat at the bar now I leafed idly through the pages looking at the alternative diversions – Byron Bay, Dorrigo National Park, the Darling Downs of south Queensland – when two words, printed small and attached to a pale and erratic blue line, leaped out at me. I had my destination. I was going to a place called Myall Creek.

It was time to consider Australia's forgotten people.

CHAPTER THIRTEEN

ONE OF THE MOST MOMENTOUS EVENTS IN HUMAN HISTORY TOOK place at a time that will probably never be known, for reasons that can only be guessed at, by means that seem barely credible. I refer, of course, to the peopling of Australia.

Until fairly recently accounting for the presence of human beings in Australia was not such a problem. At the beginning of the twentieth century, it was thought that Aborigines had been on the continent for no more than 400 years. As recently as the 1960s, the time frame was estimated to be perhaps 8,000 years. Then in 1969 a geologist named Jim Bowler from the Australian National University in Canberra was poking around on the shores of a long-dried lake bed called Mungo in a parched and lonely corner of western New South Wales when something caught his eye. It was the skeleton of a woman, obtruding slightly from a sandbank. The bones were collected and sent off for carbon dating. When the report came back, it showed that the woman had died 23,000 years ago, at a stroke almost tripling the known period of occupation of Australia. Since then, other finds have pushed the date back further. Today the evidence points to an arrival date of at least 45,000 years ago, but probably more like 60,000.

The first occupants of Australia could not have walked there because at no point in human times has Australia not been an island. They could not have arisen independently because Australia has no apelike creatures from which humans could have descended. The first arrivals could only have come by sea, presumably from Timor in the Indonesian archipelago, and here is where the problems arise.

In order to put *Homo sapiens* in Australia you must accept that, at a point in time so remote that it precedes the known rise of behaviourally modern humans, there lived in southern Asia a people sufficiently advanced that they were fishing inshore waters from boats of some sort, rafts presumably. Never mind that the archaeological record shows no one else on earth doing this for another 30,000 years. We have got to get these people waterborne.

Next we have to explain what led them to cross at least sixty miles of open sea to reach a land they could not know was there. The scenario that is invariably invoked is of a simple fishing raft – probably little more than a floating platform – accidentally carried out to sea, probably in one of the sudden squalls that are characteristic of this part of the world. This craft then drifted helplessly for some days before washing up on a beach in northern Australia. So far so good.

The question that naturally arises – but is seldom asked – is how you get breeding stock out of this. If it's a lone fisherman who is carried off to Australia, then clearly he must find his way back to his homeland to report his discovery and to persuade enough people to come with him to start a colony. This suggests, of course, the possession of nautical skills sufficient to shuttle back and forth between invisible land masses – a prowess few prehistorians are willing to grant. If, on the other hand, the trip was one-way and accidental, then it must necessarily have involved a community of people of both sexes swept out to sea, either all together on a large raft (thought very unlikely) or in a flotilla of small rafts, and after successfully weathering a storm and at least a few days at sea, they were washed up on proximate parts of the north Australian coast where they regrouped and established a society.

You don't need vast numbers of people to populate Australia. Joseph Birdsell, an American academic, calculated that a group of twenty-five founding colonists could have produced a society of 300,000 in a little over 2,000 years. But you still need to get those initial twenty-five people there – more than can be plausibly accounted for with a raft or two blown off course.

Of course all of this may have happened in any number of other ways, and it may have taken generations to get fully under way. No one can possibly say. All that is certain is that Australia's indigenous peoples are there because their distant ancestors crossed at least sixty miles of fairly formidable sea tens of thousands of years before anyone else on earth dreamed of such an endeavour, and did it in sufficient numbers to begin to start the colonization of a continent.

By any measure this is a staggeringly momentous accomplishment. And how much note does it get? Well, ask yourself when was the last time you read anything about it. When was the last time in any context concerning human dispersal and the rise of civilizations that you saw even a passing mention of the role of Aborigines? They are the planet's invisible people.

A big part of the problem is that for most of us it is nearly impossible to grasp what an extraordinary span of time we are considering here. Assume for the sake of argument that the Aborigines arrived 60,000 years ago (that is the figure used by Roger Lewin of Harvard in *Principles of Evolution*, a standard text). On that scale, the total period of European occupation of Australia represents about 0.3 per cent of the total. In other words, for the first 99.7 per cent of its inhabited history the Aborigines had Australia to themselves. They have been there an almost unimaginably long time. And here lies their other unappreciated achievement.

The arrival in Australia of the Aborigines is, of course, merely the start of the story. They also mastered the continent. They spread over it with amazing swiftness and developed strategies and patterns of behaviour to exploit or accommodate every extreme of the landscape, from the wettest rainforests to the driest deserts. No people on earth have lived in more environments with greater success for longer. It is generally accepted that the Aborigines have the oldest continuously maintained culture in the world. It is thought by some – the respected prehistorian John Mulvaney, for instance – that the Australian language family may be the world's oldest. Their art and stories and systems of beliefs are indubitably among the oldest on earth.

These are obviously important and singular achievements, too. They provide incontestable evidence that the early Aboriginal peoples spoke and cooperated and employed advanced technological and organizational skills at a time much earlier than anyone had ever supposed. And how much notice do these achievements get? Well, again, until recently, virtually none. I had this brought home to me with a certain unexpected forcefulness when, after leaving Alan and Carmel and flying to Sydney, I went for an afternoon to the State Library of New South Wales. There while browsing for something else altogether I came across a 1972 edition of the *Larousse Encyclopedia of Archaeology*. Curious to see what it had to say about the findings at Lake Mungo three years earlier, I took it down to have a look. It didn't mention the Mungo findings. In fact, the book contained just one reference to Australia's Aborigines, a sentence that said: 'The Aborigines also evolved independently of the Old World, but they represent a very primitive technical and economic phase.'

That was it – the entire discussion of Australia's indigenous culture by a scholarly volume of weight and authority, written in the last third of the twentieth century. When I say these are the world's invisible people, believe me these are the world's invisible people. And the real tragedy is that that is only the half of it.

From the first moment of contact the natives were a source of the deepest wonder to the Europeans. When James Cook and his men sailed into Botany Bay they were astonished that most of the Aborigines they saw sitting on the shore or fishing in the shallows from frail bark canoes seemed hardly to notice them. They 'scarce lifted their eyes from their employment', as Joseph Banks recorded. The creaking *Endeavour* was clearly the largest and most extraordinary structure that could ever have come before them, yet most of the natives merely glanced up and looked at it as if at a passing cloud and returned to their tasks.

They seemed not to perceive the world in the way of other people. No Aboriginal language, for instance, had any words for 'yesterday' or 'tomorrow' – extraordinary omissions in any culture. They had no chiefs or governing councils, wore no clothes, built no houses or other permanent structures, sowed no crops, herded no animals, made no pottery, possessed almost no sense of property. Yet they devoted disproportionate efforts to enterprises that no one even now can understand. All around the coast of Australia the early explorers found huge shell mounds, up to thirty feet high and covering at the base as much as half an acre. Often these were some distance inland and uphill. The Aborigines clearly had made some effort to convey the shells from the beach to the mounds – one midden was estimated to contain 33,000 cubic metres of shells – and they kept it up for an enormously long time: at least 800 years in one case. Why did they bother? No one knows. In almost every way it was as if they answered to some different laws.

A few Europeans – Watkin Tench and James Cook notably –

viewed the Aborigines sympathetically. In the *Endeavour* Journal Cook wrote: 'They may appear to some to be the most wretched people on earth, but in reality they are far happier than we Europeans. They live in a tranquillity which is not disturbed by the inequality of condition: the earth and the sea of their own accord furnish them with all things necessary for life . . . they seemed to set no value upon anything we gave them, nor would they ever part with anything of their own.' Elsewhere, he added with a touch of poignancy: 'All they seem'd to want was for us to be gone.'

Unfortunately, few others were so enlightened. For most Europeans, the Aborigines were simply something that was in the way – 'one of the natural hazards', as the scientist and natural historian Tim Flannery has described it. It helped to regard them as essentially subhuman, a view that persisted well into the twentieth century. As recently as the early 1960s, as John Pilger notes, Queensland schools were using a textbook that likened Aborigines to 'feral jungle creatures'. When they weren't subhuman, they were simply inconsequential. In the same period, a Professor Stephen Roberts produced a fat and scholarly tome entitled *A History of Australian Land Settlement*, which managed to survey the entire period of European occupation and displacement without mentioning the Aborigines once. Such was the marginalization of the native peoples that until 1967 the federal government did not even include them in national censuses – did not, in other words, count them as people.

Largely for these reasons no one knows how many Aborigines were in Australia when Britons first settled it. The best estimates suggest that at the beginning of occupation the Aboriginal population was about 300,000, though possibly as high as a million. What is certain is that in the first century of settlement those numbers fell catastrophically. By the end of the nineteenth century the number of Aborigines was probably no more than 50,000 or 60,000. Most of this decline, it must be said, was inadvertent. Aborigines had almost no resistance to European diseases: smallpox, pleurisy, syphilis, even chickenpox and the milder forms of influenza often cut swathes through the native populations. But where Aborigines remained, they were sometimes treated in the most heartless and wanton manner.

In *Taming the Great South Land*, William J. Lines details examples of the most appalling cruelty by settlers towards the natives – of Aborigines butchered for dog food; of an Aboriginal woman forced to watch her husband killed, then made to wear his decapitated head around her neck; of another chased up a tree and tormented from below with rifle shots. 'Every time a bullet hit,' Lines reports, 'she pulled leaves off the tree and thrust them into her wounds, till at last she fell lifeless to the ground.' What is perhaps most shocking is how casually so much of this was done, and at all levels of society. In an 1839 history of Tasmania, written by a visitor named Melville, the author relates how he went out one day with 'a respectable young gentleman' to hunt kangaroos. As they rounded a bend, the young gentleman spied a form crouched in hiding behind a fallen tree. Stepping over to investigate and 'finding it only to be a native', the appalled Melville wrote, the gentleman lifted the muzzle to the native's breast 'and shot him dead on the spot'.

Such behaviour was virtually never treated as a crime – indeed was sometimes officially countenanced. In 1805, the acting judge-advocate for New South Wales, the most senior judicial figure in the land, declared that Aborigines had not the discipline or mental capacity for courtroom proceedings; rather than plague the courts with their grievances, settlers were instructed to track down the offending natives and 'inflict such punishment as they may merit' – as open an invitation to genocide as can be found in English law. Fifteen years later our old friend Lachlan Macquarie authorized soldiers in the Hawkesbury region to shoot any group of Aborigines greater than six in number, even if unarmed and entirely innocent of purpose, even if the number included women and children. Sometimes, under the pretence of compassion, Aborigines were offered food that had been dosed with poison. Pilger quotes a mid-nineteenth-century government report from Queensland: 'The niggers [were given] . . . something really startling to keep them quiet . . . the rations contained about as much strychnine as anything and not one of the mob escaped.' By 'mob' he meant about one hundred unarmed men, women and children.

The wonder of all this is that the scale of native murders was not far greater. In the first century and a half of British occupation, the number of Aborigines intentionally killed by whites (including in self-defence, during pitched battles and in other rather more justifiable circumstances) is thought to be about 20,000 altogether – an unhappy total, to be sure, but much less than one-tenth the number of Aborigines who died from disease.

That isn't to say that violence wasn't casual or widespread. It was. And it was against this background, in June 1838, that a dozen men on horseback set off from the farm of one Henry Dangar, looking for the people who had stolen or driven off some of their livestock. At Myall Creek they happened on an encampment of Aborigines who were known among the white settlers of the district as peaceable and inoffensive. Almost certainly they had nothing to do with the rustled cattle. Nonetheless their captors tied them together in a kind of great ball – twenty-eight men, women and children – led them around the countryside for some hours in an indecisive manner, then abruptly and mercilessly slaughtered them with rifles and swords.

In the normal course of things, that would almost certainly have been that. But in 1838 the mood of the nation was changing. Australia was becoming an increasingly urbanized society, and city dwellers were beginning to express revulsion for the casual slaughter of innocent people. When a campaigning Sydney journalist named Edward Smith Hall got hold of the story and began to bray for blood and justice, Governor George Gipps ordered the perpetrators tracked down and brought to trial. When arrested, two of the accused protested, with evident sincerity, that they hadn't known killing Aborigines was illegal.

Despite clearly damning evidence at the subsequent trial, it took a jury just fifteen minutes to acquit the defendants. But Hall, Gipps and the urban public were not lightly pacified and a second trial was ordered. This time seven of the men were found guilty and hanged. It was the first time that white people had been executed for the murder of Aborigines.

The Myall Creek hangings didn't end the slaughter of Aborigines so much as drive them underground. They went on sporadically for almost another century. The last was in 1928 near present-day Alice Springs when a white dingo hunter named Fred Brooks was murdered in uncertain circumstances and at least seventeen and perhaps as many as seventy Aborigines were chased down and killed by mounted constabulary in reprisal. (A judge in that case declared that the police had acted within the law.) But the Myall Creek case was undoubtedly a defining moment in Australian history. Though it gets at least a mention in almost all history books these days, I hadn't met anyone who had been there or even quite knew where it was, and it seemed apparent from the descriptions I had read that the authors had drawn exclusively from historical sources. I wanted to have a look.

It takes a little finding. From Macksville the next morning I drove sixty miles up the Pacific Highway to Grafton, then headed inland on a steep and lonely road up and through the Great Dividing Range. Four hours later, in hot and empty sheep country, I reached Delungra – a petrol station and a couple of houses with long views over mostly treeless plains – and there I turned down a back road that followed a twisting, sometimes nearly washed-out course on its way to the small town of Bingara twenty-five miles to the south. A couple of miles short of Bingara, I came to a small rickety-looking bridge over a half-dry creek. A little sign announced it as Myall Creek. I pulled the car into the shade of a river gum and got out to have a look. There was no memorial, no historical plaque. Nothing at all to indicate that here, or at least somewhere in the immediate vicinity, was where one of the most infamous events in Australian history took place. To one side of the bridge was a forlorn rest area with a pair of broken picnic tables and a good deal of shattered bottles in the stubby grass around the edge. In the sunny middle distance, perhaps a mile away, stood a large farmhouse, surrounded by fields of unusually verdant crops. In the other direction, and much closer, an overgrown track led to a white building. I walked along it to see what it was. A sign announced it as the Myall Creek Memorial Hall. It wasn't much of a monument to a terrible slaughter, but at least it was something. Then on a wall of the building I noticed a hand-painted sign and discovered that it had nothing to do with the slaughter; it was a memorial for the dead of two world wars.

I drove on the last couple of miles into Bingara (pop. 1,363), a hot and listless village with a dozing main street. It looked like a place that had once known prosperity, but most of the storefronts now were either empty or taken up with government enterprises – a health clinic, an employment advice centre, a tourist information office, police station, something called a 'Senior Citizens Rest Centre'. An old and improbably large movie house still announced itself as the Roxy, but clearly had been shut for years. In the tourist information centre I was received by a pleasant-looking middle-aged lady who bobbed to her feet at the sight of a customer. I asked her if they had any information about the massacre, and she gave me a crestfallen look.

'I'm afraid I don't know much about that,' she said.

'Really?' I said, surprised. The place was full of leaflets and books.

'Well, it was a long time ago. I believe the children study about it in school, but I'm afraid it's not something visitors ask about very often.'

'How often? Just out of interest.'

'Oh,' she said and clasped her chin as if that was a real poser. She turned to a colleague who was just emerging from a back room. 'Mary, when was the last time someone asked about Myall Creek?'

'Oh,' said the colleague, equally stumped. 'I couldn't say – no, wait, there was a man who asked about it maybe two months ago. I remember now. He had a little goatee. Looked a bit like Rolf Harris. I can't remember the last time before that.'

'Most visitors want to go fossicking,' the first lady explained.

Fossicking is to hunt for precious minerals.

'What do they find?' I asked.

'Oh, lots – gold, diamonds, sapphires. This used to be a big mining area.'

'But you have nothing at all on the massacre?'

'I'm afraid not.' She seemed genuinely regretful. 'I tell you who can help you and that's Paulette Smith at the *Advocate*.'

'That's the local paper,' added the colleague.

'She knows all about the massacre. She did some kind of study on it for college.'

'If anybody can help you, Paulette can.'

I thanked them and went off to find the *Advocate*. Bingara was an oddly interesting little town. It was small and half dead and on a road to nowhere, yet it had not only a tourist office but also its own newspaper. At the *Advocate* office I was told that Paulette Smith had popped out and that I should try back in an hour. Slightly at a loss, I went into a café and ordered a sandwich and a coffee, and was mindlessly consuming both when a lady, red-haired, late-thirtyish and looking faintly breathless, abruptly slid onto the seat facing me.

'I hear you're looking for me,' she said.

'News travels fast here.' I smiled.

She rolled her eyes ironically. 'Small town.'

Paulette Smith was rather intense but with a sudden, disarming smile that would flash at odd moments, like a broken sign, and then be lost at once in the greater intensity of what she was telling me.

'We didn't learn anything about the massacre when I was growing up,' she said. 'We knew it had happened – you know, that a long time ago some Aborigines were killed out by the creek and that some white people were hanged for it. But that was about it. We weren't taught about it in school. We didn't, you know, make school trips out there or anything.' The smile came and went.

'Did people talk about it?'

'No. Never.'

I asked her where exactly it had happened. 'Nobody knows. Somewhere on Myall Creek Station.' (Station in this context means a farm or ranch.) 'It's all private property now, and they're not real friendly to trespassers.'

'So there's never been any kind of archaeological dig or anything? You don't get academics poking around?'

'No, there's not that kind of interest in it. Anyway, I don't think they'd know where to look. It's a big property.'

'And there's no memorial of any kind?'

'Oh no.'

'Isn't that odd?'

'No.'

'But wouldn't you expect the government to put up *something*?'

She considered for a moment. 'Well, you've got to understand there was nothing all that special about Myall Creek. Aborigines were slaughtered all over the place. Three months before the Myall massacre 200 Aborigines were killed at Waterloo Creek, near Moree.' Moree was sixty miles or so further west. 'Nobody was ever punished for that. They didn't even *try* to punish anybody for that.'

'I didn't know that.'

She nodded. 'No reason why you should. Most people have never heard of it. All that was different about Myall Creek was that white people were punished for it. It didn't stop them killing Aborigines. It just made them more circumspect. You know, they didn't boast about it in the pub afterwards.' Another flickering smile. 'It's kind of ironic when you think about it. Myall Creek's not famous for what happened to the blacks here, but for what happened to the whites. Anyway, you wouldn't be able to move in this country for memorials if you tried to acknowledge them all.'

She stared dreamily for a moment at my notebook, then said abruptly: 'I have to get back to work.' She made an apologetic look. 'I'm afraid I haven't been much help.'

'No, you've been a great help,' I said, then I thought of another question.

'Are there any Aborigines here now?'

'Oh, no. They're long gone from round here.'

I paid for my lunch and returned to the car. On the way out of town, I stopped again by the bridge and wandered a little way up an overgrown lane that led onto part of the station property. But there was nothing to see and I was a little afraid of snakes in the tall grass. So I returned to the car and retraced my route across the dusty plain and on towards the distant blue slopes of the Great Dividing Range.

And so to Surfers Paradise, back on the Pacific Coast Highway and another hundred miles north. Surfers Paradise is just over the border in Queensland, and I was eager to dip a toe into that interesting and erratic state. In a country where states are both few and immense, the arrival in a new one is always an event. I wasn't going to come this far and not at least slip over the border.

One thing you find if you browse much through non-fiction works on Australia is that practically every book written about the country in the last forty years, possibly more, has in it somewhere an anecdote illustrating that Queenslanders are not like other people. In *Australian Paradox*, Jeanne MacKenzie relates the story of an American guest at a rural Queensland hotel in the 1950s who was presented at dinner with a plate of cold meat and potatoes. He stared with private disappointment at the offering for a moment, then diffidently enquired whether he might have a little salad with it.

'The waitress', Ms MacKenzie reports, 'looked at him with astonishment and disdain and, turning to the other guests, remarked: "The bastard thinks it's Christmas." '

Here's another that I have seen twice. A visitor (French in one version, English in the other) is staying at a Queensland hotel during 'the wet', the rainy season that is a feature of life in northern Australia. The guest is startled, upon reaching his room, to discover that it is flooded to a depth of three or four inches. When he reports this at the front desk, the owner looks at him with pain and irritation and says: 'Well, the bed's dry, isn't it?'

All these stories have certain things in common. Generally they take place in the 1950s. Generally they involve a foreign visitor at a rural hotel. Generally they are presented as true. And always they make Queenslanders look like pricks. Most suggest that Queenslanders are just crazy, and the evidence does rather point in that direction. For almost two decades the state was under the control of Joh Bjelke-Peterson, an eccentric, right-wing state premier who at one time seriously entertained the notion of blowing up parts of the Great Barrier Reef with small atomic bombs to create shipping channels. Of late it had gained fame as the seat of a politician named Pauline Hanson, a fish-and-chip shop owner who had started a right-wing, anti-immigration party called One Nation, which had had a spell of striking success before it became evident even to her most ardent followers that Ms Hanson was a little, shall we say, cerebrally unpredictable. She wrote a book in which she suggested that Aborigines engaged in cannibalism, and produced an interestingly paranoid video which began: 'Fellow Australians, if you are seeing me now it means I have been murdered.' Her seat was the Brisbane suburb of Oxley, which inspired some genius to dub her the Oxley moron. In a word, Queensland has a reputation for being a place apart. I couldn't wait to get there.

In 1933 Elston, Queensland, was a remote and inconsequential seaside hamlet with an excellent beach, a few flimsy cottages, a popular but slightly raffish hotel and a couple of shops. Then the town fathers got a really good idea. Realizing that nobody was going to travel hundreds of miles to visit a place called Elston (and, more to the point, that nobody was travelling hundreds of miles to visit a place called Elston), they decided to give the place a peppier name, based on something novel and upbeat. Looking around, their gaze fell on the local hotel. It was called Surfers Paradise. The name had a certain ring. They decided to give it a try and see what happened. The town has never looked back.

Today Surfers Paradise is famous, while its neighbouring resort communities – Broadbeach, Currumbin, Tugun, Kirra, Bilinga – are scarcely known outside Queensland. It hardly matters because they have all coalesced into a single unsightly sprawl stretching for thirty miles from the Queensland–New South Wales border almost to Brisbane. The whole is called the Gold Coast. This is Australia's Florida.

You see it long before you get to it – shimmering towers of glass and concrete rising beside the sea and snaking off down the coastline to a distant, hazy vanishing point. When Jeanne MacKenzie passed this way in 1959, not one bit of this glitziness existed. Surfers Paradise was still a low-key, low-rise, old-fashioned sort of place. In 1962 it got its first high-rise. Another followed a year or two later. By the end of the sixties, half a dozen ten- or twelve-storey buildings stood awkwardly and a little self-consciously along the front. Then in the early 1970s a development frenzy started. Where once there were just sandy quarter-acre plots, each holding a matchbox beach cottage, today stand hotels of Trump-like splendour, balconied apartment blocks, a domed casino, verdant golf courses, water parks, amusement parks, miniature golf courses, shopping malls and all the rest. Much of this, you are told in a confidential tone, was built and paid for with money of dubious pedigree. People outside Queensland will tell you that the Gold Coast is rife with unsavoury elements – Australian drug barons, Japanese yakuza, flashy linchpins of the Hong Kong triads. This is not, you are led to believe, a place to bump a Mercedes and start an argument.

Nearly everyone you meet elsewhere in Australia will tell you: 'Oh, you must see the Gold Coast. It's awful.'

'Really?' you say, intrigued. 'In what way?'

'I don't know exactly. I've never been there myself. Well, obviously. But it's like – have you seen *Muriel's Wedding*?'

'No.'

'Well, it's like that. Just like it. Apparently.'

So I was interested on many levels to see the Gold Coast, and disappointed on nearly every one of them. To begin with, it wasn't tacky at all. It was just another large, impersonal, well-provisioned international resort. I could have been in Marbella or Eilat or anywhere else developed in the last twenty-five years. The hotels were mostly big international names – Marriott, Radisson, Mercure – and of an unexceptionably respectable standard. I parked the car on a side street and walked along to the seafront. En route I passed stores of an unexpected glitziness – Prada, Hermès, Ralph Lauren. All perfectly fine. It just wasn't very interesting. I didn't need to travel 8,000 miles to look at Ralph Lauren bath towels.

The beach, however, was exceedingly splendid – broad, clean, sunny, with lazy, manageable-sized waves rolling in from an almost painfully blue and bright sea. The air was filled with salt tang and the ozone-enriched shrieks of pleasure and children shouting and a sense of people having fun. I took a seat on a bench and just watched people enjoying themselves. I had read somewhere that the Gold Coast beaches are actually quite treacherous for rips. As it happened, drownings were much in the news lately. The Australian media cover beach mishaps the way American papers cover blizzards and hurricanes – as a seasonal event involving lots of comparative statistics. According to the papers, there had been thirty-four drownings already this year, more than most years, and the summer wasn't yet half over. Much of it was blamed on tourists who didn't know how to read the water for rips or to stay calm when they were caught in one. But a lot of it was just down to lunacy. The *Sydney Morning Herald* cited the case of a 52-year-old man at a place called North Avoca Beach, who had sternly cautioned people not to swim at a particular spot, then went in himself and drowned. Just that morning, while packing up at my motel, I had paused to watch a lifeguard from here at Surfers Paradise being interviewed on a breakfast television programme. He said that he himself had rescued 100 people the previous week, including one tourist whom he had saved twice.

'Twice?' said the interviewer.

The lifeguard grinned at the ridiculousness of it. 'Yip.'

'What, you saved him and he went back in the water and you had to save him again?'

The grin broadened. 'Yip.'

I scanned the water for troubled swimmers. I couldn't imagine how any lifeguard could spot a drowning person among all the hundreds of happy, frolicking bodies, but they most assuredly do. Australian lifeguards are unquestionably the finest in the world. In the same period that thirty-four people drowned, more than 6,000 were saved – a commendable ratio, to say the very least.

Eventually I stopped for a cup of coffee and then wandered through the business district, but Surfers Paradise was mostly just a succession of stores selling the same stuff – painted boomerangs and didgeridoos, cuddly toy koalas and kangaroos, postcards and souvenir books, rack upon rack of T-shirts. In one of the shops I bought a postcard that showed a kangaroo surfing, and asked the young lady who served me if she knew where the original Surfers Paradise Hotel was.

'Oh, I don't know,' she said and looked guilty, as if she had forgotten a secret with which she had been entrusted. 'I haven't been in the area very long,' she added.

I nodded that it didn't matter and asked her where she was from.

'ACT.' Seeing my mind whirring to little effect, she added: 'Australian Capital Territory. Canberra.'

Of course. 'So which is better,' I asked, 'Canberra or Surfers Paradise?'

'Oh, Surfers by a mile.'

I raised an eyebrow. 'It's that good, is it?'

'Oh *no*,' she said emphatically, amazed that I had misread her. 'Canberra's that bad.'

I smiled at her solemnity.

She nodded with conviction. 'I reckon if you were going to rank things for how much pleasure they give – you know? – Canberra would come somewhere below breaking your arm.' I grinned and she grinned too. 'Well, at least with a broken arm you know it'll get better.' She talked with the rising intonation common to young people in Australia, which turns every statement into a question. It drives older Australians crazy, but personally I find it endearing, and sometimes, as here, charmingly sexy.

A supervisor-type person came over to make sure we weren't enjoying ourselves too much. 'Cahn I be of assistahnce?' she said in an odd accent that suggested long devotion to a book entitled *Elocution Self Taught*. She held her head at an odd angle too, tilted back slightly as if she were afraid that her eyeballs might fall out.

'I was looking for the original Surfers Paradise Hotel.'

'Ah, that was torn down some years ago.' She flashed a satisfied smile – it reminded me exactly of William F. Buckley – though whether the smile indicated that she was happy that it had been torn down or merely pleased to be able to convey disappointing news I couldn't say. She showed me on the map in my guidebook where it had stood.

I thanked them both and, clutching my directions, found my way to the site of the famous and now irretrievably lost Surfers Paradise Hotel. Today the spot is occupied by a shopping complex called the Paradise Centre, which was much more in keeping with the modern resort, in that it was ugly and filled with overpriced shit.

In the Surfers Paradise book I had consulted in Adelaide, a photograph from the late 1940s had shown a delightfully ramshackle hotel – a place that looked as if it had been built in phases with whatever materials had come to hand – with a terrace bar on which sat many people soaking up sunshine and alcohol in careless volumes and looking awfully pleased to be there. I walked all the way around the block, then stood on the opposite corner and stared at the site for a long time, but it wasn't possible to imagine it as it had been, any more than it was possible to imagine the Myall Creek massacre from its present peaceful situation. So I returned to the car and headed out of town through the dappled stripes of sun and shade created by the big hotels and lavish palm trees. At the edge of town I rejoined the Pacific Highway and headed south.

I had a long drive to Sydney ahead of me. For the moment, my trip was over. But I would be back, of course. I wasn't anywhere near finished with this place yet.

Part Three

AROUND THE EDGES

CHAPTER FOURTEEN

'I JUST WANT YOU TO KNOW,' SAID A VOICE IN MY EAR AS QANTAS flight 406 popped cork-like out of a tower of monsoonal cumulonimbus, presenting the window passengers with a sudden view of emerald mountains rising almost sheer from a pewter sea, 'that if it comes to it you may have all my urine.'

I turned from the window to give this remark the attention it deserved and found myself staring at the solemn and rested countenance of Allan Sherwin, my friend and temporary travelling companion. It would be incorrect to say that I was surprised to find him sitting beside me because we had met in Sydney by design and boarded the flight together, but there was nonetheless a certain residual measure of unexpectedness – a kind of pinch-me quality – in finding him seated there. Ten days earlier in London, where I had stopped on my way back to America from my hike in the Middle East, I had met Allan to discuss some project he had in mind. (He is a television producer by profession; we had become friends while working together on a series for British television the previous year.) There, in a pub on the Old Brompton Road, I had told him of my experiences in Australia so far and mentioned my plans on the next trip to tackle the formidable desert regions alone and at ground level. In order to deepen his admiration for me, I had told him some vivid stories of travellers who had come unstuck in the unforgiving interior. One of these had pertained to an expedition in the 1850s led by a surveyor named Robert Austin, which grew so lost and short of water in the arid wastes beyond Mount Magnet in Western Australia that the members were reduced to drinking their own and their horses' urine. The story had affected him so powerfully that he had announced at once the intention to accompany me through the most perilous parts of the present trip, in the role of driver and scout. I had, of course, tried to dissuade him, if only for his own safety, but he would have none of it. Clearly the story was still much on his mind, judging by his kind offer to keep me in urine.

'Thank you,' I replied now, 'that's very generous of you.'

He gave me a nod that had a touch of the regal about it. 'It's what friends are for.'

'And you may have as much of mine as I can spare.'

Another regal nod.

The plan, to which he was now resolutely attached, was to accompany me first to northern Queensland, where we would relax for a day amid the fertile shoals of the Great Barrier Reef before setting off in a suitably sturdy vehicle along a bumpy track for Cooktown, a semi-ghost town in the jungle some way north of Cairns. This warm-up adventure completed, we would fly on to Darwin in the Northern Territory – the 'Top End' as it is fondly known to Australians – for the thousand-mile drive through the scorched red centre to Alice Springs and mighty Uluru. Having assisted me through the worst of the perils, the heroic Mr Sherwin would fly back to England from Alice, and leave me to continue on through the western deserts on my own. It wasn't that he thought I would be ready for this by then – for he had no confidence whatever in my survival capabilities – but that ten days was all he had to spare. For my part, I had no greater confidence in him, but I was glad of the company.

'You know,' I added reassuringly, 'I don't suppose it will actually be necessary to drink urine on this trip. The infrastructure of the arid regions is much improved since the 1850s. I understand they have Coca-Cola now.'

'Still, the offer is there.'

'And much appreciated, too.'

Another exchange of regal nods, and then I returned my gaze to the exotic verdure below our waggling wingtip. If you needed convincing that Australia is an exceptional part of the world, then tropical Queensland would be the place to come. Of the 500 or so sites on the planet that qualify for World Heritage status, only thirteen satisfy all four of UNESCO's criteria for listing, and of these thirteen special places, four – almost a third – are to be found in Australia. Moreover, two of these, the Great Barrier Reef and the wet tropics of Queensland, were right here. It is the only place in the world, I believe, where two such consummate environments adjoin.

We were lucky to be there at all. They were having a terrible wet season in the north. Cyclone Rona had recently buzzsawed along the coast, causing $300 million of havoc, and lesser storms had been teasing the region for weeks, disrupting travel. Only the day before all flights had been cancelled. It was evident from the dips and wobbles of our approach into Cairns that a lot of assertive weather was still about. The view as we came in was of palm trees, golf courses, seaside marinas, some big beachside hotels and lots and lots of red-roofed houses poking out of abundant foliage. Weather apart, it all looked very promising.

It is remarkable now, when over two million people a year come to the Great Barrier Reef and it is universally esteemed as a treasure, how long it took the tourism industry to discover it. In *Rum Jungle*, an account of a tour through northern Australia in the 1950s, the historian Alan Moorehead made venturing into northern Queensland sound like a journey to the headwaters of the Orinoco. Then, Cairns was a small, muggy coastal outpost hundreds of miles up a jungle road and occupied mostly by eccentric dropouts of a fugitive disposition. Today it is a bustling mini-metropolis of 60,000 inhabitants, indistinguishable from any community of similar size in Australia except for the humidity that falls over you like a hot towel when you emerge from the airport terminal and a certain hale devotion to the tourist dollar. It has become a hugely popular stopoff point for backpackers and other young travellers for whom it has a certain reputation for tropical liveliness. On this day the whole was pressed under an oppressive weight of low grey skies of the sort that threatened rain in volume at any moment. We took a cab into town through a long, unbecoming sprawl of motels, petrol stations and fast food establishments. Central Cairns was somewhat snugger, but it had the feel of a place that had been built only recently, in haste. Every second business offered reef cruises or snorkelling expeditions, and most of the rest sold T-shirts and postcards.

We went first to pick up our hire car. Because I had been hiking in the Middle East, I had left the arrangements to a travel agent, and I was mildly surprised to find that the agent had plumped for an obscure local firm – Crocodile Car Hire or something similarly improbable and unpromising – whose office was little more than a bare counter on a side street. The young man in charge had a certain chirpy cockiness that was ineffably irritating, but he dealt with the paperwork in a brisk and efficient manner, chattering throughout about the weather. It was the worst wet in thirty years, he told us proudly. Then he led us out to the pavement and presented us with our vehicle – an aged Commodore Holden estate car that seemed to have a decided sag about the axles.

'What's this?' I asked.

He leaned towards me and said as you might to a dementia sufferer: 'It's your car.'

'But I asked for a four-wheel drive.'

He sifted through his paperwork and carefully extracted a fax from the travel agent, which he passed to me. It showed a request for a large, standard, high-polluting car with automatic transmission – an American car, in other words, or the nearest local equivalent. I sighed and handed back the paper. 'Well, do you have a four-wheel drive I can take instead?' I asked.

'Nope, sorry. We only do town cars.'

'But we were going to drive up towards Cape York.'

'Oh, you won't get up there in the wet. Not even in a four-wheel drive. Not at this time of year. They had a hundred centimetres of rain at Cape Tribulation last week.' I had no very clear idea what a hundred centimetres was, but it was evident from his tone that it was considerable. 'You won't get beyond Daintree in anything less than a helicopter.'

I sighed again.

'The road to Townsville's been cut off for three days,' he added with yet more pride.

I looked at him again. Townsville is south of Cairns – in the opposite direction from Cape York. It appeared we were boxed in. 'So where *can* we go?' I asked.

He spread his hands in cheerful irony. 'Anywhere you like in greater Cairns.'

Allan looked at me in the happily brainless way of someone who doesn't realize disaster is afoot, irritating me further. I sighed and hefted my bags. 'Well, can you point us the way to the Palm Cove Hotel?' I asked.

'Certainly. You go back out past the airport to the Cook Highway and take the road north. It's about twenty kilometres up the coast.'

'Twenty kilometres?' I sputtered. 'I asked for a hotel in Cairns.'

He scratched his chin thoughtfully. 'Well, it's sure not in Cairns.'

'But the road is open?'

'So far.'

'You mean it might flood?'

'Always a possibility.'

'And if it floods we're stuck in the middle of nowhere?'

He looked at me with a touch of pity. 'Mister, you're already in the middle of nowhere.' The point was inarguable. Cairns was 1,100 miles from Brisbane, its own state capital, and there was nothing in the other directions but ocean, jungle and desert. 'But Palm Cove's real nice,' he added. 'You'll like it.'

And he was right. Palm Cove was lovely – really quite astonishingly so. It was a purpose-built village inserted with some care into a stretch of tropical luxuriance beside a curving bay. On one side of a beachside road stood low-rise hotels and apartments, a few cottages and a scattering of bars, restaurants and shops, all discreetly obscured by palms, spreading fronds and flowering vines, and on the other was a palm-lined walk overlooking a smooth, golden beach and the sea.

Our hotel was, in everything but name, setting and price, a motel, but it was friendly and overlooked the sea. We claimed our rooms, then went for a walk along the beach. A few other people were strolling over the sand, but no one was in the water and for a very good reason. It was the height of the season for box jellyfish, also known in Queensland as marine stingers, or just stingers. By whatever name they go, these little bubbles of woe are not to be trifled with. From October to May, when the jellyfish come inshore to breed, they render the beaches of the tropics useless to humans. It is quite an extraordinary thought when you are standing there looking at it. Before us stood a sweep of bay as serene and inviting as you would find anywhere, and yet there was no environment on earth more likely to offer instant death.

'So you're telling me,' said Allan, for whom all this was new, 'that if I waded into the water now I would die?'

'In the most wretched and abject agony known to man,' I replied.

'Jesus,' he muttered.

'And don't pick up any of the seashells,' I added, stopping him from leaning over to pick up a seashell. I explained to him about coneshells – the venomous creatures that lurk inside some of the handsomest shells, waiting for a human hand to sink their vile pincers into.

'Seashells will kill you?' he said. 'They've got lethal seashells here?'

'There are more things that will kill you up here than anywhere else in Australia, and that's saying a lot, believe me.'

I told him about the cassowary, the flightless, man-sized bird that lives in the rainforests, with a razor claw on each foot with which it can slice you open in a deft and appallingly expansive manner; and the green tree snakes that dangle from branches and so blend into the foliage that you don't see them until they are clamped onto a facial extremity. I mentioned also the small but fearsomely poisonous blue-ringed octopus, whose caress is instant death; and the elegant but irritable numb ray, which moves through the water like a flying carpet discharging 220 volts of electricity into anything that troubles its progress; and the loathsome, sluggish stonefish, so called because it is indistinguishable from a rock, but with the difference that it has twelve spikes on its back that are sharp enough to pierce the sole of a sneaker, injecting the hapless sufferer with a myotoxin bearing a molecular weight of 150,000.

'And what does that mean exactly?'

'Pain beyond description followed shortly by muscular paralysis, respiratory depression, cardiac palpitations and a severe disinclination to boogie. You might similarly be discommoded by firefish, which are easier to spot but no less hurtful. There's even a jellyfish called the snottie.'

'You're making all this up,' he said, but without conviction.

'Oh, but I'm not.'

Then I told him about the dreaded saltwater crocodile, which lurks in tropical lagoons, estuaries and even bays such as this one, leaping from the waters from time to time to snatch and devour unsuspecting passers-by. Just up the coast from where we now strolled, a woman named Beryl Wruck had been taken not so long before in a startling manner. 'Shall I tell you about it?' I offered.

'No.'

'Well, one day,' I went on, knowing that really he wanted to hear, 'a group of locals at Daintree got together for a festive pre-Christmas barbie when some of them decided to go for a cooling dip in the Daintree River. The river was known to be the home of crocodiles, but none had ever attacked anybody locally. So several of the party scampered down to the water's edge, stripped to their underwear and splashed in. Ms Wruck apparently thought better of leaping in, so she merely stepped a foot or so into the water. As she stood there watching the happy frolicking, she idly leaned over and trailed a hand through the water. Just at that instant the water split in a flash of movement and poor Ms Wruck was gone, never to be seen again. "There was no sound, no scream," reported one witness. "It was so quick that if you had blinked an eye you'd have missed the whole thing." That is what a crocodile attack is like, you see – swift, unexpected, extremely irreversible.'

'And you're telling me there are crocodiles here in this water?' Allan said.

'Oh, I don't know whether there are or not. But it's why I'm letting you walk on the inside.'

Just then from the restive skies there came a single startling crack of thunder. Abruptly the wind kicked up, sending the palm trees dancing, and a few fat splats of rain fell. Then the skies opened in a warm but soaking downpour. We hied back to our hotel where we took refuge under the veranda of the beachfront bar, ineffectually wrung out our steaming shirts and watched the rain beat down with a tumultuous fury. There was nothing so dainty as raindrops in this. It was just a cubic mass of falling water, filling the world with a fearful pounding din. I had thought that growing up in the American Midwest I was familiar with lively weather, but I am happy to concede that where the elements are concerned Australia plays in a league of its own. I had never seen anything like it.

'So let me get this straight,' Allan was saying. 'We can't go to Cooktown because we can't get through. We can't swim because the ocean's full of deadly jellyfish. And the road to Cairns might be cut off at any moment.'

'That's about the size of it.'

He blew out thoughtfully. 'Might as well have a few beers then.' He went off to get some. I took a seat at a small table on the veranda and watched the rain pour down.

One of the bar employees came and stood in the doorway. 'Worst wet in thirty years,' he said.

I nodded. 'What's the forecast?'

'Same.'

I nodded bleakly. 'We were supposed to be going out to the Great Barrier Reef tomorrow.'

'Oh, you've got no worries there. They don't cancel the reef tours unless it's a hurricane.'

'People go out to the reef in this kind of weather?'

He nodded. The water in the bay was sloshing around like a bath into which a fat man has just jumped.

'*Why?*'

'How much did you pay for your tickets?'

I had no idea – everything had been booked as part of a package – but I had the tickets with me and pulled them out of my wallet. 'A hundred and forty-five dollars each,' I squeaked in miserly disbelief.

He smiled. 'There you go.'

He went back in. A moment later Allan reappeared with the beers, looking unusually dejected. 'There is a jellyfish called the snottie,' he said in wonder. 'The barman told me.'

I gave him an apologetic smile. 'Told you.'

He stared for some minutes at the rain. On the table someone had left a copy of the local paper, the *Port Douglas and Mossman Gazette*. Allan started to move it to get at the ashtray, then something caught his eye. He read for a minute, with increasing absorption, then passed the paper to me, tapping the article he wished me to see. It was a small story at the bottom of the front page noting that the dengue fever epidemic in Port Douglas had slowed at last. The article said that since the epidemic had started 485 cases had been reported in the area. Although the pace was slowing, this was not grounds for complacency, a spokeswoman for the Tropical Public Health Unit warned.

'It's at the bottom of the page!' he said, his eyes just a trifle wild.

'That's where we're going tomorrow,' I noted with idle interest.

'Do you have any idea what a dengue epidemic would be like in Britain? People would be nailing boards over their windows. Ferries would have people hanging off the sides trying to get out of the country. The police would have to shoot people in the streets to restore order. Here they get 485 cases in a single community and it's two bloody inches on the bottom of the page! Where have you brought me, Bryson? What kind of country is this?'

'Oh, it's a wonderful country, Allan.'

'Yeah, right.'

We split up to shower and change, then reconvened in the bar for an aperitif before dinner. As the rain showed no sign of easing, we decided to dine at the hotel. At dinner, Allan ordered red snapper.

'You've not heard of ciguatera then?' I said casually.

'Of course I haven't bloody heard of it,' he replied through clenched teeth. 'What now?'

'It's nothing,' I said.

'Of course it must be something or you wouldn't have mentioned it. What is it? Am I sitting in it? Is it on my head? What?'

'No, it's a kind of toxin endemic to tropical waters. It accumulates in certain fish.'

'Like red snapper, for instance?'

'Well, especially red snapper, actually.'

He considered this with a kind of slow, catatonic nod. I think jet lag was kicking in. It can do terrible things to one's equilibrium.

'I'm sure there's nothing to worry about,' I added reassuringly. 'I mean, if there was an outbreak snapper wouldn't be on the menu, would it? Unless of course.' I stopped there.

'What?'

'Well, unless you were to be the first case. It has to start with somebody, after all. But, hey, what are the chances of that? One in a hundred? One in twenty?'

'I want you to stop this right now.'

'Of course,' I agreed at once. 'I'm sorry. Do you want to change your order?'

'No.'

'The symptoms include, but are not limited to, vomiting, severe muscle weakness, loss of motor control, paraesthesia of the lips, general lassitude, myalgia and paradoxical sensory disturbances – that is, feeling hot surfaces as cold and vice versa. Death occurs in about twelve per cent of cases.'

'I'm telling you to stop it right now.' The waitress came with our drinks. 'This snapper,' Allan said with forced casualness. 'It's all right, is it?'

'Oh, yeah. It's beaut.'

'I mean, it hasn't got – what is it, Bryson?'

'Ciguatera.'

She gave us a befuddled look. 'No, it comes with chips and salad.'

We exchanged glances.

'Would I be right in assuming you're not from around here?' I asked.

Her puzzlement deepened. 'No, I'm from Tassie. Why?'

'Just wondered.' I whispered to Allan: 'She's from Tasmania.'

He leaned to me and whispered back: 'Yes. So?'

'Their snapper are OK.'

'Is it possible to change my order, love?'

She stared at him heavily for a moment, the way young people do when they realize they are being asked to take twenty steps they hadn't budgeted for, and with a martyred air went off to find out. A minute later she reported back that permission had been granted to change his order.

'Excellent!' said Allan with sudden enthusiasm, perusing the menu anew. He considered the many alternative options. 'Do you do baked snottie?' he asked distantly.

She stared at him.

'Just joking!' he said, seeming much chirpier. 'I'll have the sirloin and chips,' he announced. 'Medium rare, please.' He turned to me. 'No horrid diseases I should know about with regard to beef? Queensland beef palsy or anything like that?'

'You should be fine with steak.'

'Steak it is then.' He handed her the menu. 'And easy on the ciguatera,' he called after her. 'And keep the beers coming,' he added further.

We had a lovely meal, and afterwards retired once more to the bar where, through the foolish wonders of alcohol, we managed to acquire nearly all the symptoms that we had so recently been at pains to avoid.

In the morning, the rain had stopped but the skies were dark and dirty and the sea full of chop. Just looking at it made me feel faintly ill. I am not enamoured of the ocean or anything within it, and the prospect of bouncing out to a rain-shrouded reef to see the sort of darting fish I could view in comfort at any public aquarium, or indeed dental waiting room, was not enticing. According to the morning paper, a 2.3-metre swell was expected. I asked Allan, who once owned a sailing boat and a captain's cap and thus fancies himself an accomplished mariner, how big this was and he lifted his eyebrows in the manner of one impressed. 'Oh, that's big,' he said. This led him to tell me many happy anecdotes of being pitched about in terrifying seas, some of them involving boats not tied to a dock. As we sat there, one of the members of the staff breezed past.

'Cyclone coming!' she said perkily.

'Today?' I asked in what was becoming a customary bleat.

'Maybe!'

Our reef tour included pick-up at our hotel and transfer by coach to the boat at Port Douglas, twenty miles up the coast. The bus drew up at eight fifty, on time to the minute. As we climbed aboard, the driver was giving a rundown on marine stingers, with vivid descriptions of people who had failed to their cost to heed the warning signs. He assured us, however, there were no jellyfish on the reef. Unaccountably, he failed to mention reef sharks, boxfish, scorpionfish, stinging corals, sea snakes or the infamous grouper, a 900-pound monster that occasionally, through a combination of testiness and stupidity, chomps off a swimmer's arm or leg, then remembers that it doesn't like the taste of human flesh and spits it out.

I can't tell you how pleased I was when we arrived at Port Douglas to find that the boat was huge – as big as an English Channel ferry or very nearly – and sleekly new. I was also pleased, for their sake and mine, that none of the crew seemed to be manifesting any of the more obvious signs of dengue fever. As we lined up with other arriving coach passengers I learned from a crew member that the ship held 450 and that 310 people were booked today. He also told me that the trip to the reef took ninety minutes and that the seas should be relatively benign. It was thirty-eight nautical miles to Agincourt Reef, where we would moor. This was, I noted with more than passing interest, the place where the American couple had gone missing.

When we got aboard they announced the free distribution of seasickness tablets to anyone who wanted. I was the first to the table.

'This is awfully thoughtful of you,' I said as I swilled down a handful.

'Well, it's better'n having people spewing up all over the shop,' said the girl brightly, and it was hard to argue with that.

The trip to the reef was smooth, as promised. What's more the sun came out, albeit weakly, turning the water from a leaden grey to an approximation of cobalt. While Allan went off to the sun deck to see if there were any women with large breasts to look at, I settled down with my notes.

Depending on which sources you consult, the Great Barrier Reef covers 280,000 square kilometres or 344,000 or something in between; stretches 1,200 miles from top to bottom, or 1,600; is bigger than Kansas or Italy or the United Kingdom. Nobody can agree really on where the Barrier Reef begins and ends, though everyone agrees it's awfully big. Even by the shortest measure, it is equivalent in length to the west coast of the United States. And it is of course an immensely vital habitat – the oceanic equivalent of the Amazon rainforest. The Great Barrier Reef contains at least 1,500 species of fish, 400 types of coral and 4,000 varieties of molluscs, but those are essentially just guesses. No one has ever attempted a comprehensive survey. Too big a job.

Because it consists of some 3,000 separate reefs and over 600 islands some people insist that it is not a single entity and therefore cannot accurately be termed the largest living thing on earth. That seems to me a little like saying that Los Angeles is not a city because it consists of lots of separate buildings. It hardly matters. It is fabulous. And it is all thanks to trillions of little coral polyps working with a dedicated and microscopic diligence over 18 million years, each adding a grain or two of thickness before expiring in a self-created silicate tomb. Hard not to be impressed.

As the ship began to make the sort of slowing-down noises that suggested imminent arrival, I went out on deck to join Allan. I had expected that we would be arriving at some kind of sandy atoll, possibly with a beach bar with a thatched roof, but in fact there was nothing but open sea all around, and a long ruff of gently breaking water, which I presumed indicated the sunken and unseen reef. In the middle of this scene sat an immense aluminium pontoon, two storeys high and big enough to accommodate 400 day trippers. It brought to mind, if vaguely, an oil platform. This was to be our home for the next several hours. When the boat had docked, we all filed happily off. A loudspeaker outlined our many options. We could loll in the sun in deckchairs, or descend to an underwater viewing chamber, or grab snorkels and flippers for a swim, or board a semisubmersible ship for a tour of the reef in comfort.

We went first on the semisubmersible, a vessel in which thirty or forty people at a time could crowd into a viewing chamber below the waterline. Well, it was wonderful. No matter how much you read about the special nature of the Barrier Reef, nothing really prepares you for the sight of it. The pilot took us into a shimmery world of steep coral canyons and razor-edged defiles, fabulously colourful and teeming with schools of fish of incredible variety and size – butterfly fish, damselfish, angelfish, parrotfish, the gorgeously colourful harlequin tuskfish, tubular pipefish. We saw giant clams and sea slugs and starfish, small forests of waving anemones and the pleasingly large and dopey potato cod. It was, as I had expected, precisely like being at a public aquarium, except of course that this was entirely wild and natural. I was amazed, no doubt foolishly, by what a difference this made. As I looked out a great turtle swam past, just a couple of yards from the window and quite indifferent to us. Then, furtively poking about on the bottom, was a reef shark – only a couple of feet long but capable of giving you a jolly good nip. It wasn't just the darting fish and other creatures, but the way the light filtered down from above, and the shape and texture and incredible variety of the coral itself. I was captivated beyond description.

Back on the pontoon, Allan insisted we go at once for a swim. At one side of the pontoon metal steps led into the water. At the top of the steps were large bins containing flippers, snorkels and masks. We kitted up and plopped in. I had assumed that we would be in a few feet of water, so I was taken aback – I am putting this mildly – to discover that I was perhaps sixty feet above the bottom. I had never been in water this deep before and it was unexpectedly unnerving – as unnerving as finding myself floating sixty feet in the air above solid ground. This panicky assessment took place over the course of perhaps three seconds, then my mask and snorkel filled with water and I started choking. Gasping peevishly, I dumped the water out and tried again, but almost immediately the mask filled again. I repeated the exercise two or three times more, but with the same result.

Allan, meanwhile, was shooting about like Darryl Hannah in *Splash*. 'For God's sake, Bryson, what are you doing?' he said. 'You're three feet from the pontoon and you're drowning.'

'I am drowning.' I caught a roll of wave full in the face and came out of it sputtering. 'I'm a son of the soil,' I gasped. 'This is not my milieu.'

He clucked and disappeared. I dipped my head lightly under to see him shooting off like a torpedo in the direction of a colourful Maori wrasse – an angelfish the size of a sofa cushion – and was consumed once more with a bubbly dismay at all the clear, unimagined depth beneath me. There were big things down there, too – fish half as big as me and far more in their element than I was. Then my mask filled and I was sputtering again. Then another small rolling wave smacked me in the face. I must confess that I liked this even less – quite a good deal less – than I had expected to, and I hadn't expected to like it much.

Interestingly, I later learned that this is quite a common reaction among inexperienced ocean swimmers. They get in the water, discover that they are way out of their comfort zone, quietly panic and faint (a Japanese speciality, apparently) or have a heart attack (a fat person speciality). Now here's where the second interesting aspect comes in. Because snorkellers lie on the water with their arms and legs spread and their faces just under the surface – that is, in the posture known as the dead man's float – it isn't actually possible (or so I am told) to tell which people are snorkelling and which are dead. It's only when the whistle blows and everyone gets out except for one oddly inert and devoted soul that they know there will be one less for tea.

Fortunately, as you will have deduced from the existence of this book, I escaped this unhappy fate and managed to haul myself back onto the pontoon. I took a seat on a deckchair in the mild sunshine and towelled off with Allan's shirt. Then I pulled out the newspaper files Alan Howe had given me on the American couple who had died out here. I had read them once before, but now that I could attach visible landmarks to the words I went through them again with particular interest.

The story, insofar as the known events are concerned, is straightforward. In January 1998, Thomas and Eileen Lonergan, of Baton Rouge, Louisiana, who had recently completed a tour of duty as Peace Corps volunteers in the South Pacific, were holidaying in Australia before returning home when they went for a day's scuba diving on the reef with a company called Outer Edge. At the end of the afternoon, they failed to return to the dive boat at the time directed. Their absence was not noted and the boat left without them. Two and a half days passed before anyone reported them missing. No trace of them was ever found.

Why the Lonergans didn't return to the dive boat and what became of them when they realized they had been stranded are necessarily matters of conjecture.

From where I sat I could see the scuba-diving boat, which a passing crew member informed me was about three nautical miles away. (A nautical mile is about a hundred yards longer than a land mile.) It looked awfully small and distant, but the Lonergans, who were experienced divers and at home in the water, should have found the swim no terrible hardship. Conditions were perfect. The sea was calm, the water temperature was 29° C (84° F) and they had on wetsuits. In addition to the pontoon, they had the somewhat easier option of swimming to St Crispin Reef, just 1.2 nautical miles away, where there were some exposed coral outcrops onto which they could clamber to await rescue. The problem, as Alan Howe had so rightly recalled, was that to reach either of these refuges meant crossing a deep-water trench known to be a haunt of large pelagics – which is to say toothy sharks and the occasional blundering grouper.

From this point the mystery deepened. A few days after their disappearance, the Lonergans' flotation jackets washed up undamaged on a mainland beach. Why two people stranded at sea would take off their flotation devices would appear to be an unanswerable question. Moreover, the absence of damage to the flotation jackets suggested that they had not been attacked by sharks. Puzzlement grew further when police examined the belongings they had left behind at the backpackers' hostel in Cairns where they had been staying. There it became clear that the polite young American couple weren't as happy as they appeared to be. Eileen Lonergan had recorded in her diary that her husband had been depressed and had said he wanted 'to end it all' on a scuba-diving trip. (Whoa!) He had suggested that he would take her with him. (Double whoa!)

There was obviously more to this than met the eye.

Allan emerged at last, looking invigorated and holding in his stomach in a manner that recalled Jeff Chandler in some of his later films, chattering with tedious gusto about what a brilliant experience it had been and what an egregious wimp I was. He slipped on his shirt and fell into the chair beside me, looking very happy. Then he sat up and patted himself extravagantly.

'This shirt's wet,' he announced.

'Is it?' I said, frowning with concern.

'It's wringing wet.'

I touched it lightly. 'Why, yes it is,' I agreed.

They were losing people all over the place in Queensland these days, it appeared. The papers the next day were full of reports of an inquest that had been convened to examine the disappearance of a young British backpacker named Daniel Nute on the Cape Tribulation promontory almost two years earlier. Nute had set off alone on a six-hour hike to a place called Mount Sorrow and had dutifully filled out the safety forms bush hikers are asked to complete to help searchers in the event that they fail to return.

Unfortunately, no one from the national park staff collected or checked the safety sheets that day. In fact, it turned out that the national park staff seldom collected or checked the safety sheets. So when Nute failed to return no one noticed and no alarm call went out. Even more puzzling was that although Nute had left a tent pitched on the grounds of a backpackers' lodge in Daintree, the staff at the lodge did not notify the authorities that he was missing for twenty-three days. An employee at the lodge told the inquest that it was 'common for people to abandon their tents and leave without telling management'.

But of course.

The upshot was that by the time a search was organized almost a month had passed. Nute's body has never been found.

All this took on a certain relevance the next morning when Allan and I drove into Cairns to run a couple of errands. Something in the window of a sportswear shop caught his eye so we went in. While he was off trying on items of clothing, I chatted pleasantly with the two middle-aged ladies who worked there. I mentioned for no reason – just making conversation really – that Cairns had been much in the news lately.

'Oh?' said one of the ladies, a little coolly.

'You know, the Lonergan case and the Chinese boat people and this poor kid who went missing at Daintree.'

'Oh, all that,' said the lady with a dismissive air. 'They always blow these things out of proportion down south.'

Her colleague nodded vigorously. 'Whenever there's a chance to make Queensland look bad, they leap on it. It was just the same with the cyclone. I was in Sydney that week visiting my sister and, do you know, they had pages of articles about it.'

'Well, it was a big story,' I pointed out.

'But they wouldn't have covered it like that if it had been in Western Australia.'

'Oh?'

'No. They do it to discourage people from coming up here, you see.'

'You really think so?'

'Oh yes. They don't want visitors to leave Sydney. They want to keep them down there. So they take any story that makes Queensland look, you know, dangerous or backward and they twist the facts about to frighten people.'

They both nodded in the sincerest agreement.

'It was same with that young couple out on the reef. It's quite evident that it was suicide, but they blew it all out of proportion—'

'All out of proportion,' seconded her friend.

'—so that they could make it look like it wasn't safe to go out on the reef.'

'And the boy at Daintree?' I ventured.

'They don't know that he's dead at all,' she said in the tone of one who has unimpeachable sources.

'But he's been missing for two years.'

'Yes, but he's been sighted all over the Cape York peninsula.'

'All over,' agreed her friend.

'I'm sorry, are you saying the papers falsely reported his death to make Queensland look dangerous?'

'I'm just saying that all the facts aren't in.' She nodded primly and crossed her arms. Her partner did likewise.

And I thought: madder than cut snakes.

As it happened, we were heading to Daintree ourselves. It was as far north as you could get on a paved road in this part of Australia, so we decided to go and have a look. By mid-morning all traces of rain had abated and the sun began to come out – tentatively at first, but then with sumptuous gusto. Queensland was transformed. Suddenly we were in Hawaii – tropical mountains running down to sparkling seas, sweeping bays, flawless beaches guarded by listing palms, little green and rocky islands standing off the headlands. From time to time we drove through sunny canefields, overlooked by the steep, blue eminence of the Great Dividing Range.

At Daintree we parked and got out to have a look around. We walked down to the edge of the Daintree River, where both the road and Beryl Wruck came to their respective abrupt terminations. We couldn't see any sign of crocodiles. Then we got back in the car and drove off down a winding side road that leads to a ferry across the Daintree to Cape Tribulation. The ferry had been shut for a week by the rains, so there wasn't much point in going down there, but I wanted to see the cape at least from across the river, and there was the off chance that we might glimpse a crocodile. To our surprise, the ferry was operating. We had been assured in Daintree that it was still shut.

'Reopened yesterday,' said the ferryman, a man of few words.

So we took the ferry across and set off on the twenty-mile drive to Cape Tribulation through Daintree National Park. The road wound up and through a mountainous and intensely beautiful rainforest. We had at last made it into the wet tropics, and I couldn't have been more pleased.

The Daintree forest is a remnant of a time when the world was a single land mass, the whole covered in steamy growth. As time passed, continents split up and drifted off to the far corners of the globe, but the Daintree, through some tectonic fluke, escaped the more dramatic transformations of climate and orientation that spurred ecological change elsewhere. In consequence, there are plants out there – whole families of plants – that survived as nowhere else. In 1972, scientists began to appreciate just how ancient and exceptional Australia's northern rainforest is when some cattle mysteriously sickened and died after grazing in the jungle's lower slopes. The cows, it turned out, had been poisoned by the seeds of a tree called *Idiospermum australianse*. What was unexpected about this was that *Idiospermum* was thought to have vanished from the earth 100 million years ago. In fact, it was doing very well in the Daintree, as were eleven other members of its family, a primitive outpost of botany called the angiosperms, from which all flowering plants are descended. That's the kind of place Daintree National Park is – dark, dense, seeming to belong to some remote epoch. It's a landscape in which it wouldn't entirely surprise you to see pterosaurs gliding through the trees or velociraptors sprinting across the road ahead.

In fact, there is quite a lot of odd life out there. This is one of the few remaining areas where you can hope to see cassowaries. They look much like emus except that they have a bony growth on their head called a casque and the infamous murderous claw on each foot. They attack by jumping up and striking out with both feet together. Fortunately, this doesn't happen very often. The last fatal attack was in 1926, when a cassowary charged a sixteen-year-old boy who had been taunting it and sliced open his jugular as it bounded across him. The reason attacks are so few is that cassowaries are exceedingly reclusive and now, alas, very few in number. No more than a thousand of them survive. The Daintree is also one of the last homes of the celebrated tree kangaroo – which, as its name suggests, is a kangaroo that lives in trees – but it is even shyer than the cassowary and almost never seen. So dense is the jungle, and so remote from the centres of academia, that much of it remains unstudied. The first scientific study of cassowaries, for instance, was begun only about a decade ago.

At length the road ended at a sunny clearing in the jungle with, incongruously, a takeaway food stand and a phone booth. Tucked away in the extravagant foliage was a campground, and beside it an arrowed sign pointed the way to the beach. This led to a boardwalk through mangroves. Little creatures plinked unseen into the swampy water as we approached. After a few minutes we emerged onto the beach. It was remarkably beautiful – a great sweep of soft white sand strewn with driftwood, palm fronds and other natural clutter, standing before a very bright blue bay. Ahead of us loomed a towering headland cloaked in green.

The spot was sunnily pristine, exactly as it must have appeared to James Cook when he first laid eyes on it more than two centuries ago. He called it Cape Tribulation because it was here that the *Endeavour* disastrously lodged on coral some twelve miles off the coast. Severely holed, it was in imminent danger of sinking, but Cook had with him a seaman who had once been in similar straits on a ship that had been saved by an unusual process known as fothering – in effect bandaging its underside by running a sail beneath it and pulling it tight to cover the hole. It was a desperate and improbable measure, but miraculously it worked.

Cook nursed the ship to shore a few miles around the headland from where we were now. The crew spent seven weeks making repairs before sailing off to England and glory. Had the *Endeavour* sunk, and Cook failed to get home, history would of course have been very different. Australia would very likely have become French – an eerie thought, to say the least – and Britain would have had to adjust its colonial ambitions accordingly. No part of the world would have escaped the effects. Melbourne might now stand on African plains. Sydney could be the capital of the Royal Colony of California. Who can possibly say? What is certain is that the global balance of power would have changed in ways beyond imagining. On the other hand, we would almost certainly have been spared *Home and Away*, so it's not as if it would have been an unmitigated disaster.

Allan and I explored along the beach for half an hour or so, then walked back to the clearing where the food stand was, and had a look at where the road continued on to Cooktown. Beyond the food stand it became at once a rough and rocky track, which climbed steeply up into the lush hills. It looked like something Harrison Ford would struggle to negotiate in an adventure movie. I had learned only the day before that the track is dangerously and unnervingly tippy even in good weather, so perhaps it was as well that Allan and I hadn't been let loose on it. In any case, it was impassable now.

Still, it did look awfully inviting in an adventuresome sort of way. Cooktown, a former gold-mining town that had once had a population of 30,000 and has just 200 now, lay seventy-five kilometres away on the other side of the mountains. It is the last town in eastern Australia. Beyond it there is nothing but a scattering of Aboriginal settlements along the 600-kilometre track to Cape York, Australia's northernmost point. But this was as far as I was going to get here.

I turned around to discover that Allan had slipped off. He reappeared after a minute from the direction of the food stand bearing two cans of Coke, one of which he passed to me.

'They didn't have urine,' he said, and we both had a good laugh over that.

CHAPTER FIFTEEN

AND SO TO THE TOP END. WE BOUNCED INTO DARWIN THROUGH THE outer strands of two minor cyclones that were bumping along the north coast, and acquired another rental car – a sleek and powerful Toyota sedan that looked as if it could cover the 1,500 kilometres to Alice Springs in a single rocket-like burst. We dubbed it the Testosterone.

The Northern Territory has always had something of a frontier mentality. In late 1998, the inhabitants were invited to become Australia's seventh state and roundly rejected the notion in a referendum. It appears they quite like being outsiders. In consequence, an area of 523,000 square miles, or about one-fifth of the country, is in Australia but not entirely of it. This throws up some interesting anomalies. All Australians are required by law to vote in federal elections, including residents of the Northern Territory. However, since the Northern Territory is not a state, it has no seats in Parliament. So the Territorians elect representatives who go to Canberra and attend sessions of Parliament (at least that's what they say in their letters home) but don't actually vote or take part or have any consequence at all. Even more interestingly, during national referendums the citizens of the Northern Territory are also required to vote, but the votes don't actually count towards anything. They're just put in a drawer or something. Seems a little odd to me, but then, as I say, the people seem content with the arrangement.

Personally, I feel that the Territorians should not be permitted to take full part in national affairs until they get friendlier hotel staff in Darwin. This might seem a curious basis on which to found a political philosophy, but there you are. Darwin's hoteliers are seriously deficient in the charm department and if it takes the withholding of certain civil liberties to get them to address the problem then I think that is a small charge to exact, frankly.

Our troubles began when we went looking for our hotel. We were booked into a place called the All Seasons Frontier Hotel, but no such establishment appeared to exist. The guidebook mentioned a Top End Frontier Hotel, and a tourist leaflet I acquired at the airport listed a Darwin City Frontier Hotel, and yet another listed an All Seasons Premier Darwin Central Hotel. All of these we spied, distantly, as we drove around for the next forty minutes, squabbling quietly in the manner of a fractious married couple. We stopped about half a dozen pedestrians, but none had heard of an All Seasons Frontier Hotel, except one man who thought it was at Kakadu, 200 kilometres to the east. With the aid of a small, inadequate map I directed Allan down a series of streets which proved always to end at a pedestrianized zone or a cul de sac of loading bays, to his increasing exasperation.

'Can you not read a simple map?' he asked in the peevish tone of a man whose happy-hour needs are going unmet, reversing into cardboard boxes and wheelie bins.

'No,' I replied in kind, 'I cannot read a simple map. I can read a good map. This map, however, is useless. Less than useless. It is the print equivalent of your driving, if I may say so.'

Eventually we stopped outside a large hotel on the seafront and Allan ordered me to go inside and seek professional guidance. At the front desk a young man who had evidently invested a recent pay cheque in a very large tub of hair gel stood with his back to me regaling two female colleagues with some droll anecdote. I waited a long minute, then went: 'Ahem.'

He turned his head to give me a look that said, without warmth: 'What?'

'Could you point me to the All Seasons Frontier Hotel?' I asked politely.

Without preamble he reeled off a series of complex directions. Darwin is full of strange street names – Cavenagh, Yuen, Foelsche, Knuckey – and I couldn't begin to follow. On the counter was a pad of maps, and I asked him if he could show me on that.

'It's too far to walk,' he said dismissively.

'I don't want to walk. I've got a car.'

'Then ask your driver to take you.' He rolled his eyes for the benefit of the girls, then continued with his story.

How I longed for a small firearm or perhaps a set of industrial tongs with which to clamp his reedy neck and draw his head close to me, the better to hear what I next had to say. It was: 'Do you think if I had a driver I would be asking directions of you? It's a rental car, you snide, irksome, preposterously glossy little shit.' I may not have said the words precisely in that order, or indeed at all, but that was certainly the emotional gist of it.

With sullen gaze and a long sigh, he took a pen and rapidly but vaguely sketched the route on the map, tore it from the pad and handed it over as if giving me a voucher to which I had no right. Ten minutes later we pulled up outside a hotel that announced itself, in large letters, as the Darwin City Frontier Hotel. We had passed it several times already, but I had confidently rejected it on each occasion. I stalked through the front doors.

'Is this the All Seasons Frontier Hotel?' I barked from an unsocial distance.

The young woman behind the counter looked up, and blinked. 'Yes,' she said.

'Then' – I came much closer – '*why don't you put a sign up saying so*?'

She regarded me levelly. 'It says it on the side of the building.'

'Well, it doesn't.'

She favoured me with a thin, metallic, supremely condescending smile. 'Yes, it does.'

'Well, it doesn't.'

Torn between her training in customer relations and her youthful certitude, she hesitated, and in a soft voice said: 'Does.'

I held up a finger in a way that said: 'Don't move. Don't go anywhere. I'm going to check this out and then come back and throttle someone. You, actually.'

I went out and ranged around the hotel in the manner of a demented building inspector, examining it from every angle and from various distances, held up a silencing finger to Allan, who watched bewildered from the driver's seat, then came back in and announced: 'It doesn't say All Seasons on it anywhere.'

She looked at me and said nothing, but I could see she was thinking: 'Does.'

I am happy to let the record show that by whatever name it goes, the Darwin City Frontier Hotel was a wondrously disappointing establishment. It was overpriced, charmless and inconveniently sited. The TV in my room didn't work, the pillows were concrete slabs and the receptionist was irritating. This was not the Australia I had come to respect and adore.

To get to the hotel bar, we discovered after much blind experimentation and a further interview with our young friend at the front desk, it was necessary to descend by a back stairway to the basement, find our way through some storage areas, leave the building and present ourselves at a pair of automatic sliding doors, which weren't working. Allan, who is not a man to let any impediment stand between him and his evening beverage, yanked them open with a vehemence that was impressive, and we squeezed through. The bar was liberally, not to say unexpectedly, arrayed with rough, boisterously drunk and dangerous-looking fellows, all with copious tattoos, long hair and beards like mattress ticking – not exactly the patrons you would expect to find drinking in the bar of a business hotel.

'Like a fucking ZZ Top convention,' Allan muttered darkly but correctly.

We procured a couple of beers and sat primly in a corner, like two old maids at an inner city bus station, and watched as two of the burlier fellows played a game of pool in which each disappointing shot – and there seemed to be almost no other kind – was accompanied by a whack of cue across something metallic or unyielding: the pool table, a chairback, the swinging light above the table. It seemed only a matter of time before flesh and bone came into the equation. We decided to repair to the rooftop restaurant on the seventh floor in search of a more serene and composed environment. The restaurant was a large room with big windows giving expansive views over Darwin by twilight. Of the perhaps fifty tables in the room no more than three or four were occupied, so it came as a surprise when the hostess informed us, with a look of stark panic, that no tables were available at the moment.

'But it's practically empty,' I pointed out.

'I'm sorry, but we've got a terrible rush on.' As if to underline the urgency of the situation she flew off.

We took a seat at the bar and had two more beers, which we coaxed out of a cheerful Indonesian fellow who sometimes wandered past, and may actually have been an employee. After another thirty minutes and further enquiries we were finally granted a table by a far window. There we sat for ten minutes more until a waitress came out and plonked in front of each of us a small standard terracotta flowerpot in which had been baked a little loaf of bread.

'What's this?' I asked.

'It's bread,' she replied.

'But it's in a flowerpot?'

She gave me a look that I was beginning to think of as the Darwin stare. It was a look that said: 'Yeah? So?'

'Well, isn't that kind of unusual?'

She considered for a moment. 'Is a bit, I suppose.'

'And will we be following a horticultural theme throughout the meal?'

Her expression contorted in a deeply pained look, as if she were trying to suck her face into the back of her head. 'What?'

'Will the main course arrive in a wheelbarrow?' I elaborated helpfully. 'Will you be serving the salad with a pitchfork?'

'Oh no. It's just the bread that's special.'

'I'm so pleased to hear it.'

Before we could take our relationship to the next stage and ask for drinks or perhaps a menu, she was gone, announcing as she went that she would be back when she could but there was a bit of a rush on.

There then followed the most extraordinary evening in which, each time we hankered for food or additional refreshment or just the sound of an Australian voice, we had to go off and stand by the kitchen doors until we caught someone emerging. Some of the other few diners were doing likewise. During one foray I asked a man with an empty beer glass if he dined here often.

'Wife likes the view,' he explained, and we looked across the room to a plump little woman who gave us a small but cheery wave.

'Service is a bit slow, don't you think?'

'Bloody hopeless,' he agreed. 'They've got some kind of a rush on apparently.'

In the morning a new man was behind the front desk. 'And how did you enjoy your stay, sir?' he asked smoothly.

'It was singularly execrable,' I replied.

'Oh, *excellent*,' he purred, taking my card.

'In fact, I would go so far as to say that the principal value of a stay in this establishment is that it is bound to make all subsequent service-related experiences seem, in comparison, refreshing.'

He made a deeply appreciative expression as if to say: 'Praise indeed,' and presented my bill for signature. 'Well, we hope you'll come again.'

'I would sooner have bowel surgery in the woods with a stick.'

His expression wavered, then held there for a long moment. 'Excellent,' he said again, but without a great show of conviction.

We went into town to look around. Darwin is in the steamy heart of the tropics, which to my mind imposes certain stylistic requirements – white buildings with verandas, louvred windows, potted palms, lazy ceiling fans, cool drinks in tall glasses presented by obsequious houseboys, men in white suits and Panama hats, ladies in floral-print cotton dresses, a little mahjong to pass the sultry afternoons, Sydney Greenstreet and Peter Lorre in evidence somewhere looking hot and shifty. Anything that falls short of these simple ideals will always leave me disappointed, and Darwin failed in every respect. To be fair, the place has been knocked about a good deal – it was bombed repeatedly by the Japanese in the Second World War and then devastated by Cyclone Tracy in 1974 – so much of it is necessarily new. Even so, there was almost nothing to suggest a particular climatic affiliation. We could have been in Wollongong or Bendigo or any other moderately prosperous provincial city. The one small local peculiarity was that there seemed to be no one about of professional demeanour. Nearly every person on the streets was bearded and tattooed and scuffed along with a wino shuffle, as if some very large mission had just turned everyone out for the day. Here and there, too, were scatterings of Aborigines, shadowy and furtive, sitting quietly on the margins of sunny plazas as if in a waiting room. While Allan went off to get some money out of a bank machine, I drifted into the vicinity of three Aboriginal people, two men and a woman, all staring at nothing. I gave them a nod and respectful g'day smile as I passed, but failed signally to establish eye contact. It was as if they were somewhere else, or I was transparent.

We had breakfast in a small Italian café, the only customers, then drove out to the Museum and Art Gallery of the Northern Territory because I had read that it had a box jellyfish on display. I had expected the museum to be small and dusty, and to detain us for no longer than it took to find and briefly examine the jellyfish display, but in fact it was sleek and modern and quite wonderful. It was improbably large for a provincial museum and chock-full of interesting stuff thoughtfully presented.

One area was devoted to Cyclone Tracy, still the most devastating natural event in Australian history. It all but blew away the town on Christmas Eve 1974. According to a recorded commentary, most people didn't expect the storm to come to much. A weaker cyclone had passed through a few weeks earlier without doing significant damage, and the leading edge of Tracy brushed over the town without leaving any hint of particular ferocity to come. Most people turned in as if it were a normal night. It wasn't until Darwin was hit by the back end of the storm system, about 2.30 a.m., that people realized they were really in for it. As the winds whipped up to 160 miles an hour Darwin's frail tropical houses began to shed pieces and then to disintegrate. Most of the housing was post-war fibreboard homes of a type called the D series, which were cheap and quick to build but could not stand up to a real hurricane. Before the night was out Tracy had blown away 9,000 homes and killed more than sixty people.

Just off the main display area was a small, darkened chamber in which you could listen to a tape recording of the storm that had been made on the night by a Roman Catholic priest. A sign on the door warned that people who had lived through the storm might find the recording distressing, which I thought perhaps a trifle overwrought until I heard it myself. Well, it was an amazingly effective way of making you realize how powerful and terrifying such a storm can be. The recording began with various lively but clearly preliminary wind noises – branches knocking, gates banging – and then rose and rose again till it was a continuous, howling, unearthly fury, with sounds of metal roofs being wrenched from their moorings and other weighty debris flying murderously through the night. Experiencing it in pitch darkness, as the locals would have done, gave it an immediacy that was inexpressibly effective. I actually found myself ducking whenever anything crashed nearby. When it finished, Allan and I exchanged impressed and drained looks, and proceeded on to the visual part of the display with a new appreciation.

On a wall outside, a television endlessly showed the original Australian Broadcasting Corporation footage of what the town woke up to the next day – namely, total devastation. The film, taken from a slow-moving car, showed street after street in which every structure was flattened.

Much of the rest of the museum was given over to cases of stuffed animals illustrating the Northern Territory's extraordinary biological diversity. Pride of place was given to an enormous stuffed crocodile named Sweetheart, who was for a time the most famous in Australia. Sweetheart – who was, despite the effeminate name, a male – had a passionate dislike for outboard engines and used to attack any boats that disturbed his peace. Unusually for a crocodile, he never harmed a person, but he crunched at least fifteen boats and their motors, bringing a certain unexpected liveliness to many a fisherman's afternoon. In 1979 when it was feared that he would do himself some serious harm – he was constantly being clobbered by propellers – wildlife officials decided to move him somewhere safer. Unfortunately, the capture was botched when a cable snagged and Sweetheart drowned. So he was stuffed and put on display in the Darwin museum, where he has been impressing visitors ever since with his very substantial heft: he stretches almost seventeen feet and in life weighed over 1,700 pounds.

Another case answered a question that must have occurred to nearly everyone at one time or another: namely, how exactly do they stuff the animals? I had always assumed they filled them with sawdust or old socks or something. Well, here I learned, by means of a small stuffed animal shown in cross-section, that in fact a mounted specimen is empty but for a spare interior framework of styrofoam balls and wooden dowels. I was touched and grateful that some curator had taken the trouble to provide this insight. Also on display were lots of snakes and reptiles, many of them quite severely murderous, which Allan regarded with particular absorption.

Perhaps the most admirable quality about the museum – and I suspect this is a real Northern Territory thing – is that it didn't mince words about the dangers of the world outside. Most museums in Australia are at pains to stress the unlikelihood of anything happening to you. The Darwin museum makes it quite obvious, with cold facts and figures, that if something does happen to you out there, you are really going to regret it. This was most potently displayed in the aquatic creatures section – and here at last we found what we had come to see: a large glass cylinder containing a preserved box jellyfish, the deadliest creature on earth.

It was remarkably unprepossessing – a translucent box-shaped blob, six or eight inches high, with threadlike tentacles several feet long trailing off beneath it. Like all jellyfish, it is all but brainless, but its lethality is unbelievable. The tentacles of a box jellyfish carry enough wallop to kill a roomful of people, yet they live exclusively on tiny krill-like shrimp – creatures that hardly require a great deal of violent subduing. As ever in the curious world of Australian biology, no one knows why the jellyfish evolved such extravagant toxicity.

Alongside were displays of other dangerous sea creatures, of which the Northern Territory has an impressive plenitude – five types of stingray, two of blue-ringed octopus, thirty varieties of sea snake, eight types of coneshell, and the usual roguish assortment of stonefish, scorpionfish, firefish and others too numerous to list and too depressing to dwell on. All these are found in shallow coastal waters, in rock pools and even sometimes on the beaches themselves. It is a wonder to me that anyone goes within a hundred feet of the sea in northern Australia. The sea snakes are especially unnerving, not because they are aggressive, but because they are inquisitive. Stray into their territory and they will come to check you out, all but rubbing against you in the manner of cats seeking affection. They are the most sweet-tempered creatures in existence. But cross them or alarm them and they can hit you with enough venom to kill three grown men. Now *that*'s scary.

As we were studying the display, a man, lean and lavishly bearded in the Darwinian style, said g'day and asked how we were going. He identified himself as Dr Phil Alderslade, curator of coelenterates. 'Jellyfish and corals,' he added at once, seeing our expressions of frank ignorance. 'I noticed you taking notes,' he added further.

I told him of my devotion to box jellyfish and asked him if he worked with them himself.

'Oh, sure.'

'So how do you keep from getting stung?'

'Basic precautions really. You wear a wetsuit, of course, and rubber gloves, and you just take a good deal of care when handling them because if even a tiny piece of tentacle is left on a glove and you accidentally touch it to bare skin – wiping sweat from your face or brushing away a fly or something – you can get a *very* nasty sting, believe me.'

'Have you ever been stung?'

'Once. My glove slipped and a tentacle touched me just here.' He showed us the soft underside of his wrist. It bore a faint scar about half an inch long. 'Just touched me, but jeez it bloody hurt.'

'What'd it feel like?' we asked together.

'The only thing I can compare it to is if you took a lit cigarette and held it to your skin – held it there a goodish long while, maybe thirty seconds. That's what it felt like. You get stung from time to time by various things in my line and I can tell you I've never felt anything like it.'

'So what would a couple of yards feel like?' I wondered.

He shook his head at the thought of it. 'If you tried to imagine the worst pain possible, it would be beyond that. You're dealing with pain of an order of magnitude well past anything most people have ever experienced.'

He did something you don't often see a scientist do: he shivered. Then he smiled cheerfully through his extravagant facial hair and excused himself to get back to his corals.

We left the museum and headed out of town through Darwin's sunny, orderly suburbs – white bungalows on tidy lawns – and at the edge of town passed a sign that said: 'Alice Springs 1479 kilometres'. Ahead, along the lonely Stuart Highway, lay nearly a thousand miles of largely unrelieved emptiness all the way to Alice Springs. We were on our way into the famous and forbidding Never Never, a land of dangerous heat and bone-white sunshine.

The road – the Track, as it is still sometimes called – was nearly empty but straight and well maintained. Ask ten people in Sydney or Melbourne whether the highway from Darwin to Alice Springs is paved or not and most will have no idea. In fact, it was paved long before most other outback roads: during the Second World War when northern Australia became a principal staging post for the Pacific campaign. These days it carries a small but growing number of tourists, a very little local traffic and lots of road trains – multi-trailered lorries up to a hundred and fifty feet long, which haul freight between the most distant outposts of Australia. To meet a barrelling road train coming at you at full throttle on a two-lane highway on which it desires all of its lane and some of yours is a reliably invigorating experience – an explosive *whoomp* as you hit its displaced air, followed at once by a consequent lurch onto the shoulder, several moments of hypermanic axle action sufficient to loosen dental fillings and empty your pockets of coins, an enveloping shroud of gritty red dust and the metallic dinks and savage thumps of flying rocks, some involuntary oral emissions on your part as the dust clears and you spy a large boulder dead ahead; and a sudden, miraculous return to tranquillity and smoothness as the car regains the highway, entirely of its own volition, and continues on its way to Alice Springs.

The only time that this part of the world had any life at all was during the Second World War, when sixty airfields and thirty-five hospitals were built along the highway between Darwin and Daly Waters, and a hundred thousand American troops were stationed in the area. The sites are still indicated with historical markers, and a couple of times we pulled off to have a look. When Alan Moorehead passed this way for *Rum Jungle*, a decade after the war's end, most of the buildings were still standing. Sometimes he came across abandoned planes and stacks of munitions quietly decomposing in the desert. I naturally hoped we would as well, but there was nothing out there now – nothing but stillness and oppressive heat and a sense of being on the edge of a boundless nullity.

In every direction for as far as the eye could see the earth was covered with spinifex, a brittle grass, which grew in clumps so closely packed as to give an appearance of verdure. It looked like land that could support a thousand head of cattle an acre. In fact, spinifex is useless – the only wholly non-edible grass in the world apparently. It is also murder to travel through because its needle-sharp points, tipped in silica, break off when brushed and become embedded in the skin, where they fester into small but horrible sores. Scattered among the spinifex were turpentine bushes and man-sized termite mounds, which stood in the desert like ancient dolmens. And that was it.

After about three hours we passed through Katherine, a dusty, inoffensive little community, and the last town worthy of the name for 400 miles. Beyond it, the landscape grew more visibly impoverished, and the traffic thinned out from little to almost none. For much of the way the highway was simply a taut line connecting impossibly distant horizons, the landscape on either side a monumental emptiness punctuated by spinifex, low bushes, lunar rocks and almost nothing else. The sky everywhere was huge, and brilliantly blue.

We had been driving for perhaps ninety minutes in a largely mindless silence when at last Allan spoke. He said: 'How are you off for urine?'

'I have all I need, thank you. Why do you ask?'

'It's just that I notice we're nearly out of petrol.'

'Truly?' I leaned over to confirm that Allan could indeed

interpret a petrol gauge – if not perhaps quite as frequently as one might wish.

'Interesting time to notice, Allan,' I observed.

'This thing just seems to suck up fuel,' he replied, perhaps just a trifle inadequately. 'So where are we?' he asked after a moment's further reflection.

'We're in the middle of nowhere, Allan.'

'I mean in relation to the next town.'

I looked at the map. 'In relation to the next town, we are' – I looked again, just to confirm – 'in the middle of nowhere.' I did some measurements with my fingers. 'We appear to be about forty kilometres from a dot on the map called Larrimah.'

'And do they have petrol there?'

'One sincerely hopes so. And do you think we have enough to get there?'

'One sincerely and, if I may just say, bloody well hopes so.'

We chugged into Larrimah on the last vapour of gas. It was an all but dead hamlet, but it did have a petrol station. While Allan fuelled up, I went in and purchased a stock of bottled water and snack foods for future emergencies. We vowed that henceforth we would jointly keep a steady eye on the fuel gauge and not let it dip below the halfway mark. There were even greater stretches of emptiness to come.

Still, the very slight brush with crisis buoyed our spirits, and we were in a triumphant frame of mind when in late afternoon we rolled into Daly Waters, our destination for the day. Daly Waters – 370 miles from Darwin, 570 from Alice Springs – was off the Stuart Highway a couple of miles down an unpaved side road and over a small ford, which added to its already palpable sense of remoteness. If you were looking for a classic outback spot, you could not improve upon it. It consisted of a few small houses, a tumbledown and obviously long-closed general store, two petrol pumps unattached to any particular building beneath a sign saying 'Outback Servo' and a utilitarian pub with a tin roof. All the rest was heat and dust.

We parked outside the pub. It had signs hung all over it. One said: 'Est. 1893. Australia's oldest licensed public house.' Nearby another sign said: 'Est. 1930. Northern Territory's Oldest Pub.' The heat when we stepped from the car was stifling. The temperature must have been pushing 110 degrees. A tourist brochure I had picked up in Darwin hinted, without actually saying, that the Daly

Waters pub provided accommodation. I certainly hoped so as we were 230 miles from the next town, with nothing but a scattered and uncertain assortment of roadhouses in between. Anyway, it's dangerous to drive through dusk in the outback. That's when kangaroos come bounding out of the gloaming and into the paths of passing vehicles, to the frequent regret of both. Trucks sweep them aside, but they can make a mess of cars, and sometimes the cars' occupants.

We stepped into the gloomy interior – gloomy because the world outside was so painfully bright and we had been out in it all afternoon. I could hardly see a thing.

'Hello,' I said to a face behind the bar that might, for all I could tell, have been a ping-pong paddle, 'do you do rooms?'

'Finest rooms in Daly Waters,' responded the paddle. 'Also the only rooms in Daly Waters.' As the form spoke, it transmogrified before my eyes into a cheerfully sweaty, bespectacled, slightly harassed-looking man of late middle years. He was sizing us up with a look that was very slightly askance. 'You want two rooms,' he said, 'or are you bunking up together?'

'Two,' I said at once.

This seemed to please him. He rummaged in a drawer and produced two keys with unmatching tags. 'This one's a single,' he said, laying a key on my palm, 'and this one's got a double bed in it – in case one of yers gets lucky tonight.' He bounced his eyebrows in a slightly salacious manner.

'And do you think that's likely?'

'Hey, miracles happen.'

The rooms were in a separate block that stood alongside the pub, ten or so of them ranged on either side of a central corridor. I insisted Allan take the double as he was far more likely to get lucky than I was.

'Out here?' He gave a hollow laugh.

'There's eighty million sheep in the outback, Allan. They can't all be picky.'

We parted to examine our rooms. Basic was the word that leaped to mind. Mine consisted of an ancient bed, a battered dresser and a raffia wastebasket. There was no TV or phone, and the illumination consisted of a bare yellow bulb dangling from the ceiling, but the solitary window held an ancient air conditioner, which shook and juddered violently when switched on but did actually seem to generate a little cool air. The bathroom was at the end of the corridor and was a touch insalubrious, with rust stains in the sink and a shower that looked actively infectious.

I went to visit Allan, who was sitting on his bed grinning inanely. 'Come in!' he cried. 'Come in. I'd offer you something from the minibar, but I don't seem to have one. Pull up a chair – oh, no! There is no chair. Well, please make full use of the wastebasket.'

'It is a little basic,' I conceded.

'Basic? It's a bloody cell. I'd show you the light, but it's burnt out.'

'I'm sure we can get a replacement for you.'

'No, no, no. I think I'll like it better in full darkness.' He pursed his lips. 'Is it too early to start drinking?'

I looked at my watch. It was only four forty-five. 'It is a bit. There's actually something I wanted to see.'

'An attraction? In Daly Waters? What can it be? Someone getting petrol? The evening sheep shag?'

'It's a tree.'

'A *tree*. Of course it is. Please lead the way.'

We went out to the car and drove a couple of miles down a hot dirt track. There on the edge of a large, barren clearing beside the road stood a sign announcing that we had found our way to the Stuart Tree, commemorating John McDouall Stuart, perhaps the greatest of all Australian explorers. A Scottish soldier of bantamweight dimensions (he barely topped five feet), Stuart led three epic expeditions through the interior, and all but killed himself in the process. The bright light of the outback severely disagreed with his vision, and on at least two of his trips he was soon seeing double – not perhaps the most encouraging affliction in someone choosing a route through an uncharted wilderness. ('So, boys, which of those twin peaks do you think we should head for? I say we go for the one under the left-hand sun.') Generally he would finish the trips effectively blind. On his second expedition, he also became crippled with scurvy, for which he seemed to have a particular susceptibility. His body became 'a mass of sores that will not heal'. The skin, one of his lieutenants noted, 'hung from the roof of his mouth, his tongue became swollen and he was incapable of talking'. Virtually insensible, he was carried on a stretcher for the last 400 miles and each day his colleagues lifted him down from his mount expecting to find him dead. Yet within a month of returning to society he was on his feet again and setting off once more into the punishing void.

His final attempt, in 1861–2, seemed fated to end in failure as well. His horses 'were much distressed' for want of water, and both men and beasts were tormented by bulwaddy, a treacherous shrub with thorny spikes. But at Daly Waters they found a stream with potable water. It was the moment that saved the venture. The men rested, rewatered and pushed on. In July 1862, nine months after setting off from Adelaide, they reached the Timor Sea and in so doing became the first to find a practical route through the heart of the continent. Within a decade, a telegraph line had been strung from Adelaide to what would eventually become Darwin, putting Australia at last in direct touch with the world.

In his delight at finding the stream at Daly Waters, Stuart carved an S into a big gum tree. It was this that we had come to see. The tree, it must be said, was not much – a fifteen-foot-high chunk of gum tree, lopped of its upper branches and long dead. Every guidebook tells you the S is clearly visible, but we couldn't find it. Still, there was a certain pleasure in being at a famous spot that few Australians visit. As we stood there, a flock of galahs, a noisy pinkish parrot, came and settled on the surrounding trees. It was a scene almost entirely without feature – a barren plain, a fat setting sun, a scattering of ragged gum trees – and yet, in a wholly uncharacteristic way, I was captivated by it. I don't know why, but I loved it out here.

We regarded it for quite a time, then Allan turned to me and asked in a respectful voice if we could go for a drink now.

'Yes we can,' I said.

Daly Waters' fame did not begin and end with the fleeting visit of Stuart and his band. In the 1920s a rather shadowy couple by the name of Pearce came to Daly Waters and opened a shop with a borrowed twenty pounds. Amazingly, they did pretty well. Within a few years they had a shop, a hotel, a pub and an aerodrome. Daly Waters became a stopoff point between Brisbane and Darwin on the run to Singapore and on to London in the early days of Qantas and the old Imperial Airways. Lady Mountbatten was among the first overnight guests at the hotel. Goodness knows what she made of the place – though I dare say she was just awfully glad to be on solid ground. In the early days a commercial flight from London involved, in addition to nerves of steel, forty-two refuelling stops, up to five changes of aircraft and a train journey through Italy because Mussolini wouldn't allow flights through Italian air space.

It took twelve days. As well as the seasonal monsoons, the flights were subject to dust storms, mechanical failures, navigational confusion and occasional pot-shots from hostile or impish bedouins. Crashes were not infrequent.

The perils of aviation in the period are neatly encapsulated in the experience of Harold C. Brinsmead, the head of Australia's Civil Aviation Department in the first days of commercial aviation. In 1931, Brinsmead was on a flight to London, partly for business and partly to demonstrate the safety and reliability of modern air passenger services, when his plane crashed on takeoff in Indonesia. No one was seriously hurt, but the plane was a write-off. Not wanting to wait for a replacement aircraft to be flown in, Brinsmead boarded a flight with the new Dutch airline, KLM. That flight crashed while taking off in Bangkok. On this occasion, five people were killed and Brinsmead suffered serious injuries from which he never recovered. He died two years later. Meanwhile, the surviving passengers carried on to London in a replacement plane. That plane crashed on the return trip.

Daly Waters claims to be Australia's oldest international airport, though I suspect many other venerable airstrips make a similar boast. It is certainly true that it was used as a stopoff point on some international flights and more regularly on cross-country flights from Queensland to Western Australia, so it was a kind of crossroads. The airport stayed open until 1947. The pub opened in 1938, so it is not by any stretch the oldest in the outback or the Northern Territory, but it is certainly one of the most extraordinary.

As with most outback pubs every inch of interior surface – walls, rafters, wooden support posts – was covered with mementos left by earlier visitors: college ID cards, drivers' licences, folding money from many nations, bumper stickers, badges from various police and fire departments, even a generous and arresting assortment of underwear, which dangled from rafters or was nailed to walls. The rest was nicely spartan: a large but basic central bar, concrete floor, bare tin roof, an assortment of tables and chairs of different vintages and styles, a battered pool table. At the bar, seven or eight men, all in shorts, T-shirts, boots and bush hats, stood drinking stubbies – squat bottles of beer – served in insulated foam holders to keep them cold. They all looked hot and dusty, but then everything in Daly Waters was hot and dusty. The atmosphere in the pub can best be described as convivially sweltering. Even standing still, the sweat dripped off us. The windows had screens, but most were full of holes and anyway the doors were wide open so flies came in freely. The men at the bar gave me compact but friendly nods as I bellied up to the bar, and obligingly made space for me to stand to order, but showed no special interest in me as an outsider. Clearly, as the souvenirs attested, visitors were not a novelty.

I acquired a pair of chilled stubbies and conveyed them to the table where Allan sat beneath a bumper sticker commemorating a visit by the 'Wheredafukarwi Touring Club'. Allan was suffused with a strange happiness.

'You like it here?' I said.

He shook his head with a kind of speechless delight. 'I do. I actually do.'

'But I thought you hated it.'

'I did,' he said. 'But then I was sitting here looking out the window at the setting sun, and it was lovely – I mean really quite astoundingly lovely – and then I turned and saw the bar with all these outback characters, and I thought: "Bugger me, I like it here."' He looked at me in the frankest wonder. 'And I do. I really like it.'

'I'm so pleased.'

He drained his beer and rose. 'You ready for another?'

Now it was my turn to be filled with wonder. I started to point out that it was a touch early to be setting such a blistering pace, but then I thought: what the hell. We had come a long way and this place was, after all, built for drinking.

I drained my bottle and handed it over. 'Sure,' I said, 'why not?'

Well, I can't pretend I remember a great deal of what followed. We drank huge amounts of beer – huge amounts. We ate steaks the size of catcher's mitts (they may actually have been catcher's mitts) and washed them down with more beer. We made many friends. We circulated as if at a cocktail party. I talked to ranchers and sheep shearers, to nannies and cooks. I met fellow travellers from around the world, and talked for some time to the proprietor, one Bruce Caterer, who told me the complicated story of how he had come to own a pub in this lonely and far-flung spot, of which confidence I have not the tiniest recollection and certainly nothing approximating a note. As the evening wore on, the bar grew almost impossibly crowded and lively. Where all the people were coming from I couldn't guess. What was certain was that there were at least fifty cheerfully committed drinkers tucked away in the bush in the vicinity of Daly Waters and at least as many visitors like us. I got comprehensively beaten at pool by at least fourteen people. I bought rounds for strangers. I called my wife and professed my lasting devotion. I giggled at any story told me and radiated uncritical affection in all directions. I would have gone anywhere with anyone. I awoke the next morning, fully clothed and on top of the bedding, with no clear memory past the catcher's mitt portion of the evening and a head that felt like a train crash.

I pressed my watch to an eyeball and groaned at the discovery that it was nearly ten o'clock. We were hours late if we were ever going to get to Alice Springs. I stumbled down to the bathroom and put myself through some cursory ablutions, then found my way blearily into the pub. Allan sat propped against a wall with his eyes closed, a cup of black coffee steaming untouched before him. There was no one else around.

'Where coffee where?' I croaked in a tiny voice.

He indicated vaguely with a weak hand. In a side room I found an urn of hot water and containers of instant coffee, tea bags, powdered milk and sugar with which to make a hot beverage. I loaded a cup half full with instant coffee powder, dribbled in some water, and rejoined Allan.

Weakly, in the manner of an invalid, I lifted the cup and introduced a little coffee to my lips. After a couple of more sips, I began to feel a little better. Allan, on the other hand, looked terminally wretched.

'How late were we up?' I asked.

'Late.'

'Very late?'

'Very.'

'Why are you sitting with your eyes closed?'

'Because if I open them I'm afraid I'll bleed to death.'

'Did I disgrace myself?' I peered around the room to see if my boxer shorts were draped from any rafters.

'Not that I recall. You were shit at pool.'

I nodded without surprise. I often use alcohol as an artificial check on my pool-playing skills. It's a way for me to help strangers gain confidence in their abilities and get in touch with my inner wallet.

'Anything else?' I asked.

'You're doing a house swap next summer with a family from Korea.'

I pursed my lips thoughtfully. 'North or South?' I asked.

'Not sure.'

'You're making this up, aren't you?'

He reached over and plucked from my shirt pocket a business card, which he presented to me. It said: 'Park Ho Lee, Meat Wholesaler' or something and gave an address in Pusan. Underneath it, in my own handwriting, it said: 'June 10–August 27. No worries.'

I placed the card, folded once, in the ashtray.

'I think I'd like to get out of here now,' I said.

He nodded and with an effort of will rose from the table, wobbled ever so slightly, and went off to gather up his things. I hesitated a long moment and followed.

Ten minutes later we were on our way to Alice Springs.

CHAPTER SIXTEEN

NOW HERE'S A STORY TO PONDER.

In April 1860, during the second of his heroic attempts to cross Australia from south to north, John McDouall Stuart reached the almost waterless centre of the continent, roughly halfway between the present sites of Daly Waters and Alice Springs. A thousand miles from anywhere, the spot was the very 'climax of desolation', as Stuart's fellow explorer Ernest Giles once nicely put it, and Stuart and his men went through hell to get there. They were sick and ragged and half starved, and it had taken months, but at least they had the satisfaction of knowing that they had become the first outsiders to penetrate to the brutal heart of the continent.

So you may imagine Stuart's surprise when, in the middle of this baking nowhere, he and his party encountered three Aboriginal men who greeted them by making a secret sign of the Freemasons. Stuart didn't say in his journal what the sign was, but it was clear from his amazed description that it was unlikely to have been coincidental. Then a few days later Stuart and his men found horse tracks following a natural course across the plains. Finally, some distance further on, the explorers were setting up camp for the night when some people from the Warramunga tribe approached. One of Stuart's party, a young man named W. P. Auld, was sitting with his boots off rubbing his aching feet when one of the Warramunga men knelt before him. While Auld watched bemusedly, the man replaced the boots on Auld's feet and carefully but deftly tied the laces for him, then sat back with a big pleased smile. It was painfully evident to Stuart that he and his men were not in fact the first white people to reach the empty centre of the country. So who preceded them? No one has ever had the faintest idea.

I mention this to make the point that the outback is an odd and unfathomable place. There is something about all that emptiness that exerts a strange hold on people. It is an environment that wants you dead, yet again and again in the face of the most staggering privations, for the meagrest of rewards, explorers ventured into it. Sometimes, as Stuart found, they didn't even bother to leave their names. It is almost not possible to exaggerate the punishing nature of Australia's interior. For nineteenth-century explorers, it wasn't just the inexpressible heat and constant scarcity of water, but a thousand other miseries. Stinging ants swarmed over them wherever they rested. Natives sometimes attacked with spears. The landscape was full of thorny bushes and merciless spinifex whose silicate pricks nearly always grew infected from sweat and dirt. Scurvy was a constant plague. Hygiene was impossible. Pack animals grew frequently crazed or lost the will to go on. Ernest Giles recorded in his memoirs how his horse once grew so delirious after an unsuccessful search for water that when they returned to camp at the end of the day the animal plunged its nose into a fire in the deluded hope that it would provide relief. In pity, Giles gave the injured animal a drink from his own meagre supplies, but it died anyway. Even camels could barely cope with the desert conditions. In *Beyond Leichhardt*, a history of Australian exploration, Glen McLaren notes how blowflies doted on the wounds of camels, laying eggs in any raw lesions, which soon erupted in horrible swarms of wriggling maggots. On one expedition, a camel's wound grew so infected that the maggots 'were scooped out daily with a pint pot'. Eventually the animal just lay down and died. When even camels can't manage a desert, you know you've found a tough part of the world. For human and animal alike, nearly every breathing moment was a living hell.

And yet over and over the explorers returned. Nearly every expedition of the nineteenth century started off with some ostensible practical purpose – to find a route for a telegraph line, to look for gold, to uncover some zone of hidden promise – but almost without exception the explorers soon became transfixed by the emptiness. Unable to resist its allure, they just pushed on and on.

Perhaps no one suffered privations more willingly and repeatedly, to less effect, than Ernest Giles. In 1874, while he was travelling with a companion named Alfred Gibson through the barren wastes of Western Australia, Gibson's horse died. Giles gave Gibson his own mount with instructions to follow their tracks 120 miles back to a place called Fort McKellar to fetch another. Gibson lost his way in the emptiness and was never seen again. (The area is now called the Gibson Desert.) Left to find his own way back on foot, Giles staggered for days over exhausting sandhills, the last sixty miles with almost no water. It was while in this desperate state, tormented by flies and half dead with hunger, that he famously spotted a baby wallaby and fell upon it, devouring it raw, fur, skin and all.

These were not exceptional experiences, you understand. This is what awaited you when you went into the outback. When Robert Austin and his men, lost in the featureless wastes of Western Australia, drank their own and their horses' urine, there was nothing terribly unusual about that. Lots of people did likewise in the desert. When Giles found and devoured the baby wallaby, he thought himself exceedingly lucky – not just at that moment but for years afterwards. 'The delicious taste of that creature I shall never forget,' he wrote with sincere and telling enthusiasm in his memoirs. Stuart and his men retained equally fond memories of a time when, on the brink of starvation, they found a clutch of dingo puppies and boiled them up in a pot. They were, he wrote, 'delicious!'

Why people repeatedly subjected themselves to such ordeals is a mystery that surpasses understanding. Despite the extreme travails he experienced on the fatal expedition with Gibson, Giles returned almost at once to his compulsive wanderings. Stuart did likewise; almost continuously for four years he hurled himself at the unyielding interior until he succeeded in breaking through. Worn out by the effort, he retired to London and died soon after.

It is impossible to say who endured the greater hardships, Stuart or Giles, but there is no question that Giles did it for less reward. No explorer was ever unluckier. In the same year that he lost Gibson in the desert and stumbled 120 miles through appalling heat, Giles also explored the central regions around the area known as Yulara. One day, he struggled up a small rise and was confronted with a sight such as he could never have dreamed of finding. Before him, impossibly imposing, stood the most singular monolith on earth, the great red rock now known as Uluru. Hastening to Adelaide to report the find, he was informed that a man named

William Christie Gosse had chanced upon it a few days ahead of him and had already named it Ayers Rock in honour of the South Australia governor.

Eventually, too old to explore, Giles ended up working as a clerk in the gold fields of Coolgardie, where he died in obscurity in 1891. Today he is almost entirely forgotten. No highway bears his name.

And so the doughty Mr Sherwin and I proceeded through the hot and inexhaustible desert. As we travelled south from Daly Waters, the landscape became more sparsely vegetated. It began to feel eerily as if we had left Planet Earth. The soil took on a reddish glow, more Martian than terrestrial, and the sunlight seemed to double in intensity, as if generated by a nearer, larger sun. Even on a smoothly paved highway, in the comfort of air conditioning, you are not entirely robbed of the sense of what the explorers must have gone through. The discomforts can't be fully imagined but the scale can, and it was awesome.

To the left were several thousand square miles of stubbled nothingness called the Barkly Tableland, which eventually merges into the Simpson Desert, probably the toughest ranching country in the world. So unyielding is the land that ranches have to be vast to support a single operation; the largest of them, at a place called Anna Creek, is bigger than Belgium. To the right, unbelievably, the land was even harsher. This was the infamous Tanami Desert, an area of hellish dryness that even now is largely uncharted. On my map, not a feature was indicated – not a dried creekbed or old dirt track – for 300 miles to the Western Australia border. Beyond that, it was virtually as bleak for 600 miles more.

Even along the Stuart Highway, with its life-bearing traffic, the 550-odd miles between Daly Waters and Alice Springs could boast just one small town, an old gold-mining community called Tennant Creek, three or four clustered habitations that made Daly Waters look cosmopolitan, and a roadhouse perhaps once every eighty miles. And that was it. I had never been out in such a boundless blank. Eventually, some hills began to rise in the middle distance: the MacDonnell Ranges. Very occasionally – once or twice an hour – a road train would bomb past. Once we saw an approaching car, the driver evidently sedated by monotony, leave the road and bang wildly along the rough shoulder for perhaps two hundred feet, pulling in its wake a long speed ramp of dust. As he neared us –

stirred possibly by Allan's honking – the driver jerked to startled wakefulness and veered reflexively, but much too sharply, for the pavement and thence, to our shrill amazement, into our path. It was absurd: in an area of inexpressible emptiness the only two pieces of moving metal were about to bang together in a very big way. There passed an instant made up in equal parts of horn blare, muted shrieks and wild, tight swerves. For the strangest moment, time went into arrest and I could see perfectly our unwitting assailant, frozen as if in a candid photograph, looking at us with a mixture of bewilderment and apology. I shouldn't wonder that it's a moment all people are given when they are about to die suddenly. Then all was blurred swiftness again. The cars passed without hitting – goodness knows how – and I turned full in the seat to watch our adversary shooting away into the distance behind us, soberly attentive to his lane. I watched until he was a dot at vanishing point, then turned to Allan.

'Well, I don't know about you,' he said brightly, 'but I'm ready for a cup of coffee and a change of underpants.'

'Excellent plan,' I agreed, and I joined him in scanning the horizon for a lonely but welcoming roadhouse.

The great virtue about driving through emptiness is that when you come to anything – anything at all – that might be called a diversion you get disproportionately excited. In mid-afternoon we saw a signpost for something called the Devils Marbles and, with the briefest exchange of glances, followed a side road a mile or so to a parking area. And there we saw something really quite fabulous – enormous piles of smooth granite boulders, many as big as houses, stacked in jumbled piles or scattered over an immense area (1,800 hectares, according to a signboard). Every one brought to mind something else: a jelly bean, a bread roll, a bowling ball – except that they were immense and often perched on impossibly fine points. Imagine a boulder maybe thirty feet high and nearly spherical standing on a base little larger than, say, a manhole cover. Needless to say, there wasn't a soul around. Put these stones anywhere in Europe or North America and they would be world famous. In every family album would be a photograph of mom and the kids having a picnic against a backdrop of fantastic rocks. Here they were a lost wonder, off the road in the middle of a boundless nowhere. We wandered around for half an hour, as amazed by the solitude as much as by the rocks, then congratulated ourselves on our good fortune and good sense in stopping, and returned to the road in a state of elevated contentment.

Ten hours and 903 kilometres after leaving Daly Waters we arrived, dry and dusty, in Alice Springs, a grid of ruler-straight streets set like an enormous helipad on a plain beside the golden slopes of the MacDonnell Ranges. Because it is so bang in the middle of nowhere, Alice Springs ought to seem a miracle – an actual town with department stores and schools and streets with names – and for a long time it was a sort of antipodean Timbuktu, a place tantalizing in its inaccessibility. In 1954, when Alan Moorehead passed through, Alice's only regular connection to the outside world was a weekly train from Adelaide. Its arrival on Saturday evening was the biggest event in the life of the town. It brought mail, newspapers, new pictures for the cinema, long-awaited spare parts and whatever else couldn't be acquired locally. Nearly the whole town turned out to see who got off and what was unloaded.

In those days, Alice had a population of 4,000 and hardly any visitors. Today it's a thriving little city with a population of 25,000 and it is full of visitors – 350,000 of them a year – which is of course the whole problem. These days you can jet in from Adelaide in two hours, from Melbourne and Sydney in less than three. You can have a latte and buy some opals and then climb on a tour bus and travel down the highway to Ayers Rock. The town has not only become accessible, it's become a destination. It's so full of motels, hotels, conference centres, campgrounds and desert resorts that you can't pretend even for a moment that you have achieved something exceptional by getting yourself there. It's crazy really. A community that was once famous for being remote now attracts thousands of visitors who come to see how remote it no longer is.

Nearly all guidebooks and travel articles indulge the gentle conceit that Alice retains some irreproducible outback charm – some away-from-it-all quality that you must come here to see – but in fact it is Anywhere, Australia. Actually, it is Anywhere, Planet Earth. On our way into town we passed strip malls, car dealerships, McDonald's and Kentucky Fried Chicken outlets, banks and petrol stations. Only a scattering of Aborigines strolling along the dried bed of the Todd River gave any hint of exoticism. We took rooms in a motor inn on the edge of the modest town centre. My room had a balcony where I could watch the setting sun flood the desert floor and burnish the golden slopes of the MacDonnell

Ranges beyond – or at least I could if I looked past the more immediate sprawl of a K-Mart plaza across the road. In the two million or more square miles that is the Australian outback, I don't suppose there is a more unfortunate juxtaposition.

Allan was evidently held by a similar thought, for a half-hour later when we met out front he was staring at the same scene. 'I can't believe we've just driven a thousand miles to find a K-Mart,' he said. He looked at me. 'You Yanks have a lot to answer for, you know.'

I started to protest, in a sputtering sort of way, but what could I say? He was right. We do. We have created a philosophy of retailing that is totally without aesthetics and totally irresistible. And now we box these places up and ship them to the far corners of the world. Visually, almost every arrestingly regrettable thing in Alice Springs was a product of American enterprise, from people who couldn't know that they had helped to drain the distinctiveness from an outback town and doubtless wouldn't see it that way anyway. Nor come to that, I dare say, would most of the shoppers of Alice Springs, who were no doubt delighted to get lots of free parking and a crack at Martha Stewart towels and shower curtains. What a sad and curious age we live in.

We strolled through the centre of town looking for somewhere to eat. Alice's central business district was sufficiently compact that it took little time to exhaust its modest possibilities for sustenance and diversion. When we realized that we were walking the same streets twice, we repaired more or less by default to a Chinese restaurant we had passed a few minutes earlier from the other direction. It was nearly empty.

While we waited for our food, Allan gazed critically at the flock wallpaper and gaudy fixtures as if these alone might explain Alice's disappointing inadequacies. For a moment he seemed even to be gazing at the background music. 'So how long are we here for?' he asked at last.

'Well, we're here tomorrow. And then we go to Uluru. And then we come back here for a day. And then you fly back to England.'

He nodded thoughtfully. 'So two days here altogether?'

'Yup.'

'And what is there to do for two days in Alice Springs?'

'Quite a lot, in fact,' I said encouragingly, and pulled out a brochure I had taken from a rack in the motel. I flipped through it. 'There's the Alice Springs Desert Park, for one thing.'

He inclined his head a fraction. 'What's that?'

'It's a nature reserve where they've carefully recreated a desert environment.'

'In the desert?'

'Yes.'

'They've recreated a desert in the desert? Have I got that right?'

'Yes.'

'And you pay money for this?'

'Yes.'

He nodded contemplatively. 'What else?'

I turned the page. 'The Mecca Date Garden.'

'Which is?'

'A garden where they grow dates.'

'And they charge money for this as well?'

'I believe so.'

'Is that it or is there more?'

'Oh, much more.' I went through the list of other attractions – the old telegraph station, Frontier Camel Farm, Old Timers' Folk Museum, National Pioneer Women's Hall of Fame, Road Transport Hall of Fame, Minerals House, Chateau Hornsby Winery, Sounds of Starlight Theatre, Strehlow Aboriginal Research Centre.

Allan listened intently, sometimes requesting a soupçon of elaboration, and considered all this for some moments. Then he said: 'Let's go to Ayers Rock.'

I thought for a moment. 'Yeah, all right,' I said.

And so in the morning we rose early and set off for mighty Uluru. Alice Springs could wait.

Uluru and Alice Springs are so inextricably linked in the popular imagination that nearly everyone thinks of them as cosily proximate. In fact, it is almost 300 miles across a largely featureless tract to get from the one to the other. Uluru's glory is that it stands alone in a boundless emptiness, but it does mean that you have to really want to see it; it's not something you're going to pass on the way to the beach. That is as it should be, of course, but it is equally a fact that when you have just completed a thousand-mile passage through barren void, you don't really require another five hours of it to confirm your impression that much of central Australia is empty.

Well into the 1950s Ayers Rock was inaccessible to all but the most dedicated sightseers. As late as the late 1960s, the number of annual visitors was no more than 10,000. Today Uluru gets that many every ten days on average. It even has its own airport, and the resort that has sprung up to serve it, called Yulara, is the third largest community in the Territory when full. Yulara stands a discreet and respectful dozen or so miles from the rock itself, so we stopped there first to get rooms. It consists essentially of a lazy loop road along which are tucked a range of accommodations, from campgrounds and a youth hostel up to the most sumptuously de luxe of resort hotels.

With nothing better to do, we had passed much of the five-hour drive working out a programme for ourselves for our stay. Essentially this had established that we would spend the afternoon studying the rock in a calm and reflective manner, then divide whatever remained of the day between a cooling dip in the hotel pool, drinks on a terrace while watching the setting sun gorge the rock with the red glow for which it is famed, a little stroll through the desert to stretch our legs and look for dingoes, wallabies and kangaroos, and finally a dinner of refinement and quality beneath a sky of twinkling stars. We had, after all, just driven 1,300 miles in two and a half days. If ever anyone was entitled to a little desert R&R it was us. So there was a certain real excitement as we turned off the highway and entered the cosseted confines of Yulara.

We went first to the Outback Pioneer Hotel, which sounded moderately priced if dangerously likely to have chandeliers made of waggon wheels and an all-you-can-eat buffet for people in baseball caps. In fact, it proved on approach to be rather grand and clearly very nice, but unexpectedly busy. Stacks of luggage were being unloaded from two tour buses out front and there were people everywhere, nearly all white-haired and pear-shaped, standing around squinting or fiddling with cameras and video recorders. Allan dropped me out front and I trotted inside to enquire about rates. I was amazed at the amount of hubbub in the lobby. It was early afternoon on a weekday out of season and the place was a circus. The check-in area brought to mind a mustering station on a foundering cruise ship. I asked a guy at the concierge desk what was going on.

'Nothing in particular,' he said, joining me in considering the unattractive chaos. 'It's always like this.'

'Really?' I said. 'Even out of season?'

'There is no out of season here now.'

'Are there any rooms here, do you know?'

'Afraid not. The only place with rooms left is the Desert Gardens.'

I thanked him and hied back to the car.

'Problem?' said Allan as I climbed in.

'Very poor dessert selection,' I said, not wishing to alarm him. 'Let's try the Desert Gardens Hotel. It's much nicer.'

The Desert Gardens was vastly more swank than the Pioneer Outback, and mercifully less crowded. Only one person, a man of about seventy, stood between me and the check-in clerk. I arrived just in time to hear the clerk say to him: 'It's three hundred and fifty-three dollars a night.'

I swallowed hard at this.

'We'll take it,' said the man in an American accent. 'How big is it?'

'I beg your pardon?'

'How big is the room?'

The clerk looked taken aback. 'Well, I'm not sure of its dimensions exactly. It's a fair size.'

'What's that mean? "Fair size".'

'It's amply proportioned, sir. Would you like to see the room?'

'No, I want to sign in,' the man said shortly, as if the clerk were needlessly delaying him. 'We want to get to the rock.'

'Very good, sir.'

As he signed in he asked a million subsidiary questions. Where was the rock exactly? How long did it take to get there? Was there a cocktail lounge in this hotel? Where was that exactly? What time was dinner served? Could you see the rock from the dining room? Was it worth seeing the rock from the dining room? Where was the pool? Through which doors? *Which* doors? And what about the elevator – where was that? *Where?*

I looked at my watch unhappily. It was getting on for two o'clock, and we didn't even have rooms yet. Time was speeding away.

'So is it good, this rock?' the man was saying in what might have been an attempt at levity.

'I beg your pardon, sir?'

'The rock. Is it worth coming all this way?'

'Well, as rocks go, sir, I think you could say it's first class.'

'Yeah, well, it'd better be,' the man said darkly.

Then his wife joined him and to my dismay *she* began asking questions. Was there a hairdresser's? How late was it open? Where could they mail postcards? Did the gift shop accept travellers' cheques? These were US dollar travellers' cheques; was that OK?

And how much are postage stamps for America? Is there an iron and ironing board in the room? Where'd you say the gift shop is? And what about my brain? Have you seen that anywhere? It's about the size of a very small walnut and never been used.

Eventually they shuffled off and the clerk turned to me. With a regretful air, he informed me that the gentleman ahead of me had taken the last room. 'There might be dormitory space at the youth hostel,' he said, and allowed this deeply unappealing proposition to sit there for a moment. 'Shall I check?'

'Yes, please,' I murmured.

He consulted his computer and looked suitably doleful. 'No, I'm afraid even that's full now. I'm sorry.'

I thanked him and went out. Allan was leaning against the car with a hopeful face, which fell when he saw mine. I explained to him the situation. He looked crushed.

'So no swim?' he said.

I nodded.

'No wine on the terrace? No sunset over the rock? No elegant room with downy pillows? No complimentary fluffy dressing gown and tinkling mini-bar?'

'The dressing gowns never fit anyway, Allan.'

'Not quite the point.' He fixed me with a frank gaze. 'And instead of these things we will be . . . ?'

'Driving back to Alice Springs.'

He removed his focus to the wider world while he allowed this thought to settle. 'Well,' he said at last, 'I suppose we'd better go and see if this bloody rock is worth a 600-mile round trip.'

It was.

The thing about Ayers Rock is that by the time you finally get there you are already a little sick of it. Even when you are a thousand miles from it, you can't go a day in Australia without seeing it four or five or six times – on postcards, on travel agents' posters, on the cover of souvenir picture books – and as you get nearer the rock the frequency of exposure increases. So you are aware, as you drive to the park entrance and pay the ambitiously pitched admission fee of $15 a head and follow the approach road around, that you have driven 1,300 miles to look at a large, inert, loaf-shaped object that you have seen photographically portrayed a thousand times already. In consequence, your mood as you approach this famous monolith is restrained, unexpectant – pessimistic even.

And then you see it, and you are instantly transfixed.

There, in the middle of a memorable and imposing emptiness, stands an eminence of exceptional nobility and grandeur, 1,150 feet high, a mile and a half long, five and a half miles around, less red than photographs have led you to expect but in every other way more arresting than you could ever have supposed. I have discussed this since with many other people, nearly all of whom agreed that they approached Uluru with a kind of fatigue, and were left agog in a way they could not adequately explain. It's not that Uluru is bigger than you had supposed or more perfectly formed or in any way different from the impression you had created in your mind, but the very opposite. It is exactly what you expected it to be. You *know* this rock. You know it in a way that has nothing to do with calendars and the covers of souvenir books. Your knowledge of this rock is grounded in something much more elemental.

In some odd way that you don't understand and can't begin to articulate you feel an acquaintance with it – a familiarity on an unfamiliar level. Somewhere in the deep sediment of your being some long-dormant fragment of primordial memory, some little severed tail of DNA, has twitched or stirred. It is a motion much too faint to be understood or interpreted, but somehow you feel certain that this large, brooding, hypnotic presence has an importance to you at the species level – perhaps even at a sort of tadpole level – and that in some way your visit here is more than happenstance.

I'm not saying that any of this is so. I'm just saying that this is how you feel. The other thought that strikes you – that struck me anyway – is that Uluru is not merely a very splendid and mighty monolith, but also an extremely distinctive one. More than this, it is very possibly the most immediately recognizable natural object on earth. I'm suggesting nothing here, but I will say that if you were an intergalactic traveller who had broken down in our solar system, the obvious directions to rescuers would be: 'Go to the third planet and fly around till you see the big red rock. You can't miss it.' If ever on earth they dig up a 150,000-year-old rocket ship from the Galaxy Zog, this is where it will be. I'm not saying I expect it to happen; not saying that at all. I'm just observing that if I were looking for an ancient starship this is where I would start digging.

Allan, I noted, seemed similarly affected. 'It's weird, isn't it?' he said.

'What is?'

'I don't know. Just seeing it. I mean, it just feels weird.'

I nodded. It does feel weird. Quite apart from that initial shock of indefinable recognition, there is also the fact that Uluru is, no matter how you approach it, totally arresting. You cannot stop looking at it; you don't want to stop looking at it. As you draw closer, it becomes even more interesting. It is more pitted than you had imagined, less regular in shape. There are more curves and divots and wavelike ribs, more irregularities of every type, than are evident from even a couple of hundred yards away. You realize that you could spend quite a lot of time – possibly a worryingly large amount of time; possibly a sell-your-house-and-move-here-to-live-in-a-tent amount of time – just looking at the rock, gazing at it from many angles, never tiring of it. You can see yourself in a silvery ponytail, barefoot and in something jangly and loose-fitting, hanging out with much younger visitors and telling them: 'And the amazing thing is that every day it's different, you know what I'm saying? It's never the same rock twice. That's right, my friend – you put your finger on it there. It's awesome. It's an awesome thing. Say, do you by any chance have any dope or some spare change?'

We stopped at several places to get out and have a look, including the spot where you can climb up it. It takes several hours and much exertion, which comfortably eliminated it from our consideration, and in any case the route was closed for the afternoon. So many people have collapsed and died on the rock that they close it to climbers when the weather is really warm, as it was this day. Even when it's not too hot, lots of people get in trouble from fooling around or taking wrong turns. Just the day before a Canadian had had to be rescued after getting himself onto some ledge from which he could not get either up or down. Since 1985, ownership of the rock has been back in the hands of the local Aboriginal people, the Pitjantjatjara and Yankunyjatjara, and they deeply dislike visitors (whom they call 'minga', or ants) clambering all over it. Personally I don't blame them. It is a sacred site to them. I think it should be for everyone, frankly.

We stopped at the visitors' centre for a cup of coffee and to look at the displays, which were all to do with interpretations of the Dreamtime – the Aborigines' traditional conception of how the earth was formed and operates. There was nothing instructive in a historical or geological sense, which was disappointing because I was curious to know what Uluru is doing there. How do you get the biggest rock in existence onto the middle of an empty plain? It turns out (I looked in a book later) that Uluru is what is known to geology as a bornhardt: a hunk of weather-resistant rock left standing when all else around it has worn away. Bornhardts are not that uncommon – the Devils Marbles are a collection of miniature bornhardts – but nowhere else on earth has one lump of rock been left in such dramatic and solitary splendour or assumed such a pleasing smooth symmetry. It is a hundred million years old. Go there, man.

Afterwards we had one last drive around the rock before heading back to the lonely highway. We had been at the site for barely two hours, obviously not nearly enough, but I realized as I turned around in my seat to watch it shrinking into the background behind us that there never could be enough, and I felt moderately comforted by that thought.

Anyway, I'll be back. I have no doubt of that. And next time I'm bringing a really good metal detector.

CHAPTER SEVENTEEN

SO WE DROVE ALL THE WAY BACK TO ALICE SPRINGS. TO COMPENSATE for our setback at Uluru, we decided to stay at one of Alice's fancy outlying resort hotels and hang the expense. Imagine then our surprise and gratification when we pulled into the oasis-like splendour of the Red Centre Resort and discovered that it was $20 a night less than we had paid for much less at the town-centre Best Western the night before. This alone, we agreed at once, was almost worth a 600-mile drive.

The Red Centre was really just a very large motel with a bit of landscaping, but it was friendly and welcoming and at its heart was a pool with a terrace and an adjoining bar and restaurant. Needless to say, this is where we were to be found thirty seconds after arrival. There we were told by the kindly staff that we were too late for dinner, but that they could probably rustle us up a couple of steak sandwiches or something. We told them we would be grateful for whatever they could give us, particularly if it was accompanied with drink, then took a table by the pool's edge, where we sat watching the tranquil shimmer of the water and savouring the delightfully warm and wholesome desert air, under a sky spread with stars.

Suddenly life seemed pretty good. Our driving was behind us now. We had seen Uluru – too briefly, perhaps, but sufficient to appreciate its wonders. And here at the Red Centre we appeared to have landed on our feet.

Allan announced his intention to spend his final day in Australia sitting in a lounger beside the pool, reading inferior fiction and working on his tan.

'How very shallow of you,' I said.

He accepted the criticism with imperturbable equanimity.

'So you're not coming to see the desert park?' I said.

'Nope. Nor the telegraph station, nor the sand dune hall of fame, nor the fig farm . . .'

'It's a date garden.'

A pause to stand corrected. 'Nor anywhere else. I'm going to sit right here beside this pool and pass my day in a vain and idle manner. And you?'

'I'm going to see the sights, of course.'

'Well, then I will meet you afterwards and you can tell me all about it, no doubt in excruciatingly boring detail.'

'You can count on it.'

And so the following morning I emerged from my room in a clean summer shirt, clutching a notebook with a pen tucked into the spiral, and went off in a dutiful frame of mind to see what Alice had to offer. I called first at the telegraph station, on a patch of sunny high ground a mile or so outside town. In its early days Alice Springs was a repeater station, one of twelve between Darwin and Adelaide, which were needed to boost signals on their way across the country. What a forlorn and tedious existence that must have been, stuck in the middle of a suffocating nowhere, endlessly tapping out second-hand messages involving people you would never see or know, living in places you could only dream about. Outside the station was the reedy pool of water from which Alice Springs takes its name. The Alice in question was the wife of the director of telegraphs in Adelaide, and originally it was only the station that was called Alice Springs. The town that slowly rose in the valley below was called Stuart, after the explorer. For some reason people found this confusing, and in 1933 the whole became known as Alice Springs. So the most famous town in the outback is named for a woman who had no connection with it and, as far as I know, never saw it.

This done, I made a tick beside 'Telegraph Station' on my list of things to do, then drove on to the Alice Springs Desert Park. My expectations frankly were not high, but in fact it was splendid. It's run by the Parks and Wildlife Commission of the Northern Territory. What they have done is recreate over a large area three primary desert habitats – one that is very dry, one that gets a little moisture, and one that is normally dry but occasionally is swept by flash floods. This alone provided a worthwhile lesson – it makes you realize that deserts in their quiet, arid way are as varied as other environments – but I was also grateful to find various shrubs and other plants labelled and explained. It was a pleasure to be able to say: 'Ah, so *that*'s kangaroo paw. Well, I never. And let's see if this spinifex really does hurt as much as Ernest Giles said. Why, yes, it does!'

Scattered at intervals were large walk-in enclosures containing birds and other small desert animals – bandicoots and bush-tailed possums and so on – with labels detailing their habits. Best of all was a large nocturnal house where all manner of night creatures endlessly prowled and hopped and sniffed the air in a succession of night-time dioramas. The display area was so faintly illuminated that it was actually possible to walk into walls and glass panels, but as my eyes slowly adjusted I was able to pick out an amazingly diverse and rewarding range of small marsupials – potoroos and bettongs and bilbies and numbats and quolls and much more.

Because Australia is so vast and arid and difficult a landscape to study, and because the modest population base produces comparatively few scientists for the amount of ground to be covered, and because, above all, the animals within it are often small, furtive, nocturnal and sometimes mysterious, even now nobody really knows quite what is out there. Any list of Australian wildlife is arrestingly punctuated with qualified comments like 'possibly extinct' or 'thought to be endangered' or 'may survive in some remote areas'. The difficulties are well illustrated, I think, by the uncertain fate of the oolacunta, or desert rat kangaroo. Nearly everything that is known about this interesting creature is owed to two men. The first was a nineteenth-century naturalist named John Gould, who studied and described the animal in 1843. It had, according to Gould, the shape and manner of a kangaroo but was only about the size of a rabbit. What particularly distinguished it was that it could move at very high speeds for unusually long distances. Since that one initial report, however, the oolacunta had not been seen. Enter Hedley Herbert Finlayson.

Finlayson was a chemist by profession, but devoted much of his life to searching for rare native animals. In 1931 he led an expedition that travelled on horseback deep into the interior, to the perpetual furnace that is Sturt's Stony Desert. Upon arriving, Finlayson was surprised to discover that the little desert rat kangaroo, far from being on the verge of extinction or possibly gone altogether, was both visible and clearly thriving. The animal's speed and endurance were just as Gould had reported. Once when Finlayson and his colleagues gave chase on horseback a desert rat kangaroo ran twelve miles without pause through the searing heat of day, exhausting three horses in the process. Ounce for ounce, the little oolacunta may well have been the greatest runner (or bouncer, actually) the animal kingdom has ever produced. Returning to society, Finlayson reported his exciting find and naturalists and zoologists everywhere dutifully amended their texts to account for the desert rat kangaroo's rediscovery. Over the next three years Finlayson made further expeditions, but in 1935 when he returned once more he was nonplussed, as you may imagine, to discover that the little desert rat kangaroo had quietly vanished – as utterly as it had after Gould's single sighting in 1843. It hasn't been seen since.

The chronicles of Australian fauna are amazingly full of stories such as this – of animals that are there one moment and gone the next. A more recent casualty of the phenomenon was a frog called *Rheobatrachus silus*, which was around for such a short time that it didn't even manage to attract an informal name. What was extraordinary about *R. silus* (and it almost goes without saying that there would be something) was that it gave birth to live young through its mouth – something never before seen in nature inside Australia or out. It was discovered by biologists in 1973 and by 1981 it had disappeared. It is listed as 'probably extinct'.

My favourite animal disappearance story, however, harks back to a somewhat earlier age. It concerns a nineteenth-century naturalist named Gerard Krefft, who in 1857 caught two very rare pig-footed bandicoots. Unfortunately for science and for the bandicoots, Krefft soon afterwards grew hungry and ate them. They were, as far as anyone can tell, the last of the species. Certainly none has been seen since. Krefft, incidentally, was later appointed head of the Australian Museum in Sydney, but was invited to seek alternative employment when it was discovered that he was supplementing his salary by selling pornographic postcards. I am sure there must be a moral in there somewhere.

From the Desert Park, I went to the Strehlow Aboriginal Research Centre. This was a quietly boring display concerning a man born on the Hermannsburg Mission, an Aboriginal reserve outside Alice, who devoted his life to studying Aborigines. He collected a huge stock of spiritual artefacts, but because they are sacred and not allowed to be seen by the uninitiated, they cannot be put on display.

What you get instead are lots of old photographs of life at Hermannsburg and more detail on the life and work of Theodore Strehlow than a reasonable person could wish.

However, as I was walking back to the car, I noticed a small aviation museum in an old hangar next door. Curiously, no one was in attendance, but the door was open so I stepped inside and had a look around. The museum had a fairly predictable assortment of old engines and walls of yellowing photographs, but in a separate building there was something I had no idea still existed and certainly never expected to see. No guidebook I have ever seen draws attention to it; even the local tourism literature contained no hint that it is there. But for a few fretful days in 1929 it was the most famous and sought-after object in Australia – and here it was in a small aviation museum in Alice Springs, of all places. I refer to the remains of a light aircraft known as the Kookaburra, which went down in the desert while searching for a lost pilot named Charles Kingsford Smith.

Kingsford Smith was not only the greatest Australian aviator of his age, but possibly the greatest aviator ever. He held more records than anyone else and tackled infinitely more daring challenges. Just a year after Charles Lindbergh made his historic solo flight across the Atlantic, Kingsford Smith became the first to cross the Pacific – a far more ambitious enterprise, not simply because the scale was greater but because flying conditions were much, much tougher and far less well understood. At the time of his Pacific attempt, only ten months had passed since the first aeroplane had successfully flown to Hawaii in a race sponsored by a Hawaiian pineapple magnate – and that event had claimed the lives of ten airmen. So when, in 1928, Kingsford Smith set off with a crew of three from San Francisco aiming to reach Brisbane by way of Honolulu and Suva in Fiji, the undertaking was widely held to be impossible and insane, and so it nearly proved. Six hundred miles out from Hawaii, Kingsford Smith flew into a belt of meteorological liveliness known as the intertropical convergence zone – an expanse of boiling clouds, towering storms and the sort of winds that could blow a moustache off. As his small craft began to bounce about like some kind of elasticated toy, Kingsford Smith had no idea what to expect, or when it might end, because no pilot had ever flown into such a system before.

This was, bear in mind, in a frail, spruce-framed, cloth-covered 1920s Fokker so elemental in design that the seats weren't even bolted down. For hours Kingsford Smith fought to hold the plane steady and in one piece. When at last it popped into clear air, he and his men were perilously low on fuel and faced with the problem of finding Fiji – a dot in an all but infinite ocean – before their engine ran dry and they fell into the sea. This and a hundred other alarming obstacles Kingsford Smith tackled with courage, skill, resolution and wit. Crossing the Pacific was possibly the most daring organized feat of aviation ever.

Kingsford Smith always flew with a co-pilot, and generally with a navigator and radioman as well, so it is unfair to compare his achievements with the solitary heroics of Charles Lindbergh. Nonetheless it is fair to observe that Lindbergh never flew through anything as ferocious as Kingsford Smith's Pacific storm. Indeed, after 1927 Lindbergh scarcely made another notable flight. Kingsford Smith, on the other hand, flew on and on, establishing records all over. He became the first to fly the Atlantic from east to west (again much tougher because it was against the jet stream), first to fly from Australia to New Zealand and back again, and first to cross the Pacific in the other direction. He also held a fistful of records for fastest flights between Australia and England, and for various legs along the way.

Which brings us to the Kookaburra. In March 1929, with a crew of three, Kingsford Smith set off to fly from Sydney to England. Over northwest Australia, along the Kimberley coast, they hit bad weather, grew hopelessly lost (not altogether surprisingly: for guidance they had only a couple of admiralty charts and a map of Australia torn from a standard *Times Atlas*) and made a forced landing on a coastal mudflat, with almost no fuel left and hopelessly short of supplies. Almost all they had was a flask of coffee and some brandy, which could be combined to make a drink called a coffee royal. Thus what followed became known, somewhat darkly, as the Coffee Royal Affair.

Luckily for Kingsford Smith, he and his men were in an area with plentiful fresh water and some adequate if unappealing sources of food (mud snails mostly). However, because the plane's radio was broken, they had no way of telling the outside world where they were. When news of the disappearance reached Sydney, two of Kingsford Smith's associates, Keith Anderson and Bob Hitchcock, decided to mount a rescue. In the little Kookaburra they took off from Mascot Airport in Sydney, flew by stages to Alice Springs, and finally set off from there on what was supposed to be the final leg early on the morning of 12 April 1929. Soon afterwards, while crossing the parched emptiness of the Tanami Desert – the area that Allan and I had skirted in the car on our drive from Daly Waters to Alice Springs – the engine began to sputter and backfire and they were forced to make an emergency landing in the desert. In their haste to depart they had packed no food and only three litres of water. Unlike Kingsford Smith, they landed in a place that offered no succour.

They were dead by the third day. That is how unimaginably murderous the outback is. I don't wish to seem obsessive about this, but they drank their own urine, too. Nearly everybody does who gets stuck in the outback. (It's actually counterproductive because the salts in urine accelerate thirst.)

At almost the moment when Anderson and Hitchcock were wretchedly expiring, Kingsford Smith and his cronies were rescued by someone else. They returned to civilization looking so fit and rested that some people began to suspect (and some newspapers to speculate) that it had all been a publicity stunt. The whole thing grew rather ugly. Kingsford Smith was subjected to the humiliation of a public inquiry into his character (he was ultimately exonerated). Meanwhile, the nation waited breathlessly for news that Anderson and Hitchcock had been found alive. Alas, they were not. In late April, a search plane spotted the downed Kookaburra with their bodies nearby, and a few days later a rescue party recovered the remains and brought them back to civilization. Hitchcock's family opted for a quiet funeral in Perth, but Anderson was given a state funeral of the most grave and magnificent pomp in Sydney. For days beforehand people in their thousands stood in line for hours to view the coffin. On the day of the funeral, thousands more lined the streets to watch the cortège or gathered at the burial site. It was the biggest funeral in Sydney to that time, possibly the biggest ever.

Today, it almost goes without saying, Anderson and Hitchcock are completely forgotten, inside Australia as well as out. So, too, for a long time was the Kookaburra. It sat in the desert, rusting and unnoted, for half a century before it was finally collected and taken to Darwin for restoration. About ten years ago, it was placed in a special small building at the aviation museum at Alice Springs, where it appears to attract no attention whatever.

Kingsford Smith returned to flying, setting yet more records. In 1935, while flying home from England, his plane crashed into the sea off Burma, taking him with it. Today, he is fitfully remembered in Australia (Sydney's airport is named after him) and not at all elsewhere. In 1998, the American writer Scott Berg produced a 600-page doorstop biography of Charles Lindbergh, which naturally ranged over the whole story of aviation's early days. Of Charles Kingsford Smith it contained not a mention.

Allan and I dined that evening on the patio of the Red Centre, where I told him in great detail about my many exciting discoveries of the day. As we sat enjoying the warm evening and lazily finding our way to the bottom of our second bottle of very nice Western Australia Cabernet Sauvignon, as if on cue a wallaby hopped up to the perimeter fence on the far side of the swimming pool, regarded us for a moment with a general air of unconcern, and began nibbling the shrubs that were planted there. It was the first time since my crossing of the country on the Indian Pacific many weeks earlier that I had seen a distinctive Australian animal in the wild. It was the first time Allan ever had, and he was thrilled.

Whether for this reason or some other, he announced that he thought Australia a very fine place.

'Do you?' I said, pleased, but just a little surprised for he had seen little of it but desert.

He leaned towards me very slightly and said, as if sharing a confidence: 'It's very roomy.'

I looked at him. 'Yes, it is.'

'It's a very roomy country.'

On reflection, I think it may have been our third bottle.

In the morning I drove him to Alice's small but handsome airport, where we had a cup of coffee and sat quietly, for we were both a trifle hung over. I saw him to his gate, where we exchanged the usual rushed and fatuous expressions of thanks and goodwill, and he disappeared down the walkway. I watched him go, then turned and walked back to the car. I had a day to kill before flying on to Western Australia, and I wasn't at all certain how I was going to fill it. I headed into town for the business district to find a bank machine and buy a newspaper, but en route I passed a sign for the School of the Air, down a side street, and impetuously I decided to have a look.

I didn't expect a great deal, but it was terrific. What a lot of nice surprises Alice Springs was throwing up. The School of the Air was in an anonymous building on a residential street. It consisted of a reception area where the children's work was displayed on tables and around the walls, two small studios, a large meeting room and that was about it. Although there are seventeen schools of the air in Australia now, Alice Springs is the grandmother of them all and still covers the largest and emptiest area. It was a Saturday, so no lessons were in progress, but a very nice man was happy to show me around and tell me how it worked.

The idea was simple enough: to provide formal schooling and some sense of classroom experience for kids growing up on cattle stations or other lonely spots – something it has been dutifully doing since 1951. Lonely is certainly the key word here. With a catchment area of 468,000 square miles – that is an area roughly twice the size of France – the Alice Springs school has just 140 pupils spread between kindergarten and the early teens. I retain a strangely vivid and influential memory of watching a film about it at school when I was eight or nine, and of being extremely taken with the notion of being hundreds of miles from your teacher, entrusted with your own microphone and shortwave radio set, and free to sit there buck naked with a plate of cookies if you chose since no one could see you. All of these seemed incalculable improvements on the situation that prevailed at Greenwood Elementary in Des Moines, Iowa. So the romance of radio learning has never quite left me. I was disappointed, therefore, to discover that the radio portion has only ever been a tiny and incidental part of the programme. The School of the Air is and always has been essentially a correspondence course, which doesn't sound anything like as appealing.

Even so, the place had a very real charm and air of goodwill. The noticeboards were filled with illustrated essays from kids of about eleven describing life on their stations and what a typical day was like for them. I read every one with absorption.

'Would you like to listen to a lesson?' the man in charge asked me.

'Very much,' I said.

He took me into a side room and put on a tape recording of a day's lesson for five-year-olds. It consisted mostly of a perky teacher going through the roll-call, saying: 'Good morning, Kylie. Can you hear me? Over.'

After a moment there would be a faint crackle, as of a transmission from a very distant galaxy, and sounds almost recognizable as human speech but much too indistinct to be deciphered.

'I say good morning, Kylie. Are you there? Can you hear me? Over.'

This time there would be a pause and no response at all, just a rather poignant interval of dead air. Then: 'Well, let's try Gavin then. Good morning, Gavin. Are you there? Over.'

More crackle and then a small, tinny voice would come back: 'Good morning, Miss Smith!'

And so it went, with some voices coming in loud and clear, but many others fading in or out or proving totally unreachable. As I listened to this, I also read a little booklet I had bought where I was frankly taken aback to discover that each child spends only half an hour a day (actually, 'up to half an hour a day') on the radio, plus ten minutes a week in a private tutorial with their teachers – hardly a lavish amount of personal attention. For the rest, they are expected to spend five to six hours a day working under the supervision of a parent or nanny. The students also make use of televisions, VCRs and personal computers, but I didn't see any sign of them. The conclusion to which you are reluctantly but inescapably drawn is that it is forever 1951 at the School of the Air.

The real surprise, however, was that there seemed to be no Aboriginal children involved – certainly none were evident in the photographs. The population of the Northern Territory is about 20 per cent Aboriginal overall, but in the far outback the proportion is much higher. I asked the man about that on my way out.

'Oh, there are some,' he said. 'I'm not sure how many just at the moment, but there are a few. The problem is that the pupils have to be supervised by a competent adult, you see.'

I waited a moment, then said: 'I'm sorry, I don't see.'

'They need a reliable, conscientious adult with core language and reading skills.'

'And Aboriginal parents don't have that?'

He looked unhappy, as if this was a route we really shouldn't be travelling down. 'No, I'm afraid not. Not always.'

'But if you're not giving the kids the lessons because the parents can't help them, then those kids, when they become parents, won't have the core skills either, will they?'

'Yes, it's a problem.'

'And so it will just go on for ever?'

'It's a very big problem.'

'I see,' I said, though of course I didn't really see at all.

Afterwards, I continued into town. I bought a newspaper and took it to an open-air café on Todd Street, a pedestrian mall. I read for a minute or two, but then found myself just watching the passing scene. It was quite busy with Saturday shoppers. The people on the street were overwhelmingly white Australians but there were Aborigines about, too – not great numbers of them, but always there, on the edge of frame, unobtrusive, nearly always silent, peripheral. The white people never looked at the Aborigines, and the Aborigines never looked at the white people. The two races seemed to inhabit separate but parallel universes. I felt as if I was the only person who could see both groups at once. It was very strange.

A very high proportion of the Aborigines looked beaten up. Many had puffy faces, as if they had wandered into a hornet's nest, and an almost absurdly high number sported bandages on shins, elbows, foreheads or knees. A label at the Strehlow exhibition which I had seen the day before had been at pains to stress that the most ruined Aborigines were those one saw in towns. The idea, I guess, was to inform visitors like me that one shouldn't judge all Aborigines by these mild wrecks seen shuffling through the streets. Nonetheless, it struck me as an odd and paternalistic thing to say, in that it seemed to imply that Aborigines had two choices in their lives: to stay on the missions and prosper, or come into town and fall into penury and dereliction.

It made me think of a line I had seen penned by a famous outback character named Daisy Bates, who came to Australia from Ireland in 1884 and for years lived among and studied the indigenous peoples of Western Australia. In *The Passing of the Aborigines*, published in 1938, she wrote: 'The Australian native can withstand all the reverses of nature, fiendish droughts and sweeping floods, horrors of thirst and enforced starvation – but he cannot withstand civilization.' In 1938 that may have qualified as sympathetic and enlightened comment, but it was disheartening to see it presented in modified form at an Aboriginal research centre in 1999.

You don't have to be a genius to work out that Aborigines are Australia's greatest social failing. For virtually every indicator of prosperity and well-being – hospitalization rates, suicide rates, childhood mortality, imprisonment, employment, you name it – the figures for Aborigines range from twice as bad to up to twenty times worse than for the general population. According to John Pilger, Australia is the only developed nation that ranks high for incidence of trachoma – a viral disease that often leads to blindness – and it is almost exclusively an Aboriginal malady. Overall, the life expectancy of the average indigenous Australian is twenty years – *twenty years* – less than that of the average white Australian.

In Cairns, quite by chance, I had been told about a lawyer named Jim Brooks who has worked for years for and with Aborigines, and I had managed to meet him for a cup of coffee in town just before Allan and I had flown on to Darwin. A calm, easygoing, immediately likeable man with just a hint of the earnestness that must have led him to devote his working life to fighting for the disaffiliated rather than piling up money in private practice, he runs the Native Title Rights Office in Cairns, which helps native peoples with land issues, and was one of the members of a human rights commission set up in the mid-1990s to investigate an unfortunate experiment in social engineering popularly known as the Stolen Generations.

This was an attempt by government to lift Aboriginal children out of poverty and disadvantage by physically distancing them from their families and communities. No one knows the actual numbers, but between 1910 and 1970 between one-tenth and one-third of Aboriginal children were taken from their parents and sent to foster homes or state training centres. The idea – thought quite advanced at the time – was to prepare them for a more rewarding life in the white world. What was most amazing about this was the legal mechanism that enabled it to be done. Until the 1960s, in most Australian states Aboriginal parents did not have legal custody of their own children. The state did. The state could take children from their homes at any time, on any basis it deemed appropriate, without apology or explanation.

'They did everything they could to eliminate contact between the parents and children,' Jim Brooks told me when we met. 'We found one woman whose five children were sent to five different states. She had no way of keeping in touch with them, no way of knowing where they were, whether they were sick or well or happy or anything. Have you got kids?'

'Four,' I said.

'Well, imagine if a government van turned up at your house one day and some inspector came to the door and told you they were taking your children. I mean seriously imagine how you would feel if you had to stand by and watch your children taken from your arms and put into a van. Imagine watching the van driving off down the road, with your kids crying for you, looking at you out the back window, and knowing that you will probably never see them again.'

'Stop,' I said with an uneasy stab at jocularity.

He smiled sympathetically at my discomfort. 'And there is not a thing you can do about it. Nobody you can turn to. No court that will take your side. And this went on for decades.'

'Why did they do it in such a heartless way?'

'They didn't see it as heartless. They thought they were doing a good thing.' He passed me a précis of the rights commission's report, which he had brought for me, and showed me a quotation from early in the twentieth century by a travelling inspector named James Isdell, who wrote of the dispossessed parents: 'No matter how frantic [their] momentary grief might be at the time, they soon forget their offspring.'

'They sincerely believed that indigenous peoples were somehow immune to normal human emotions,' Brooks said. He shrugged at the hopelessness of such thinking. 'Very often the children were told that their parents were dead; sometimes that the parents no longer wanted them. That was their way of helping them cope. Well, you can imagine the consequences. There was a lot of grief-related alcoholism, stratospheric levels of suicide, all that kind of stuff.'

'What became of the kids?'

'Well, the kids, meanwhile, were kept in care until they were sixteen or seventeen, and then turned out into the community. They had a choice of staying in the cities and trying to cope with the inevitable prejudices, or returning to their traditional communities and resuming a way of life that they could barely remember with people they no longer really knew. The conditions for dysfunction and dislocation were bred into the system. You don't get rid of that overnight. You know, some people will tell you that the removal of children only affected a small proportion of indigenous families. That is both wrong – there was scarcely a family in the land that wasn't affected at some profound and immediate level – but even more tragically to miss the point. Taking children away destroyed a whole continuity of relationships. Just because you stop that practice doesn't mean that all that damage is going to be magically undone and everything will be fine.'

'So what can you do for them?' I asked.

'Help to give them a voice,' he said. 'That's all I can do.' He shrugged, a little helplessly, and smiled.

I asked him if there was still much prejudice in Australia and he nodded. 'Huge amounts,' he said. 'Really quite huge amounts, I'm afraid.'

Over the past twenty years, successive governments have done quite a lot – or quite a lot compared with what was done before. They have restored large tracts of land to Aboriginal communities. They have returned Uluru to Aboriginal stewardship. They have spent more money on schools and clinics. They have introduced the usual initiatives for encouraging community projects and helping small businesses get started. None of this has made any difference at all to the statistics. Some have actually got worse. At the end of the twentieth century, an Aboriginal Australian was still eighteen times more likely to die from an infectious disease than a white Australian, and seventeen times more likely to be hospitalized as a result of violence. An Aboriginal baby remained two to four times more likely to die at birth depending on cause.

Above all, what is perhaps oddest to the outsider is that Aborigines just aren't *there*. You don't see them performing on television; you don't find them assisting you in shops. Only two Aborigines have ever served in Parliament; none has held a Cabinet post. Indigenous peoples constitute only about 1.5 per cent of the Australian population and they live disproportionately in rural areas, so you wouldn't expect to see them in vast numbers anyway, but you would expect to see them *some*times – working in a bank, delivering mail, writing parking tickets, fixing a telephone line, participating in some productive capacity in the normal workaday world. I never have; not once. Clearly some connection is not being made.

As I sat now on the Todd Street Mall with my coffee and watched the mixed crowds – happy white shoppers with Saturday smiles and a spring in their step, shadowy Aborigines with their curious bandages and slow, swaying, knocked-about gait – I realized that I didn't have the faintest idea what the solution to all this was, what was required to spread the fruits of general Australian prosperity to those who seemed so signally unable to find their way to it. If I were contracted by the Commonwealth of Australia to advise on Aboriginal issues all I could write would be: 'Do more. Try harder. Start now.'

So without an original or helpful thought in my head, I just sat for some minutes and watched these poor disconnected people shuffle past. Then I did what most white Australians do. I read my newspaper and drank my coffee and didn't see them any more.

CHAPTER EIGHTEEN

CONSIDER THE PLATYPUS. IN A LAND OF IMPROBABLE CREATURES, IT stands supreme. It exists in a kind of anatomical netherworld halfway between mammal and reptile. Fifty million years of isolation gave Australian animals the leisure to evolve in unlikely directions, or sometimes scarcely to evolve at all. The platypus managed somehow to do both.

When word reached England in 1799 that there existed in Australia a toothless, venomous, fur-covered, egg-laying, semi-aquatic animal with a duck-like bill, the tail of a beaver, feet that were both webbed and clawed, and a strange orifice called a cloaca, which served both reproductive and excretory purposes (a feature, as one taxonomist delicately noted, that was 'highly curious but not well adapted for popular details'), it was received, not altogether surprisingly, as a hoax. Even after a careful examination of a shipped specimen, the British Museum's anatomist, George Shaw, found it 'impossible not to entertain some doubts as to the genuine nature of the animal, and to surmise that there might have been practised some arts of deception in its structure'. According to the natural historian Harriet Ritvo, the original specimen still bears the scissor scars where Shaw snipped and fiddled to determine whether a hoax had been perpetrated.

For most of the next century, scientists argued – and argued heatedly, for it was an age obsessively devoted to exactitude – over how to classify the animal before putting it and its cousin the echidna (a creature similar to a hedgehog) in a family of their own: the monotremes. (The name means 'one hole', in reference to the distinguishing cloaca.) Unresolved, however, was the question of whether the monotremes were to be regarded as primarily mammal or reptile. It was evident from their peculiar anatomy that monotremes laid eggs, a reptilian trait, but it was equally evident that they suckled their young, a mammalian characteristic. A further vexation was that for almost a century nobody could find a monotreme egg. So we may envision the murmur and buzz that swept the auditorium when, in 1884, at a meeting of the British Association, the delegates were read a cable just arrived from a young British naturalist in Australia named W. H. Caldwell.

Caldwell's message in full read: 'Monotremes oviparous, ovum meroblastic.'

Well, the murmurs were prodigious, the buzz electric. What Caldwell was announcing with such elegant pith was that he had found platypus eggs and they were unquestionably reptilian in nature. In the end, Caldwell's find didn't make a lasting difference. The monotremes ended up in the mammalian camp, though for a while it was a close-run thing.

I mention all this to give a little context to the very real excitement I felt the following day when, freshly arrived in Perth, I happened upon a monotreme of my own: an echidna crossing a path in a lonely corner of Kings Park. I was already, I have to say, in pretty high spirits. Perth is a lovely city and one of my favourites in Australia. I have perhaps an inflated fondness for it because on my first visit there, in 1993, I arrived by way of Johannesburg, where I had just been robbed in a fairly hair-raising manner, in broad daylight in the city centre, by a party of cheerfully menacing youths with twitchy knives, and it was such a relief to find myself in a city where I could wander without fear that I might be bundled into an alley, liberated of my possessions and liberally incised with sharp instruments.

Even without arriving fresh from an incident of criminal excitement, Perth is a cheery and welcoming place. There is first of all the delight in finding it there at all, for Perth is far and away the most remote big city on earth, closer to Singapore than to Sydney, though not actually close to either. Behind you stretches 1,700 miles of inert red emptiness all the way to Adelaide; before you nothing but a featureless blue sea for 5,000 miles to Africa. Why 1.3 million members of a free society would choose to live in such a lonely outpost is a question always worth considering, but climate explains a lot. Perth has glorious weather, *good-natured* weather – the kind that sets the postman to whistling and puts a spring in the step of delivery people. Architecturally, Perth has no particular distinction – it is a large, clean, modern city: Minneapolis down under – but its sharp and radiant light makes it a beauty. You will never see bluer city skies or purer sunlight bouncing off skyscrapers than here.

But what especially sets Perth apart is the possession of one of the world's largest and finest parks, Kings Park. Spread across a thousand comely acres on a bluff above the broad basin of the Swan River, Kings is all those things a city park should be – playground, sanctuary, strolling area, botanical garden, vantage point, memorial – and so big that you can never feel as if you have seen it all. Most of it is arrayed in a conventional manner – undulant lawns, paths, flower beds – but a substantial corner, constituting perhaps a quarter of the whole, has been left as unimproved bush. It was while strolling down a sunny path through this little-visited zone that I saw a small furry hemisphere, rather like the brush portion of a floor polisher, emerge from the undergrowth on one side of the path and proceed with a stately lack of haste towards identical undergrowth on the other side.

Sensing me, it stopped. It had glossy black quills pointing straight back and had curled itself roughly into a ball so I couldn't see its pointy snout, but it was clearly an echidna. It could be nothing else. I couldn't have been more thrilled. It was a little pathetic, I grant you, when you consider that this was my most exciting moment of engaging a creature in the wild in Australia. In a country filled with exotic and striking life forms my high point was finding a harmless, animated pincushion in a city park. I didn't care. It was a monotreme – a physiological anomaly, a wonder of the reproductive world, an oddity from the loneliest branch on the mammalian tree. When the echidna sensed that I had retreated to a respectful distance, it unfurled and continued on its waddling way into the bush.

Thrilled to my cloaca, I followed the path around and back into the park proper, where I came after some time to a long, lovely avenue of tall white gum trees planted long ago to commemorate the fallen of the First World War. Each tree bore a small plaque giving bare details – unexpectedly moving when read one after another down a long walk – of an abbreviated life. 'In honour of Capt. Thomas H. Bone, 44th Batt.,' said one. 'Killed in action

Passchendaele 4th October 1917 aged 25. Dedicated by his wife and daughter.' It is a fact little noted outside Australia – and I think worth at least a mention here – that no other nation lost more men as a proportion of population in the First World War than Australia. Out of a national population of under five million, Australia suffered a staggering 210,000 casualties – 60,000 dead, 150,000 injured. The casualty rate for its soldiers was 65 per cent. As John Pilger has put it: 'No army was as decimated as that which came from farthest away. And all were volunteers.' Only a few days earlier, in one of the weekend papers I had read a review of a new history of the First World War by the British historian John Keegan. In passing, the reviewer had noted, with an all but palpable sigh, that Keegan's 500 pages of densely observed text had failed to include a single mention of the Australian forces.

Poor Australia, I thought. Other countries produce unknown soldiers. It produces unknown armies.*

Beyond this sombre avenue lay the much perkier and sunnier realm of the botanical gardens, and this I approached now with unusual devotion, for Australia's plants are exceptional and there is no place where you will find them more handsomely displayed. Australia really is the most amazingly fecund country. It is thought to contain something of the order of 25,000 species of plants (Britain, for purposes of comparison, has 1,600 species) but that's really only a guess. At least a third of what is out there has never been named or studied, and new stuff is turning up all the time, often in the most unlikely places. In 1989 in Sydney, for instance, scientists found an entirely new species of tree called *Allocasuarina portuensis*. People had been living around these trees for 200 years, but because they weren't very numerous – just ten have been found – no one had noticed them before. In much the same way, in 1994 in the Blue Mountains some botanist out for a walk happened on another of those unexpected relic species long presumed to be extinct. Called wollemi pines, these were not modest shrubs hidden among tall grasses but stout and imposing trees up to 130 feet tall and ten feet around. It's just that with such a lot of land to survey and only so many botanists to go round, it took a while for the two to intersect. Nobody can guess, of course, what else might

* Weeks later, in London, I checked the Keegan book, and it was full of references to the Australian army. The conclusion to draw from this, I guess, is that Australians so expect to be overlooked that they sometimes overlook not being overlooked, so to speak.

be out there awaiting discovery. This is what makes Australia such a fundamentally exciting place to engage in the natural sciences. In Britain or Germany or America, you might with great luck find a new strain of mountaintop lichen or some sprig of previously overlooked moss, but in Australia take a stroll through the bush and you can find half a dozen unnamed wildflowers, a grove of Jurassic angiosperms and probably a ten-kilo lump of gold. I know where I'd be working if I were in science.

The question that naturally occurs in all this is why Australia, which so often seems singularly hostile to life, has produced such an abundance of it. Paradoxically, half the answer lies in the very poverty of the soil. In the temperate world, most plants can prosper in most places – an oak tree can grow as productively in Oregon as it can in Pennsylvania – and so a relatively few generalist species tend to predominate. In poor soils, on the other hand, plants are driven to specialize. One species will learn to tolerate soils containing, say, high concentrations of nickel, an element that other plants find distasteful. Another will become tolerant of copper. Yet another might learn to tolerate nickel *and* copper, and perhaps prolonged drought as well. And so it goes. After a few million years, you end up with a landscape filled with a great variety of plants each favouring very specific conditions and each master of a patch of ground that few other plants could abide. Specialized plants lead to specialized insects, and so on up the food chain. The result is a country that seems on the face of it hostile to life but in fact is wonderfully diversified.

The second, more obvious factor in Australia's variety is isolation. Fifty million years as an island clearly sheltered indigenous life forms from a great deal of competition and allowed certain of them – eucalypts in the plant world, marsupials in the animal world – to prosper uncommonly. But no less important in terms of species diversity is the isolation that has long existed *within* Australia. In general terms, Australia comprises scattered pockets of life separated by great zones of harshness. And nowhere is all of this more true than in southwestern Australia. According to David Attenborough (in *The Private Life of Plants*), this one corner of Australia 'contains no less than twelve thousand different plant species and 87 per cent of them grow nowhere else in the world'.

Which makes it alarming to report that many of these singular plants are in trouble from a terrible and little-understood malady called 'dieback'. Dieback comes from a fungus family called

Phytophthora, which is related to the fungus that caused the potato blight in Ireland. It has been in Australia for a century and has affected plants all over the country, though the source wasn't identified by science until 1966. It is especially a worry in south-west Australia, partly because it thrives there as nowhere else and partly because the southwest has such a density of rare and vulnerable plants. I discovered now, from an informative signboard, that even banksias are under threat. The banksia (named for its discoverer, Joseph Banks) is perhaps the most adored flower in Australia. It's a bit of an oddity – the flowers look uncannily like toilet brushes – but Australians love it because it is striking and it is everywhere and it is theirs alone. So it was discouraging to read that seven species of banksia are on the endangered list and could well become extinct in the wild in the next few years. Twelve more species are under threat. Perhaps it's my natural pessimism, but it seems that an awfully large part of travel these days is to see things while you still can. The most disturbing thought of all, I suppose, is that with so much still unrecorded many plants could disappear before they are even found.

All of this was of some moment because I was about to go off on a small botanical quest of my own. First, however, I had a day at leisure in Perth. I had nothing very particular in mind, but a few minutes later as I sat on the shady terrace of the park's central café, decorating my face with a chocolatey froth of cappuccino and reading the *West Australian* newspaper, I came upon a news article that planted the possibility of an idea.

The article was to do with a man named Lang Hancock, about whom I had lately been reading. Hancock was a rancher in the remote north of Western Australia who had the exceptional good fortune to be at the heart of one of the greatest mineral booms in modern history. Anyone who doubts that Australia truly is a lucky country has only to review the story of the country's mineral discoveries in the 1950s and a little beyond. Up until that time, conventional wisdom held that Australia was deficient in almost all natural resources. Iron ore, for instance, was considered to be in such short supply that for two decades it was illegal to export it. Then in 1952 Lang Hancock made an important discovery. While piloting a light aircraft over the trackless emptiness of the Hamersley Range near the north coast he lost his bearings in a sudden storm and made a forced landing in a zone of flat rock known to geology as the Western Shield. Stepping from his aeroplane, he realized that he was standing on almost solid iron.

Looking into the matter further, he discovered that he owned a 100-kilometre-long block of nearly solid iron ore. From almost nothing in 1950, Australia's estimated reserves of iron ore rose to 20 billion tonnes in 1960. By the end of the 1960s, Hancock alone controlled iron ore reserves greater than those of the United States and Canada combined. That is a lot of iron ore.

But it was only the beginning. In dizzying succession mineral deposits were found all over the place – bauxite, nickel, manganese, uranium, copper, lead, diamonds, tin, zinc, zircon, rutile, ilmenite and many others that most of us have never heard of. Almost overnight, people with mining interests made fortunes that were embarrassing to contemplate and impossible to spend. The stock markets went crazy as investors scrambled to grab a piece of the action. In Sydney one broker lost an ear – an ear! – in the frenzied trading that accompanied the constant reports of new discoveries. It was a heady period, and it transformed Australia's fortunes. From a sleepy, good-natured producer of wool, it became a mining colossus, the world's biggest exporter of minerals. As many of the biggest finds were in Western Australia, much of the wealth settled in Perth, the state capital, which is what accounts for all its skyscrapers.

Lang Hancock, the man who started it all, was called to the great iron mountain in the sky in 1992 but in his dotage, it appears, he did that thing that brings dread to the hearts of rich children everywhere: he married his housekeeper, a lady from the Philippines named Rose. According to the morning paper, Hancock's daughter had filed a lawsuit alleging that the widow Rose and the late Mr Hancock had 'lavishly and improperly spent money that was not their own'. Helpfully the article provided a sidebar in which Mrs Hancock's principal assets were listed. These included a $35-million house in a Perth suburb called Mosman Park, complete with the address. It was apparently the grandest residence in the city; the chandeliers alone had cost $3 million. Looking at my map of the city, I realized that Mosman Park was at the far end of a clutch of famously well-heeled suburbs running all the way to Fremantle, and as it was a fine day and I was feeling perky, I decided to walk out.

Well, it's a long way from central Perth to Mosman Park and beyond, that's all I'm saying. I walked for hours, through the leafy sprawl of the University of Western Australia campus and around the sunny foreshore of the Swan River estuary, tracing the sweep of sunny bays and yacht-cluttered coves, and made my way at length into residential zones of startling, showy wealth – Nedlands, Dalkeith, Peppermint Grove – where palatial houses basked in the penetrating sunshine. These neighbourhoods went on for miles – just street after foot-wearying street of trophy homes, with big gates beside broad drives, patios adorned with Grecian urns on ornate plinths and garages for fleets of cars. It was a stunning demonstration of the proposition that money and taste don't always, or even often, go together. These were the houses of lottery winners, of retailers of the sort who appear in their own television commercials, of people for whom the words 'Peppermint Grove' in an address would not be an embarrassment. I would not suggest for a moment that Australia's nouveaux riches are more distant from refinement than the people of other lands, but the absence of a distinctive architectural vernacular in Australia does mean that people can take their styles from a wider range of sources – principally drive-in banks, casinos, upmarket nursing homes and ski lodges. To see it massed over a spread of miles as in the western suburbs of Perth is certainly an absorbing experience.

I had been walking for nearly three hours when I arrived at a landmark called Chidley Point and realized I had found Mosman Park. I delved in my bag for the newspaper to check the address, and discovered that I had evidently left it on the table at the café in Kings Park. Never mind. I had walked eight or nine miles by now and had seen enough extravagant real estate to last me a lifetime. I vaguely recalled the Hancock house as being on Wellington Street, so I found my way to this sedate thoroughfare and strolled along it. En route I saw perhaps eight houses that looked as if they might contain many million dollars' worth of bricks, mortar, garden ornaments and tinkling chandeliers, but nothing that announced itself unequivocally as the grandest pile in the metropolis. As I stood there, a young woman in shorts and a matching top – a professional dog walker, I supposed – came along behind a frisky dog not much smaller than a pony. She wasn't so much walking the dog as skiing behind it on the soles of her shoes. I stepped into the street to keep from being eaten, but asked as she passed if she knew the Hancock house and she pointed to a place about three doors up. I went and had a look. Considering the cost, I have to say I had expected rather more – a sort of San Simeon meets Liberace's dream mausoleum is what I believe I had in mind – but this was on a smallish lot and was neither particularly tacky nor outstandingly ornate. I studied it for a few minutes, struck by the somewhat tardy thought that although I had voluntarily invested a good deal of exertion to get here, I didn't actually care in the tiniest degree where Rose Hancock dwelled. This notion absorbed, I turned with a thoughtful countenance and continued on my long march to the sea.

Fremantle is an interesting and likeable place. In gold-rush days it was a port of cosmopolitan liveliness, but then it sank into a long period of decrepitude. In the 1970s, it underwent a gentrifying revival as people realized the commercial potential of its large stock of neglected Victorian buildings. So today it is a trendy hangout, a place of latte and gelato and little shops selling things of an arty nature. Everybody is fond of Freo, as they call it. So am I normally, though my enthusiasm was wilting swiftly this day. The afternoon was uncomfortably warm, with no sign of the ameliorating ocean breeze they call the Fremantle Doctor (because it makes you feel better, of course). I had already walked far enough to make my feet smoke when I realized that I still had a good four miles to go, nearly all of it along the busy, charmless, mercilessly shadeless Stirling Highway.

By the time I flopped into central Fremantle, it was late afternoon and I was comprehensively bushed. I went into a pub and downed a beer for medicinal purposes.

'You all right?' said the barmaid.

'Yeah,' I replied. 'Why?'

'Seen your face?'

I knew at once. 'Am I sunburned?' I asked bleakly.

She gave a frank, sympathetic but essentially deeply amused nod.

I peered past her into the mirror behind the bar. Looking back at me, mockingly attired in clothes to match my own, was a cartoon character called Mr Tomato Head. I allowed myself a small sigh. For the next four days, I would be a source of concern to every elderly Western Australian and of amusement to all else. Then for three days more, as my skin flaked and peeled and I took on the look of someone just escaped from a leprosarium, the mood would change to universal horror and revulsion. Waitresses would drop trays; gawkers would walk into lamp-posts; ambulance drivers would slow as they passed and look me over carefully. It would, as always, be a quiet ordeal. In another three or four hours I would be in tender pain. Meanwhile, I was already a small wreck. My feet and legs hurt so much that I wasn't sure they would ever be of service to me again. I was as dirty as a street urchin and rank enough to be buried. And all of this so that I could see a house I had no actual interest in seeing and then walk on to a place that I was now too tired to explore.

But I hardly minded at all. And do you know why? I had seen a monotreme. Life could throw nothing at me that would diminish the thrill of that. Sustained by this thought, I drained my beer, lowered myself gingerly from the bar stool and limped through the staring crowds to see if I could find a taxi to take me back to the city.

In the morning, I took custody of another rental car and set off on the penultimate of my Australian quests. I was on my way to the great jarrah and karri forests of the southwest peninsula. If that sounds a trifle dull, then bear with me please, for these are exceptional trees. They are to the Australian arboreal world what the giant worm of Gippsland is to invertebrates: large, under-appreciated, and mysteriously occurring in only one small area, the southwest corner of Western Australia below Perth. Karris are Australia's sequoias. They attain heights of over 250 feet, but it is their amazing girth – they can be up to fifty feet around and scarcely taper on their climb to their distant crowns – that gives them their majesty. Think of the mightiest, most graceful sycamore you have ever seen, then triple it in every dimension and you have pretty well got a karri.

The dominant species of the region, however, is the handsome and noble jarrah, slightly less massive than the karri, but still enormous and arresting. It is something of a miracle that jarrahs are left at all, for it is just about the unluckiest tree alive. The specialization that allowed it to flourish in the first place was also its tragic undoing, for jarrah has the poor luck to thrive in soils rich in bauxite, and bauxite is a very valuable mineral. In the 1950s mining companies discovered the connection and came almost simultaneously to the exhilarating realization that they could knock down and sell the jarrah for quite a lot of money, then dig out all that gorgeously commercial bauxite underneath, thus getting two lots of income from one plot of land. Life doesn't get much better than that – so long, of course, as your conscience can bear the thought of removing large stands of prime forest of a type that occurs nowhere else and replacing them with large, unsightly gashes. Mining engineers – these people are so ingenious –

got around this problem by having no consciences at all. Brilliant!

In this they were long aided by their colleagues in the forestry industry. Australian foresters, it must be said, do rather like to chop down a tree. You can't entirely blame them – it is after all how they make their livelihood – and unquestionably they are less reckless than in former times, but they were allowed to get away with so much for so long that they still need the most attentive watching. These are people, you must understand, who could describe clear-cutting as 'the full sunlight method of regeneration' and not blush. Just to ease you into a sense of perspective here, Australia is the least wooded continent (Antarctica excluded, of course) and yet it is also the world's largest exporter of woodchips. Now I am no authority, and for all I know this is all managed with the most exacting care (that is certainly the impression the Australian Department of Conservation and Land Management strives to create), but it does seem to me that there is a certain mathematical discrepancy between having very few trees on the one hand and the world's liveliest chip-exporting industry on the other. Anyway, there is much less jarrah forest than there once was, and even a good deal less of the rare and clearly irreplaceable karri forests. According to William J. Lines, between 1976 and 1993 Australia lost a quarter of its karri forests to woodchipping. To woodchipping! I repeat: these people need watching.

Even without its singular forests, the southwest corner of Australia would be an area of interest. Stretching for about 180 miles from Cape Naturaliste on the Indian Ocean to Cape Knob on the Southern Ocean, it is another of those unexpected intrusions of comparative lushness that occur in Australia from time to time. It's rather like the Barossa Valley of South Australia, but so obscure and unassuming that it doesn't even have a name. Nearly everywhere you go in Australia you are provided with a handy label to fix your bearings – Sunshine Coast, Northern Tropics, Mornington Peninsula, Atherton Tablelands – but the zippiest appellation I saw for this region was 'the Southern corner of Western Australia'. I think they need to work on that a little. However, of the land itself and the seas beyond, no improvements are necessary.

Perhaps it was because my Australian adventure was nearly at an end and I was feeling consequently affectionate, or maybe because I had spent so much of the previous couple of weeks at large in arid landscapes, or perhaps simply because I knew almost nothing of the area (hardly anyone outside Western Australia does) and thus had no expectations to disappoint, but I was charmed at once. It was as if it had been assembled from the most pleasant, least showy parts of Europe and North America: lowland Scotland, the Meuse Valley of Belgium, Michigan's upper peninsula, Wisconsin's dairyland, Shropshire or Herefordshire in England – nice parts of the world but nothing you would normally travel vast distances to savour. This wasn't a world-class landscape, but it was an engagingly snug and wholesome one. I dubbed it – and offer it here for free pending the invention of something better – the Pleasant Peninsula. ('Where everything is . . . *rather nice*!')

So I spent an agreeable day – a pleasant day – motoring through woods and rolling fields, past orderly orchards and bottle-green vineyards, on winding country roads forever running down to a blue and sunny sea. It was a blessed little realm. I stopped often in the country towns – Donnybrook, Bridgetown, Busselton, Margaret River – to sit with a cup of coffee or browse through stacks of second-hand books or take a walk along a wooden pier or duney foreshore.

I stayed the night in Manjimup, on the edge of the southern woodlands, and in the morning rose early and refreshed, and set off without delay in the direction of Shannon and Mount Frankland national parks. Within minutes I was in cool, green forests of erect and stately grandeur. This was very promising indeed. I was headed for a place called the Valley of the Giants, to a recently developed tourist attraction that I had been told not to miss. It's called the Tree Top Walk, and as the name suggests it is an elevated walkway that wanders through the canopy of a grove of tingle trees – yet another of the rare outsized species of eucalypts unique to the region. I had assumed it was essentially a gimmick, but in fact I discovered that tingle trees, for all their immensity, are quite delicate and reliant on the few nutrients to be found in the soil at their bases, and that the constant trampling of visitors' feet was interfering with the breakdown of organic matter, imperilling their well-being. The Tree Top Walk thus not only provided visitors with a novel diversion and an unusual perspective, but also kept them conveniently out of harm's way.

The Tree Top Walk stands a mile or two into coastal forest near the small town of Walpole. I arrived at opening time, but already the car park was crowded and filling fast. A lot of people were gathered by the entrance and milling around in the little shop.

The whole thing is run by the Department of Conservation and Land Management and, like the Desert Park at Alice Springs, it was an impressive example of a government department doing something innovative and doing it extremely well. We could do with these people back in the Known World.

Well, all I can say is that the Tree Top Walk deserves to be world famous. It consists of a series of cantilevered metal ramps, like industrial catwalks, wandering at exhilarating heights through the uppermost levels of some of the world's most beautiful and imposing trees. The Tree Top Walk is an impressive erection. It runs for almost 2,000 feet and at its highest point stands 120 feet above the ground – a goodly height, believe me, when you are peering over the edge of a waist-high railing. Since the walkway surface is an open grid that lets you look straight down – indeed, more or less compels you to – there is a certain element of rakishness and daring in proceeding along it. I loved it. There are larger trees than the tingle (even the ashes of eastern Australia grow a little higher) and doubtless there are more beautiful trees than the tingle, but I cannot believe that there are any trees in the world that are both. Redwoods may reach giddier heights, but their canopy is nothing – like a broom handle with nails hammered into it. Tingles, because they are broad-leafed, spread out with luxuriant profusion. Makes all the difference. You simply won't find a better tree.

I went around twice, charmed and appreciative. It wasn't until I was halfway around the second time that I realized that actually it was quite crowded and that, like everyone else, I was sharing the experience with those around me, pointing out things to strangers and in turn allowing them to point things out to me. I am seldom drawn to strange children but I found myself now talking to two young boys – bright young brothers, about ten and twelve, on holiday from Melbourne with their parents – trying to decide between us whether there were koalas in Western Australia and whether we might therefore spy any up here in the treetops. Then their father joined us and we discussed it with him. Then the mother came along and took one look at me. 'You know, you're awfully sunburnt,' she said with concern, and offered me some cream from her bag. I declined, but was touched nonetheless.

It was oddly heart-warming to realize that we were all having this experience together, sharing our observations and pharmaceutical products. It reminded me very much of my stroll through the parks of Adelaide on Australia Day when hundreds of people seemed to be – effectively were – picnicking together. This had that same spirit of shared undertaking. In the most interesting and elemental anthropological sense, this was a social occasion.

Even then, it didn't quite register with me how important a component this is in Australian life until I descended to ground level and strolled through an area called the Ancient Empire. This consisted of a protective boardwalk path that made a large and inviting loop through another part of the same woods. It was in its way nearly as diverting as the Tree Top Walk – to stand at the foot of a circle of tingle trees, head craned to take in their impossibly remote heights, is an experience almost as dizzying as wandering on foot through the leafy canopy – but because the boardwalk wasn't novel and lofty, no one came here. I had it entirely to myself, but rather than feeling pleased to have found solitude, as I normally would, I felt suddenly quite lonely. 'Hey, everybody!' I wanted to call. 'Come down and see this! It's great. Come down and be with me! Somebody! Please!!'

But of course I said no such thing. Instead I had a long and respectful look around. It struck me in a moment's idle thinking that this forest was quite an apt metaphor for Australia. It was to the arboreal world what Charles Kingsford Smith was to aviation or the Aborigines were to prehistory – unaccountably overlooked. It seemed amazing to me, in any case, that there could exist in this one confined area some of the rarest and mightiest broad-leafed trees on earth, forming a forest of consummate and singular beauty, and hardly anyone outside Australia has even heard of them. But that is the thing about Australia, of course – that it is packed with unappreciated wonders.

And with that thought in mind, I set off now for what was, in its quiet way, one of the most amazing wonders of all.

CHAPTER NINETEEN

EARLIER ON THIS TRIP, WHILE DRIVING BACK TO SYDNEY FROM SURFERS Paradise, I stopped for coffee in a pleasant college town called Armidale in northeastern New South Wales. Indulging myself in a brief amble through its attractive streets, I happened on an official-looking building called the Mineral Resources Administration and – I don't know why exactly – I went in. I had long wondered why there is such an abundance of mineral wealth in Australia and not, say, in my back garden, and I went in thinking maybe somebody could tell me. One of the delights of poking about journalistically in a cheerful and open society like Australia's is that you can just turn up in places like the Mineral Resources Administration with nothing very particular in mind, and people will invite you in and answer any questions you care to put to them.

The upshot is that I spent a half-hour with an obliging geologist named Harvey Henley who told me that in fact Australia is not really fantastically overendowed with mineral resources – at least not on the basis of mineral wealth per square metre. It's just that Australia has a lot of square metres, relatively few people and a short history, so that much of the country is still unexplored and unexamined. To put matters in perspective for me, he took me through to his work area to show me what he does for a living. He makes geological maps, large, impressively detailed ones, rolled like blueprints, which he spread across a table with a certain respectful care, as if they were old prints. Even an untrained eye could see that they recorded every lump and ruffle on the landscape, with particular emphasis on pools of mineralogical splendour. Each, he explained, covered a portion of New South Wales sixty kilometres long by forty wide and took ten to fifteen man-years to produce. The Armidale team was in the process of surveying eighty such blocks.

'Big job,' I said, impressed.

'You bet. But we're finding new stuff all the time.' He drew back one map to expose the one beneath. 'That', he said, tapping a portion of the map shaded in a restful pastel tone, 'is a new mine at a place called Cadice Hill near Orange. It contains about 200 million tonnes of mineral-bearing sands.'

'And that's good, is it?'

'That's very good.'

'So,' I said thoughtfully, trying to get a grasp on all this, 'if it takes ten to fifteen man-years to produce one map covering a block of land sixty kilometres by forty, and if there are eight million square kilometres in Australia, then how much of the country has been properly surveyed?'

He looked at me as if I had asked a very basic question. 'Oh, hardly any.'

I found this quite an arresting thought. 'Really?' I said.

'Sure.'

'So,' I went on, still thoughtful, 'if you parachuted me into some random spot in the outback, into the Strzelecki Desert or something, I would be landing on a patch of land that had never been surveyed?'

'Formally surveyed? Almost certainly.'

I gave a moment to taking this aboard. 'So just how much mineral wealth might be left out there to be discovered?'

He looked at me with the happy beam of a man whose work will never be completed. 'No one knows,' he said. 'Impossible to say.'

Now hold that thought just for a moment while I take you with me onto the lonely coastal highway from Perth north towards Darwin, 4,163 kilometres away. Here, near the coast, there are a very few towns and quite a lot of visible farming, but head inland over the low, pale green hills to the right and with amazing swiftness you will find yourself in a murderous and confusing emptiness. And nobody really knows what is out there. I find that a terribly exciting thought. Even now people still sometimes make the sort of stupefying, effortless finds that can only happen in uncharted country. Just recently, some beaming fellow had come in from the western deserts cradling a solid gold nugget weighing sixty pounds. It was nearly the largest such nugget ever found, and it was just lying in the desert. Goodness!

Mining experts may study satellite images and the sort of charts generated by repeated aeroplane passes at low altitudes ('fantasy maps' as Harvey Henley termed them for me, just a touch dismissively), but up-close investigations, the kind that involve wandering through dried riverbeds and taking rocks away for later analysis, have barely begun. The problem lies not just in the vastness of Australia – though that is daunting enough, goodness knows – but in the risks involved in wandering into unknown country. As the British palaeontologist Richard Fortey has written: 'Tracks appear briefly, only to disappear into ambiguous washes, where the bewildered and anxious passenger is instructed to hang out the window to look for broken twigs which might indicate where a vehicle has passed before . . . It is appallingly easy to get lost.'

In such an environment rumours of fabulous, unexploited finds naturally proliferate. The most famous story concerns a man named Harold Bell Lasseter, who in the 1920s claimed to have stumbled on a gold reef some ten miles long in the central deserts thirty years before, but for various reasons beyond his control had neglected to return to claim it. Although it seems an unlikely tale, the story evidently had greater plausibility than a bare description would suggest. In any case, Lasseter managed to persuade several sceptical businessmen and even some large corporations (General Motors, for one) to underwrite an expedition, which set off from Alice Springs in 1930. After several weeks of confused and fruitless tramping around, Lasseter's backers began to lose confidence. One by one his team members abandoned him, until Lasseter was on his own. One night his two camels bolted. Lost and on foot, he died a lonely and wretched death. I dare say he drank some urine. In any case, he never found the gold. People are searching for it yet.

Although Lasseter was almost certainly either sorely deluded or a charlatan, the idea of there being a vast reef of gold just sitting in the desert is not at all beyond the bounds of reasonable possibility. Nor is it as implausible as it seems that people might make such a fabulous find and then, as it were, mislay it. Others far more meticulous and attentive than Lasseter have misplaced important discoveries in the desert. Such was the case of Stan Awramik, a geologist who was poking about in the low, irregular, exceedingly hot hills of the Pilbara, a region of northwestern Australia still largely unexplored, when he came upon an outcrop of rocks bearing tiny fossilized organisms called stromatolites dating back to the dawn of life some 3.5 billion years ago. At the time of Awramik's discovery they were the most ancient fossils yet found on earth. From a scientific point of view, these rocks were the equivalent of Lasseter's elusive gold reef. Awramik collected some samples and made his way back to civilization. But when he returned to the Pilbara to pursue his searches, he couldn't find the rock outcrop again. It had just vanished into an endless sameness of low hills. Somewhere out there those original stromatolites still wait to be rediscovered. It could as easily have been gold.

Since that time other stromatolite beds of similar or greater venerability have been found elsewhere, both in Australia and further afield. Meanwhile, however, in the warm, shallow waters of Shark Bay, on a lonely stretch of the Western Australian coast, scientists found something no less extraordinary, and even more unexpected. They found a community of *living* stromatolites – colonies of lichen-like formations that quietly but perfectly replicate the conditions that existed on earth when life was in its infancy. It was this that I was on my way to see.

It's about an eight-hour drive from Perth north to Shark Bay. In early afternoon, near a place called Dongara, the road curved down towards the sea and I began at last to get glimpses of blue ocean. This section of Western Australia is called the Batavia Coast, which, as it happens, was something else I was interested to look into. At Geraldton, the only town worthy of the name (certainly the only place with more than one set of traffic lights) for 600 miles, I stopped for coffee and parked by chance outside a small maritime museum in the town centre. I hesitated by the door, torn between the need to keep moving and a curiosity to see what was in there, then impulsively stepped in, and how glad I was I did, for the museum was devoted in large part to the little-known story of the ship that gave the coast its name – a forgotten merchant vessel called the *Batavia*, which blundered onto Australian shores in 1629 and in so doing set in motion one of the more bizarre and unlikely episodes in the annals of maritime affairs. Most Australian histories give it no more than a footnote (Manning Clark does not mention it at all), which is a little surprising because it was the first sojourn by Europeans on Australian soil, and it remains the greatest slaughter of white people in Australian history. But I get ahead of myself.

In 1629, when our story begins, Dutch mariners had only recently discovered that the swiftest way to the East Indies from Europe was not to make a beeline across the Indian Ocean after rounding Africa's Cape of Good Hope, but to drop down to the fortieth parallel – the famous Roaring Forties – and let those lively winds convey you eastward. The approach worked well so long, of course, as you managed not to crash into Australia. Alas, this was the fate that befell Captain Francisco Pelsaert, two hours before dawn in early June 1629, when the *Batavia* ran aground on some sandy impediments called the Abrolhos Islands off Australia's west coast. Almost at once the ship began to break up.

Many of the 360 people aboard drowned in the confusion, but 200 or so managed to struggle ashore. As the sun came up, they found themselves on a desolate sandbar with a few salvaged provisions and exceedingly dim prospects. They were 1,500 miles from Batavia (now Jakarta). Pelsaert ruminated for a while, then announced that he would take a party of men in a longboat and try to row to Batavia – a faint hope but their only one.

He left in charge a man named Jeronimus Cornelisz. What happened next is not entirely certain, but it appears that Cornelisz was both a madman and a religious fanatic – always a dangerous combination. What is certain is that over the next few days he and a few faithful followers slaughtered the bulk of the survivors – 125 men, women and children in all. The few they spared became their slaves – the women to cook and provide sexual favours, the men to fish and toil – except for a small group who escaped to another sandbar a couple of hundred yards away across a difficult channel. There they made such weapons as they could fashion from shells and driftwood, and built a fort to stave off the attacks that Cornelisz and his men occasionally flung at them.

Pelsaert, unaware of the turmoil he had left behind and with quite a lot on his mind already – he had, after all, wrecked a brand new ship, the pride of the Dutch merchant fleet – rowed on to the Timor Sea and miraculously reached Batavia. There his dumbfounded superiors listened to his tale, gave him another ship and ordered him to return at once for survivors.

Five months after all his troubles started, Pelsaert arrived back at the Abrolhos Islands. There, the ever-blundering captain, finding the survivors engaged in a civil war, came within a whisker of supporting the wrong side and losing his ship to the crazed Cornelisz and his desperate band. Eventually, however, he managed to sort out what had happened and to introduce order and justice to the murderous little sandbar. Cornelisz and six henchmen were swiftly hanged. Most of the others were whipped or keelhauled and clapped in chains to be taken back to Batavia for further corrective treatment. But for reasons unknown, Pelsaert decided to go to the considerable trouble of having two of the miscreants – a marine named Wouter Looes and a cabin boy named Jan Pelgrom – rowed to the mainland and marooned there.

On 16 November 1629, they were set down at a place called Red Bluff Beach. What became of the two Dutchmen after that no one knows, but two things are certain. They were the remotest Europeans in the world and the first white Australians.

Red Bluff Beach, I learned from the helpful museum staff, is at a place called Kalbarri, a couple of hours further up the coast, and since it was on the way to Shark Bay I decided to stop there for the night. Kalbarri lies about forty miles down a side road off the North West Coastal Highway, across a green plain covered to every horizon in heathery scrub. It was getting on for evening when I arrived – too late to go looking for the Dutchmen's landing place – so I got a room in a motel near the beach and contented myself with a stroll around the town. Kalbarri was an appealing little place. It dates only from 1952, when some fishermen discovered that the waters offshore teemed with lobster. Until the mid-1970s, when the road in from the North West Coastal Highway was paved, it was essentially cut off from the outside world except by sea. Today fishing remains at the heart of community life, but it has also grown into a small resort. The two seem to coexist very well.

The setting could hardly be bettered. It stands on a big bay, sheltered by long white sandbars. I walked to the front through warm end-of-day sunshine. The Abrolhos Islands were sixty kilometres out to sea – well out of sight of the mainland – but I could clearly see, only a couple of miles down the coast, the headland called Red Bluff, where the two mutineers were marooned.

As I strolled along the front, two things caught my notice – that a few hundred yards out in the bay a boat, half sunk, was being towed very slowly into the harbour through a narrow channel between the sandbars, and that crowds of people were gathering to have a look. The biggest cluster of onlookers was on the jetty at what appeared to be the commercial side of the harbour about a mile away. Here on the resort side of the harbour there were lots of people, too – sitting on the bonnets of cars parked along the beach, gazing from the balconies of seafront homes and apartment houses, coming out of shops and pubs to stand and watch. About it all, there was a strange, almost eerie silence.

I asked a man sitting on a car bonnet what was going on. 'Oh, it's a fishing boat that got holed on a reef last night,' he explained. The accident had happened at two thirty in the morning, far out to sea, and for a time it looked as if the boat might be in serious peril. To add to the tension, the skipper had his seven-year-old son with him – evidently taken out with him as a treat. Three other local fishing boats had gone out to rescue them. I looked at my watch. They'd have been at it for sixteen hours by now. I remarked on this to my informant and he gave a small smile, as if in apology. 'It's been a long day for the town,' he said. 'We've been on a bit of a knife-edge. Still, it seems to have turned out all right.'

Kalbarri has a year-round population of 1,500, and I would guess that two-thirds of the town was there. As the boat came through the sandbars and its safety seemed assured at last, people from all sides of the harbour clapped warmly, as if welcoming home the winner of a regatta, and called encouragement. I thought that was wonderful – that a whole town would turn out to watch a stricken local fishing boat brought in. If I handed out fivers, I'm sure I couldn't find a thousand people to watch me limp into port after a night of peril. I decided I liked Kalbarri very much.

In the morning, I rose early and drove the couple of miles along the coast to Red Bluff Beach where I had been told I would find a cairn marking the spot where the two naughty Dutchmen had been left to their lonely fate. It was a dramatic spot – a very large rock platform bashed by waves, which threw spray everywhere. Leading off to one side was a long duney beach marked at intervals with signs saying: 'Caution – Dangerous Rips'. The ocean was a bright turquoise, and the long beach was being pounded by a fury of big waves.

I had a good hunt around the area but couldn't find the cairn anywhere, and there was no one out at this hour to ask except for a couple way down the beach exercising a bouncy dog. It hardly mattered. Whoever built the cairn had to have done so long after the fact and was almost certainly guessing. So I just enjoyed the sunshine and sea-freshened air, and realized with a touch of surprise that the idea of being stranded here wasn't entirely without appeal. It was a lovely spot. The sea was lavishly fruitful and the hills behind abounded in materials for building. Looes and Pelgrom – again for mysterious reasons – were quite generously endowed by Pelsaert. They were left with a small boat, some food and water, a few tools and some trinkets with which to trade with the natives, if any could be found. There were certainly far worse places in the world to see out your days – not least a fetid and malarial dungeon in Batavia, which was their alternative fate. Assuming cordial relations with the natives, you could make quite a nice life for yourself here.

I was quite taken with the notion – not least because it was so patently a real possibility here. The coastline of Western Australia north from Perth is astoundingly beautiful and almost entirely untouched by development. Beyond Kalbarri there is not a single town for some 200 miles to Carnarvon, and just one side road to the sea – the one I was heading for at Shark Bay. Beyond Carnarvon, it's much the same for another 1,800 miles to Darwin – just a coastline of undisturbed splendour dotted at distant intervals with small communities. Altogether, Western Australia has some 7,800 miles of coastline and only about three dozen coastal communities, even including those along the southwestern peninsula from which I had just come.

That is, of course, why it took so long to discover the stromatolites at Shark Bay. Though they are there on the edge of an accessible shell beach, for any fool to see, they weren't noticed by anyone until 1954, and not identified by science for another decade. But then with almost 23,000 miles of Australian coastline to investigate, it takes time to get to it all.

From Kalbarri it was forty miles back to the North West Coastal Highway – there is still just the one road in and out – and then another hundred or so miles on to Shark Bay. In two and a half hours I passed just three other cars and a solitary barrelling road train. At one point I saw a couple of mysterious dots in the road far ahead. It turned out to be two workmen, digging a hole in the middle of the highway and protected from either direction by a single orange plastic cone placed in the centre of the road about five feet from where they worked. This was, you understand, the main west coast highway. It was an arresting reminder of just how far from anywhere I was. This was about as far from the main population centres as you can get in Australia. By road from where

I was now, it was over 4,000 kilometres to Sydney and nearer 5,000 to Brisbane. Even Alice Springs, the nearest town to the east, was 4,000 highway kilometres away, because of the way the roads ran. At length, in the middle of a featureless nowhere, I came to the turnoff for Shark Bay. I followed a newly paved side road for a few miles to another, unpaved side road, which passed through a marshy landscape for another mile or so. It ended at an old telegraph repeater station at a place called Hamelin Pool – a complex of white wooden buildings, one of which now announced itself as a museum, another as a café and gift shop.

The car park had only two or three other cars in it, but as I stood reading an information board two coaches pulled up in convoy, wheezed to a pneumatic halt and almost at once began disembarking streams of passengers – all white-haired, camera-toting and blinking confusedly under the impossible glare of sun. They appeared to be from all over – America, Britain, Holland, Scandinavia. Having come this far, I didn't wish to share the experience with a hundred twittering strangers, and I set off for the beach in a brisk stroll along a chalky track. It was amazingly hot. A breeze was running in from the sea, but it seemed only to bring more heat. After about half a mile the track brought me to a sumptuously sunny bay, flat calm and of the deepest aquamarine. At some distance across the water a long sandbar ran in a lazy curve out to sea. This, I gathered, was the Fauré Sill – a thirty-mile-long dune barrier that nearly encloses the bay and gives it its special character, namely warm, shallow, very saline waters of the sort that once prevailed across the planet when stromatolites were king.

Nowhere in any direction was there a sign of human intrusion except directly ahead where a nifty wooden walkway zigzagged for 150 feet or so out into the bay over some low, dark, primeval-looking masses that didn't quite break the water's calm surface. I had found my living stromatolites. Eagerly I boarded the walkway and followed it out to the first cluster of shapes. The water was as transparent as glass and only three or four feet deep.

Stromatolites are not easy to describe. They are of so primitive a nature that they don't even adopt regular shapes in the way, say, crystals do. Stromatolites just, as it were, blob out. Nearer the shore they formed large, slightly undulant platforms – rather like very old asphalt. Further out they were arrayed as individual clumps that brought to mind very large cow-pats, or perhaps the dung of a particularly troubled elephant. Most books refer to them as club-shaped or cauliflower-shaped or even columnar. In fact, they are shapeless grey-black blobs, without character or lustre.

It has to be immediately conceded that a stromatolite formation is not a handsome or striking sight. I can almost guarantee that your reaction upon seeing a bed of living stromatolites for the first time will be to say 'Hmm' in the vague, ruminative, cautiously favourable tone you would use if you were given a canapé that tasted better than it looked but not so good that you wanted another right away, or possibly ever. It is a sound that says: 'Well, I'll be.'

So it's not the sight of stromatolites that makes them exciting. It's the *idea* of them – and in this respect they are peerless. Well, imagine it. You are looking at living rocks – quietly functioning replicas of the very first organic structures ever to appear on earth. You are experiencing the world as it was 3.5 billion years ago – more than three-quarters of the way back to the moment of terrestrial creation. Now if that is not an exciting thought, I don't know what is. As the aforementioned palaeontologist Richard Fortey has put it: 'This is truly time travelling, and if the world were attuned to its real wonders this sight would be as well-known as the pyramids of Giza.' Quite right.

Stromatolites are rather like corals in that all of their life is on the surface, and that most of what you are looking at is the dead mass of earlier generations. If you peer, you can sometimes see tiny bubbles of oxygen rising in streams from the formations. This is the stromatolite's only trick and it isn't much, but it is what made life as we know it possible. The bubbles are produced by primitive algae-like micro-organisms called cyanobacteria, which live on the surface of the rocks – about three billion of them to the square yard, to save you counting – each of them capturing a molecule of carbon dioxide and a tiny beat of energy from the sun and combining them to fuel its unimaginably modest ambitions to exist, to live. The by-product of this very simple process is the faintest puff of oxygen. But get enough stromatolites respiring away over a long enough period and you can change the world. For two billion years this is all the life there was on earth, but in that time the stromatolites raised the oxygen level in the atmosphere to 20 per cent – enough to allow the development of other, more complex life forms: me, for instance. My gratitude was real.

The chemical process involved in this makes the little cells very slightly sticky. Tiny motes of dust and other sediments cling to their surfaces and these slowly bind and accrete into the rocks I was looking at now. The stromatolites thrive here not so much because the conditions are particularly amenable to them as because they are discouraging to other creatures. The reason stromatolites don't exist elsewhere is that they would either be washed away by stronger tides or eaten. Here nothing else can survive the bitter salt waters, so there is nothing to graze the stromatolites away.

That stromatolites gave rise to life on earth, then became a food themselves and were eaten out of existence has a certain irony, of course. Something not entirely unlike that happened to me now, for as I stood studying the crystalline waters the elderly day trippers could be heard coming down the track, and a few minutes later the spryer among them began to arrive on the boardwalk. A woman in a Miami Dolphins eyeshade took a position beside me, stared at the water for some moments, waved away a couple of flies, then regarded her husband and in a voice that would have drowned the clang of a steelworks said: 'Are you telling me we just crossed a *continent* for *this*?'

I was feeling charitably disposed, so I turned to her with an understanding smile and with all the gentleness and tact I could muster I endeavoured to ease her into a position of appreciation for this marvel that lay at our feet. I saluted her perceptiveness in recognizing that stromatolites were not much to behold, but explained how their diligent, infinitesimal chemical twitchings, over a span of unimaginable duration, made the world the green and lovely place it is. I pointed out too that at only two other places on earth have such living formations been found – one elsewhere in Australia, the other off a remote coral cay in the Bahamas, both much smaller and practically inaccessible – so that this was the only place in the world where visitors could with relative ease examine these singular creations in their full understated glory. So in fact, I concluded – and here I offered my warmest, most ingratiating smile – this really *was* worth crossing a continent for.

She listened with what I can only call an air of startled submissiveness, never taking her gaze from my face. Then she touched a hand to my forearm and said: 'Did you know that you have the most terrible sunburn?'

I took a walk along the neighbouring shell beach until the flies made it impossible to persevere, then wandered back to the telegraph station. The museum was locked and in darkness, so I went to the café. The trippers, I gathered, had stopped for refreshments because the lady in charge was busy rounding up cups and plates. I wondered in passing how she managed out here to feed coachloads of people 140 miles from the nearest supermarket.

'Yes, love?' she said brightly as she passed.

'I was wondering if it's possible to see the museum.'

'Course it is. I'll get Mike to take you.'

Mike was Mike Cantrall, an equally cheery middle-aged fellow with a raffish earring and an easygoing manner, who emerged from the kitchen wiping his hands on a tea towel and looking pleased to be excused dishwashing duty. He took me to the museum and with some difficulty unlocked the door. The museum was small and airless and felt as if it hadn't been opened for months – he told me that not many visitors asked to see it – but entirely charming. One room was devoted mostly to stromatolites. It had a fish tank with a stromatolite quietly bubbling away in it – the only one in the world in captivity, apparently. On an old TV and VCR he showed me a four-minute video, which gave a concise rundown on what stromatolites were and how they were formed. Then he picked up a brick-sized fragment of old stromatolite and passed it to me and I made the appropriate expressions of surprise at how heavy it was.

The rest of the museum was given over to its days as a telecommunications outpost – first for telegraph and then for telephones. It was a great deal more appealing than I had expected it to be, not least because one of the walls was dominated by a large photograph of a linesman, Adgee Cross by name, standing at the top of a ladder buck naked, repairing a telegraph line and looking for all the world as if this were absolutely the correct attire for telegraph repairs in the outback. He was naked, Mike told me, because he had just swum the Murchison River with his ladder and didn't want to get his clothes wet. I didn't say anything, but the thought crossed my mind that wet clothes would dry out in minutes in the desert, whereas boots – the one thing he had kept on – would stay wet for hours. My suspicion is that Adgee Cross did his line repairs naked because he liked to. To which I say: why not?

I also learned the happy story of Mrs Lillian O'Donahue who was a telephone operator here in the days before automated telephone exchanges. At Carnarvon up the road was a big satellite dish that NASA used until the 1970s to track spacecraft as they passed over the Indian Ocean. During a mission in 1964 the communications link between the Carnarvon dish and a tracking station near Adelaide broke down, and all messages had to be routed through Mrs O'Donahue and her ancient equipment. Through one long, hot night Mrs O'Donahue sat at her switchboard, carefully recording strings of coded messages from one outpost and passing them on to the other. Each time the Gemini craft passed over southern skies the fate of the mission – I just love this – was in the devoted hands of an unassuming little old lady sitting in a small white building miles down a dusty track on the west Australian coast. She made $6 in overtime money, Mike told me. I loved that, too.

When we emerged and Mike had locked the door, we walked together across the car park. I asked him how he had come to be in this lonely place. He told me that he and his wife, Val – the cheery lady behind the counter – had been there just three weeks. They were novice grey nomads – retirees (often these days early retirees) who sell up, buy a motorhome of some description and spend their lives on the open road, stopping from time to time to earn a little money, but never tied to anywhere and essentially ever on the move. Six months earlier this would have seemed to me the dreariest punishment imaginable – endlessly driving across a landscape that is mostly hot and dry and empty. But now I understood completely. All that emptiness and dazzling light has a seductive quality that you might actually never tire of – an amazing thought. Besides, Australia is just so full of surprises. There is always something just down the road – a treetop walk, a beach harbouring ancient life forms, museums celebrating improbable Dutch shipwrecks or naked telegraph repairmen, really nice people like Mike and Val Cantrall, a fishing village turning out to see a stricken ship limp home. You never know what it's going to be but it is nearly always pretty good. Maybe it was just my mood at the time, but I felt I could keep this up for a good long while yet.

So I thanked Mike for showing me around and returned to my glinting vehicle. Even from a distance I could see it was going to be unbearably hot inside, so I opened the doors to air it a little and went with my book of maps to the shade of a bent tree beside the track to the beach. I don't know why I bothered exactly because the only way back to Perth was the way I had come, along the long and empty North West Coastal Highway. But as I stood there, I flipped idly through the other pages of Western Australia – it's so big it needs several – and my eye was caught by a patch of highlighted landscape very near the Northern Territory border. It was a range of hills called, with unimprovable melody, the Bungle Bungles. I had only lately read about these. The Bungle Bungles are an isolated sandstone massif where aeons of harsh, dry winds have carved the landscape into weird shapes – spindly pinnacles, acres of plump domes, wave walls. The whole extends to about a thousand square miles, yet, according to the book *Australia: A Continent Revealed*, these extraordinary formations 'were not generally known until the 1980s'. Think of it. One of the natural wonders of the world, covering an area the size of an English county, was unvisited and essentially unknown until less than twenty years ago.

I had a sudden powerful impulse to go there. When would I be this close again? Besides, it would be a chance to drive into the Pilbara and visit little Marble Bar, famous as the hottest town in Australia. I could see the landscape where Stan Awramik found and lost his fossilized stromatolites. From there it was but a hop along the Victoria Highway to Darwin. The wet season would be over soon, so I could go to Kakadu National Park – said to be a wonder, but a virtual lake when I had been in the area – and maybe even cross Queensland to visit Cooktown at last. Why, I could do this for ever.

But of course this was just a fantasy, born of perhaps a little too much sun, a natural longing not to have to retrace my steps along 450 miles of lonely highway back to Perth, and a genuine reluctance to bring this adventure to a close just yet. I made callipers of my fingers to measure the distance and was both appalled and hardly surprised at all to find that it was 1,600 miles to the turnoff for the Bungle Bungles – plus another hundred miles or so over rough back-country tracks on which I was neither insured nor safe. Here I was halfway up the west Australian coast, on the very edge of the world, and there was still 1,600 miles of emptiness to an attraction in the same state. What a preposterously outsized country this was.

But that is of course the thing about Australia – that there is such a lot to find in it, but such a lot of it to find it in. You could never see the half of it. Idly I wondered what my wife would say if I called home and announced: 'Honey, we're selling the house and buying an Australian motorhome. We're off to see the Bungle Bungles!' I didn't think it would fly, frankly, so I shut the car doors, climbed into the driver's seat and began the long journey back to Perth.

I drove in the gloomy frame of mind that overtakes me at the end of every big trip. In another day or two I would be back in New

Hampshire and all these experiences would march off as in a Disney film to the dusty attic of my brain and try to find space for themselves amid all the ridiculous accumulated clutter of half a century's disordered living. Before long, I would be thinking: 'Now what was the name of that place where I saw the Big Lobster?' Then: 'Didn't I go to Tasmania? Are you quite sure? Let me see the book.' Then finally: 'The Prime Minister of Australia? No, sorry. No idea.'

It seemed a particularly melancholy notion to me that life would go on in Australia and I would hear almost nothing of it. I would never know who ended up with the Hancock millions. I would never learn if anyone found out what became of that poor American couple stranded on the Great Barrier Reef. Chinese immigrants might wade ashore and ask for cabs, and I would never hear of it. Crocodiles would attack, bush fires would rage, ministers would depart in shame, amazing things would be found in the desert, and possibly lost again, and word of none of this would reach my ears. Life in Australia would go on and I would hear nothing, because once you leave Australia, Australia ceases to be. What a strange, sad thought that is.

I can understand it, of course. Australia is mostly empty and a long way away. Its population is small and its role in the world consequently peripheral. It doesn't have coups, recklessly overfish, arm disagreeable despots, grow coca in provocative quantities or throw its weight around in a brash and unseemly manner. It is stable and peaceful and good. It doesn't need watching, and so we don't. But I will tell you this: the loss is entirely ours.

You see, Australia is an interesting place. It truly is. And that really is all I'm saying.

BIBLIOGRAPHY

Attenborough, David, *The Private Life of Plants*. Princeton: Princeton University Press, 1995.
Bates, Daisy, *The Passing of the Aborigines*. New York: Pocket Books, 1973.
Berndt, R. M. and C. H., *The World of the First Australians*. Sydney: Lansdown Press, 1981.
Berra, Tim, *A Natural History of Australia*. Sydney: University of New South Wales Press, 1998.
Blainey, Geoffrey, *Triumph of the Nomads: A History of Ancient Australia*. Sydney: Pan Macmillan Australia, 1982.
——, *A Land Half Won*. Melbourne: Sun Books, 1983.
——, *A Shorter History of Australia*. Sydney: Random House Australia, 1997.
Bowden, Tim, *Penelope Goes West: On the Road from Sydney to Margaret River and Back*. Sydney: Allen & Unwin, 1999.
Boyd, Robin, *The Australian Ugliness*. Melbourne: Penguin Books, 1980.
Charles-Picard, Gilbert (ed.), *Larousse Encyclopaedia of Archaeology*. London: Hamlyn, 1972.
Clark, Manning (abridged by Michael Cathcart), *Manning Clark's History of Australia*. Ringwood, Victoria: Penguin Books, 1995.
Diamond, Jared, *Guns, Germs, and Steel: The Fates of Human Societies*. New York: W. W. Norton, 1997.
Edwards, Hugh, *Crocodile Attack in Australia*. Marleston, South Australia: J. B. Books, 1998.
Fagan, Brian M. (ed.), *The Oxford Companion to Archaeology*. New York: Oxford University Press, 1996.
Flannery, Tim, *The Future Eaters: An Ecological History of the Australasian Lands and People*. Sydney: Reed New Holland, 1997.
—— (ed.), *1788: Comprising a Narrative of the Expedition to Botany Bay and a Complete Account of the Settlement at Port Jackson by Watkin*

Tench. Melbourne: Text Publishing, 1996.
—— (ed.), *The Explorers*. Melbourne: Text Publishing, 1998.
Fortey, Richard, *Life: An Unauthorised Biography*. London: HarperCollins, 1997.
Gould, Stephen J., *Bully for Brontosaurus: Reflections in Natural History*. London: Hutchinson Radius, 1991.
Gunn, John, *The Defeat of Distance: Qantas 1919–1939*. St Lucia, Queensland: University of Queensland Press, 1985.
Gunther, John, and William H. Forbis, *Inside Australia*. New York: Harper and Row, 1972.
Hall, Timothy. *Flying High: The Story of Hudson Fysh. Qantas and the Trail-Blazing Days of Early Aviation*. Melbourne: Methuen of Australia, 1979.
Hermes, Neil, and Anne Matthews, *Australia: A Continent Revealed*. London: New Holland (Publishers) Ltd., 1996.
Hiddins, Les, *Bush Tucker Man: Stories of Exploration and Survival*. Sydney: ABC Books, 1996.
Hornadge, Bill, *The Australian Slanguage: A Look at What We Say and How We Say It*. Melbourne: Mandarin Books, 1986.
Hough, Richard, *Captain James Cook: A Biography*. New York: W. W. Norton, 1995.
Hughes, Robert, *The Fatal Shore: A History of the Transportation of Convicts to Australia, 1787–1868*. London: Pan Books, 1988.
James, Clive, *Flying Visits: Postcards from the Observer, 1976–1983*, London: Picador, 1984.
Keneally, Thomas, *Outback*. Sydney: Hodder and Stoughton, 1983.
Lacour-Gayet, Robert, *A Concise History of Australia*. London: Penguin Books, 1976.
Laseron, Charles Francis, *The Face of Australia: The Shaping of a Continent*. Sydney: Angus and Robertson, 1953.
Lewin, Roger, *Principles of Evolution*. Oxford: Blackwell Science, 1997.
Lines, William J., *Taming the Great South Land: A History of the Conquest of Nature in Australia*. Sydney: Allen and Unwin, 1991.
——, *A Long Walk in the Australian Bush*. Athens, Georgia: The University of Georgia Press, 1998.
Low, Tim, *Feral Future: The Untold Story of Australia's Exotic Invaders*. Sydney: Viking, 1999.
Luck, Peter, *Australian Icons: Things That Make Us What We Are*. Melbourne: William Heinemann Australia, 1992.
McGregor, Craig, *Profile of Australia*. London: Penguin Books, 1968.
McIntyre, K. G., *The Secret Discovery of Australia*. London: Souvenir Press, 1977.
MacKenzie, Jeanne, *Australian Paradox*. Melbourne: F. W. Cheshire, 1961.
Mackersey, Ian, *Smithy: The Life of Sir Charles Kingsford Smith*. Sydney:

Little, Brown and Co., 1998.
McLaren, Glen, *Beyond Leichhardt: Bushcraft and the Exploration of Australia*. Fremantle: Fremantle Arts Centre Press, 1996.
Malouf, David, *A Spirit of Play: The Making of Australian Consciousness*. Sydney: ABC Books, 1998.
Marshall, Sam, *Luna Park: Just for Fun*. Sydney: Luna Park Reserve Trust, 1995.
Moorehead, Alan, *Rum Jungle*. New York: Charles Scribner's Sons, 1954.
——, *Cooper's Creek*. London: Hamish Hamilton, 1963.
——, *The Fatal Impact: An Account of the Invasion of the South Pacific, 1767–1840*. New York: Harper and Row, 1966.
Moorhouse, Geoffrey, *Sydney*. Sydney: Allen and Unwin, 1999.
Morris, Jan, *Sydney*. London: Viking, 1992.
Morrison, Reg, *Australia: The Four Billion Year Journey of a Continent*. Sydney: Weldon Publishing, 1988.
Mulvaney, John, and Johan Kamminga, *Prehistory of Australia*. Sydney: Allen and Unwin, 1999.
Nile, Richard, and Christian Clerk, *Cultural Atlas of Australia, New Zealand and the South Pacific*. Oxford: Andromeda Books, 1996.
O'Connor, Siobhan (ed.), *The Book of Australia*. Sydney: Watermark Press, 1997.
Pilger, John, *A Secret Country: The Hidden Australia*. New York: Alfred A. Knopf, 1991.
Powell, Alan, *Far Country: A Short History of the Northern Territory*. Melbourne: Melbourne University Press, 1982.
Rich, P. Vickers, *Wildlife of Gondwana*. London: Reed, 1993.
Ritvo, Harriet, *The Platypus and the Mermaid and Other Figments of the Classifying Imagination*. Cambridge, Massachusetts: Harvard University Press, 1998.
Rolls, Eric, *They All Ran Wild: The Animals and Plants That Plague Australia*. Sydney: Angus and Robertson, 1969.
Sampson, Anthony, *Empires of the Sky*. London: Hodder and Stoughton, 1985.
Seal, Graham, *The Lingo: Listening to Australian English*. Sydney: University of New South Wales Press, 1999.
Sheehan, Paul, *Among the Barbarians*. Sydney: Random House Australia, 1998.
Spearritt, Peter, *Sydney's Century: A History*. Sydney: University of New South Wales Press, 2000.
Terrill, Ross, *The Australians*. New York: Simon and Schuster, 1987.
Vizard, Steve, *Two Weeks in Lilliput: Bear-Baiting and Backbiting at the Constitutional Convention*. Sydney: Penguin Books, 1998.
Ward, Russell, *The History of Australia: The Twentieth Century*. New York: Harper and Row, 1977.

White, Mary E., *Australia's Prehistoric Plants*. Sydney: Methuen, 1984.
——, *The Greening of Gondwana: The 400 Million Year Story of Australia's Plants*. Sydney: Reed Australia, 1994.

ACKNOWLEDGEMENTS

Among the many people to whom I am indebted for help in the preparation of *Down Under*, I wish to express particular thanks to Alan Howe and Carmel Egan for so generously sharing their time and hospitality even knowing that I was about to put them in one of my books; Deirdre Macken and Allan Sherwin for their astute observations and sporting participation; Patrick Gallagher of Allen & Unwin and Louise Bourke of the Australian National University for the very generous and thoughtful provision of books and other research materials; and Juliet Rogers, Karen Reid, Maggie Hamilton and Katie Stackhouse of Random House Australia for their conscientious and ever-cheerful help.

I am also much indebted in Australia to Jim Barrett, Steve Garland, Lisa Menke, Val Schier, Denis Walls, Stella Martin, Joel Becker, Barbara Bennett, Jim Brooks, Harvey Henley, Roger Johnstone, Ian Nowak, the staff of the State Library of New South Wales in Sydney, and the late, dear Catherine Veitch.

Further afield, I am especially grateful to Professor Danny Blanchflower of Dartmouth College for much statistical assistance; my longtime friend and agent Carol Heaton; and the kindly, peerless talents at Transworld Publishers in London, among whom I must mention Marianne Velmans, Larry Finlay, Alison Tulett, Emma Dowson, Meg Cairns and Patrick Janson-Smith, who remains the best friend and mentor any writer could ask for. Above all, and as always, my profoundest thanks to my dear, patient, incomparable wife, Cynthia.